JUTLAND

THE UNFINISHED BATTLE

SKAGERRAK ✚ JUTLAND

1916

100 YEARS

DEDICATION

To Patricia, Zoë and Francesca for their great patience
as well as thoughts and advice on how to write a better book.

To my father, George, in loving memory.

To Ron Horabin, whose model of the *Iron Duke* will
always remain a tribute to his great generosity of spirit.

JUTLAND
THE UNFINISHED BATTLE

Nicholas Jellicoe

FOREWORD BY
Prof Dr Michael Epkenhans

Copyright © Nicholas Jellicoe 2016

First published in Great Britain in 2016 by
Seaforth Publishing,
An imprint of Pen & Sword Books Ltd,
47 Church Street, Barnsley, South Yorkshire S70 2AS

www.seaforthpublishing.com
Email info@seaforthpublishing.com

Reprinted with corrections 2016

Published and distributed in the United States of America and Canada by
the Naval Institute Press, 291 Wood Road, Annapolis, Maryland 21402-5043

www.nip.org

Library of Congress Cataloging Number: 2016931555

British Library Cataloguing in Publication Data
A catalogue record for this book is available from the British Library

ISBN 978 1 84832 321 6

Designed and set by David Rose

Printed and bound in Great Britain by
CPI Group (UK) Ltd, Croydon, CR0 4YY

Contents

Illustrations

The German flag hoist for torpedo attack, the red pennant of the 'Stander-Z' by Willy Stöwer (1864–1931). Flotilla torpedo attacks were thoroughly rehearsed by the German navy. (Courtesy of Hamburg International Maritime Museum © 2016, ProLiterris, Zürich)

In Jellicoe's mind, the chief function of British destroyers was to fend off German torpedo-boat attacks, and in an attempt to obtain a degree of control the flotillas were commanded from larger 'leaders' like *Broke* seen here. However, during the confusion of the night actions on 1 June, *Broke* collided with *Sparrowhawk,* one of her own 4th Destroyer Flotilla. (N03104 © National Maritime Museum, Greenwich, London)

The 935-ton destroyer *Spitfire* colliding with the 20,000-ton battleship *Nassau* in the early hours of 1 June. (Courtesy of Alan Bush)

The heavily damaged *Spitfire* entering the Tyne at 14:00 GMT on 2 June. (Courtesy of Alan Bush)

The battleship *Malaya* burying her dead at sea, 1 June. (Author's collection)

The German poet Johann Kinau (1880–1916), is better known under his nom de plume Gorch Fock. He died on the light cruiser *Wiesbaden.*

Repairing *Warspite*'s battle damage at Rosyth. Shown is a 12in shell hit beneath the after Y turret. (N16494 © National Maritime Museum, Greenwich, London)

A lone sailor stands silhouetted in the gaping shell hole on *Derfflinger,* one of the German ships most heavily damaged at Jutland. (Courtesy of the German Bundesarchiv)

Sir John Jellicoe bidding farewell to the Grand Fleet, leaving to take up the position of First Sea Lord, 29 November 1916. (Author's collection)

Sir Hugh Evan-Thomas (*left*) with Admiral Beatty after being awarded the KCB by King George V using Beatty's sword, 25 June 1917. (Courtesy of Martin Bourdillon)

John Jellicoe was laid to rest on 3 December 1935 in Nelson's shadow in the crypt of St Paul's. The procession passing Ludgate Hill. (Courtesy *Illustrated London News*)

On the news of Jellicoe's death, the flags of three nations' navies, including that of Hitler's Kriegsmarine, were lowered. (Author's collection)

Maps

———

(Drawn by Peter Wilkinson)

Foreword

———

A hundred years ago, on 31 May/1 June 1916, the Grand Fleet and the German High Seas Fleet clashed in the North Sea. Within the space of twelve hours, two hundred and fifty warships fought the biggest naval battle in history. Although both navies had always longed for *Der Tag* – the day of reckoning – before 1914 neither was willing to risk the potential losses. As a result, the Grand Fleet established a distant blockade, keeping the High Seas Fleet at arm's length and, at the same time, helping force Germany to its knees by cutting off its access to world trade. The High Seas Fleet, in return, had no intention of facing the Grand Fleet in an open encounter in the northern North Sea. Any attack against the Grand Fleet in those waters would, most likely, end in a catastrophe as German naval manoeuvres had shown on the eve of war.

The German decision to risk no open encounter was further underscored by the loss of three light cruisers after a British surprise attack near Heligoland (28 August 1914). As a result, hoping to lure out parts of the Grand Fleet and whittle down its strength, the High Seas Fleet reverted to a hit-and-run strategy. This, however, also proved a disaster. At the Battle of Dogger Bank (24 January 1915), British battle-cruisers surprised the German Fleet, sinking the armoured cruiser *Blücher*. Seeking to avoid any risk of more losses, the High Seas Fleet stayed in harbour for more than a year. In spring 1916 the new Commander-in-Chief of the High Seas Fleet, Vice Admiral Reinhard Scheer, decided to resume this strategy. Thus he hoped to prove the existence of the navy as well as to contribute to the overall German war effort. The first sortie of this strategy eventually ended in the battle now commonly known as the Battle of Jutland.

This battle, which is described in Nick Jellicoe's book, was a unique event. It occurred almost precisely at the midpoint of World War I. In this respect, it was an exceptional event, and the protagonists on both sides would have preferred it to have been a normal one.

The long duration of the war, before and after the battle, suggests that it was a superfluous battle, one that only served to confirm the status quo. And yet it claimed an alarming number of casualties by today's standards – nearly ten thousand dead and wounded on each side. In comparison with the battle of the Somme, begun a few weeks earlier and which cost the lives of far more combatants – three hundred thousand to be exact – these losses were minor. But the Battle of Jutland contained other 'superlatives'. Unlike the mass killing on the Western Front, this battle was a showdown between the most highly developed battle technologies, with what were essentially state-of-the art weapons that had been the achievements of domestic industrial ability and had been developed and produced over many years and at great expense.

Nick Jellicoe marvellously describes all the events and developments which eventually led to the great naval encounter of Jutland. Both from the German and British points of view, he tells us why the German navy challenged the Royal Navy before 1914 and how the latter responded. He combines the analysis of events with a vivid description of the mentality of naval leaders and leadership on both sides of the North Sea, without which it would be difficult to understand what happened during the war. His description of the battle itself is a masterpiece of historical writing. Always trying to offer a fair and unbiased judgement, he gives the reader deep insight into an event which has, ever since, attracted the attention of millions of people all over the world although it had changed nothing. On the day, the High Seas Fleet fought with outstanding bravery and skill, yet it had only been able to knock at the gate of its golden cage without successfully opening it.

Nick Jellicoe's book not only describes the battle's origins, he also gives the reader a view from both above and below deck and a sense of the ordeal of naval action. And finally he explores the aftermath, the lessons learned by admirals on both sides, and the way in which naval officers and the public commemorated and symbolised the battle, known in Germany as the *Skagerrakschlacht*, back then but also today. This very contemporary approach, which is based on a wide range of both well-known as well as some new documents, makes reading his book a real pleasure.

PROF DR MICHAEL EPKENHANS
Centre for Military History and
Social Sciences of the Bundeswehr, Potsdam

Preface

The Battle of Jutland was the largest, and last, dreadnought engagement in history. Two hundred and fifty ships battled against each other for twelve hours, through day and night, in a struggle that dwarfed the battle of Trafalgar. Every tenth sailor, whether British or German, died, but unlike the war in the trenches, officers led from the front with their men and for the British, three admirals paid the ultimate price.

The century that followed Trafalgar was one in which no other nation came close to challenging British sea power until Kaiser Wilhelm II, emboldened by a deep jealousy and hatred of his British birthright, set Germany on a course that would inevitably lead to war.

The significance of Jutland is in danger of being lost, its importance over-shadowed by the monumental slaughter of the land war, rather than being put into the wider strategic context of, and impact on, the First World War as a whole. The battle was one of the decisive turning points in the First World War, promoting a complete turnaround in German naval strategy, one that brought Britain to its knees and close to defeat in 1917, as shipping vital to the nation's survival was methodically destroyed by unrestricted German submarine warfare.

Even so, the German navy's strategic shift proved to be a huge miscalculation on Germany's part. It brought American manpower and resources into the war and helped tip the balance of the war to favour the Allied cause. The incarceration of the German surface fleet and its eventual scuttling at Scapa Flow had other unforeseen results. It accelerated the collapse of morale in the German navy, exacerbating the social tensions between ranks, and fomenting the growing revolutionary movement in Germany by providing committed and seasoned recruits to its cause. With the loss of the fleet as a bargaining chip at the Versailles peace negotiations, the reparations exacted by the Allies only fuelled German bitterness after the end of the war. That bitterness ultimately contributed to the years of civil strife and to Hitler.

Acrimony followed the battle's end. The British public had expected another Trafalgar and when the German fleet was not annihilated, the search for a scapegoat began. Admiral Sir John Jellicoe, the British commander-in-chief, was the first victim. A war of words between two rival camps comprised of zealous supporters of the two British admirals who fought on the day – Sir John and Vice Admiral Sir David Beatty, commander of the Battle Cruiser

Fleet – dragged on for decades, although neither faction wanted a public debate which both knew was liable to tarnish the Royal Navy's reputation. And yet, even today, the unhealthy, nationalistic debate continues. For Germany it was different. The *Skagerrakschlacht*, as the battle became known, served as the key act in the German navy's fight to restore its honour. The battle became a well of heroic and courageous propaganda. In Wilhelm II's words, German valour at Jutland had broken the spell of Trafalgar.

The battle was complex. Its story must be set against the context of the times, and the story of its tactics, technology and personalities told through both British and German eyes. It is a story of how the two most powerful navies were shaped by the larger-than-life personalities of men like Tirpitz and Jacky Fisher, men who were, in turn, both limited and empowered by the shifting structure of European alliances and domestic political debate. It is the story of the commanders at sea and how their choices shaped the battle as it unfolded about them. Jutland was the first real test for the tactics and naval and military technologies which had been developed in the years of peace and not yet proven under the stress of war. It was a test faced by two very different navies, one only a generation old, the other steeped in, and bound by, the traditions of centuries.

For me this story is also a personal journey, as John Jellicoe was my paternal grandfather. I have discovered a man whom I never knew: a complex, sometimes flawed figure, but one whom I have come to greatly admire. My family ties have given me both a sense of responsibility in helping keep the epic of Jutland alive, as well as opening many doors, giving me wider and privileged access to many British and German sources.

I have tried to bring to light the many viewpoints that exist in a balanced, transparent and fair manner. I owe a great deal to the mass of written material that has already been published on the battle, but still find it a great pity that much of the German point of view has never been translated, or that the role of the ordinary seamen in the German navy has not received more focus. There is significant value to be found in the different national perspectives. I hope the centenary will shed some new light and understanding on a story that has all too often been mired in deep controversy.

Rarely has a battle been so written about, discussed and disputed as has Jutland. I hope to have made a valued contribution by bringing more understanding to a wider public.

NICHOLAS JELLICOE
Jongny, Switzerland, August 2015

Acknowledgements

In the course of researching and writing the book I received a huge amount of help and goodwill from many people who willingly gave me their time and the benefit of their knowledge. I owe them all a large debt of gratitude.

Eric Grove was the first historian to whom I spoke. It was as a result of our first meeting in Blackpool in 2011 that I then met – one introduction leading to another – Prof Dr Michael Epkenhans, Kapitän zur See Dr Werner Rahn, Dr Stefan Huck of the Wilhemshaven Marine Museum and Dr Jann Witt of the Laboe Memorial, all of whom I now regard as friends and colleagues. I am especially grateful to Robert Massie, who visited my father while writing *Castles of Steel* and who then reciprocated, this time inviting me to visit his Hudson River home to discuss my ideas.

A chance meeting in a Geneva bookshop with the American writer, Matt Stevenson, led to months of his thoughtful advice as well as contacts. I introduced myself because, at the time, I overheard him talking with another close American friend, John McCarthy. It was John's mother's generosity that made the McCarthy Nelson Gallery at the National Museum of the Royal Navy possible, and John was the one person my father said I must look up when I went to work in Geneva. He has beed a friend and supporter for more than twenty years. My sincere thanks to Don Walsh, who in 1960 as captain of the *Trieste* took man to the deepest part of our known oceans at the very bottom of the Marianas Trench. It was Don who, late one night as we talked, laid down the gauntlet and got me on the road to writing seriously. I thought of his exploits in the deep while on the surface of the North Sea visiting the Jutland wreck sites in the spring of 2015. The M/S *Vina* expedition was led by Gert Normann Andersen, founder of the new SeaWar Museum in Thyborøn, Denmark. Naval archaeologist Dr Innes McCartney, someone who has dived more Jutland wrecks than anyone, was the main adviser. We surveyed thirty-two square kilometres of the North Seabed and visited all the known Jutland wrecks, many with close ROV inspection. It was extraordinarily generous of Gert to include me and to be able to witness first-hand the weather conditions similar to those on the actual day of the battle, 31 May 1916.

My extended family came through in spades. Many illuminating conversations about Trafalgar were spent with my cousin Richard Latham, ex-RN. Phillip Wingfield shared with me some personal Jellicoe artefacts that I was able to take with me to the area where John Jellicoe made the deployment decision. James Loudon gave me full access to all the admiral's obituaries and newspaper clippings. It was James who found the photo of the Kriegsmarine flag being lowered to mark the admiral's death in 1935. Christopher Balfour contributed with some extensive research on the funeral attendees. My sincere thanks to Dominic Gibbs of The Cayzer Trust company, without whose financial and moral support much of the editing would not have been possible, and very sincere thanks to Elizabeth Gilmour (Cayzer) for her deep interest and extensive support. The writing of this book brought me in closer contact with all my cousins and helped rebuild an important family link, which has been a wonderful, unexpected gift for me.

Tony Lovell, whom I met in Boston in 2011, let me try a hand-held Barr and Stroud range-finder on the Harvard River to give me a feel for the intricacies of range-finding. I was embarrassingly bad. Tony also made me an editor on the *Dreadnought Project* (as it turned out, a remarkably quiet one) which, in turn, opened more doors to a group whose deep knowledge has been a source of great insight: Dr John Brooks, Brooks Rowlett, Byron Angel, Dr Simon Harley, Steve McLaughlin, Dr Matthew Seligmann and Bill Jurens, to name but a few.

Over the last five years there have been many sources of help from different parts of the world: Mike Pitschke from Monterey whose photos, together with the Barton collection, will make fine materials for the Fleet Air Arm museum in Yeovil; Rear Admiral James Goldrick RAN (ret'd), David Stevens and Dr Alex Kolloniatis (whose help on Jutland signals has been invaluable) from Australia, and Prof Paul Halpern and Tobias Philbin from the United States. James Goldrick, who has just published *Before Jutland*, graciously gave me his time whenever I asked.

Among the naval and military museums in Britain and Germany have come many other friendships and encouragement: Dr Kevin Fewster (NMM), who has encouraged me since the start of the Jutland Centenary Initiative; Dr Quintin Colville, who helped me connect with Sir Hugh Evan-Thomas's family. Martin Bourdillon was kind enough to entrust me with full access to family records of the great admiral's life. And, of course, Andrew Choong at the National Maritime Museum's Brass Foundry, who is the keeper of Aladdin's Cave: the ships' plans. To others: I give thanks to Alan Bush, grandson of the *Spitfire*'s Lt Athelstan Bush, and Dave Smith who made me an honorary member of the Equal Speed Charlie London Society. And I thank Dr Andrew Gordon, whose *Rules of the Game* is considered by many as seminal a work on Jutland as Marder's were, for his advice and support. We can disagree, but as friends.

The many friendships that I have made in Germany as a result of this book have been a source of great pleasure: Jörg Wehmer, Dr Wolf von Tirpitz, grandson of the great Alfred Tirpitz, Hans Koever for his Room 40 work, Christian Jentsch from the Mürwick Naval Academy, Peter Kram from the Wilhelmshaven Bilddienst, Peter Schenk, the historian, and Karl-Heinz Jockel of the deutsche-marinearchiv.de. Peter knew my father, George, well from his work on the German invasion of Leros where he lost one of his closest friends. After having given his *parole*, George was allowed to search for the body but it was in vain. Given the many close German friendships of my grandfather, the admiral, I have always maintained that the 2016 Jutland Centenary Memorial should be a joint British and German affair. Hopefully, we have learnt some lessons from what happened so that we don't stumble again into such an abyss.

I must also acknowledge the access to photos from the Blohm und Voss, Hamburg Archives and for the kind and generous help that I received at both the Liddle Archives in Leeds and the Churchill Archives in Cambridge. And of archives and archivists, I only have the highest praise for Susan Scott of The Cayzer Trust Archives who generously went well beyond the call of duty to help make this a better book.

Some connections are just being made now: to reconnect with the Scheer and von Hase families. Even though nothing came of it at the end, my thanks to Ernst Lahner for the many hours that he spent trying to see how we could join the two stories of HMS *Spitfire* and SMS *Nassau* together.

Jutland: The Unfinished Battle is but one part of the Jutland Centenary Memorial Initiative. Many people have been quietly and generously working behind the scenes to commemorate properly the memory of the men who died at Jutland. A website will be accessible online and will be useful to refer to alongside my book. My thanks to Clément Lador of Ergopix in Vevey for his help in designing the site, Guillaume Goutchtat from A46 in Montreux for sound engineering all the animation voice-overs and podcasts, and Caroline Buechler for her ideas on the podcast concept. A very special thanks to my old friend and respected colleague, Rupert White, whose Munich agency, White Communications, helped with all the preparations of the first museum presentation on *Skagerrakstag* 2014 and whose family looked after me on many Munich visits for the animation work with Peter Pedall. Oberst Dr Matthias Rogg of the Dresden Militarische Museum, Dr Jann Witt from Laboe, Dr Stefan Huck from the Wilhelmshaven Marine Museum and Dr Dominic Tweddle from the National Museum of the Royal Navy all came to share ideas on how or where we might be able to work together fruitfully.

Other people who helped in the presentation did so as they shared my passion – the Frameworks agency was responsible for the beautifully executed film introduction to the meeting. Thank you, Terry Brissendon, Lawrence James and Simon Fairweather, a great friend from my Rolex creative days. And thanks go to Crispin Sadler who, together with Innes McCartney and myself, is now working on a Jutland documentary.

Apart from this book a great deal of effort has been focused on creating the Jutland Centenary Initiative website, built as a learning resource around an animation of the complex battle. I wish to thank Peter and Alissa Pedall in Munich, for their work which will engagingly communicate with a younger generation to keep Jutland and its lessons alive and relevant. They have both worked long hours on the project's behalf. There have been some fun projects too. We will have a special commemorative edition of Scapa Scotch. Pernod-Ricard has generously agreed that all the proceeds will be donated to the Royal National Lifeboat Institution. The 1st Earl of Scapa would have, I am sure, very much liked the idea. Thank you Eric Benoist, Nikki Burgess, Clarisse Daniels and Alison Perottet. And Tom Muir of the Kirkwall Historical Museum, Orkney. The Royal Hospital School, where my grandfather laid the foundation stone in 1927, gave me one of my most treasured opportunities: working with school pupils on how best to communicate Jutland in a meaningful way to a younger generation through the work of profiling the more than one hundred school alumni who died in the battle. I am deeply grateful to former headmaster, James Lockwood, project evangelist Rob Mann, Monty Callow, history master David Barker, business development manager Lucy Pembroke and, of course, for the enthusiasm of the RHS pupils.

As a result of my brother, John Jellicoe, the Venerable Peter Sutton, Archdeacon of the Isle of Wight, agreed that the Union Flag which flew on the *Iron Duke* will see another day on the North Sea in 2016. We just found out (through Knud Jacobsen in Denmark) that the admiral had given it to the Church of Holy Trinity in Ryde in October 1916, when he had been unable to personally attend his own mother's funeral because of his duties of command. Instead, he asked his eldest sister, Edith, to take the Union Flag from his flagship. It was a highly symbolic gesture. And, of course, thanks to my elder brother, Paddy, who has generously given me the portrait of the admiral that Sir Arthur Stockdale Cope painted as a study for the National Portrait Gallery's larger *Naval Officers of World War One*. It will be seen by many around the various Jutland exhibitions in the coming years.

My most heartfelt thanks are to my wife, Patricia, and our two daughters, Zoë and Francesca, all of whom have left their mark on my work – to Zöe for the exhausting task of re-reading the final manuscript and to Francesca for all her design input for the Jutland Centenary Initiative. But most of all, thanks go to each for all their understanding and patience with a project that often seemed never-ending: almost like the unfinished battle.

In closing, my sincere thanks to Rob Gardiner of Seaforth for his continuous but always patient explanations to a neophyte writer and to James Woodhall, my editor, who spent more time with me at one point than my family, though when we worked together at my family's house we discovered another passion in common: great wine.

It is inevitable that with such a large work there will be errors, especially since I am neither a professional historian nor writer. Nor have I had the years of experience needed for a real historian's grasp of all the facts, but I only ask a reader's understanding when these occur but their presence (and their correction) is my responsibility alone.

Abbreviations

Gun classification

Throughout this work, a gun's calibre will refer to the metric or non-metric diameter of the shell size; British capital ship weaponry ranged from 12in to 15in calibre for the main armament. A gun on HMS *Iron Duke* could be described as being 13.5in/45 (/45 refers to the barrel length – it is 45 x 13.5in shell calibres in length, ie 607.5in). German guns were classified in metric measurements, so that the main eight guns on SMS *Lützow* might be referred to as 30.5cm SK L/50 ('SK' referring to *Schnellfeuerkanone,* or fast-fire artillery); L/50 is comparable to the British barrel length.

Time

The times used are (unless specified) GMT and in military, 24-hour format (00:00). German literature often uses either Berlin *summer* time (GMT +2) or central European time (GMT +1).

Rank equivalency: The Royal Navy and the High Seas Fleet

Admiral of the Fleet	Großadmiral
Admiral	Admiral
Vice Admiral	Vizeadmiral
Rear Admiral	Konteradmiral
Commodore	Kommodore
Captain (senior)	Kapitän zur See
Captain (junior)	Fregattenkapitän
Commander	Korvettenkapitän
Lieutenant Commander	Kapitänleutnant
Lieutenant (senior)	Oberleutnant zur See
Lieutenant (junior)	Leutnant zur See
Sub Lieutenant	Oberfähnrich zur See
Naval Cadet/Midshipman	Seekadette/Fähnrich zur See

Additional abbreviations

AdC	Aide-de-camp
CB	Companion of the Most Honourable Order of the Bath
C-in-C	Commander-in-chief
CMG	Companion of the Most Distinguished Order of Saint Michael and Saint George
CVO	Commander of the Royal Victorian Order
DF	Destroyer Flotilla
DSC	Distinguished Service Cross
DSO	Distinguished Service Order
Frhr	Freiherr (title in the Prussian nobility, equivalent to baron)
GFBO	The Grand Fleet Battle Orders (Jellicoe)
GFBI	The Grand Fleet Battle Instructions (Beatty)
HMS	His Majesty's Ship
KCB	Knight Commander of the Most Honourable Order of the Bath
KCMG	Knight Commander of the Most Distinguished Order of Saint Michael and Saint George
KCVO	Knight Commander of the Royal Victorian Order
MVO	Member of the Royal Victorian Order
SMS	Seiner Majestät Schiff (His Majesty's Ship)
TOD	Time of Dispatch
TOR	Time of Receipt
1SL	First Sea Lord
2IC	Second-in-command

Digital resources

Digitally animated maps of the Battle of Jutland, the official British and German track charts, as well as a large amount of other reference materials (gunnery and signal logs, ship data, Jutland-related events and artefacts around the world, teaching and academic resources) are available to view on line at **www.Jutland1916.com**. These make understanding the evolution of this complex battle considerably easier for the reader.

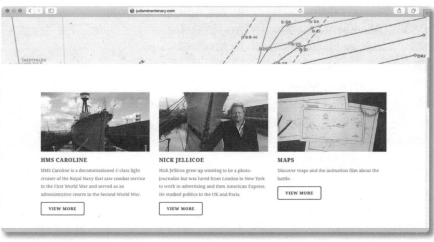

Introduction

There were many battles within, and around, the Battle of Jutland. There was the initial battle-cruiser action from which the British came out decidedly the worse off. There was the 'run to the north', in which Rear Admiral Hugh Evan-Thomas's *Queen Elizabeth*-class battleships, the latest and most heavily gunned British ships of the time, evened up the score, in some senses rescuing the equally heavily gunned but faster, lightly armoured battle-cruisers of his immediate but temporary superior, Sir David Beatty, from the jam in which they had become enmeshed. There was also the Grand Fleet deployment, a dangerously slow but in the end decisive manoeuvre, putting the British between their opponent's forces and their home bases. Finally, there were the night actions, so often overlooked, yet rich with stories of extraordinary smaller-ship courage – and equally extraordinary for the lack of signals and personal initiative, particularly by major British ships.

The Battle of Jutland, fought at the end of May 1916, pitted two nations' power, and had been awaited by the British and the Germans with equal impatience. For more than a hundred years after Nelson's victory at Trafalgar in 1805 the British had basked in a period of unbroken naval supremacy. No nation came close to challenging them. Britain's naval reviews were an awesome and premeditated display of imperial maritime power. Yet there was an inherent flaw in the apparently impregnable hardware: too much washed teak and gleaming brass, and not enough modernity, speed and professionalism.

Ever since 1897, when Kaiser Wilhelm II brought Alfred Tirpitz to the helm of the German naval ministry, Germany's path towards *Der Tag*, its day of reckoning, was navigated by these two men. The smaller German fleet was professional and single-mindedly built for one purpose alone, that of ending Britain's stranglehold on Germany's close sea-lanes in the North Sea. Ship for ship, it was of the highest quality. Jutland thus brought to a head a twenty-year arms race, the accelerator of which was Britain's launching of HMS *Dreadnought* in 1906. The advent of this fast, well-armoured and very heavily gunned battleship was a military game-changer.

By 1909 the race had reached a critical point. This was the year in which Britain's naval establishment first felt that it could no longer rely on what was publicly voted for in Germany to act as the guide by which it needed to make sure it always held the competitive edge in ships. Strong rumours were circulating that Germany was secretly stockpiling key elements – for example, turrets and barrels – and was speeding up the annual building programme to try to gain an upper hand in the balance of dreadnoughts.

The year 1909 was also the one in which Britain's Admiralty first asked for six dreadnoughts, and came up against David Lloyd George's and Winston Churchill's fierce opposition, based on their strong, populist, Liberal agenda: the Navy should, the two insisted, accept four. The Navy fought back and, in the context of increased fears not only of Germany's intention to build a bigger, stronger fleet of dreadnoughts to counter Britain's, but also the prospect of other naval powers joining the dreadnought-building race, eight were finally agreed upon.

When the two rival forces, Germany's High Seas Fleet and Britain's Grand Fleet, met early on the evening of 31 May, it seemed as if the North Sea climax had finally arrived. Yet the first engagement had taken place over the preceding three hours. The two fleets' scouting elements, the British Battle Cruiser Fleet, and the Germans' First and Second Scouting Groups, had met up with sudden ferocity. When the massed dreadnoughts came within reach of each other's guns, British sea power had already received a bloody nose.

Sir David Beatty's force of six battle-cruisers, the greyhounds of the British Navy, along with four of the most powerful ships on the sea that day on either side – the 15in-gunned battleships of Hugh Evan-Thomas's 5th Battle Squadron – were lured by Admiral Franz Hipper's supposed flight into a full-scale and disastrous chase, ending with the sinking of two British battle-cruisers, *Indefatigable* and *Queen Mary*, and the loss of more than two thousand British sailors' lives. Beatty's and Evan-Thomas's ships had faced a numerically far inferior German force. However, at the end of the 'run to the north', Beatty was able to lure Hipper and Scheer into the guns of the Grand Fleet. It was a courageous and brilliant run, designed to give the impression that he was fleeing Hipper's forces, but one also that was dearly paid for.

The outcome of the battle of Jutland was not one with which the British were in any way happy. The German fleet had got away. It had been badly mauled, but inflicted higher losses of life and tonnage on the British than the British on its enemy, and Germany had successfully spun to the world the story of its victory at sea. Britain's sailors came home and were jeered at, spat on and booed by the public. Rightly, they felt that they had given their best, but in the minds of a nation bathing in the glory of naval supremacy and having awaited a second Trafalgar, they had seriously let their compatriots down.

The aftermath of the battle became a race to regain the public's confidence in the Royal Navy and correct what had been seen to be at fault, as well as a public hunt for a scapegoat. That scapegoat was found in John Jellicoe, not in Jellicoe's second-in-command, David Beatty. The truth lay somewhere in between, but Beatty's charisma easily won the public's hearts and support.

The irony of Jutland is that its seemingly indecisive outcome – neither side definitively annihilated the other's naval presence – is key to its real meaning. Admiral Reinhard Scheer, Jellicoe's German opposite number, realised that Germany should now never build its hopes on defeating the Royal Navy in a pitched fleet encounter. Jutland was proof for Scheer that only unrestricted submarine warfare against Britain would bring Germany's adversary to its knees, and when launched in February 1917 such warfare was deadly. Germany hoped to destroy Britain's lifeline: its trade. Within months, millions of tons of shipping had gone to the bottom of the sea; in April 1917 alone more than 800,000 tons of Allied shipping were lost. Sounding more defeatist than realist in war council, Jellicoe warned that unless solutions could be found, Britain would have to sue for peace with Germany.

In this sense Jutland was very much a *decisive* battle. It was the moment at which Germany questioned its naval strategy, and which led, ultimately, to the declaration of unrestricted submarine war, a decision which in the end brought the US entry in to the war. It is important not to focus too closely only at the tactical level of the battle itself; as a contemporary account put it: 'It is absolutely necessary to look at the war as a whole; to avoid keeping our eyes only on the German fleet. What we have to do is to starve and cripple *Germany*, to destroy *Germany*. The destruction of the German fleet is a means to an end and not an end in itself.'[1]

The British had lost overall supremacy of the seas. It was a dramatic moment, but it was not the case that Jellicoe was 'dead against' the convoy system, a system by which unarmed merchant ships were taken across hostile waters under the watchful eye of a protective screen of destroyers.[2] He just did not come out overwhelmingly in favour of it before two conditions were met: he felt that it *could* work, but he did not then believe that the British could find the destroyers to meet the challenges of convoy. He came to the conclusion after 120 days at the Admiralty that wide scale convoy protection should be undertaken as a *defensive* measure. It was his failure to see the *offensive* potential of convoy destroyer screens that might be more accurately criticised.

Here he was let down by the bureaucratic mentality within the Admiralty (to which he had gone only in December 1916) and erroneous assumptions about how many destroyers would be needed. It is also not true that it was a visit to the Admiralty by Lloyd George on 30 April 1917 that pushed it into line, as he always maintained, though it certainly helped – as one of Jellicoe's biographers, John Winton, stated – to focus minds.

Jellicoe had already given Beatty the go-ahead for a test of the system in Scandinavian waters before a larger, more formal one was carried out in May 1917, with a convoy leaving Gibraltar. In other words, practically within one 'quarter', Jellicoe and Rear Admiral Alexander Ludovic Duff had reviewed what was working and what was not; by October 1917, with additional destroyers having come from America in July, as well as from British shipyards, not only were the losses stemmed but, equally important, U-boats were being sunk at a significantly increased rate.

Jellicoe was not an impassioned innovator by nature, but he was far from inflexible. 'He was a man of great ability and strength of character, but he was a developer not an innovator.'[3] In the same way that he changed his mind on numerous strategic and tactical issues in the two years of wartime command of the Grand Fleet up until the end of 1916, he was adamant about keeping his mind open about solutions to the submarine threat in the first five months of 1917.

When it came to managing his image he was his own worst enemy. Beatty was far more adroit in recognising the benefits of good press relations. Many of his contemporaries, even supporters, spoke of Jellicoe as having been a weak delegator, and he was a mediocre presenter of his ideas in Cabinet. He overworked himself and got involved in the minutiae of detail. When you read Beatty's Grand Fleet Battle Instructions (GFBIs) after Jellicoe's rather turgid orders, the contrast between the latter and Beatty's simplicity could not be starker. But Jellicoe saw that a move from fleet operations to an anti-submarine offensive was needed. Not surprisingly, once in command of the fleet and bearing the same responsibilities, Beatty became, in practice, as conservative as Jellicoe had been on the preservation of the Britain's overwhelming dreadnought ratio.

Jellicoe's command of the Grand Fleet spanned the vital months of wartime retraining before the day of the battle. It was the same for his subsequent twelve months at the Admiralty during a period of decisive strategic change that took the war under the seas and away from a surface fleet action. Beatty's command, by contrast, came after the shift from a fleet-to-fleet encounter, while his eight-year role as First Lord came with peace. His great reforms of the Navy were born when timely reflection during peacetime was possible. In the first months of 1917 circumstances were turbulent.

What made the outcome of Jutland so important? And if it was that important, what actually happened? What – alongside 'who won?' – are the other important questions to ask? I hope this book will help enlarge on an already well-trodden path.

THE CONTEXT

—

1

The Emergence of German Economic and Naval Power

On 31 May 1916 the early twentieth century's two great rival naval powers, Germany and Great Britain, met in combat in the North Sea. The Battle of Jutland, or, as the Germans still call it, the *Skagerrakschlacht*, was fought through the night and into the morning of 1 June. The conflict had been building broadly for nearly five decades, but had really taken its grip on the two nations in the late 1890s.

In 1856, at the end of the Crimean War, the last shot fired in action by the British battle fleet opened up the next half-century of unchallenged dominance. At the naval review of 26 June 1897 more than 165 ships steamed past Queen Victoria's stand, in five columns that each stretched over five miles. Moreover, 'not a single post abroad had been weakened to make the strong show at Spithead. Only the modern units in home waters were used.'[1] Such was the visual impact of this show of naked power that the British freely used it to impress their message on other nations invited to attend as guests.*

Yet Trafalgar's outcome in many ways sowed the seeds of the Royal Navy's later demise. Much British innovation was simply blocked by a growing feeling of invulnerability. Too much pomp emerged from military inaction. The marine-engineering innovator, Charles Parsons, whose turbines were later to power many British and German battleships at Jutland, was able to demonstrate the innovation of his new engine only by an audacious publicity stunt, running the small 34.5-knot *Turbinia* steam yacht between the lines on that June day and getting away without being caught by the smaller, slower picket boats on duty. The *Turbinia* was by far the fastest boat afloat on that occasion. The powers-that-were did not want Parsons there. He rocked the boat in which too many were getting fat off easy profits.

---

* James Goldrick commented on the strained overseas resources of the Royal Navy before the outbreak of hostilities in August 1914. The Royal Navy 'now mustered some twenty dreadnought battleships and eight battle-cruisers ... Yet, apart from the three battle-cruisers in the Mediterranean, the Australian navy's *Australia* in the Pacific, and single pre-dreadnoughts in the East Indies and China, there were no capital ships outside British waters' (Goldrick, *Before Jutland*, p21).

In Germany, the half-century leading up to 1900 had seen bewilderingly profound changes. In forty short years its population had exploded, growing by twenty-four million to total, in 1910, around sixty-five million. This new, united Germany was now the largest nation in Europe. In the same period production had soared: coal output went up seven times, and iron and steel even more. By 1893 its steel production surpassed Britain's.[2] Paralleling industrial production, food consumption also climbed, supported largely by imports.[3]

With economic growth came demands for better education, housing, living conditions and benefits, creating political pressure on hard choices between 'guns or butter'. Colonial resources were sought to feed these needs: these became Germany's 'place in the sun'. In 1884 Otto von Bismarck added Togoland, the Cameroons, the Marshall Islands, German Southwest Africa and German East Africa to the colonial portfolio.

A new force in Germany

Against a backdrop of tremendous industrial and social change, Germany's naval strength in 1897 ranked her in only fifth or sixth position.[4] This is not surprising: the navy had been in existence for just over two decades. It was founded in 1871, the year of the unification of Germany.

When Wilhelm became Kaiser in June 1888, following the death of his father after a reign that lasted only ninety-nine days, the die was cast for a radical change in army–navy policy. Wilhelm had been greatly impressed by his reading of Alfred Thayer Mahan's *The Influence of Seapower upon History* and the overt show of British naval power visible every time that he visited Cowes. Wilhelm's desire to match the British grew from an inferiority complex that was fired up every time he was in the presence of his British family:

> I had a peculiar passion for the navy. It sprang to no small extent from my English blood. When I was a little boy … I admired the proud British ships. There awoke in me the will to build ships of my own like these some day and, when I was grown up, to possess a navy as fine as the English.[5]

Determined not be outshone, he would greet the British Ambassador in the full regalia of a British Admiral of the Fleet. 'Fancy wearing the same uniform as St Vincent and Nelson. It is enough to make one giddy,' the Kaiser once exclaimed. Wilhelm had a fetish for uniforms and he made '37 changes to their design between 1888 and 1904'.[6] He himself rarely dressed in anything but military attire. This obsession with the navy even went so far as his signing all the promotions right down to the rank of lieutenant and planning winter manoeuvres. Challenged on whether this was correct for his position, he reacted petulantly:

I am tired of these discussions. I simply command and that is that. I am always supposed to ask Tom, Dick and Harry, and only sign what the Republic Navy decides is good. I am finally tired of this. To hell with it! I am the Supreme War Lord. I do not decide. I command.[7]

In fact, he was not only a Grand Admiral of the German Imperial Fleet but an Admiral of the Imperial Russian Fleet, as well as the fleets of Norway, Sweden and Denmark – and even of the Royal Greek Navy. His fascination for all things naval was such that he would even submit his own designs to the Imperial German Naval Office. One such design was along the lines of the eventual British battle-cruiser.

The Kaiser's early ideas on the composition of his navy reflected his desire that Germany should be seen around the world: a German naval presence would be used to send a signal. In Michael Epkenhans' opinion, 'he was convinced of the relationship between naval power and world power, which was the prerequisite of national prestige, economic wealth and social stability'.[8]

Tirpitz's ideas

The early focus on cruiser construction came from Wilhelm's desire to underline Germany's growing importance. Conveniently, this was also cheaper. In the opinion of Alfred Tirpitz, however, the cruiser solution was wholly impracticable (see the following chapter for a full account of Tirpitz's part in the story of the German navy). Germany did not possess the required coaling stations and its real need – to confront and defeat British sea power – could only be attained by constructing a fleet that could take the challenge directly to the British: a battleship fleet. Without a strong navy, Tirpitz was convinced that Germany would never be the world power that it strived to be. It was not merely a case of defensive naval power or naval deterrence in protecting German interests. Tirpitz was an instinctive aggressor: 'Those who consistently advocate the defensive often base their argument on the premise that the offensive enemy will present himself to do the decisive battle whenever that might suit us'.

It is not always clear what Tirpitz's strategy was primarily aimed at. According to Patrick Kelly, 'His post-war writings give the strong impression that he expected war against Britain from the beginning; his pre-war actions indicate, however, that he wanted much more to deter the British than to fight them'.[9] Tirpitz's ideas were built around the so-called 'risk theory' that suggested that Britain would – at a certain point – face a huge risk in trying to defeat Germany: every ship lost in that confrontation would weaken it against the 'two-power standard' – the British policy of maintaining a navy larger than the next two largest combined, at this time the French and Russian navies. But to reach the necessary size, Germany would have to pass through a period in which it would find itself in a kind of 'no man's land', when its navy was not large enough to deter, but might actually even encourage, a pre-emptive strike by the British – what Admiral Lord Fisher essentially, privately, referred to as a 'Copenhagen strategy'.*

From the start, the chief of the Admiralstab, the Kaiser's Imperial German Admiralty, ran the navy militarily (subject to the Kaiser) and politically (subject to the Reichstag and the Chancellor). Wilhelm wanted more control, even if he hated taking decisions. This need led to the creation of a very complex system of command. His naval 'direct reports' numbered eight, already a dangerously high number. Von Müller, head of the Marine Kabinett, was the most influential. Being responsible for personnel appointments and promotions put him in a powerful position and it was understandable that, having the Kaiser's ear, this proximity to power became very much part of his character. It eventually turned him into the worst kind of courtier. But it was Tirpitz's position as head of the Reichsmarine Amt (RMA) that was the all-powerful position in the German peacetime navy as it was from his office that all the budgeting, design, construction, supplying and manning of the Kaiser's ships emanated. However, operational authority, especially in times of war, was split between the Inspector-General of the navy and the regional commands (the Baltic and North Sea station chiefs, the commanders of the High Seas Fleet and the East Asia Squadron) as well as the head of the Admiralstab, the replacement organisation to the old Naval High Command under Hugo von Pohl. Added to this complexity was the Kaiser's brother, Prince Heinrich of Prussia, a serving naval commander, who kept control where he wanted to. He would often, for example, be responsible for special units like the Flandern Marine Korps (even if direct command was exercised by Ludwig von Schröder).

In a little under twenty years Germany had succeeded in building a fleet that the British naval establishment took as a very serious threat. From the day when Wilhelm brought the forty-eight-year-old Rear Admiral Tirpitz to the helm of the German Imperial Naval Office, Germany was steered towards a day of reckoning with Britain.[10] The German fleet might have been smaller than Britain's but, ship for ship, it demonstrated high quality and great professionalism. It was a fleet built for one purpose: ending Britain's stranglehold on the North Sea.

---

* Fisher's private comments were taken up publicly by the then Lord Commissioner of the Admiralty, Arthur Lee. A 'Copenhagen strategy' was so named after James Gambier's 1807 pre-emptive attack on the Danish fleet. In a speech on 3 February 1905, Lee rather unwisely talked about getting the British Navy's 'blow in first, before the other side had time even to read in the newspapers that war had been declared' (Hough, *First Lord*, p248).

2

The Fleet Builders:
Fisher and Tirpitz

———

John 'Jacky' Fisher and Alfred Tirpitz: the two names are resonant of a bygone age, a naval arms race that characterised Anglo-German relations in the early years of the twentieth century, an inevitable descent into the open conflict in a manner of Christopher Clark's *The Sleepwalkers*. Both were cunning politicians and careful cultivators of future naval leadership. Their legacies shaped their countries' navies for decades: Fisher dragged an out-of-date Royal Navy into the new century against fierce opposition; Tirpitz created Kaiser Wilhelm's High Seas Fleet.

Not everything about them was comparable and much in each was not particularly likeable. Tirpitz was a shrewdly manipulative man, recognising his sovereign's obsession with what he saw as Germany's rightful place in the world order. Reinhard Scheer, later Commander-in-Chief of the High Seas Fleet at Jutland, commented that he 'had no doubt of the overwhelming stature of statesmanlike greatness' in Tirpitz. Meanwhile, Robert Massie praised Tirpitz for being, after Bismarck, 'the most able, most durable, most influential and most effective minister of imperial Germany'. Of Fisher, Jameson said 'that he was a great man is indisputable – a figure of almost Churchillian proportions with the same gift for expressing himself in vivid language, the same prophetic vision and the same dominating personality'.[1]

Yet Fisher left as much destruction in his wake as any man ever did. Rather than seeking consensus, he divided. Tirpitz was the opposite: he sought alliances whenever he could, though both he and Fisher would often sound out junior officers' opinions over those of more senior men. Whichever way they went, they were bound to ruffle feathers. As obsessive as Tirpitz was in building his own vision of a German fleet, Fisher was just as dogged in protecting what he saw as Britain's dwindling capability to maintain its imperial bearer of power.

Fisher's early life and career

John Arbuthnot Fisher was born in 1841 in Ramboda, Ceylon (now Sri Lanka), of British parents, the eldest of eleven siblings, four of whom did not survive their early years. His mother, Sophie (or Sophia), the daughter of a church-man, had in 1840 married a British army officer, Captain William Fisher, who was serving as aide-de-camp (AdC) to the governor of Ceylon, Sir Robert Wilmot-Horton. Fisher's father had decided to buy a coffee plantation. It was not an auspicious beginning: the coffee market collapsed that year.

Fisher grew up to be a stocky man. His rather bulbous eyes and pouting lips were not characteristics of classic good looks; nevertheless, throughout his life women found him attractive and he learnt how to best play his allure to his advantage.

In 1847, aged just six, Fisher was sent to school in London; he never saw his father again. Whenever Captain William sent him funds (usually meagre), Fisher maintained occasional contact. He applied himself to his studies and to other interests: he enjoyed fishing and shooting, although one day he took a shot at the butler and claimed that he had mistaken the poor man for game.

Fisher was lucky enough to be taken under the wing of the Ceylon gover-nor's wife, Lady Wilmot-Horton, a woman with a handsome fortune. In part, through her acquaintance with one of the last surviving of Nelson's captains, Sir William Parker, Fisher was able to enter the Royal Navy. Fisher was also coincidentally supported in his application by another Nelsonian connection, the Lord High Admiral's niece. At the time a senior officer usually had at his disposal a commission that he could give away how he liked. Parker had two commissions – one he gave to Fisher.

From the grave, Nelson's influence on the younger Fisher lived on. On 12 July 1854, when he was thirteen, his first ship's posting was to HMS *Victory*. Though she was still an active warship (and had been made ready for the Crimea), life on the *Victory* was almost as it had been a half-century before. One of the more colourful surviving traditions was in the turning of the cap-stan, the spoked winch on decks that teams of sailors pushed around to heave in a ship's anchor cable and raise the anchor itself: the rhythm of work was still set to a fiddler's rhythmic tune.

Just how little the Royal Navy had changed by 1854 becomes stark when one looks at the make-up of the seaborne force that was to bombard Sebas-topol: of twenty-seven ships, only six were driven by screw-propulsion; the rest were powered by sail. It was small wonder that gunnery had advanced so little. Indeed, the bombarding force came off badly, with two of its ships being badly damaged and 340 sailors dead.

After a short stay on *Victory*, Fisher transferred to *Calcutta* on 29 August. She was an 84-gun ship of the line, so-called because designed to fight in the line of battle (the 'line of battle ship' is the origin of the term 'battleship'). Im-mediately, the teenage Fisher made his mark by the manner of his arrival.

Maybe not fully aware that the man to whom he was addressing himself was an admiral, he handed the old, gold-braided gentleman before him his letter of introduction with such an air of self-confidence that he was invited to dine that same evening. The following January, Fisher set sail for the Baltic on *Calcutta* but by March 1855 he was already back in Plymouth and on the 2nd joined the 91-gun *Agamemnon*, also a ship of the line that combined steam with sail.

In July 1856 Fisher was made a midshipman, joining a 21-gun corvette, the very next day heading out for China. Her Majesty's Ship bore an auspicious name: *Highflyer*. On the ship, Fisher crossed paths with a man who left a deep impression on him, Captain Charles Shadwell. To the end of his life, Fisher wore without exception the cufflinks gifted to him by the captain. On them were inscribed the Shadwell family crest with the motto '*Loyal à la mort*'. Those cufflinks, and the gift of Shadwell's library of leather-bound books, symbolised the deep bond that was to grow between the two.

In June 1857 Fisher finally saw action, at the Battle of the Peiho Forts in northern China, near the city of Tianjin (once Tientsin). In his own words he was 'armed to the teeth like a Greek brigand, all swords and pistols'.[2] By October the duties of watch officer were his, a sure sign that he was being singled out for greater things. As the year came to an end, Canton fell. This was, needless to say, an extraordinary opening chapter for any sixteen year old.

By 1859 Shadwell's favourite midshipman became the captain's aide-de-camp. It was a posting normally reserved for a more senior officer, so the move was unusual, but little was usual about young Jacky Fisher. He was once again back in the thick of it. When envoys were sent on their way to Tientsin to ratify the treaty ending the Second Opium War, Shadwell led a party ashore through the mudflats to try to capture the Taku Forts that guarded the entrance of the Peiho River. It turned into a rout and four of the seven gunboats were sunk. The badly wounded Shadwell was, unfairly, forced to resign, an easy scapegoat for the press.

The fighting had been fierce. In Fisher's words:

> You sank up to your knees at least every step, and just fancy the slaughter going 500 yards in the face of that fire … right in front of you and on each flank … They had horrid fireballs firing at us when we landed. I saw one poor fellow with his eye and part of his face burnt right out. If a piece struck you, it stuck to you and regularly burnt you away till it was all gone.[3]

Shadwell took care of his protégé. In 1860 when he passed on command to Rear Admiral Sir James Hope he made sure that Fisher was taken in under the new commander. Hope would be his second mentor, a man who would similarly and significantly shape his young protégé's career. He had, as he put it, 'got into such a good berth', that his shipmates were 'very jealous' of him. On his nineteenth birthday, 25 January, Fisher was examined for and awarded his commission as a lieutenant (under the acting rank of mate) on board HMS *Cambrian*.

> I went up on January 25th on board the *Cambrian* before the three captains, and they gave me a regular bounce-out. It took altogether three days and, as I told you last mail, I had the satisfaction of getting a first-class certificate. Well, I came on board the *Chesapeake* and handed in my certificate. After a short time the Admiral [Hope] sent for me and told me he was very pleased to see I had passed such a good examination, and that as a reward for it and on account of old Shadwell's report of me, he should take me as his Flag Mate, and that he would take care to look out for me always.[4]

In March, Fisher was offered a lieutenancy on *Esk*. He turned this down, as *Esk* was not bound for action. Four days later, on the 28th, he received his lieutenancy and instead joined a ship he described a 'horrid old tub', *Furious*. On *Furious*, Fisher obtained his certificates in gunnery and navigation, both first class, with 963 out of a possible 1,000 for navigation – some of the highest marks seen in years. For his efforts he was awarded the Beaufort Testimonial (named after Rear Admiral Sir Francis Beaufort, whose Beaufort Scale became for geographers the accepted measure of wind speed) – a prize for the best results in navigation. By the time he arrived back in Portsmouth a year later in 1861, his commanding officer, Sir W A Bruce was unequivocal in his praise: 'As a sailor, as an officer, a navigator and a gentleman, I cannot praise him too highly'.[5]

As a result, Fisher's commission was also backdated by twelve months, which would make a considerable difference to his seniority in the 'lists' and the extra pay was very welcome. In January 1862 he was appointed to HMS *Excellent* as a gunnery staff officer. The Admiralty had by now started to focus on improving gunnery performance, to which end every gunnery lieutenant had to undertake six months of training at the Royal Naval College. Until he passed he remained only a lieutenant, third class. Not to anyone's surprise, Fisher passed with a first-class certificate.

He was starting to be noticed where it mattered. On a regular visit to the ship, an Admiralty board member was overheard asking whether Fisher was as good a sailor as he clearly was a gunnery officer. Not one to miss an opportunity at self-promotion, Fisher stepped up: 'My Lords, I am Lieutenant Fisher, just as good a seaman as a gunnery man'.[6]

In March 1863 he got the prize that he was after, that of gunnery lieutenant on *Warrior*, one of the most advanced ships in the fleet. Innovative for the age, the 14-knot ship was the world's first iron-hulled seagoing armoured ship. She was well-armed and one of the first in the Royal Navy to have breech-loading guns. Fisher stayed with the ship for over three years.

Born in 1849 in Küstrin in what was then Brandenburg (today Kostrzyn nad Odrą in Poland), son of Rudolf Tirpitz, Alfred was almost a decade younger than the man who would figure so prominently in his later life. Family tradition had it that the origins of the family's name (thought to have been 'Czern von Terpitz') were Silesian and Bohemian, and that their ennoblement had been lost in the passage of the Thirty Years War.* Whatever the truth, Alfred Tirpitz would eventually return 'von' to the family name when he was ennobled by the Kaiser on New Year's Day, 1900.

While Fisher's star was on the rise, Tirpitz did not shine at school, where he had not displayed any of the particular aptitudes that Fisher had. He did not stand out and found study hard, mathematics especially. The story goes that when his teacher complained to his father in a conversation that he lacked intelligence, Tirpitz's attitude – when he found out about it – was one of delight. If the expectations were so low, he figured he wouldn't have to work so hard. When he was fifteen in 1864, his overall grade was ranked *mäßig* (moderate) and his father started genuinely to worry that his son would not make it into university.

Early on in 1865 Tirpitz decided that he had had enough. It was to be either the army or navy, but no more school. Curt von Maltzahn (with whom Tirpitz formed a lifelong friendship) had just joined the navy and this made up Tirpitz's mind. In April, after his father had provided tutors with whom he could work to catch up, Tirpitz was able to enter Prussian military service as a cadet. Rudolf Tirpitz had not, in fact, been that keen on the idea of naval service for his son, but eventually reluctantly agreed. Much to his own surprise, Tirpitz passed the exams, fifth among twenty-four.

A month later he was aboard *Arcona*, based in the recently conquered port of Kiel, captured by Prussia in the war for Schleswig-Holstein against Denmark, and in June, under the command of Captain Otto Batsch, he boarded the *Niobe* training ship purchased from England just three years previously. It speaks to both the quality of the candidates and to the education they received that six of Tirpitz's classmates from the 1865 class on *Niobe* would reach the rank of admiral.[7]

Once at sea Tirpitz visited the newly captured ports of Schleswig-Holstein, continued to the Skagerrak and from there to England. That October of 1865 *Niobe* made the open Atlantic trip in very heavy weather to the Azores. For the young cadet, it was exciting, but very much a baptism of fire. However, while

* In a short but charming meeting in Munich with Dr Wolf von Tirpitz on 31 May 2015, *Skagerrakstag*, he dismissed this rumour, saying that his father, Rudolf, had always found it far-fetched.

the seafaring was gruelling, performance in the primary art, warfare, was un-impressive. In gunnery drills, shooting at a stationary target at 300m (330yds), they only managed two hits in thirty-six shots.

Tirpitz's first visits to Plymouth attest to the admiration he had for the Royal Navy: 'As a sea cadet I soon found from my own experiences that Prussians were still esteemed in England … Our tiny naval-officer corps looked up to the British navy with admiration and our seamen sailed in those days quite as much in English-built ships as in German.'[8] In fact, the nascent Prussian navy relied on the British for guns, dockyard repairs, coaling and supplies. None of these could be done in home ports – Germany did not have the resources.

In 1866 *Niobe* continued to Cadiz and on to Lisbon where rumours reached them about the possibility of war between Prussia and Austria. Nervous that she had been spotted in the channel by an Austrian warship, the ship quickly made her way back to Plymouth and thence to Kiel, where it was learnt that the ship they had seen was, in fact, Norwegian. Tirpitz, manning the guns, felt a certain disappointment at having seen no action. When war was declared, he had to report to a new ship, the *Gazelle*. On it he saw no action either but, already a sea cadet, was now promoted to midshipman.†

In his new life he was learning fast and becoming a man. Like Jellicoe, off the Tripoli coast he also nearly lost his life, launching a boat to rescue a fellow sailor who had fallen overboard. He was not a strong swimmer and when his own rescue boat capsized he almost drowned. By the time he was picked up he was unconscious.

At the end of 1866 Tirpitz was appointed watch officer to another Brit-ish-built vessel, the training-ship *Musquito*. In the company of *Niobe* and another, *Rover*, the three ships left for Plymouth. On the trip Tirpitz displayed his navigation skills when he confidently and correctly announced that the nav-igation officer was almost a hundred miles off course. Tirpitz had calculated the ship's correct location to be off Cape Finisterre.

Like Fisher, Tirpitz had also to be thrifty to get by. He discouraged his father from sending his usual 10 marks a month when he could.

Tirpitz continued in his cadet training – in 1867 on *Thetis*, yet another ship bought from the British. It was badly run and a new commander, Lieutenant Commander Eduard von Knorr, was brought on board to clean things up. The captain's wife even made unsuccessful advances on Knorr to try to win him over to the ship's lax ways.

The North German Confederation now included Hamburg and, as a

† This was the war with Austria that ended with the dissolution of the German Confederacy and Prussia's dominance over Austria symbolised by the founding of the North German Confederation.

consequence, had 'the world's third largest merchant marine'.[9] In the new Reichstag, a ten-year programme was approved for the construction of sixteen armoured ships and a host of support vessels. The next year, in August 1868, Tirpitz was able to leave *Thetis* after he had successfully completed his artillery exam. He began two years in Kiel at the naval school, which had itself only just been opened two years previously by Prince Adalbert. The routine was packed: twenty-two lectures a week, each of them ninety minutes long. Tirpitz was also now starting to get more confident as his work improved. He passed eighth out of forty-six; two of the eight were already sub lieutenants.

Fisher was promoted to the rank of commander on 2 August 1869, aged thirty-two. In November he was given command of *Donegal*, commissioned on the 25th. A year later, in June 1870 he was transferred to *Ocean*, the flagship of Vice Admiral Sir Henry Kellett, Commander-in-Chief, China.

The young German navy was starting to grow and now possessed three armoured frigates, among which was *König Wilhelm*. At 9,800 tons she was, on paper at least, the world's most powerful warship. On this vessel Sub Lieutenant Tirpitz reported, in May 1870, as watch officer: she had a crew of 750 sailors and mounted eighteen 24cm and five 21cm guns, but she was not well-maintained and the ship that could normally easily manage 14 knots was reduced to 10 knots because of the drag created by the heavy mass of barnacles (60 tons of them) that she was carrying on the hull.

A year later, in May 1871 Tirpitz was able to get off *König Wilhelm* and join a small gunboat, *Blitz*, as first officer. It turned out to be a comfortable summer. The boat was used as a kind of chauffeur service by Prince Friedrich-Karl, a nephew of Kaiser Wilhelm I, and it gave Tirpitz an important entrée into royal circles. At the end of the year, *Blitz* took up watch duty on the River Elbe. A long season of balls and shooting ensued.

In summer 1871 Rudolf sent Tirpitz a copy of Captain Reinhold Werner's pamphlet, *The German Reich Navy*. It got him thinking about what sort of navy Germany should build and why. Werner had also lobbied for the acquisition of Helgoland, a small but significantly-placed island off the Jade Basin, from the British, an exchange that Fisher later used as an example of British short-sightedness when it came to the emerging German naval threat. Heligoland, as it was known to the British, dominates the approaches to the German Jade Basin and if in British possession during the First World War, while difficult to maintain, it could have been of enormous value.

The minimal role that the new navy played in the Franco-Prussian war – apart from Knorr's actions in the gunboat *Meteor* off Havana and the corvette *Augusta*'s commerce-raiding in the Bay of Biscay – left a deep mark in the minds of many German officers.* The proud traditions of Prussia's military turned the navy's growing sense of inferiority into an open sore.

Aged thirty-two, Tirpitz was promoted to full Leutnant at the end of May 1872. That summer he was ordered into the North Sea to protect German herring boats off the coast of Aberdeen. He could learn first-hand that without sea power even the simple activity of herring fishing could be harassed and impaired by British supremacy on the water. This threat was barely concealed. At the end of the year, Tirpitz was transferred to an armoured frigate *Friedrich Karl* as watch officer. He was captained by the pamphleteer Captain Werner, whose works Rudolf had sent Alfred the previous summer. Tirpitz started to wonder if he was up to the challenge – such thoughts would never have entered Fisher's mind, but Tirpitz often had moments of real doubt and suffered severe depression.

With a corvette (*Elizabeth*) and a gunboat (*Albatross*), Tirpitz was about to embark on a year-and-a-half cruise around South America, Japan and the Caribbean on debt-collection assistance, a typical role in colonial navies. With him was Curt Maltzahn – seven years previously his inspiration to enter the navy – who now served under him.

When *Friedrich Karl* had already sailed across the Atlantic, she was ordered back. The abdication in 1873 of the King of Spain, Amedeo, had put the property and lives of German nationals there at risk, and *Friedrich Karl* was to 'fly the flag' for the young Germany. She even landed a substantial shore party of 1,200 German sailors at Cartagena, giving Tirpitz some military experience. Surprisingly, Werner himself ended up in the dog-house: Bismarck accused him of exceeding his orders and he was replaced. When *Friedrich Karl* made her way back to Wilhelmshaven, Werner (who was acquitted of any misconduct) made his report on Tirpitz: 'I only consider him suited for higher positions if he can prove that he fully understands how to be a better subordinate'.[10]

Tirpitz was not one to be silenced by officers senior to him if he felt that his ideas were right. Another officer's conclusions were different, but based on the same observations, Admiral Gustav von Senden foresaw the greatness ahead: 'Tirpitz has too big a head of steam not to be a leader. He is ambitious, not choosy about his means, and of a sanguine disposition … He has never had a superior who could match him.'[11] The rest of the year saw him take a short position on *Musquito*, from which he transferred with the captain and the crew to *Nymphe*, escorting Prince Friedrich-Karl on his tour of Scandinavia.

Tirpitz prepared for his entry to the naval academy. Initially he struggled,

---

* The so-called 'Battle of Havana' was a minor affair but it was one of the very few engagements with the French in which the Prussian navy actually played any part at all. Hence it was played up in Prussia and Knorr was awarded the Iron Cross, 2nd Class, for his part in an action on 9 November 1870 against the French dispatch boat, the *Bouvet*.

but with the notification of his promotion to lieutenant commander in the autumn of 1875 soon gained the confidence needed for success. He was also able to survive financially without his father's subsidy, and started to think of marriage. The next year, 1875, as a battery commander aboard *Hansa*, Tirpitz was able to show off his new skills in full view of Admiral Albrecht von Stosch, despite being momentarily blinded in one eye following an accident.

Von Stosch was one of the two most important men who shaped the new German navy. He started the young navy's modernisation right after the Franco-Prussian war, in 1872 creating the new navy academy in Kiel and founding two new corps more reflective of the times: the Machine Engineer Corps and the Torpedo Engineer Corps. Before he left office in 1873 he had embarked the navy on a ten-year building programme that his successor, Leo von Caprivi, took over. Caprivi, a distant relative of Rudolf Tirpitz, was also an army man. His hand was evident in the furtherance of the navy's torpedo arm, with the introduction of the first torpedo division in Wilhelmshaven in October 1897 and the second in Kiel. He is also credited with far-sightedness in launching the first work on the Kiel Canal, completed ten years later, in 1895, although the story of the Kiel Canal has been somewhat mythologised. Commercial pressure led to its rebuilding and re-routing, not innovative naval planning. In Mürwik, the site of today's German navy's officer training school, the busts of Stosch and Caprivi stand side by side with Hipper and Scheer. But not Tirpitz: his later life caused his fall in favour.

In May 1876 Tirpitz took up a position in Wilhelmshaven as battery officer on the frigate *Kronprinz*. He did not like the town, describing it as 'desolate', but he did not, at least, compromise his performance. His squadron commander, Batsch, now a rear admiral, noted his proficiency and used his influence to get Tirpitz transferred to the *Kaiser*, an 8,900-ton, English-built ironclad frigate. Years later, when he was at the Oberkommando in Berlin, he again served under its commander, Max von Goltz.

Tirpitz was now about to initiate a critical phase in his career, reporting to Berlin to the Torpedo Experimental Commission. It had been set up a few years earlier by Admiral Stosch under Commander Alexander von Monts with a hundred of the newly designed torpedoes purchased from the English inventor, Robert Whitehead, and his armaments company, the Firma Stabilimento Tecnico in Fiume, Italy. Tirpitz was in charge of warheads and detonators.

Unlike Fisher, at this early stage Tirpitz was not convinced by the new weapon. The 'whole torpedo story seems to me to more and more regrettable'.[12] Nevertheless, he became adept with the weapon and soon concluded that 'compared to the gun it is a very cheap means of destruction'. As torpedo officer on *Zieten*, he scored three direct hits on a stationary target at a (what seems now ludicrously short) range of 730m (800yds). Stosch called Tirpitz's after-action report 'exemplary'.

Before Fisher was appointed to the ironclad *Hercules* in January 1877, his career had run in parallel with that of Tirpitz. He had been transferred in 1872 to head of torpedo instruction on *Excellent*, which was the navy's gunnery school. Even though the technology was young and not yet widely trusted, it gave Fisher, like Tirpitz, the opportunity to develop a name for himself as an expert in what he considered to be one of the most potentially important technological developments of his day. Four years later, in 1876 he wrote, 'the issue of the next naval war will chiefly depend on the use that is made of the torpedo, not only in naval warfare but for the purposes of blockade'.[13] Tirpitz had been somewhat more sceptical but became as strong a convert to the new weapon as Fisher. In some ways he went further, putting as much, if not more, emphasis on the development of the launch platform, the torpedo boat. It was looked down on by the more establishment officers, but its affordability as a weapons system was much of its appeal to Tirpitz.

The new weapon, which by Jutland could hit targets at 14,000m (15,300yds), was still in its infancy and had teething problems. With a single screw it tended to run in a curve and had a tendency to sink. No one had thought that the lower salinity levels compared to the Fiume testing waters would make a difference, but they did, considerably lowering torpedo buoyancy. Tirpitz started to think about the design of the actual boats from which this new weapon would be launched, and about how to make them smaller, cheaper and faster to build.

Stosch was pleased with how Tirpitz was systematically developing the torpedo's potential. When Tirpitz succeeded in getting Whitehead in 1878 to take back a number of the earlier defective units, Stosch promoted him to director of torpedo development on *Zieten*. His previous commanding officer, Eduard von Heusner, was sent to the Admiralstab in Berlin to be head of the torpedo department. The twenty-nine-year-old Tirpitz felt fortunate to be 'uninterruptedly in positions of independence', and he recognised that the weapon would be significant only after years of focused development.

Careers at mid-point

Fisher now started a period of being moved from posting to posting. He was appointed to *Hercules* in January 1877 where he served until March. On the 2nd he took up the important position of flag captain to Vice Admiral Sir Astley Cooper Key, Commander-in-Chief, North America and the West Indies, on the armoured battleship *Bellerophon*. It was a prestigious command. Two new commands followed in 1878, first to *Hercules* and then to *Valorous*. The moves continued into 1879. Fisher went for a short time to the *Pallas*, where his attention was focused on committee work revising a gunnery manual, until he took up another command on *Northampton* at the end of September. The training regimen that he gave his men was hard. In fact, Fisher was notorious. It is said that in ten days he made his crew practise torpedo runs 150 times 'when the whole navy had only done 200 in a year'.[14]

Around the same time, midsummer 1880, Tirpitz participated in the first public torpedo demonstration in Germany. He was able to sink an old target vessel at 200m (220yds) with two hits. It was a promising start in the development of the new weapon. Based on his success, Stosch decided immediately to equip some large battleships with steam launches. The following day Tirpitz hit the *Barbarossa* amidships at 400m from a speeding boat; it was also the first hit from an underwater tube.

It was clear that this performance by Tirpitz, as Stosch's protégé, had made his boss look good in front of Prince Heinrich of Prussia, the Kaiser's brother and the crown prince. Through his superior Graf Schack von Wittenau, Stosch sent Tirpitz his congratulations: 'To lead and carry out a military manoeuvre with such skill as you have is excellent'.[15]

Breaking the Whitehead monopoly was important for Tirpitz and it reflected in his later dealings with contractors. He awarded a contract to Schwarzkopf to develop a German torpedo at its depot in Friedrichsort. It would be cheaper, faster and longer-ranged than Whitehead's weapon.

Back in England, Fisher took up command of *Duke of Wellington* in January 1881 before transferring to the battleship *Inflexible*, newly commissioned in July. The ship, seven years in the making, was one of the largest gunned and most heavily armoured in the Navy. But she was also an anomaly. Her muzzle-loading guns were slow and her sails rarely used. Even though she had such innovations as electrical lighting and torpedo tubes, the internal design of the ship was a nightmare – so maze-like that crew regularly became disorientated and lost. Fisher came up with the novel idea of painting the many decks and areas of the ship in different colours, with direction arrows helping guide the sailors running around in confusion below.

During this time, *Inflexible* was in the Mediterranean. Fisher had an opportunity to meet Queen Victoria when she visited Menton. With her was a grandson, Prince Heinrich. The Queen did not like the Navy and made no bones about it – the Admiralty had stupidly refused to make Prince Albert an Admiral of the Fleet and the insult stuck – until she met Fisher. As was his way with women, Fisher was able to win her over with devotion and flattery.

During the siege of Alexandria in July 1882, Fisher took command of a landing party and eventually ended up being billeted in the Khedive's palace, the Ras-el-Tin. A British force had been sent to protect its financial interests against a populist rising aimed at removing the Khedive, whose ties to the British and French were resented. Many thought that Seymour, the commanding admiral, had overplayed the threat, but the unilateral action (the French refused to participate and moved its fleet to Port Said) pushed Britain into a military occupation which lasted until 1936. Needing reconnaissance information, Fisher designed a rather unusual solution: armour-plated protection mounted on a train. Its originality and effectiveness won Fisher press exposure in Britain and catapulted him into the public eye. But he became badly ill. His bouts of malaria would give his face a curious hue: his skin toned yellow, tinted with the effects of the fever. He was not well-off and could not afford to go home at his own expense. In the end, none other than the First Lord of the Admiralty, Lord Northbrook, intervened: 'we can get many *Inflexibles*, but only one Jack Fisher'.

In September the same year – 1881 – Tirpitz was promoted to commander. The promotion had been long awaited, but it was made immediately on the spot after he had successfully torpedoed *Elbe* at 400m. From *Blücher*, Tirpitz had carried out the demonstration in front of *Hohenzollern*, Wilhelm's royal yacht. As a result, the 1883 construction plans were changed to include ten large and twelve small torpedo boats, a number that Tirpitz himself would never have recommended for the same class construction. He felt that more testing was needed, but it was a sign of a growing confidence in this new weapon's platform.

Early in 1883 Jacky Fisher was invited to the Queen's private residence, Osborne House in the Isle of Wight, a house that she and Prince Albert adored, a place where she could learn languages, and he could paint. This was a mark of how far Fisher had come. The Queen made allowances for Fisher, even permitting him to wear trousers (instead of the normally mandatory tights) for dancing, which he did with vigour and barely restrained enjoyment. Even his often slightly risqué jokes were appreciated by the sovereign: 'With royalty he always had a marvellous talent for taking light-hearted banter to the very edge of that delicate boundary between respect and disrespect'.[16] When the French visited Portsmouth in 1891 he told the Queen, concerned about the need to bolster friendship with the old enemy, 'Yes, Your Majesty. I have arranged to kiss the French admiral on both cheeks!' – at which point the Queen roared with laughter. In April he took up the command of *Excellent*, which he held for two years.

In March 1883 Stosch offered the Kaiser his resignation. His successor was not, as many expected it to be, Admiral Batsch. It was another military man, Leo von Caprivi. Many in the German navy were upset at not having one of their own, but for Tirpitz it was a stroke of good luck. He overtly referred to the new navy head as 'Uncle Leo', as the count was, in fact, a distant relation of his father's, but that is where the relationship between the two men ended, even if Caprivi was a great supporter of the torpedo and Tirpitz's natural ally. Caprivi's ideas were very much opposed to those of Tirpitz. Because of the construction time needed for the larger ships, he pushed all his efforts into smaller-ship development, away from the big-gun fleet. Tirpitz now had a superior who believed that the torpedo boat was almost a substitute for larger capital ships: Caprivi favoured a fleet for coastal de-fence with torpedo boats, rather than one that could take the battle to the enemy. He assumed that the enemy would come to him at a time of his choosing.

At the end of 1884 Tirpitz married Marie Auguste Lipke, the daughter of the liberal politician Gustav Lipke; they were to have four children. Gustav helped the couple substantially, paying for a house in Kiel. Tirpitz's admiration for the English and everything English, meanwhile, ran deep. He was fluent in English, read the English papers daily and felt it important that his two daughters, Ilse and Marie, be educated at Cheltenham Ladies' College.

Fisher had married twenty years earlier, taking as his wife a Portsmouth girl, Frances Broughton, daughter of the Reverend Thomas Delves Broughton. Both Tirpitz and Fisher were self-made men and had waited till they felt financially confident enough to take on heavier responsibilities, but both marriages were happy ones (Fisher stayed together with Frances till her death in 1918).

In Sankt Blasien, in the country house that he built on land that was given by the Grand Duke of Baden, Tirpitz spent much of his time thinking about the right type of boat to construct, and for this he could choose from different suppliers in Britain and in Germany. He was, like Fisher, never in great health but, unlike Fisher, was seen by his family as a hypochondriac. He suffered from a bad back, rheumatism and problems with his lungs.

Contracts were awarded to British and German shipbuilders and compar-ative trials were held in September with the British firms of Thornycroft and Yarrow as well as with Weser, Vulkan and Schichau.* The weather was appall-ing, but for Tirpitz this was a plus – more like battle conditions. Tirpitz himself took command of one of the damaged Schichau boats that had a bent propel-ler, eventually bringing her to safety in Danish waters. But he was so dirty and shabby after the sea trials that he and the torpedo boat's commander, Lieutenant August von Heeringen, were initially refused hotel rooms. Tirpitz was thence-forth known as 'der Kossackenhetmann', the Cossack chief.

In June 1885 Fisher's command of the Excellent came to an end. Again, his health was bad and he took the time off to visit the spas in Marienbad. In June and July he briefly commanded Minotaur in the Baltic, but spent the rest of the year back on Excellent and did not to return to a seagoing command for another dozen years.

---

* German torpedo boats were designated according to the yard where they were built. Hence the 'S' class was Schichau, 'B' class Blohm, und Voss, 'G' class, Germania, and 'V' class, Vulkan.

Tirpitz's exploits at sea with the torpedo boats had placed him centre stage. He went to Berlin to take over the Admiralstab posting as head of the torpedo department. He formalised the position of the torpedo boats as being best to operate on a divisional basis, unattached to individual large ships.

In those years the design of torpedo boats – and not only Germany's – started to evolve and a lot of effort went into looking at variants. Torpedo-boat tonnage ranged between 98 and 113 tons; speed was fixed at around 20 knots. Tubes were mounted at deck level and above water. Schichau also built a larger, 300-ton vessel that could accommodate the extra staff needed to lead a flotilla, in line with Tirpitz's idea of independent torpedo flotillas.

At the end of 1886 Fisher moved into the post of Director of Naval Ordnance (DNO), a position in which, like John Jellicoe years later, he was responsible for the Navy's guns and ordnance (even though gun manufacture was still under the control of the War Office and not yet independently controlled by the Royal Navy). The position put him in close contact with industry and the large armaments companies, so it was not unnatural that he formed a friendship with Josiah Vavasseur of the Armstrong company. Later his only son Cecil was adopted by Vavasseur, and his stately home, Kilverstone Hall, passed into the Fisher family as the seat and title. Fisher's proximity to the Queen, meanwhile, ended in his being appointed the sovereign's AdC in 1887 and a rear admiral that August.

The year 1888 started well for Tirpitz. His chief, Caprivi, asked for views on tactics from his senior officers. As usual, Tirpitz's twenty-page response was well-documented, well-argued and well-presented; Tirpitz impressed Caprivi. In November he reached the rank of Kapitän zur See, but he was worried about the effects of Wilhelm's bureaucracy changes on the unified command, and therefore on the future of the torpedo boat.

British naval policy at this point was based on the assumption that the British would face either the French or the Russians as adversaries, or a combination. This led to the adoption of the two-power standard, a battle-fleet weight that would equal that of the next two strongest naval powers together. What had been informal was now written into policy in the Naval Defence Act of 1889.

While Tirpitz was eventually unsuccessful in preventing a split – as was the case for the rest of the navy – between the command and administrative functions of the torpedo units, the torpedo 'school' would still come to be strongly represented later in the war years. Three High Seas Fleet commanders – Ingenohl, Scheer and Hipper – and five chiefs of the Admiralty staff – von Büchsel, Fischer, von Heeringen, von Pohl and Bachmann – were from the ranks of the famed 'sea-cossacks', the nickname by which German torpedo men came to be known. In April, Tirpitz took command of an armoured frigate,

Preußen. The 7,700-ton vessel had been built sixteen years earlier, but was re-fitted in 1885 with torpedo tubes and became part of the 2nd Division of the so-called manoeuvre fleet (a self-contained unit that can operate freely without having an impact on other units) under the command of Rear Admiral Frie-drich Hollmann, later to be one of his great critics.

Once more at sea on board *Preußen*, Tirpitz accompanied the Kaiser to Greece and Turkey, and on his return took command of an armoured corvette, the 7,800-ton *Württemberg* in 1890. While the junior officers took to him be-cause he always included them in tactical discussion, he was not considered a good sea captain and was referred to as '*ein schlechter Fahrer*', a bad helmsman.

Caprivi had thought to put Tirpitz in charge of dock work, to get him to learn more about construction. Instead, in the summer he gave him a posting in the Baltic Station as chief of staff to Vice Admiral von Knorr, 'Red Eduard' (as was he fondly known because of his proneness to blush), the hero of Havana in 1870. Knorr had the greatest respect for Tirpitz, but later commented that Tirpitz had used this posting merely to 'gather things he could then use for later opportunities'.[17]

In May 1891 Fisher took up the important post of admiral superintendent of Portsmouth dockyards. The roles of Fisher and Tirpitz almost overlapped. Fif-teen years later the skills and experience that Fisher gained here would strongly influence the record construction of *Dreadnought*. Here, he succeeded in cut-ting 30 per cent off the three-year construction time of *Royal Sovereign*. He used every trick in the book, including memorising the name of at least one worker in a team, so that it would seem that he knew many workers by name when he pulled the name out of the air to compliment the unsuspecting man. His atti-tude was that anything could be achieved if one just set one's mind to it: 'When you are told a thing is impossible, that there are insuperable objections, then is the time to fight like the devil'.

Tirpitz used his time thinking about policy issues in the navy. He wrote three papers, one arguing for a strong Oberkommando, another on the consid-erations for the purpose and design of the navy, and a third on fleet organisation and manning.[18] It was more than likely that these papers directly influenced the choice to put him into the chief of staff role at the Oberkommando.

After leaving the Portsmouth posting, Fisher moved to the Admiralty in 1892 as the Controller of the Navy (Third Sea Lord on the Admiralty Board). In this position he was responsible for the ships and equipment of the Navy, and for the design, building and repair of the great ships of the fleet. The British Ad-miralty was a curious institution. It was, in fact, a board, both a civil (political) and professional institution designed to run the Royal Navy. At the time of Jut-land, the professional naval group was headed by the First Sea Lord (1SL) who worked with a group of three other Sea Lords. Each had a specific role: the 1SL was the operational head of the Navy; 2SL was responsible for personnel; 3SL for warship design and construction and known as the Controller; and 4SL for logistics – supply, transport and warehousing. A secretariat was made up of two further admirals. The political head, appointed by the ruling government, took the title of First Lord of the Admiralty and was himself supported by a junior Member of Parliament and a naval assistant.*

Fisher championed the development of what he called the 'destroyer', the torpedo-boat destroyer. When the leading torpedo-boat builders Yarrow and Thornycroft approached him to get his backing to develop more powerful boats to counter French designs, Fisher not only approved the idea but also took the challenge to other builders. He tried to have water-tube boilers introduced into new designs.

With these kinds of action Fisher also made enemies. He was bound to – he was challenging the comfortable, uncompetitive relationship that the Navy had always had with its suppliers. He wanted efficiency, competition and value for money. He bulldozed through what he saw as waste and corruption to get his way. His work and proximity to the Queen also won him royal recognition, and some protection. He became a Knight Commander of the Order of the Bath.

In 1892 Tirpitz took up the position of chief of staff in the Oberkommando, moving his family to Berlin for the start of the year.[19] In the OK, as it was known, he started to make his views on the importance of naval strength very clear. While Caprivi had been pushing for war readiness Tirpitz focused on the bigger picture. Naval strength meant, for him, a longer vision requiring patience and cunning. His arrival was felt immediately. Fleet exercises reduced the gaps between ships, to concentrate fire; lights were dimmed so that a little more of the disorientation of a night action could be felt. As expected, complaints abounded. Serious thinking about how to fight – whether at close quarters or in a longer-range artillery duel – started to be the order of the day. For Tirpitz, Germany's future strength as a nation would be dictated by its industry, access to raw materials, colonial acquisitions and military might, naval especially.

> A state which has oceanic, or – an equivalent term – world, interests must be able to uphold them and make its power felt beyond its own territorial waters. National world commerce, world industry, and to a certain extent fishing on

---

* My grandfather, Sir John Jellicoe, became First Sea Lord at the end of 1917 while his son, George, my father, was – if I am not mistaken – the *last* First Lord of the Admiralty in October 1963. The writer, Graham Greene was closely related to Sir William Graham Greene who, at Jutland, was Secretary of the Admiralty. His granddaughter is my neighbour. Another friend who lives nearby in Switzerland is a close relation of Sir Edward Carson, who was First Lord of the Admiralty when my grandfather was 1SL. Small world.

the high seas, world intercourse and colonies are impossible without a fleet capable of taking the offensive. The conflicts of interests between nations, the lack of confidence felt by capital and the business world will either destroy these expressions of the vitality of a state, or prevent them from taking form, if they are not supported by national power on the seas, and therefore beyond our waters. Herein lies by far the most important purpose of the fleet.[20]

In the design of the *Flottenbauprogramm* (fleet construction programme), Tirpitz faced a choice between a fast cruiser force and a slower, more heavily armed battleship configuration. At best, the cruiser force would be able only to suggest the idea of German power around the world. It would never ultimately be able to demonstrate it.

By 1894 Tirpitz's position on the issue had been concretely formed. In a paper, 'General Considerations in the Determination of Our Fleet by Vessel Class and Vessel Types', he rejected the cruiser programme. It would have no impact on the decisive battle that, in his mind, would take place in the North Sea. By reducing the number of cruisers and favouring more heavily armoured battleship construction, Tirpitz was clearly building a navy that would be able to be successful in 'its most difficult task', that of taking on a new adversary in the North Sea, and winning. At this point he did not name the British but it was clear about whom he was talking.

Winning for Tirpitz did not necessarily mean what it later came to be in the minds of the British public – far from it. If the sensitive ratio of superiority could be shifted just far enough, British supremacy was under threat through the 'risk' of alliance. British thinking was based on the defeat of a threat from the combined forces of the next two naval powers (the two-power standard). However, it was Germany's potential combination with another naval power, a third-rate one, that could now pose a formidable threat to the British. This was the basis of Tirpitz's 'risk theory': the idea that, in challenging Germany, Britain would be going out on a huge limb. Even if Britain managed to defeat Germany, enough damage would have been suffered by its fleet, he believed, that the British Navy's oceanic dominance would be seriously jeopardised by the possible entrance of a second, albeit of tertiary importance, naval power on Germany's side.

In the first part of the war at sea, German strategy was very much tied to an eventual fleet meeting, with an emphasis on actions in the North Sea, as well as in the far-flung reaches of the British Empire, thus dispersing Britain's naval forces or trying to catch small, unsupported elements of the British fleet and overwhelm them. Tirpitz was clear that the best form of defence or deterrence would be an offensive role for the German fleet:

Advocates of a defensive fleet proceed from the assumption that the enemy fleet will come to them and that the decision must take place where they wish it. But this is only the case very infrequently. Enemy ships need not stay close to our coasts … but they can stand out to sea far from one's own works. Then our fleet would have only the choice between inactivity, ie more self-annihilation and fighting a battle on the open sea.[21]

These were profoundly prophetic words.

In the *Dienstschrift IX*, a series of writings documenting tactical lessons from fleet exercises and published in 1894, Tirpitz took the opportunity to define the fleet size based on an assumed 30 per cent superiority over whichever would be the largest fleet: the Russian Baltic fleet or the French North Sea fleet. The resulting numbers provided for a seventeen-battleship fleet made up of two squadrons of eight, with a flagship. In support would be six first-class cruisers, twelve third-class cruisers and six torpedo flotillas.

With the replacement of Max Goltz by Eduard Knorr as commanding admiral, things started to go badly for Tirpitz. The two men clashed and eventually Tirpitz was removed from the OK, leaving in September 1895. In November the OK published its 'Draft Plan for the Renewal and Expansion of Fleet Material'. Behind it lay Tirpitz's thinking, and to achieve his 30 per cent margin Knorr wanted to spend around 420 million marks annually between 1896 and 1908, adding twelve more battleships and three armoured cruisers. Kaiser Wilhelm jumped in. He was in favour of battleship construction but would not countenance the loss of second-class cruisers from the programme.

In 1896 Fisher was promoted to vice admiral (Tirpitz had himself been made a rear admiral the year before) and the following year, 1897, was made commander-in-chief of the North America and West Indies Station, a post that he had accepted the previous December. Life was made a little easier as his wife was able to join him. While he was at sea on board his flagship, *Renown*, she stayed at Admiralty House in Bermuda. *Renown* was his first seagoing command since *Inflexible*. Fisher was happy. He had a ship that had all he wanted: the 'lightest big gun and the biggest secondary gun'.[22]

He might have been happy with his ship, but his treatment of junior officers left much to be desired. He had a penchant for publicly humiliating subordinate officers if they slipped up over even the most seemingly trivial of matters. On one occasion he signalled his displeasure to an officer who had forgotten to include in an order that the men should wear their hats for an early-morning review. Fisher made sure that the whole squadron knew about it. He enjoyed the act of humiliating a fellow officer.

Wilhelm II had arrived at a point in his reign when a sea-change in Germany's world standing was necessary. To bring this about he made two important appointments: Prince Bernhard von Bülow as Foreign Secretary and Alfred Tirpitz as Secretary of the Admiralty. Tirpitz's task would be to give Germany the navy that it needed, while Bülow should initially calm the climate around him as his new weapon was being built and, once he had it, pursue the more expansionist foreign policy that Wilhelm had always wanted.

In March Tirpitz was summoned back from Asia and the Kaiser outlined the challenge: 'We have a Navy Bill ready but we need you to put it into operation'.[23] Tirpitz was strong enough to stand up to both the Kaiser and Admiral Wilhelm Karl von Büchsel, saying that their ideas lacked the structure of a policy framework.

Taking over from Friedrich Hollmann, Tirpitz had immediate aims to focus on the British threat and, of course, limit the influence of his old chief, Knorr, at the OK. Hollmann and the Kaiser wanted to build cheaper cruisers that would be more suitable for coastal defence. For those used far away – in China, for example – this made little sense, as Germany did not possess the necessary coaling stations.

In his memoirs Tirpitz declared that the sole purpose of the Bill was 'the strengthening of our political might [and] importance against England'. 'For Germany, the most dangerous enemy at the present time is England. It is also the enemy against which we must urgently require a certain measure of naval force as a political power factor'.[24] His views had an extremely long horizon. Until his fleet was ready he would rely on Bülow's maintaining the peace.

That being the case, the 'fleet must be so constructed', Tirpitz said, 'that it can unfold its greatest military potential between the Heligoland and the Thames'.[25] In Tirpitz's mind the decisive battle of the battleship war – the *Entscheidungsschlacht* – would be in the North Sea where he could field a superiority that Britain could not easily match. His adversary's resources would be always be stretched to the limit while his fleet would be fighting in home waters with few other responsibilities. The fleet that he had to build, therefore, would be made up of 'home-water' ships, for short distances. With the same reasoning, Tirpitz maintained that Germany should not try to match Britain's worldwide strengths by building a cruiser-raider fleet: without strategically located coaling stations, this would be folly.

He had thus decided what the German navy's role should be, where it should fight, and what type of ships it should be composed of. It should inflict just enough damage on the major adversary, the British, that they would face difficulties from either of the next most powerful fleets or a combination of them, and hence the importance of alliance strategy focusing on a partner who possessed a strong navy. This became a key diplomatic consideration of the decade.

Tirpitz went to work with his team with a fury. His leadership was Nelsonian: 'My method of work always had Nelson's "We are a band of brothers" for its motto'. Like Fisher he understood the power of press and public opinion. He saw as vital the need to publicise his ideas and create a groundswell of public opinion during legislative debates in the Reichstag. A special news bureau, a public-relations funnel, was created and a magazine, *Marine-Rundschau*, popularised.[26]

Tirpitz's first Navy Law

On 19 August 1897 Tirpitz presented his new Navy Bill to the Kaiser. His aim was to get the Reichstag to pass a law that would, without its understanding it, limit its power as the years progressed by legally binding it to a pre-determined programme of new construction and ship replacements: 'I needed a Bill that would protect the continuity of the construction of the fleet … it intended to make the Reichstag abandon the need to interfere each year afresh in technical details, as it had hitherto done when every ship had become an "exercise for debates"'.[27]

By defining the expected fleet size in terms of ships, men and active service, and the time in which this was to be reached and the replacement of existing ships (the working life for a battleship was, for example, set at twenty-five years), Tirpitz 'knew that any Reichstag which passed such a law would necessarily tie itself more tightly in moral terms than it ever could have done by any monetary obligations'.[28] But there were other purposes behind the law: to guard against the Kaiser's constant interference as well as that of the navy itself. The Kaiser wanted to build a fleet that would show the flag around the world. He maintained his core belief in the offensive need of such a fleet: 'I believe that the enemy will not come and that we would wait with our fleet while France cuts us off from two-thirds to three-quarters of our imports by blockade in the Channel and off northern England'.[29]

Tirpitz's plan initially foresaw a 1905 fleet of nineteen battleships (including the existing eight smaller coastal defence ships) and forty-six cruisers (eight armoured cruisers, and twelve large and thirty light cruisers). He did not include all the Kaiser's wishes – for example, the medium-class *Hertha* cruisers. The building programme was based on a seven-year period from 1898 to 1905. Eight older battleships would still be operational in 1905, so the construction need was for eleven new ships across a '*Bautempo*' (build rate) of 2:2:1:2:1:1:2 – two ships in years one and two, one in the third, and so on. Tirpitz was able to speed up his building programme by concentrating on fewer classes of ships but, surprisingly, with better protection – as Jonathan Steinberg put it, 'a smaller but more powerfully armed fleet with fewer classes, costing less, more quickly'.

The task was huge: there was no officer corps, little shipyard infrastructure and a yet-to-be-built alliance with industry. To save money, Tirpitz limited ship size (battleships to 11,000 tons, cruisers to 9,000) and men (reduced to 1,100 from an annual intake of 1,700). The limitation in size was also restricted by the shallow-water facilities that Germany had and the existing width of the Kiel Canal. Wherever he could, Tirpitz looked for savings that he could hoard away into projects, such as the expansion of the dockyards in Wilhelmshaven, that would support the longer and larger vision that he had. Additionally, he moved the torpedo boat construction budgets to the regular estimate process and out of the legal framework of the Navy Law, saving 44 million marks. With that, the total budget amounted to 410 million marks, a small increase of 10 million per annum on what Hollmann had proposed.

With the Kaiser's blessing, Tirpitz set up meetings with all the important parties whose support would be needed: Treasury Secretary Thielmann, the Chancellor Hohenlohe, individual Bundesrat members, such as his old benefactor the Duke of Baden, and even the ageing Bismarck, who could wield considerable influence in the background. In the Reichstag the support of Ernst Lieber's Centre Party was critical. Tirpitz agreed to meet the parliamentarian in secret to work out an agreement, even paying for his travel (and a little more) out of departmental funds.

In his relations with the Reichstag, Tirpitz would lean heavily on two men: Commander Eduard Capelle and Commander August von Heeringen. Both were 'torpedo gang' members.[30] Tirpitz at first criticised Capelle for being nothing more than a 'calculator', but later came to see him as 'indispensable' in working with the budgets. Heeringen would head the Nachrichtenabteilung, usually known simply by its initial, N – the 'section for news and parliamentary affairs', in other words Tirpitz's propaganda machine. Parallel to the budget work, von Heeringen published *Die Seeinteressen des deutschen Reiches*, showing how, since 1871, imports had doubled, exports tripled and German merchant shipping increased tenfold.

By March 1898, despite strong opposition from the Conservatives and the strongly anti-imperialist Social Democrats, who were very opposed to the vast amounts of money that these laws represented, the Reichstag accepted Tirpitz's proposals.[31] It accepted, at face value, Tirpitz's proposition that the fleet had 'the function of a protective fleet', since he had put a cap on spending that was designed to put to rest their fears about Wilhelm's 'limitless fleet plans'. On 10 April 1898 the legislation passed into law.

Even if Tirpitz was clear about his battleships, he also clearly understood the role of scouting in the new German navy: 'A battle fleet does not only consist of battleships but requires today, as it did in earlier times, scouting ships and escorts'. For the next decade Tirpitz single-mindedly pursued the same goal; his thinking was tied up in three more naval amendments – known as 'Novelles' – passed in 1906, 1908 and 1912 respectively. Each one followed a period of intense diplomatic tension.

British reactions

In Britain, the passing of this first German Navy Law did not have the effect that Tirpitz feared it might have. British relations nearly broke down again with the French; the British were more concerned about the effect of the law on spurring on Russian and French construction rather than their own.

The British had dealt with one regional threat – with victory in 1898 at the Battle of Omdurman – and another now reared: a French challenge to their claims in the Sudan. Four hundred miles to the south, at Fashoda (now called Kodok), a small force had been spotted, commanded by a Frenchman, Captain Jean-Baptiste Marchand. French plans had been talked about openly for months, so the British were ready and waiting.

With his troops, Marchand had marched northeast across half of Africa, from Brazzaville in the Bay of Guinea to Fashoda, south of Omdurman. The French thus moved eastwards across Africa from Senegal, and the British came south from Omdurman to meet the French threat. The French were interested because they thought that with control of the Upper Nile they would be able to exert pressure on Egypt by leveraging valuable water supplies. The Fashoda crisis bought to the surface the old Anglo-French imperial rivalries. The British even considered responding to the French threat with a bombardment of Brest.

Luckily, Queen Victoria was quite against a war 'for so miserable and small an object', and Lord Salisbury rightly guessed that the French would not go through with their venture. When the British sent forces to intervene (Beatty and his gunboats by water, Kitchener by land), it was enough to convince the French that the British were serious and would take military action; on 11 December they pulled back. For the Kaiser it was a real disappointment. Anything that could split the French and the British apart would give him more room for manoeuvre and eventual expansion. Fisher came up with his own novel contribution to the affair: to rescue Captain Alfred Dreyfus from Devil's Island and bring him back to France to act as a British-placed agent provocateur. It never happened, of course.

With the Americans, by contrast, Britain's relations were good. During the Spanish-American War, begun in 1898 when Cuba struck out for independence from Spain, Fisher frequently hosted his American naval counterparts in Hamilton, Bermuda. Tirpitz was helped by the fact that the French proposed substantial navy budgets at just the moment when the Reichstag debate was starting. The British, from whom he would have anticipated opposition, had their hands full in South Africa with the revolt of the Boers. It had been clear for the Germans that both the 'impotence of Spain and France' was a direct result of 'their naval inferiority'.[32]

At the Hague Convention of 1899, Fisher was sent to press for Britain's interests in the question of naval arms. Few of the leading nations even wanted the convention. It was really the Russians who, having suffered countless military defeats in the Far East, wanted to slow down the arms race. Their military had fallen significantly behind. The Germans wanted no restrictions. They were pushing for expansion, while Britain and France hung between the two, with Fisher declaring that Britain's continued naval supremacy was 'the best security for the peace of the world'.

Tepid British support for a slowdown was self-interested. Sir Edward Grey, Britain's Foreign Minister, was sent an Admiralty memorandum that nicely summed up the British position: 'From the standpoint of pure opportunism ... our present naval position is so good that we might express our adhesion to the principle [of armaments limitation] on the condition that other countries were willing to do likewise'.[33]

Fisher, however, never forgot – and it made an indelible impression on him – the visible militarism that the Germans displayed. His heart was not particularly aligned with the spirit of the conference: 'You might as well talk about humanising hell,' he said.[34] His 'sole object [he said] is peace. What you call my truculence is all for peace.'[35] The thought was illustrated by an example of how he would treat neutral shipping if he thought that an enemy could benefit:

> Some neutral colliers attempt to steam past us into the enemy's waters. If the enemy gets their coal into his bunkers, it may make all the difference in the coming fight. You tell me I must not seize these colliers. I tell you that nothing that you, or any power on earth can say, will stop me from sending them to the bottom.[36]

Fisher was rewarded for Lord Salisbury's decision on sending him to The Hague by being promoted to the Navy's plum posting, Commander-in-Chief of the Mediterranean Fleet. Based in Gibraltar and Malta with his old flagship *Renown*, the command guarded one of the jewels of the empire, the Suez Canal. It was (in David Wragg's words) 'the most important seagoing appointment in the Royal Navy'.

Fisher set about reforming the prestigious but moribund command with his usual gusto, setting up a committee of captains and commanders to tease out new thinking and challenge the traditions. It was very like what Tirpitz or even Hipper would have done. Fisher always put on a show, with the largest and

highest pennant flying. He was a champion of opening up the Navy to the talents of the nation. For him an officer 'who had not stooped to oil [his] fingers'
(in other words worked in the engine room) was useless.[37] 'Knowledge is power,'
he would say, 'When you have been a kitchen maid no one can tell you how to
boil potatoes.' With Lord Selborne, First Lord of the Admiralty, he championed
the cause. Cadets could now enter at twelve, and be thoroughly educated in
naval and general subjects. Engineering and executive officers would train together to form a cohesive social unit. The challenges to social relations between
decks that Fisher faced, the German navy faced in spades.

The development of the torpedo, seen as the weapon of the underdog, now
started to have an impact on gunnery. Ranges started to extend to 5,000yds
(4,600m). Fisher trained his people relentlessly. Lord Hankey described how
it went:

> It is difficult for anyone who had not lived under the previous regime to
> realise what a change Fisher brought about in the Mediterranean Fleet ...
> Before his arrival, the topics and arguments of the officers' messes ... were
> mainly confined to such matters as the cleaning of paint and brass work ...
> These were forgotten and replaced by incessant controversies on tactics,
> strategy, gunnery, torpedo warfare, blockade, etc. It was a veritable renaissance
> and affected every officer in the navy.[38]

Admiral Lord Charles Beresford, Fisher's most aggressive critic in later
years, said that in being around him he had 'learnt more in the last week than
in the last forty years'.

Tirpitz's second Navy Law

On the back of the first Navy Law's success, Tirpitz was promoted to rear admiral in mid May 1899. The previous November, Tirpitz had already been
thinking of a *Novelle* and had raised the idea with the Kaiser. Nevertheless, Tirpitz always wished to proceed with great care, finding alliances and feeling out
potential adversaries.

Wilhelm let the cat out of the bag a year later in a speech in Hamburg at the
launch of *Karl der Große* ('We bitterly need a strong German fleet').[39] Tirpitz
was dumbfounded. Because the second Navy Law would bring about a really
significant acceleration of the German fleet-building programme, he was trying
to fly very low under the radar. The Kaiser's words strongly hinted at what Tirpitz wanted to hide. Only because the British were so heavily engaged in South
Africa did Tirpitz maintain the charade.

That, along with Spanish America, helped him. South Africa gave
him the emotional charge that was needed to rouse public opinion. The

Spanish-American War showed that German ships would be under-armed; an increase in costly armour protection was needed to make sure that if ships were built they would be strong enough to achieve the objectives set for them.

The Boer War brought German antagonisms with the British to the surface. As early as January 1896 Wilhelm had made his position clear. His open support for the 'enemies of my enemy' became even clearer when he congratulated President Paul Kruger on the defeat of Leander Starr Jameson's British-backed raid on the Transvaal of 1895/6. The British reacted immediately and sent a flying squadron down to the Cape. Wilhelm yearned to be able to do this himself and now understood that he could never act like a great power without a navy to back him up. He told a British visitor at the time: 'I realised that unless I had a navy sufficiently strong that even you would have to think a little bit before you told me to "Go to hell out of it" my commerce would not progress as I wanted it to, and so I determined to build a navy which would at least command respect'.[40]

After the first Navy Law, private enterprise started to lobby more heavily, seeing a goldmine down the road. Krupp, who had himself been asked by Tirpitz to support him, sponsored the German Navy League (*Deutscher Flottenverein*), helping Viktor Schweinburg, editor of Krupp's newspaper, the *Berliner Neuesten Nachrichten*, to found the Flottenverein, where its clear commercial interests could find a voice.[41] Schweinberg expressed its purposes to be:

> the arousing, cherishing, and strengthening in the German people of an understanding for and interest in the meaning and purpose of the navy ...
> The Navy League considers a strong German navy a necessity, especially for securing the coasts of Germany against the danger of war, for maintaining Germany's position among the world powers, for protecting the general interests and commercial relations of Germany, as well as the honour and security of her citizens engaged in business abroad.[42]

Tirpitz joined the Flottenverein (and officers and naval staff were encouraged to do so), but always maintained a tense oversight, worrying that its activities could upset his carefully laid manoeuvres – his 'enthusiasm waned when he felt that it pushed his agenda to the detriment of his own nuanced approach'.[43] Membership, the basis for the subscription to its newspaper, *Die Flotte*, started to grow slowly at first, then by leaps and bounds, stimulated by overseas crises and Anglo-German tension. There were a few thousand in 1898, 130,000 in mid 1899, 250,000 in early 1900 and almost a million by 1906.[44] The company even published the original 'nothing book': it was called *What Parliament Has Done for the Navy* and was full of blank pages.

Events in South Africa continued to help create the right atmosphere for Tirpitz's and the Kaiser's plans. In the first month of the new year of 1900 the British stopped and searched three steamers, suspecting that they were carrying supplies to the Boer forces. German public opinion was outraged. Tirpitz got all that he needed from this growing Anglophobia to put a second Navy Bill on the table: 'Now we have the wind we need to blow our ship into port; the Navy Law will pass'.

On 12 June 1900 the second Navy Law did so, without much debate. A parliamentary commission recommended that rather than pass this legislation as a *Novelle*, the old 1898 law should be repealed and this new version take its place. On the day that the *Novelle* became law Wilhelm raised Tirpitz to the nobility in recognition for the successful passage of the laws.

The new law aimed at doubling the fleet size – from nineteen to thirty-eight battleships, and to twenty armoured cruisers and thirty-eight light cruisers – by 1917. There would be two flagships, and four battle squadrons each with eight battleships, with a further four in reserve to be built over seventeen years. The cost was huge: 1,306 million marks (up from 410 million) or 81.6 million marks a year (up from 58.6 million). The planning was considerably more far-seeing and more dangerous than that allowed by the first law.

The German legislation did not go unnoticed in Britain. Lord Selborne was alarmed:

> The naval policy of Germany is definite and persistent. The Emperor seems determined that the power of Germany shall be used all over the world to push German commerce, possessions and interests. Of necessity it follows that German naval strength must be raised so as to compare more advantageously than at present with ours. The result of this policy will be to place Germany in a commanding position if ever we find ourselves at war with France and Russia ... Naval officers who have seen much of the German navy lately are all agreed that it is as good as can be.[45]

Fisher finally attained the rank of full admiral in November 1901. He constantly pressured the Admiralty for more resources: after the course of Tirpitz's second Navy Law, the Royal Navy was more and more of the opinion that the real future enemy would be Germany, not France or Russia.

In the middle of 1902 Fisher went back to the Admiralty as Second Sea Lord. Like Grand Admiral Alfred von Tirpitz, Fisher was concerned to integrate the new officer branches, specifically engineering officers, into the service. He started by including engineering cadets into the curriculum. While the Admiralty initially resisted Fisher's idea, it eventually came around. Cadet training was extended from two to four years. New quarters were established at Osborne for the fuller ranks.

While the British Cabinet still argued over who would be the enemy, Lord Selborne was still convinced of his reading of German intentions. In October he was unequivocal:

The more the composition of the new German fleet is examined, the clearer it becomes that it is designed for a possible conflict with the British fleet. It cannot be designed for the purpose of playing a leading part in a future war between Germany and France and Russia. The issue of such a war can only be decided by armies on land, and the great naval expenditure on which Germany has embarked involves deliberate diminution of the military strength which Germany might otherwise have attained in relation to France and Russia.[46]

The British now referred increasingly to the two-power standard: their benchmark for fleet strength was to be as powerful as the next two foreign fleets combined. They added that it was desirable to have at least a 10 per cent (or six-battleship) advantage over the second-nation threat. Concerned to restore more weight to the European and Mediterranean theatres, Britain signed an alliance with the Japanese in 1902, potentially releasing ships from the Far East, and started to work hard at cementing relations with the French.

Tirpitz went to the United States for the third and last time in February and March 1902, accompanying Prince Heinrich. Along with him were two officers of the torpedo gang: Captain Georg Alexander von Müller, who worked in the Marinekabinett, and Lieutenant Commander Adolf von Trotha, from the Reichsmarineamt's central department.

Fisher went back to Portsmouth in 1903. This time *Victory* became his flagship, in his new role of Commander-in-Chief, Portsmouth. At the end of October 1904, he took up the supreme command of the Navy as First Sea Lord. His arrival brought a whirlwind of reform and drastic, but much-needed, measures. He had prepared for the post and while he had no particular love for the French he was convinced that it was from Germany that danger came.

Tirpitz did not want to act in ways that would underline the fact. When in June 1904 Edward VII visited Germany for Kiel Week – the Kaiser's attempt at mimicking his grandmother's rather grander affair at Cowes – Tirpitz was visibly upset with Wilhelm for putting on for the occasion such an ostentatious display of German naval power. It was unnecessarily provocative.

Tirpitz and Fisher were now effectively 'head to head'.

The Fisher reforms
In December, less than two months after arriving in Whitehall, Fisher initiated the most fundamental change in the distribution of British fleets since the Napoleonic Wars. Over the previous hundred years, the political alliances and

structure of Europe had changed dramatically, but the Royal Navy had not kept pace. For Fisher, the threat had decisively moved north, from the Mediterranean to the North Sea. The old Channel Fleet was renamed the Atlantic Fleet and moved to Gibraltar, from where it could steam northeast to reinforce the North Sea or to the southeast and the Mediterranean. The old Home Fleet was renamed the Channel Fleet and strengthened with ten battleships and support vessels. Fisher's point was that a defeat in the North Sea would be catastrophic, in foreign waters a mere setback.

To crew the new forces, Fisher cut drastically. Ninety ships were paid off and a further sixty-four put into reserve, at a stroke of the pen. They were, in Fisher's words, 'too weak to fight and too slow to run away'. The cuts and redeployments were unpopular within the service, Fisher becoming a kind of magnet of antagonism for Lord Beresford – Beresford continued to hold the threat of a Franco-Russian naval alliance a higher danger than the one emerging to the north. He pushed for joint Army–Navy planning. The army was, he said, 'a projectile to be fired by the navy. The navy embarks it and lands it where it can do most mischief! … We should be employing ourselves in joint naval and military manoeuvres.'

Fisher was so perturbed about the growing threat of the German navy that he now started to recommend a 'Copenhagen' strategy of attacking the holed-up fleet in a pre-emptive strike. The King said that he was mad to think in such terms. At a diplomatic level the British were, at the same time, able to put a second alliance cornerstone into place: the Entente Cordiale between Britain and France was signed on 8 April 1904.

Patrick Kelly points out that Tirpitz's refusal to upset the apple-cart by insisting on not sending too large a fleet contingent to China during the Boxer Wars, or being more forceful about German rights to Chinese port access, was paradoxical. But Tirpitz did not want to allow premature grandstanding to get in the way. He was also opposed to a possible Russian alliance in 1904; in a naval war the Russians would contribute little to counter the British threat. This had been amply demonstrated in the Russo-Japanese War, which broke out in February 1904.

In February 1905 an Admiralty Civil Lord, Arthur Lee, echoed Fisher's private threats but did so publicly, declaring that Britain should 'get its blow in first, before the other side had time even to read in the papers that war had been declared'.[47] The comment did not make that much of an impact in Britain but it did cause waves of concern in Germany.

Now Wilhelm reacted. He decided to use the colonial status of Morocco as a means of raising tensions between France and Britain, whose relationship was so dramatically and charismatically repaired only the previous year by Edward VII's visit to Paris. The Kaiser visited Tangier in March 1905 to show his support for the Sultan, Abdelaziz, and his quest for independence. When Abdelaziz rejected French efforts to seek a compromise with reform, Wilhelm put forward the idea of a German-sponsored conference that the French Foreign Minister, Théophile Delcassé, rejected, in turn causing Germany's Chancellor, Bernhard von Bülow, to threaten war over the issue. Even as the French called up their reserves, they caved in and agreed to attend an international conference. Edward VII called it 'the most mischievous and uncalled-for event which the German Emperor has ever been engaged in since he came to the throne'.[48] The Kaiser's behaviour only reinforced the feeling that the real enemy was not the traditional one directly across the channel. It was Germany.

In September Fisher was promoted to Admiral of the Fleet. His impact was soon felt on the 1905 naval estimates. Not only achieving far greater efficiency, he was also able to reduce the budget by £3.5 million to £36.8 million. The Admiralty Committee[49] on Designs* would spearhead two of Fisher's great innovations: the *Dreadnought* and the new battle-cruiser, *Invincible*.

In retrospect, neither were well thought-out moves. The *Dreadnought* revolutionised battleship design and threw down the gauntlet to rekindle the Anglo-German naval arms race with a vengeance. For Jan Morris, this was 'a moment when naval architecture seem[ed] suddenly to change gear'.[50] It also put Britain and Germany on an equal footing, as it made Britain's power – based as it had been on the sheer numbers of ships available – obsolete.

The Naval Race: Comparative Fleet Growth in Tonnage

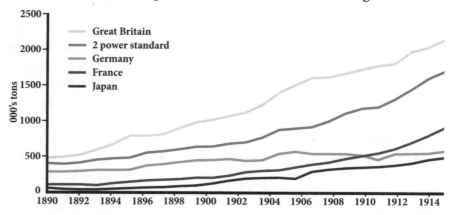

Source: Deutsche Museum, Munich. All figures approximate.

---

* This committee was formed at the end of 1904 to push forward the design of new battleships. Its members included Philip Watts (Director of Naval Construction), Lord Kelvin, R E Froude of the Admiralty Experimental Works, Henry Gard, Sir John Thornycroft, Prince Louis of Battenberg, John Jellicoe, Reginald Bacon, Captain Henry Jackson and Rear Admiral Alfred Winslow.

For the Liberals, this was a red rag to a bull, Lloyd George describing the new ship as 'a wanton and profligate ostentation'.[51] But the *Dreadnought* was Fisher's baby and, because she was 'precisely the same length as Westminster Abbey', he thought that she would be divinely protected. Working in 11½-hour shifts, a workforce of three thousand men took exactly one year and one day to make her ready for trials.[52] The second design resulted in a ship, the battle-cruiser, that could not fulfil its basic function as a fast battleship. The death of thousands of British sailors at Jutland resulted from the lack of armoured protection without the necessary radical gunnery or speed advantage.

In December 1905 when Arthur Balfour resigned and Sir Henry Campbell-Bannerman formed a new government, a wind of liberal reforms brought in political constraints on those working on a more modern navy. With it came increasing pressure on military expenditure, with a growing confidence in Britain's partnership with France and the reduced pressure in the Far East because of the alliance with Japan.

The 1906 *Novelle*
The conference that Wilhelm had promoted as the wedge between France and England during the Morocco crisis turned out to be a disaster for Germany. Of the thirteen nations that attended the Algeciras Conference, only Austria-Hungary supported Germany, while Spain, Italy, Russia, Great Britain and the United States firmly supported France's claims and continued confrontation was only avoided by the Germans accepting a face-saving compromise and signing an agreement on 31 May, whereby French control of the local police ceased.

For the British, Lord Grey was at one point quite ready to give the Germans what they really wanted out of any planned compromise: coaling stations that could support their flag carrying fleet around the world. Fisher would have been livid had the Germans walked away with these, as fuel was *the* critical factor in supporting a fleet in foreign waters. But, even if it had become clear that among the British there was not 100 per cent support for France's position, the damage done by the Moroccan Crisis was tangible. It pulled Germany's potential enemies closer together rather than forcing them apart.

1906 was a turning point in Anglo-German relations, particularly naval relations. Against the background of Morocco, Britain was to throw down a gauntlet – in fact, two. *Dreadnought* was launched and the keel laid for the second of Fisher's revolutionary ships, HMS *Invincible*. Wilhelm was worried that Germany was about to be outdone.

In May 1906 a new draft of the *Novelle* was ready to be presented to the *Reichstag*. It even provided a small amount for U-boat development, although Tirpitz was not a supporter of submarines, derisively calling them pieces of '*altes Eisen*'

– old iron. Young officers at the head of the nascent submarine arm, men like Kapitän Lothar Persius, found themselves distinctly cold-shouldered during this period. So were proponents of cruiser warfare, which Tirpitz felt was a distraction from the main task of the navy: big-ship confrontation. 'Young officers who associated too closely with cruiser or submarine tactics could be assured of short careers in the Imperial Navy'.[53] For this reason Tirpitz even spoke out against Wilhelm's taking up the Fisher 'fast capital ship' cause, thinking that it was too close to the cruiser position that was a challenge to what he really wanted to build: battleships.

By the end of the year the draft of the *Novelle* was complete. Tirpitz found himself under increasing pressure from the Flottenverein to strengthen the *Novelle*; they wanted a reduction in a battleship's life of twenty-five years, something that would not happen until the 1908 Navy Law. The eventual bill foresaw eighteen battleships, thirteen large cruisers and twenty small cruisers. After the Moroccan Crisis, Wilhelm was angry that Tirpitz had backed down from an even larger request to the Reichstag for funding.

The different approaches of Tirpitz and his sovereign, the Kaiser, resurfaced. The always more cautious Tirpitz did not want to overdo the parliamentary request. He wanted to show the legislators that he was acting responsibly and spending their monies wisely. Wilhelm took the opposite view: '*Flaußen! Man hat nicht genug seinerseits gefordert und fühlt nun, daß die darauf hinweisen, recht haben.*' ('Humbug! We did not demand enough. Now we feel that the people who advised us asking more were correct.')[54] When Tirpitz heard about Wilhelm's criticism he offered his resignation. It was rejected by the Kaiser and Tirpitz came crawling back. Threatening resignation was something that both Fisher and Tirpitz did regularly. Fisher would even threaten the *mass* resignation of the Admiralty board if his wishes were not respected.

Despite the scare ignited by rumours going around about Fisher's new battle-cruiser class (*Invincible*), Tirpitz decided against a race based mainly on calibre. Nevertheless, costs were rising sharply and Germany's first *Invincible*-type battle-cruiser, SMS *Von der Tann*, was to cost 36.6 million marks. And now, with news that the French were moving major fleet elements down to the Mediterranean, the conclusion for the Germans was that the French and the British had come to a secret agreement to manage naval resources in tandem, adding even more pressure on Tirpitz's planning.

In June 1906, taking full advantage of the anti-British sentiment following the failure of the Algeciras Conference, he got the Reichstag to pass the third Naval Law. With it, six large cruisers were added to the fleet. The Kaiser's attempt to find a way to prise open cracks within the Entente Cordiale came to an end.

Work on widening the Kiel Canal was taken by the British as a sign of German intentions to provide a way to move heavier and broader-beamed battleships between Kiel and Wilhelmshaven. Fisher guessed the eventual date of the start of the war with extraordinary accuracy. He thought that it would be in 1914, because that was the estimated completion year of the canal, and it would occur after harvests had been brought in. Furthermore, it would occur on a bank holiday: 4 August 1914 was just that.

Despite these forebodings the British government was committed to its programme of social welfare, particularly the introduction of pensions, and in July the new First Lord, Lord Tweedmouth, let the axe fall. Two of the four capital ships in the 1907/8 building programme were dropped. But the dreadnought project was concluded, in true Fisher style, in record time. In October 1906 *Dreadnought* set off on her sea trials. She was, however, a double-edged sword because overnight she rendered all other fleets obsolete, including a significant proportion of the Royal Navy's strength. Patrick Kelly maintains that *Dreadnought* was Fisher's anticipation of what the Japanese or United States navies would do, but it was with Germany, in the first decade of the twentieth century, that she directly spurred the naval arms race.

In the short term, Fisher's innovation paid dividends. By November 1909, Britain had seven commissioned dreadnoughts, Germany had two and Japan one. But Germany had eleven under construction against Britain's projected ten. Other countries, too, were about to jump into the race: the United States, Russia, France and Italy.

Tirpitz spent much of the summer months of 1906 pondering how best to respond to the dreadnought threat. It posed a series of quite different challenges to him. In Tirpitz's mind Fisher had, in fact, made a mistake. By launching the dreadnought he had 'wiped the slate clean'.[55] 'The huge British superiority in pre-dreadnoughts would become increasingly irrelevant as both sides built more dreadnoughts.'[56] The fact that the race was now more even, lending each side a more sporting chance, gave Tirpitz hope that he really could win after all.

Cost was, of course, one challenge. It was not the canal-widening cost that bothered him. This would be taken by the Interior Ministry. But he would have to face the cost impact on the docks at Kiel. Tirpitz wanted to limit the displacement of the actual ships being built, as construction costs were dramatically increasing. His first agreement was to build a ship of around 15,000 tons. What he ended up with was nearly 19,000 tons, costing 37.3 million marks, two-thirds of what the annual construction spend was estimated to be in the first Navy Law.

Tirpitz could also match British technology. He was quick to copy where he could and exploit weaknesses where he saw them. German design took a different approach to armament. Hans Bürkner, the chief designer of the *Nassau* class (Germany's first post-dreadnought class, laid down between June and August 1907), purposely increased belt armour to match turret calibre. The *Nassau* class's sixteen watertight compartmental divisions were also subsequently increased to nineteen on later classes, resulting in a wider beam and, therefore, more stability for a battleship in its primary role as a gunnery platform.

In the end, the new *Nassau* class displaced 18,873 tons and mounted twelve 28cm (11in) guns, two more than *Dreadnought* herself had at launch. But Tirpitz's rejection of the new turbine engines meant that the maximum speed was, critically, limited to 19 knots and therefore to a lesser role. At 37 million marks this was an expensive mistake.[57]

The next major ship to be laid down, Germany's first battle-cruiser *Von der Tann* at the Blohm and Voss yards in 1908, used a Parsons turbine power plant, the same design that had been first used on *Dreadnought*. With the new power plant *Von der Tann* was able to reach a speed of 27 knots, 6 knots faster than *Dreadnought*. She was a formidable ship.

The last alliance cornerstone – the Anglo-Russian Entente – was put in place. Germany, encircled, was getting increasingly nervous that Fisher would, in fact, be responsible for the British Navy 'doing a Nelson', 'Copenhagening' the German fleet while in harbour. In 1907 Kiel schoolchildren were kept at home for two days and the stock exchange was in crisis: fear was mixed with rumour that 'Fisher [was] coming'. No other British naval man provoked collective anxiety in the Germans in quite the way that Fisher did.

As the year headed for its close, Fisher made a speech at the Lord Mayor's banquet that he would come to regret. He assured his audience that Britons could sleep soundly in their beds. Just days later, on 18 November, the news from Germany was that the shipbuilding programme was accelerating. Its fleet would supposedly increase by 25 per cent over the next five years and would also include five new battle-cruisers.

The 1908 *Novelle*

Constant rumours of a pre-emptive British naval strike (that Fisher was again to threaten in 1908) increased the Reichstag's receptivity to new propositions from Tirpitz. The fourth *Novelle* was passed on 28 March 1908. By reducing the active life of a battleship from twenty-five to twenty years, replacement production was sped up. Without knowing it, the Reichstag was painting itself into a corner and giving Tirpitz what he needed faster. Indeed, the suggestion to reduce the life of a battleship had been made by Reichstag deputies eight years earlier. They thought that this would merely limit the number of years that they would have to live with Tirpitz's laws on the books. The opposite was the case: it built into law the replacement of the older ship with a new one on a more accelerated timetable.

In the inner circle there was considerable debate over whether Germany should adopt a three or four *Bautempo*. The Etatsabteilung (the estimates department of the Reichsmarineamt known as the RMA) was strongly against the dangerous signals that a four *Bautempo* would send the British:

> If we go to the four tempo we would be tarred with the stigma of starting an arms race and even worse the Liberals in England would likely be replaced by the Conservatives. Thus, even if there is a majority within the bloc, we must have a four tempo, and therefore it would be better to stabilise [ie perpetuate] the three tempo and make us independent for all time from political accidents.[58]

David Lloyd George was, for one, full of suspicion about the German naval construction rumours and treated the reports as pure propaganda, designed to whip up national fervour to heighten the pressure for increased naval estimates. German naval planning called for twelve dreadnought keels to be laid down in three years: four in 1908, four in 1909 and the last four in 1910. Churchill, trying to avoid being tied down to building more dreadnoughts, argued that the quality of British ships counted for more than merely increasing their numbers. As in Germany, national sentiment carried the day. The cry went up in the country for a bigger British dreadnought building programme to maintain the safety margin over Germany: 'We want eight and we won't wait'. The press whipped up the frenzy, the *Observer* announcing, 'The Eight, the whole Eight, and nothing but the Eight'.[59]

The Liberal government tried to resist. Sir Henry Campbell-Bannerman's administration had come to power calling for 'peace, retrenchment and reform', and saw 'militarism, extravagance and protectionism' as 'weeds which grow in the same field'. In his mind, the monies needed for social reform could not support an ongoing shipbuilding race with Germany.

The British Admiralty proposed a programme for 1908 that had already been cut back: one battleship, a battle-cruiser, six light cruisers, sixteen destroyers and some submarines. When Campbell-Bannerman cut the programme by £1.3 million there was no way out but for the battleship to be scrapped. The consequences for the naval armament value chain, Fisher felt, would be catastrophic. Armour-plating expertise would be lost. At the very moment when the Germans were building up the munitions and armaments infrastructure, Britain was talking about dismantling hers.

The tussle over the question of how many dreadnoughts continued, with various creative options being put on the table. One was to build four and allow for another four contingent battleships if reports from Germany warranted it. By July 1908 the contingent ships became part of the build plan. The British government could no longer oppose public pressure.

Fisher's fortunes were on the wane.

The 1909 naval scare

John Jellicoe, one of Jacky Fisher's rising stars, heard that the Essen Krupp works were turning out artillery at a pace which would be consistent with a four *Bautempo*. The nickel market was heating up as Germany started to stockpile the essential ingredient for armour-grade steel. Claims that materials for the 1909 building programme had already been purchased in 1908 ahead of Reichstag sanction were made.

Doing the calculations, the British Admiralty became nervous. It looked like the ratio between the British and German fleets could by 1912 be, optimistically, 18:13. But if the Germans had reduced construction time they could have as many as eighteen or even twenty-one ships. Britain would be at a severe disadvantage. The Admiralty wanted eight ships and not the six authorised for the 1909 estimates.

The manoeuvring was intense. The Liberal administration did not want to be pushed into surrendering its pension programmes. Lloyd George was scornful of the reliability of the Admiralty reports and openly poured cold water on them. But the spirit in the nation was jingoistic; in the words of Churchill, 'The Admiralty had demanded six; the economists wanted four and we finally compromised on eight'.[60] More importantly, if in the end Tirpitz did not shorten the building cycles, the British had really been unnerved. Negotiations about an imperial contribution began (leading, ultimately, to the addition of the battle-cruisers HMAS *Australia* and HMS *New Zealand*).

In 1909 Fisher accepted a barony from the King, becoming Baron Fisher of Kilverstone and adopting the motto 'Fear God and dread nought'. Asquith's words were kind and referred to 'the great work – unique in our time – which [Fisher had] accomplished in developing and strengthening the navy, and in assuring the maritime supremacy of Great Britain'.[61]

The following year, on 26 January, Fisher left the Navy: his life should now have become roses, golf and correspondence. But even in retirement in Kilverstone Hall he continued to be able to influence and have an impact on people and events around him. One of the causes that he took up was that of pushing for social change in the Navy, trying to make it easier for those from the ranks to attain commissions. Churchill espoused the same cause.

By 1912 the British were preparing for the inevitable. There was a need to concentrate forces where the fleets' meeting was likely to take place, the North Sea. Echoing what Fisher had initiated years before, the Mediterranean now became a French theatre of operations. To confirm earlier moves, the entire French Atlantic fleet was indeed moved from Brest, south to Toulon.

Fisher's 1912 chairmanship of the Royal Commission to inquire into liquid fuel was significant. The commission's findings, completed in six months, paved the way for the initial conversion of the Royal Navy from coal to oil. It held and still holds huge sway on British strategy and diplomacy, with the British moving to secure oil resources in the Middle East. Churchill's 15in *Queen Elizabeth*-class battleships were the first to run exclusively on oil-fired boilers. The change would have profound consequences, as it shifted Britain's global focus to future oil supplies and away from domestic coal.

The 1912 *Novelle*

In Germany, General Helmuth von Moltke considered war inevitable and was pushing for a faster engagement than was comfortable for Tirpitz, who still did not have the advantage in fleet-to-fleet ratio that he wanted. He was getting there, fast, but Moltke was worried that Russia would also pick up the pace. He wanted to pre-empt the strength that he feared was coming from the east.

The crisis was brought about by another North African confrontation in 1911 and the obvious snub to the Kaiser that resulted from it.[62] For Tirpitz, it was further affirmation that more visible naval strength was needed. He was now keener than ever to show the British and French that he was not a man to be trifled with. A fifth *Novelle* was being passed in June, with three new battleships proposed for the *Flottenbauprogramm* but, importantly, adding Zeppelins and a small fleet of seventy-two submarines.

Each diplomatic failure that Wilhelm precipitated, as he had just twice done in the space of five years with Morocco, directly benefited Tirpitz. With this final pre-war *Novelle*, Tirpitz envisioned a fleet of sixty-one heavy ships that would be ready in 1918, but Moltke would not give him the time. The year 1914 started with Tirpitz's promotion to the rank of grand admiral. It ended in war.

Fisher was brought back by Churchill to the Admiralty for a second term as First Sea Lord, ironically in October, the very month that he had predicted as being the date for the outbreak of war. (His predecessor, Lord Louis Battenberg, had resigned because of his German name. This was before George V had taken the decision to change his own family name to Windsor.) Fisher's relations with Churchill fell apart after the failure of the Gallipoli assault in 1915. He had never been a great supporter of the Dardanelles plan and had preferred the idea of an assault directly on German territory in the Baltic, but he had served Churchill as well as he could.

Two months before Jutland, Grand Admiral von Tirpitz retired from active military service. Having worked closely with his emperor for over a decade in building the High Seas Fleet into a forbidding fighting machine, he ended up disagreeing fundamentally with the Kaiser who, now that he had his fleet, did not dare to use it.

3

A Contradiction, Not A Team:
Jellicoe and Beatty

If you were to look for two officers to take command of the Grand and Battle Cruiser Fleets in August 1914, it would be hard to find two admirals more different than John Jellicoe and David Beatty. Everything that Beatty was, Jellicoe was not. One man's strengths were often the other's weaknesses and each had been sponsored and nurtured in their positions of command by forces greater than themselves.

Beatty's chance meeting with Winston Churchill during the Sudanese campaign, at the Battle of Omdurman in 1898, led to a friendship born of shared experience, though Churchill was the younger. Jellicoe was one of Fisher's anointed and a member of his inner circle of Young Turks known collectively as the 'Fishpond'. Jellicoe probably would have got to where he did without Fisher's support; Beatty, without Churchill's, probably not, and certainly not without a war to accelerate promotion.

They were, wrote Keith Yates, 'a study in contrasts, not just in their physical appearance and dress, but in their temperament, strengths and weaknesses. While Jellicoe was calm, deliberate and realistic in assessing his own forces and those of his enemy, Beatty was highly strung, impatient for action, and supremely confident of his superiority over his enemy.'[1] The quiet Jellicoe was intellectually brilliant, modest and warm-hearted. Beatty was known for his flamboyance and vanity, but also for his courage and charisma. With supreme command at sea, both men became increasingly cautious. Though their paths crossed in the years leading up to Jutland, the individual journeys were very different.

The two officers can be looked at in quite distinct ways. Amid the increasingly unstable events of the late nineteenth and early twentieth centuries their paths touched, then drew apart again. This pattern gives an idea of how their characters and careers were formed, of the influences in the early stages of their careers, and how these same continued to shape them in later years.

John Rushworth Jellicoe was born on 5 December 1859. It was a time of great change within the British Empire. The year 1859 also, coincidentally, saw the birth of the future Wilhelm II. Jellicoe's lineage left no doubt that the sea was his calling. His father, John Henry Jellicoe, had been at age twelve already at sea in a merchant ship, and by twenty-one he had his first command. Through his marriage to Lucy Henrietta (née Keele), John Henry entered a family with a naval tradition that went back to Nelson.

John Jellicoe's maternal great-great-grandfather, Philip Patton, had fought at La Hogue in 1692, the decisive sea battle of the Nine Years War, and his son, another Philip, rose to the flag rank and was Second Naval Lord at the Admiralty at the time of Trafalgar. Jellicoe's second name, Rushworth, was also from one of Lucy's ancestors, a Royal Navy captain, Edward Rushworth, who died in 1780 in Barbados. Captain John Henry, Jellicoe's father, was an outstanding officer in the Southampton-based Royal Mail Steam Packet Company, where diligence and natural abilities helped him rise through its ranks to become commodore and a member of the board of directors. Southampton thus became John Jellicoe's home for the first ten years of his life.

David Richard Beatty was eleven years Jellicoe's junior. Born on 17 January 1871, the future admiral came into the world out of wedlock. This remained a closely held secret that his nephew (and one of his biographers), Charles Beatty, claimed had a profound impact throughout his life, saying that David lived 'under a family bane which dogged him until high office became a burden and private life a cage'.[2] Indeed, had it become known, the social costs for Beatty would have been enormous and probably adversely affected his eventual brilliant naval career.

Technically, David Beatty could have been disinherited by younger, legitimate siblings. As it was, his elder brother Charles inherited the estates; later, they fell to the admiral's nephew when Charles died in 1917 after a riding accident. David's father's military career was not a harbinger of his son's later achievements. As was the practice at the time, David Longfield Beatty had purchased his commission in the 4th Hussar Regiment and when he retired a captain he had never actually seen active service. David's father was also a dark influence on the boy – in Robert Massie's words, 'eccentric, irascible, and tyrannical and ... a heavy drinker'.

His birth was registered by his father simply writing his mother's name as 'Edith Catherine Beatty', when she was still Katherine (or Katrin) Edith Chaine (née Sadleir), the wife of a fellow officer – in fact, David's father's colonel – in the 4th Hussars. The circumstances of the two future officers were thus very different. Jellicoe's father's achievements had been won the hard way, while Beatty came from the moneyed Anglo-Irish. The Jellicoe house in Southampton, 1 Cranbury Place, was modest. Beatty grew up in large houses, surrounded by servants.

Even if Jellicoe's family struggled to pay for their promising boy's schooling (and at one point came close to abandoning it because of the hardships that it was causing), his intellect got him noticed. His break came when he was given a recommendation to the Navy by a family friend of his father's, Captain Robert Hall, then Naval Secretary to the Admiralty. The recommendation was soon justified. In 1872 the young 'Jack' passed his entrance exam, second in a class of thirty-nine pupils. In the static training ship *Britannia* he could not have done better. Jellicoe was awarded a first in each of his four terms and finally passed out with a first-class certificate in 1874 with more seniority and was promoted in July to midshipman.*

Jellicoe's first ship duty was on the port ship, the hulk of the once mighty wooden three-decker *Duke of Wellington* in Portsmouth. A strange coincidence was that forty years later his flagship would be *Iron Duke*, the name by which, of course, the victor at Waterloo came to be known.[3] But it was not until *Newcastle*, a fully rigged frigate that also had auxiliary steam power, that he experienced his first ocean-going duty. After a ten-day sail to Gibraltar, Jellicoe went on to St Helena, Rio de Janeiro, the Falklands, Bombay and Japan. He was discovering the world and his sea legs.

These two and a half years under sail must have been magical days. To the end of his life Jellicoe loved to sail and even ended up having a small class of dinghy named after him when, after the war, he went out to New Zealand as governor general. It would be the same for Beatty, who spent toughening-up tours on a small wooden steam corvette, *Ruby*. All four major commanders at Jutland – Scheer, Hipper, Beatty and Jellicoe – learnt the ropes, their tactics and command of men, under sail.

Jellicoe's second sea appointment was in July 1877, the mighty 10,600-tonner *Agincourt*. She was a five-masted, broadsided, armour-plated ship, a kind of 'super *Warrior*': the flagship of the Channel Squadron. The squadron relied on sail rather than on their inefficient steam engines to give the necessary range to what was the Navy's strategic reserve.

While the conditions on *Agincourt* were tough and onboard duties disciplined, Jellicoe started here to make friendships that lasted all his life. With him as fellow midshipmen were his cousin, Charles Rushworth, and Cecil Burney, who would later became his second-in-command in the Grand Fleet. When the ship was sent out to reinforce the Mediterranean Fleet during a war between Russia and Turkey, Rushworth was drowned, and as a consequence Jellicoe's workload increased. Soon he was in charge of the ship's steamboats and cutters,

---

* On my desk at home is a silver inkwell that my father gave me. It reminds me daily of the type of man my grandfather was: it was awarded for the 1874 *Britannia* First Admiralty Study Prize.

as well as acting as one of the three signals officers and AdC to the admiral. He learnt to ride well; occasionally he used the admiral's horse to take messages between ships anchored around the bay in the Gulf of Xeros, the other side of which, at Gallipoli, would be so hard fought-for thirty-seven years later.

Later in 1877 Jellicoe did a short stint in the sailing sloop *Cruiser*, after which he sat his sub lieutenant exams, coming third in maths out of 109 candidates. On his nineteenth birthday he passed his seamanship examinations before going to Greenwich for the sub lieutenants' course at the Royal Naval College. He then went on to Portsmouth for specialist gunnery and torpedo instruction.

Two years later, in March 1880 Jellicoe was appointed to the centre-battery ironclad *Alexandra*, the flagship of the Mediterranean Fleet. Beatty too would start his career on *Alexandra* six years hence, but Jellicoe had got there by hard slog, not connections. When he left the ship in August, he travelled back to England via Italy. It was not the romantic grand European tour he imagined: he came down with dysentery and was forced onto half-pay for three months.

Fit again by February 1881, he was appointed for a second time to *Agincourt*, where he had to serve for a year of watch-keeping duties before he could apply for any specialisation in the Navy, but he already knew that it was going to be gunnery. It was an exciting post: the ship was sent out to the Mediterranean, again as reinforcement. She reached Port Said by way of Alexandria, where Jacky Fisher made a name for himself in Admiral Sir Beauchamp Seymour's bombardment. Jellicoe joined *Orion,* an armoured ram recently acquired from Turkey, but his real adventure started when he was sent back with a message for the admiral. Disguised as a refugee, Jellicoe travelled clandestinely by canal boat delivering the admiral's messages.

While Jellicoe was in the Middle East, Beatty was growing up in Irish fox-hunting country. His grandfather died in 1881 and his father took over the running of the eighteenth-century family mansion, Borodale, in County Wexford (that David eventually took as the association with his title, although the house burnt down in the 1930s). Beatty's initial career steps contrasted strongly with Jellicoe's. Knowing that he wanted to get into the Navy but also aware that he was not greatly gifted academically, Beatty was enrolled in 1882 at Burney's Naval Academy in Gosport, a crammer, to get him over the initial career hurdle. Jellicoe, meanwhile, having chosen his specialisation, began the 'long course', first at Greenwich and then at Whale Island, Portsmouth, to study to become a gunnery lieutenant. Typically, at Greenwich he came out top of his class; at Portsmouth too he became a gunnery lieutenant, first class.

Jellicoe's appointment to the staff at the Whale Island Gunnery School on *Excellent* in 1884 brought him together with Fisher. As captain, Jacky Fisher took an active interest in Jellicoe from this moment on; his patronage would shape Jellicoe's career in giving him the best grounding in technical know-how, as well as the active fleet service that was needed for highest command. This was the path to the aforementioned Fishpond, Fisher's cabal of young officers who would so decisively influence the future of the Royal Navy in matters such as gunnery and fire control. This included men such as Percy Scott, one of gunnery's radical thinkers: 'I don't care if he drinks, gambles and womanizes; he hits the target,' exclaimed Fisher of his protégé.[4]

Beatty followed Jellicoe to *Britannia* at the start of 1884 aged almost thirteen, the age of entry having been reduced. He passed tenth in his class of ninety-nine.[5] Beatty did make his mark at Dartmouth, but not in a positive way – in fact, for bullying, although a supportive biographer put it this way: 'rigid discipline and endless routine clashed with his lively, sociable character'.[6] When Beatty passed out two years later, his performance was average: he was placed eighteenth out of thirty-four pupils.[7]

Jellicoe now had his first real chance of combat. A war scare in 1885 with Russia, whose southern expansionist ambitions were slowly but inexorably bringing it closer to confrontation with Great Britain, led to Admiral Hornby assembling a fleet in the southwest of Ireland to threaten St Petersburg. He took Fisher with him on *Minotaur*, *Agincourt*'s sister ship, 'for service with the squadron ... to report on points connected with gunnery'. Jellicoe in turn was chosen by Fisher 'for experimental duties during cruise', and later went on to serve as gunnery officer on *Monarch* under Captain Edmund J Church in the Channel Squadron.[8]

With the performance that Beatty had put in at the *Britannia*, it was not surprising that he was initially posted to the 'undesirable' China Station.[9] More impressive was his mother's immediate and effective lobbying with Charles Beresford, which resulted in his gaining the 'navy's prime midshipman appointment' to *Alexandra* in February 1886.

This was the trajectory of Beatty's early career. The time spent on *Alexandra* gave him important connections, the sort that would help him later: Stanley Colville, Colin Keppel, Walter Cowan, Richard Phillimore and Reginald Tyrwhitt, and the Duke of Edinburgh's eldest daughter, Marie, which gave him a key advantage at court. Within months, in May 1886 he won his promotion to midshipman and assignment to Colville on watch-keeping duties.

In April 1886 Jellicoe was transferred to the turret ship *Colossus*, the most modern ship afloat and armed with breech-loading 12in guns;[10] though she had two masts, she carried no sail as the masts were used purely as signalling and observation platforms. While serving on *Colossus* Jellicoe rescued a seaman who had fallen overboard during rough weather. After Captain Cyprian Bridge had congratulated him, he went about his business, returning quietly to his cabin to change into dry clothes.

Time on ship was not exciting – mostly endless drills, deck- and brass-cleaning – and to keep the men fit and focused the officers needed constantly to organise activities like inter-ship sports competitions. Jellicoe's idea had a twist: to ensure that the sailors were at their peak, some say he invented a field-gun exercise that would become the predecessor of the competition held annually at London's Royal Tournament (subsequently known as the British Military Tournament) until the end of the twentieth century.

In December 1886 Jellicoe embarked on eighteen months as the experiments officer on *Excellent*. The work here helped the development of the new, standard 4.7in and 6in quick-firing (QF) guns that revolutionised naval warfare through their ability, by sheer volume of fire, to increase the chances of hitting other ships in engagements at sea.

When Jellicoe's mentor Fisher became Director of Naval Ordinance in September 1889 he took the young lieutenant with him as his assistant. Long hours would become a daily routine, but the experience gained was valuable, for here he was responsible for the development and testing of all new gunnery ideas – that is, guns, ammunition and mountings – for the Navy.

While Jellicoe worked on gunnery development, Beatty was learning seamanship on *Ruby*, after which he continued shore training at Greenwich. Beatty is said to have taken full advantage of being so close to the exciting social life of London and his studies probably suffered as a consequence. Nevertheless, his first in the torpedo course earned him a posting to a torpedo boat.[11] It was not necessarily a high road to promotion, but maybe because of this experience, and an obvious interest in the torpedo as a weapon, Beatty always placed a higher priority on the offensive potential of the torpedo-boat destroyer (or TBD). Like Scheer and Hipper he was captivated by the excitement of the fast, aggressive weapons. Jellicoe, on the other hand, would end up reversing the position of his then commander-in-chief, Admiral George Callaghan, when he took over the Grand Fleet from him in 1916. While Callaghan stressed the role of the 'destroyer' to attack an enemy's line, Jellicoe was inclined to the opposite: he preferred to see the main role for the destroyer as defending his own line.

Jellicoe's career started to pick up. Only thirty-one in 1891, he was promoted to commander and his first return to sea duty was to serve as executive officer on *Sans Pareil* under Captain A K Wilson (later Admiral Wilson, fondly known as 'Tug' and, maybe less friendly, as 'old 'ard 'eart'). Kenneth Dewar's criticism would be that Jellicoe 'only had 16 months in a seagoing ship between the ages of twenty-three and thirty-three [sic]'. Looked at another way, this shows that Jellicoe's reputation was already such that this did not count against him. In fact, the real figure for the amount of time Jellicoe had spent at sea was considerably higher: around thirty months if you include the ten that he served as the commander of the *Sans Pareil* before turning thirty-three; if you add on his service on *Handy*, *Excellent*'s tender, it was closer to forty-eight.

After the torpedo-boat destroyer experience Beatty was assigned to the battleship *Nile* in January 1892 and then, in July, to the Royal Yacht, *Victoria and Albert*. It was not a particularly enjoyable posting as the Queen was in mourning for Prince Albert (he had died more than thirty years previously). Beatty was probably quite happy to rejoin *Ruby* in August.

After little more than a year, at the request of Admiral Sir George Tryon, Jellicoe took up the post of executive officer on *Victoria*, a sister ship of the *Sans Pareil*, the flagship of the Mediterranean Fleet in 1893, at the time that the Mediterranean was considered a potential conflict zone, with France and Russia closing ranks, and with the recent advent of a Russian squadron. Tryon, with a formidable intellect, was regarded as one of the stars of intricate naval manoeuvre.

The naval disaster of the century place off the Tripoli coast in 1893, between the two battleships *Victoria* and *Camperdown*. Admiral Tryon had tried to accomplish a manoeuvre at sea that involved a course-reversal of two lines of ships steaming in parallel, effected by the two leading ships turning inwards concurrently to initiate the turn of each of their lines. It is still not known whether Tryon intended that at the end of the manoeuvre each ship would resume a parallel course (albeit in the opposite direction), or whether the resulting parallel lines would be inverted, but they just got much closer. There was simply not enough room in which to accomplish the tricky endeavour and, despite repeated requests to abort from *Camperdown*'s captain, Rear Admiral A H Markham, Tryon persisted. He and 357 others went to their graves when *Camperdown* rammed *Victoria*.

Jellicoe was below decks on *Victoria* with a fever of 103 degrees and suffering a bad case of piles. His subsequent immersion saved his life and cured his fever. Had it not been for the intervention of a young midshipman who offered help,* he would probably have drowned, so weak was he from the fever.[12] He was one of 291 men who got off safely. He even managed to get his clothes back: his chest of drawers was spotted bobbing on the surface and pulled in.

The disaster was later satirised, in a cinematic depiction of the cult of blind obedience in the Victorian Navy.[13] Beatty's nephew biographer says that this was

---

* The young midshipman was probably Philip Roberts-West, whom Jellicoe later intervened to save during the First World War when his nerves had the better of him; Prof Temple Patterson maintained that Jellicoe never really recovered from the effects of the immersion. Some have used this conclusion to suggest that this 'terror' was what lay behind the turn-away. I doubt it.

the moment when 'there began [his] lifelong friendship with Jellicoe,[14] as Beatty was transferred to *Camperdown* in September. They would not have been long together: Jellicoe was soon away, appointed to a new battleship, *Ramillies*, the very next month. I have never seen any evidence to support this notion of friendship. Stephen Roskill wrote that this was a period in which Beatty's enthusiasm for the Navy waned because of all the spit and polish. He yearned for something more, something through which to prove himself. Nevertheless, he was to stick it out for another two years until he transferred to *Trafalgar* in 1895.

On *Ramillies* Jellicoe enjoyed visits to Malta, with range-shooting and athletics. He later said that it was 'pleasant to recall those days when keen competition served to cement friendships'. *Ramillies* had strong competitors from the old *Agincourt* and the modern first-class cruiser, *Hawke*, both commanded by friends, Stanley Colville and Cecil Burney, while Sir Michael Culme-Seymour's flag lieutenant on *Ramillies* was Hugh Evan-Thomas, later to command the 5th Battle Squadron at Jutland. Culme-Seymour's naval service was a long and important one. He was to hold all the top positions: Commander-in-Chief of the Atlantic, Mediterranean and Channel Fleets as well as of Portsmouth. Francis Bridgeman, his flag captain, was also already acquainted with Jellicoe as he had been on *Excellent* when Jellicoe was on its junior staff.

Jellicoe praised the *Ramillies*, a high freeboard battleship of the latest design and one of the finest in the world at the time. He admired the ship because of her speed of coaling and performance in team sports. Viewed from the perspective of the continuous gunnery transformations of the early twentieth century, her fighting capacity was limited: 'Gunnery efficiency in the modern sense was I fear non-existent. An annual competition in prize firing was carried out off Malta at a range of some 1,600 yards and fire control was unheard of, as was long-range practice … Gunnery work took rather a back seat in considering the smartness and efficiency of a ship's company.'[15]

What, meanwhile, Beatty yearned for – action – finally came in 1896 when an Anglo-Egyptian expedition led by General Sir George Herbert Kitchener embarked on the reconquest of the Sudan and the avenging of General Sir Charles Gordon's death at the hands of the Mahdist rebels in 1885 at Khartoum.

A naval element was needed to bring supplies to the army and make sure that river communications were under their control. Kitchener thought that Colville would be a wise choice to lead the expedition and since the latter knew Beatty not only from the Royal Yacht but also from before, it was natural that he should ask for him. Yet it was not an obvious choice. Beatty was 'a twenty-five-year old navy Lieutenant of no particular distinction', but his spirit and character must have made a distinct impression.[16] It was, in Andrew Lambert's words, Colville who 'made Beatty's career'.[17]

What perhaps was not known was that Kitchener had actually asked for Jellicoe to fill this role but his commander at the time, Culme-Seymour, said that he could not be spared (without consulting Jellicoe: he was at sea, on target practice) and that because of his bouts of Malta fever he probably would have been unsuitable anyway. Colville went in his place, something that upset Jellicoe considerably. He wrote that he was 'deeply disappointed'. It was another occasion on which the Jellicoe–Beatty paths could have crossed.

During the campaign there were moments when Beatty displayed extraordinary courage. One occasion was when his gunboat, the *Abu Klea*, was hit and an unexploded shell lay in her magazine. Beatty did not hesitate. He picked it up and threw it overboard. Then, after Colville was seriously wounded at Wadi Halfa, Beatty took over command and managed to get further downstream in preparation for Kitchener's last push in this first part of the campaign; he was also in command of the successful attack on Dongola.

As a result of his actions, Beatty was awarded the Distinguished Service Order after Kitchener had praised the role of the river gunboats in his first dispatch in October; Kitchener could not 'speak too highly of this officer's behaviour'.

In January 1897 Jellicoe returned to England where he was promoted to captain after his commission on *Ramillies* had ended. While Beatty was in the Sudan, Jellicoe was to develop further skills and experience in ordnance. In January he was appointed to the Ordnance Committee, having previously served, as we know, as the assistant to the DNO. At this point the committee was still managing armaments for the army and the Navy, with a view that this would simplify research and production. It was also heavily engaged in the testing of the Vickers 6in breech-loading gun, which would emerge in one version or another as a standard armament for cruiser-size Royal Navy ships until well into the Cold War.

More important things were afoot, however. One was Jellicoe meeting his future wife, Gwen Cayzer, daughter of the very successful British shipowner, Sir Charles Cayzer. Another was his being asked by Vice Admiral Sir Edward Seymour to come as his flag captain to the China Station to which he had just been appointed. Jellicoe enthusiastically accepted, taking up the position on *Centurion* in December.[18]

In China, Jellicoe really established his first German naval connections. He became friends with Prince Heinrich, the younger brother of the Kaiser. It was an important connection: Prince Heinrich was Hipper's principal mentor and sponsor in the imperial navy along with Henning von Holtzendorf. Later, Jellicoe's younger daughter Prudence (my Aunt Prudie and the sibling to whom my father George was probably closest) went out with Crown Prince

Wilhelm's fourth son, Prince Friedrich of Prussia, better known as Fritzi.* At the time, Prince Heinrich was in command of the German East Asia Squadron, covering the growing colonial presence in China that the Kaiser and the German Reichstag was expensively funding. Jellicoe also got to know one of the future commanders-in-chief of the High Seas Fleet and chief of the German naval staff, Captain Henning von Holtzendorff, as well as Captain Guido von Usedom; Usedom later took over Jellicoe's role as Edward Seymour's chief of staff and became responsible for the docks in Kiel.†

Beatty was still in the Sudan. After a short leave, he returned at Kitchener's explicit request. Overall command of the gunboats passed to Colin Keppel, and Beatty served alongside Walter Cowan (a partner in crime on *Britannia*) and the Honourable Horace Hood. His boat, *El Teb*, capsized on a cataract, and he and most of her crew of fifteen were swept along in the hazardous and swift currents of the Nile. Taking command of *Fateh*, Beatty continued downriver, seizing targets ahead of Kitchener's land army. He was able to watch Churchill's famous charge at Omdurman from the crow's nest. When Churchill later asked Beatty what he had seen, Beatty's only reply was that 'it looked like plum duff: brown currants scattered about in a great deal of suet'.[19]

Eventually, after the Battle of Omdurman, Khartoum was retaken. The battle is now most notably connected with Churchill's vivid descriptions of one of the last cavalry charges of the British Army, that of the 21st Lancers in 1898. Churchill is said to have met Beatty when, drawing close to his gunboat, he inquired if they had something to drink. A bottle of champagne was thrown over to land, safely, at Churchill's feet, cushioned by the sand.

Then came the reaction of the British to what they felt was a French challenge to their regional security. After the flare-up subsided, Beatty's role was lauded and he was promoted to commander. Jellicoe had had to wait until he was thirty-one; Beatty was twenty-seven. He had served only half of the time that was normal for the rank: six rather than twelve years. He came back to Britain a hero, and there met his future wife, American heiress Ethel Field Tree, daughter of Marshall Field, the millionaire department-store owner.

In China the carving-up of substantial territories by the Western imperial powers continued. Britain had recently leased Weihaiwei, the Germans Tsingtao, the Russians Port Arthur and the French Kwangchou. Against this foreign invasion, the Society of Righteous and Harmonious Fists – the Boxers – reacted. It was a rebellion that could easily have been turned against the Empress

---

* Fritzi was later to become my cousin James Loudon's, Prudie's son's, godfather.

† My mother had a small silver German officer's peaked cap, gifted by von Usedom to my grandfather, but sadly lost by one of my siblings.

Dowager Tz'u-hsi, but in fact it was being cleverly turned against the foreigners by her and particularly against the religious zealotry of the Western
missionaries.

Jellicoe was enjoying these last days of the nineteenth century before the
twentieth was welcomed in. He held shooting matches with Prince Heinrich
and usually won. He visited Japan and the Philippines, which had just been an-
nexed by the Americans despite fierce, local guerrilla resistance.

On the other side of the world in Africa, a territorial dispute between France
and Britain over Fashoda had the effect of cooling relations with the French,
and Britain diplomatically manoeuvred against its traditional rival. And even
though it was rebuffed, an overture to Berlin was made in 1899 by the Colonial
Secretary, Joseph Chamberlain, for a closer working relationship. The mood in
Germany, however, was changing. The Kaiser had a vision for his country that
was echoed in what the foreign minister, von Bülow, called 'Weltpolitik': the
desire to assert itself globally.

Germany struck out on a new path, becoming an imperialist force, intent
on altering, challenging and upsetting the international balance of power. The
Kaiser had his own dreams. Impressed by the British Diamond Jubilee naval
review, Germany and her new leader, the Kaiser, set out on the creation of a
fleet with the hope of forcing Britain into an alliance on the former's terms and
the way that the passing of Germany's first Navy Law the following year saw the
beginnings of a new North Sea battle fleet that would eventually lead to a naval
arms race with Britain and to war, not an alliance.

In China, however, the Europeans opted more for co-operation than competition. It was to their mutual benefit to push their demands as a united threat.
Beatty now came to China as well. In April he was appointed as executive officer
of Barfleur, the flagship of Rear Admiral James Bruce, second-in-command of
the China Station. Again, Beatty's superior was Stanley Colville, with whom
he had served on Alexandra and Trafalgar, and most recently on the Nile
riverboats.

What had started north in Shantung province spread south in 1900 to
Peking, where foreigners felt increasingly under threat. A step-change came
with the murder of the top German diplomat, Clemens von Ketteler. Fearing
for their lives, foreigners barricaded themselves into the foreign legation quarter. They felt more and more isolated and cut off, especially when the rail link
southeast to Tientsin was cut. Then the Chinese army switched sides. The dowager empress had found a way to use the hatred that the Boxers felt towards
foreigners to her advantage.

On 28 May the British ambassador in Peking, Sir Claude MacDonald, asked
for help and succeeded on the 30th in getting permission from the Tsungli

Yamen, an office established by the imperial government to deal with foreigners, for troops to enter the capital. The next day Seymour took his British squadron to join the other allied ships at anchor at the Taku Forts. Russian, French and German battleships joined up, and numbers were increased by additional units from the Japanese, the Austrians and the Italians, these last arriving on the trot resplendent in their long-plumed Bersaglieri helmets. As Seymour was the senior officer present, they agreed to merge forces under his command.

On 4 June the last successful escape was made from Peking. Thereafter, no one could get out to reach the allied expeditionary force. Jellicoe was sent to Tientsin to gather intelligence and on 9 June he heard from Peking that unless the foreign quarter was speedily relieved, the worst could be expected. He did not hesitate and signalled back to Seymour that landing parties should be prepared. Beatty, meanwhile, had landed 150 troops from the *Barfleur* the day after Seymour left for Tientsin, where he found a garrison of 2,400 surrounded by 15,000 Boxers.

As Roskill wrote, Seymour 'proceeded to act with more courage than judgement'.[20] A mixed expeditionary force of 2,129 British, Americans, Russians, Germans, Japanese and Italians set out on 10 June for Peking and the besieged legation. Jellicoe was commander of the British contingent, the largest, 915 strong. With them they had seven field guns and ten machine guns.

Almost immediately they ran into trouble as the railway line had been torn up. The Taku Forts were taken after a short bombardment, ensuring that the allied ships could still reach the port. In the fighting around the railway station Beatty was wounded, twice, in the left arm below the shoulder and in the left wrist. He was hospitalised but discharged himself after a few days without permission and still clearly in considerable pain.

On 19 June, after hearing from a German officer that the lines had been taken up behind them, cutting the expedition off from Tientsin, Seymour ordered that the Peking relief force be turned around; it could make no further headway. The expeditionary force had been advancing up both sides of the river, pulling junks carrying the wounded. The advances on either side were, not unnaturally, uneven and often one side's flank was exposed. At one point an advancing party of 150 cavalry attacked the British left flank. They were mistaken for Russian but turned out to be Chinese.

From the village ahead, Peitsang, two cannons also opened up. Jellicoe, together with ten sailors from the *Centurion*, charged the village with fixed bayonets, hoping to flush out the Boxers. Coming round a corner he was hit hard with a bullet, which spun him around. Piercing his left lung, he was soon coughing up blood and his assisting doctor did not think he would make it. With Jellicoe injured, Guido von Usedom, who had taken over the rear-guard, was nominated by Seymour to take over as chief of staff. Later he too was wounded in the knee. Jellicoe, believing that he might die after the British doctor, Sibbald, had indicated he probably would, wrote a six-line will leaving everything to his mother.

With the help of Beatty's and Christopher Cradock's men, Seymour managed to get Jellicoe and some two hundred other wounded out safely on the night of 22 June, taking them downriver by junk where they stumbled on a great arsenal at Hsiku. Met by a wall of fire, Seymour organised two attacks, one by the British from the northwest, the other by the Germans from the southwest. After an hour they had taken the fort. It was bursting with stores, tons of rice and seven million rifle rounds, and even some Krupp field and Maxim machine guns. The supplies allowed them to hold out. Several counter-attacks were launched during the night. All were repulsed but not without quite serious casualties. Food began to run low.

Jellicoe was evacuated to Weihaiwei, where he slowly recovered, but the wound seriously weakened him in the years to come. Like Beatty, he temporarily lost the use of his left arm and until later in life often suffered painful cramps. My father always felt that it was the bullet that had remained lodged in his lung that probably caused his death in 1935, when he caught pneumonia.

Seymour's troops made it back but losses were heavy. Out of the party of 228, there were sixty-eight casualties. The names of the German dead can be seen carved onto impressive marble tablets hung on the wall of the Marinekirche in Wilhelmshaven.

This was Jellicoe's second encounter with Beatty. Both encounters had seen Jellicoe in mortally dangerous circumstances. The action must have brought him closer to Beatty, but most of the evidence seems to point more to the ties that he felt for the German soldiers with whom he fought so closely. They were, of course, to be his future adversaries.

Aged twenty-nine and newly promoted captain, Beatty held equal rank to Jellicoe, a man four years his senior in the Navy List. 'He had been placed ahead of 291 commanders whose average age was forty-three.'* Beatty received great praise from Seymour and from Captain Edward Bailey, his shore commander.

Beatty helped in the defence of Tientsin, relieved on 13 July, and would have liked to go on to Peking in the successful relief (commanded by Count von Waldersee), but his own wounds were more serious than he made out and he was strictly forbidden. Instead, he went back to England, arriving in

---

* Gibson and Harper, p36; also Roskill, p34. Beatty was promoted to captain on 9 November 1900, having served only two years in the previous rank.

Portsmouth to be given letters from Ethel suggesting that their liaison should continue, but that he should first mend physically. Beatty underwent a difficult operation to regain the use of his left arm, although he never fully recovered the use of two of his left-hand fingers.

Beatty's affair with Ethel Tree was conducted with great caution. Signing his letters to her from China 'Jack', he waited patiently while her divorce from Arthur Tree was in progress. Despite considerable opposition within Beatty's family, from his father and even his sister 'Trot', who felt the move could damage his career, the two, David aged thirty and Ethel aged twenty-seven, married on 22 May 1901 at Hanover Square registry office, just ten days after Ethel's divorce had come through. In so readily agreeing to it, she had not contested Arthur's accusations of adultery and on that basis lost custody of their son, Ronald. On the Tree side of the family it was the same – it was some time before Ronald was reconciled with Beatty. Eventually, he became a great admirer.

Back from China, Jellicoe found his reputation and public profile worked in his favour. He was asked by Admiral Sir William May, Third Naval Lord and Controller, to come to the Admiralty as his assistant. Jellicoe accepted and started in November 1901. The post took responsibility for all the ships of the Navy – their design, construction and repair. The engineer-in-chief, the director of naval construction and the director of dockyards reported to May. Again, the Navy took advantage of his talent and expertise, and in each post he had served with distinction and merit. Scheer, the man destined to be his opposite number, was enjoying a similar path and was now commanding the pre-dreadnought *Elsass,* the German equivalent to HMS *Queen.* This was between Berlin assignments and a later appointment as Chief of Staff of the High Seas Fleet, a stint in the Admiralty and command of a battle squadron.

There was no better post from which Jellicoe could gain an intimate understanding of the technology of the Royal Navy. Travelling around the country was part of the job – visiting ports, shipbuilding yards and repair docks. When in Glasgow he would sometimes stay at Sir Charles Cayzer's house, in Ralston. It was a chance for Jellicoe to get to know Cayzer's daughter, Gwen, better.

The Beattys, however, faced a certain amount of social stigma because of Ethel, being a divorcee, and an American one to boot. Shane Leslie talked of her in a way that made it clear that the situation often drove David to despair. 'I have paid dearly for my millions', was his comment in later life. She was very strong-willed and had a streak of arrogance, born of her great inherited wealth, which left many astonished.

She also hated David's being in the Navy and had often stood in the way of decisions that he needed to take. On one occasion, when he commanded the battle-cruisers, she tried to get their cruising plans changed so that she could more conveniently meet her 'Jack' (a rather ironic choice of nickname, given that this was the name by which John Jellicoe, the man she came to despise as standing in her husband's way, was also known). Beatty chided her angrily: 'You must not bother Prince Louis [of Battenberg] or Winston [Churchill] by asking them where we are going and asking them to send us here or there because you want to spend Whitsuntide with me. It won't do. The Admiralty have a good deal to do without having to consider which port will suit the wives best.'[21]

Jellicoe came to the conclusion that Gwen Cayzer was the one for him when he sprained his knee while on one of Sir Charles's ships that was fitting out. Naturally, he went back to Ralston to be nursed back to health by Gwen. She was almost twenty years younger than the forty-two-year-old captain whose heart she soon captured. Theirs was to be a strong bond. In July 1902 they got married and set up house in an apartment above Harrods. It was far above Jellicoe's income. His captain's pay was £410 per annum and the rent £400, but it did not pose a problem, as Gwen had her own funds. 'My married life was one of the most perfect happiness ... Our love grew if possible stronger as the years passed by,' John Jellicoe recounted later.

Beatty recovered from his wounds and in May 1902 was pronounced fit for sea duty. In June he took command, as captain, of the cruiser *Juno*, part of the Channel Squadron under the command of Arthur Wilson. By the time that he left the ship in December, the *Juno* had dramatically improved her gunnery performance. Looking forward, it was unfortunate that Beatty was not to have the time needed to bring the Battle Cruiser Fleet's gunnery up to a similar standard.

In August the following year, Jellicoe went back to sea as captain of the first-class cruiser *Drake*, a very long, 500ft, four-funnelled armoured ship that could steam at just over 24 knots. He had actually visited *Drake* when he was working for the controller and on his first days on board he warned his officers to make sure that doors were properly locked down. This was timely. The doors leaked and repairs had to be made. One recommendation that came out of the experience was to place the main armament of the classes of armoured cruiser laid down in the 1904/5 programme on the upper deck to avoid too much water intake in heavy seas – the *Drake* had suffered considerable flooding through the lower 6in casemates at sea.

In November 1903 Beatty was given command of *Arrogant*. Andrew Lambert quipped of the matching of man to name, 'Clearly someone in the Admiralty had a sense of humour'.[22]

In March 1904 Jellicoe was joined by his wife in Bermuda. With her came her younger sister, Constance, or Connie. Here she met one of the other captains, Charles Madden (who would later become Jellicoe's chief of staff at Jutland). They were married two years later.

The *Drake* was meanwhile in harbour undergoing repairs on her steering gear when an unfortunate incident took place. As the Russian fleet sailed for the Far East, it came across a collection of British fishing boats out of Hull near the Dogger Bank. The Russians somehow believed them to be Japanese torpedo boats, and opened fire. There was substantial damage and death and the British public clamoured for action. Only adroit diplomacy kept the situation from sparking a war.

With Fisher becoming First Sea Lord (the first time that this new title was used), Jellicoe returned to the centre of technological development. In October 1904 he was brought into the team that would design the *Dreadnought*. Fisher had told Lord Selborne that he wanted 'the five best brains in the navy below the rank of Admiral' to work on the project that would include Jackson, Jellicoe and Bacon.[23] He could vouch for them as he had 'tested each of them for many years'.

Besides Jellicoe, the group also included Captain Henry B Jackson (soon to be controller), Captain Reginald Bacon (Jellicoe's future biographer and soon to become naval assistant to the First Sea Lord), Captain Charles Madden, Captain Wilfrid Henderson and Henry Gard, chief constructor at Portsmouth. Alexander Gracie of Fairfield Shipbuilding and Engineering provided industrial advice.

The earliest results of the work of the group was the launching of the *Dreadnought* in 1906. Her 12in guns, normally the single longest construction element, were Jellicoe's work. He managed to get them in time. One story was that he did this by taking them from *Lord Nelson* and *Agamemnon*, but this was unlikely as the tender offers for the mountings were only received in June 1905. More probably, he was able to steal materials from a number of mountings in the early stages of production for a number of other ships.[24] Fisher's simultaneous reforms of the Navy were discussed in the previous chapter.

Beatty was elsewhere; Ethel joined him in October when he went to the first-class armoured cruiser *Suffolk*. In February 1905 Jellicoe relieved Rear Admiral Barry as DNO. Here he managed to wrest control of manufacturing away from the War Office and, as the newer guns delivered increased range, started to focus more and more on spotting and range-finding issues. He worked closely with Percy Scott, the man most closely associated with revolutionising British naval gunnery performance, appointed as inspector of target practice in March in the knowledge that he had to find new, innovative solutions to the increasing issues of long-range gunnery.

The shortcomings of British ammunition at long range was another issue also begging to be settled, but Jellicoe had been moved on before any action could be taken. It was a mistake. Before leaving the post of DNO Jellicoe had requested the Ordnance Board to design and produce a new armour-piercing shell effective at ranges at which future sea battles were likely to be fought.

> In order to determine the effectiveness against armoured ships of the shell supplied for the various guns I arranged for extensive firing trials to be carried out in 1910 against the old battleship *Edinburgh*, which had been specially prepared by the addition of modern armour plates. As a result of these trials, before the end of my term of office as Controller, the Ordnance Board were asked in October 1910 to endeavour to produce an armour-piercing shell which would perforate armour at oblique impact and go on in a fit state for bursting.[25]

However, '[b]efore the matter was resolved, Jellicoe departed and subsequent Controllers allowed it to drop.'[26] The issue of faulty ammunition would come back to haunt the British within a decade.

We have seen in Chapter 2 how the Kaiser's interference in the situation in Morocco in an attempt to drive a wedge between Britain and France, which may have seemed a storm in a teacup, had been dangerous nevertheless. Two European power ministers were immediately at loggerheads: Théophile Delcassé, the French foreign minister, declared that there was no need for the international conference for which Bülow was pushing, even though by June Germany was threatening war over the issue. Although by April 1906 the Moroccan crisis had been settled, it had taken Europe to the very brink, with the French mobilising troops on Germany's borders and the Germans calling up the reserves. Britain had sided with her old cross-Channel foe but there was a strong feeling that the country's possible entry into a war was being decided not in Whitehall, but in the ministry on the Quai d'Orsay. When the Treaty of Algeciras was signed, Germany had been heavily outplayed: it was now increasingly behaving like the rogue state of Europe.

No sooner had one crisis for Germany been resolved than another came along: none other than the *Dreadnought*. With a single event, Britain had changed the rules of naval competition. Jellicoe's view, mirroring that of Fisher, was that this type of innovation was not to be viewed in the same way as an arms race. He saw it as maintaining peace:

> In peace strategy, the initiative is probably as important as in war. So long as we maintain the initiative we keep our rivals in a chronic state of unreadiness, confuse their building policy and, by maintaining a perpetual superiority in each individual unit, tend to preserve peace by postponing the moment when they could make war an advantage.[27]

Many say that he was wrong. *Dreadnought* sparked a fire of catch-up by

Germany. Tirpitz's response was to use the natural public reaction of fear successfully to get his third Navy Law passed, making it clear that Germany would now build 'all big-gun' ships of its own, to keep up in the naval race.

In 1907 Jellicoe was promoted to rear admiral, then asked if he would take a position of command in the Atlantic Fleet. This he did in August, joining the pre-dreadnought *Albemarle*, whose sister ship *Exmouth* served as the flagship of the commander-in-chief, Admiral Sir Assheton Curzon-Howe. With him came William Goodenough as flag captain. Nine years later Goodenough would provide the key tactical intelligence to support Jellicoe's situational awareness at Jutland. The reputation and zeal that Jellicoe brought to each new assignment had earned him a Commander of the Victorian Order in 1906, then a Knight Commander after that year's Cowes Regatta. He was now Rear Admiral Sir John Jellicoe.

While with *Albemarle* in Quebec in 1908, Jellicoe received instructions from the First Lord, Reginald McKenna, offering him the post of Third Sea Lord and Controller. Perhaps, for the first time in his career, Jellicoe hesitated. He knew that the post would put him right in the centre of political controversy – whether national investment should be in dreadnoughts or social welfare. He replied saying that, while he would take the position, he would prefer to have stayed second-in-command of the Atlantic Fleet. He made his conditions known to McKenna: the country needed a strong dreadnought and destroyer construction programme. In 1908 the dreadnought programme had been halved and now, for 1909, Jellicoe proposed four such vessels. As soon as he was back in England, he took six weeks' leave, knowing that his new post would demand all of his energy and talents.

In April Winston Churchill entered the Cabinet as President of the Board of Trade and immediately allied himself with David Lloyd George, the Chancellor of the Exchequer, in opposition to the Admiralty proposals. Jellicoe's unease stemmed from his belief, not entirely well-founded, that the German programme was accelerating and that its ships were generally of superior quality to their British equivalents. Krupp was building gun mountings and outpacing British production. Since the critical factor in how long a battleship needs for construction is not the ship itself but the provision of her guns, this was a serious issue.

He also repeatedly tried to persuade Churchill to focus not only on gun calibre, but on the total displacement of a ship. If ships of equal displacement were compared, it was clear that the ratio of weight in British ships was biased toward gun weight and higher calibre rather than armour; armour was what German ships had. They were coupled with better watertight subdivisions and generally wider beams: he concluded that this had to give them a distinct advantage.

Beatty was appointed captain of the pre-dreadnought *Queen* in the Atlantic Fleet. Ethel did not bother to see him. She hated Gibraltar and this was one of the principal reasons why, years later, when offered the command of the Atlantic Fleet Beatty turned it down. His career was not going well and it was only due to Jacky Fisher's personal intervention that it caught a second wind. Not having held a fleet captain's command for long enough precluded Beatty from flag rank. Fisher managed to get through an Order in Council – legislation often used in emergencies in place of normal parliamentary process – to make an exception. On 1 January 1910 Beatty became the youngest flag officer since Nelson. *The Times* commented: 'Rear-Admiral Beatty will not only be the youngest Officer on the Flag list, but will be younger than over 90% of the Officers on the Captain's List'. He was close on Jellicoe's heels.

That same summer Jellicoe was invited by Usedom to the Kiel regatta. Usedom was now, as an admiral, in command of the Kiel naval base and for Jellicoe this was an ideal opportunity to get to know the man whom he believed would be his eventual foe a little better. They had been comrades in arms ten years before in China, but Usedom was wary nonetheless.

As a result of this trip Jellicoe returned with a better understanding of the investment that the Germans had made in dry docks (initially constructed for non-military purposes) and went on to win the argument about having a floating dock constructed at Cromarty (albeit not as wide as he would have liked). Still, the strengthening of the new bases, such as the one at Rosyth, was much slower than he thought wise. The need arose from the changing alliances that Britain was building. With Germany emerging as Britain's principal enemy, the northern bases were becoming key.

Jellicoe also came back to an issue he had looked at when he had been DNO, namely the quality of British armour-piercing shells. Tests were carried out against an old battleship that had been strengthened with additional armour plates for the test. Again it was found that the shells burst on impact rather than after penetration. But Jellicoe's term in office was once more too short and his successor dropped the issue. He was successful in arguing the case for parallel engine rooms so that a ship's speed could be maintained even if a torpedo hit had put one set of engines out of action.

In December 1910 Jellicoe took command of the Atlantic Fleet, flying his flag in the pre-dreadnought *Prince of Wales*. The following year started with a terrible personal tragedy. While he was at sea, his daughter Agnes Betty died, aged just five, of a mastoid infection.* The cruel news came by telegram. It must

---

* Betty, as she was known in the family, was christened Agnes Betty Gardiner Jellicoe, named after Gwen's mother, Lady Agnes Elizabeth Cayzer. She was buried at St John's Church, Cranmore, Middlessex, in a grave beautifully adorned with carved angels.

have been shattering for him. Yet it was difficult for him to grieve; all around him matters were coming to a head.

In mid 1911 relations with Germany broke down, nearly to crisis point. This was brought about by France moving troops into the interior of Morocco in April. By doing so France had broken with the terms of the Treaty of Algeciras and the Franco-German Accord of 1909 that had ended the first Moroccan crisis, and essentially set out the basis of equilibrium between France and Germany. France would be allowed her territory if Germany's commercial interests were respected.

As we saw in Chapter 2, the Kaiser's attempts to use the Agadir Crisis to break up the Triple Entente had not been successful. However, Germany's gunboat diplomacy in sending the *Panther* to Agadir had escalated tensions and a planned meeting between the Atlantic Fleet and the German High Seas Fleet was cancelled. The Kaiser was furious and, through Prince Heinrich, conveyed his feelings: Jellicoe, now as wary as Usedom had been earlier, did not now feel comfortable giving the real reason or explanation to the Kaiser's brother.

Ethel continued to make David Beatty's life hell. She threatened him with an end to his life in the Navy unless he found a way to get her presented at court. He did this through Eugénie Godfrey-Faussett's husband. He was naval AdC to George V and had nurtured a close relationship with Prince Albert, the future King George VI, whose boredom with London gave the Godfrey-Faussetts the means to curry favour. After Jutland, Prince Albert came back to London and, along with his wife, Godfrey-Faussett did what they could to alleviate the ennui of the young prince. On 29 January 1916, for example, they took him to the London Hippodrome with Portia Cadogan, whom the prince had three times suggested be present, even if she was, in fact, already close with his elder brother. Godfrey-Faussett was successful in getting Ethel presented. For his pains, Beatty ended up taking Godfrey-Faussett's wife as his own lover.†

Ethel simply would not have her husband in Gibraltar as second-in-command of the Atlantic Fleet. Rear Admiral Beatty turned down what would have been a significant promotion. Unsurprisingly, the reaction of the Navy was not one of great understanding. The naval secretary to the First Lord, Captain Ernest Troubridge, wrote to Beatty: 'The fact is that the Admiralty's view is that officers should serve where the Admiralty wish and not where they themselves wish'. But this was Beatty, supremely confident to the point of arrogance. At best his pay would be docked, not that it mattered that much to him. This also signalled another close brush with Jellicoe's career, as Beatty would have served

---

† There is a story – but I do not know whether it was actually true or merely the idle gossip of ill-wishers – that Beatty kept the correspondence of various girlfriends on his desk, arranged in small piles with colour-coded paperweights on each.

as Jellicoe's second-in-command. The experience of working together would have served them both well.

The thirty-nine-year-old Winston Churchill became First Lord of the Admiralty. Beatty asked for an interview, which was granted. Instead of being thrown out for having turned down a promotion, Beatty was offered a position as Churchill's naval secretary. It was the critical appointment of his career. Churchill was struck by Beatty – by 'the profound sagacity of his comments expressed in a language free from technical jargon'.[28] But soon enough Beatty sounded like Jellicoe: 'I hope to be able to squeeze some sense into him'. It was inevitable that Beatty and Churchill should lock horns occasionally – both were young and displayed the cockiness of their age – but eventually theirs became a strong working relationship.

In December 1911 the honour of Knight Commander of the Order of the Bath was bestowed on Jellicoe. This was followed six months later by his inclusion in the Coronation honours list, with a promotion to vice admiral. In September 1912 he was promoted to command the 2nd Battle Squadron of the Home Fleet, his flag hoisted on the new dreadnought *Hercules*, serving in this role as Sir George Callaghan's second-in-command.

This finally gave him the command experience of a battle squadron as well as the hands-on command of a dreadnought. Jellicoe exerted a considerable degree of independent thinking and innovation in battle exercises. Temple Patterson cited him dropping the single line-ahead formation, taking 'successful independent action with his squadron against the rear of the "enemy"', Sir George subsequently approving'.[29] Was it a refusal to delegate or a desire for action that got Jellicoe up from his sick bed in August 1916 when the German Fleet was out again off Sunderland?

At this point he was also very much in favour of fast divisions and the principle of offensive destroyer actions. There were also criticisms. Sir Francis Bridgeman (from whom Sir George had taken over) at the time made an astute comment on Jellicoe: 'He must learn to work with his captains and staff more and himself less ... At present he puts himself in position of, say, a glorified gunnery Lieutenant. He must trust his staff and captains and if they don't fit, he must kick them out'.[30] In my own opinion, Jellicoe was, in fact, a keen supporter of his staff, but he was also a workaholic and not known as a delegator.*

Jacky Fisher was aware that he owed Churchill much for getting Jellicoe the second-in-command role: he had been promoted over twenty-one other vice admirals. Jellicoe was not fully aware of why be was being moved to the Home

---

* This is arguably a curious comment from Bridgeman. Jellicoe was a key figure in developing staffs afloat when he became Second Sea Lord and was later criticised by one of his admirals for having too large a staff when he was in command of the Grand Fleet.

Fleet and actually asked to remain in command of the Atlantic Fleet. He did not know that Fisher was grooming him for the ultimate role. As Fisher rather melodramatically declared, 'If war comes in 1914 then Jellicoe will be Nelson at the Battle of St Vincent. If it comes in 1915 he will be Nelson at Trafalgar.' Jellicoe loathed that kind of talk.

Outside his fleet duties Jellicoe was also a member of the committee enquiring into the supply and sourcing of liquid fuels. This would have far-reaching results. He also closely followed the tests on *Thunderer* of the director-firing system. Invented by Scott and first fitted on *Neptune*, it essentially centralised the task of spotting and firing the guns from a director position mounted high above the ship. For Jellicoe, the comparative *Thunderer/Orion* tests where the two ships were pitted against each other were conclusive and he lobbied strongly for the system, even though there was still considerable opposition both within the fleet and from the Admiralty.[31] This was probably why, in 1914, only eight capital ships had been fitted, although Jellicoe sped up the implementation so that all but two had the system by the time of Jutland. In December he was back again at the Admiralty as Second Sea Lord. He continued to run up against Churchill, who unfailingly took an over-keen personal interest in all things technical.

Speaking of Churchill, Jellicoe said:

> It did not take me very long to find out that Mr Churchill was very apt to express strong opinions upon purely technical matters. Moreover, not being satisfied with expressing opinions, he tried to force his views upon the board. His fatal error was his entire disability to realise his own limitations as a civilian … While his gift (wonderful argumentative powers) was of great use to the Admiralty when we wanted the naval case put well before the government, it became a positive danger when the First Lord started to exercise his powers of argument on his colleagues on the board.[32]

In March 1913 Beatty joined the 1st Battle Cruiser Squadron. It must have been a moment with a great sense of personal achievement, but the manner of his assumption of command remained pure Beatty. He was late, unprepared to cut short a holiday in Monte Carlo. As his flag lieutenant he took on Ralph Seymour. It was a decision that had little to do with his skills or reputation: Beatty had not known him before. In all probability it had more to do with the fact that Seymour was very socially well-connected and that his sister was a close friend of Churchill's wife.

That May, three years before what both sides would call *Der Tag*, the day of reckoning between the British and German fleets, Jellicoe was invited to Berlin to what would be the last formal meeting of the kings and emperors of

Europe; the occasion was the marriage of the Kaiser's daughter, Victoria Louise of Prussia, to Ernest Augustus of Hanover (once Victoria Louise's husband, he became the Duke of Brunswick). Jellicoe got to meet Theobald von Bethmann-Hollweg, the German chancellor, see the working of a Zeppelin reconnaissance airship up close and dine privately with the Kaiser and Tirpitz. Talking after dinner, the latter politely declined Jellicoe's invitation to stay with him in Britain saying that he 'would certainly be murdered if he were to visit England', as his shipbuilding programmes had so raised public ire. Two months later, in July, Jellicoe out-manoeuvred his own commander-in-chief, Sir George Callaghan, in a battle exercise. Jellicoe's Red Fleet simulated a possible German invasion of the Humber Estuary which was cut short 'for fear of giving useful information to the Germans'.[33] Eric Grove feels that it was probably Jellicoe's success at these manoeuvres that singled him out as Churchill's choice to replace Callaghan as the commander of the Grand Fleet in the first days of war and not to wait for the previously agreed timing at the end of the year.

The men and their marriages

Beatty and Jellicoe had both married into considerable wealth, but Beatty regretted the penalty that he had to pay. His was an unhappy marriage and one from which his career seemed constantly under threat, although it miraculously remained immune. Ethel's influence and outspoken comments on Jellicoe were quite another matter. That the two men would eventually come to represent different schools of naval thinking was a matter of course, but she brought a shameful degree of acrimony.

This was perhaps inevitable for a number of reasons. One was certainly Beatty's personality. He had a streak of vanity and was very sensitive to criticism or failure. His sense of frustration at not being seen as another Nelson when victory had been snatched from his grasp at the Battle of Dogger Bank in 1915, then again at Jutland and in the action-less aftermath, was tangible. (At Dogger Bank, Beatty had successfully managed to sink the armoured cruiser *Blücher* but signals that had been meant to order a pursuit of the rest of the German force had been muddled; the pursuit halted to pound an already crippled ship.) Where Jellicoe naturally tried to understand the lessons of Jutland, Beatty became increasingly concerned with his image and career. To this he sacrificed any relationship that he had built to that point with Jellicoe.

One of Beatty's biographers, Andrew Lambert, heartily praised Beatty who came to be known as the first 'modern' admiral (Roskill called him 'the last naval hero'), mainly for his eight-year term as First Lord of the Admiralty, Lambert was also forthright, though, in his criticism of his character. Of his wartime accomplishments, he wrote searingly:

His career was advanced by fortune, publicity and money; his reputation reflected an image rather than reality; his victories only existed in the pages of wartime newspapers. In later life he waged a devious, if not downright dishonest campaign to maintain the illusion of glory by traducing the reputation of another officer, splitting the navy right down the middle in the process.[34]

The physical appearance of each of these two admirals painted a portrait of contrasts. Jellicoe was diminutive, his large nose not the most attractive of features, but his eyes were sparkling, and full of energy and intelligence. Beatty was broad-shouldered and square-jawed, a handsome man – a rake. He always wore his hat at a slight angle and insisted on having six buttons on his naval tunics, not the regulation eight. No one else in the Navy did that, not even the King. Beatty had the Irish side in him, Jellicoe was thoroughly English.* Mountbatten would call Jellicoe's looks similar to those of a tapir, while of Beatty, (he) 'loved the man, cap jauntily aslant, really going for the enemy, giving the order to close Hipper's ships after two of his own had been blown up'.[35] It was not surprising with his looks, his elan, his dash and charisma that Beatty came to be seen and hero-worshipped as the Nelson of the twentieth-century Navy. Jellicoe's only proximity to any Nelson-like characteristic, Andrew Gordon concluded in a 2015 BBC programme, was the 'intimacy with his men'.

Beatty had an aura 'which radiated in part from his genuine accomplishments and in part from his successful exhibitionism'. Jellicoe, almost consistently, was remembered for his soft-spoken nature, his kindness and his modesty.

There is a telling description of Beatty's and Jellicoe's behaviour on *Iron Duke*, a ship that Beatty later described as having 'too much Jellicoe in it' when he moved his flag to *Queen Elizabeth*, more fondly known as the 'Big Lizzie'. To reach the bridge often meant going through the ratings' galley. Jellicoe would walk through, his presence only obvious by the click of his steel heels on the plates and his occasional 'Excuse me', as he passed a rating; Beatty would be preceded by a group of armed men.†

Such were the two sailors in whose hands the fate of the nation lay in May 1916.

---

* Beatty had talked to a fortune-teller, a Mrs Robinson, about his future prospects and sometimes would be heard to wonder out loud about what the omens might hold. It was surprising for so strong and confident a man.

† Gordon quoted an electrician who, I believe, was called Joe Cockburn: 'An electrician who served on Jellicoe's *Iron Duke*, named Joe, recalled that in his cabin, he had some partitions taken down and an enormous table fitted with holes in the middle where he could get up through. On it he had a model of every naval ship in Europe, and he would spend hours working out all his various moves, one in particular called the "Grid Iron". I made some ship models for him for his operations table, and he just said, "Thanks Joe". That was the kind of officer he was.'

4
Men From the Same Mould: Scheer and Hipper

The two German commanders with whom the British would join battle, Reinhard Scheer and Franz Hipper, were born in 1863. In the same year the future Kaiser Wilhelm II, then aged four, made his first visit to his royal cousins in England for the marriage of Victoria's eldest son Bertie, later Edward VII, to Princess Alexandra of Denmark.

Born on 30 September, Scheer had a middle-class upbringing. His father, Julius, was a minister in Obernkirchen in Lower Saxony and also, as rector of the town's school, a teacher. From his mother, Marie Rheinhart, Scheer inherited his name, though it is said that his real name was Arthur.

Hipper was also born in September, on the 13th. His family was from Weilheim, a small town around forty miles south of Munich, close to the Alpine village of Oberammergau. Hipper's father Anton was, like Scheer's, middle-class and ran a hardware store. Hipper's father died when the boy was just three, leaving his widow Anna to care for Franz and his three brothers, who were brought up in a Catholic school that Franz attended from the age of five.

The 1870s were tumultuous years for the new Germany. The victorious war against her neighbour sowed the seeds of a deep French bitterness and a longing for revenge that would play its part in the final weeks before war broke out in August 1914. Two years after Bavaria joined the newly created German Reich, the ten-year-old Hipper was sent off to Munich to attend *Gymnasium*, home for the next six years.

On 22 April 1879 Scheer joined a training ship, a small sailing frigate, SMS *Niobe*, as an officer cadet. He was following closely in the footsteps of Tirpitz, who had trained on the same ship fourteen years before. Built in 1848, *Niobe* had in 1859 been sold by the Royal Navy to the nascent Prussian navy. Scheer spent three months on her, learning basic navigation and engineering. When he came back in September he went straight to the Kiel naval academy.

Meanwhile, Hipper was finishing *Gymnasium* and decided to skip *Abitur* – the equivalent of today's A-levels – and leave with a qualification of *Obersekunda*. This was specifically designed for those following a technical career path. He joined the *Einjährigfreiwilliger*, an organisation that fed the ranks of the reserve-officer class.

Like Jellicoe, Scheer excelled. In the 1880 sea-cadet exams in Kiel, his marks earned him second spot. Considering that he had only achieved a 'satisfactory' rating entering as a cadet, it was a clear sign of his subsequent application. After graduation and promotion to sea cadet in June, he spent six months studying gunnery, torpedo warfare and infantry tactics. It was perhaps unsurprising that infantry tactics should be included, as the Kiel academy was modelled on the Prussian military academy and the navy headed mostly by army officers.

Scheer joined another old British ship, this time the 91-gun *Renown*, followed by a stint in the armoured frigate *Friedrich Karl*. In his last year as a cadet, Scheer joined *Hertha* on a world tour to Australia (Melbourne), Japan (Yokohama and Kobe) and China (Shanghai).

Hipper decided, too, that the navy would be the best place for him. He had become obsessed with the idea through a friend of his who had been in the merchant marine. He secretly underwent the medical examinations required for all cadets. When found to be in fit state, he confronted his mother with his decision. Though she did what she could to dissuade him, she never regretted his decision and lived long enough to see the honour of the Kaiser's ennoblement of her son following the *Skagerrakschlacht*. She would die four months after the battle.

A cadet candidate until he was eighteen, Hipper joined the navy on 12 April 1881, and like Scheer and Tirpitz before him started on the *Niobe*. He had passed his exams with thirty-four others, most of whom had not needed to sit them as they had finished their education in higher schools. With him in class was the future Admiral Souchon. He would become Commander-in-Chief of the Mediterranean Squadron, and lead the dramatic episode of *Goeben* and *Breslau* at the start of hostilities.* The future Admiral Schultz was also a classmate – he would lead the 4th Squadron of the High Seas Fleet in the Baltic. For a man 'born neither to influence nor to wealth'[1], Hipper was moving in an increasingly select circle. In September he went back to the naval cadet school.

In March 1882 Hipper graduated and was sent to attend gunnery school on the training ship *Mars*, before joining *Friedrich Karl* and then the frigate *Leipzig*. The latter would take him on a two-year world cruise. At the end of his time on

---

* Souchon was in the Adriatic at the outbreak of war and feared that he would be boxed in. He fought his way through to Istanbul with *Goeben* and *Breslau*, and handed them over to the Turkish navy. Turkey was most receptive, as two of their own capital ships – those that became HMS *Erin* and HMS *Agincourt* – had been seized by the British. Souchon was named commander-in-chief of the Tukish navy and *Goeben* assisted considerably in closing the Bosphorus to international maritime traffic.

the *Mars*, he became Midshipman Hipper, someone who could command the lower deck. The newly recommissioned *Leipzig* was to 'proceed to Yokohama, when the work of commissioning the ship is complete, and to take up station in Japanese waters for the protection of German interests'.[2] As soon as she was at sea, she ran into trouble when her gun ports badly leaked in a heavy sea. Eventually she ran into harbour at Yarmouth, where she received extensive repairs in the local yard, the cadets using the time to be shown around the town. Hipper was back in Kiel in October 1884 and spent the winter at the naval officer school, after which he became responsible for recruit training in the 1st Naval Battalion.

Scheer was commissioned into the navy, taking up the first of two postings to the East Africa Squadron from 1884 to 1886. He served on the corvette *Bismarck* as a newly appointed Leutnant. On *Bismarck*, the squadron flagship of Eduard von Knorr, he made a connection that would stand him in good stead through his career: this was with Leutnant Henning von Holtzendorff, later to become commander of the High Seas Fleet. Holtzendorff would bring along Scheer, by then a captain, as his chief of staff. During his time on *Bismarck* Scheer took part in an armed landing against a pro-British chieftain in Cameroon.

In December 1885, Scheer was promoted to Oberleutnant. Scheer and Holtzendorff would again serve together, Holtzendorff as his superior officer on the cruiser *Prinzeß Wilhelm*. A cruise had been organised for a group of officers to observe the Sino-Japanese War of 1895/6.

In April 1885 Hipper was assigned as division officer to drilling recruits of the 1st Naval Battalion in Kiel and on 19 December he received his promotion to Unterleutnant and took some well-deserved leave. The leave was short, however, and in January 1886 Hipper was assigned as division officer to the 2nd Seaman's Artillery Division, where he remained until early March. At this point he made an immediate switch to *Friedrich Karl* as watch officer, a key promotion as it only came through direct recommendation from the commanding officer. The appointment soon paid off, and his service record noted that he was a 'very fine ship handler and navigator'. Other assignments, on *Prinz Adalbert*, *Stein* and *Stosch* followed in quick succession.

Scheer returned home in 1886 and from January to May 1888 undertook a six-month training course in torpedo tactics on *Blücher*. He put his newly acquired skills to immediate use as torpedo officer on the corvette *Sophie* in the East Africa Squadron.

That summer, Hipper was promoted to Leutnant. As winter approached he joined the small dispatch boat *Wacht*. It turned out to be quite an important move in that he came under the eye of Commander von Baudissin, who would captain SMS *Hohenzollern* (the royal yacht) and be Chief of Naval Staff and

Commander-in-Chief of the North Sea Station. Always on the move, however, Hipper left *Wacht* in 1889 and on Christmas Eve joined the battleship *Friedrich der Große*. After this short interlude, for his foreign service was at an end, he arrived back in Wilhelmshaven the following spring.

In 1890 Scheer was establishing himself as a torpedo specialist and was appointed as an instructor at the Kiel torpedo school in June. Scheer's career path took a dramatic turn when in Kiel he met Alfred Tirpitz, who was later to bring him to the RMA to continue his work on torpedoes.

While Scheer was honing these skills, Hipper was pulled in two apparently unhelpful directions. The first was as watch officer on the coastal battleship *Siegfried*. The second posting was to the armoured gunboat *Mücke*, which was essentially a floating gun platform, armed with a single 30.5cm gun as well as two bow-mounted torpedo tubes. *Mücke* was 'a kind of movable coast fort which in war could be stranded at the ebb on the sand banks of the North Sea estuaries, where they [the coast forts] settled down like a clucking hen and re-floated at the flood'.[3]

Yet being on *Mücke* facilitated an important move for Hipper: he was transferred to another ship of the 2nd Reserve Division, *Blücher*, which was stationed alternately at Kiel and Flensburg. On this ship Hipper became immersed in torpedo tactics and technique. All the individual torpedoes in the training ship had nicknames based on how they would perform, such as 'Twisting Franz' or 'Diving Emil'.

In October 1891 Hipper rejoined *Friedrich der Große* as torpedo officer. He was 'responsible for the efficiency of torpedoes, torpedo armament and all that pertains to it: torpedo charges, explosive equipment, including charges and mine-clearing gear, and for the administration and maintenance of torpedo stores'.[4] After *Friedrich der Große* came another torpedo position, this time as torpedo officer on SMS *Beowulf*. In April 1892 he was made company commander of the 2nd Torpedo Unit based in Wilhelmshaven. From then until September 1894 Hipper made frequent position changes and commanded a total of nine torpedo boats.

Excellence in torpedo tactics did not at this time necessarily help Hipper. Alexander von Monts, who succeeded Caprivi as head of the Admiralstab in 1888, 'had an undisguised dislike of torpedo boats, which indeed was shared by almost all the older officers at the time'[5], yet it was a service within the service, with an incredible *esprit de corps*.

While serving on the battleship *Wörth*, commanded by Prince Heinrich, Hipper was promoted in 1895 to lieutenant commander. The design of *Wörth* was noteworthy. She was heavily gunned, with six 28cm guns down the centre-line. He had come aboard as a watch officer but also served in gunnery and navigation roles. It was these all-round abilities that made him interesting to the prince, who was by now quietly promoting him.

His next torpedo assignment was as commanding officer of a torpedo reserve unit, the 2nd, in September. His chief biographer, Hugo von Waldeyer-Hartz, stated that this was 'the decisive step which led to Hipper's brilliant career'.[6] Among his men – around four hundred in the company – there was great camaraderie. Hipper was immensely popular and well-respected. A leutnant on *S.73* commented: 'He was extraordinarily attractive, a slim, wiry officer who knew exactly what he wanted, and was a splendid leader'. Hipper regularly used to appear with his men, all dressed in similar straw hats with black ribbons on which, emblazoned in red, was '*Stander-Z*', the German naval signal for attack.

With Tirpitz's shaping of the future German navy, and his appointment to the torpedo section in the RMA in 1897, Scheer's outlook took a dramatic change for the better in a career which was in many ways shaped by his association with Tirpitz; in Gary Weir's estimation, it was at this time that he 'absorbed the Tirpitz doctrine'[7].

In 1898 Hipper temporarily took up another position in the torpedo divisions, as navigating officer under Admiral Thomsen on SMS *Kurfürst Friedrich Wilhelm*, a sister ship of *Wörth*. In September the following year Hipper joined the royal yacht *Hohenzollern* as navigator. The post would last three years, which, as Waldeyer-Hartz pointed out, was a solid endorsement of the esteem in which Hipper was now held. At this time she was captained by the Kaiser's naval AdC, Commander Count von Baudissin.

For a vessel transporting such an important passenger, *Hohenzollern* was badly equipped and quite unseaworthy (according to Erich Raeder she was a 'monstrosity') yet Hipper was in good company, able to rub shoulders with anyone who was anyone in naval circles.

Scheer went back to sea in 1900, this time as the commander of a destroyer flotilla. It was an excellent opportunity for the man to form his ideas about these craft, which would later play such an important part at Jutland. That same year, his daughter Marianne was born.*

Hipper and Beatty shared a common experience of service on a royal yacht (Beatty had served on *Britannia*), but the duty afforded Hipper closer contact

* In 1933 Marianne Scheer would christen the 'pocket battleship' *Admiral Scheer*. She married a naval officer and had a son, Helmut Scheer-Besserer, in 1921. Helmut's son, Mathias, born in 1956, is the admiral's surviving bloodline. Scheer married twice and in August 1916 adopted Rudolf Hennings as his son, changing his name to Rudolf Scheer-Hennings. His grandson, Reinhard, and I are now re-establishing the friendship that Jellicoe had wished to restore in 1928, when the German admiral died.

with his sovereign than was the case with Beatty. Hipper made some long and sometimes quite dangerous trips together with the Kaiser on *Hohenzollern*.

At the start of 1901, along with HM Yachts *Victoria and Albert* and *Osborne*, *Hohenzollern* went to the Isle of Wight off the south coast of England as part of the funeral cortège of Queen Victoria following her death. The start of 1902 saw another significant trip for *Hohenzollern*. Against Baudissin's advice, the Kaiser wanted her to travel to America to see, among other things, the imperial yacht *Meteor* race. Sailing via St Thomas, she arrived in New York harbour, covered in ice, on Lincoln's birthday. Social activities brought the Kaiser and Hipper close together. The Kaiser was not a drinker – he normally had orange juice in a silver goblet – and he was keen on physical exercise. There is even a photo of the Kaiser, Hipper and Baudissin all doing callisthenics on the deck of *Hohenzollern*.

After a direct endorsement of Hipper's qualities by the Kaiser's brother, who arrived to join them in New York on the Norddeutscher Lloyd liner *Kronprinz Wilhelm*, Hipper was given the command of the 2nd Torpedo Unit in October, with *Niobe* as flotilla leader. He was based in Wilhelmshaven, nicknamed 'mud town', 'the roughest of all North Sea bases', but his friendship with the Kaiser meant that the latter would often visit him informally on the ship.[8]

Training was vigorous. Admiral Zeye, inspector of destroyers, had a favourite test for young destroyer captains. They had to grab a bottle of champagne hanging off the stern boom of the flagship at high speed. It captures the wonderful spirit of a young renegade group within the more conservative naval ranks. Hipper himself would time his own boat's performance as she sped through narrow and difficult passages, each time trying to shave off precious seconds. After eight months bringing *Niobe* up to seaworthiness, Hipper transferred his flag to a torpedo boat, *D.8*. He also tried out *G.110*, *G.112*, *S.102* and *D.9*.

In 1903 Scheer was brought back off sea duty by Tirpitz, this time as chief of the central division of the RMA. With his promotion to Korvettenkapitän in 1904, he took command of the light cruiser SMS *Gazelle*. *Gazelle*, which had been launched at the end of 1898, was on a goodwill visit to New Orleans.

Scheer's next promotion came in March 1905 when he was given the rank of Kapitän zur See. The past few years had witnessed a prolonged period of promotion: lieutenant commander in 1900, commander in 1904, captain in 1905. Hipper had commanded the 2nd Torpedo Unit for more than thirty-five months during which, on 5 April 1905, he was promoted to commander. He now took up a new position on the staff of the commandant of the North Sea Station, attending two gunnery courses on *Prinz Adalbert* and SMS *Schwaben*.

In April 1906 Hipper took up the command of the cruiser *Leipzig*, which was larger than *Niobe* and had served as escort to *Hohenzollern*. When *Leipzig* departed for the Far East, Hipper returned to *Friedrich Karl* in September as her commander. Once again he found himself under the watchful eye of Prince Heinrich. His performance was notable: the ship gained the Kaiser's gunnery prize. Moreover, Hipper was mentioned in 1907's manoeuvre reports and *Friedrich Karl* classed as outstanding. This second encounter with Prince Heinrich led to Hipper's becoming flag officer of torpedo boats when the position became available, 'recommended for battleship command and for higher independent commands'.

In April, Hipper was promoted to Kapitän, received high awards and was present at the meeting between the Kaiser and the Tsar. But as always he was averse to the paperwork and administration that went with senior posts. He had, in Waldeyer-Hartz's words, a 'distaste for pen and paper'.

For Scheer, battleship command finally came. He was given command of *Elsass* and spent the next two years on her. His evaluation report was complimentary: 'Filled the position well, very accomplished in gunnery. Should be well-suited for a high staff position.'

Hipper took command of the newly commissioned SMS *Gneisenau* in March 1908, preparing her for the East Asia Squadron and in October got what Prince Heinrich had had in mind for him: command of the 1st Torpedo Boat Division in Kiel. The Kaiser read his report and underlined one phrase: '*große Dienstfreundigkeit*' – 'tremendous enthusiasm for the service'. Hipper was being recognised in very high places. So it was with the British, whose naval attaché in Berlin commented on the German torpedo-boat forces: 'there is no reason to suppose that personnel or materiel are anything but first class'.[9]

On 1 December 1909 Scheer was promoted to Admiral von Holtzendorff's chief of staff. Within six months, aged forty-seven, he was a Konteradmiral. He went back to the RMA as Chief of the General Naval Staff in 1911, while Hipper, now a commodore, was made commander of the 10,200-ton armoured cruiser SMS *Yorck* and then appointed chief of staff to the deputy flag officer of the reconnaissance forces, or *Aufklärungsgruppe*, the service branch in which he would really make his name and the command of which would bring him face to face with Beatty five years later.

In January 1912 his senior, the deputy flag officer, Rear Admiral Gustav von Bachmann, was made flag officer. Hipper moved up. On the 27th, the day after taking up this new position – it was the Kaiser's birthday, too – the forty-nine-year-old became Rear Admiral Franz Hipper, rising star of the Kaiser's navy, responsible for all the torpedo boats of the scouting forces and the cruisers of the 2nd Scouting Group. It was a huge achievement: 'A man who had never been inside a ministry, never attended the naval academy, never held an Admiralty appointment. A fighting officer pure and simple.'[10] He would be praised by his immediate superior officer, Bachmann, and the overall fleet commander-in-chief, Holtzendorff.

Hipper attained a higher profile in 1912, perhaps higher than he bargained for. The Kaiser had proposed a new staffing policy for the High Seas Fleet, in which the entire crew – officers and men – of a battleship would be changed every three years. Since this followed the organisational precedent set in the torpedo forces, Hipper was asked to look at the issue. He did so, and courageously voted against the Kaiser's proposal. Bachmann and Admiral Friedrich von Ingenohl supported him but that might have been scant comfort for Hipper, who was out on a limb. 'I believe that an experiment with this [three-year] system in the fleet would be of extremely dubious value. The low battle readiness of the particular ship which is in its first year would decrease the battle readiness of the whole fleet.'[11]

Despite this, the new system was pushed through. One of the first ships to be affected was the newly commissioned battleship *Prinzregent Luitpold*. She soon got a bad reputation and, almost to prove the point, was the ship on which the first mutinies later broke out in August 1917.

As 1913 was closing, Scheer was promoted on 9 December to the rank of Vizeadmiral. In January he took the command of the six battleships of the 2nd Battle Squadron. Later that month he was given the 3rd Battle Squadron, the prize squadron of the German navy with the latest and fastest ships, the powerful *Kaiser*- and *König*-class dreadnoughts.

When Bachmann took up command of the Baltic forces, his recommendation that Hipper take his position was acted upon and on 1 October 1913 Hipper took overall command of the scouting forces. Erich Raeder, who would later become Hitler's supreme naval commander, is worth quoting: 'Our new commander was an energetic and impulsive individual, with quick perception and a keen "seaman's eye" but unlike his predecessor he had risen exclusively through performance in the fleet'.[12]

Hipper's ideas for the battle-cruisers came from what Bachmann had started, namely the battle-cruiser charge. It was a manoeuvre that Bachmann had developed in 1912 to cover the possible emergency extraction of the main battle fleet. Hipper also developed an idea of a battle-cruiser breakthrough in which the battle-cruiser's role would be as a hammer blow to do exactly that: break through the cruiser and destroyer screens that the British would have. In some ways it was a precursor of the '*Schwerpunkt*' thinking at which German armoured forces became so adept in the Second World War: to identify the enemy's weak point, then push everything against that point until it broke. The breakthrough and charge tactics were known to be dangerous, and would result in substantial battle-cruiser damage, but they would also protect the battle squadrons.

Scheer was bitterly disappointed with his commander, Friedrich von Ingenohl, when in 1915, after raids on Hartlepool, Whitby and Scarborough had successfully lured out the Grand Fleet, the vice admiral failed to close the trap. Tirpitz at the time wrote that Ingenohl could have dealt the British a heavy blow. 'On 16th December, Ingenohl had the fate of Germany in the palm of his hand. I boil with emotion whenever I think of it.'[13] Even the British could not believe how close they had come to a possible defeat. At the time, a British naval staff monograph stressed:

> Here at last were the conditions for which the Germans had been striving since the beginning of the war. A few miles away on the port bow of the German High Seas Fleet, isolated and several hours steaming from home, was the most powerful homogeneous battle squadron of the Grand Fleet, the destruction of which would at one blow have completed the process of attrition and placed the British and German fleets on a precisely even footing as regards numerical strength.[14]

James Goldrick echoed the sentiment: 'Never again would such an opportunity to redress the balance present itself to the Imperial Navy'.[15]

Hipper had no qualms about the loss of civilian life caused by the raids. He viewed it 'entirely as a war measure and therefore as a task imposed upon him by duty. It is a regrettable but obvious fact that modern war is blind: it involves both combatants and non-combatants, slaying indiscriminate'.[16] From the outcome, it was clear that Scheer's and Hipper's strategy was logical and predictable.

Then, after the loss of the *Blücher* at Dogger Bank, the Kaiser moved against Ingenohl – but replaced him with the excessively cautious Hugo von Pohl. Throughout the rest of 1915, the High Seas Fleet, if it sortied, remained closely offshore under the protection of the Heligoland Bight and was never further than 120 miles from home shores.

On 8 January 1916 von Pohl was hospitalised, suffering from liver cancer. On the ships of the High Seas Fleet, bottled up in Wilhelmshaven and Kiel, there was little sympathy for the ailing commander-in-chief. The past year had provided little action.

When, ten days later, a new commander-in-chief was named, the anticipation of a fresh wind was almost palpable. Unlike Pohl, Scheer reckoned that a 'fleet in being' did not mean languishing in the safety of a home port. It meant actively seeking out contact with the enemy. Scheer was not afraid of making his case to the Kaiser. In mid 1915 Admiral Georg Alexander von Müller, the chief of the naval cabinet, had noted in his diary that he considered Scheer the dark-horse candidate to take over the High Seas Fleet. Interestingly, Tirpitz had also been considered for this position, but his vacillation about engaging the High Seas Fleet at the start of the war, and his politicking, robbed him of the position. Scheer brought with him the 'calm and deliberate' Captain Adolf von Trotha as chief of staff and the 'brilliant and impulsive' Captain Magnus von Levetzow to direct operations.[17]

On 26 March Hipper applied for sick leave. He had been having painful bouts of sciatica and for most of the time was unable to sleep. The next day, on board SMS *Seydlitz* Scheer approved command being temporarily handed over to Konteradmiral Friedrich Bödicker. Hipper had little but disdain for him – he did not like the same music as Hipper did (Hipper was a fan of Wagner and would often have the ship's band play his favourites). But the differences did not last: later, at Jutland, he and Bödicker worked closely.

Behind his back, even if he had approved his leave, Scheer tried to get Hipper removed. 'Vice Admiral Hipper no longer possess[es] the qualities of robustness and elasticity'[18] needed for command of the scouting groups. Hipper frequently took time off at spas. His sciatica flared up chronically with the stress of his position. It was only Holtzendorff's and Müller's staunch rejection that staved off what would have been a fatal organisational blunder.

Scheer firmly believed in the strength of integrated naval operations: using all the means at his disposal, and not just the battleships and battle-cruisers. He laid out his vision in *Guiding Principles for Sea Warfare in the North Sea*, a manual that the Kaiser approved at the end of February in a meeting on the flagship *Friedrich der Große*, anchored in the waters of Wilhelmshaven. The Kaiser brought to the meeting his brother, Prince Heinrich, Tirpitz and Holtzendorff.

> First of all, I have the High Seas Fleet ... These ships alone would not
> be enough, in view of the enemy's dreadnought strength. But I have one
> hundred excellent submarines ... and a number of Zeppelin airships
> for scouting purposes. When I consider my fleet as a whole, I cannot
> argue that I am weak. I am strong – stronger than the enemy. My
> strength, however, will do me no good unless I attack with all weapons
> simultaneously ... Only if I use, simultaneously, every naval weapon
> that I have will the total of my offensive power be greater than Britain's
> resistance, and I shall win.[19]

Scheer was popular, quick-witted and handsome: what better combination for the new commander? Known as 'the man in the iron mask' because of his imperious looks, Scheer was also a strict disciplinarian. Trotha summed him up:

One could not find a better comrade. He never stood on ceremony with young officers. But he was impatient and always had to act quickly. He would expect his staff to have the plans and orders for an operation worked out exactly to the last detail … He was a commander of instinct and instant decision who liked to have all the options presented to him and then as often as not chose a course of action no one had previously considered. In action he was absolutely cool and clear.[20]

Pointers to Scheer's vanity lie there in Trotha's praise. Raeder talked of Scheer's 'practical common sense and a keen sense of perception, but he also possessed that rare commodity, a delight in responsibility'.[21] He had a sense of humour too. Von Weizsäcker said that he had the nickname '*Bobschiess*', because of 'his likeness to a fox terrier, which he was fond of provoking to bite his friends' trousers'.[22]

Much of Scheer's post-war life was spent writing, starting with the publication in 1919 of his history of the German fleet, *Germany's High Seas Fleet in the World War*. Published in English in 1920, it was the other side of Jellicoe's 1919 *The Grand Fleet*. Neither makes terrific reading but of the two, Scheer's is probably the more approachable.

In 1920 Scheer's life went into a tailspin. One evening at home in Weimar, in a villa that stands today, Scheer asked his maid to fetch another bottle of wine from the cellar. When she did not come back, his wife Emilie went to look. When Emilie failed to reappear, his daughter Else went to investigate. A robber had been caught in the act by maid and wife: he had shot the maid dead and mortally wounded Emilie. Else was also severely injured but survived. Emilie died on the way to hospital. She and Reinhard had been married thirty-one years. The effect of the loss on the admiral was profound and he became a recluse.

Scheer published his autobiography at the end of 1925, *Vom Segelschiff zum U-Boot* (*From Sailing Ship to Submarine*). In 1928 Jellicoe reached out to his old adversary and invited him to his country house on the Isle of Wight. Scheer accepted but, aged only sixty-five, died at Marktredwitz, near Bayreuth in Bavaria, before he could make the trip. One can only speculate – with more than a certain amount of frustration – what an extraordinary meeting this would have been. Their discussion on the tactics of Jutland or the change of naval strategy and the launch of unrestricted war would have been a unique and fascinating opportunity to have heard the old foes explore the wide ranging issues. Frost concluded: 'He [Scheer] was willing, contrary to Jellicoe, to leave something to chance'.[23] I am no great fan of Frost's writings but here, like Beatty, he may have a point. However, I strongly disagree with Frost's comparison of Jellicoe to the American General McClellan, who would endlessly drill his men but was not very strong as a commander when it came to battle. It sounds very much like

Admiral Sir Heworth Meux's letter to King George's private secretary: 'Practically the whole of the fighting was done by our battle-cruisers, and our battle fleet only fired a very few rounds ... Jellicoe has done splendid work as an organiser and driller of the fleet, but as yet I am sorry to say he has shown no sign of being a Nelson'. It could not have been more misleading.

Scheer's simple tombstone stands under the shade of trees in the quiet cemetery of Weimar. The words *'Hier rührt Admiral Scheer'* (Here rests Admiral Scheer) are a quiet testament to the man, in the navy at sixteen and without the social or financial assets associated with the officer class, who nearly brought Britain to its knees.

On 25 May 1932, a week before the sixteenth anniversary of Jutland, Hipper died. Unlike Scheer he chose to be buried not where he had lived but where he was born, in Weilheim. Hipper was the only Bavarian to have broken into the hold of northern and central German officers on the High Seas Fleet.

It was actually more of an accomplishment than might appear, given that Austria – Bavaria's neighbour – chose to fight Prussia in 1866, a mere five years before the establishment of the new German empire in 1871. Maybe for this reason, Tirpitz always felt that the navy was the melting pot of the German people. Hipper was the sole commander-in-chief from the southern state. Among the four major admirals at Jutland, he was also the only one who did not have political posts in either Whitehall or Berlin.

Hipper, the Jutland commander with the least experience in staff and administrative functions, was probably, of all the battle's commanders, the most instinctive. Like Beatty, he was a natural leader of men. Unlike Jellicoe and Scheer, he lacked the political acumen acquired though staff and policy positions. But like Jellicoe he was a technician. Jellicoe's expertise was gunnery, Hipper's the torpedo. During his career, Hipper spent more than ten years as a 'sea hussar' in positions where he was teaching, in direct command of, or working with torpedoes. His service as a watch officer was equally important, not only because he was under the direct eye of Prince Heinrich, but also because watch-officer duties were such that they put him in direct control of a ship's handling and management. The only exposure that Hipper had to strategy was on the short Admiralstab staff cruise in 1897. He never attended the Marineakademie. As a partial result of this, he knew little about politics or economics, nor did he speak a foreign language.

But where it mattered, Hipper shone. Hough summed up his role at Jutland: he 'played the part of a maestro ... He manoeuvred his ships superbly, kept his nerve under the most daunting and intimidating circumstances, and extricated his ships from the famous "death ride" following his C-in-C's second turnabout. He and his captains deserve the highest credit.'[24]

5

The Naval Non-War

———

Persuaded by the Kaiser that his fleet should not be put at risk, German naval commanders were also instinctively cautious. They felt that a fleet-to-fleet engagement with the British was to be avoided at all costs, at least until their superiority at sea could be whittled down.

In the early twentieth century Britain's dominance of world trade remained enormous, even though it was in relative decline. In 1913 her merchant fleets totalled something in the region of eight thousand ships and just over eleven million tons.[1] The Germans knew that, as a net importer, Britain's dependency on trade could be used against it, directly and indirectly. As Churchill pointed out, 'Britain imported almost two-thirds of its food and, usually, did not maintain a stock of more than four to six weeks of food and of raw materials for its manufacturing industries in stock at any one time'.[2] Germany's attack on Britain's sea-lanes took three forms: long-range cruiser hit-and-run, submarine warfare, and, indirectly, the power of the High Seas Fleet.

Share of World Merchant Tonnage, June 1914

	Tons Net (000s)	Percentage
United Kingdom	11,538	44.4
British Dominions and Colonies	902	3.5
Total British Empire	12,440	47.9
Germany	3,096	11.9
United States	1,195	4.6
Norway	1,153	4.4
France	1,098	4.2
Japan	1,048	4.0
Netherlands	910	3.5
Italy	871	3.4
Other	4,179	16.1
	25,990	

Source: Hawkins, *The Starvation Blockades* (see Bibliography).

To wear Britain down, a number of options were available: anti-commerce cruiser operations, to divert resources from the North Sea, mines, submarine warfare, and, finally, scouting groups to lure smaller sections of the British fleet into well-prepared traps, at which point they would be pounced on by larger German supporting forces of the High Seas Fleet.

Not only did the British have to contend with these threats: the Royal Navy was also charged with taking over German colonial territory, defending Britain's worldwide bases and patrolling the oceans. Fisher once famously asked, 'Do you know there are five keys to the world? The Straits of Dover, the Straits of Gibraltar, the Suez Canal, the Straits of Malacca, the Cape of Good Hope. And every one of these keys we hold. Aren't we the lost tribes?' But the Navy's task made colossal demands on already stretched resources.

The North Sea blockade

Britain's geographical position gave it a natural 'breakwater effect' in the North Sea, set astride the seaways to Germany. Nothing could get through to Germany by sea without passing British shores, either through the Channel or the narrow gap between the Orkney Islands and the northwest Danish coast. With the increasing threat of submarines and the unseen danger of minefields, the British finally decided on a 'distant' rather than a 'close' blockade (the latter had always been used against her enemies in the past).[3]

Up to as late as 1911 – with destroyers off the German coast – the British were still considering a close inshore blockade, which were the tactics that had been employed in the Napoleonic Wars. This changed in 1912, with recognition of the growing mine, torpedo and submarine threat, by an Order in Council to build a more distant blockade. Gary Staff has called it an 'observational' blockade. As such it was designed, after early warnings of German activity, to give the Grand Fleet time to put to sea. Only just before the start of the war in 1914 was a 'far-distant' blockade finally adopted, and none too soon.

Less than fifty days after the declaration of war, on 22 September three old cruisers had been on blockade duty off the Flanders coast. A lone German submarine, *U.9*, on her way back to base, spotted the targets. HMS *Aboukir* was first to be struck. Her commander, Captain Drummond, asked the other two ships for help in picking up survivors; he thought that his ship had hit a mine. On the surface, *U.9* fired again: two torpedoes were aimed at *Hogue* which, despite opening fire, was hit and sunk within ten minutes. *Cressy* was also struck by two torpedoes after she came back to pick up survivors.

It was a wake-up call for the Royal Navy. By the time that British destroyers arrived, 1,397 men and sixty-two officers had paid the ultimate price. The Germans celebrated the victory of one of their new weapons and decorated *U.9*'s commander: Kapitänleutnant Otto Weddingen received the Iron Cross, first class. If the real dangers had not been fully appreciated, these early British losses brought the stark truth home: Germany's sea lanes, unlike those of France, had either to pass by the closed funnel of the Dover Straits or through the gap between Scotland and Norway. For this reason the Grand Fleet was moved north, to the unprotected but distant anchorage at Scapa Flow in the Orkneys.

When war was declared, as much enemy shipping as possible was impounded. Around twenty German vessels unlucky enough to be in British waters or ports were immediately seized.[4] 'By November a larger picture emerged: 221 German merchant vessels lay idle in German ports, 245 had been detained in allied ports, and a further 1,059 in neutral ports. The bulk of Germany's maritime fleet was paralysed for the duration of the war.'[5]

To the south, Commodore Tyrwhitt's Harwich Force patrolled the east coast, with additional flotilla craft in the Straits of Dover that became known as the Dover Patrol. To the north, the 10th Cruiser Squadron was formed to patrol the 270-mile gap. It was ill-equipped to do its job. The vessels were the old 7,000-ton *Edgar*-class cruisers. While reasonably well-armed (they had two 9.2in and twelve 6in guns), at 17–19 knots they were really too slow to be in a position for the chase. At times only three out of eight ships were on patrol, so prone were they to mechanical failures. By December 1914 they were replaced by armed merchant cruisers, mostly converted liners, and four radio-equipped trawlers.

Britain recognised, too, that a trade war could be the basis of whittling away not only Germany's capability to fight, but also its will. Britain thus chose to adopt a naval blockade not only to try to force a naval encounter, but also to subdue Germany through economic pressure. The Navy was to provide the resources for trade protection or trade blockade in the natural choke-point of the North Sea.

The Royal Navy also had other specific roles beyond the control of commerce. Coastal protection and naval gunfire support might seem two sides of the same coin, but one is inherently more offensive than defensive. The British did not like to use the term 'blockade', as they were running a distant blockade. If their actions had been those of a close blockade that cut off specific enemy ports, things would have been different. The Declaration of London, the outcome of discussions held in London in 1908 to define the laws of the sea, particularly as they might apply in war, upheld the principles of international law, stating that a blockade should not extend beyond the coast or to ports belonging to or occupied by the enemy. Present at the discussion had been Great Britain, France, Germany, Austria–Hungary, Italy, Japan and Russia but since the declaration was never ratified by any government, it never actually took on the force of law. Despite this crucial flaw, the United States continued insisting that Germany and Britain should honour its aim of protecting neutrals in time of war.[6] Since Britain could not easily intercept coastal commerce between German ports and other countries – for example, the Netherlands – what it was doing could not actually be termed a 'blockade'.

Instead, the British talked about the seizure of 'contraband'. They had declared the entire North Sea a war zone and so claimed a right to stop and search neutral ships entering that zone, and, if the cargo manifest was complex, to tow them back to a harbour for a search to be carried out there. The British definition of what constituted war materiel or contraband was wide, because of the issue of the secondary usage of most materials. Cotton, for example, could be used in ammunition manufacture, as well as for clothing and bandages. On the *Lusitania,* one dive expedition found copper ingots, substantiating the German claim that the ship was carrying dual-purpose, contraband military cargo (more overtly, the ship was also supposed to have been carrying around 4,200 cases of ammunition).* These, then, were considered 'war materiel' and, as such, labelled 'conditional contraband'. But if the latter went to a neutral port, the British, technically, could not seize it.

It did not take long for the British to change the rules. On 20 August, with an Order in Council, the British said that they would now also seize conditional contraband even if consigned to a neutral port. In September iron ore, copper, lead, glycerine and rubber were added to the British list of what was considered conditional contraband. While diplomatic efforts by the Americans were able to rescind the British rights of seizure on conditional contraband, the British merely enlarged the list of what they considered 'absolute contraband'.

These practices infuriated neutral nations and British methods were, no doubt, seen as extremely dubious and a double standard. Cotton and copper were key American exports that the Allies wanted to control. It was not surprising that there was business pressure in the US for the country to change its allegiance in favour of Germany in protest at British actions of seizure. Comments such as Lloyd George's, 'Nations fighting for their lives cannot always pause to observe punctilios', did not go down well.[7] The British, nevertheless, managed to tie up 95 per cent of American copper exports by pressure on neutral countries, saying that they would maintain the supplies only to the level needed by that neutral country if re-export to Germany was guaranteed to be blocked.[8]

While there were some notable exceptions to the Allied success in cutting down Germany's supply of much-needed resources – for example, coal,

---

* The Greg Bemis expedition was filmed on the National Geographic Channel (*Dark Secrets of the Lusitania*), while *The Week* under an equally uncreative heading (2 May 2015 'Secrets of the *Lusitania*') made the allegations about carrying ammunition.

which was additionally sourced from newly conquered territory in Belgium and northern France – Germany's overall import–exports certainly suffered. After a year of war, imports had fallen by 55 per cent and exports were at 53 per cent of what they had been. A large quantity of materials reached Germany through the neutrals, such as Holland or the Scandinavian countries. If you compare the two months of December and January 1913/14 against the same period 1914/15, there was an explosion of exports to Germany. There was an eightfold increase from Sweden, while from Norway and Denmark it was fivefold.[9]

In planning the war, Germany's leaders did not think that there would be food shortages. The country's high use of fertilisers would give it wheat and meat independence (it was thought), as '85–90 per cent of her essential food' was domestically produced.[10] Nevertheless, wheat had not been stockpiled and soon the country began to feel the effects. An ersatz economy grew up: bread was made with a mixture of turnips and potatoes. The problem of food shortages would not just be limited to the civilian population: a major reason for the decline in morale in the navy (as we will later see) was lack of food. Some studies have suggested that shortages of food and fuel would eventually cause the death of more than 400,000 Germans.[11]

The navy's commanders, Ingenohl and his chief of staff, Pohl, both felt that Germany should turn the tables and 'wound England most seriously by wounding her trade ... the whole British coast, or at anyway a part of it, must be declared to be blockaded ... the gravity of the situation demands that we should free ourselves from all scruples which certainly no longer have any justification'. In vain they tried to persuade the German Chancellor von Bethmann-Hollweg. He would not change his position as he feared the international consequences. But there was support from the Kaiser himself, who preferred not to risk his precious surface fleet and from German submariners, wanting to prove the newest arm of the fleet.

Commerce-raiding

Germany was initially extremely successful in using a small cruiser force for commerce-raiding: sending small groups of fast cruisers out onto the major shipping lanes worldwide to wreak havoc. Before the war the Admiralty feared the large-scale use of armed merchantmen (civilian vessels with decks strengthened for gun mountings). They were well-suited to the task of commerce-raiding, being fast and having a lot of free stowage area for captured cargo, or for the more urgently needed coal supplies (the British were able to coal at many more ports). However, this never really came about. Of the sixty available, forty had already been impounded when war broke out.

One armed liner that did manage to break out of a German port was *Kaiser Wilhelm der Große*, which had won the Blue Riband on her maiden Atlantic voyage in 1887. Heading south, she encountered two passenger liners, *Galician*, on her way back from South Africa, and *Arlanza*. Kapitän Reymann at first thought about sinking both, but spared them as they had so many women and children on board. In a gesture of gratitude, *Galician*'s Captain Day gave the Germans 300 cigars and 1,200 cigarettes. These were early days. *Kaiser Wilhelm der Große* was eventually sunk by the cruiser HMS *Highflyer* on 26 August off the west African coast. Despite being outgunned, Reymann had chosen to fight: 'German warships do not surrender'. Before being fired upon, however, the captain put his British prisoners in boats to get them to safety (Reymann had earlier sunk three other vessels: *Tubal Cain*, *Kaipara* and *Nyanza*).

Opening Actions – German Commerce Raiders

Raider	Type	Ships captured	Gross registered tonnage (GRT)
Karlsruhe	Cruiser	17	76,609
Emden	Cruiser	15	66,023
Kronprinz Wilhelm	Armed liner	15	60,522
Prinz Eitel Friedrich	Armed liner	11	33,423
Leipzig	Cruiser	4	15,279
Dresden	Cruiser	4	12,960
Kaiser Wilhelm der Große	Armed liner	3	10,685
Königsberg	Cruiser	1	6,601
	TOTALS	70	282,102

Source: Hewitt, *The Kaiser's Pirates* (based on *British Vessels Lost at Sea*, HMSO 1919).

Perhaps the best-known of the naval raider actions were those of Vice Admiral Maximilian Reichsgraf von Spee, who commanded the four cruisers of the East Asia Squadron based in what is today Tsingtao – it was then a German colony. Spee split up his force and sent SMS *Emden* to the Indian Ocean while he took the armoured cruisers *Scharnhorst* and *Gneisenau* with the light cruiser *Nürnberg* across to the Pacific Ocean. There, he was joined by a merchant supply ship, *Prinz Eitel Friedrich*. However, of the eight supply ships that were to have joined Spee, half were intercepted and fell victim to British or French guns.

It was a formidable force, not least since *Scharnhorst*'s and *Gneisenau*'s gunnery was top-notch and the two had vied for first place in the 1913 and 1914 Kaiser's gunnery prize. The German force started causing as much damage and interference as it could. *Nürnberg* cut telegraph lines on Fanning Island and Tahiti was bombarded, but Spee was desperately cut off from supply. There was hardly anywhere where he could re-coal, though he was informed by Berlin that Chile would probably supply Spee's squadron. After stopping at Easter Island, he was joined by *Leipzig* and *Dresden*, both under the command of Fregattenkapitän Haun.

Britain's first great naval defeat of the First World War was at the Battle of Coronel, off the Chilean coast. Rear Admiral Sir Christopher 'Kit' Cradock, on his flagship, *Good Hope*, had come round from the Atlantic chasing *Dresden*, then dashed north in pursuit of his foe, leaving behind him the 12in guns of the pre-dreadnought *Canopus*. He had heard signals from *Leipzig* and thought that he would be engaging only light forces, at best. The Germans, however, were passing all their signals back through this one ship.

Cradock was totally outgunned: *Good Hope*'s two 9.2in guns faced *Scharnhorst*'s and *Gneisenau*'s sixteen 8.2in guns. *Good Hope* went down with all hands lost – more than 1,500 men, including Cradock. Another of his ships, *Monmouth*, continued north. The fact that she survived even for another hour was surprising, as her crew were completely green reservists and they had only managed to fire a few practice rounds before being pitted against the real thing. The shooting from *Scharnhorst* and *Gneisenau* took its toll, but it was left to *Nürnberg* to finish off *Monmouth*. A pause offering the British a chance to surrender was not heeded. *Monmouth*'s guns were useless; her list was so heavy that the guns could not be trained. She sank with all hands. The British lost 1,600, the Germans none (three on *Gneisenau* were wounded).

But Cradock had achieved something. Spee had used up almost all his ammunition and lamented: 'I cannot reach Germany; we possess no secure harbour; I must plough through the seas of the world doing as much mischief as I can, until my ammunition is exhausted'.[12]

Churchill reacted immediately, sending two fast battle-cruisers, *Invincible* and *Inflexible*, to seek revenge, while a third, *Princess Royal*, went to guard the Panama Canal. Under the command of the fifty-five-year-old Vice Admiral Sir Frederick Doveton Sturdee, the British force was coaling in the Falkland Islands when the German raiders came into sight on 8 December. Despite having had their keels cleaned to give them more speed, the battle-cruisers had proceeded across the Atlantic at only 10 knots to preserve fuel.[13]

Spee ordered the light cruisers off back to South America, while blocking the British with *Scharnhorst* and *Gneisenau*. Initially, *Gneisenau* was able to obtain hits after only her third salvo against *Invincible*, but gradually Sturdee turned the action around and soon *Gneisenau* was listing. *Scharnhorst* was on fire: she suddenly stopped firing, rolled over and sank; there were no survivors. Two hours later, *Gneisenau* joined her, sinking with only 200 of her crew making it to the water, most of whom died of exposure, even after rescue.

Haun could not escape on *Leipzig*. Eventually, HMS *Glasgow* caught up with her. Only after he had expended all his ammunition and fired off his torpedoes did Haun order the sea-cocks opened. Seven officers and eleven ratings survived; Haun went down with his ship. *Nürnberg* was eventually caught by the nominally slower HMS *Kent* and sunk, even though the latter was peppered with nearly forty hits herself.

In extraordinary scenes, British seamen jumped over the sides of *Kent* trying in vain to rescue German sailors. There were twenty-five survivors from the combined crew of 580 from the two light cruisers: eighteen from *Leipzig*, seven from *Dresden*. *Dresden* alone escaped, but was caught later when her radio transmissions gave away her position. She was sunk near the island of Más a Tierra in Chilean waters.

To the west, on the Indian Ocean, *Emden*'s forty-one-year-old captain, Fregattenkapitän Karl Friedrich Max von Müller, was extremely successful, sinking fifteen ships in addition to bombarding Penang, where he sailed into the harbour unchallenged and managed to torpedo the Russian light cruiser *Zhemchug* from under 400yds (460m).

The Australian cruiser, HMAS *Sydney*, eventually caught up with him, sinking *Emden* on 9 November near the Cocos Islands. The Australian ship had taken heavy fire and after ten hits in the first quarter of an hour, was on the point of succumbing to an ammunition explosion, when a young sailor picked up a live shell and threw it overboard, suffering terrible burns in the process. Only after nine of *Emden*'s ten guns were put out of action was the white flag run up. Almost half her crew, 122 men, had been killed.

Müller was an audacious and chivalrous commander. He had on several occasions erected a false fourth dummy funnel made of canvas to give his ship the appearance of a typical British cruiser. He 'earned the admiration of his crew and the gratitude of his victims'.[14] But the top-scoring ship was *Karlsruhe*, whose captain, Erich Köhler, was responsible for seventeen sinkings before his ship mysteriously blew up on 4 November, probably from faulty ammunition.

Germany had secretly built much of its passenger liner fleet with a dual military role in mind. Decks were reinforced in anticipation of guns being mounted later, and they were given very fast turbines to chase down enemy merchant ships. Around sixty had been designated for this purpose but when war broke out many were caught in Allied-controlled ports. Around ten were not. Two in particular, *Prinz Eitel Friedrich* and *Kronprinz Wilhelm*, became successful commerce-raiders. Between them they took twenty-six merchantmen before being interned in the United States in April 1915. A T Mahan's summation of the difference between fleet actions and trade destruction is illuminating: 'The essence of one is concentration of effort, whereas for commerce destroying diffusion of effort is the rule. Commerce destroyers scatter that they may see and seize more prey.'

In all, the raiders sank around 280,000 tons of merchant shipping. While Spee's squadron accounted for only one British merchantman (and two warships), the propaganda effect was large. Yet despite Müller's success, total tonnage lost was not large in the light of what happened later during unrestricted submarine warfare, nor did it really achieve what Tirpitz had wanted: a significant diminution of British North Sea presence. What *was* remarkable was that during this episode of maritime chivalry, when over sixty merchant vessels had been sunk by the raiders, it is said that not a single crew or passenger life was lost.

Mining

> While its cruisers were conducting a campaign on the seven seas with punctilious regard for the Hague Conventions and the sanctity of human life, minelayers in the North Sea and in the Channel were depositing their deadly cargoes in waters where they inevitably took a toll on civilian lives from belligerent and neutral nations alike.[15]

In its opening actions of the war Germany did not employ the Kaiser's precious fleet. They focused instead on using mines – cheaper, deadly but indiscriminate.

On the night of 5 August 1914, the day after war was declared, HMS *Amphion* reported seeing a vessel 'throwing things overboard'. It was the German converted ferry *Königin Luise* – she was laying mines. *Amphion* gave chase but her adversary's captain decided that if he could not outrun his pursuer he would at least scuttle his ship. *Amphion* stood by and picked up forty-six of her 100 crew but then, ironically, fell victim to her defeated enemy, being struck by several German mines. She went down with her captured German sailors unfortunate enough to have been rescued and then die as a result of their own actions. Contrary to the gentlemanly manner in which the commerce-raiding war was managed, this attack not only targeted Germany's new enemy but, being far off the Suffolk coast, was also aimed at neutral shipping. It caused quite a backlash against the Germans in the world's press.

Two weeks later, the German light cruisers *Mainz* and *Stuttgart*, accompanied by a specially fitted minelayer, SMS *Albatross*, laid minefields thirty miles off the Humber and Tyne ports. Admiral Lord Charles Beresford made serious efforts to combat mines, employing fishing vessels. At the start of the war there were eighty-two trawlers operating in this manner; within a month another 250 vessels were added. By the end of 1914 a clean shipping lane – 800yds (730m) wide and two hundred miles long – was cleared twice daily along the east coast of England. The work involved was monumental.

It was felt, as time passed, that even neutral vessels were dangerous and could be active minelayers. The pre-war offshore territorial limits were unilaterally expanded by the British to between thirty and one hundred miles from the shoreline. Any neutral vessel within these limits was treated as belligerent.

German coastal raids

A new approach by the Germans in their playing of the '*klein Krieg*' (little war) – by which they meant warfare on a lesser scale than fleet actions – was coastal bombardment. It was specifically designed to lure the British out into mine traps and ultimately into the hands of the High Seas Fleet. This helped 'to some extent the dispositions of the British fleet', as the attacks were planned to overpower a smaller battle-cruiser force before the battleships could catch up in support.[16] As was the case with mining, civilians were caught in the line of fire, but the coastal raids were different. They were specifically conceived of to cause a public outcry, thereby putting increased pressure on the Royal Navy for a prompt response, one that might give Germans the chance of catching a small force off-guard and luring them into a trap.

The day after the British declared the North Sea a war zone, the Germans sortied in a long-planned attack, but one designed more as a propaganda coup than one with any real military benefit. Great Yarmouth was only 280 miles from Heligoland, an easy night's cruise. Arriving offshore early on the morning of 3 November 1914, Hipper's 1st Scouting Group (the battle-cruisers *Moltke*, *Seydlitz*, *Von der Tann* and the armoured cruiser *Blücher*) commenced a rather ineffective bombardment. As the Germans withdrew, they laid mines in which an attacking British submarine, *D.5*, was caught, as was also, ironically, one of the German armoured cruisers, *Yorck*. Hipper had given the British notice that the Royal Navy was incapable of defending its shores, let alone dominating the North Sea.

The next raid, on 16 December, was different. It was better planned and resulted in high British casualties. One group attacked Scarborough and Whitby, the other Hartlepool where, over almost an hour, around 1,500 heavy shells were fired, causing the loss of 600 houses, killing 119 men, women and children, and wounding 300. Scarborough, utterly defenceless apart from an old cannon dating back to the Crimean War, was hit by around 500 shells. In half an hour seventeen were dead. Whitby, with three killed, was the least damaged.

Hipper had succeeded in luring out the battle-cruisers, but not quite as he expected. Alerted by Room 40 intercepts, the British ships had already been at sea at midday on the 15th in anticipation of the raid. Room 40 in the

Admiralty was where the British housed their cryptographic resources, decoding intercepted German naval messages before passing the results on to the Admiralty's operations staff. The existence of this capability was a closely guarded secret and so the information would never be passed on without a consideration given to covering the tracks of where the information might have been garnered, something that would have dire consequences for the night action at Jutland. Not wanting to indicate that they had any knowledge of German intentions, the British played along, hoping, as later at Jutland, to turn the trap on its head. And as at Jutland, the British were unaware of Admiral von Ingenohl's presence with the main battle fleet; he, unlike Scheer, turned tail and left Hipper to defend himself, to Tirpitz's fury. At Jutland the consequence of waiting to batch signals together to form the basis of information sent to the fleet at sea would have equally negative consequences. The result of the raid was that the battle-cruisers were moved south to Rosyth, better placed there for a future interception.

Six weeks later they got their chance. Again the British were waiting, having received advance warning through radio intercepts, this time off the Dogger Bank. This is a large, elongated stretch of shallow waters, sixty miles off England's northeast coast, that stretches 160 miles towards the northern Danish coast. The Germans were caught by surprise, turned away, and were immediately involved in a prolonged stern chase from Beatty's ships.

The older, slower, armoured cruiser *Blücher* was badly damaged and clearly not far from her end but due to a mix-up on the heavily damaged *Lion*, caused by Beatty's signals officer, Ralph Seymour, the British stopped to finish off *Blücher* rather than continue the chase. Beatty felt that only two of his battle-cruisers, *New Zealand* and *Indomitable*, were needed to do the job. *Blücher* sank with 880 lives lost, but Beatty was bitterly disappointed. The bigger prize had got away: Hipper had been on *Seydlitz*, which was badly battered and suffered a turret explosion. Ingenohl, holding off at distance with the battle fleet, did not come to Hipper's aid. Rather, he turned tail. He was replaced as commander-in-chief by his chief of staff, Hugo von Pohl; this should have happened after the Scarborough raid.

Submarines: the short-lived gentlemen's war

At the outbreak of war, neither the British nor the Germans knew the potential power of a relatively new weapon: the submarine. At first, British merchantmen losses were minimal. The war was fought with chivalry. A U-boat would surface, fire a warning shot or threaten its target ship. Papers would be exchanged, and the crew taken off and usually towed to safety. These were the accepted rules of the sea. In fact, when the first merchant ship *Glitra* was sunk by *U.17*, her commander, Kapitänleutnant Feldkirchner did not know whether he would be reprimanded or treated as a hero. Yet it was as a result of his actions that the British declared the war zone that triggered unrestricted submarine warfare. In January 1915 the Germans sent out three submarines, *U.19*, *U.20* and *U.21*, specifically to target merchant shipping. While the conduct of *U.19* and *U.21* was impeccable, Kapitänleutnant Droescher's on *U.20* was not. His third target, SS *Oriole*, was torpedoed with the loss of all her crew.

At first, submarines were not thought of by the British as easily employable against commerce at all, and their operating range had been badly underestimated. The British soon woke up. The war was only four days old when *Monarch* reported spotting a U-boat five hundred miles north of Heligoland, south of Fair Isle. The next day, on 9 August, the same U-boat (*U.15*) was rammed and sliced in two by HMS *Birmingham*. Another U-boat failed to return home from this first sortie across the North Sea.

The toll on the Germans was high, but the British were alarmed. Up until now it had not been thought that the fleet anchorages this far north could be threatened. Now, without adequate countermeasures such as depth-charging, or even adequate detection, such as sonar, the British felt vulnerable. On 3 September HMS *Pathfinder* was struck by *U.21* not far from the mouth of the Forth River after her commander, Kapitänleutnant Otto Hersing, had reached the Forth Bridge without detection a few days before. However, as detailed earlier, the real shock came three weeks later, on the 21st, when Kapitänleutnant Otto Weddingen's *U.9* sank *Aboukir*, *Cressy* and *Hogue*.

Jellicoe was unnerved and decided to keep the Grand Fleet moving for much of the time, out of the unprotected, tempting, but still dangerously open waters of Scapa Flow until the anchorage was protected. He moved the fleet to Loch Ewe in the west of Scotland and to Lough Swilly on the northwest coast of Ireland in County Donegal, so when Kapitänleutnant von Hennig's *U.18* managed to enter Scapa Flow by following a steamer through the Hoxa Sound boom, the British were not there.

It was clear that U-boats could be used effectively, but the force was tiny (Germany started the war with around twenty-four) and losses since the start of war were heavy (seven; four were replaced). On 4 February 1915 Pohl put the world on notice by declaring that the Germans now considered 'the waters around Great Britain and Ireland a military area', and that 'every enemy merchant vessel encountered in this zone will be destroyed' and 'neutral vessels also will run the risk in the war zone': any merchant shipping in these areas might be fired upon. As Pohl put it, neutral vessels might be 'destroyed without it being always possible to avert the dangers threatening the crews and passengers on that account'.

The British reacted a month later. On 11 March the Reprisals Order in Council said that now 'commodities of any kind' would be prevented from 'reaching or leaving Germany'. As the prime minister declared, Britain was not going to allow its efforts at survival to be 'strangled in a network of judicial niceties'.

On 27 March an act by a German submarine commander, Kapitänleutnant Freiherr von Forstner on *U.28*, fundamentally changed the course of the submarine war. After sinking a merchantman, *Aguila*, he then fired on crew and passengers. The next day he sank a 5,000-ton liner, *Falaba*: in the 104 lost was an American. The accusation that the baron and his crew jeered at the dying burnt a deep scar into the American public conscience.

Thus with potentially grave political consequences, this early sortie into unrestricted submarine warfare did not last long. On 25 April Germany announced that such warfare, directed at neutral shipping, would be halted and that 'before an enemy or neutral vessel could be torpedoed, she must be stopped and searched, and the presence of contraband in her cargo definitely established'.[17] The German politicians had learnt something important: actions of this kind would almost inevitably lead to immense diplomatic tensions. The navy had not. The 'fears of the Reich Chancellor that neutral ships might become involved were brushed aside by the Chief of the Admiralty Staff, and later fleet commander, Admiral Hugo von Pohl, in the mistaken belief that U-boat commanders would be able to tell neutral ships from British ships without stopping them'.[18] In the year 1915 only 21 per cent of German submarine sinkings were without warning.[19]

One such case – but one that would echo around the world – was the sinking of the *Lusitania*. The passenger ship had received numerous warnings of U-boat activity south of Ireland and had taken precautions, such as sailing dark, having lifeboats ready in the davits and closing watertight doors. But the liner's captain, William Thomas Turner, went in too close to shore, thinking that he was safer there than further out to sea. Enhancing the risk of the captain's chosen course, the Navy had not provided the escort support promised.

Late in April, *U.20* lay in wait. The submarine's commander, a thirty-year-old Berliner named Walther Schwieger, was well-respected (even Tirpitz would ask for his opinion), and he had been given orders to expect 'large English troop transports'. On the morning of the fateful attack, 7 May, *U.20* was actually lost. There was a thick fog and so she used the opportunity to surface and pull fresh ocean air into the dank and putrid bowels of the boat. Soon, however, the weather improved. *U.20* now had clear blue skies and a calm sea. Schwieger tried to get a shot in against an old cruiser, *Juno*, that came temptingly close; he failed. But his disappointment vanished when at 13:30 petty officer Max Valentiner spotted a 'forest of masts and stacks'. The first thought was that this meant several ships, but then the great prize came fully into his sights, steering directly for him, in fact. Schwieger fired a torpedo at 700m (770yds). The battle diary recorded the event: 'Unusually great detonation with large white cloud of smoke and debris shot above the funnels. In addition to the torpedo, a second explosion must have taken place.'

Schwieger's pilot, Lanz, is said to have exclaimed as he was closing the periscope, 'My God, it's the *Lusitania*'.[20] But, on closer examination, the scene feels rewritten for public consumption. One historian, Diana Preston, holds that 'there is good reason to suspect that *U.20*'s war diary was doctored after Schwieger returned to port'.[21] Unlike his other diaries, this report was neither on a printed form nor double-sided as was common practice. The style somehow felt different and, strangely, only on one day – 7 May, the day of the sinking – was Kapitänleutnant Walther Schwieger's signature missing.

Among the 1,134 lives lost there were 128 Americans, including Alfred Vanderbilt, reportedly last seen helping children into lifeboats. It was a huge affront to the American public, but the outcry was not yet powerful enough that Woodrow Wilson, a pacifist at heart and a man who wanted to be seen as the peace broker for Europe, could be persuaded into risking war. A hundred years after the event, it is clear that the British had exceeded their rights, as there were Canadian soldiers on board, as well as ammunition stowed below decks. The sinking nonetheless had huge propaganda value for the Allies and contributed to America's eventual entry into the war. Theodore Roosevelt scorned Wilson: 'For many months our government has preserved between right and wrong a neutrality which would have excited the … admiration of Pontius Pilate'.

The *Lusitania* incident led to another important change in how the Germans employed submarines in the commerce war. In future, the submarine would destroy a vessel only while on the surface, by torpedo or gunfire from newly fitted deck guns. This allowed the crew to disembark in lifeboats and survive. Neutral ships would be spared if they were not found to be carrying 'contraband'.

It was an extremely unpopular decision for the U-boat crews. First, it gave away their most important weapon: concealment. Secondly, the Allies increasingly used the opportunity that this gave to fight back with defensive weapons now added to merchant ships or, even more dangerous to the Germans, with ships specially made to appear like unarmed merchant ships: they were in fact naval-manned vessels called Q-ships, which carried a heavy concealed armament.

Scheer was furious with the policy reversal and protested to Berlin that a most important element in German sea power was being thrown away. He had always believed that a well-laid torpedo trap could cut down an enemy's forces before surface ships joined battle. As a demonstration of German power, he now wanted to ring the British bases with submarines, and use Zeppelin reconnaissance to avoid serious entrapment of the High Seas Fleet and battle-cruisers.

In 1917, when Scheer was able to reinstate the unrestricted type of warfare, the inevitable reaction was kept in mind, and it was fully understood that this time it might lead to America's entry into the war. That outcome was a calculated risk. Germany banked on the hope that, with a concentrated effort, it could finish off Great Britain before the benefits of American participation could be felt. However, the unrestricted submarine warfare lobby would have to wait until 1916 to gain momentum. Immediately following Jutland, Scheer knew that a fleet engagement would never bring Britain to its knees, so he returned to thinking about the weapon, the U-boat, that he would eventually and fully unleash against the British. With increased production and the British unable to find effective means of destroying them, Germany was able to reach a force of around 130 U-boats by the time that unrestricted submarine warfare was launched on 1 February 1917. Though only roughly a third would be available for patrol duty around Britain at the start of this policy, this was enough in the first month to yield a doubling of tonnage sunk and by the third month a staggering 811,000 tons.

The U-boat was a far deadlier threat to Britain than a battle fleet. It was a weapon of total war. Not one only aimed at a military victory, its aim was – like the British blockade – to starve the nation of both military resources and food.

THE BATTLE

—

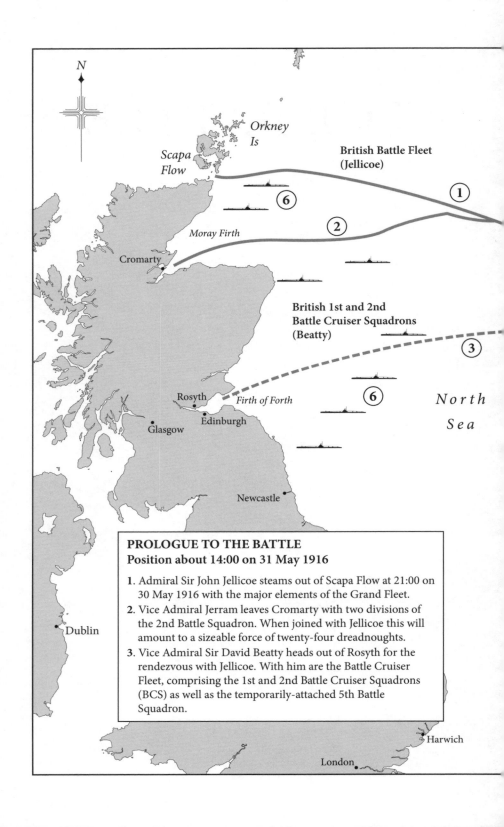

N

Orkney Is

Scapa Flow

British Battle Fleet (Jellicoe)

(6)

(1)

(2)

Moray Firth

Cromarty

British 1st and 2nd Battle Cruiser Squadrons (Beatty)

(3)

Rosyth   *Firth of Forth*   (6)

Edinburgh

Glasgow

North Sea

Newcastle

Dublin

Harwich

London

PROLOGUE TO THE BATTLE
Position about 14:00 on 31 May 1916

1. Admiral Sir John Jellicoe steams out of Scapa Flow at 21:00 on 30 May 1916 with the major elements of the Grand Fleet.

2. Vice Admiral Jerram leaves Cromarty with two divisions of the 2nd Battle Squadron. When joined with Jellicoe this will amount to a sizeable force of twenty-four dreadnoughts.

3. Vice Admiral Sir David Beatty heads out of Rosyth for the rendezvous with Jellicoe. With him are the Battle Cruiser Fleet, comprising the 1st and 2nd Battle Cruiser Squadrons (BCS) as well as the temporarily-attached 5th Battle Squadron.

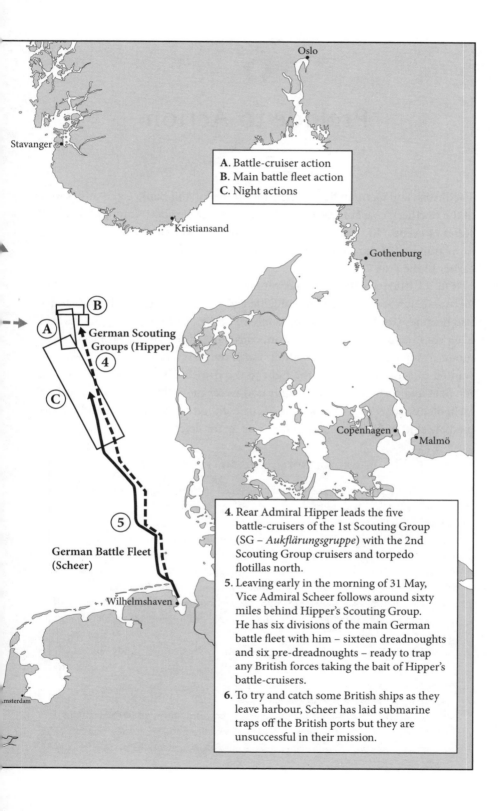

Oslo

Stavanger

Kristiansand

Gothenburg

A. Battle-cruiser action
B. Main battle fleet action
C. Night actions

Ⓑ

Ⓐ

**German Scouting
Groups (Hipper)**

④

Ⓒ

Copenhagen
Malmö

⑤

**German Battle Fleet
(Scheer)**

Wilhelmshaven

Amsterdam

4. Rear Admiral Hipper leads the five
   battle-cruisers of the 1st Scouting Group
   (SG – *Aukflärungsgruppe*) with the 2nd
   Scouting Group cruisers and torpedo
   flotillas north.

5. Leaving early in the morning of 31 May,
   Vice Admiral Scheer follows around sixty
   miles behind Hipper's Scouting Group.
   He has six divisions of the main German
   battle fleet with him – sixteen dreadnoughts
   and six pre-dreadnoughts – ready to trap
   any British forces taking the bait of Hipper's
   battle-cruisers.

6. To try and catch some British ships as they
   leave harbour, Scheer has laid submarine
   traps off the British ports but they are
   unsuccessful in their mission.

6

Prelude to Action

The British and German fleets finally met at the Jutland Bank, eighty miles west of the northern coast of Denmark. The meeting came about through a curious series of events. To start with, each admiral planned to lure the other into the same trap on the same day. It was the culmination of a pattern that had begun earlier in the year.

On 22 February 1916 the terminally ill and ageing commander of the German High Seas Fleet, Hugo Pohl, died. On 18 January the frail commander had been replaced by a new man, Reinhard Scheer. Until that point Scheer had been commanding the 3rd Squadron, consisting of the High Seas Fleet's most modern ships. An eager anticipation was in the air. His views were known. He wanted to get out and bring the fight to the British. During Pohl's command the fleet had sortied eight times only and never more than 130 miles north of Heligoland. Scheer was known for his orientation towards action and an immediate shift in German naval policy was up for discussion.

Life at Anchor: Scapa, Rosyth and Kiel

The morale of sailors at anchor was a critical factor in their performance at sea. Conditions for the officers and men of the ships – great and small – of the two navies could not have been more different.

For both sides life quickly became dull. The much hoped-for '*Entscheidungstag*' that the Germans had been waiting for drifted out of sight and imagination. '*Es wird mächtig langweilig. Man stellte sich den Krieg immer so vor, also er nach der Kriegerklärung, gleich Hurrah käme, Angriff und dann Schluß ... ein Feind finds nichts su zehen.*'[1] (Rough translation: 'It was unbelievably boring. One imagined that with the declaration of war there would be cheers, battle and then an end ... but we can't even find the enemy.)

One officer, Knobloch, even started to question why Germany had built a navy: '*Wozu eigentlich haben wir die dicken Schiffe?*'[2] (Rough translation: 'By the way, why on earth do we even need these big, fat ships?')

There was utter joy felt by the German sailors when the British were spotted. They had been champing at the bit for this day. As the commander of Seaman Richard Stumpf's ship, SMS *Helgoland*, Korvettenkapitän Walter Zaeschmarr described it: '*Es herrschte bei uns am Bord aufrichtige Freude, also die ersten feindlichen Mastzeichen* über *der Kimm auftauchten*.[3] (Rough translation: 'When the first characteristically shaped enemy mast was seen over the horizon, all on board had a real sense of joy.') Stumpf himself spoke of the mix of feelings: *'Ich müßte lügen, wenn ich sagen würde, daß ich Angst gehabt habe. Nein, es war ein undefinierbares Gemisch von Freude, Angst, Neugierde, Gleichgültigkeit und noch etwas, das mit dem Worte Tatendrang vielleicht nicht ganz richtig ausgedrückt ist'.*[4] (Rough translation: 'I'd be lying if I said that I was afraid. No, it was an indefinable mix of joy, fear, inquisitiveness, indifference and something which I can't adequately put into words.')

For the German navy, technology, ship design and armaments had all strongly advanced. But its very heart, the ship's crew, was to become the source of the navy's destruction. The social divisions were more extreme than on British ships where, at least, the back-breaking ritual of coaling brought officer and rating together. The food in the German navy was already of low quality and significantly declined as the war continued, while in the British Navy this was never a cause for conflict or resentment.

Life in Scapa Flow – a place that is hauntingly beautiful in the late spring and the summer months – was dismal in the winter, when it became a grey, cold and windy prison for the sailors. As inventive as the officers and men were in entertaining themselves with sports, crafts, theatre, opera and the like, it became numbingly boring. What made it worse was that the Grand Fleet crews knew that the battle-cruiser life was so much better in Rosyth, with all that near-by Edinburgh could offer.

See Malcolm Brown and Patricia Meehan, *Scapa Flow: The Reminiscences of Men and Women who Served in Scapa Flow in the Two World Wars* (Allen Lane, 1968).

Up to the early spring of 1916, German strategy had been to tie up the Royal Navy, holding back resources that could have been released elsewhere. Scheer's decision was to upset the balance of naval power with the combined weight of his scouting forces and his dreadnoughts, the High Seas Fleet. As we have seen, Scheer believed he had contrived the perfect trap for the British Navy. 'The fatal flaw in Scheer's reasoning,' Eric Grove writes, 'was that surprising the Grand Fleet was much more difficult than he thought. Thanks to the feats of the cryptanalysts in Room 40 at the Admiralty, the British had prior warning of many of Scheer's intentions.'[5]

In April 1916 Scheer had put his strategy into play with the attacks on Lowestoft and Yarmouth. The image of the Royal Navy, for which the public had been asked to spend today's equivalent of billions of pounds over a decade, was badly tarnished. Scheer's major lesson from the raids was that he would be better off moving the scouting group target just far enough north to tempt Beatty out of Rosyth, but not so far that it would make it easy for Jellicoe's forces, coming from the far northern Orkney base in Scapa Flow, to get there in time as effective support.

Scheer's third attempt was to coincide with the Irish Easter Rising; he was looking for a point of maximum political and military distraction for the

British. His top priority was to keep his 'fleet in being', posing a significant enough threat to the British that they constantly had to guard against any German action, resulting in the tying up of significant British resources in men and materiel. He was not looking for any major naval action, but rather one in which he could lure out a small group of British ships and safely overpower them. Scheer was a great believer in integrated naval operations and prepared a number of strategically located submarine traps. These were deployed to critical points where ships could be torpedoed by U-boats.

Scheer had ordered two boats, *U.34* and *U.44*, to lie in wait for Jellicoe's forces to sortie from the Pentland Firth separating Caithness and the Orkneys; eight U-boats were to wait for Beatty in the Firth of Forth to the south. On 20 May *U.27* was sent to the latter to head in as far as the Isle of May. Three U-boats were to lay mines. On 13 May *U.72* was to lie off the Firth of Forth, on 23 May *U.74* off the Moray Firth and, the next day, *U.75* off the Orkneys; another was off Peterhead. *U.21* and *U.22* were off the Humber, as British warships had been (incorrectly, as it turned out) reported there and two more, *U.46* and *U.47*, were west of the island of Terschelling off the Dutch coast, to guard against a possible intervention by Commodore Tyrwhitt's Harwich Force. The submarines could be operational until 31 May.[6] Scheer had ordered ten to be deployed to the North Sea, with orders to patrol from 17–22 May.[7] The British picked up on this and responded with increased patrols. Three U-boats turned back.[8]

Scheer's planning ran into more difficulties: he had to postpone his operation because of machinery problems in the 3rd Squadron, then because of news that repairs to *Seydlitz* would take another week. This delayed the operation from the 17th to the 23rd, and finally until the 30th. Scheer had also planned extensive reconnaissance by Zeppelins but the date chosen, 29 May, turned out to be too windy. As a result of reconnaissance not going ahead, Scheer dropped his targeting of Sunderland, replacing it with a sortie to the Skagerrak, the stretch of water between the southern end of Norway and the northwestern tip of Denmark. With that decision, the fleet was informed by the coded signal '31 May GG 2490'. *U.66* and *U.32* alone received it.

Jellicoe had his own plans for the High Seas Fleet. He would send a squadron of British battleships and eight light cruisers to appear off the Danish coast, at Skagen, on 2 June and move into the Kattegat. He banked on the news getting to Scheer – with Scheer undoubtedly then sending units to try to cut them off. Jellicoe held the Grand Fleet south, at the Horns Reef, shallows about ten miles off the westernmost point of Denmark, and used the planes of *Engadine*, the Grand Fleet's sole carrier, to deter Zeppelins and so keep Scheer in the dark about its presence. Jellicoe deployed British submarines north for his particular trap.

Fleet composition

The fleet that Jellicoe took to sea was numerically very strong. He had twenty-four dreadnoughts in the line, with varying degrees of hitting power. Two had 15in guns, one had 14in, eleven, including *Iron Duke*, had 13.5in and ten had 12in. But the fleet also had its weaknesses: Jellicoe had decided to keep with the current formation two squadrons of obsolete, pre-dreadnought, armoured cruisers.*

Jellicoe was missing the added punch of the thirty-five destroyers from Tyrwhitt's Harwich Force. Rear Admiral Henry Oliver, chief of staff, was convinced that real danger lay in the Germans feinting and rushing the Straits of Dover. According to Correlli Barnett, 'this is where [Jellicoe's] ... superiority was at its narrowest'.[9] Tyrwhitt had actually set sail at 17:10 on his own initiative, only to be pulled back by terse instructions from the Admiralty: 'Return to base at once and await orders'. They never came.

Fleet Composition August 1914

Ship Type	Royal Navy	Imperial Navy
Battleships in commission	22	15
Battleships under construction	13	5
Battle-cruisers in commission	9	5
Battle-cruisers under construction	1	3
Pre-dreadnought battleships	40	22
Old armoured cruisers	40	7
Small/light cruisers	20	16
Torpedo boats/destroyers	330	205
U-boats/submarines	73	31

Source: Wolz, *Imperial Splendour*, p17. Missing are the seaplane carriers.

---

* The 1st Cruiser Squadron consisted of the last of the pre-*Invincibles*. *Defence* had been laid down almost ten years previously in February 1905, and was completed in 1909. Her two sister ships, *Edinburgh* and *Black Prince* were completed even earlier (in 1906). They were badly limited in armour and armament, and effectively obsolescent. The 2nd Cruiser Squadron was also outmoded: *Minotaur* and *Shannon* had been completed in 1908, while *Cochrane* and *Natal* were commissioned in 1907. These ships were the cruiser equivalents of pre-dreadnoughts.

Comparative Fleet Composition at Jutland

Ship Type	British (151)	German (99)
Dreadnought battleships	28	16
Pre-dreadnought battleships	0	6
Battle-cruisers	9	5
Armoured cruisers	8	0
Light cruisers	26	11
Destroyers	79	61
Seaplane carriers	1*	0

*HMS *Campania* should also have sailed with the battle fleet but did not receive her initial sailing orders and was ordered back to port by Jellicoe, who would not spare destroyers for a separate escort. She would have added ten aircraft.

On the German side, Scheer made errors of composition similar to Jellicoe's, including in the 2nd Battle Squadron the six famously slow *Deutschland*-class pre-dreadnoughts under pressure from his old friend, Rear Admiral Franz Mauve. Steaming at a maximum speed of 17 knots, these old models were known as the *Fünf-Minuten-Schiffe* (five-minute ships), their effect being seriously to reduce the German fleet's overall speed – and there was not a single super-dreadnought in it when it sailed. The new 15in SMS *Bayern* would not be completed until a month after Jutland and the first 13.8in battle-cruiser, *Mackensen*, not launched for another year.

Scheer's battle-cruisers were, by contrast, well-balanced ships – the force created, in Grove's words, 'excellent combinations of speed, power and protection'.[10] Scheer was fortunate to have *Seydlitz* as part of the battle-cruiser squadron; water-tightness repairs had only just been completed on 29 May. She was a large vessel, having twenty-seven boilers, eighty-four furnace doors and 200 sq yds (170 sq m) of heating surface. 'The bunkers hold 3,600 tons of coal, a railway train 380 wagons long.'[11]

The German fleet numbered 99 ships with 900 guns in total, against Jellicoe's 1,700 guns on 151 ships. British firepower massively outweighed the adversary: the British would be fielding 324 heavy guns on each broadside, against 196 German heavy guns; the broadside weight ratio was approximately 400,000lbs (181,000kg) to the Germans' 200,000lbs.

Battleship Design

In 1906, a revolutionary point in the middle of the naval age of steam, HMS *Dreadnought* was launched. Thereafter one talked of earlier 'pre-dreadnoughts' or 'super-dreadnoughts' with heavier guns that followed. Generally, the *Dreadnought* sacrificed armour in favour of speed and broadside weight.

She was a weapons platform, with a broadside of eight 12in guns, each capable of hurling an 850lb (350kg) shell 17,990yds (16,450m) across the sea while knifing through the water at over 20 knots, powered by the new Parsons turbines. This had replaced the old reciprocating engine, increasing her speed from 16 knots to around 21, but reducing maintenance. As a new weapons platform, she also demanded improved gunnery. It was another of Fisher's protégés, Admiral Percy Scott, who revolutionised naval gunnery, introducing training with moving targets, spotting and director firing.

By contrast, the German fleet was primarily developed for short-distance operations. Short ranges meant less fuel. Less fuel meant more space, with lighter guns and more armour or armament weight. German ships tended to be lighter-gunned, slower but far more heavily armoured as a ratio to total displacement. And crews often slept ashore while in harbour. Even coaling spaces were used very effectively for increased protection. When they inspected many German ships at Scapa Flow straight after the end of the war, British commentators saw for themselves their strength of construction: after Jutland, *Seydlitz* limped back with 5,300 tons of water on board, *Derfflinger* with 3,000 tons.

So, one way to compare the relative strengths of British and German ships is to look at the ratio of total displacement to armour:

> *Queen Mary*: 27,000 tons displacement, of which 3,900 tons was armour (a ratio of 14 per cent armour to displacement).
>
> *Seydlitz*: 24,600 tons displacement, of which 5,200 tons was armour (a ratio of 21 per cent armour to displacement)

German ships were broader beamed, allowing more side armour as well as superior performance as a stable gun platform. Here are some examples of comparative beam (measured in feet):

> *Iron Duke*: 90   *König*: 97   *Lion*: 88   *Derfflinger*: 95

The broader German beam came about because the British did not invest in the prize tool that was Britain's protection in war: its Navy. In this particular instance, the issue was the many dry-dock facilities that would require widening.

At Trafalgar, Nelson had supreme confidence in his ships. He knew that at close quarters the Spanish and French ships would be no match. For Jellicoe, it was different. Technically, he was exceptionally knowledgeable about ship construction and had seen much of the German yards up close. Temple Patterson writes that 'as Jellicoe was at least in part aware, there were many matters in which the German Navy was the equal or superior of our own. Its capital ships had better armour protection and the more complete water-tight sub-divisions made possible by their lesser sea-keeping needs and by their broader beam which their roomy docks allowed them rendered them more difficult to sink, especially in view of the inferiority of British shells'.[12] Jellicoe knew his ships' weaknesses.

The initial deployment

At 17:40 on 30 May, after the Admiralty had learnt at around noon of a possible German sortie, a signal was sent to Jellicoe to warn him. The Grand Fleet was to deploy at 'the Long Forties', a hundred miles east of Scotland's east coast.

Between 22:00 and 23:00 five British battle-cruisers passed from their base at Rosyth under the imposing arches of the Forth Bridge into the North Sea. The 1st Battle Cruiser Squadron was led by Beatty on *Lion*. With him were *Princess Royal*, *Queen Mary* and *Tiger*; the 2nd Battle Cruiser Squadron was commanded by Admiral Sir William Pakenham on *New Zealand*, along with *Indefatigable*. *Kempenfelt* and nine destroyers of the 11th Flotilla accompanied them. *Australia* was absent as she was in dry dock following a collision with *New Zealand* (which, unfortunately, led to a great feeling of bitterness between the two ships' crews).[13] Finally, the new 15in *Queen Elizabeth*-class battleships of the 5th Battle Squadron, with Rear Admiral Evan-Thomas on the flagship *Barham*, led *Valiant*, *Warspite* and *Malaya*. Beatty's force was accompanied by three light cruiser squadrons (1st, 2nd and 3rd) and twenty-seven destroyers of the 1st, 9th, 10th and 13th Flotillas, led by two light cruisers. One of Scheer's submarines, *U.32*, fired a torpedo at *Galatea*, flagship of the 1st Light Cruiser Squadron under the command of Commodore Edwyn Alexander-Sinclair, as she put to sea, but without success.

Once at sea, Beatty's battle-cruiser forces split into two components, the 5th Battle Squadron sailing slightly to the north, and the 1st and 2nd Battle Cruiser Squadrons to the west of it. As noted earlier, the Harwich Force was turned back by Rear Admiral Oliver, who believed that there was a threat to the Straits of Dover without it in reserve. Further south, Rear Admiral Horace Hood had the 3rd Battle Cruiser Squadron join up with Jellicoe's fleet midway. Normally, Hood would have been with Beatty but his ships – *Invincible*, *Inflexible* and *Indomitable* – were at Scapa Flow on a gunnery exercise. They had switched places with Evan-Thomas's battle squadron.

By 20:00 on 30 May Jellicoe was clear of Scapa Flow and heading out to sea. With the fleet were the 4th and 12th Destroyer Flotillas, *Castor*, and four destroyers of the 11th Flotilla. Passing the Hoxa Boom, the main anti-submarine net that barred the southern entrance to the anchorage at Scapa Flow, *Gentian* was fired on by a German submarine (*U.32*) but, as with *Galatea*, the torpedo missed.[14] In fact, Scheer's submarine deployment had not really yielded any really significant benefits or intelligence.[15]

Jellicoe's Grand Fleet headed to the agreed rendezvous point in the Long Forties at a measured 15 knots, as 'he wished to conserve the limited fuel carried by his destroyers'.[16] At 12:48, an hour after an exercise 'action stations' had been called, and crews then sent off for painting and more training, Jellicoe received from the Admiralty the first of what was going to prove to be a long string of misleading signals: 'No definite news of the enemy. They made all preparations for sailing early this morning. It was thought that the Fleet had sailed but "directionals" place Flagship in Jade [river] at 11:10 GMT. Apparently they have been unable to carry out air reconnaissance which has delayed them.'[17]

Captain Thomas Jackson, director of the Operations Division of the Admiralty, had gone to Room 40 and put one question to them: where were they picking up Scheer's flagship *Friedrich der Große*'s call-sign, 'DK'? He was told: in the Jade. Jackson assumed that this meant that Scheer's flagship was still at anchor in what was known as the *Jadebusen*, the protected basin or bay of the Jade River that eventually opens out to the North Sea.

In fact, Scheer's 'harbour' call-sign, when he went to sea, was transferred to land to disguise it. Room 40 knew about this practice, which Scheer had put in place during the Scarborough and Lowestoft raids, but either because of how Jackson was perceived by the Room 40 staff, and he had supposedly put the question, or because he had not actually asked the right one, Room 40 gave the misleading response that led Jellicoe and Beatty to think only the German battle-cruisers were at sea.

Jackson's feelings, that 'these chaps could not possibly understand' the implications of all intercepted signals, were well-known to the Room 40 staff. One description of Jackson has him as 'ridiculous', 'angry', 'blustering', 'insufferable' and a 'buffoon'.[18] Jackson had been to Room 40 only twice before – both times to complain. He was not well-liked.

Jellicoe and Beatty were out on the North Sea ahead of Scheer and Hipper, but as a direct consequence of the information from Room 40, Jellicoe steamed on to the Long Forties meeting point very slowly, hoping, as just noted, to conserve fuel. This would cut down the fighting time, and on that particular day, time was what was most in need.

At around 03:00 on 31 May Hipper's battle-cruisers had weighed anchor, after spending the night in the approaches to the Jade Bay and Wilhelmshaven, known as the Schillig Roads, beside the entrance to the *Jadebusen*. Having passed the island of Sylt and to the side of their protective minefield, the massed High Seas Fleet steamed north with Hipper's battle-cruisers out ahead.

Hipper and Scheer knew from their intelligence sources that something large was afoot: Hipper's war diary states that he was told at 03:56 by *U.32* that it had spotted two dreadnoughts, two cruisers and many torpedo boats heading southeast (probably Beatty's). Neumünster had also told Hipper at 08:00 that two dreadnought or battle squadrons had left Scapa Flow at 22:00 the night before, accompanied by destroyers. At 08:44 *U.66* signalled from Quadrant 132B III that eight British dreadnoughts with cruisers and destroyers had been sighted heading northeast. That was the last information until *Elbing*, steaming out ahead of Hipper's 2nd Scouting Group (under Vice Admiral Friedrich Bödicker), sighted British forces on the day of the battle itself. This should have been enough to alert Hipper and Scheer that this was going to be a sortie, in force, by the British. Probably, Scheer and Hipper's mindset at this point of the war was that the High Seas Fleet had to do something to justify its existence.

At 14:00 on 31 May there was a long roll on the drums of the battle-cruiser *Derfflinger*, a signal to clean guns. Georg von Hase, the gunnery commander, inspected all the guns, along with his trusted warrant officer, Włodarczek, nicknamed 'The Goblin' (he had an uncanny knack for knowing what was needed before needing to be asked). The combined German and British forces, which were now unbeknownst to each other converging, constituted the biggest concentration of armoured shipping ever seen – 250 ships manned by 95,000 sailors. Each was planning to trap the other.

The Grand Fleet sailed in divisions: the 1st was led by *King George V*, followed by the 2nd and 3rd, with Jellicoe's flagship, *Iron Duke*, followed by the 4th, 5th and 6th. A cable's length[19] separated each ship and about 1,000yds (900m) lay between the divisions themselves.

On one ship, *St Vincent*, there was a staff officer from the 4th Hussars, Major Claude Wallace.[20] *St Vincent*'s captain, William Fisher, by now used to endless trawls through the North Sea with the Grand Fleet, made a plea: 'We have tried to do this so often but without bringing the Germans to book; but today is a little different. We have a Staff Officer who has come direct from the trenches. Please God, may the shells follow him here: he may bring us luck.'[21]

Wallace had been having premonitions of a great sea battle for months. He was determined to be aboard for it – he was sure there would be action. For most it felt like yet another North Sea sweep, although Lieutenant Bowyer-Smith on the turret of *Marlborough* described how this time there was a feeling that it might actually be different: 'The men were laughing and joking, but one could see that mixed with the relief of at last getting a rap at someone, there was a certain amount of nervousness and wondering what it would be like.'[22]

7

The Battle-Cruiser Debacle

The disturbing feature of the battle-cruiser action is the fact that five German battle-cruisers engaging six British vessels of this class, supported after the first twenty minutes, although at great range, by the fire of four battleships of the *Queen Elizabeth* class, were yet able to sink the *Indefatigable* and the *Queen Mary*.

> Temple Patterson, *Jellicoe*, quoting J E T Harper

The truth is that if it had not been for the blowing up of the *Indefatigable* and the *Queen Mary*, which was due to superior German shell, not shooting, the first phase would have ended differently.

> Marder, *From the Dreadnought to Scapa Flow*

By the early afternoon of 31 May the two main arms of the British forces had steamed to their agreed rendezvous point in the Long Forties, close to the Scandinavian coastline.* Beatty's battle-cruisers, protected by flotillas of fast scouting cruisers both ahead and astern, proceeded in two columns at around 25 knots on a southeasterly bearing. To Beatty's northwest, and around five miles behind his two battle-cruiser squadrons, were the most powerful guns on the North Sea that day. They belonged to the four modern *Queen Elizabeth*-class dreadnoughts of Evan-Thomas's 5th Battle Squadron. While enemy contact was expected to the southeast, Beatty had positioned the most powerful but slowest element of his force to his northwest.† He had split his forces.

In the fifteen minutes after quarter past two in the afternoon, everything changed. A lone neutral steamer, the Danish *N J Fjord*, was spotted by the German cruiser *Elbing*, scouting ahead of Hipper's force. Two fast destroyers, *B.110* and *B.109*, were sent ahead to search.

---

* The Long Forties is an area of deep water, around 40 fathoms (73m), that runs across the North Sea from just above Aberdeen to the southern tip of Norway.

† Ahead of the battle-cruisers, on their port, was the 9th Flotilla with *Dublin* and *Nottingham* further east. On the starboard bow steamed the 13th Flotilla headed by *Champion*. Slightly to their south were *Southampton* and *Birmingham*.

THE BATTLE-CRUISER ACTION
Up to 17:35 on 31 May 1916

1. Beatty heads his forces south to get ahead of Hipper's ships. He wants to cut them off from a route home. With him are six battle-cruisers and four *Queen Elizabeth* 15in-gunned battleships of Rear Admiral Evan-Thomas's 5th Battle Squadron. The *Queen Elizabeth*s are the most powerful ships on the sea on 31 May 1916.
2. The 5th Battle Squadron does not understand the instructions from Beatty's flagship, *Lion*. They continue on their previous course before finally following Beatty south. The gap between them has considerably widened.
3. 15:48. The German battle-cruisers are the first to open fire. Beatty's ships answer thirty seconds later, but their range and speed advantages have been lost.
4. *Indefatigable* is hit and sinks at 16:01. There are only three survivors, one of whom, the captain, dies in the water; 1,015 others go down with the ship.
5. 16:26. *Queen Mary* erupts in a massive mushroom cloud from a magazine explosion. 1,258 men die with only eight surviving the explosion.
6. Commodore Goodenough on *Southampton* spots sixteen German dreadnoughts coming north. At 16:38 he signals the intelligence to Beatty. At 16:40 Beatty orders a turn around, making the manoeuvre look like a flight but, in fact, leading the German fleet to Jellicoe.
7. At 16:58, eighteen minutes later, the 5th Battle Squadron also turns around and follows Beatty's remaining four battle-cruisers. They take a large amount of fire from both the German battle fleet and battle-cruisers but give Beatty a temporary respite.
8. 17:35. As Beatty pushes north, he begins to bend his line to the east, blocking the German view of Jellicoe's approaching dreadnoughts.

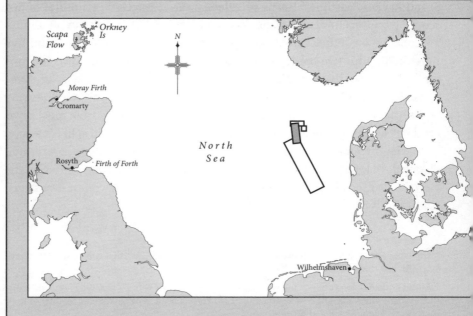

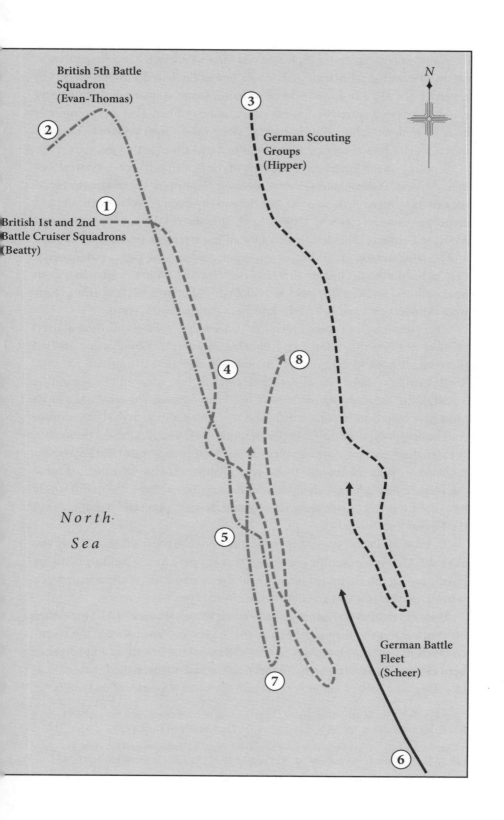

British 5th Battle
Squadron
(Evan-Thomas)

②

③

German Scouting
Groups
(Hipper)

①

British 1st and 2nd
Battle Cruiser Squadrons
(Beatty)

④

⑧

North·
Sea

⑤

German Battle
Fleet
(Scheer)

⑦

⑥

N

A stationary ship on the high seas was often of enough concern as an indication of possible submarine activity. As one of the two destroyers stood off, covering her, *N J Fjord* was ordered to let off steam so that a boarding party could carry out a search and, if necessary, impound her. This was commonly done by both sides but more so by the British (given their greater freedom of movement), who were trying to stop war materiel from getting through.

Scouting on the extreme eastern wing of the British battle-cruisers were two light cruisers, *Phaeton* and *Galatea*.[1] Because *Galatea* had been late in receiving orders to turn north, so as to stay close to the main redeployment, she had continued to steam closer to *N J Fjord* and, unknown to them, Hipper's forward scouting elements. The British also spotted the steamer's smoke, and *Galatea* and *Phaeton* headed off to investigate. When they saw the German destroyers, they radioed the information to Beatty on *Lion*. Eight minutes later they both opened fire with their 6in guns at 11,000yds (10,000m).[2] The opening shots were the overture to what became known as the Battle of Jutland.

The German destroyers turned back to rejoin *Elbing* and then started to head north, with *Galatea* and *Phaeton* in pursuit. *Elbing* also signalled the contact back to Hipper, but mistakenly reported the British ships as 'battle-cruisers';[3] later, one of her signals was further misread to suggest that 'twenty-four to twenty-six battleships' had been sighted. The muddled signals must have caused some consternation on the latest addition to the battle-cruiser Aufklärungsgruppe, *Lützow*, Hipper's flagship. *Elbing*'s gunnery was better than her signalling: at almost seven miles she opened fire and one of her 5.9in shells hit *Galatea* under the bridge.[4] It was very accurate shooting and the first hit of the battle, causing 'a certain amount of damage but nothing to what it would have done if it had burst'.[5] *Falmouth*, further down the line and out of range of the *Elbing*'s fire, was luckier.

As soon as *Galatea* spotted more funnel smoke to the northeast, Beatty was alerted.* Alexander-Sinclair confirmed that Hipper's forces had turned to the north, adding much-needed detail about the composition of the enemy force. It was clear that this was an enemy sortie in strength.†

Beatty's reaction was swift. He ordered air reconnaissance at 14:51 and then ordered his ships to turn southeast so that he could come between the enemy and their bases.[6] The air reconnaissance was one of the first times seaplanes had been employed in this capacity. To that point, it had not been used in naval warfare. *Engadine* hoisted her only plane into the water a quarter of an hour later.[7]

---

* Signal time 14:39. 'Urgent. Have sighted large amount of smoke as though from a fleet bearing E.N.E. My position Lat. 56° 50' N., Long. 5° 19' E. *(Received in Iron Duke 14:35.)*'

† 'Urgent. My 14:35. Smoke seems to be seven vessels besides Destroyers and Cruisers. They have turned North. My position Lat. 56° 52' N., Long. 5° 33' E. *(Received in Iron Duke 14:41).*'

This vessel did not look much like a warship – she had been converted from a cross-Channel ferry with a hangar rather crudely built on abaft her two funnels. She should have been supported by a second such ship which might have led to a very different outcome to the day – and a different outcome could have more clearly indicated the potential of air reconnaissance.‡

Just before 15:10, Flight Lieutenant Frederick J Rutland took off in a Short Type 184 floatplane, accompanied by his observer, Assistant Paymaster G S Trewin. The conditions were far from ideal and Beatty had been warned: 'Sea suitable for getting off but not for landing. Impossible to distinguish where mist ends and water begins in coming down to sea. Will be all right if horizon clears.'

The bad visibility forced Rutland to fly dangerously close to the sea, within easy range of Hipper's ships' secondary armament. The small plane came under intense and accurate fire from three German light cruisers, *Pillau*, *Frankfurt* and *Elbing*, all in the van of the German battle-cruiser fleet. Extreme courage and honed skills were needed. Rutland certainly had both. After they spotted Hipper's ships, Trewin tried to get a signal back at 15:30, but was unsuccessful. After around half an hour's flight time, one of the oil pipes burst, but Rutland managed to coax the plane down.[8] The Short had been hit seven times. Back on *Engadine* a signal with details of what they had seen was written up for Beatty, but even from *Engadine* nothing ever got through. The whole venture was a dismal failure: one carrier only, no successful signals contact. It was frustrating for Rutland after an exceptionally harrowing and brave flight that his efforts were for nought; more sadly, his Jutland exploits were to be completely over-shadowed by his activities with the Japanese and his later imprisonment on charges of espionage.[9]

Finally, the British battle-cruisers spotted the German line itself. *New Zealand* was the first. Ten minutes later Beatty's *Lion* could also see the line of German battle-cruisers as well. They, in turn, were spotted by *Lützow*, on whose bridge Hipper was standing. Then, from *Seydlitz*, the telltale tripod masts of two specific ships, *Indefatigable* and *New Zealand*, were made out. From the air Rutland was able to see the German battle-cruiser turn and radioed back the information.[10] Of the four detailed messages that he sent over fifteen minutes, three were received by the *Engadine* but, because of the fleet radio ban, attempts to pass the vital information to Evan-Thomas were made only by searchlight signals. It was an inauspicious beginning for such a promising new capability.

Hipper immediately understood that Beatty was going to try to cut him off from his home bases. He signalled his light cruisers in the north as he reversed

---

‡ Jellicoe had ordered the second carrier available with the fleet, *Campania*, back to harbour at 16:41 because she had misunderstood the sailing time orders and her delayed departure would have needed additional destroyer protection.

onto a southeasterly track but, unlike Beatty's actions with the 5th Battle Squadron, slowed his fleet down to 18 knots to allow his scouting and screening forces to catch up. At around 15:30 his forces turned 180 degrees and headed south, running along the same track they had used to go north.

Hipper wanted to make it look as though he had been caught off-guard and was in full retreat back to the Jade: the Germans could read Beatty's character perhaps better than Beatty realised; they knew the character of a fox-hunting man. They knew that he would run into the chase and that this was their chance to lure a portion of the British naval forces into the waiting guns of Scheer, heading north not far behind with the main battle fleet.

Beatty sensed the opportunity and increased speed to close with his foe. The two battle-cruiser fleets – still fourteen miles apart – started to close the gap rapidly, Beatty at 25 knots, Hipper at 26. Beatty's orders even called for the 5th Battle Squadron to increase speed to 25 knots to close the gap. This was easier said than done, because 'his best speed was only 24 knots, and if the battle-cruisers increased to their own full speed they would have a four-knot advantage over the battleships'. It had always been assumed that the *Queen Elizabeth* class would have roughly a 4-knot advantage over the *König* class but it turned out to be untrue and by April 1915 Jellicoe had already realised that their speed had been over-rated. He told David Beatty: '*Warspite* is only good for about 23½ knots – no use to you.'[11] Already, as the British forces headed east with Beatty leading the charge, this was the point at which he should have taken a clear decision about how he wanted to deploy the powerful guns of the 5th Battle Squadron.

One of Jellicoe's biographers, Reginald Bacon, seized upon what he saw as Beatty's first major error:[12] failing to stop to think first, before dashing off at high speed. Even Hipper had just shown that he would wait for his further scouting forces. 'Clearly the first thing for the admiral to do was to close up his capital ships. This he did not do. In twelve minutes, he could have repaired the original error of dispersion.'[13] The distance between the 5th and Beatty's 1st and 2nd Battle Cruiser Squadrons actually then increased from five to ten miles.

Beatty later laid the blame for what was about to happen at Admiral Evan-Thomas's feet, saying that 'an admiral commanding a squadron sighting, or in touch with, the enemy would anticipate that his supporting squadrons would close without further orders'.* Considering that Beatty had not conferred with, or even talked to Evan-Thomas during the eight days before the departure

---

* It is ironic that Beatty blamed Sir Hugh Evan-Thomas for the mix-up over signals, as the latter was always regarded as a signals expert and had commanded the Signals School in Portsmouth. In Andrew Gordon's words, 'he was one of the Royal Navy's high priests of signalling with all the punctilious, pedantic regard endemic in that abstruse craft' (Gordon, *The Rules of the Game*, p38).

from Rosyth, it was a manifestly unfair judgement; it tried to shift the focus of attention after the battle from bad signalling and fleet management to lack of initiative – in effect, a 'tilt of the hat' to more defensible territory, to the memory of Nelson. But for many in the post-battle discussion, Evan-Thomas's failure was being put forward as an example of the Edwardian Navy's inability to do anything without direct orders.

Jellicoe later commented that after the *Galatea* had spotted the first signs of Hipper's forces and had signalled the information back, there was more than enough time for Beatty to organise his forces before rushing south. 'There was now an excellent opportunity to concentrate his forces. The enemy was streaking towards our battle fleet so that the loss of two or three miles by the battle-cruisers was immaterial. But the opportunity was not taken.'[14]

Jellicoe had not been at all keen on giving the 5th Battle Squadron to Beatty, but with Hood's 3rd Battle Cruiser Squadron on gunnery training he had no alternative: 'The stronger I make David Beatty, the greater is the temptation for him to get involved in an independent action.'[15] Horace Hood felt the same: 'This is a great mistake. If David Beatty has these ships with him, nothing will stop him from taking on the whole German fleet if he gets the chance.'[16]

If one is of the opinion that the failure to concentrate his forces was Beatty's first major error of judgement, a second now occurred. When Beatty felt that the optimal spot had been reached, he sent a 'general' signal that the fleet should prepare to alter course to the southeast to form a battle line in preparation for the opening engagement of Jutland, the battle-cruiser duel. After seven minutes, Beatty's signal was hauled down and made executive, meaning that ships that had been signalled had now to execute the command. Beatty's signal ordered a 'complicated manoeuvre whereby his ships would all turn together to form a compass line of bearing north-west while pursuing an east-south-east course'.[17]

As *Lion* turned, her signals were badly obscured by her thick, black funnel smoke, and the flags were impossible to read across five miles of grey water made worse by low-hanging cloud. *Barham*'s officer of the watch, Lieutenant Alfred Philips, knew that there was a signal, but he could not make out the message. Evan-Thomas is said to have assumed that Beatty's other ships' manoeuvres were just a continuation of anti-submarine zigzagging that had been in force while steaming east; and so, despite the muddled signals from Beatty, he slightly altered his course away to port, which in itself would exonerate Evan-Thomas from Beatty's accusation that he did not respond.

Tiger was also responsible. She failed to pass the signal on to *Barham* by searchlight. With wireless telegraphy blacked out and flags clearly not working, this would have been the only option. *Tiger* would have understood the importance of the signals and should have acted on that knowledge. And every minute counted. Each minute that Evan-Thomas continued towards Jellicoe added another two-thirds of a mile of distance between himself and the rest of Beatty's forces.[18]

There was disagreement on *Barham*'s bridge about Evan-Thomas's decision not to follow Beatty's ships.[19] Captain Arthur Craig and the flag commander, Wilfrid Egerton, both tried to persuade the rear admiral but to no avail.* Evan-Thomas was confused about his orders. He had seen the earlier one to turn, but not the 'executive' one. He saw the battle-cruisers turn off, but at this point was not sure whether he should not maintain his earlier orders and continue to look for Jellicoe's forces from the north, thus forming a 'bridge' between the two fleets. At this – what turned out to be – critical moment, Rear Admiral Evan-Thomas did not know why Beatty was turning south.

Without clear orders from a superior officer, who had not up to this point been explicit in communicating his intentions, Evan-Thomas had to rely on inference. Beatty had, as will be recalled, not even met with Evan-Thomas. In his defence, Evan-Thomas said that there were other considerations on his mind and that it was not for him to assume what Beatty's intentions were:

> The only way I could account for no signal having been received by me was that the Vice-Admiral [Beatty] was going to signal another course to the Fifth Battle Squadron – possibly to get the enemy's light cruisers between us. Anyway, if he wished us to turn, the searchlight would have done it in a moment. It was not until the *Tiger* asked *Lion* by wireless whether the signal to turn was to be made to the *Barham* that the Vice-Admiral seemed to realise the situation.[20]

Whoever was to blame, it meant that the powerful 15in guns of the 5th Battle Squadron would not be able to contribute broadside weight or any support to Beatty until twenty-three minutes after he had initially opened fire. Geoffrey Rawson continued to defend Beatty's positioning of the 5th Battle Squadron, quoting Jellicoe's Grand Fleet Battle Orders (GBFOs) which actually called for a ten-mile separation and pointing out that Beatty had already dropped that to five miles.[21] Rawson suggested that had Beatty done more he would never have even joined action with Hipper. His reasoning was that since 'Hipper was averse to meeting Beatty with five battle-cruisers to the British six; he would certainly decline action the moment he became aware that he was also in the presence of the 5th Battle Squadron.'[22] It is not an unreasonable point but it must be remembered that Hipper's objective in the action was to run – not to

---

* Craig and Egerton 'endeavoured to persuade our admiral to turn and follow Beatty' (Gordon, p82).

join action. To lure Beatty – generally a more powerful but smaller force at the end – into the awaiting guns of the High Seas Fleet. So in this instance, Rawson's argument does not hold much water. Bagging the 5th Battle Squadron as well might have been an even more welcome larger prize.

Signalling at the Time of Jutland

The ineffectiveness of existing signalling and how signalling was used in the battle – a mixture of flag (using the semaphore alphabet), searchlight and (the least used) wireless – is evident.

Wireless telegraphy (WT) could have freed the British from many of the disadvantages of visual signalling. But it also had its drawbacks. It could be jammed (the Germans did this quite successfully); it sometimes gave away vital information on an enemy's strength and, indirectly, on the type of ship, as signal strength was different from small destroyer to battleship; it could be interrupted if the aerials were down (as happened on *Lion* in the initial battle-cruiser actions), or if electrical supplies were similarly interrupted. Lastly – the matter that most concerned Jellicoe – these signals could be read. It was also not that fast. Getting a signal out required many people's intervention. At Jutland, WT was still pretty much an orphan. It was not even considered a part of signalling and was taught alongside electrical disciplines at the Torpedo School, HMS *Vernon*, until 1907. From July 1908, signals training incorporated a rudimentary knowledge of WT. It was only from 1914 that it was fully incorporated into the main signals curriculum.

Flags had been part of the navy's core skill-set since the Napoleonic Wars and required no technology; they were obviously susceptible to visibility conditions, either natural or man-made, like cordite and funnel smoke. Because signals were a visual method, they had the effect of 'bunching' fleets, so keeping them from wider dispersal, particularly disadvantageous to scouting duties. Given that the visual distance between larger ships was around fourteen miles, this was a short reaction time for fleets converging at a combined rate of 50 knots, as was the case when the Grand Fleet met the High Seas Fleet before the Jutland deployment. This had a considerable impact on the flagship's (hence the name) position in a line of battle. After the 1910 sea trials, the common assumption was that its best position was in the middle so that signals could travel, forward and aft, up and down a battle line. *Lion*'s signals went no further than *Tiger*. She should have passed them on but did not. Flags also took time to distribute commands: to pass a message back along twenty-four capital ships – the number that would be fighting at Jutland, creating a continuous line of ships almost eight miles long – could take, at worst, up to half an hour.

Bringing a dreadnought to a full stop took some distance. Shutting off the engines at 15 knots required a mile and a half. In many ways it was with the smaller, more mobile ships – the destroyers – that this problem of control was most keenly felt. Commodore Charles Le Mesurier, commander of the 4th Light Cruiser Squadron, put it like this: 'you *must* leave things to individual initiative in these very high-speed little ships – there is no time to make signals'.[23] Beatty hated the symbolic slavishness of the flag system: commanders losing their sense of initiative and needing a signal to tell them what to do. Consequently, Beatty used flag signals sparingly. Admiral Sims said that Beatty went considerably further: 'that it was generally reported that he [Beatty] had ordered all torpedo flags – an emblem displayed to warn ships to change course, if torpedoes were seen – to be destroyed.'[24]

Searchlight signalling was as fast as flag signalling, and had the advantage of being more readable in low light and bad visibility, but like WT was subject to electrical failure and battle damage. Given the lack of initiative and of radar, and the slow speed of flag signalling, Jellicoe probably had no option other than to keep a tight rein on the fleet. His caution over signals security was perhaps imbalanced. He would have profited handsomely had he made the message clear: relaying enemy positions back to the commander during fast-moving actions essentially outweighed any idea of compromising the sender's position.

Considering the amount of signals traffic that came from *Iron Duke* in the hours of darkness, it was extraordinary that so little intelligence had been passed back by officers of either the Grand Fleet or Beatty's battle-cruisers. In fact, according to Harper, between 21:17 (when the last flag signal was made by *Iron Duke*) and 02:20 (when it was light enough again for flag signalling), no fewer than forty-two WT and eighty-five lamp signals were sent out.

To the northeast of Beatty, just before *Invincible* was to turn south to join her old squadrons, *Indomitable* signalled Rear Admiral Hood that she had picked up 'very loud' *Telefunken* signals.[25] It was a sure sign that the Germans had heavy ships in the area. Hood's first reaction to the earlier *Galatea* sighting was to turn his own three-ship squadron east-southeast and increase speed to 22 knots.[26] If there were to be any German ships using the Skagerrak as a fast way home, he thought, his squadron –some of the best gunners in the Navy – would be waiting.

Jellicoe had another idea. He signalled Hood to join Beatty to the south with the 3rd Battle Cruiser Squadron. Just after 16:00, Hood, fifty miles away, moved the squadron onto a south-southeast course.[27] Fifty minutes later, racing to support Beatty at 26 knots, he sent a message to *Lion* asking for position, course and speed to tighten up his planned RV point.[28] He did not receive a reply.

As the 'action stations' was sounded on the ships of the Battle Cruiser Fleet, well-rehearsed drills sprung into action.* The routines started with all decks being hosed down so that hot splinters and shrapnel would have less chance of starting fires. Steel doors were closed up and 'dogged' – clamped from both sides to make them absolutely watertight.[29] Emergency medical preparations were put underway to receive the wounded. Fire hoses were unwound, and

---

* The 'action stations' alarms are sounded by a bugler leaving out the beginning G notes that denote an exercise.

boxes of sand prepared and placed near ammunition stores. The glass panes from the bridge windscreens were removed. Shoring-up spars and reserves of electrical and hydraulic gear were readied. Inside the turrets, urinal buckets were taken out. If they had the time, sailors donned clean clothes to avoid contamination if wounded. All over the ships of the battle-cruiser force, white ensigns were strung from all available points, on halyards and behind funnels. The sight was magnificent.

Going into battle also brought out all sorts of superstitions. On *New Zealand* her captain, John 'Jimmy' Green, donned the traditional Maori costume and put the greenstone tiki around his neck. This, he had been assured, would protect the ship and her crew if worn during battle. It was quite a sight: a Royal Navy captain on the bridge dressed in a black and white piu-piu skirt over his navy blues. But Green had done this before, at Dogger Bank, and *New Zealand* had come out unscathed. He was not one to take any chances. *New Zealand* would also emerge from Jutland with neither death nor damage.

Accessing the Battle Maps on Jutland1916.com

This is the point at which the reader may find it helpful to access accompanying materials on the Jutland1916.com website. You will not only find useful animations of the battle showing the movements of the main forces, but also other resources such as the official German maps as well as Harper's own maps, marked-up copies of which are in the British Library (these are clean ones, the BL's not). For those more interested in following the gunnery or signals, you can do so, minute-by-minute. Either use the Jutland.com link on a Google search (in Germany, Skagerrakschlacht. com will get you there) or capture the QR code below on a tablet device to access these resources.

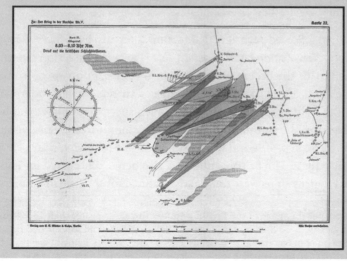

The distance between Hipper's and Beatty's ships closed to around ten miles. It was 15:40. The British had formed a single line of six battle-cruisers steaming south on a course that was slowly but surely converging on their five German counterparts. Then something strange happened. Beatty held off from opening fire, even though he had the range advantage. The 13.5in guns could manage ranges of up to 24,000yds (22,000m); the German battle-cruiser guns, depending on the ship, up to something like 19,000–21,000yds (17,400–19,200m). It is often said that this was when Beatty could have exercised his range superiority over Hipper, or at least 'try ranging shots as he had done successfully at Dogger Bank'.[30] Instead, the British guns stayed silent. Everyone on board was expecting them to open up but nothing happened.

This has always been a curious point in the opening battle-cruiser action. As a midshipman on *Lion*'s compass platform observed: 'I could not bring myself to realise that we were in the presence of the enemy. What struck me as being rather strange was that while the range of the enemy on sighting them was only about 23,000 yards, we did not open fire until the range was 18,500 yards on the gun sights.'[31] There was, however, considerable confusion about what exactly the range was.*

From the bridge of *Lützow*, Hipper saw that he was outnumbered, outrun, outranged and outgunned. His fastest ships were one or two knots slower than Beatty's fastest. On the conning tower on *Derfflinger*, Hase described what he could see:

> How menacing they appeared, magnified fifteen times ... It was a stimulating, majestic spectacle as the dark-grey giants approached like fate itself. The six ships, which had at first been proceeding in two columns, formed one line ahead. Like a herd of prehistoric monsters, they closed on one another with slow movements, spectre-like, irresistible.[32]

Lion was leading, followed each at 500yd (450m) intervals, by *Princess Royal*, *Queen Mary*, *Tiger*, *New Zealand* and *Indefatigable*. The wind direction did not favour the British: with the breeze blowing from the west, gun smoke would be pushed to the front of the British battle-cruisers' turrets. Beatty ordered a deployment 'on the right echelon', meaning that each successive ship would be slightly pulled back on the starboard quarter of the ship in front. This would present a narrow torpedo profile and would still allow the following ship a clear view of the enemy targets. The British ships were also better silhouetted for Hipper's guns, while Hipper's ships were not clearly outlined for the British gunners.

---

* Some commentators put the range of the British response fire at far nearer than 18,000yds. Chalmers said that 'Beatty, as advised by his gunnery officers, believed he had opened fire at 18,000 yards, when in point of fact the range was only 15,500 yards'. Ernle Chatfield, Beatty's flag captain on the bridge of *Lion*, maintained that it was closer to 16,000yds. Others put it even less.

So much of the gunnery achievement on the day – British or German – owed its success as much to the weather conditions, as to range-finding and targeting methods. As seen (albeit a little later) from *Southampton*, the leading ship of the 2nd Light Cruiser Squadron, the weather conditions generally really favoured the German gunners: 'The Germans were almost entirely merged into a long, smoky cloud on the eastern horizon, the sort of cloud that presages a thunderstorm, and from this gloomy retreat a series of red flashes darting out in our direction indicated the presence of five German battle-cruisers'.[33] Indeed, Erich Mahrholtz, *Von der Tann*'s gunnery officer, specifically said that the 'hazy weather conditions' were strongly in favour of his own side's gunners.

The British line also still had a number of destroyers on what would become the engaged side, the ones that were too slow for the rapid speed increase to 26 knots – *Lydiard*, *Liberty*, *Landrail* and *Laurel*.[34] Their presence on the wrong side of the battle line – or at least in the wrong place – would add another obstacle to British firing and block clean gunnery views. Kapitän Harder on *Lützow* actually thought that the destroyers might have been there specifically to interfere with German spotting:

At 6pm SMS *Lützow* received the first hit but I was not informed of its location. The enemy now stationed a destroyer on the engaged side of each ship: the former generated dense smoke and thus spotting was at times impossible. I gained the impression that this smoke cloud was made each time after we fired and that it then gradually disappeared. Only the fire control top of the opponent was visible above this smoke.[35]

Beatty himself was frustrated by the funnel smoke, even if the presence of destroyers possibly helped protect the British line from torpedoes: 'It would appear that at this time [16:08] we passed through a screen of submarines ... Though causing considerable inconvenience from smoke, the presence of *Lydiard* and *Landrail* undoubtedly preserved the Battle-cruisers from closer Submarine attack'.[36] By contrast, the breeze had the opposite effect for the German gunners. It cleared before their guns and drifted to their non-engaged side.

Seven miles behind – the gap had only slightly reduced – were Evan-Thomas's four ships, *Barham*, *Valiant*, *Warspite* and *Malaya*, impatient to engage but not able yet to support Beatty.

The Germans open fire

Across the gap stood Hipper in the armoured conning tower of *Lützow*, calmly smoking a cigar as he looked through the periscope at the British line. He gave the order to open fire. It was 15:48. The thunderclap of the first German shells sounded the opening of the Battle of Jutland.

Günther Paschen, the gunnery commander on *Lützow*,[37] described the countdown to the moment:

> Our range-finders gave us good ranges commencing at 240 Hm* and it seemed an eternity; actually it was twenty minutes before we had reached our range of 190 Hm. Even then we had to wait for the *Seydlitz* until the range was further reduced. 5 points – 57 degrees is the enemy's bearing. Estimated speed 26 knots; course 110 degrees.† This made the rate of closing four Hm a minute. At a range of 167 Hm by our calculations the first turret salvo from A and B turrets was fired at 4.48. Time of flight: twenty-two seconds.[38]

This meant that the Germans had waited and closed in from 26,000yds (23,800m) to 20,700yds (18,900m) while finally firing at 18,200 yards (16,600m). Both *Lion* and *Princess Royal*'s guns had been ranged at 23,820yds (21,780m). If 18,200yds is taken as the distance at which *Lützow* opened fire, Beatty had lost the advantage of around 5,620yds (5,140m). Beatty's hesitation in opening fire meant that the Germans' opening salvos were all well within their operating ranges: *Moltke* the shortest, at 15,500yds (14,200m), *Derfflinger* and *Seydlitz* at 16,400yds (15,000m), *Lützow*, only slightly longer, at 16,800yds (15,400m) and *Von der Tann* the longest, at 17,700yds (16,200m).[39]

Range-finding

British coincidence range-finding equipment was supplied by Barr and Stroud The most common model was the 9ft (2.7m) FQ2 while the larger 15ft (4.6m) FT24 was more suitable for the longer ranges of which British guns were increasingly capable. The FT24 was first mounted on the 1912 *Queen Elizabeth*-class ships whose powerful 15in guns could range up to 24,000yds (22,000m). By 1915, forty-five had been delivered; by the following year, eighty-four. But in the Grand Fleet, only *Orion*'s 13.5in guns were supported by the FT24.

It is difficult enough to use a hand-held coincidence range-finder, even in ideal conditions in sunlight, stationary, with no interfering cordite smoke blowing across your view. Imagine being on a rolling, pitching battleship in the mists or low cloud conditions of the North Sea, with spray and shell splashes drenching you, with engine vibration thrown in for good measure.

The Karl Zeiss stereoscopic optics used by the Germans had – as is still the case – a formidable reputation for quality. For an operator to focus on a hazy object without hard defined edges, Zeiss reputedly performed better, but the Barr and Stroud split-

---

* *Hektometer*, or hectometre in English; 1hm is 100m (320ft).

† A compass point is equivalent to approximately 11½ degrees. A full circle has 32 points so a 16-point turn – 184 degrees – is a course-reversal.

screen system – if provided with a hard, well-defined edge – also worked well but caused less eye strain for the operator. It was often remarked that at Jutland the Germans were better at finding the initial range, but this fell off as the engagement wore on.

Now comes the second part: testing the ranges. The German 'ladder' system of ranging salvos proved extremely effective and seemed, in the initial engagements, to find an adversary's range more quickly. The approach required salvos being rapidly fired from successive turrets while the shells from the previous turret were still in flight at ranges that were purposely separated by around 400 yards (370m). They were then able rapidly to 'ladder' up or down depending on 'spotting': the reading and plotting of the fall of shot by the shell splash.

After Jutland the British were quick to adopt a variation on the 'ladder'. The British system was changed to allow for two salvos to be in flight simultaneously towards a target – the first spread for deflection, the second for range. Later, director-firing methods were implemented for secondary armament and the equipment also fitted with gyro-stabilisation to counteract a ship's roll. There is a wealth of technical literature on the related issues of course plotting and fire control. For how these came into play at Jutland see John Brooks, Georg von Hase, Arthur Pollen, Dreyer and Jon Sumida.[40]

Hipper was very clear about the benefit that he had been given by Beatty's decision to let the gap close:

The fact that the English battle-cruisers, (possibly) on account of bad light conditions or perhaps forming the line of battle too late, delayed opening fire allowed us too to withhold our fire until the enemy was in effective gun range (15,000–16,000 yards). The possibility of obtaining a rapid gunnery superiority … is principally to be attributed to this delay in opening fire which compelled the enemy to remain a longer time within effective gun range.[41]

Each German battle-cruiser was instructed to target its British counterpart, meaning that Beatty's first five ships (*Lion, Princess Royal, Queen Mary, Tiger* and *New Zealand*) were each individually targeted; *Indefatigable* was not.

Fire distribution in the British line was a problem: Beatty had been misunderstood. He had intended that the first German ship of the line, *Lützow*, be engaged by two ships, then that every ship of the line take its opposite number counting from the rear. What happened was otherwise. *Lion* and *Princess Royal* both correctly engaged the *Lützow*, but the others that received the message counted from the front of the line. *Queen Mary* fired on *Seydlitz* rather than the second in line, *Derfflinger*. As a result *Derfflinger* was allowed to fire unmolested for a full ten minutes.‡ *Tiger* and *New Zealand* fired on *Moltke*, made

‡ Surprisingly, no mention is made, in either the text or the footnotes of the infamous 'Narrative of the Battle of Jutland', of the fact that the initial fire allocation left *Derfflinger* unfired on for ten minutes (Narrative, pp151–61).

a little easier to identify as the latter 'had her second funnel painted bright red, a great blessing, as it made her very easy to distinguish from the other enemy ships'.[42]

Indefatigable and *Von der Tann* got into a gunnery duel at the rear of the line. Korvettenkapitän Erich Mahrholtz, first artillery officer on *Von der Tann*, complemented Hase's vivid descriptions of the battle from the turrets. When fire opened on Beatty's line, *Von der Tann* was supposed to have fired at both the two last British ships of the line, *Indefatigable* and *New Zealand*. 'Since the secondary artillery was still out of range, I had to consider splitting my main artillery, two turrets fore, two aft. But this would mean only two splashes for each salvo which I wanted to avoid. So I decided to keep my battery together and annihilate one ship after another.'[43]

The order to fire came at 162 hectometres (hm), extreme long range (17,700yds). The fire and observations were directed at the bow section, so that, first, course changes could be more easily detected and, secondly, 'longs' that were also ahead of the ship could also be 'spotted'. Every time *Indefatigable* veered off course, range was lowered or increased by 1hm, about 110yds.

On *Derfflinger* Hase was amazed at his good fortune:

What astonished me was that so far we had apparently not been hit once. Only quite rarely did a shot stray near us. I observed the gun turrets of our target more closely and established that the ship was not firing at us. She too was firing at our flagship. I observed the enemy ship for a moment; by some mistake we were being left out. I laughed grimly and then I began to engage our enemy with complete calm, as at gun practice, and with continually increasing accuracy.[44]

This was a repeat performance of Dogger Bank. There, *Tiger's* captain, H B Pelly, fired on *Seydlitz* leaving *Moltke* free, on that occasion, to fire at will. The British seemed doomed to repeat a large number of errors made in January 1915. It is ironic that the German ships actually hitting at the start were *Moltke* and *Lützow*. Both of these German battle-cruisers had been mistakenly double-targeted by the British. But both German ships, in the midst of heavy shelling from two enemy ships, were still able to target very effectively.[45]

Paschen's first shells from *Seydlitz* landed just 300yds (275m) short, according to a gunner in *Lion's* Q turret. For an opening salvo at more than 16,000yds (14,600m), it was an incredible feat of gunnery. The same high standard was true of *Derfflinger*, which targeted *Princess Royal* and within six salvos had successfully straddled her.[46] *Lion* was hit twice within three minutes of fire being opened.

Eventually, it was Ernle Chatfield, *Lion's* captain, who gave the command to fire from the British side, thirty seconds after the Germans themselves had fired. He ordered that the 'five flag' be hoisted – the signal to 'engage the enemy'.[47] Beatty was apparently off the bridge at the time and sending a signal to Jellicoe. The flag was raised by *Lion*'s signals officer, Ralph Seymour.[48]

> The enemy battle-cruisers were rapidly closing us steering south-westerly. The range receiver on the bridge showed 20,000 yards. I was on the compass platform ... Beatty ... was on his own bridge below me with his staff ... I wanted him to come to the compass platform and sent a message ... [to him] that the range was closing rapidly and that we ought almost at once to open fire ... But I could get no reply: the Vice-Admiral was engaged in an important message to the Commander-in-Chief. Eighteen thousand yards. I told Longhurst [*Lion*'s gunnery officer] to be ready to open fire immediately. The turrets were already loaded and trained on the leading enemy ship, the *Lützow*. At 3.45, the range was 16,000 yards. I could wait no longer and I told Longhurst to be ready to open fire. At the same time the enemy did so ... [Then] Beatty came on to the compass platform.[49]

Generally speaking, incredible gunnery from *Lützow* aside, German opening fire was too short, British too long.* British gunnery was also inaccurate compared to the Germans', with some salvos going over their targets by as much as three miles. Shells from the British battle-cruiser line were even falling close to *Regensburg*, which was some distance off, on Hipper's port wing.

Beatty's feeling might have been that at the greater distances British fire would be so inaccurate as not to warrant the waste of ordnance. He might have also lacked confidence in British ability to score decisive hits. The delay has been questioned ever since.

British accounts seem to give a longer opening distance. Chatfield reported fire opening at 18,500yds (16,900m), but the description of Beatty being off the bridge talks about the range having been at 16,000yds (14,600m) at 15:45. This must have either widened or been a mistake. *Queen Mary* probably opened at around 17,500yds (16,000m); according to a survivor (of the latter's sinking), *Tiger* and *New Zealand* did so at 18,100yds (16,550m). *Tiger* was almost immediately straddled by two salvos from *Moltke*, one 'long', the other 'short'.[50] The very next minute she was hit, twice: once on the forecastle and the other on the shelter deck: 'A blinding flash through our gun port and the rattle of a hail of shell splinters on our ship's side told us that Jerry was already straddling us with a near miss.'[51]

---

* A 'short' was more useful for spotting purposes than a 'long', as it could be more clearly seen – if the deflection was correct – against the intended target, while a 'long' was usually hidden by the target itself and difficult to use as an indication of range adjustment needed.

Three minutes later at 15:54, when *Moltke* had increased her rate of fire to a salvo every twenty seconds, *Tiger* was hit again, this time more critically. The hit took off the sighting hood on Q turret,[52] killing one officer and three men, badly wounding another officer and many men. It was only through the skill of the turret officer, Petty Officer Fitzgerald, that the turret could be brought back into action. 'Very suddenly, amidst deafening noise, our ship heeled over to the hammer of a tremendous shock and my mind rolled and spun like quicksilver. Then she seemed to shake herself like a dog with a bloody nose and then belted on at the speed of the fleet.'[53]

Victor Hayward, who served on *Tiger*, described the feeling, saying that the ship seemed to 'lift bodily sideward':

> We received the worst hit we had until then. Just one shell had exploded underneath the warrant officer's mess, through the ship-side armoured belt, and into a storeroom below. A great fire raged around the ammunition passages and the port after a 6-inch magazine had to be flooded to save the ship from blowing up. The German 12-inch shell did an immense amount of damage and almost brought the ship to a standstill.[54]

After *Tiger*'s Q turret was put out of action, she was hit again at 15:55, as was X turret. At the same time, German fire from *Lützow* had started to straddle *Lion* from 15:54, the salvos bunched into close groups of four projectiles each. One shell hit the inboard side of *Lion*'s 4in (10cm) armour, the other the upper deck causing casualties in the 4in-gun crew. *Derfflinger* hit *Queen Mary* three times with 12in (30.5cm) fire; *Von der Tann* scored a number of hits on *Indefatigable*; *Seydlitz* likewise on *Queen Mary* (although *Derfflinger* claimed the hit). While it had taken *Lützow* just five salvos to get on target, *Lion* took nine.[55]

Course Plotting

Fed into the fire-control tables was data on the range and bearing of a target. With the firing ship's course and speed, these tables would compile the critical input, known as a 'firing solution', required to set the constantly changing gun elevation and bearing needed to hit moving targets.

This was one of the supporting dramas of Jutland, mostly played out in the pre-war years: the battle between the rival systems of Arthur Hungerford Pollen, who offered his services in monopoly to the Royal Navy, and Jellicoe's flag captain on *Iron Duke*, Frederic Dreyer, considered one of the Navy's top gunnery experts. Dreyer copied many of Pollen's ideas, but in Dreyer's system range and bearing were plotted separately, simultaneously in Pollen's. The Dreyer Mark II system used Pollen's Argo Clock Mark IV. This instrument mechanically combined target and firing ship's courses, bearing and speeds to present the firing solution but, by the time of Jutland, only six Argo clocks were on British ships.

All British ships' gunfire was controlled by a single master sight on the director tower, hence the system's name, 'director firing'. Here was mounted a Barr and Stroud coincidence range-finder system. On the platform itself were four petty officers and twenty men; in the transfer room there were one petty officer and twelve men; in the switch room, one warrant officer and three gunnery mechanics; in the magazines, one petty officer and eighteen men; and in the cartridge magazine, one petty officer and around fourteen men.

The Dreyer tables were slow to enter service. At the outbreak of war only one was fitted in a 12in dreadnought, although they were then quickly installed in the rest. However, the Dreyer Mark I (actually a variant that used a Vickers rather than an Argo or Dreyer clock) was less reliable. Its simplicity made it easier to produce, but the same characteristic made it less reliable and particularly problematic at longer ranges. So by Jutland, while all the 15in dreadnoughts had the superior Dreyer clock, one-third of the Grand Fleet battleships and half the battle-cruisers used the less reliable equipment type.

Turning to the German systems, Hase wrote a very useful description of how gunnery was organised on *Derfflinger*. She was equipped with four 30.5cm (12in) guns, mounted two aft and two forward, and, as was the practice in the German navy, they were named, from bow to stern, Anna, Bertha, Caesar and Dora. (On a British ship, the equivalents were the rather less romantic A, B, X and Y, with the occasional Q thrown in for good measure; A and B were the fore and X and Y the aft turrets; Q was a midship turret.)

The secondary armament consisted of fourteen 15cm (5.9in) guns, mounted in equal numbers on each side of the ship. Ammunition was stored in around fifty separate magazines scattered throughout the ship. Organisationally, Hase had three lieutenant commanders, three lieutenants, four sub lieutenants, four midshipmen, six warrant officers, and around 750 petty officers and men: around 50 per cent of the entire complement of *Derfflinger*, in fact. Each turret was under the command of a turret officer, normally a lieutenant commander or lieutenant, a *Stückmeister*, to work the turret, and seventy-five petty officers and men.

The guns were controlled from what Hase described as an 'armoured chamber', forming the rear portion of the ship's conning tower. During action Hase worked the main guns from this position using an observation periscope to afford him some protection, while the three gunnery officers were responsible for the secondary batteries, with a sub lieutenant and three petty officers manning the range-finder, and a further three petty officers on the director, and five men who were responsible for getting the orders to the various points of the ship. They did this through the transmitting stations that were directly below the conning tower, but below *Derfflinger*'s armoured decks.

Range-finding equipment was provided by seven Zeiss stereoscopic finders that could measure accurately up to 200hm. Each finder had two *Basisgerät* men (*BG Männer*), one to read the range, the other to set the figures in hectometres on the gunnery telegraph. This was then sent to the BG-transmitter that took an average from all the reports. The German Zeiss 3m range-finder system hugely magnified

targets and could more accurately be used in hazy conditions. Combined with efficient 'ladder' bracketing, the German system tended to find enemy targets more
quickly, but in time, as operators reputedly tired faster with eye strain, German
range accuracy fell off during engagement.

Derfflinger also carried a new invention called the *Entfernungs-unterschieds
Peilschreiber* (*EU Anzeiger*) that the first gunnery officer of *Lützow*, Commander
Günther Paschen, had designed, the equivalent to the Royal Navy's Dumaresq.
Ranges from separate stereoscopic range-finders were averaged, passed to the transmitting station, combined with elevation data and sent to the gun layers to calculate
the required 'deflection' for a successful shot. A clock, the AW-Geber C12, was used
to keep the range-rate data.

Being on the receiving end of heavy fire was a horrifying combination of
expectation, noise, paranoia:

> With each salvo fired by the enemy, I was able to see distinctly four or
> five shells coming through the air. They looked like elongated black spots.
> Gradually they grew bigger, and then – crash! They were here. They exploded
> on striking the water or the ship with a terrific roar. After a bit I could tell from
> watching the shells fairly accurately whether they would fall short or over.[56]

An officer on *New Zealand* talked of the same feeling, almost that you were in
the cross-hairs of a sniper's rifle:

> I was surprised to find that, in addition to being able to follow the flight
> of one's own projectiles with spotting glasses, the enemy's projectiles also
> appeared as dots getting larger and larger, till they burst short or droned past
> and fell beyond us. They always seemed to be coming straight for one's eye.
> Ricochets were also clearly visible, turning end over end, and making a noise
> like the rumbling of a distant train.[57]

Not until 15:55 did *Queen Mary* – third in the British line and considered
a crack gunnery ship – finally score the first hit from the British side, two on
Seydlitz, one just in front of the foremast.[58] *Seydlitz* and *Queen Mary* started to
duel, but at the very moment that *Queen Mary* scored her hit, she was herself
hit in the aft 4in battery. Two minutes later *Queen Mary*'s shooting scored another hit, this time on her opponent's barbette armour in the aft super-firing
gun. The turret was holed and an ammunition fire broke out, but it was not as
serious as at Dogger Bank. There, a small burning splinter had ignited 13,000lbs
(5,900kg) of cordite and killed 190 in the turret; this time, the damage was limited to twenty dead and the turret being put out of action.[59]

Seven minutes had passed since action had been engaged: seven minutes in
which German gunnery had been accurate from the first ranging shots. Beatty

signalled 'increase the rate of fire' and let Jellicoe know that he was engaged with the enemy but gave no further detail.[60] This penchant for an increased rate of fire plagued the Royal Navy during this period. Its requirements – feeding the guns with propellant and shell as fast as possible – produced lax and dangerous munitions-handling procedures; it led to cordite-stacking outside the magazines and to flash-proofing precautions being over-ridden.

Two minutes before four o'clock, *Princess Royal* was hit by two 12in shells from *Derfflinger*. The latter had just laid down a heavy barrage of five salvos in three minutes. The second 'caused the electric training of the Argo Tower to fail, and the hand gear was found to be set up. Control was turned over to B turret for ten minutes, and then resumed by the Argo Tower' where the range-finder was out of action. The switch of director command to the *Princess Royal's* B turret was ordered till 16:14.[61]

At this point, the British destroyers passed up the line on the engaged side of the battle-cruisers. As if the battle-cruisers were not having enough problems, now their gunnery was even more obscured by belching funnel smoke. To lessen the effect and regain his balance, Beatty slightly altered course to the south-southeast to open the range with the Germans. The move was not signalled and, as a consequence, seemed to cause some confusion among the destroyers.

> The sudden switch to the south-south-east threw the destroyers out of station. We had been assembled ahead of the *Lion* but the rapid 70 degree change turn to starboard left us trailing and there was a mad scramble to regain our battle position in the van. Most of our flotilla mates steamed up the disengaged side of our battle-cruisers, but *Obdurate* and *Morris* found themselves on the engaged side and as we crept up between the battle lines we were much inhibited by the necessity to moderate our speed so that excessive funnel smoke would not obscure the big ships' view of the enemy.[62]

Beatty wanted to run ahead of Hipper, but he also wanted to get out of range of the Germans' smaller secondary armament, the lighter 5.9in guns that *Seydlitz* had been using for six minutes after opening up main weapons fire. He felt that if he could successfully out-run his opponents, he could also swing back over to his port to cross their 'T'.

Hipper also turned off to the southeast and – with Beatty already turning away – this put considerably more distance between the two lines than either commander might have intended. However, a minute later, after the turn-away, at 15:59 both *Derfflinger* and *Lützow* were hit. *Lion*, who struck the latter, was finally able to avenge some of the harsh treatment that she had received earlier. Although both hits landed on the forecastle, little damage actually resulted.

Lion's hit was the final of the first eleven minutes of the action in which five German battle-cruisers, outnumbered by Beatty's six, managed to land twice as many hits on their opponent: at least fifteen against eight, and probably many more. *Tiger* herself had probably taken nine hits by this point.

Lion continued taking heavy fire. Lieutenant Chalmers saw a lifeboat explode 'in a cloud of splinters'. He could not tell through the 'white mist' what was happening with the enemy.[63] At 16:00, as she was trying to close the gap caused by the double turn-away, *Lion* received a critical hit. *Lützow* had managed to land a 12in shell on Q turret's weakest point. The turret top was ripped wide open, killing all but three of the turret crew instantaneously. Had the shell hit 6in (15cm) either side, it would have glanced off or exploded on the exterior.

The destructive power of a shell hit is described by an eyewitness on *Lion* in Massie's *Castles of Steel*:

> No further confirmation was necessary: the armoured roof of Q turret had been folded back like an open sardine tin; thick yellow smoke was rolling up in clouds from the gaping hole, and the guns were cocked up in the air awkwardly. All this happened within a few yards of where Beatty was standing and none of us on the bridge had heard the detonation. The destructive power was enormous but, oddly, in the maelstrom of the battle, completely unregistered on the bridge.[64]

The comment is extraordinary in its attempt to convey the noise and mayhem of a sea battle. The explosion must have been violent, like a thunderclap and yet nothing was registered. From *Birmingham* the hit looked terminal:

> She was heavily hit and I saw a large plate which I judged to be the top of the turret, blown into the air. It appeared to rise very slowly, turning round and round, and looking very much like an airplane. I should say it rose some 400 or 500 feet and looking at it through glasses I could distinctly see the holes in it for the bolts. My attention was drawn from this by a sheet of flame in her second funnel, which shot up about sixty feet and soon died down but did not immediately disappear.[65]

On *Lion*, her crew felt that they had just had an extremely close escape, though Chalmers noted that it was 'strange that this should have all happened a few yards from where Beatty was standing and none of us on the bridge [had] heard the explosion'.[66]

Then, between the flashing lines, came the strangest sight. During this hell-fire, a large sailing barque with all sails set lay becalmed between the two fleets, amidst this firestorm of steel and death. It was all the more extraordinary as the very same thing had happened a year earlier at the Dogger Bank action.

On *Lion* one disaster had been narrowly averted only for another quickly to follow. A shell that had been in the breech fell back out with the powder charge. About ten minutes after the initial shell had landed, the cordite ignited. The explosion was strong enough to flatten some of the marines who were cleaning up after the initial turret hit. Marine H Willons takes up the story:

> And then the chief gunner came along to see if everything was in order. Finding the turret out of action, he ordered several of us to put out fires on the mess deck. Just as he and I got clear, the ignition of the cordite occurred and the blast pushed us along. [67]

The turret fire had ignited the charges that were in the loading cages. The flash went right through the handling room but, because it found a way through the 'escape trunk' onto the deck, the explosion was not mortal. It was only because of the Royal Marines turret officer, Major Francis Harvey, that *Lion* survived. He had lost both legs, but he had somehow crawled to the voice pipe and ordered the magazines to be flooded and doors closed; it was just in time. Three of the turret crew survived. Harvey had sent his marine sergeant, his face 'black from fire, his hair singed, his clothes burnt', directly to the bridge to report in person to Chatfield and Beatty.[68] Later, Harvey's body was found by the voice pipe. His action saved the ship and his shipmates. He was posthumously awarded the Victoria Cross.

Now severely wounded, *Lion* staggered out of the line and *Princess Royal*, which had also just received another close hit from *Derfflinger*, took over the van.[69] The Germans were throwing everything that they could at the British, including *Moltke*, which loosed four torpedoes. The torpedoes had no effect, but the steadily overwhelming pace and accuracy of German gunnery, and now the addition of torpedoes, must have substantially shaken the British. On the German side, *Lützow* was also hit, but out of the thirty-one salvos in the seventeen minutes of action, Günther Paschen counted six hits. By contrast the Germans had been hit just three times.[70] It was a sign of how badly things were developing.

The loss of *Indefatigable*
Princess Royal shifted her fire onto *Derfflinger* and successfully hit her. *Von der Tann* continued to target *Indefatigable* at the rear of the British line. The latter's forty or so 12in shells seemed to have had no noticeable effect on the German battle-cruiser's ferocious rate of fire. After she found the British battle-cruiser's range, *Von der Tann* registered three consecutive hits from a four-gun salvo, her 11in shells hitting the forward A turret and forecastle. Encouraged by her success, *Von der Tann* laid down a massive barrage. Fifty-two 11in and

thirty-eight 5.9in shells were fired, at ranges varying from 14,000–18,000yds (12,000–16,500m); four salvos straddled *Indefatigable*. Finally, at 16:02, at a range of around 16,000yds, the German shells tore through the thin plating just above the armoured belt by X turret and exploded in the magazine. A second salvo hit A turret and may have caused a cordite fire. Thirty seconds after the superstructure was hit, a ripple of fire seemed to race from the bows right the way back down the 19,000-ton battle-cruiser as her magazines exploded.

Beatty pulled away a second time, but *Indefatigable* was unable to follow *New Zealand* and, instead, started slowly to sink by the stern. Fourteen minutes after opening fire, 'the deadly blow struck the enemy'. Looking through the direction finder (*Richtungs-weiser Rohr*), Mahrholtz 'saw the arrival of a salvo, followed by a gigantic explosion in the aft turret.'[71]

> [A] bright sheet of flame shot out of the turret roof and expanded along the entire aft section. Debris whirled through the air, possibly fragments from the turret's roof. A monstrous black cloud of smoke rose into the air, to twice the height of the top mast … apparently we had hit an oil tank.

More fire was unnecessary. *Indefatigable* 'slipped below the waves'. Looking back from *New Zealand*, around 150yds (140m) from her when it happened, the sinking *Indefatigable* could be seen by British sailors to shudder from the repeated hits that she sustained.

> She was about 500 yards on our starboard quarter, in full view of the conning tower. While he [the admiral's secretary] was still looking at her through his glasses she was hit by two shells, one on the fo'c'sle and one on the fore turret. The shells appeared to explode on impact.
>
> Then, there was an interval of about thirty seconds during which there was absolutely no sign of fire or flame or smoke, except the very little actually formed by the burst of the two shells, which was not inconsiderable. At the end of the interval of about 30 seconds the ship completely blew up, commencing apparently from forward. The main explosion started with sheets of flame followed immediately afterwards by a dense, dark smoke which obscured the ship from view. All sorts of stuff was blown high into the air, one fifty-foot steam picket boat, for example, being blown up about 200 feet, apparently intact, though upside down.[72]

One thousand and fifteen officers and men went down with *Indefatigable* but since she was the last ship in the line, most British sailors did not know what had happened. The officers and crew on *Lion* were certainly not aware.

There were only two survivors from the massive explosion, Able Seaman Elliot and Leading Signalman Falmer.[73] Both were picked up by a German destroyer, either *S.68* or *S.16*, later that evening just before eight.[74] The two sailors had not been able to keep the only other survivor, the ship's captain, Charles Sowerby, alive. He died before rescue came. Falmer was atop the mast:

> A message came through that the flags were entangled round the mast –
> somebody must go up. So I took my sea boots off, climbed out the port-top,
> went up the Jacob's ladder right to the very top. I unfolded the flag and I sat
> on the wireless yard, looking around. I could see all the German fleet and I
> made out roughly forty ships. There were six of us, and I suppose we'd been
> in action about an hour and a half or so when a shell or something hit the
> magazines. There was a terrific explosion, the guns went up in the air just like
> matchsticks – 12-inch guns they were – and she began to settle down, and
> within half a minute she was gone. I was thrown I suppose, well, I was 180
> foot up, you understand, and I was thrown well clear of the ship, otherwise I
> would have been sucked under.[75]

In an interview in 1963, Falmer described how he had somehow managed to survive:

> I see the guns go up, bodies and everything. Within half a minute the ship
> turned right over. Threw me in the water. Luckily I was top of the mast
> otherwise I would have been sucked under … turning over … Nothing to be
> seen ... German battle-cruisers started coming along. German shells which
> was dropping short I could feel myself in the water.[76]

Beatty's second course correction again widened the gap between the fleets, this time to between 20,000 and 21,000 yards (18,300–19,200m). The Germans were, with the loss of *Indefatigable*, getting an impression of the British line starting to lose battle cohesion. In fact, what seems to have happened was that some of Beatty's ships thought that they had spotted a submarine and started rapid course changes. It was more likely jitters. This widening of the gap between the lines – maybe wider than Beatty planned, as his radio had been destroyed – gave the British ships some welcome respite from German shells,[77] although *Lion* continued to receive intermittent fire from 16:10 to 16:16 during which, at 16:14, *Lützow* hit her again.

After *Indefatigable* sank, *Von der Tann* wasted no time and switched her fire onto a new target: *New Zealand*. For *Von der Tann*, in Mahrholtz's words, 'the ensuing battle was far more challenging' (than the duel with *Indefatigable*).[78] Beatty's numerical superiority had now been equalised by Hipper and he now held the upper hand. Beatty had been engaged since 14:48; he had lost one of his capital ships with a horrendous loss of life, but he had also, more crucially, lost the advantage. Hipper now outgunned him in terms of turrets – twenty-one to fifteen. On his own flagship Beatty had narrowly escaped a similar fate by one man's sacrifice. By 16:07 *Lützow* had hit *Lion* at least six times.[79]

Beatty, entering with a superior force, had been mauled. He had fought this action with 56,000lbs (25,000kg) of broadside weight.* With Evan-Thomas's 15in guns – the most powerful in the British Navy – Beatty would have doubled his firepower by adding a further 61,000lbs (28,000kg). Hipper would not have stood a chance.

To the north, Evan-Thomas had somehow managed to coax the maximum 24½ knots out of his squadron and was starting to close the gap with his commander. At around eight miles, the trailing ships of Hipper's line finally became visible to the naked eye. At the start of the action, when Hipper had made his initial 180-degree turn, starting the battle-cruiser action that would become known as the 'run to the south', one thing that he should have done was to place his light cruisers on the German line's engaged starboard side. He did the opposite and consequently they were not best placed to act either as scouts or more importantly as attackers.

Then Evan-Thomas's arrival came as a shock. The range between the steadily closing van of the 5th Battle Squadron and the rear of Hipper's line was now around 19,000yds or almost eleven miles (17km). Sub Lieutenant Eric Brand of *Valiant* was on the Dumaresq when he finally caught sight of the German line:

> I saw a German ship and exclaimed, 'My God, it's the *Von der Tann!*', and got busy estimating her 'inclination' and speed. As soon as we could, we opened fire at a range of 22,000 yards, or at any rate the time of flight was around 45 seconds. In those days we only fired one four-gun salvo and waited to see the splash before making any corrections to the range and firing the next salvo. Nobody had thought of double salvos separated by a definite amount of range in those days. That was one of the lessons we learnt that day.[80]

In the two minutes between 16:08 and 16:10, the 15in guns of the 5th Battle Squadron opened fire on the rear of the German line where *Von der Tann* and *Moltke* had taken up position.[81] The danger of the squadron's arrival for Hipper was immediately obvious. At 16:09 one of *Barham*'s 15in shells hit near *Von der Tann*'s water line and smashed through a number of decks. With the amount of water flooding in – almost 600 tons rushed through the holed stern – her engines began to run hot and she started to list badly, although she courageously remained in the line to draw fire away from her still lightly-damaged sister ships.

---

* The broadside weight is simply calculated by taking the weight of each shell and multiplying it by the number of guns being brought to bear. Broadside weight per minute based on the rate of fire can then also be calculated.

The effect of a 1,920lb (870kg) 15in shell in a gunnery duel was devastating. The guns of the *Queen Elizabeths* could hurl a massive, one-ton projectile (0.9 tons to be exact) across 24,400yds (22,300m) of open sea against an enemy target with an initial muzzle velocity of nearly 2,500ft (760m) per second.[82] After the hit, which seriously damaged *Von der Tann's* steering system, Seaman Carl Meims was sent to investigate and reported back:

> There was lots of damage and a few dead. Lots of blood everywhere. A young sailor crouched on the floor looking very bad, losing a lot of blood, he had been hit in the arm. He was trying to bandage his own arm. I tried to help him but he said 'No' in a very weak voice. 'Go upstairs and fight.'[83]

Almost six minutes after the destruction of *Indefatigable*, the first shell hit *Von der Tann* and penetrated the armoured belt below the water line close to Section No. 1. The impact was felt throughout the ship: it 'made the hull vibrate like a tuning fork, five to six times the ship's end swayed back and forth, and the bending of the ship damaged the radio antennae between the masts'.[84] Now the visibility was also 'degrading and the initially clear horizon getting hazy'. *Von der Tann* was being massively straddled by the arrival of 15in shells from the powerful *Queen Elizabeths* finally joining the action. A neighbouring torpedo boat said that the ship was 'scarcely visible among the shell splashes'. Two more hits landed: 'Turret Alsen does not reply'; then, 'Turret Culm does not reply'. A messenger reported that they were full of smoke and gas, and that the magazine had been flooded as a precaution.

At 16:10, as the *Queen Elizabeths* closed in on their quarry, Evan-Thomas allocated fire on the two German vessels to two British ships in pairs: *Barham* and *Valiant* to concentrate on *Moltke*, *Warspite* and *Malaya* on *Von der Tann*. The 5th Battle Squadron's fire was almost immediately accurate although, even with the larger Barr and Stroud range-finders, visibility was bad and very difficult for the gunners:

> To realise our difficulties you must try and visualise the light and position. The range was about ten to eleven miles. Behind the enemy were blue-black clouds and a low-lying mist and behind us was the sun and a sharp clear horizon with no mist. The actual sun was behind clouds high in the sky so they had no glare in their glasses. Thus you will see that the Germans were almost invisible and we were silhouetted against a bright clear background so they could get good readings from their range finders and also mark their fall of shot. Neither of these things could we do.[85]

Moltke was hit at around 16:16 on her side armour. There was an explosion in a coal-bunker that set the coal dust afire. A 5.9in gun had also been put out of action and a number of the gun crew killed.

Three minutes later, there was another case of submarine jitters. *Princess Royal* thought that she had spotted a torpedo track passing from her disengaged starboard side, which led to the (erroneous) conclusion that German submarines were also operating along with their surface fleet. Scheer later confirmed that there were no German submarines operating in the area; they had been deployed around the British port exit points. But, while nobody actually saw a German submarine, the effect was to push Beatty to steer off more to port and so close with the German battle-cruisers once again.

Evan-Thomas's ships had saved the day. Three days after the battle, Beatty wrote effusively about the 5th Battle Squadron's performance:

> Just a line to thank you from the bottom of my heart for your gallant and
> effective support on Wednesday … Your coming down in support and
> poor Hood's magnificent handling of his squadron will remain in my mind
> forever.[86]

Sadly, it did not remain long. After the battle, Evan-Thomas later became the brunt of Beatty's criticism when the dust had settled, and Beatty was feeling the frustration of having been robbed of the victory and recognition that he felt should have rightfully been his.

The loss of *Queen Mary*

The loss of *Lion*'s main aerials was making the job of maintaining control over his two squadrons considerably more difficult for Beatty. It was imperative to get communications back. A young telegraphist, Arthur Lewis, was sent up the rigging to put something together to re-establish basic wireless telegraphy (WT). It was a hazardous task:

> It was a particularly bad time, shrapnel bursting all around, shells whistling
> overhead; our speed, approximately 26 knots, did not make the task any
> easier. My hat was whisked away and landed in one of the picket boats; it was
> then that I felt really scared and prayed that I might be spared to be able to get
> down into the 'comparative safety' of 'below decks'.[87]

In the first twenty-five minutes of the encounter, from the moment the German line opened up at 15:48 to around 16:20, the British had managed to land only three hits: two from *Queen Mary* and one from *Lion*. It was a particularly poor record.

But for a short while the British seemed to regain the upper hand. At 16:15 *Lion* and *Princess Royal*, firing on *Lützow*, achieved some hits. *Princess Royal*'s shooting was creditable, her first shot hitting between the forward turrets, the second the armour belt. *Lion* continued to suffer problems with her range-finding and over-shooting, her 'longs' landing as far out as 23,000yds (21,000m). The next minute, fire from the 5th Battle Squadron hit *Moltke* and put one of her 5.9in guns out of action.

More importantly, the far-off *Barham* had joined the fray, and at around 16:12 a 15in shell had critically damaged *Von der Tann*'s steering gear. In the German official history, Otto Groos wrote of the significance of *Barham*'s intervention: 'the greatest calamity of a complete breakdown of the steering gear was averted, otherwise the *Von der Tann* would have been delivered into the hands of the oncoming battleships as in the case of the *Blücher* during the Dogger Bank action'.[88]

New Zealand prematurely shifted her fire to *Moltke*, thinking that *Von der Tann*, enveloped in a cloud of smoke, was in a critical condition and *Moltke* was hit twice. Despite this she managed to hit back at *Tiger*. Now *Von der Tann* sought and had her vengeance, hitting *New Zealand* at around 16:20 after the latter had clearly taken her eye off the ball.

At 16:17 *Queen Mary* hit *Seydlitz*, putting a 5.9in casemate out of action, but instead of staying trained on the same ship, she moved her fire to *Derfflinger*. Meanwhile, *Derfflinger* and *Seydlitz* concentrated fire on her, even though Hase was initially under the impression that he was still firing against her sister ship, *Princess Royal*.[89] After *Lion* had been hit earlier and moved out of the head of the line, Hase had confused his targets. During the melee *Lion* was hit again and completely shrouded in smoke.

Things now started to go badly for *Queen Mary*, considered the best gunnery ship of the Royal Navy. *Derfflinger* landed a shell but this would prove minor to what would come later:

Everything was going beautifully until 4.21, when Q turret was hit by a heavy shell and the right gun put out of action. We continued firing with the left gun for two or three minutes and then a most awful explosion took place, which broke the ship in half by the foremast. Our left gun broke off outside the turret and the rear-end fell into the working chamber; the right gun also slid down. The turret was filled with flying metal and several men were killed. A lot of cordite caught fire below me and blazed up and several people were gassed.[90]

At 16:25 or 16:26, *Queen Mary* was hit again, by salvos. In the magazine of one of the forward turrets, the cordite detonated. Petty Officer Ernest Francis, one of the survivors, later recalled what he remembered happening:[91]

Then came the big explosion, which shook us a bit, and on looking at the pressure gauge, I saw the pressure had failed. Immediately after that came what I call the 'big smash' and I was dangling in the air on a bowline which saved me from being thrown on the floor of the turret.[92]

Francis got out to see what had happened. There was no panic, just consternation and confusion. As soon as he put his head up he saw that the 4in battery was completely smashed and that the ship was listing badly. Donning a respirator, Francis got as many men as he could out of the turret as the ship's bows began to go down rapidly.

For Midshipman John Lloyd Owen, trapped in X turret, it was the same: getting permission from the turret officer, Lieutenant Ewart, he scrambled out at as fast as he could. The ship had already developed a heavy 45-degree list to port, but Francis was prevented from sliding down by two of his turret crew, who came to help him: turret trainer AB Long and left-gun number 4, AB Lane. *Derfflinger* started to rapidly increase her rate of fire and, at 15,000yds (137hm), managed to straddle the listing *Queen*. One salvo was fired every twenty seconds and the range closed to around 14,400yds (132hm): six complete salvos in three minutes.

The awful and complete suddenness of the death of *Queen Mary* was captured in the words of a gunlayer from *Tiger*:[93]

> Every shell that the Germans threw seemed suddenly to strike the battle-cruiser at once. It was as if a whirlwind was smashing a forest down, and reminded me very much of the rending that is heard when a big vessel is launched and the stays are being smashed ... The *Queen Mary* seemed to roll slowly to starboard, her masts and funnels gone, and with a huge hole in her side. She listed again, the hole disappeared beneath the water, which rushed over her and turned her completely over. A minute and a half, and all that could be seen of the *Queen Mary* was her keel, and then that disappeared.[94]

Hase was stunned by the suddenness of the change of fortune:

> The *Queen Mary* was firing less rapidly than we were but usually full salvos. I could see the shells coming and I had to admit that they were shooting superbly. As a rule, all eight shells fell together, but they were almost always over or short ... but the poor *Queen Mary* was having a bad time. In addition to the *Derfflinger*, she was being engaged by the *Seydlitz* ... At 4.26 she met her doom ... First, a vivid red flame shot up from her forepart. Then came an explosion forward, followed by a much heavier explosion amidships. Black debris flew into the air and immediately afterwards the whole ship blew up with a terrific explosion. A gigantic cloud of smoke rose, the masts collapsed inwards, the smoke cloud hid everything and rose higher and higher. Finally nothing but a thick, black cloud of smoke remained where the ship had been. At its base, the smoke

column covered only a small area, but it widened towards the summit like a monstrous pine tree.[95]

Tiger was following closely astern. Able Seaman Victor Hayward talked of the curious scene as paper started to unravel and flutter in the North Sea air.

Rolls and rolls of white paper came streaming out of her aft hatch situated on her quarter deck. These must have been the spare rolls of Dreyer's chart paper, because her gunnery office was situated close to her after hatch. It went trailing over the boiling sea like a shaking toilet roll. When quite a few men were already in the water, the second explosion occurred.[96]

This explosion reached a thousand feet above her and the hull split into two. An officer from *Tiger*'s bridge had a grandstand view:

I saw one salvo straddle her. Three shells out of four hit … The next salvo straddled her and two more shells hit her. As they hit, I saw a dull red glow amidships and then the ship seemed to open out like a puffball or one of those toadstool things when one squeezes it. Then there was another dull red glow somewhere forward, and the whole ship seemed to collapse inwards. The funnels and masts fell into the middle, and the hull was blown outwards. The roofs of the turrets were blown 100 feet high, then everything was smoke, and a bit of the stern was the only part of the ship left above water. The *Tiger* put her helm hard-a-starboard, and we just cleared the remains of the *Queen Mary*'s stern by a few feet.[97]

As she sank, her propellers were still turning.

The officers and men lost numbered 1,258; only a handful survived. Among the eight who did were clerk Lloyd Owen, Petty Officer Francis and a midshipman, Storey, who even in the water nearly did not make it as enemy shells were landing short. As he recounted, the worst part for him was seeing many of his friends and fellow sailors giving up as British destroyers raced past and were not able to stop. All officers, except for four midshipmen, were lost. Hase wrote that a Japanese prince, Commander Chiusuke Shimomura, an IJN observer and naval attaché in London was among the dead.[98] A very small group of survivors who had somehow managed to stay alive were picked up by *Laurel*, the one destroyer that did stop.

Tiger and *New Zealand* steamed past the wreck to continue battle. *Princess Royal* continued to be heavily straddled. The captain of *Tiger*, Henry Pelly, reported that as she passed through the cloud of smoke, 'there was a heavy fall of debris on her decks'.[99] As *Tiger* was only 400yds behind, she passed *Queen Mary*'s stern within a few feet, 'but so thick was the pall that most of them were completely blinded'.[100]

At this moment, Vice Admiral Beatty turned to his captain, Ernle Chatfield, on the bridge of *Lion* and made his now famous comment: 'There seems to be something wrong with our bloody ships today!'[101]

Protecting a Ship's Magazines

The dangerous practices of stacking ammunition outside protective magazines and leaving anti-flash doors open during battle were a direct result of an obsession with gunnery speed. It is probably no coincidence that the fastest gunners in the British navy were on *Invincible* and *Queen Mary*, both ripped apart by magazine explosions and each going down with almost all hands. Of the 6,094 British sailors who lost their lives at Jutland, 38 per cent were from these two ships alone. Add in the 1,017 deaths from the sinking of *Indefatigable* and more than half the deaths at Jutland resulted, in part at least, from this tragic belief in gunnery speed and also, possibly, from the over-confidence in British battleship design.

It has now been confirmed by inspections of the wrecks of *Queen Mary*, *Invincible* and *Indefatigable* that the silk cordite bags had been brought up from the magazines and stacked in the passageways below the guns. British cordite was not stable and actually became even less so with age. The silk bags in which it was packed caught fire easily.

German charges, by contrast, were quite different. For a start, they were stored in machined brass tubes. The Germans had learnt lessons from Dogger Bank and quickly applied them. After the disastrous experience on *Seydlitz*, where 120 men had been killed in a turret explosion, but where magazine detonation had luckily been avoided, the Germans immediately tightened up. Stacking propellant in the turret was limited and anti-flash doors were redesigned.

Magazine protection was largely ignored on many British ships, especially in the Battle Cruiser Fleet. Later, Beatty wrote little about this as a possible factor in the brutal battle-cruiser losses, but his Battle Cruiser Battle Orders (BCBOs) were changed. His own near-death experience on *Lion* no doubt added a new perspective and, ironically, Beatty owes much to his chief gunnery officer, A C Grant, who had been brought up in the practices of the Grand Fleet and had actively limited the open stacking of cordite against considerable opposition. When Grant arrived on *Lion*, it did not take long for him 'to realise what a pitiful mess' the cordite was in. When cordite was introduced, he maintained, handling explosive charges 'became unconsciously considerably relaxed, even I regret to say, to a dangerous degree'. Dress regulations (against wearing hobnail boots that could spark on metal) were relaxed, as was access to the locked magazine. Cases were opened in preparation for action as this made the handling faster, but also created a large hazard. Cordite was stacked both in turrets and in passages in excessive quantity, for the same reasons.[102]

After Jutland, investigations into what went wrong started in the fleet and at the Admiralty. Ernle Chatfield headed the fleet committee. The Admiralty one set up to investigate and recommend on 'the causes of explosions in British warships when hit by heavy shell' included 3SL, Admiral Sir Frederick Tudor, the DNO Rear Admiral

Morgan Singer and the DNC, Tennyson d'Eyncourt. They corroborated what Grant had found, that cordite was often stacked within turrets, so that 'each turret became its own magazine' (Nicholas Lambert, *Our Bloody Ships*). The BCF took action immediately. Beatty wrote to Jellicoe about the dangers of 'open magazine doors in turrets', saying that it was 'imperative to maintain a small stock of cordite in handling room for magazine (and) doors being kept closed with one clip and opened only for replenishment of handling room'. On 5 June a circular went around the BCF saying that only four rounds were allowed outside the magazines at any one time (including the two in the breech).

The report was sent to the Admiralty. When Jackson resigned and was replaced by Jellicoe, the report was suppressed by the new 1SL, along with Beatty, 'anxious not to damage the morale of the fleet any further', as this would have clearly placed the blame in the hands of officers who condoned such a practice. Jellicoe even sent a letter of apology to Beatty at the implied criticism of his men's conduct during the battle. The ensuing actions were more to do with armour correction than magazine practice – the new *Howe* class (HMS *Hood* was actually just being laid down) would add another 3,000 tons of armour protection.

It was clear that the practice had been condoned. Dannreuther says this of *Invincible*. Lt Victor Shepherd said the same of *Agincourt*, able to shoot off 144 shells in the short battleship engagement, probably as a direct result of this stacking of cordite in passageways. *New Zealand* must have done the same. She shot a record of 422 shells during the battle.

At 16:28, nearly a full half-hour since *Lion* had been hit on her Q turret, a huge flame roared up. 'Doubtless some burning clothing fell from one of the ramming numbers into the open cage and caught the cordite afire. Owing to the fact that the top of the turret was partially blown off, there was no explosion, but the flames travelled right through the turret and the adjacent compartments.'[103]

Four minutes before, as *Derfflinger* and *Seydlitz* carried on their grim destruction of *Queen Mary*, *Lützow* had also very effectively barraged *Lion*, hitting her three times in thirty seconds at 16:24, covering the ship entirely in smoke. *Lützow* then shifted her fire to *Princess Royal*. That small respite may have saved *Lion*. On *Lützow*, there was 'a moment of complete silence, then the calm voice of the gunnery observer announced, '*Queen Mary* blowing up', at once followed by the order, 'Shift target to the right', given by the gunnery officer in the same matter-of-fact tone as at normal gunnery practice'.[104] Hase also turned *Derfflinger*'s guns (as did *Seydlitz*'s gunnery officer) onto *Princess Royal*, which had – in the same momentous episode of gunnery – just been hit by *Lützow*. After sixty-five seconds the first salvo struck home. By any standards, it was remarkable shooting. *Barham* was then hit by *Von der Tann*, but this salvo put her starboard waist turret out of action. The guns had overheated and would not slide back into firing position. The heat was terrific: as the barrels got hotter and hotter, the grey paint darkened and turned brown.[105]

At this point Hipper's position was mixed. He knew that the High Seas Fleet was close at hand, to the south. He faced Beatty's four remaining ships and Evan-Thomas's powerful 5th Battle Squadron was still some way off. Things so far had not gone well for the British.

> It is unpalatable – extremely unpalatable – but nevertheless an indisputable fact that, in this first phase of the battle, a British squadron, greatly superior in numbers and gun-power, not only failed to defeat a weaker enemy who made no effort to avoid action, but in the open space of fifty minutes, suffered what can only be described as partial defeat.[106]

The reasons were a failure to concentrate the available forces, poor gunnery, lamentable signalling, and a failure, too, to use the advantages of speed and range. But, in defence, the light was strongly in the German favour. Many years after the Harper record, Ernle Chatfield countered the inferred superiority of German gunnery by saying that the 'partial defeat' here was due more to the inferiority of British projectiles than a poor performance in the battle-cruisers' gunnery. This was a sideways swipe at Jellicoe – once briefly DNO – but it also omitted his own consternation at the time that Beatty had not used the advantages in range that he evidently had.

The Problem with British Shells

Much of the 'failure' at Jutland can be found in the poor quality of British ordnance, the shells used. Certain types of shell tended to explode outside the armour shield rather than penetrate and burst within the target ship. Most British testing was done at long range with shells 'plunging', hitting deck armour rather than the belt armour of a ship's hull. The effects of hitting belt armour at an acute angle was not highlighted. It is also worth making a cautionary note: blaming ordnance took much of the focus away from gunnery and training, so unbalancing any debate there was.

The problem of British cordite, usually packed in four 'quarter-charge' silk bags as the propellant for armour piercing (AP) charges – already dangerously unstable – was compounded by the lyddite used in the AP rounds as a 'burster'. On surface impact these tended to detonate prematurely, rather than within an enemy ship and at angles greater than 20 degrees to the horizontal the result was even worse. Even range performance could significantly differ depending on the particular production batch.

On the back of disturbingly unsuccessful gunnery trials using HMS *Edinburgh* as target, Jellicoe requested the Ordnance Board in October 1910, to 'produce designs of AP shells for guns 12 inches and above which at oblique angle would perforate thick armour plate in a fit state for bursting'.[107] His lobbying for realistic trials was also unsuccessful. Jellicoe was not able to finish the job. He was transferred back to sea duties. Two months later, in December 1910 Jellicoe was posted to the Atlantic Fleet on *Prince of Wales*. His successor as DNO, Admiral Sir Charles Briggs (Fisher dubbed him 'the old sheep farmer') did not pursue the issue with any great sense of urgency.[108] Meanwhile, reports from French gunnery trials were showing that their nickel-chrome steel AP shell was successfully breaking through the armour layer and bursting inside.

The debate on shell quality that Jellicoe had supported was stifled by politicians like Churchill who spoke in Parliament, saying, 'Although the German shell is a most formidable instrument of destruction, the bursting, smashing power of the British projectile is decidedly greater'.[109] Even in July 1914, a mere few weeks before the outbreak of war, Jellicoe had delivered another pessimistic report to Churchill, much to the latter's displeasure.

In the end, argues Iain McCallum, it was the Ordnance Board's decision to stay with lyddite rather than use TNT that meant that a superior shell solution was impossible; furthermore, orders for lyddite high-explosive (HE) and AP had already been placed. With the likely cost of AP being three times that of 'common' (a designation used for shell with a low-explosive mixture), the board was even more inclined to try to improve the existing shell rather than design a completely new one.

Before Jutland, there were several incidents which should have persuaded the British to revisit the issue: (a) In the Falklands the Germans ran out of ammunition. It still took three hours to sink *Scharnhorst* while *Gneisenau* did not sink as a result of gunfire, even though she had received more than fifty hits. She sank because she was scuttled by her crew. (b) At the Dogger Bank *Blücher*, hit with sixty heavy shells, did not sink till torpedoed. Even the damage from *Seydlitz*'s turret hit explosion was limited. Later, captured enemy officers openly spoke of the poor performance of British ordnance: 'Twelve-inch shell seemed to go right through the ship without exploding in most cases'.[110]

After Jutland, Beatty is said to have discovered how laughable the Germans supposedly thought British munitions were, through the dinner remarks of a Swedish naval officer in August 1916.[111] Even Dreyer said that, with a better shell, the British could have expected to claim considerably more sinkings between 17:00 and 17:30: 'three or four battle-cruisers and four or five battleships'.[112]

German shells used a more stable substance, trotyl (TNT), which also had a fuse system with better time-delay characteristics, resulting in more internal explosions on British ships. The closer grouping of salvos might also indicate this more stable and consistent characteristic. The British AP shell known as a 'Green' finally replaced the old shell (called a 'Yellow') that had been the cause of so much heated debate. But it was not introduced into the fleets till 1918, too late to make an impact.

Between 15:48 and 16:36 – between fire being opened by the Germans, and fire being checked and action temporarily halted – the Germans scored forty-four hits (forty-two on the battle-cruisers and two on *Barham*), while in return they received only seventeen hits (eleven from the battle-cruisers and six from the 5th Battle Squadron).[113]

German and British Hits in the Run to the South

British (hits sustained)		German (hits sustained)	
Lion	9	Lützow	4
Princess Royal	6	Derfflinger	0
Queen Mary	7	Seydlitz	5
Tiger	14	Moltke	5
New Zealand	1	Von der Tann	3
Indefatigable	5		
Barham	2		
Valiant	0		
Warspite	0		
Malaya	0		
TOTAL	44		17

Source: Tarrant, *Jutland: The German Perspective.*

The Dewar brothers would, at first, pen a vitriolic account published internally as the *Naval Staff Appreciation*. That account, in its only slightly watered-down version, concluded that 'the damage done to the German battle-cruisers in this phase of the action was considerable';[114] this seems very far-fetched or, more as I feel, an out and out distortion of the opening actions of the battle of Jutland given the facts. Better call a spade a spade: these fifty minutes had, for the British, seen one disaster and one error after another.

Beatty's revenge: the run to the north

At this point of the day, visibility for the main German fleet coming north was good: a cloudless sky, a calm sea and a light breeze[115] and at 16:28 *König*, the leading dreadnought of the High Seas Fleet, sighted vessels in action to the north-northwest. A few minutes later, at 16:35, lookouts on *Southampton*, part of a scouting force running ahead of Beatty, spotted the advancing German battleships.

Along with three other light cruisers, Commodore Goodenough took *Southampton* further south and to 13,000yds, well within range of the enemy's line.[116] Surprisingly, the Germans did not fire, but it was because they assumed that, since Goodenough's forces were steaming so close, he must be one of their own. He stared at the German fleet laid out before him. One of his officers commented at the time: 'Look, sir, this is the day of a light cruiser's lifetime. The whole High Seas Fleet is before you.'[117] While Goodenough knew that he quickly needed to inform Jellicoe, before he did so he consciously did not respond to Beatty's recall so that he could get closer – and thus gain a better idea of the German line's strength.

> We saw ahead of us first smoke, then masts, then ships … sixteen battleships with destroyers around them on each bow. We hung on a few minutes to make sure before confirming the message. Then my commander, efficient and cool, said, 'If you're going to make that signal, you'd better make it now, sir. You may never make another.'[118]

Goodenough signalled back the vital intelligence at 16:38: 'Have sighted enemy battle fleet south-east. Enemy's course north. My position is 56 degrees 34 minutes north 6 degrees 20 minutes east.'

In his book *North Sea Diary*, Stephen King-Hall (then a young lieutenant on *Southampton*) specifically noted the details of what they had sighted and it seems curious that this intelligence was not included in the signal: 'As we got closer, I counted 16 or 17 battleships with the four *König* class in the van and the six older pre-dreadnoughts in the rear.'[119] At the very least this would have given Jellicoe an indication for future reference of the effect that Rear Admiral Mauve's pre-dreadnoughts – the 'five-minute wonders' – would be having on slowing the German line in order to keep the 17-knot ships with them.

For five minutes Beatty held his course and then, once he had confirmed for himself what had been received from Goodenough, signalled his intention to turn his fleet sixteen points to starboard and made a 180-degree turn starting the 'run to the north'. The time was 16:40.

Jellicoe and Beatty were both taken totally by surprise. Neither expected Scheer to be at sea. The arrival of Scheer's dreadnoughts was the last thing either anticipated and it destroyed their confidence in the Admiralty intelligence they had received to that point. 'What am I to think of OD [Operations Division] when I get that telegram and in three hours' time meet the whole of the German High Seas Fleet well out at sea?'[120] Beatty had to get away, but he very much needed his run to the north to be seen by both Scheer and Hipper as a desperate turn-tail escape away from the certain defeat that the arrival of the German battle fleet would bring. It was his big chance to lure his foe back up towards Jellicoe's guns. Beatty had to do now what Hipper had himself just done, so convincing Hipper that this was a real run would no doubt have been a major concern of Beatty's.

Then *Southampton's* luck ran out. As soon as she and her accompanying three ships put the helm over, fire was let loose from the heavy guns of the German dreadnought line. It was going to be rough:

We knew the time of flight was twenty-three seconds, and the sub had a wristwatch with a prominent second hand – we almost agreed to throw it overboard after three-quarters of an hour shelling; at the twenty-third second the sub would make a grimace, and as if in reply a series of splitting reports and lugubrious moans announced that the salvo had arrived. Frequently they were so close that torrents of spray from the splashes splattered down on the boat deck. Each shell left a muddy pool in the water, and appeared to burst on impact.[121]

The crew compared notes and reckoned that in one hour around sixty shells 'fell within 100 yards of the ship',[122] more than one impact every sixty seconds.

At 16:41 the flag signal was hauled down on *Lion*'s halyard and her orders became executive, but by ordering a turn in succession, Beatty gave the German gunners a much-appreciated gift – an unchanging aiming point. They simply had to concentrate their fire on one fixed point on the seas to be certain that a target would move into their guns' fields of fire. The turning point became a hellish picture of towering shell splashes as the concentrated fire lashed the sea. So much so that when it came to *New Zealand*'s turn she did not wait; she turned early, before she had reached the designated point.

For the second time that day, *Barham* could read neither *Lion*'s signal nor that of *Tiger* (whose continued duty it was to pass signals on). At 16:48 a second signal by flags for *Barham* to change course was made but Seymour[123] again did not make it executive for a further six minutes at 16:54.[124] During the delay, the 5th Battle Squadron ships steamed 4,000yds closer to the German guns. It was unfortunate that even now *Lion*'s signal book was not able to provide an explanation of the delay:

> 4.55 – most of the records of the outgoing visual signals were lost and destroyed in the action. The records had been sent down to the port signal stations to be logged but, on account of bursting shells and smoke and fire, they got lost or destroyed. This log was preserved with difficulty, not before a hose had been turned on it.[125]

Even as esteemed a naval historian as Andrew Gordon was surprised.[126]

Given the earlier confusion that he had caused, it is odd that Beatty could even countenance Seymour's continued service on *Lion*. Now that we see the 5th Battle Squadron repeating mistakes made earlier in the day, no matter where the source of the error lay, it is little short of incredible. Maybe Evan-Thomas was also somewhat to blame. He continued southward, passing Beatty coming north, not questioning anything. It was almost as if he were either in complete denial of Beatty's command, or insisted on receiving specific orders. Nevertheless, this time he could see what was happening. While the first signals muddle seems more explainable, this time, Evan-Thomas's continued steaming does not speak so well for the rear admiral.

With *Lion* steaming north at 25 knots, the battle-cruisers and the 5th Battle Squadron passed each other in opposite directions at 16:50, *Barham* still heading south at 24 knots; the effective speed of separation was nearly 50 knots. What is more, Beatty's earlier signals also ordered him to repeat the same manoeuvre of turning in succession on the same point. There was real confusion on the British line. As the executive officer on *Warspite* commented:

> I suddenly saw our battle-cruisers coming closer by about half a mile away, going in the opposite direction and I realised that they had turned back. I noticed that *Queen Mary* and *Indefatigable* were …[missing] but never realised that they had been sunk ... X turret of *Lion* was askew and trained towards us (that is, away from the enemy), the guns at full elevation, several hits showing on her port side ... Then we turned ... Very soon after the turn, I saw on the starboard quarter the whole of the High Seas Fleet – masts, funnels and an endless ripple of orange flashes all down the line ... I felt one or two very heavy shakes but it never occurred to me that we were being hit ... I distinctly saw two of our salvos hit the leading German battleship ... I know we hit her hard.[127]

Finally, at 16:55 Evan-Thomas hoisted the signal flags 'T' and 'A' (that warned of rapid turns in succession or changes of speed).

For Hipper, however, the sands were shifting. Of his five ships, only four were now in fighting order. *Von der Tann*'s only functioning waist turret was thus useless, since it was on her disengaged starboard side, but Kapitän Zenker bravely decided to keep her in the line: 'In spite of this failure, I decided to keep with my division to prevent the enemy from noticing anything and re-distributing fire so that the other ships would not come in for worse punishment.'[128]

The weather also started to deteriorate, adding another looming issue to Hipper's balance of power. According to Waldeyer-Hartz, Hipper was becoming increasingly unsure of the conditions once the run to the north had started. He felt that there could be hidden surprises in the mists that would now work in favour of the British: 'Mark my words, Harder, there's something nasty brewing. It would be better not to get ourselves in too deep.'[129] Scheer himself now also felt a victim to the increasingly difficult weather conditions:

> Meanwhile, the previously clear weather had become less clear; the wind had changed from north-west to south-west. Powder fumes and smoke from the funnels hung over the sea and cut off all view from north and east. Only now and then could we see our own reconnaissance forces ... The cessation of

firing at the head of the line could only be ascribed to the increasing difficulty of observation with the sun so low on the horizon, until it finally became impossible.[130]

Even after Goodenough delayed the implementation of the signal to turn back north because of wanting to confirm more details about the composition of Scheer's force, he also hoped to deliver a torpedo attack 'on the long crescent-shaped line of heavy ships that was stretched round on our port bow'.[131] After signalling back more intelligence at 16:45, Goodenough turned his ships at the same time as signalling Jellicoe. All throughout, his small light cruiser squadron was being massively straddled by German fire that was only around 14,000yds (12,800m) off to his port.[132]

> Urgent. Priority. Course of Enemy's battle fleet, north, single line ahead. Composition of van *Kaiser* class. Bearing of centre, east. Destroyers on both wings and ahead. Enemy's battle-cruisers joining battle fleet from northward. My position lat. 56 degrees 29 minutes north, long. 6 degrees 14 minutes east.

Three minutes after receiving Goodenough's vital information Jellicoe signalled the Admiralty at 16:51 with the warning: 'Fleet action is imminent'.

All the fire from the German battle fleet was now focused in a deadly hot stream of steel against *Southampton* and the 5th Battle Squadron, but she somehow managed to escape.[133] One officer commented on their luck: 'I can truthfully say that I thought each moment would be our last ... How we escaped amazes everyone from the commodore downwards.'[134]

The helmsman 'chased the splash' to avoid getting hit, a practice that involved guessing the enemy's range corrections and steering a course to the last shell splash on the basis that the next fire would be corrected from that spot. *Southampton's* gunnery officer, Lieutenant (later Admiral Sir) Harold Burrough, described the sensation of being the sole target of Scheer's massed guns: 'half drowned by spray from shots falling in the water alongside the ship. The spray rises about eighty or one hundred feet and then we steam through the column of falling water. We seemed to have a charmed life.'[135]

The 2nd Light Cruiser Squadron now brought up the rear on the port quarter as Beatty's Battle Cruiser Fleet pulled out ahead, steaming north-northwest at 25 knots, not slowing for any reason. After 16:46 Beatty's ships also came into range of Scheer's guns on *König*, *Großer Kurfürst* and *Markgraf*, all successfully straddling *Tiger* and *Princess Royal*. *Lion* raced north as fast as she could, parallel to *Lützow*, and continued to receive more hits.

The other British ships also began to take punishment. Between 16:58 and 17:02 *Barham* was hit four times, all by *Derfflinger*. Until now she had been lucky, the only hit registering at long distance at 16:23 on the run south from *Von der Tann*. At 16:58 she was hit first on the no. 2 starboard 6in gun, then again three minutes later on the superstructure; the third was at 17:08 on the aft side, and the fourth at 17:10 was almost a repeat of the 16:58 hit, landing within 20ft (6m).

> I saw all four rounds of the salvo which hit *Barham* in mid-air as they came. One hit penetrated the deck six feet from where I stood. It went on to explode below without doing too much harm. Another hit below the water line and blew a hole in the opposite side of the ship, causing jagged edges which may have slowed us up. It wiped out a torpedo detachment.[136]

Warspite also took three hits (probably also from *Derfflinger*) at around 16:58. The turret officer of *Malaya* witnessed the scene:

> When we turned I saw our battle-cruisers proceeding north at full speed, already 7,000 or 8,000 yards ahead of us. I then realised that just the four of us of the battle squadron would have to entertain the High Seas Fleet – four against perhaps twenty.[137]

At this point, the light was still definitely to the Germans' advantage (as opposed to what Hipper immediately feared). A bridge officer from *Southampton* described it: 'our ships were silhouetted against a bright western sky, but the sun being hidden, there was no glare, whereas to the eastward there was still a dark cloudy background, against which the German ships' outlines were not clearly visible.'[138] From *Valiant* the impression was the same: 'We had great difficulty seeing them but they could easily see us against the setting sun. It was not unadulterated bliss seeing the flash of their guns and wondering whether the shell would touch you or not.'[139]

In Beatty's line, *Lion* and *Tiger* were hit by *Seydlitz* and *Lützow* simultaneously, a minute before 17:00. *Seydlitz* had expended a large amount of ammunition – around three hundred 11in shells (from 15:48 to 17:10) – and she continued to throw more at *Tiger*. One shell caused a cordite fire in the aft 4in battery, while two other shells landed in and near the sick bay. Even if *Seydlitz* was low in the stern and the ship appeared to leave the line, Beatty turned *Lion* away in an attempt to throw the German gunners off. He was also trying to buy some time for much-needed repairs to *Lion*'s turrets, to get fires under control and the decks cleared of the debris of shrapnel and torn metal, and, most urgently, to treat the wounded. Gradually, *Lion*, at 24 knots, bent her course away from German fire. *Tiger* switched fire to *Derfflinger*.

By this point *Lion* had been hit thirteen times and *Tiger*, third in line, seventeen. The *Princess Royal* had also been hit heavily. Only *New Zealand* seemed to have been unscathed. *Queen Mary* and *Indefatigable* were, of course, gone.

The 5th Battle Squadron divided the tasks between the four ships. *Barham* and *Valiant* targeted the five leading German battle-cruisers ahead of them, *Warspite* and *Malaya* the four *König*-type battleships that were chasing them. At the head of the German dreadnought line, Rear Admiral Paul Behncke led the *König*-class battleships: the name-ship, *Großer Kurfürst*, *Kronprinz* and *Markgraf*.

Malaya, in the rear, was the prime target for these dreadnoughts. She turned 16 points to starboard and followed her sister ships north, at 16:59:

> When it was time for the *Malaya* to turn, the turning point was a very 'hot corner' as the enemy had, of course, concentrated on that point. The shells were pouring in very fast, and it is doubtful whether we, the last ship of the line, could have got through without a very severe hammering if the captain had not used his initiative and turned the ship early.[140]

Initially, *Malaya* was being targeted by two dreadnoughts, *Prinzregent Luitpold* and *Kronprinz*. After a further quarter of an hour, the salvos started to 'arrive thick and fast round us at a rate of six, eight or nine a minute'.[141] From 17:17 *Malaya* was under constant threat for twenty minutes and was hit nine times. *König* at the head of the line was the first successfully to score a hit at 17:17 on *Malaya*'s forward turret.

Almost immediately, after *Barham* turned to follow Beatty, the rest of the German 3rd Squadron turned its guns on *Malaya*. She was hit at the lower edge of the armour belt, below the water line, abreast of B turret. As the loading cages were jammed, the guns were temporarily out of action. The hit also broke the steam pipe feeding the siren and the noise from the steam escaping at high pressure made effective communication with the fore control top almost impossible.

Ten minutes in, *Malaya* was bracketed for another ten, during which six separate hits were registered; all came from the 3rd Squadron. The first of these landed on the aft X turret, putting the range-finders out of action. *Malaya* was firmly in the enemy's sights:

> A German battleship took up position on our right and let us have it broadside on with everything she had. Shells ripped through the armour plating like a knife through cheese. One shell dropped amidships, came down through the deck head and exploded. It ignited our ammunition charges throwing every man off his feet. We lay half stunned ... It was soon roaring like a furnace and we were trapped by watertight doors.[142]

The order was given to depress and fire the 6in guns close by the ship so as to obscure her profile and confuse enemy spotters. She would have surrounded herself with close-in shell hits and spray. But even before this could be done, two more hits landed, putting the whole starboard battery out of action, and killing 102 men and officers. It was a terrible scene: 'Everything was dark chaos. Most of the wounded had been taken away but several of the killed were still there [and] the smell of burnt human flesh remained in the ship for weeks giving everybody a sickly nauseous feeling.'[143]

Minutes later, there were another two shells. This time they hit below the waterline, by the forward boiler room. Fifty feet of compartments were flooded and the *Malaya* listed 4 degrees starboard, reducing the effective elevation against her enemy targets. Finally, ten minutes after the start of this ordeal came a hit on her 6in side armour. The dread feeling of being left at the back was overwhelming: 'During this time we never had less [*sic*] than three ships firing at us and sometimes more.'[144]

For those whose duty lay below decks it must, in many ways, have been much worse, a dark terror mounting in each man as the ship shuddered from hits, never knowing when the bulkheads would come crashing in. It must have felt like slowly being buried alive.

> The salvos fell at very irregular distances from our ships. Nevertheless, we suffered bad hits, two or three heavy shells striking us during this phase. When a heavy shell hit the armour of our ship, the terrific crash of the explosion was followed by a vibration of the whole ship, affecting even our conning tower. The shells which exploded in the interior of the ship caused rather a dull roar, which was transmitted all over the ship by voice pipes and telephones.[145]

From the start of the run to the north, the volume of firepower aimed at *Malaya* was heavy. In the first two minutes (after 17:10), *König* fired seven salvos and *Kaiser*, while checking fire at 17:35, had by that point expended twenty-seven salvos in twenty-five minutes. *König* actually hung on for another five minutes. *Kronprinz* was one of the first to drop out (at 17:21), claiming the range had become too extended for her guns, only coming back for around six minutes at about half-past five. The last two shells that could have done some serious damage just passed over and landed near the port-side 6in battery at 17:36. Then the pressure eased.

By now, however, the *Queen Elizabeth*s were starting to hit back. From 17:00 *Seydlitz*, *Großer Kurfürst* and *Markgraf* were all struck, *Seydlitz* three times by *Valiant*, hitting her a number of times on her forecastle. With *Barham*, *Valiant* had mauled *Großer Kurfürst* (17:09) and *Markgraf* (17:10). But, as fire from the German battle-cruisers lessened against Beatty's line at around 17:10, the guns were retrained. *Barham* and *Valiant* took on the German battle-cruisers, while

Malaya and *Warspite* focused on the German dreadnoughts, especially the 5th Division. Effectively, Evan-Thomas's four *Queen Elizabeth*s were outnumbered two to one and holding their own against nine German aggressors.

As Beatty continued to drive his force north as fast as he could, fire on his line started to die out. His turn north-northwest and fast run at 24 or 25 knots seemed to have worked, but had left some of his forces behind struggling to regain position.

Lützow and *Derfflinger* were hit heavily at 17:30, as was *Markgraf* at the end of the line. On *Lützow*, with no WT, searchlight now became the sole means of communication. The only German ships to have escaped damage during this phase were *Moltke* and *Von der Tann*.

Beatty ordered Evan-Thomas to 'prolong the line by taking stations astern'. For the 23½-knot, slower-moving 5th Battle Squadron to catch up was no easy task. Nevertheless, at 17:10 Evan-Thomas ordered 25 knots.[146] *Barham* was around 4,000yds (3,600m) behind *New Zealand*, the last ship in the battle-cruiser fleet line. The 5th Battle Squadron turned 3–4 degrees to the starboard and ran a course of 0°: true north. The squadron had to pass over Beatty's wake onto his engaged side, thus to form a protective screen, falling in behind *New Zealand*, whose 12in guns were now out of range, although there is some disagreement on this.

The courage of Evan-Thomas's act went unrecognised in Beatty's dispatches. Evan-Thomas's version has been discounted by a few commentators, but Gordon strongly believes that Evan-Thomas was on the starboard, engaged side, stating that those who felt otherwise were simply 'wrong'. Andrew Gordon cites Marder's charts. John Campbell, Stephen Roskill and Julian Corbett all put Evan-Thomas on Beatty's disengaged side.[147] However, both Evan-Thomas himself and the German official account support the assertion that Beatty's force was shielded by the 5th Battle Squadron:

> It was not long before they vanished from our view in the mist and smoke …
> After [their] gradual disappearance we were still faced with the four powerful
> ships of the 5th Battle Squadron: *Malaya*, *Valiant*, *Barham* and *Warspite* …
> this part of the action, fought against a numerically inferior but more
> powerfully armed enemy who kept us under fire at ranges at which we were
> helpless, was highly depressing, nerve-wracking and exasperating.*

Such a statement would not make sense had the 5th Battle Squadron fallen in behind the port wing of Beatty's ships. Indeed, even the account by *New*

---

* Evan-Thomas in 1923 in an explanation to the Director of Training and Staff Duties when he said that changes in the course were 'necessary to get *on the enemy side* of *Lion*' (quoted Gordon, p406).

Zealand's gunnery officer supports Evan-Thomas's picture of events, saying that the 5th Battle Squadron 'held on southwards longer than the battle-cruisers, [and] finally turned up on our *starboard* [my italics] quarter, where they now took the brunt of the action, coming under very heavy fire from German battle-cruisers and battle fleet'.[148] In the action, according to Hase, the four battleships of Evan-Thomas' gallant 5th BS was under fire from 'at least nine German ships, five battle-cruisers and from four to five battleships'.[149] This was a far braver action than was reported in Beatty's commentary, in which Evan-Thomas's ships were merely placed 'astern'.[150]

With shell falling all around them, at 17:14 the 5th Battle Squadron turned north-northwest to line up with the heading of Beatty's own Battle Cruiser Fleet. Beatty had lost sight of the German battle-cruisers while the 5th Battle Squadron continued to bear the brunt of the fire. The speed of Beatty's northward haul prompted strong and, maybe, rather unfair comments, such as: 'The battle-cruisers ran out of the action'.[151] But for the men of the 2nd Light Cruiser Squadron, following much further astern to the south, the attack up to 18:00 was pretty terrifying.

> Then followed an hour in which I can truthfully say that I thought each succeeding minute would be our last. For a solid weary hour, we were under persistent 11-inch shell-fire from the rear of the German battle fleet, that is to say from all the German battleships who could not quite get [ie hit] the 5th Battle Squadron and therefore thought they might as well while away the time by knocking us out.[152]

Sub Lieutenant Haworth-Booth, the officer mentioned earlier whose watch timed the shells coming in every twenty-three seconds from sighted muzzle flash to target, summed it up: 'I would say (and this is a carefully reasoned and considered estimate) that 40 large shells fell within 75 yards of us within the hour'.[153]

Hipper started turning northwest at around 17:27 and soon after *Derfflinger* and *Lützow* started receiving hits again. With Beatty now edging to starboard towards him, Hipper feared that his van would be crossed and he had little alternative other than to also swing away to starboard. On *Von der Tann* the last turret was now declared out of action due to a mechanical failure.

The British had been lucky. It was through a combination of their own speed and the bad visibility the Germans now had to contend with, that Beatty was able to come out of the engagement with Hipper without any further loss. The conditions were now turning against the German battle-cruiser commander and becoming too dangerous for his line. He temporarily pulled his ships out of the pursuit.

I had to work against a blinding sunset in the western sky and devastating enemy artillery. The sun stood deep and the horizon was hazy and I had to fire directly into the sun. I saw absolutely nothing of the enemy, who was behind a dense cloud of smoke – the gunnery officers could find no target although we made a superb one ourselves. There was nothing else to do but take the ships out of the battle for a while.[154]

But Beatty's accomplishment was a very significant one. He had managed to obscure the Grand Fleet coming south from behind him on his port beam. The bending of his line starboard in turn threatened Hipper's own so that he was forced to 'follow suit'. Hase was very complimentary:

He [Beatty] accomplished the famous 'crossing the T', compelled us to alter course, and finally brought us into such a position that we were completely enveloped by the English fleet and the English battle-cruisers.[155]

The big prize that Hipper and Scheer had wanted was a stern chase that ended with the annihilation of a smaller force. Now the boot was on the other foot.

But, in summing up, 'If the cruiser action had stood alone', wrote Charles Cruttwell in 1934, 'it would have been beyond dispute one of the severest defeats recorded in the annals of the British navy'.[156] Harper went further than calling the outcome a 'partial defeat'. He pointed the finger at Beatty's failure to concentrate his line and the poor gunnery performance of his ships, saying that this combination led to 'regrettable results' – results which could only be termed 'disastrous'.[157] He might have been correct on the first, but it has become more clear that gunnery was terribly – and sequentially for each side – adversely affected by the haze.

Beatty accomplished what he understood his mission to be – to bring the German battle fleet to Jellicoe – but at a very high cost and having sent virtually no communications back to the C-in-C, who continued to be in the dark until the very last moments.

At around 17:40 *Derfflinger* and the battle-cruisers turned eastwards by 6 points as a heavy attack was launched against them by destroyers and light cruisers. Fifteen minutes later they were heading almost directly eastwards as Beatty succeeded in bending the line. As Hipper pulled off to the east, Beatty temporarily lost contact but when *Lützow* re-sighted Beatty's ships, Jellicoe's battle-cruiser commander was not able to report the sighting back to his commander-in-chief, as his radio had been blown away.

The British spring the trap

At 17:43 firing from the British battle-cruiser line was recommenced. In the next quarter of an hour, a large amount of damage was inflicted on their opponents: seven hits within nine minutes. At 17:46 *Lützow* was hit by *Princess Royal*; *Markgraf* was hit at 17:51, *Seydlitz* twice at 17:53 and again two minutes later at 17:55 by 15in shells. The hits that she received came in around her forecastle and, from the British line, she appeared done for. *Derfflinger* was hit twice at 17:55, also by 15in shells. One hit landed just above her torpedo room and the damage caused heavy flooding.

The range between the parallel battle-cruiser lines was now around seven miles, 14,000yds. Even in the midst of the carnage and death, there were lighter moments. Before the meeting of the battle fleets, the paymaster on *New Zealand* came up on deck to take some fresh air. As he stretched and breathed in, he was suddenly surprised to find himself standing on deck with no trousers – they had been pulled off by the immense effect of the guns being fired. 'He was standing on the fore superstructure when P turret opened fire, and deprived him by its blast of his very necessary garment. Decency demanded an immediate retreat.'[158]

Hipper started to see groups of other ships, destroyers and light cruisers. At 17:45 the Grand Fleet was spotted from *Lion* – she seemed to be almost on a parallel course.

> The four battle-cruisers were being heavily shelled by an invisible foe to their starboard, and I could see the numerous columns of water made by the falling shells. They continued on their easterly course for six or seven minutes, and during this time the *Lion* was heavily hit forward, amidships, and aft: fires seemed to break out on board.[159]

Beatty's line was obscured from Hipper while the latter also could not see the Grand Fleet, which was hidden by Beatty's line. It was a masterly manoeuvre.[160] Hipper was forced to turn his line to starboard or risk having his 'T crossed'.

On the bridge of *Iron Duke*, Jellicoe found himself decidedly uninformed about the events of the past few hours. Apart from commanders such as Goodenough, most did not feel that it was their duty or even their responsibility to relay information to the commander-in-chief. On *Malaya* Captain Algernon Boyle was in a position to see what was happening. He gave his point of view as to why this kind of information was not being sent back to Jellicoe on *Iron Duke*:

> [I doubt] whether the various observations of enemy ships made by ships of our battle fleet ought to have been reported to the Commander-in-Chief. I was on the bridge all night with my admiral and we came to the conclusion

that the situation was well known to the Commander-in-Chief and that the attacks were according to plan. A stream of wireless reports from ships in company with the Commander-in-Chief seemed superfluous and uncalled for. The unnecessary use of wireless was severely discouraged as being likely to disclose our position to the enemy ... This may have been an error in judgement but cannot be termed 'amazing neglect'.[161]

Maybe, then, an 'amazingly' bad error in judgement, especially for a commander! Mistakes happen. That was clear. Even Goodenough had confused the situation by giving a wrong bearing by mistake when he signalled at 17:40 that the enemy battle-cruisers bore southwest of the enemy battle fleet when actually they were northeast.

Jellicoe's biographer Reginald Bacon was also exceptionally critical of Beatty's deficiency in the basics of fleet command, such as the almost total lack of signalled instructions to his force during this phase: 'except for a signal to the battleships at 15:35 to alter course to the east (three minutes after the same signal had been made to the battle-cruisers), not a single signal was made specially to the battleships until after the turn to the north had been carried out by the battle-cruisers; nor was a single signal made especially to the light cruisers between 15:00 and 17:47; their existence was practically ignored.'[162]

Shortly after 18:00 another British torpedo attack drove the German battle-cruisers south. Hase described what confronted him and the German line when the cruisers came back north twelve minutes later: 'a terrific struggle began. Within a short time the din of battle reached a climax. It was perfectly clear to us that we were faced with the whole English fleet. I could see from her gigantic hull that I had engaged a giant battleship.'[163] At this point, nothing much was visible from *Derfflinger* apart from the burning wreck of *Wiesbaden*.

The outcome – bringing the German fleet to the Grand Fleet – was the desired one but the cost had been extremely high. 'The results cannot be other than unpalatable,' wrote Jellicoe. A British squadron, 'greatly superior in numbers and gun power', had succumbed to 'a weaker enemy' to produce what Bacon called 'a partial defeat'.[164] Captain J E T Harper, whose report was the Navy's first official attempt to analyse the battle, came to the following unpalatable – and therefore highly controversial – conclusion:

The disturbing feature of the battle-cruiser action is the fact that five German battle-cruisers engaging six British vessels of this class, supported after the first twenty minutes, although at great range, by the fire of four battleships of the *Queen Elizabeth* class, were yet able to sink the *Queen Mary* and the *Indefatigable*. It is true that the enemy suffered heavily later and that one vessel, the *Lützow*, was undoubtedly destroyed, but even so the result cannot be other than unpalatable. The facts which contributed to the British losses were, first, the indifferent armour protection of battle-cruisers and deck plating, and second the disadvantage under which our vessels laboured as regards to light ... But it is also undoubted that the gunnery of the German battle-cruisers in the early stages was of a very high standard. They appeared to get on to their target and establish hitting within two or three minutes in almost every case, and this at very long ranges of 18,000 yards. Once we commenced hitting, the German gunnery fell off, but – as was shown by the rapidity with which the *Invincible* was sunk at a later stage – their ships were still able to fire with great accuracy even when they had received severe punishment. The fact that the gunnery of the German battle fleet when engaged with our battle fleet did not show the same accuracy must not, I think, be taken as showing that the standard was not so high as with their battle-cruisers, as I am inclined to the opinion that we then had something of an advantage in the way of light, although it was very bad for both sides.[165]

8

The First Destroyer Melee

___

In the *Naval Staff Appreciation*, the Dewar brothers put great emphasis on the massed torpedo attacks launched from the opposing battle lines by both Beatty and Hipper in the middle of the run to the south,[1] saying that the British vice admiral's actions 'exercised considerable influence on the battle.'[2] It was a very fast, violent affair. The waters separating the fleets became a boiling inferno, the sea churned by the speeding destroyers, trailing cockerel plumes of foam, along with the bubbling wakes from the forty-odd torpedoes let loose during this short but extremely aggressive and lightning-fast conflict.[3]

Anticipating the need by around twenty minutes, *Lion* had already sent a WT to *Champion*, the 13th Flotilla leader, at 15:55 to warn her to get ready for an attack: 'Opportunity appears favourable for attacking'. The enemy battle-cruisers were around eight miles off on the port beam, but little more could be made out except for the flash of their guns. A minute later Beatty let his destroyers off their leash: 'Proceed at your utmost speed'. Maybe it was because he saw no obvious reaction that at 16:09 he signalled again: 'Attack the enemy with torpedoes', the message being received by *Champion* through *Princess Royal*, presumably because *Lion*'s WT was out of operation.

But the disposition of Beatty's destroyers made it difficult to field the forces he wanted to. The 13th Flotilla was way off to the starboard, disengaged side of the battle-cruiser line. Six 9th Flotilla destroyers – *Moorsom, Morris, Liberty, Landrail, Lydiard* and *Laurel* (along with one straggler from the 13th, the *Obdurate*) were on Beatty's engaged side. They were receiving 'shorts' but they did at least protect his line from potential German torpedo. A minute later, Beatty ordered them to clear his line of sight which they were obscuring with their smoke. Only *Moorsom* and *Morris* held position.

At around 16:15, just as *Lion* scored a hit on *Lützow*, Captain James Farie, the 13th Flotilla commander, relayed the orders from *Champion* to the group under the command of *Nestor*'s captain, Barry Bingham. Out in front were *Nestor, Nicator, Nomad, Narborough* and *Pelican*. First, Bingham ran southwards to gain a better position, then raced across the gap between the opposing battle lines. But almost immediately *Nestor, Nomad* and *Nicator* were cut off from the rest of the group when one of the 2nd Light Cruiser Squadron, *Nottingham*, cut through the destroyer line, obliging *Petard* to take immediate and violent evasive action, and breaking up the attack. The leading group of five went on; eventually *Narborough* and *Pelican* doubled back to join *Champion*.[4]

Nestor, Nicator and Nomad

At 16:40 the three destroyers of the first group (Bingham on *Nestor*, Jack Mocatta on *Nicator* and Paul Whitfield on *Nomad*)[5] turned and raced back north at a fast 35 knots to head into a kind of no-man's-land towards the German battle-cruiser line. Following them were *Petard*, *Nerissa*, *Termagant*, *Moorsom* and *Morris*.[6] Most of this group chased other German destroyers that had been sighted five minutes after setting off from the British line, about 7,000yds (6,400m) off. *Nestor*, *Nicator* and *Nomad* stuck to their plan to go after the battle-cruisers themselves.

Heavy secondary fire from the German battle-cruisers, as well as from a single cruiser, possibly *Wiesbaden*, zeroed in on the three. At around 16:45 *Nomad* was badly hit.[7] Her boilers were now out of action after the steam pipes were damaged. She hauled out to port and wheeled around the stern of *Princess Royal* and came to a complete stop behind the battle-cruiser, herself heavily under fire. Even though Captain Whitfield's boat was starting to go down by the stern, two torpedoes ran right under her, but the boat's sinking condition did not prevent Whitfield from launching two of his own torpedoes before the list became extreme. Then he weighed down the destroyer's confidential documents in ammunition boxes and threw them overboard. Meanwhile, *Nestor* and *Nicator* continued, wheeling over to the east to line up an attack; the *Nicator* fired one torpedo, at 6,000yds (5,500m), and a second, slightly closer at 5,000yds (4,600m). These ships' captains pressed home their attacks in the face of intense enemy fire.

Together the two destroyers made the high-speed dash and reached to within about 3,500yds of what turned out to be *Lützow*, 'devilishly close' in Hase's words.[8] Each fired two torpedoes, but after all their efforts, neither was lucky enough to score a single hit.[9] They then made a second run, this time getting in as close as 3,500yds (3,200m). Bingham even managed to get off a third torpedo and the two boats turned 180 degrees and headed west back towards the British lines which had, at least for the battle-cruisers, made the 16-point turn and were steaming back north, making Hipper think that he had them on the run.[10]

Twelve British destroyers had gone out to attack the German lines: *Nestor*, *Nicator*, *Petard*, *Nerissa*, *Nomad*, *Turbulent*, *Termagant*, *Obdurate*, *Moorsom*, *Morris*, *Narborough* and *Pelican*. All except *Pelican* attacked and launched torpedoes, *Nomad* from a stationary position after being damaged. Together they had launched twenty-one torpedoes, ten each at the battleship and battle-cruiser lines, hitting *Seydlitz* and knocking out *V.27*.

With their flagship *Lützow* under direct attack, the German torpedo boats reacted fast: 'Seeing the plight of their leader [ie *Lützow*] the German torpedo-boat flotilla commanders decided, on their own initiative, that they must go into the attack to relieve the situation.'[11] Fifteen destroyers under the command of *Regensburg* were sent to meet the British attack, eleven from Commander Herbert Goehle's 9th Flotilla and a further four from the 2nd Flotilla. Eighteen torpedoes were launched at the British line at the extremes of close range: between 1,000 and 1,500m (1,100–1,640yds). While not a single one hit, Scheer credited the attacks with forcing the 5th Battle Squadron to turn away. The battle squadron did, in fact, turn 2 points away and because of this it was not able to keep up with the speeding, northward-bound British battle. Evan-Thomas's turn away was the first of a number of turns away during the day, intended to protect slow manoeuvring battleships from torpedo attack.

The Germans were not so lucky. They lost two of their boats, the 810-ton *V.27* and *V.29*. The former, hit amidships, had received significant damage to her engine room. *V.29* had had her bottom ripped off by one of *Petard*'s torpedoes, launched as the two passed each other at high speed. After *Petard* saw that she had crippled *V.29*, the former circled back to finish her off with 4in gunfire. At this point – it was about 17:00 – *Nestor* was hit twice from a range of around 3,000yds (2,700m), but it is not known whether this was from *Regensburg* or from one of the battle-cruisers in the van. Her boilers badly damaged, *Nestor* still managed to steam a further four miles, but half an hour later stopped not far from *Nomad*.

Mocatta on *Nicator* swung back to try to help Bingham and *Nestor*, but was bravely waved off by Bingham. 'I was obliged to refuse,' he wrote later, 'for I could not see my way to involving a second destroyer in a danger which probably only applied to one, for at the time we were still under fire and able to steam slowly.'[12] After he could not help Bingham, Mocatta acted on Beatty's recall order and headed *Nicator* back to rejoin *Champion*.

On the way back, *Nomad*, which had also stopped between the lines like *Nomad* and *Nicator*, was also spotted by the enemy in whose direct path she now lay helplessly. The German battle fleet came into view, very close – at 3,000yds – smothering the two wounded British destroyers with a rain of heavy-calibre fire. Eventually, Whitfield's luck ran out. His boat *Nomad* had been badly shot up by four battleships as they passed by. Along with another officer and seven ratings, Whitfield was critically wounded. He made the decision to abandon ship: *Nomad*'s signalling gear was smashed and there was no way that he could get any information, however vital, back to the commander-in-chief.

Nestor was in trouble too. She fired off her last torpedo while under heavy shellfire, about 10,000yds (9,100m) off from the approaching battleships. Of Bingham's crew, two officers and four men were killed. Bingham was later awarded the Victoria Cross for his actions. Bingham himself had also tried to help one destroyer from the second wave, *Petard*, but had been waved off in much the same manner as he had done to Mocatta on *Nicator*. The German *S.16* rescued the eighty surviving crew members from *Nomad* – who heroically but unsuccessfully tried to keep her afloat – and seventy-two men from *Nestor*. The gallant ship had also picked up her own, crews from *V.27* and *V.29*.*

Petard and *Obdurate*

Petard[13] and *Obdurate*[14] set out to attack the enemy's battle-cruisers together, but they were joined by *Nerissa*, *Termagant*, *Morris* and *Moorsom*, a mix of 13th and 10th DF boats.† *Nerissa* and *Termagant* decided to go after *Von der Tann*. *Petard* and her group targeted *Seydlitz*. Before they could even get close, they were engaged by an incoming group of German destroyers and a light cruiser.

Petard had aimed one high-speed torpedo at the head of the line, set the running depth for 6ft and fired. It hit the German destroyer amidships and then *Petard*'s guns were also brought to bear as she swooped past her opponent, now stopped dead in the water, 'her upper deck awash and obviously sinking'. While *Obdurate* could not get into a position to fire her torpedoes, *Petard* could. Having loosed off three at the 'second or third' ship in the battle-cruiser line from around 7,000yds (6,400m), the British destroyer turned northwards to rejoin her lines. On the way she stopped where *Laurel* had heaved to beside a large patch of oil. It was where *Queen Mary* had gone down. Passing by, *Petard* was able to spot and then pick up one lucky survivor, the turret officer, Petty Officer Ernest Francis. With Francis safely on board, she made her way up astern of the 5th Battle Squadron to rejoin *Champion*.[15]

Harry Oram, serving as a young sub lieutenant on *Obdurate*, described the scene. It was one of utter, deadly confusion:

> By sheer coincidence the hounds on both sides had been unleashed simultaneously to steam at full speed into a fierce melee between the lines.

---

* The German destroyers *V.26* and *S.35* stopped to take their crews off: four officers and sixty-eight men. It is not quite known how many were killed on *V.29*. The estimates range from forty-three to thirty-three. It is not thought that there were men killed on *V.25*, despite heavy casualties.

† Hodgson in *Moorsom* had joined the destroyer actions, but when part of the group went hunting the battle-cruisers, he was unable to join and, instead, tried to make a run for the van of the High Seas Fleet itself. *Moorsom* was very heavily shelled and water got into one of the oil tanks, abruptly slowing her. Only a quick switch to an undamaged fuel line was able to get her out of harm's way.

The opposing forces were evenly matched and their combat was spectacular, highly exciting and chaotic – thirty ships at 30 knots weaving about in a restricted area striving to find a way through to a torpedo-firing position and hotly engaged in frustrating enemy craft. The approaching German torpedo boats with gushing funnels, high bow waves and sterns tucked down in foaming wakes looked sinister and menacing. I remember feeling that they were a pack of wolves that must, at all costs, be killed.[16]

It must have felt like hand-to-hand fighting, swift, deadly and merciless. 'Events,' Oram continued, 'moved far too quickly for stereotyped gun-control procedure and we let fly at anything hostile that came within our arc of fire.' *Obdurate* herself was damaged, hit twice by 4in fire, but none of her crew was wounded. Eventually she found herself too far off to use her torpedoes on the battle-cruisers and fell back.

The immense gallantry of the 13th and 10th Flotillas did not go unrecognised. While Bingham was responsible for two torpedo hits during the brief hours of the battle-cruiser action and himself received a VC, other destroyer captains received Distinguished Service Orders: Paul Whitfield (*Nomad*), E C O Thompson (*Petard*), John Coombe Hodgson (*Moorsom*), Cuthbert Blake (*Termagant*), Jack Tovey (*Onslow*), Roger Alison (*Moresby*), Jack Mocatta (*Nicator*) and Montague Legge (*Nerissa*).

Seydlitz is torpedoed

Originally, two destroyers, *Moresby* and *Onslow*, had been sent to screen and protect *Engadine*.[17] Once Rutland had completed his reconnaissance flight and had managed to bring his plane safely back down, Lieutenant Commander Tovey on *Onslow* could hold off no longer, now that he saw the battle-cruiser engagement going on. At 16:12 he signalled *Engadine* asking if he and Lieutenant Commander Alison's *Moresby* could be released so that they could join the fray (he rather charmingly asked if *Engadine* could 'dispense with [his] services').[18]

By 16:55 the two destroyers were heading south-southeast at 30 knots. As Beatty had started coming north again following his 16:40 signal, they found themselves about three miles off on his engaged side (most of the other destroyers had re-formed to the disengaged side). From around 18,000yds (16,500m), they saw no cruiser or destroyer screen protecting the enemy battle-cruisers and they decided to make their run. Then four German light cruisers were spotted coming out, getting in between the two British destroyers and their targets. A 'heavy and very accurate fire' was opened on both before they decided to separate to present less of a target.

On *Moresby* Alison headed back around and took station astern of the 1st Battle Cruiser Squadron line, spotted the van of the German battle fleet, decided to head in, and between 17:05 and 17:10, at what he estimated was between a 6,000 and 8,000yds (5,500–7,300m) range, let loose a high-speed torpedo at the third dreadnought in the line. He missed and was severely straddled for his pains.[19] As the torpedo attack was carried out, *Seydlitz* was under 15in fire, most probably from *Valiant*, and hits were being made on the forecastle. Just as he was moving off, Alison saw a commotion; a torpedo fired by someone else (it had been from *Petard*) had hit home somewhere on the line.[20]

Moresby and *Onslow* received a fair amount of fire. *Lützow* fired on both of them at 17:08 with her 5.9in guns and at 17:12 *Von der Tann* added fire from her main 11in armament. The German battle-cruiser fired six rounds in three minutes, but had to cease fire when her guns jammed. The shooting was so good that Alison said that 'had they fired double salvos they would have hit'.[21] He reported that German defensive fire was well organised and that 'enemy ships appeared not to fire after a certain bearing, but the fresh ship starting seemed to straddle with almost the first salvo, though not again'.[22]

Returning to the British line, *Moresby* was mistaken by *Tiger* for an enemy destroyer and fired upon. Diplomatically, no mention of it was made in Alison's report to Captain Farie, though a young sub, de Salis, clearly recalled the event:

We must have been steaming nearly bows on to the *Tiger* who, taking us for a German destroyer attack under the famous smoke screen, opened a brisk fire upon us with her 6-inch guns ... A piece of shell was picked up on the upper deck afterwards – unmistakable service yellow-brown and subsequently produced to taunt the control office of the *Tiger*'s starboard battery.[23]

Onboard *Onslow*, Tovey, who had taken up position behind the 1st Light Cruiser Squadron, saw a three-funnelled enemy cruiser and 'decided to attack her to endeavour to frustrate her firing torpedoes at our battle-cruisers'.[24] Attacking at a range that closed from 4,000 to 2,000yds (3,600 to 1,800m), *Onslow* fired fifty-eight rounds, many of which Tovey saw hit home on the German ship, but as he went in, the battle-cruisers were spotted and Tovey decided to target them instead. He had intended to fire all his remaining torpedoes but just as he gave the order to fire at 8,000yds, his destroyer was heavily hit starboard amidships.

Sub Lieutenant Moore found that only one torpedo had actually left the tubes. When the enemy light cruiser was seen again, apparently stopped, Tovey ordered another torpedo launch. The two men saw the hit below the conning tower. Before turning away, they fired the two remaining torpedoes, but they must have crossed harmlessly through the German lines. The damage sustained meant that the offer of a tow from *Defender* was readily accepted and the *Onslow* made her way back home at 10 knots, arriving in Aberdeen two days later at 13:00 on 2 June.

After she had successfully avoided *Moresby's* torpedo, *Seydlitz* was badly hit below her forward turret by the third of the British torpedoes, launched in the earlier attack by *Petard*.

> Our foretop reported first one, and then more torpedo tracks. We tried to avoid them by sharp turns, but finally one got us a bit forward of the bridge. The blow was much softer than gunnery hits or near misses, no loud report, but only a rattling noise in the rigging ... The torpedo bulkhead held but it was seriously strained, as were parts of the armoured deck.[25]

The outer bottom of the forward barbette was destroyed over a length of 40ft and around 13ft high (12m x 4m).[26] Parties of men worked to repair the damage. It turned out to be in almost the same area where the ship had been damaged by a mine weeks earlier.

Even if her speed was unimpaired, conditions on *Seydlitz* deteriorated quickly. A third of her electrical generating power was lost and stokers, electricians and engineers worked below decks in horrendous conditions, in the dark, to try and restore power. In the dynamo room temperatures reached 72°C and gas-masked crew members fainted from heat exhaustion. The flooding had spread to around 90ft (27m), probably, according to David Brown, because of poor repairs from the previous mine damage. Eventually they succeeded and steering was regained.

> The stokers and coal trimmers deserved the highest praise, for they had to wield their shovels mostly in the dark, often up to their knees in water without knowing where it came from and how much it would rise. Unfortunately, we had very bad coal that formed so much slag that the fires had to be cleaned after half the usual time, and the grates burnt through and fell into the ash pits. The spare ones had to be altered in the thick of battle because even the beams supporting the grates were bent by the heat.*

Seydlitz continued being straddled and hit. In Bruno turret the starboard gun layer was killed and while the battery was back in action after three salvos,

---

* In fact, the quality of coal could make substantial difference to the speed of a ship. Welsh coal was considered some of the best available and was extensively used by the Royal Navy and stocked at the Navy's worldwide bunkering points. If the coal was not pure – Australian coal supposedly contained 15 per cent earth – the boiler tubes would clog up which would require more docking for boiler cleaning.

because visibility was so bad, Commander Richard Förster, *Seydlitz's* gunnery officer, could only occasionally fire back.

Seydlitz's helmsman stood his post for twenty-four long hours. It was his expert handling that would bring the wounded battle-cruiser back to safety. He was to be the only able seaman in the German fleet to later receive the Iron Cross, first class – and his stripes were restored (he had lost them because of being habitually drunk).

Before 17:30 British destroyers had launched between twenty-two and twenty-six torpedoes, but the verdict on torpedoes, at least at this stage of development, seems to have been that they had been over-rated. In Peter Kemp's view, 'They had, it is true, proved deadly against the thin plating of a destroyer but the armour and internal watertight subdivision of a capital ship had defeated their full destructive power. In the *Seydlitz* only one compartment had been flooded as a result of the *Petard's* hit and she was still fully able to continue the fight.'[27] However, Kemp does not mention the distraction that these attacks caused, often making commanders change course or dangerously forcing individual ships out of line. While the destroyer attacks might not have been able to claim what they hoped for – a battle-cruiser or at least a cruiser – the effect of the British torpedo strikes, in much the same way that Scheer himself claimed for the actions on the German side, persuaded Hipper to pull away and helped relieve the gunnery pressure on Beatty at a critical moment.

THE BATTLE FLEET ACTION
Up to 21:00 on 31 May 1916

1. From 17:40 onwards, Beatty bends his battle-cruiser line to starboard. It effectively hides the Grand Fleet's approach from Hipper's view.
2. Anticipating Beatty's arrival with the German main battle fleet in pursuit, Jellicoe's fleet reorganises itself into a single line-of-battle with the deployment to port at 17:40.
3. The British armoured cruiser *Defence* is sunk at 18:20 as she goes to attack the German light cruiser *Wiesbaden*. There is not one survivor from her 903-man crew.
4. By 18:25 *Wiesbaden* herself is under heavy fire and sinking, and when she also finally sinks there is only one survivor, the stoker Hugo Zenne.
5. At 18:31 *Invincible* is hit and blows up. There are only six survivors while the captain and 1,019 crew members go down. British sailors at first cheer as they pass the wreck, mistaking it for an adversary.
6. Scheer turns his fleet around at 18:30, away from the concentrated fire of Jellicoe's battleships which have 'crossed his T'. At 18:55, surprising Jellicoe a second time, Scheer turns back.
7. 19:15–19:26. Fifteen minutes later, torpedo boats are ordered to attack the British line by Commodore Heinrich. It is then followed by Scheer's general order, which includes the battle-cruisers. Under cover of the attack, Scheer escapes with his battle fleet.
8. At 19:21 Jellicoe turns away from the thirty-one torpedoes fired at the British line. Not one hits a British target.
9. Jellicoe rearranges the fleet into night-cruising formation, wishing to avoid any night action. He wants to be prepared to fight as daylight returns.
10. Brief contact is made by the two light cruisers *Caroline* and *Royalist* but they are left unsupported by Rear Admiral Sir Martyn Jerram's 2nd Battle Squadron. He thinks the enemy line is Beatty's battle-cruisers.

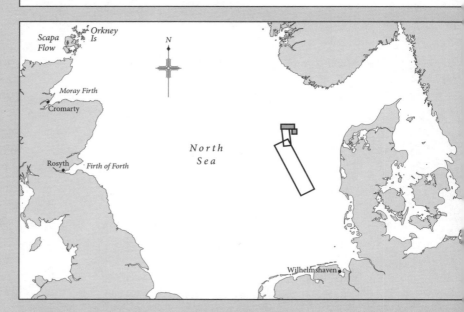

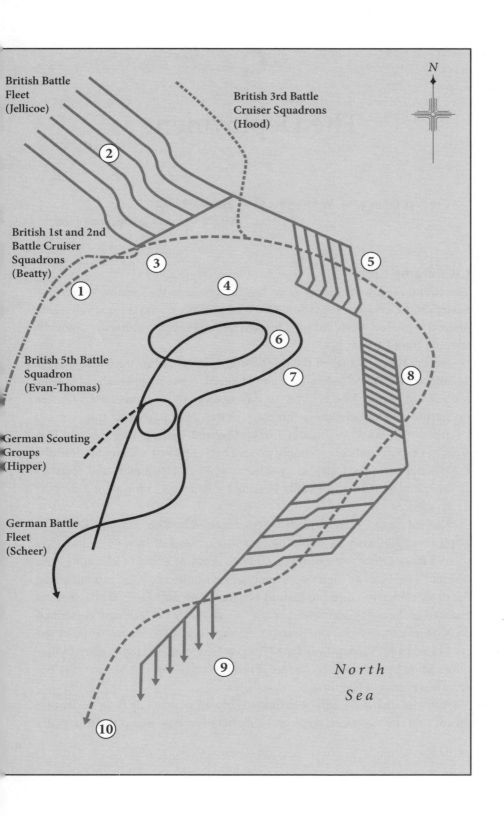

British Battle
Fleet
(Jellicoe)

British 3rd Battle
Cruiser Squadrons
(Hood)

N

British 1st and 2nd
Battle Cruiser
Squadrons
(Beatty)

British 5th Battle
Squadron
(Evan-Thomas)

German Scouting
Groups
(Hipper)

German Battle
Fleet
(Scheer)

North

Sea

9

The Deployment

The peak moment of the influence of sea power on history.
Marder, *From the Dreadnought to Scapa Flow*

Converging fleets

The Grand Fleet was heading from two directions to the meeting point with Beatty's battle-cruisers. From Scapa Flow came Jellicoe, with the main elements of the Grand Fleet, while Admiral Martyn Jerram brought further dreadnought strength from Cromarty.

Horace Hood had taken the three battle-cruisers of the 3rd Battle Cruiser Squadron – *Inflexible*, *Indomitable* and *Invincible* – twenty miles ahead of Jellicoe to act as a scout. Hood's force was accompanied by the light cruisers *Chester* (to starboard) and *Canterbury* (on port), as well as by four boats from the 4th Destroyer Flotilla: *Shark*, *Acasta*, *Christopher* and *Ophelia*. The moment that *Galatea*'s signals indicating enemy presence were picked up, preparations for the meeting were put into gear in earnest. At 15:13 Hood increased speed to 22 knots and at 16:00 to 24 knots, bearing south to meet up with and support Beatty's forces.

The 3rd Light Cruiser Squadron (commanded by Rear Admiral Trevylyan Napier on *Falmouth*) was scouting four miles ahead of *Lion* when lookouts spotted *Black Prince* to the northwest, herself scouting ahead of Jellicoe's forces. It would have been an ideal opportunity to get significant information back to the commander-in-chief, but instead Napier simply signalled: 'Battle-cruisers engaged to the south-south-west of me'.[1] *Black Prince* misleadingly elaborated on Napier's earlier signal and passed a message to Jellicoe: 'enemy battle-cruisers bearing south five miles'. Thankfully, Jellicoe had already received other information by the time that he read this, so he knew that this was actually Beatty's force and not Hipper's.

A cumulative error inherent in navigational plotting by dead reckoning meant that the two fleets were probably between eleven and thirteen miles apart.* The error was inevitable. Dead reckoning meant calculating one's current position by relying on a fixed, known point, then calculating one's relative position, given speed, elapsed time, course and currents. Beatty was still engaged. Navigational precision always suffers in action.

Finally, at 17:56 Beatty sighted the Grand Fleet itself. For over an hour, since 16:45, he had been out of contact with Jellicoe and even during the lulls between the shooting he had not thought it worth his while to pass on information needed by his commander-in-chief so that he could plan the most appropriate deployment of the fleet from the bridge of *Iron Duke*. Beatty had failed in the important mission of acting as the eyes of the Grand Fleet. At that moment, he had actually lost contact with the main German battle fleet.

Chester's lucky escape

Ahead of his three battle-cruisers, Hood's scouts pushed on to report back to their admiral, who was now rushing to back up Beatty. *Chester* was out on the starboard beam, *Canterbury* on the port, with four destroyers directly ahead of the fleet as a protective submarine screen. By 17:00 light was failing fast and the additional onset of mist made visibility increasingly difficult. In some directions, it stretched eight miles, in others only two. It was typical North Sea weather where, on average, visibility can be anywhere between three to eight miles.[2]

By 17:30 the rapid-fire sound of the guns from Hipper and Beatty's fierce engagement carried north. Aboard *Chester* all ears were cocked, eyes strained. Robert Lawson, her captain, signalled *Invincible* while he turned for a closer investigation. Six minutes later the silent silhouettes of enemy ships were spotted in the murk around 11,000yds (10,000m) off. One was a three-funnelled cruiser, the other two ships, destroyers.

Chester did not know it but the cruiser was *Frankfurt*, of the 1st Scouting Group. She was steaming five miles northwest of Hipper's battle-cruisers' disengaged side, grouped together with *Wiesbaden*, *Pillau* and *Elbing*. Working with Hipper's main force, they had been chasing Evan-Thomas's 5th Battle Squadron and Beatty's battle-cruiser force. *Chester* signalled a challenge. She thought that she had received the correct response, so, innocently unsuspecting, she had approached, cutting the intervening distance down by 5,000yds (4,600m). She was a newly commissioned ship, not completely battle-ready, so was entirely

---

* Harper, *The Truth*, pp76–7. Following *Southampton's* message giving the first indications of the position of the German High Seas Fleet, there follows a flow of contradictory information, making Jellicoe's deployment decision extremely complex. *Iron Duke's* position was put at four miles out: *Lion's* (since she had been heavily engaged in battle) nine miles, the combined total thirteen miles. Similarly, the dead reckoning (DR) between the 3rd BCS and the BCF was eighteen miles out, according to Gibson and Harper, p163.

unprepared for the withering fire let loose by what turned out to be Germans. Within three minutes most of her ten guns had been hit. Three were out of action; the forward one was the first to go.

> Many of the men in her guns' crews had their legs shorn off at the ankles as they stood behind the un-turreted guns. An officer reported that in the central ammunition passage these wounded men – cheerful Cockneys, for she had a Chatham crew – sat smoking cigarettes, the bloody stumps of their tourniqueted legs out in front. An hour or so later most of them would be dead from shock.[3]

On duty by the 5.5in gun was a boy, first class. The sixteen-year-old Jack Cornwell held great responsibility.[4] Firing orders from the bridge came to him through his headphones and with that information he set the gun's sights. In these opening moments, despite what turned out to be mortal wounds, the young boy – in our age, not yet old enough to smoke or drink – refused to abandon his post. Later, in his dispatches, Beatty wrote about his exemplary courage: 'Boy (1st Class) John Travers Cornwell of the *Chester* was mortally wounded early in the action. He nevertheless remained standing alone at a most exposed post, quietly awaiting orders till the end of the action, with the gun's crew dead and wounded all round him.'

His mother had him buried with a simple headstone, a wooden peg with the number 323 in Square 126 in Manor Park cemetery. The *Daily Sketch* picked up the story and launched the campaign that would bring Cornwell the recognition his courage warranted: 'England will be shocked today to learn … that the boy-hero of the naval victory has been buried in a common grave.'[5] In July Boy Cornwell was reburied in a public ceremony in Manor Park. His coffin was carried by six other *Chester* boy seamen his age, and the grave heaped high with wreaths and flowers from both the community and the ship's company. The Admiralty was represented by the financial secretary, Dr E J Macnamara. It was a ceremony designed to capture the nation's imagination and win back some honour for the Navy after the battle.[6] Today, YouTube footage gives a sense of national loss as the coffin made its way to Cornwell's final resting place, the pall-bearers shouldering his small coffin through huge, thronging and visibly upset crowds of mourners. Cornwell was posthumously awarded the Victoria Cross, Britain's highest military award for valour.

Severely wounded, *Chester* turned and made a dash back up northeast to rejoin Hood's main force. It had been a very uncomfortable nineteen minutes, the British ship defending herself against four attackers. But somehow she had survived.[7] *Chester* eventually got back to the port of Immingham on the Humber. She had been hit seventeen times, and came out of the action with two officers and thirty-three men dead. A further three officers and thirty-nine other men were wounded. Jutland had been, in the most literal sense, a mortal baptism of fire.

After receiving the earlier reports, Horace Hood had, meanwhile, largely closed the gap and had turned to starboard at 17:40.

The loss of *Defence*

Back with the main body of Jellicoe's battle fleet, the horde of British ships of all types were going through the deployment to port. It was a manoeuvre that risked disaster at any moment, either from collision or from being hit by the earlier than anticipated arrival of the Germans.

Without warning, Rear Admiral Sir Robert Arbuthnot's 1st Cruiser Squadron – *Defence*, *Warrior*, *Black Prince* and *Duke of Edinburgh* – steamed ahead of *Iron Duke* and raced dangerously across Beatty's speeding path. During the same moments, Beatty was heading up the battleship line to get across east with his own four remaining battle-cruisers (*Lion*, *Tiger*, *Princess Royal* and *New Zealand*) to join forces with Hood's 3rd Battle Cruiser Squadron (*Invincible*, *Inflexible* and *Indomitable*). Hood had been ordered earlier at 16:05 to join up with Beatty. In the event, neither *Duke of Edinburgh* nor *Black Prince* could make it through the line fast enough and would spend the rest of the day trying to join up with friendly ships.

The track that Arbuthnot chose to steer was so tight that *Lion* actually came close to ramming the second ship in the line, *Warrior*. She only avoided a collision by abruptly heading off to starboard. Arbuthnot, who had promised not to turn in a 'dull' performance on the day, was described by Keith Yates as a 'pugnacious individual who was itching to get into action. He had missed one splendid opportunity to come to grips with the enemy when his ship had been too late to join Sturdee at the Falklands in 1914, and he was determined not to miss another.'[8]

From his vantage point on the flagship *Defence*, Arbuthnot spotted *Frankfurt* and her accompanying ships. He opened fire, but *Defence*'s firing was short. Friedrich Bödicker's forces fell back into the safety of the mists and fog. Arbuthnot also saw *Wiesbaden* (already seriously wounded by *Invincible*'s gunnery and now burning) and was able, as he passed, to land a few more salvos onto the crippled German cruiser, setting her on fire and leaving her listing heavily.

On *Wiesbaden* Kapitän zur See Harder ordered his guns to fire and, with a 5.9in salvo, he hit *Defence*'s turret at around 18:16. Adding to *Wiesbaden*'s own limited but surprisingly effective fire, given her dire circumstances, many ships from Scheer's own line, including *Friedrich der Große* and *Lützow*, opened up on *Defence* with all that they had. At least three large shells seemed to land true.

Nothing was visible from *Derfflinger*, except the fires raging fiercely on *Wiesbaden*, but she added her weight of fire to that of *Lützow*. After two salvos, her shells struck home, although some say that the final salvo was from *Lützow*. At 18:20 it seemed as if one of *Defence*'s magazines exploded. She was done for. An eyewitness described the scene of devastation, the third large British loss of the day: 'She blew sky high, her picket boat performing a giant Catherine wheel right above a gigantic mushroom cloud of flame and smoke'.[9] There was, however, quite some confusion on *Derfflinger* and one of Hase's gunnery officers, Lieutenant Commander Hausser, asked if she was indeed an English ship, as her four-funnelled appearance closely resembled that of SMS *Rostock*. After Hase's assurance that she was indeed British, *Derfflinger*'s secondary armament, which had until that point been concentrating on repelling the destroyer attacks, joined with their added fire. *Derfflinger* turned away. The combined fire of *Derfflinger* and *Lützow* eventually blew the 14,800-ton armoured cruiser out of the water. Hausser's concern was very much the same as *Iron Duke*'s gunnery officer, who not soon after, had the same concerns as to whether *König* (the British flagship's target), was not a friendly.

Not one of the *Defence*'s 903 crew survived. *Defence*'s grim death took place right before the eyes of the Grand Fleet, though not much detail could be seen, the weather had become so poor. On *Iron Duke* it must have been particularly painful for Jellicoe, a close friend of Arbuthnot. In fact, it was almost surreal: 'Twenty-four hours earlier Arbuthnot had been playing tennis at Cromarty with Lady Jellicoe'.[10] An eyewitness on *Warrior* said that *Defence* 'suddenly disappeared completely in an immense column of smoke and flame, hundreds of feet high. It appeared to be an absolutely instantaneous destruction, the ship seeming to be dismembered at once.'[11] Nevertheless, archaeological inspections on the site have shown that what was seen of the explosion on the surface was misleading.[12]

As an opening to the great meeting of fleets it was not an encouraging sight.

The slow death of *Wiesbaden*

As the sounds of *Chester*'s engagement with *Wiesbaden* and the 1st Scouting Group was carried through the mists across the water, Hood's 3rd BCS came to her scout's rescue. At 17:53 *Invincible*'s 12in guns opened fire at 8,000yds (7,300m) and two minutes later *Inflexible* and *Indomitable* joined in at 12,000yds (11,000m).

Wiesbaden, last ship in the line, was hit as she turned to run: one of *Invincible*'s massive shells had burst through the side in the engine room, riddling the steam pipes and turbine casings with shrapnel. Both engines were badly enough damaged that *Wiesbaden* came to a dead stop; the same for *Pillau*, whose speed had already also been reduced to 24 knots when four of her boilers were badly damaged by a shell from *Inflexible*'s 12in guns.

Wiesbaden was now a sitting duck: every ship that passed took a shot. First, the 3rd Light Cruiser Squadron, then *Onslow*, on *Lion*'s starboard bow, pumped another fifty-eight salvos into her before moving on. An astonishing 200 shells would be fired at the fiery wreck of *Wiesbaden* before her end. Why she had not already sunk was anybody's guess, but the British fire was really wasted effort: a massive over-kill and needless ammunition expenditure. She needed no more attention. Even later, when the Grand Fleet passed her by, *Iron Duke* also fired on her.[13] On *Onslow*, Captain Tovey 'decided to attack [*Wiesbaden*] to endeavour to frustrate her firing torpedoes at [Beatty's] battle-cruisers'. He fired one and succeeded – at 3,500yds (3,200m) – in putting it just below the conn. Tovey now turned his attention to the larger prize.

Five miles off was the brunt of the German battle-cruiser fleet, coming up northwards leading Scheer's battleships. Hipper ran into within 8,000yds but then turned away, avoiding both of *Onslow*'s torpedoes. *Lützow*'s secondary armament damaged both *Onslow* and *Acasta*, which both abandoned their attacks. The poor *Wiesbaden*, which had only come into service the previous August, courageously fought on. When she did eventually go down, she took 543 ratings and twenty-seven officers with her. One of those who escaped the wreck was Chief Stoker Hugo Zenne, who was set adrift on a raft and not picked up till thirty-six hours later.[14] Zenne, who had started out with ten other sailors who had also managed to leave the stricken ship, was the sole survivor after all his companions slowly gave in to death's embrace.[15]

The fate of Johann Kinau, better known by the name he used as a writer and poet, Gorch Fock, was very different: his body eventually washed up on the shores of a small Swedish town, Fjällbacka, just north of Gothenburg. It is the same small town where Ingrid Bergman's ashes were also scattered. Today, Fock's body lies interred next to the graves of British sailors on the small island of Stensholmen, but his spirit lives on in the training ship of the Bundesmarine named in his memory.

The decision to deploy to port

Jellicoe was confused by Beatty's appearance on his starboard beam. It was the same for Hood. Between Beatty and Hood the distance was around eighteen miles out.[16] Not only were *Lion*'s calculations wrong, so too were those on *Iron Duke*. On Beatty's part, one would certainly have expected some inaccuracy, as he had been heavily engaged. This was not so much the case for *Iron Duke*.

At this point the latter's dead reckoning after crossing the North Sea, initially zigzagging to avoid the expected submarine trap, was out by around four miles.

Lion's reckoning was around seven miles off: this meant eleven miles total error in position. It was not surprising that either's position was out in the first place. There was little celestial navigation available because of the very poor light conditions. But Beatty's over-sensitivity to any form of criticism obliged him to comment on the issue in Harper's writing:

> Owing presumably to errors in either ciphering or deciphering, or to operators' errors, and also owing to the small unavoidable discrepancies in the dead reckoning of the ships making the reports, and also those receiving the reports, the actual position of the enemy's fleet relative to *Iron Duke*'s position must have been somewhat conjectural.[17]

The lack of accuracy in dead reckoning meant that reported enemy positions sighted from Beatty's ships – and unseen from *Iron Duke* – were not easy to use or depend upon for the deployment decision that was now facing Jellicoe. It was better to be able to see the reporting ship. This gave him more confidence in her reports.

Jellicoe had received some information at 17:40 from *Southampton* stating her position and estimating that the enemy was north-northwest, but then, ten minutes later at 17:50, north. Differences in dead reckoning also put *Southampton* further east of *Iron Duke*. And again, other destroyer reports seemed to be contradictory. As a result, Jellicoe was not sure if the enemy battle fleet was on his starboard beam or, in fact, dead ahead in the Grand Fleet's path.

This was the critical moment of the second phase of the battle. Jellicoe was not in the best of positions to be able to calculate accurately how to deploy to their greatest advantage the huge forces he commanded. In any manoeuvre now, he would want to maximise the number of heavy guns that his twenty-four dreadnoughts could bring to bear on the enemy. Otherwise, he could be caught without effective broadside firepower and himself over-powered. He calculated that it would take him a minimum of around eighteen minutes to deploy the dreadnoughts from cruising formation to battle line if he were to choose an unequal speed manoeuvre. So the manoeuvre's timing was absolutely critical. Here, Jellicoe lacked just about all the essential data.

What about Beatty? His two roles were to act as fast reconnaissance for his commander-in-chief and to attack the enemy's battle-cruiser scouting force. Between 16:38 and 17:00 Jellicoe received a number of reports of Scheer's position: two from Commodore Goodenough, one from *Champion*, one from Beatty and one from the Admiralty. The two from Goodenough (at 16:48 and 17:00) were misleading on three counts. First, and most importantly, they did not give an accurate picture of the actual enemy position, because *Southampton*'s calculation of her own position was between nine and ten miles out. Secondly, the course was reported as 347 degrees, whereas it was actually 325. Lastly, the reports were received in reverse order. The 17:00 report came in before the 16:48 signal. With the different positions given for the *Southampton* it was clear that she must have miscalculated her position.

The signal from Beatty was sent through at 16:45, though *Princess Royal*'s was muddled. It was wrong on the enemy disposition as well as its location ('26–30 battleships, probably hostile, bearing 145 degrees, steering 122 degrees'). It also sounded as if the Germans were at full disposition, in other words with eighteen dreadnoughts and ten pre-dreadnoughts. *Lion*'s own position was erroneously reported as seven miles too far to the east. By contrast, the German 1st Scouting Group requested and received, within twenty-four minutes, its own battle fleet's precise grid location after informing it of the disposition of Beatty's battle-cruisers.

The 16:48 message from *Champion*, leader of the 13th Destroyer Flotilla, strangely gave the enemy course as east-northeast, in other words heading off. The last signal, the one from the Admiralty, was sent at 17:00 and referred to a directional intercept at 16:09 (an hour before). It was discarded by Jellicoe after the fiasco of the false morning signal still putting *Friedrich der Große* in the Jade. It was a pity, because the Admiralty information turned out to have been only four miles out. Between these reports and 17:40 there were no updates.

At around this time the two British fleets, Jellicoe's Grand Fleet and Beatty's Battle Cruiser Fleet, sighted each other.[18] From *Benbow*, leading the 4th Division, Midshipman Roger Dickson (whose brother had been on *Queen Mary*) described the scene:

> [They] suddenly burst through the mist. They were a wonderful sight, these
> great ships, tearing down across us, their huge funnels silhouetted against
> a great bank of red cordite smoke and lit up by sheets of flame as they fired
> salvo after salvo at the enemy whose flashes could be seen in the distance
> between the ships.[19]

Jellicoe was starting to pace. He had signalled *Marlborough* asking, 'What can you see?' (TOO 18:00) and the reply was only *Lion* leading the battle-cruisers. A minute later (TOO 18:01) he signalled Beatty, 'Where is the enemy B.F.?'. Beatty's reply that the enemy battle fleet was 'bearing S.S.W' was received at 18:14 on *Iron Duke*: no other detail.

To the officers on the bridge of the *Iron Duke*, Beatty was now clearly in sight, but 'engaged with an enemy invisible to us'.[20] At exactly the same moment, *Southampton* reported that she had now 'lost sight of the enemy battle-fleet', though a destroyer signalled an early visual contact: 'Whole Hun battle-fleet coming up, steering N by E', which was another superlatively uninformative report. Then five minutes later (TOO 18:06) came Beatty's less than helpful reply: 'Enemy battle-cruisers bearing south-south-west'. Jellicoe signalled again: 'Where is the enemy *battle fleet*?' Finally, at 18:14 Beatty's earlier (18:01 TOO) message was received on *Iron Duke*. Beatty had regained at least some visual contact with the target that the Dewar brothers later described as having been 'delivered' into Jellicoe's 'lap', but it was *Barham* who eventually gave Jellicoe the visual fix that he needed, when she signalled by flags at 18:10 that the 'Enemy's battle fleet S.S.E'.

Bacon traced the battle-cruisers' return to the north from 16:40 up to the point when Beatty led the Germans to Jellicoe's battleships. It is clear that for much of the time from 16:40 to 18:01, Beatty had, in fact, lost touch with the German battle fleet, hence Beatty's wording – 'have sighted' – in his reply to Jellicoe's first request (TOO 18:01), which was only seen after Beatty's other message regarding the German battle-cruisers had been received on *Iron Duke*. It was not until TOO 18:18 (a message not dispatched till 18:27) that *Lion* started to fill in some of the blanks: 'Enemy battle-fleet in sight bearing south, the nearest ship is distant 7 miles'. Jellicoe's battle fleet had already been engaged for a full ten minutes.

It was small wonder that Bacon was contemptuous of the absurdly exaggerated wording, in an article by Alexander Bell Filson Young that was published in the *Daily Express* the following Sunday, 4 June: 'With that risk throughout, he [Admiral Beatty] played throughout this marvellous fighting chase towards and from the south-east of Jutland, when he brought back the whole German High Seas Fleet and laid it, as a cat brings you a mouse, at Jellicoe's feet'. In *The Jutland Scandal*, in words dripping with sarcasm, Bacon wrote: 'This is delightful! The cat ran away from the mouse and lost sight of it in twenty minutes and never saw it again. When asked where the mouse was the cat had to confess it didn't know'.[21]

Leading up to the deployment, this lack of precision was extraordinary. As Jellicoe would later describe his own frustrations to Beatty:

> My great difficulty ... was due to the difference in reckoning between *Lion*, 2nd Lt CS [Light Cruiser Squadron] and *Iron Duke*. This caused me to find the enemy and you in a totally unexpected direction and made deployment very difficult, and as the first thing I saw was firing from right ahead to abaft the beam, it was important to guess the position of the enemy battle fleet. In fact, I did not know it till some time after deployment.[22]

The deployment that Jellicoe had to decide upon could actually have been a number of distinct manoeuvres or one fluid one. He had to take the fleet from its boxed cruising formation, in which each division steamed in parallel to another, to one in which a battle line would allow as many guns as possible to bear on the enemy: a formation pretty well unchanged since Nelson's time. Even without the pressure of an unseen enemy fleet bearing down, it was a complex procedure in good visibility, but what Jellicoe faced that day was a lack of information, low visibility brought about by heavy curtains of mist mixed with cordite and funnel smoke, and a very fast-changing picture as the forces raced to a final point of convergence. He had practised many variants of the manoeuvre – at least ten times in the first six weeks of the war. During his command of the Grand Fleet, his ideas had evolved. It was clear to Jellicoe that the principle upon which he would take the decision was one which would be arrived at, not in the brief intensity of battle, but after deep and reflective consideration.

As commander-in-chief, Jellicoe did not want to remain either in the van or in the rear. He wanted to be in the centre. This was a practical matter and had been concluded as the best policy for a commander's position following the 1909 fleet sea trials under Admiral Lord Charles Beresford's direction. If Jellicoe were to maintain some manner of control over his fleet, issuing signals from the centre was faster than having them passed down an entire line, in either direction. He wanted to make sure that his opponent would not be able easily to run from the field of battle, as indeed had happened in December 1914 after the Scarborough raid and, again, in January 1915 after the Dogger Bank action. On both occasions the Germans had escaped south to Heligoland.* Whether or not they would be seeking an engagement (and this was a point itself on which thinking had evolved), the escape route south had to be blocked.

If Jellicoe assumed that the main German battle fleet would be coming from a south or southeasterly direction, his options, broadly, were these. He could deploy to the east, towards the Skagerrak, to hold the foe off the coast, or he could deploy to the west to close faster. There were variations within this. He could even deploy on the centre, although this manoeuvre had neither been contemplated nor practised. He could also move his columns to a new formation in an equal-speed manoeuvre or he could do so in an unequal-speed one.

In an equal-speed approach, each column of ships would turn 90 degrees in succession in the wake of the division leader, who would – eventually – follow the stern of the last ship of the neighbouring column on the wing on which the deployment would be made. Ships in cruising formation were normally 500yds

---

* Helgoland (Heligoland to the British) was the heavily defended island that protected the strategic entry point into the Jade Estuary; occupied by the British for most of the nineteenth century, they had exchanged it for Zanzibar in 1890. The agreement added a useless colonial acquisition but gave away the controlling point – even if it would have been very difficult to garrison or guard – to the German safe haven at Wilhelmshaven.

(460m) apart (roughly two and a half cables' length), measured stern to stern.*

In an unequal-speed manoeuvre, divisions would change course 90 degrees (or 8 points) at declining speeds as one moved from the wing that would become the van and at ever-increasing distances, so that the end battle line was actually a staggered echelon formation, with each successive line slightly off-centre of the preceding division's line of ships. The time taken for the deployment was significantly faster for an equal-speed method: four minutes against eleven to twenty for an unequal-speed deployment.[23]

As gunnery ranges increased, the speed of deployment into a battle line meant the critical minutes of added broadside could be let loose on an enemy at ranges longer than the ones they could employ to hit back. British assumptions were that the Germans would want to fight a closer-ranged battle than them. Fisher's intentions had always been to push for speed and range under the premise that the need was to 'hit first, hit hard and keep on hitting'. Weather, therefore, had a decidedly important role to play. Not only would low visibility blunt British long-range gunnery superiority, but wind, current, sun intensity and direction would also play their parts too.

The decision to deploy to port would be based on a number of factors. While it meant that action would not be joined so quickly, it put the Grand Fleet in an advantageous gunnery position, with the Germans silhouetted against the western horizon. Jellicoe had asked Dreyer's opinion on this and he was unequivocal: 'The most favourable direction was to the southward, and would draw westward as the sun sank'.[24] With a westerly wind blowing, it would also mean that smoke from their guns would drift to the disengaged side of British ships. Scheer's ships would be silhouetted against the western sun while Jellicoe's would be hidden by the intervening haze and a dark, eastern backdrop. The smoke would drift ahead and to the front of the German guns.

Jellicoe calculated that a deployment to starboard, while possibly bringing him closer to the enemy and therefore allowing him to open fire quicker, would, in all likelihood, have placed his fleet in much higher danger of having its own 'T' crossed.[25] This has often been characterised as a deployment 'away from the enemy'. It is a misleading phrase in the sense that it immediately suggests that Jellicoe lacked the Nelsonian spirit of 'closing with the enemy'.

The port deployment would also put the fleet in a better blocking position

* Because the British ships were turning at 90 degrees, the distance between the columns was always set as a multiple of the number of ships in the column times the interval plus the additional interval needed between divisions, usually an additional cable's length. So if there were four ships in the column, this would mean ten cables plus one additional cable gap between the divisions, ie eleven cables in total. A very helpful paper on the deployment is Stephen McLaughlin's 'Equal Speed Charlie London. Jellicoe's Deployment at Jutland'.

if the Germans were trying to take the eastern route through the Skagerrak as the closest one. At Jutland, Jellicoe had considerably increased the broadside power of the battle line, raising it by around a quarter from just over 200,000lbs (91,000kg) to more than 270,000lbs (120,000kg). More importantly, while increasing the number of columns from five to six, he rebalanced the broadside weight from the starboard to the port. In 1914, the two outer starboard columns had over 51 per cent of the broadside weight – in 1916, the *combined* weight of the three starboard columns was less than 45 per cent.[26]

Comparative Allocation of Broadside Weight at the Deployment: 1914 versus 1916

August 1914

1st Division	2nd Division	3rd Division	4th Division	5th Division
Marlborough 10 x 13.5in	*St Vincent* 8 x 12in	*Iron Duke* 10 x 13.5in	*Orion* 10 x 13.5in	*King George V* 10 x 13.5in
Hercules 10 x 12in	*Superb* 8 x 12in	*Dreadnought* 8 x 12in	*Monarch* 10 x 13.5in	*Ajax* 10 x 13.5in
Colossus 10 x 12in	*Vanguard* 8 x 12in	*Temeraire* 8 x 12in	*Conqueror* 10 x 13.5in	*Audacious* 10 x 13.5in
Neptune 10 x 12in	*Collingwood* 8 x 12in	*Bellerophon* 8 x 12in	*Thunderer* 10 x 13.5in	*Centurion* 10 x 13.5in
39,500lbs	27,200lbs	34,400lbs	50,000lbs	56,000lbs

May 1916

1st Division	2nd Division	3rd Division	4th Division	5th Division	6th Division
King George V 10 x 13.5in	*Orion* 10 x 13.5in	*Iron Duke* 10 x 13.5in	*Benbow* 10 x 13.5in	*Colossus* 10 x 12in	*Marlborough* 10 x 13.5in
Ajax 10 x 13.5in	*Monarch* 10 x 13.5in	*Emperor of India** 10 x 13.5in (*Royal Oak*)	*Bellerophon* 8 x 12in	*Collingwood* 8 x 12in	*Revenge* 8 x 15in
Centurion 10 x 13.5in	*Conqueror* 10 x 13.5in	*Canada* 10 x 14in	*Temeraire* 8 x 12in	*Neptune* 10 x 12in	*Hercules* 10 x 12in
Erin 10 x 13.5in	*Thunderer* 10 x 13.5in	*Superb* 8 x 12in	*Vanguard* 8 x 12in	*St Vincent* 8 x 12in	*Agincourt* 14 x 12in
56,000lbs	50,000lbs	50,660lbs	34,400lbs	30,600lbs	49,760lbs

* The difference on the day was that *Royal Oak* (8 x 15in) replaced *Emperor of India*, as the latter was in dry dock in Invergordon, while *Superb* and *Canada* exchanged places.

Source: McLaughlin, 'Equal Speed Charlie London', the organisation of the cruising formation as outlined in the May 1916 GFBOs.

Watched closely by his staff, Jellicoe mulled over the decision but quickly ordered Dreyer to 'commence the deployment'. Two short blasts signalled the turn to port. Jellicoe's signal to the fleet was originally given as 'Hoist Equal Speed Pendant south-east'. The fleet's signals officer, A R W Woods, questioned the order and asked, 'Would you make it a point to port, sir, so they will know that it is on the port wing column?' Jellicoe agreed: 'Very well, hoist equal-speed pendant south-east-by-south'. The signal, which became famous, is now better known now as 'Equal Speed Charlie London'.*

Most commentators (not, obviously, Beatty or Churchill) thought the deployment a stroke of genius. Julian Corbett called it 'the supreme moment in naval war',[27] Arthur Marder 'the peak moment of the influence of sea power on history'.[28] Andrew Gordon uses few superlatives, saying that the decision was as good as could have been expected, given the lack of time and information.[29] For me, while it may be personally appealing to hear this, both Marder's and Corbett's comments seem too flamboyant. It was a carefully thought-out and calculated decision, but to describe this as a 'supreme moment' smacks of the kind of black-and-white position one would not expect from a non-partisan account, although one could conclude that within the space of a quarter of an hour, the two British admirals Jellicoe and Beatty had both displayed a certain brilliance: Jellicoe in his deployment and Beatty in bending the van and hiding the Grand Fleet's approach from Hipper.

The alternatives were scarce. Churchill, under the influence of his naval secretary, Kenneth Dewar, wrote that a deployment on the centre would have been the best manoeuvre. It also could have been an extremely dangerous one (Dewar eventually dropped his support of the idea) as it also would have put the commander-in-chief at the van of the battleship line, not a good position for equidistant flag signals to the line. Whichever way one looks at it, it was an extraordinarily significant decision, given the minimum amount of information Jellicoe had at the critical moment. His own comment summed it up nicely: 'I wish someone would tell me who is firing and what they are firing at'.[30]

The scene at the deployment was remarkable, one ship passing over another's track as 144 captains steered their ships through the complex manoeuvre

---

* The meaning of the Equal Speed Pendant is summarised as follows: 'When altering course by Equal Speed Pendant to form single-line ahead, the column which becomes the leading column alters course in succession to the point indicated, the remaining columns alter course "Leading Ships together. The rest in succession", so as to form Astern on the Leading Column'. The letter(s) below the pennant were selected from the compass table, in which one letter represented the major points in the compass, and two letters represented the minor points in the compass. Thus: A was north, AA was north ¼ east, AB was north ½ east, AC was north ¾ east, AD was north by east, AE was north by east ¼ east, etc. Jellicoe's final signal read 'Equal Speed Charlie London'.

with a minimum of sea room between them.[31] The water was a churning mass of bubbling brown, criss-crossed with fantails and propeller wash.

> The sea was white with fountains kicked up by German shells. There didn't seem room for a ship to escape but lots of us were there and came out smiling though unfortunately we got a big splinter which damaged one of our big forced-draught fans putting one boiler room out of action and forcing us to reduce our speed for some time to 18 knots, so we had to trot along with the battleships.[32]

It did not all go quite to plan. On *St Vincent*, Major Claude Wallace, permitted to sail with the ship at the last moment, reported that she slowed to 9 knots.[33] Some ships even stopped dead in the water because the lanes just became so crowded. As the 2nd Light Cruiser Squadron joined at the rear, *Southampton* had to slow so much that in the end she turned 32 points and even then nearly collided with one of the *Queen Elizabeth*-class battleships (probably *Malaya* or *Valiant*).[34] *Warspite* turned inside *Valiant* (at around 18:15) and *Malaya*, and was hit by a 12in shell from *Kaiserin*.

Being small was not always to one's advantage: *Galatea* actually passed right beside *Agincourt*, just as the latter opened fire, feeling the full impact of the guns' pressure wave. And all this was happening when the exact position of the German fleet was still unknown: 'The signal was actually hauled down at 18:15. We still had not sighted a German ship, but [the Germans] were obviously very close.'[35]

Evan-Thomas assumed that Jellicoe would deploy to starboard and wanted to place his ships at the van. Instead, he decided that it was better to tuck in behind *Agincourt*, the last ship in the line behind *Marlborough*.† But even then there would be some real challenges to face.

> We in the 5th Battle Squadron took station in the rear of the 1st Battle Squadron. In doing so we must have been going too fast, for we ran up on to the last ship of the line and were actually overlapping each other, thus presenting an excellent target to the Huns, who were extremely quick in taking advantage of it … Amidst this perfect deluge of shells, the light cruisers and destroyers were twisting and turning, endeavouring to avoid each other and the big ships who were themselves manoeuvring violently. There were no collisions, and a few ships hit: a wonderful display of seamanship and clear-headedness.[36]

---

† *Agincourt* was also known amongst British sailors as 'A Gin Court' because of its luxurious interior decoration, if one can call it that on a battleship. She had been built for the Turkish navy and although her toilets had to be redone as they were of the squat variety, there were also copious amounts of beautiful Turkish carpeting.

With all ships crossing each other as units attempted to reform into a new battle line, the place aptly became known as 'Windy Corner'. It was hardly the 'parade ground' mentioned by Filson Young in his *Daily Express* criticism:

> ... one can find no technical fault with Admiral Jellicoe's deployment, which was strictly according to the rules. The only problem lay in the fact that at 18:15 in the evening, and in the midst of a battle, there is not always time to observe the rules of the parade ground. The opportunity was there but opportunity did not wait long enough for Admiral Jellicoe.[37]

There was considerable confusion, particularly around the 12th Flotilla, which had been posted as an anti-submarine screen at the rear. The battle-cruisers came so close that *Faulknor* (the flotilla leader) had to stop engines and 'several 12th Flotilla destroyers had to go astern to avoid a collision'.[38] Seven miles away were the German battleships and battle-cruisers. From his post on *Marlborough*, Lieutenant Bowyer-Smith described the difficulty that the low visibility presented: 'We tried to engage them [*Lützow*] but owing to the mist failed to get the guns off ... We engaged her [*König*] immediately, opening fire without being able to get the range due to the mist, and hit her with our fourth and fifth salvos.'[39]

Finally, the line of British ships started to stretch out like a long snake: *King George V, Ajax, Centurion, Erin, Orion, Monarch, Conqueror* and *Thunderer*. In the centre were *Iron Duke, Royal Oak, Superb, Canada, Benbow, Bellerophon, Temeraire* and *Vanguard*.[40] At the rear were *Colossus, Collingwood, Neptune, St Vincent, Marlborough, Revenge, Hercules* and *Agincourt*.

This deployment has been the focus of heated debate ever since. Even if the fleet had practised a deployment of this nature, the conditions would not have been anything close to those faced by Jellicoe's massed formations on the actual day. Somewhere in Jellicoe's mind might also have been a dark memory: his near-drowning in Libyan waters twenty years earlier in 1893 during Admiral Tryon's attempt at a relatively simple two-ship manoeuvre that led to the cata-strophic sinking of the *Victoria*.[41] But I certainly do not think it produced what some have described as a lifelong dread of drowning. What Jellicoe was now attempting was a manoeuvre that required total precision under the very real threat of being caught mid-manoeuvre by the enemy.

Churchill, as mentioned earlier, later criticised the deployment on either flank, suggesting that valuable time and distance were thrown away, and of-fered the alternative of a deployment on the centre, an idea that was not even covered by the GFBOs: as also pointed out, no such manoeuvre had been prac-tised by the Grand Fleet. In the best of conditions – good visibility being key – the equal-speed manoeuvre would have been complex, as many of the ships following their division leaders would have the tendency to cut corners; so speed changes were – as was the case on the day – inevitable.

Gordon makes specific reference to the fact the deployment was probably developed by Sir Arthur Wilson, in the Channel Fleet, and frequently practised as early as 1903.[42] He also noted that it was thought up when gunnery ranges were considerably shorter; by the time of the longer ranges of Jutland, it became necessary for the manoeuvre to be initiated before sighting the enemy, otherwise the manoeuvre would be completely carried out under fire. With an unseen enemy, the time must have seemed like an 'eternity'. Jellicoe managed to maintain an extraordinary composure in what was – and here I do not feel it an exaggeration to describe it like this – one of the most decisive single moments of the war.

The line was nearly caught by enemy fire in mid-manoeuvre, although the initial fire falling among the battleships were more likely 'overs': enemy fire that had passed 'long' over the battle-cruiser line and was falling on the line of battleships behind. Beatty later wanted the reference in the Harper record to 'longs' falling among the battle fleet taken out altogether, and was supposedly heard to remark sarcastically at a 14 July 1920 text review meeting with Harper: 'Well, I suppose there is no harm in the public knowing that someone in the battle fleet got wet, as that is about all they [the battleships] had to do with Jutland'.[43]

It was with comments like these that Beatty – probably unintentionally – stoked the fires of the post-Jutland controversy, playing up the role of the battle-cruisers, and dismissing the contribution and later important role of Jellicoe's battle fleet. Its also raises a question: had it not been for bad visibility on the day, might the Grand Fleet have suffered a different and potentially much nastier fate? Similar to the battle-cruisers? Even the young Prince Albert, the future George VI, who was on *Collingwood* as a gunner, felt the potential for slight: 'Bertie is very proud of being in action but he is sorry that his ship was not hit (although she was straddled by several salvos) as she has nothing to show that she has been in the fight'.[44]

Gordon also explains the danger of deploying on the closest wing to an advancing enemy line. It would present a convex line of targetable ships, while on the wing further away the unravelling line would present itself as a concave one. The former would present itself as a 'T' to be crossed by the enemy, the latter as an arc that would be able to cross the enemy's 'T'. This is what Admiral Sturdee had proposed, saying he would have done it had he been in Jellicoe's shoes. Churchill approved of this approach because it meant closing with the enemy faster, even if he might not have considered that the enemy battle line would have been in the advantageous position.

If Windy Corner was confusing for many British captains, on the bridge of *Friedrich der Große*, the sensation must have been closer to terror. Scheer,

apparently, did not have 'the foggiest idea of what was happening'.[45] His strag-
gling, stretched-out line of dreadnoughts and pre-dreadnoughts had suddenly
and decisively been caught in a trap. They had steamed into the Grand Fleet's
'T' and were now facing an arc of massed guns from twenty-four British dreadnoughts, tightly deployed in a six-mile line, his own line, by some accounts,
stretching out nearly four times the length to seventeen miles.

All the histories talk of *Lion* heading off eastwards after *Defence* blew up.
Beatty was trying to get to the van of the battle fleet once contact with the Grand
Fleet had been made. This would account for the official explanation by Corbett
that *Lion* and the battle-cruisers actually later, inadvertently, blocked the Grand
Fleet's fire, but Major Wallace was absolutely adamant – even if he seems to be the
only one who believed it – that after *Defence* blew up the battle-cruisers made a
16-point turn and went west.[46] Wallace even cited the testimony of an observer,
Reginald Foort, ex-lieutenant of Royal Naval Volunteer Reserve, from *Temeraire*:

> I was the Dumaresq worker in the foretop of the *Temeraire* throughout the
> action, so I had a grand circle view of everything that took place, and I do not
> remember seeing the battle-cruisers between the enemy ships and the Grand
> Fleet at any time during the action. They were certainly not there when the
> *Defence* blew up practically on our starboard beam, nor were they there while
> we were firing at a three-funnelled enemy ship of the *Wiesbaden* type, nor
> when we fired salvos of 12-inch into the enemy destroyer flotilla.[47]

The fact is that during an action like this, even people from the same ship
at different vantage points often disagreed with one another. During the later
night actions, this would become even more so.

The loss of *Warrior* and *Warspite*'s escape

Warspite now faced a new threat. She had been sitting at the rear of Evan-
Thomas's 5th Battle Squadron's line when she suddenly developed severe
steering problems. The rudder began to give trouble after the bearings ran hot,
and after some over-zealous manoeuvring finally jammed, stuck fast in a tight
10-degree starboard turn. She could not be steered in a direction other than
right into the firing zone, passing just astern of the *Valiant*, and heading directly
towards the enemy. She might have taken the heat off the smaller British targets
and allowed them to get away but she herself paid a high price.

> The whole leading enemy division concentrated on us during this circling, and
> we got very heavily hit, and everybody thought that we had gone. The Huns
> thought so too, and ceased firing, luckily for us, but they could no doubt not see
> us for splashes, spray and smoke. There was a heavy pall of smoke everywhere.[48]

Warspite's captain, Edward Phillpotts, did what was best, given the inevitability of where his ship was heading. He kept her in the turn rather than trying to fight it and regain control. It was better to increase speed rather than stall. *Warspite* had been shipping water because of the damage sustained from the roughly twenty-seven shell hits she had taken, thirteen of which had been received during the two turns. Whenever she went faster than 16 knots, she increased the damage to the bearings and the intake of water.

Warrior also came under intense fire. A contemporary account by Engineer Commander Henry Kitching described how unnerving it was below decks:

I heard a tremendous explosion at the after end, a heavy jar went through the whole fabric and most of the lights went out. Immediately afterwards there was a heavy roar of water and steam and my impression was that we had been torpedoed. Several men came running forward from that end, one of them with blood streaming down his face … At first the men didn't know what to do, as the ladders at the after end were inaccessible … but I shouted to them to go up the midship ladder and hustled all towards it in front of me. As soon as it appeared that they had all gone up, I followed them myself, but by that time all the lights had gone out and it was pitch dark. When I got to the top, knowing it was hopeless to go aft, I turned forward and felt my way by the handrails along the platform at the tops of the cylinders towards the door at the fore end, which communicated with the port engine room and with the mess deck. When I got there, however, a stoker told me that we could not get through there, as the mess deck was on fire, and when I tried to do so I was met with a rush of thick smoke and blinding fumes that drove me back. At this moment with this in front and the roar of steam behind me I felt like a trapped rat, for there seemed to be no possibility of lifting the heavy armoured hatches overhead, and a spasm of sheer terror came over me; but just then I realised that the man was calling my attention to a glimmer of light above, and the next minute I found myself climbing out through a torn rent in the deck.[49]

Warrior got away from *Wiesbaden*'s fire and was saved by *Warspite*'s giddy high-speed turn. Both ships now managed to escape the area, but only one survived the battle: *Warspite*, though she was now severely damaged. Her crew managed to get her steering back under control and she retreated northwards and later on at 21:07 was ordered back to port by Evan-Thomas.

Warrior also headed back west but sank at 08:25 the next day, 1 June, just 160 miles from Aberdeen after she had been towed by the *Engadine*. Her crew was taken off after the gallant effort to save her failed; 675 officers and men were transferred safely to the carrier, but when the seriously wounded were being taken over another mortal accident almost happened. A severely wounded man rolled off his stretcher between the two ships and very nearly drowned. Rutland – the pilot who had had to land his shot-up plane after nearly changing the course of the start of the battle with the information that he had carried – saved the drowning man. He jumped in and pulled him out. Rutland was awarded the Albert Medal, 1st Class, for this act of bravery, after he had already won the DSO for the courage of his earlier reconnaissance. So it was all the more surprising that this same man, soon to become famous as 'Rutland of Jutland', was to be later imprisoned, accused of spying for the Japanese.

The battle fleets engage

But, after all the planning, it was the ships of the 6th Division, the rear division of the battle line that were the first to come into action.[50] With *Marlborough* the first of the line to open fire at 18:17, closely followed by *Revenge*, the division still represented around 49,000lbs (22,000kg) of broadside. The leading German ships were around 12,000yds (11,000m) off, but the line, while it had closed up a little, stretched back nearly nine miles.[51] This actually meant that the only ships within range were Rear Admiral Behncke's 5th and 6th Divisions. Fire was returned by Behncke's guns, straddling *Hercules* as she was deploying, as well as bringing *Vanguard* and *Revenge* under fire. Gradually the British line uncoiled.

At 18:23 *Iron Duke,* from where Jellicoe was watching, opened fire. Initially, she targeted the unfortunate *Wiesbaden* at which every passing British ship was hurling steel. She was even mistakenly being hit by her own side.[52] Then, after seven minutes, *Iron Duke* transferred her fire to a more important target, *König*. Within minutes the former scored seven hits, and was said to have started hitting from her third salvo. The fire was so intense that even Behncke in *König's* armoured conning tower was severely wounded.[53] *Iron Duke's* fire was supported by *Benbow, Colossus, Orion, Monarch* and *Thunderer,* but by few others in the vast line of dreadnoughts because visibility was so poor. Torpedoes were also launched from the light cruisers *Falmouth* and *Yarmouth,* as well as from the destroyer *Ophelia*.

Below decks was different. There was little connection with, or comprehension of, what was going on above. Their own guns were only the indication that huge salvos were being hurled at the van of the German line. On *Thunderer,* for example, despite her firing over forty 13.5in shells, this disconnected sense of being in another world seemed to be permeating. 'Of course, like so many of the ship's company, we could see nothing and hear nothing beyond the thump of our own guns.'[54]

The German battle fleet had steamed straight into the 'T' without even realising that Jellicoe's fleet was there: 'The shock to Scheer was stupendous.'[55]

Marder's words are probably an understatement. Otto Groos talked of 'the belching guns of an interminable line of heavy ships, [and] salvo followed salvo almost without intermission, an impression which gained in power from the almost complete inability of the German ships to reply, as not one of the British dreadnoughts could be made out through the smoke and fumes'.[56] The paintings by Claus Bergen[57] give this visual feeling well. You feel yourself in the centre of a firestorm and all you can see on an indiscernible horizon are gun flashes: nothing else, no shape of any ship at all.

At 18:29 Jellicoe signalled a change in course to south-southeast, although this was cancelled as there was so much bunching up at the rear of the line (caused by Beatty's battle-cruisers heading across to the front in an effort to take up their agreed position in the van).

> This passage across the front of the battle fleet, to which Beatty was unavoidably committed, marred to some extent a very promising opening of the general action, and prevented full advantage being taken by Jellicoe of his position. At the moment of the deployment, when the rear divisions were nearest the enemy, they were being masked by the battle-cruisers, and later on, as the head of our line came into a suitable position to inflict damage, it was prevented from doing so.[58]

Right ahead of *Marlborough*, *St Vincent* (leading the 5th Division) was getting straddled by German fire – falling in the gap between her, *Marlborough* and *Neptune*. By the time that *St Vincent* was able to return fire, they had closed in to only 9,500yds (8,700m).[59] By 18:30 all the divisions except the 1st were engaged. There, *King George V*, in the 2nd Battle Squadron of the 1st Division, found the targets completely obscured by the mist. Nevertheless, it was a formidable concentration of fire: 266,000lbs (121,000kg) of broadside launched from over 230 guns, half of which were the heavier 13.5in calibre. In the next ten minutes, collectively they managed to land a dozen heavy shells on the leading German battleships and battle-cruisers. It was not long before the German line was reeling from the repeated blows. *Lützow* herself had taken twenty heavy-calibre hits and *König* was listing 4½ degrees.

The loss of *Shark* and the fate of *Acasta*

After Jellicoe's orders to Hood on *Invincible* at 16:00, sending his group forward to support Beatty, the latter hauled off at 16:12 at 25 knots. As he raced south, the weather became far worse – extremely variable and patchy: 'On some bearings we could see 16,000 yards, while on other bearings visibility was down to 2,000 yards'.[60] On his port side were the four destroyers of the 4th Flotilla:

Shark, her sister ship *Acasta, Ophelia** and *Christopher,* acting together as an anti-submarine screen. *Canterbury* was out ahead, leading the small force, with *Chester* even further off.

After *Chester* had engaged with some of Hipper's scouts, she had been able to get away because *Invincible* arrived in the nick of time. Hood's flagship had seen the flashes of the engagement at 17:40. The destroyers of the German 2nd Scouting Group were also spotted by his accompanying 4th Flotilla destroyers, which passed from port to starboard to make an attack and protect the battle-cruiser squadron and ten minutes later at 17:50, at a range of 5,000yds (4,600m), *Shark* fired her torpedoes. Shortly afterwards, around 18:00 *Shark* and *Acasta* opened fire at a cruiser and battle-cruiser.

Trying to load a torpedo, *Shark* was hit by a shell that had detonated the last torpedo while still in the tube. Instantly, 440lbs (200kg) of amatol exploded, wreaking havoc on the small destroyer. *Shark's* torpedo coxswain, Petty Officer William Griffin, himself severely wounded in the head, was one of the survivors and later related what had happened. He recounted how the fore 4in gun had been blown clean off the deck but, manning the midship 4in gun, its crew had carried on the fight against the German destroyers that had come out to aid other damaged vessels. The Germans had closed in to 600yds (550m), all the while keeping *Shark* trapped within a withering fire. At one point he was about to order the sinking of his own ship, but saw that he still had one serviceable gun. At the gun were a midshipman and two able seamen. Charles Howell, the gunlayer, was soon hit in the leg and Loftus Jones, the ship's commanding officer, had his right leg blown off.

Despite *Shark* being heavily damaged, her commander refused help from *Acasta.* He fought on until he was brought down by two torpedoes launched by *S.54* and his ship started to sink. Jones ordered the survivors from the thirty-man crew to abandon ship. Fifteen clambered onto the two Carley floats (small life rafts named after their American inventor, Horace Carley) but many of them soon died of exhaustion and exposure. The next morning seven survivors were picked up by a Danish freighter, *Vidar.* One who had survived till that point, Chief Stoker Newcombe, died on *Vidar's* deck.[61]

Jones's injury was fatal. Before dying and going down with his ship he had asked Charles Hope to replace the torn and tattered ensign on the gaff (the diagonal spar that projects aft from the crosstree on a mast). Hope and Charles Smith carried out his last wish. Loftus Jones was awarded a posthumous VC for his heroism that night, but only after his family had lobbied hard for the very

---

* HMS *Ophelia* had not given her crew much time to get used to the new ship. She has only been completed the day before the battle, on 30 May.

deserved recognition.† His body was not found until a few weeks later, having washed up on the Swedish coast and he was given a traditional Viking burial and a memorial erected to his honour in Fiskebackskil.[62]

Acasta continued on her way. *Lützow* was spotted on the port quarter and Lieutenant Commander John Barron turned *Acasta* to attack. Coming in close, he launched his torpedoes at 4,500yds (4,100m). He thought that he had hit with the first torpedo, but it was more likely a random shell exploding. At this close range, however, German fire was formidable and, inevitably, *Acasta* was hit in the engine room, killing or wounding the engineering officer and four crew members. She started to drift dangerously and ended up in the dreadnought lanes of the Grand Fleet, the great leviathans passing on either side. From *Valiant* her commanding officer was seen on deck: 'On her bridge was Sinclair with a pipe stuck in his face, roaming up and down his bridge as though he was on shore waiting for a tram or something'. Bravely, a signal flag was fluttering.[63]

St Vincent passed *Invincible* and then, on her starboard, *Acasta*:

She was so near to us that I could distinguish clearly the faces of the sailors, who, as we passed, raised a rousing cheer. It was such a demonstration of pluck and grit as fired every one of us on board the *St Vincent* with a fiercer desire than ever to get to real grips with the enemy.

Iron Duke also passed by and was cheered on particularly heartily by the small but courageous crew of *Acasta* as she passed the flagship.[64] From her yardarm flew a blue and yellow flag: the number '6' let others know that she was no longer under control.[65]

Galatea and *Fearless* stayed a moment with *Acasta* but then needed to move on, southwestward, into the night. Twice a burning German cruiser was spotted: nothing else. On the morning of 1 June the crew of *Acasta* was finally picked up by a destroyer, *Nonsuch* who, after taking her in tow around noon, arrived in Aberdeen on the evening of 2 June. The third of the four destroyers, *Ophelia*, was taken south by her captain, Commander Lewis G E Crabbe, and made a torpedo run at 8,000yds (7,300m) that, though abortive, kept up pressure on the enemy's battle-cruiser line.

---

† Nothing was mentioned in the immediate aftermath of the battle of the need to recognize Loftus Jones's bravery. Instead, the Navy first gave a gold watch to the captain of the *Vidar* and some money to crew members for their part in the rescue of the *Shark*'s crew. Since Jones had died, the only award with which he could be recognised was a posthumous Victoria Cross. At first the Navy balked. But Margaret Jones, Loftus's wife, interviewed all the crew members she could find and wrote up an account which she sent to an officer in the flotilla, a Captain Gladstone. He, in turn, wrote to Commodore Hawksley, who organised a series of further interviews and then made an appeal directly to Beatty who had just taken over as C-in-C of the Grand Fleet after Jellicoe had left on 29 November (1916). Beatty agreed immediately, calling it a 'fine story'.

Peter Kemp credits these two attacks with more significance than one might have at first thought appropriate: 'It had been the attack of the *Acasta* and the *Ophelia* that had led [Scheer] into that costly error, by giving him the belief that Jellicoe was much further advanced to the southward than, in fact, was the case'.[66] Even with the death of *Shark*, the remaining three British destroyers had managed to even up the score and had taken out one of their opposite number, a destroyer, *V.48*.

Hood's 3rd Battle Cruiser Squadron kept pushing forward. It had come with Jellicoe's force from Scapa Flow and was fresh from gunnery practice, having arrived from Rosyth a week before on 22 May in temporary exchange for the 5th Battle Squadron, which joined Beatty's forces. The sun was in its favour and soon both *Derfflinger* and *Lützow* were targeted by the squadron's 12in guns. Their shooting was first-class.[67] *Indomitable* hit *Derfflinger* three times and the otherwise largely undamaged *Seydlitz* once. Scheer and Hipper now believed that the 3rd BCS was, in fact, the van of the battle fleet itself because they could not see the extent of the line stretched out towards the northwest. One report even came in 'counting four dreadnoughts of the *Queen Elizabeth* or *Iron Duke* class'.

After the threat that *Wiesbaden* and her three companions had posed came another danger: thirty-one destroyers of the German 9th, 2nd and 12th Flotillas. Starting at 17:55, they launched an attack on *Invincible*'s squadron. Hood's four destroyers and *Canterbury* fought wildly to disrupt the German destroyers. The German attack, which could have been decisive, became disorganised. While the five destroyers of the 12th Half-Flotilla were able to launch at a range of 6,500yds (5,900m) and got six torpedoes into the water, the other attacks did not go well. Another ten destroyers from the 9th Flotilla also prepared to fire, but then got mixed up with the 12th Half-Flotilla boats as they were coming back. They only managed to fire three torpedoes. The 2nd Flotilla action was the worst. Its four destroyers could launch only one torpedo between them, at a range of roughly 7,000yds (6,400m). At 18:18 Scheer recalled his battle-cruisers.

The loss of *Invincible*

At 18:13 *Invincible*'s captain, Arthur Cay, turned the great ship hard to starboard, away from the torpedo attack. But in doing so, her helm jammed and she had to come to a full stop to clear the problem. Up in the conn, Commander Hubert Dannreuther saw some of the torpedoes heading in his direction, to pass by harmlessly. But they were close; one was within six yards of the port side.

Seven minutes later Hood spotted Beatty's ships almost head-on, around 4,000yds (3,700m) off. Cay swung *Invincible* around through a 180-degree turn to starboard, which brought her neatly into position around 3,000yds (2,700m) ahead of *Lion* on a southeasterly course. Beatty made a final dash at *Lion*'s rated 26 knots and got his battle-cruisers across the front of the Grand Fleet to take up position behind Hood (if Hood had taken station astern of Beatty, Jellicoe's fire would have been obstructed again).

Invincible was now running parallel with Hipper's battle-cruisers, divided by a gap of around 9,000yds (8,200m). At 18:26 *Invincible* opened fire on *Lützow*. *Inflexible* supported her firing while *Indomitable* completely focused her 12in guns on *Derfflinger*. And from astern, Beatty's ships engaged the rear of the enemy's line. *Lützow* was soon in deep trouble. She started to flood severely and had lost radio communications: 'Several 38-centimetre shells squarely hit their mark, wreaking terrible havoc. The first hit the wireless department. Of the twelve living men who a moment ago were seated before the apparatus there is nothing more to be seen.'[68]

The pounding from the head of the British battle-cruiser line 'riddled her forward part, reduced her bows and her forecastle to a waste of crumpled, battered metal – her ability to stay afloat was a tribute to her design and construction'.[69] *Invincible*'s second shot had pierced the fore part of the ship and the entire space, as far as the diesel motor room, was wrecked. Hipper sheered off to his starboard, giving up any attempt to reach the crippled *Wiesbaden*.

From his observation position on *Derfflinger*, Hase recorded the moment they first saw their adversary:

> At 18:29 the veil of mist in front of us split like a curtain at a theatre. Clear and sharply silhouetted against the horizon, we saw a powerful ship … at an almost parallel course at top speed. Her guns were trained on us and immediately another salvo crashed out, straddling us completely.[70]

With the damage that British guns had inflicted, *Derfflinger* was herself in difficulties. Kapitän Johannes Hartog then did the unthinkable. He ordered a complete stop so that the riggers could get to her trailing torpedo nets and cut them off, as they were in grave danger of fouling her propellers. Every second counted. They would have been sitting ducks had they been spotted. It gives the reader an idea of how heavy the fog must have been lying, that Hartog could even have contemplated such a dangerous decision.

At around 18:30 *Invincible* was firing flat out and pumping shells, about fifty, at *Lützow*. Below the gun turrets the silk cordite bags had been taken out of their containers so that the gun crews could keep up with the firing rate and avoid 'starving' the guns. *Invincible*'s performance was superb. She scored eight hits in eight minutes at a range of around 9,600yds (8,800m). Two of the eight hits punched holes in *Lützow*'s bow section below her waterline. The massive strikes caused instant flooding and she took on around 2,000 tons of water. These were the most damaging hits on *Lützow* in the whole day. As a flagship, Hipper's *Lützow* had become useless. At 18:37 he ordered her 'out of action' and to return to Wilhelmshaven.

Hood was pleased with *Invincible*'s gunnery and wanted to let his gunnery officer know. Through the voice pipe he complimented him: 'Your firing is very good. Keep at it as quickly as you can. Every shot is telling.'[71] His praise was justified but terribly timed. *Lützow* swung her own guns on to target *Invincible*, already under fire from *Derfflinger*: the tables were turned. With Captain Hubert Dannreuther on the foretop was the range taker, Able Seaman Ernest Dandridge, and Chief Petty Officer Walter Thompson, who recalled the moment: 'The first German salvos fell about 1,200 yards short, but they gradually fell closer until they were straddling the *Invincible*, deluging the ship with shell splashes while pieces of shrapnel buzzed over the ship.'[72]

The first hit, in Captain Francis Kennedy's recollection from the bridge of *Indomitable*, was on the ship's aft, with little damage. Ninety seconds passed and after *Derfflinger*'s third salvo Hase successfully scored hits against *Invincible*'s Q turret at 18:31.[73] Bryan Gasson, on the range-finder in Q turret, was sure that the shell hit the turret between the guns. It penetrated the 7in armour, killed all Gasson's fellow marines and blew off the turret's armoured roof.

Either this shell set up a flash that penetrated the magazines or another shell landed: the ship exploded in a huge fireball. In the one photograph of the actual explosion the ship can be seen totally enveloped, with only her bridge and the director platform silhouetted against the wall of flame; to the front, it looks as if fire is shooting up from the ship's foremost turret, A turret. Dannreuther, another officer and three ratings, up on the fire-control platform, survived only because the huge explosion severed the tripod and they were hurled from the ship. All that was left were the two hull sections, each reaching up into above the water, hanging there vertically, each section resting the bottom of the North Sea. As the depth there was only 180ft, the 567ft hull section was split in two, each visible 100ft above the surface.

The few survivors cheered their fellow countrymen as *Indefatigable* and *Indomitable* surged past, as did, unwittingly, the sailors from the Grand Fleet: they could not believe that one of their own had been blown up. They assumed it was a German ship:

> [We] could have almost chucked a heaving line aboard her. She was broken in two with her bows and stern sticking out of the water. *Benbow*'s men jumped up and down on top of their turrets and cheered heartily. The idea that it could be any other than a German ship had never entered their heads. Then

we passed about half a cable distance and saw her name, and the cheering ceased suddenly ... our Admiral [Sturdee] was very upset about it – she was his flagship in his last great fight off the Falklands.[74]

A nineteen-year-old midshipman on *Bellerophon* talked of the horror of the sudden realisation:

During the lull we came out of the turrets to get some fresh air and there, floating around us, was a whole mass of bodies and debris – some of our sailors were cheering because they thought they were Germans, but unfortunately they were from the *Invincible*. It was a terrible experience and my first experience of death.[75]

As *St Vincent* passed the wreck her crew, like the others before, had no idea of her identity. They too assumed that the ship was German. For her captain, William Fisher, the realisation was of a profound, personal sadness. His brother Charles, whom he worshipped, had been a young lieutenant on *Invincible*. He would carry 'this poignant memory of that quarter of an hour' before 'he realised it was the wreck of the *Invincible*' with him for the rest of his life. 'He closed his binoculars knowing he would never see his brother again.'[76]

For the British, the latest phase of battle of Jutland had not got off to a good start.

At 18:40 *Badger* was ordered aside by Beatty to pick up the survivors. Hood and Captain Cay, along with 1,019 crewmembers, were dead.* There were only six survivors. *Colossus* saw two of them in the water by one of the propellers as she passed by at 19:02.[77] One of these was Hubert Dannreuther. He later talked of his narrow escape: he merely 'stepped off into the water when the foretop came down'.[78] He was uninjured and the water was 'quite warm' with 'no shortage of wreckage to hold on to', and he was soon safely aboard *Badger*.[79]

With Dannreuther were Lieutenant Cecil S Sandford, Gunner Private Bryan Gasson, Able Seaman Ernest George Dandridge and Chief Petty Officer Walter Thompson. Another was Yeoman of Signals Walter Maclean Pratt, who had also been on the director platform. Gasson in Q turret was the only one not in the fire-control top, at the top of the tripod foremast. In another photograph, *Badger* is hove-to off to the north, forlornly looking for more survivors, with *Invincible*'s two broken hull sections standing vertical in the water.

The last man to see the wreck floating was probably not an Englishman. More likely it was the Kapitän of *U.75*, Lieutenant Commander Curt Beitzen.

---

* Tarrant, *Battle-cruiser Invincible*, p128, lists the lucky ones who escaped their meeting with death. There were four officers and men on leave plus another five men listed as deserters on 31 May.

He had seen the bow section through his periscope after the Grand Fleet had passed by. Jellicoe had, in fact, following British success in recovering secret documents from SMS *Magdeburg* earlier in the war, ordered a British submarine out, if necessary, to torpedo the still floating sections when at 18:55 he [Jellicoe] passed the wreck.

Even though *Invincible* was not the only casualty of this engagement – *Princess Royal* was hit by two 12in shells from *Markgraf* – the German torpedo-boat commander, Commodore Michelsen, understood, from his post on the bridge of *Rostock,* the danger of the position into which Scheer and Hipper had led their ships. Grouping together the 3rd Torpedo-Boat Flotilla with the 1st Half-Flotilla, Commodore Wilhelm Hollmann led the combined forces through the German lines to launch another torpedo attack and had approached to within 7,000yds (6,400m) of the British lines when he was recalled by Michelsen. Scheer had decided to pull his ships out and needed Michelsen's boats to cover the manoeuvre.

The first German battle turn: the turn-away to starboard

Even with the German success against *Invincible*, Scheer clearly understood that his fleet was in a perilous situation and courting certain destruction if he continued to be pulled further into Jellicoe's 'T':

> It was now obvious that we were confronted by a large portion of the
> English fleet. The entire arc stretching from north to east was a sea of fire.
> The flash from the muzzle of the guns was seen distinctly through the mist
> and the smoke on the horizon, although the ships themselves were not
> distinguishable.[80]

Despite – maybe because of – the horror of facing an extended six-mile line of British battleships, the Germans fought back hard. Prince Albert, the future King George VI, was in A turret of *Collingwood*, a fact that would, as the Prince of Wales wrote, 'buck him up a lot', despite the possibility of death.[81] 'The shell was plainly visible, a reddish brown, probably an armour-piercing. When I saw the shell flying towards us I remarked to Midshipman Stoneham, "That shell is going to hit A turret". It did not. It passed over the forecastle and fell into the sea close on the port side.'[82]

Right at the head of the 'T', *König* was taking a heavy pounding. She was in the sights of not one but twelve British dreadnoughts: *Agincourt, Bellerophon, Conquerer, Thunderer, Hercules, Colossus, Benbow, Iron Duke, Orion, Monarch, Revenge* and *Royal Oak*. Rear Admiral Behncke saw Hipper's battle-cruisers sheer off to the southeast and followed suit. He did not need much encouragement. Way back in the middle of the line, Scheer on *Friedrich der Große* had a different picture. He could not see what was happening, but had just received reports from the interrogation of the rescued prisoners from *Nomad*, who talked about sixty dreadnoughts being in the area, and feared the worst. *Nomad*'s commander, Paul Whitfield, and seventy-two men had been plucked from the icy waters by their adversaries.

At around 16:34 Scheer signalled from *Friedrich der Große* for his forces to make the first of his famous battle turns, the *Gefechtskehrtwendung nach Steuerbord* (battle about-turn to starboard), a manoeuvre practised many times by the High Seas Fleet for just such an occasion, but which supposedly took the Grand Fleet by surprise.[83] Each German ship turned 180 degrees immediately on its own axis. *Westfalen*, last in line, commenced the manoeuvre, then all remaining twenty-one turned, each initiating the turn once the ship astern was seen to move out of line. With a simple signal Scheer had, without losing speed, managed (in one description) a 'hand-brake turn'. It was probably close to what a skidding turn would have looked like, and as the line turned Michelsen's torpedo boats crossed their sterns laying a thick smokescreen.[84] The British were blinded.

Observers on *Canterbury* and *Falmouth* witnessed some part of the turn-away but did not think to report it to the bridge of *Iron Duke*. *Iron Duke* herself could not during the engagement see more than four ships at any time. Four minutes later there was no sign of the German fleet; the battle turn-away had happened so fast. Jellicoe's deployment of the Grand Fleet took twenty-five minutes: Scheer's of the High Seas Fleet, four. The confusion was understandable but also unforgivable. The Navy was still trained not to think but only do what it was told to do. While the British had used the short engagement to its fullest potential, it was a bitter pill to swallow.

During this brief encounter the British scored twenty-three heavy shell hits on the enemy's leading ships. *König* was hit eight times by 13.5in shells from *Iron Duke* and *Monarch*, and suffered severe damage. *Markgraf* received only two hits, but one of these was a near-miss by *Orion* that bent a propeller shaft and put one of her engines out of action. *Lützow* was hit no fewer than ten more times, due mostly to the superb gunnery of Hood's battle-cruisers. It was one devastating hit by either *Invincible* or *Inflexible* that led to her eventual loss. The already battered *Derfflinger* and *Seydlitz* also received more damage, mainly from *Indomitable*. In return, Scheer's battleships had only been able to register a single hit on any of Jellicoe's battleships, and only two on *Princess Royal*. Even Hipper's accurate gunners could only manage five hits, all of them on *Invincible* during those brief moments of clear visibility.[85]

In terms of materiel, the British losses were not significant. *Defence* and *Warrior* were obsolete: both had been in service for the critical decade in which battleship design was revolutionised by the arrival of the *Dreadnought*. With

9.2in guns both were badly under-gunned for their role at Jutland. *Invincible* was, meanwhile, the 'oldest and weakest of Beatty's battle-cruiser force' and was, therefore, a 'sustainable loss'.[86] The loss of life – the death of almost 2,000 sailors – was another matter entirely.

To cover the turn-away Hipper ordered a torpedo attack. It was a relatively small-scale affair and did not cause Jellicoe to turn away.[87] Nevertheless, when at around 18:40 lookouts on the British line started spotting torpedoes running, it seemed that Jellicoe's nightmare was about to become reality. Indeed, on *Revenge* a loud, heavy shock was felt, but the weapon failed to explode and bounced off the waterline armour. By 18:45 firing had ceased altogether. The German fleet had successfully disappeared right in front of their antagonists behind a smokescreen into a seemingly impenetrable North Sea mist.

The British were now fully deployed in a line of thirty-three capital ships: six battle-cruisers followed by the twenty-four ships of the Grand Fleet itself and, at the rear of these, the three operational 5th Battle Squadron *Queen Elizabeth*-class super-dreadnoughts. At the very point that Jellicoe had completed his own deployment, there was no sign of his opponent.

Jellicoe explained: 'I imagined this disappearance of the enemy to be due merely to the thickening of the mist, but after a few minutes had elapsed, it became clear that there must be some other reason and at 18:44 I hauled up one point to south-east'.[88] His critics need to imagine – for a moment – what might have happened if he had received just a titbit of information from *Canterbury* or *Falmouth*. The later debate centred on his supposed lack of Nelsonian aggression: his failure to chase Scheer into the mists and to stay close to the enemy. Having no clue as to what had happened, Jellicoe would have been foolhardy to do the latter. Bacon did not mince his words:

> If he had chased the German fleet by turning straight towards where they had last been seen, as some lunatics have suggested that he should have done, not only would he have seriously endangered the Grand Fleet, without a prospect of damaging the enemy, but he would actually have been further from the German fleet at dark than he eventually was.[89]

More to the point (Bacon added), little would be gained by listening to arguments from people who failed 'to grasp that an enemy who [ran] away [could not] be overtaken unless the ships chasing him [had] great speed and sufficient time in which to overtake'.[90] Had Jellicoe charged into the mist in hot pursuit of the German battle fleet, as his critics would have liked him to have done, the results would have most likely been disappointing. The distance that Jellicoe would have had to cover to catch Scheer would have simply been too great without a significant speed advantage.[91]

With no German battle-cruisers or battle fleet in view, the guns of the Grand Fleet were retrained on the one target still there for the taking: the wreck of *Wiesbaden*. The sheer courage of her remaining crew was inspiring, even to the British. Surrounded by the dead and wounded, with carnage and everything in flames, the crew somehow managed to load and fire one torpedo tube. *Marlborough*'s track and the missile now whizzing through the water were on a convergent destiny. She was hit at 18:54. A huge 20ft foot gash was torn in her side, 25ft below the deep waterline right by the boiler room and the starboard diesel and hydraulic engine rooms.[92] A further 70ft of framing was distorted by the blast. It was just abaft of the B-turret magazine.

The fire in the four boilers was put out almost immediately within ten minutes. By 19:30 the boiler room had been pumped and the flooding brought under control. But with the flooding came an increasing 7-degree list to starboard. Her speed was cut dramatically. Miraculously, only two men were killed: Stokers 1st Class Edgar George Monk and William Rustage. They were the only casualties on any of the Grand Fleet dreadnoughts at Jutland. Just after *Marlborough* was hit *St Vincent* also spotted a torpedo in the water:

> I observed the wake of one, about 300 yards away, coming dead for the *St Vincent*. Instantly, on my telling him, the officer in command reported its presence to Captain Fisher, with the result that the ship turned to port to avoid it ... Hit though she was, and listing badly, the *Marlborough* was by no means out of action ... I saw her guns being elevated to counteract the list, and she continued to fire broadside after broadside so long as there was anything to fire at.[93]

That the German fleet was allowed to disappear with neither vital intelligence being passed on to Jellicoe, nor shots being fired by larger ships, speaks volumes about both the state of technology at the time and the stifling legacy of a Navy trained in Victorian values. The lack of initiative of some commanders was near-baffling, given what was at stake. The performance makes all the more valuable the vital role played by commanders such as Goodenough. In his look at the British Navy in *Before Jutland*, Goldrick makes two very key points about British naval officers' pre-war operational experience: first, that it was almost always ashore (this was certainly the case for my grandfather), and, more tellingly, 'the sustained demonstrations of initiative were in detached command, well away from authority'. For Goldrick, the appearance of WT on the scene 'was moving this syndrome into virtual reality, with units on manoeuvres failing to exercise initiative because of their assumption that the remote authority knew better'.[94]

At the head of Jellicoe's line was Rear Admiral Trevylyan Napier's 3rd Light Cruiser Squadron. It did nothing. Alexander-Sinclair's 1st Light Cruiser

Squadron was at the rear of the British battle fleet and, therefore, badly positioned to perform any useful function, but Charles Le Mesurier's* 4th Light Cruiser Squadron did, in fact, move southwest to try to find the enemy, but was unable to see anything through the fog. The battle-cruisers, whose speed would have served them well for keeping contact, were effectively disabled through a gyro-compass failure and the loss of six critical minutes. This failure became the source of considerable tension after the war in the Harper record.[95]

Goodenough's 2nd Light Cruiser Squadron, on the other hand, was an exception. As the firing died out at 18:45 he steamed south and managed to catch the rear of the retreating enemy ships. He was heavily shelled but held his position and even saw Scheer's second turn, around which he signalled back to Jellicoe at 19:00: 'Urgent. Priority. Enemy battle fleet steering ESE. Enemy bears from me SSW. Number unknown. My position Lat. 57° 02' N, Long. 0° 07' E.' All that Jellicoe could do was order a 34-degree turn towards the last known enemy position.

In such circumstances Jellicoe ordered the Grand Fleet to bend around, turning 3 points to starboard a minute after Goodenough's signal was received on *Iron Duke*, hoping to catch Hipper. He then ordered a second bend to starboard, realising that Hipper must have made a wider and larger turn-away. The course was now altered 45 degrees with the fleet heading on a southerly bearing in echelon formation, one division blanketing the other. Jellicoe was still cautious – he did not want to chase either Hipper or Scheer into the mist and leave the outcome to chance – but his southerly course meant that he was better positioned to cut Hipper off from a return to his base.

The second German battle turn: the turn back and the run east

A quarter of an hour later at 18:55 Scheer ordered a second battle turn to starboard. His ships surged back to the line of British dreadnoughts to try to get across where he imagined the end of the line to have been.

At this point a curious incident occurred. Beatty's ships had raced ahead again, and in fact, were probably too far ahead of the main battle fleet to serve as the function of the van. Harper would insist that the battle-cruisers turned a full circle. In the post-war debate, Beatty was most concerned to represent the manoeuvres of his command in the best light. He countered Harper's supposition by saying that the charts were muddled and confused, and that the actual

---

* Charles Le Mesurier was related to the actor John Le Mesurier, who brought us the wonderful Sergeant Arthur Wilson in *Dad's Army*. His family had been a very old Alderney family (a namesake was governor general in 1922). I believe I heard that, when the Germans invaded, the family had to leave everything behind.

manoeuvre was a double 'S' rather than a full 360-degree circle: in other words, he and *Lion* did execute 360 degrees of turn but not as a continuous, unbroken turn in one direction. There was also, apparently, a gyro-compass failure on *Lion*, but Beatty vociferously denied that the 360-degree turn took place at all and then produced track reports that appeared to have been doctored.

But effectively Beatty denied the evidence, always maintaining that he had done two semicircular turns, one to port, followed by another to starboard. Much doubt was cast on his word when he produced what he represented as the charts drawn up and signed by him in 1916; on closer inspection, they turned out to bear the signature that he had started to use later, in 1920.

Lion's navigator, Commander Strutt, referred to the 360-degree turn in his voice-pipe commentary to Lieutenant Chalmers in the chart house below the compass platform.[96] *New Zealand* also reported – in Andrew Gordon's words, 'defiantly' – the full turn on her track chart.[97] And behind Beatty, Napier's 3rd Light Cruiser Squadron apparently followed the manoeuvre. On *Tiger*, Captain Rudolf Bentinck, Beatty's chief of staff, was allowed to take the conn as he was about to take over the ship's command from Henry Pelly. Gordon succinctly summarised the event: 'The battle-cruisers astern [of *Lion*] followed her round, while the two ahead [*Inflexible* and *Indomitable*] turned in imitation and took the opportunity to tag onto the end of the line. Napier's 3rd Light Cruiser Squadron, also ahead, copied the circle.'[98]

Most commentators today maintain that Beatty lied, but the reasons are still not clear. Maybe it added to the impression that Beatty had lost contact with the enemy. He certainly would not have made such a turn if it were still in sight. In any case, the 'full, lazy 360 degree circle ... allowed the Battle Fleet to reduce the gap with the Battle Cruiser Fleet, and caused the latter to lose bearing on the enemy'.†

Why did Scheer suddenly change course again? Many find the decision to place the battle-cruisers in the van, given their low armour protection, incomprehensible. Scheer himself said that what he had done would have been frowned on in peacetime. His comments on his own actions at the time and later, after the war, are worth quoting. He wanted neither to be seen to retreat nor to have fought a stern-chase action that had nearly destroyed the 5th Battle Squadron earlier in the day.[99] 'If the enemy followed us, our action in reversing

---

† *Lion*'s original track chart showed the 360-degree turn. The revised one, dated 17 July 1916, changed this to an 'S' manoeuvre initiated by a 180-degree turn to starboard followed by the same to port and completed at 19:01. 'The turn had brought the van of the battle fleet two miles nearer but it had also wasted seven valuable minutes – for at 19:01 *Lion* was back in the position she had been at the commencement of the turn at 18:45. This valuable seven minutes could have been better spent probing westward for the enemy' (Gordon, p457; Irving, pp145–6).

course would have been classed as a retreat and if any of our rear ships were damaged, we would have to sacrifice them. Still less was it feasible to disengage, leaving it to the enemy to decide when he would meet with us in the morning.'[100] His post-war comments were slightly different:

> The fact is I had no definite objective ... I advanced because I thought I should help the poor *Wiesbaden*, since the situation was entirely obscure because I had received no wireless reports. When I noticed that the British pressure had ceased and that the fleet remained intact in my hands, I turned back under the impression that the action could not end in this way and that I ought to seek contact with the enemy again. And then I thought that I had better throw in the battle-cruisers in full strength ... The thing just happened – as the virgin said when she got a baby.[101]

Scheer's explanations lack credibility. If he was going for a full-out attack on the British fleet, there are questions as to why he would place his weakest elements in the van, and why he would allow Jellicoe to cross his 'T' once again. Would this have made 'disengagement for the night' any easier? Going back for the crew of *Wiesbaden* seemingly 'defies common sense'.[102] Apart from putting the whole fleet in danger for a single ship, it is also clear that Scheer did not want to get pushed progressively further west. That would only have meant a longer passage back to Wilhelmshaven and the higher likelihood that he would get caught on the open seas in daylight the following morning. Scheer did send torpedo boats back in an attempt to rescue *Wiesbaden*'s crew, and two of them, *V.73* and *G.88*, took the opportunity to let loose their torpedoes on the British.

By now, *Lützow* had taken a tremendous beating:

> The bow is crushed and is entirely submerged. The four screws are already sticking out of the water so that the *Lützow* can only make 8 to 10 knots an hour, as against the normal 32 ... The *Lützow* is now a complete wreck. Corpses drifted past. From the bows up to the first 30-centimetre gun turret the ship lay submerged.[103]

Hipper was forced to leave his flagship. He was visibly affected. At first, he resisted Chief of Staff Erich Raeder's attempts to persuade him to transfer ship but eventually he gave in: Raeder had at one point even suggested that Hipper move his flag to a *König*-class battleship, but he declined, saying that he felt it would be badly viewed by the squadron. Raeder later recalled:

> A kind of paralysis seemed to descend on Hipper ... [He] issued no orders. It was the first time that he had nothing to say. 'We can't lead the squadron from *Lützow* any more, your excellency.' 'But I can't leave my flagship.' 'We're unable

to signal by wire and anyway our speed isn't enough.' ... 'The squadron needs your excellency.' Finally Hipper succumbed to the inevitable. 'You're right.'[104]

Hipper signalled *G.39* to take him off and as soon as he was clear, *Lützow* broke out of line and headed south, back to German waters, with torpedo boats of the 12th and the 1st Half-Flotillas forming a smokescreen to protect her. Just as Leutnant von Löffen on *G.39* took Hipper off the stricken vessel and left in search of another flagship, *Lützow* was hit again on B turret. She then received four more hits from Rear Admiral Leveson's *Orion*-class battleships of the 2nd Division.

Hipper first tried to transfer to *Derfflinger*, but she was in no condition to act satisfactorily in the flagship role. She had taken around twenty heavy shells and two plates had been ripped off her bow, putting her under a real threat of flooding. Hipper quickly changed his mind and decided on *Seydlitz*. To cover her escape south, the remainder of *G.39*'s half-flotilla and the 12th laid a smoke-screen. *Von der Tann* was in equally bad condition as none of her turrets were fit for firing. Even so, Kapitän Zenker felt that he had to remain in the line. In spite of defining this battle damage a 'failure', the commander decided to keep with his division 'to prevent the enemy from noticing anything and redistributing his fire so that the other ships would come in for worse punishment'.[105]

Led by Kapitän Hartog on *Derfflinger*, the German battle-cruisers started the steam south. They ran into problems almost immediately, steering too close to the battle fleet, and causing a considerable amount of bunching up: 'in some cases they were forced to stop their engines and even to go astern to avoid collision'.[106] It was not long before Scheer was back in as fatal a position as he had been before, in a British 'T'. By 19:15 the fire from the British line was deadlier and more effective than before. Scheer's leading battleship was only 12,000yds (10,900m) away, his leading cruiser 10,000yds (9,100m) from *Colossus*.[107]

> Within five minutes, no less than seventeen of Jellicoe's battleships and four of Beatty's battle-cruisers had opened fire on the enemy van at ranges from 9,000 to 14,000 yards. To make things worse, there were now several 15-inch-gunned super-dreadnoughts of the *Royal Sovereign* class in action to add to Evan-Thomas's *Queen Elizabeth*s ... Fifteen of the British battleships managed to score at least one hit on an enemy ship, while none of Scheer's battle fleet made a single hit.[108]

The leading ships of Behncke's 3rd Squadron – *König*, *Großer Kurfürst*, *Markgraf* and *Kaiser* – were all hit, as was the 1st Squadron's *Helgoland*. *Monarch*, *Iron Duke*, *Centurion*, *Royal Oak*, *King George V*, *Temeraire*, *Neptune* and *Superb* all registered hits. As she was engaged with *Seydlitz*, even the damaged *Marlborough* saw four of her fourteen salvos hit.

During this action, German gunners could see hardly a thing, let alone find an aiming point. Only one British battleship, *Colossus*, was hit twice by *Seydlitz's* fire. Five of her crew were wounded. *Seydlitz* was fighting it out not only with *Colossus*, but also *Hercules*, though she was sustaining little overall damage from British fire. *Derfflinger* was under fire from four British ships: *Hercules*, *Neptune*, *St Vincent* and *Revenge*. This last was also engaging *Moltke*.

König had been hit just under her midships turret, and was full of gas and smoke as a consequence. *Großer Kurfürst* was hit four times in two minutes. *Helgoland*, the fourth ship in line, was also hit as the fusillade reached further down the German line. *Derfflinger's* entire port side was badly damaged and no 5.9in casemate guns were working. After that, another heavy 15in shell ripped into one of her aft turrets. *Lützow*, with her four escorting destroyers, carried on but was hit again in rapid succession. With her main battery dead, she could no longer fight back. For a second time the line started to buckle at the van.

British Gunnery Performance at Jutland

The British relied more on speed than careful calculation, and even if Jellicoe himself was not of the 'speed school', Beatty was. Dreyer and Madden probably were too. In late 1915 Jellicoe spoke about the constant push for gunnery speed, telling Beatty that he felt that it was 'being carried to excess'. His fears that the system of anti-flash doors would be compromised by this obsession with speed were justified.

The first time that the German 'T' was crossed saw very effective gunnery. Within minutes of transferring fire to *König*, *Iron Duke* scored seven hits. By 18:30 five out of the six divisions were engaged with the German line. In the next short ten minutes, collectively they managed to land twelve heavy shells on the leading German battleships and battle-cruisers. Badly mauled already, *Lützow* by now had taken twenty heavy-calibre hits and *König* was left with a bad list.

During this brief encounter, the British scored twenty-three heavy shell hits on the enemy's leading ships. *König* was hit eight times by 13.5in shells from *Iron Duke* and *Monarch* and suffered severe damage. *Markgraf* received only two hits, but one of these was a near miss by *Orion* that bent a propeller shaft and put one of her engines out of action. *Lützow* was hit no fewer than ten more times, due mostly to the superb shooting of Hood's battle-cruisers. One devastating hit by either *Invincible* or *Inflexible* led to her eventual loss. The already battered *Derfflinger* and *Seydlitz* also received more damage, mainly from *Indomitable*. In return, Scheer's battleships had only been able to register a single hit on any of Jellicoe's battleships, and only two on *Princess Royal*. Even Hipper's accurate gunners could only manage five hits, all of them on *Invincible* during those brief moments of clear visibility.[109]

Despite the sinking of *Invincible*, *Defence* and *Warrior*, the punishment following Jellicoe's first successful tactical bottling of the German line, and the fact that

Scheer now realised the danger of the position he had got his fleet into, directly led to Scheer's decision for the first battle turn-away.

The second crossing of the 'T' was even more effective. Scheer realised by now that pushing west could be a bad decision. He was steaming further away from the German coast and, in his eyes, this action could in later years be looked on as a German retreat. That he went back for *Wiesbaden* was pure fantasy (although attempts to rescue her crew were made), but there is certainly some strength in the idea that this took Jellicoe by surprise. Scheer's second turn-away was covered by his destroyers and battle-cruisers in the 'death ride' that was to come. Once again the Grand Fleet's gunnery was overpowering and the damage to Scheer's battle-ships heavy. *Markgraf* was hit five times, *Großer Kurfürst* eight and *König* ten times. *Markgraf*'s damage was critical; this would reduce Scheer's overall speed. *König* then shipped 200 tons of water, *Großer Kurfürst* more than 800.

In the hour before sunset, British hits on German ships were forty-nine (versus three). In the battle-cruiser action's first hour it was four against fourteen. The Grand Fleet's gunnery performance was – during its limited engagement – demonstrably better than that of the 1st or 2nd Battle Cruiser Squadrons. This was successfully buried at the time. Some of Beatty's ships' performance was lamentable. *New Zealand* and *Tiger* collectively fired 723 rounds. *Tiger* made five hits, *New Zealand* fewer. In contrast some of the best shooting ships were *Invincible*, *Inflexible*, *Barham*, *Valiant* and Jellicoe's flagship, *Iron Duke*.

At Scapa Flow a protected gunnery range was available for the Grand Fleet battle-ships. The battle-cruisers at Rosyth had none. The elements of the Grand Fleet that did open fire were able to concentrate their fire not once but twice on the German 'T', and also fire significantly more accurately than many of Beatty's ships.

The third German battle turn: the battle-cruiser 'death ride'

The pressure on Scheer was tremendous. While he claimed that his actions took the British by surprise, the truth is that it was he who was surprised, not Jellicoe:

> Admiral Scheer had realised the danger to which we were exposed. The van of our fleet was shut in by a semi-circle of the enemy ... There was only one way to escape the unfavourable tactical situation: to turn the line about and withdraw on the opposite course. Before everything else, we must get out of the dangerous enemy envelopment.[110]

Scheer now prepared for a third battle turn by hoisting the signal on *Friedrich der Große* at 19:12. It was held on the signals halyard for a full six minutes. As soon as it was lowered, all captains complied and executed the flagship orders. Again, the ships at the head of the line taking the concentration of British fire slowed down, with a severe concertina effect on the battle line. At least one of Scheer's subordinates, *Ostfriesland*'s Vice Admiral Erhardt Schmidt, commanding the 1st Squadron from the centre of the line, decided to turn his ship around without waiting for Scheer's order to become executive, rather than risk annihilation. Even *Friedrich der Große*, the flagship, was forced to circle to port in order to give herself enough space. There was not enough sea room for such a manoeuvre and the risk of a serious collision loomed large; *Kaiserin* was actually even squeezed out of the line. *Markgraf* – followed by *Großer Kurfürst* – headed off south to try to avoid the concentration of British fire, while out in front *König* laid down as much thick smoke as she could to protect the others.

It did not take long for Scheer to react to the extreme danger. At 19:13 he ordered his torpedo boats and the four remaining battle-cruisers to race forwards at the Grand Fleet as a diversion. The action became known as the 'death ride', 'the most splendid and least intelligent moment in the short history of the Imperial Navy'.[111] Four badly damaged German battle-cruisers were sent against thirty-three capital ships, but Scheer signalled his obedient commanders to hold nothing back. '*Größe Kreuzer. Ran an der Feind. Voll einsetzen!*' ('Battle-cruisers at the enemy. Give it everything!').* With Hipper still on *G.39* looking for a new flagship, Hartog led *Derfflinger* from the van, courageously attacking at 20 knots together with all except *Lützow*, by now too badly damaged to join any concerted action.

Eighteen British battleships had opened fire on the enemy battle-cruiser charge: the entire British line was strafing the Germans, who were facing 'the greatest concentration of naval gunfire any fleet commander had ever faced'.[112] In the ten minutes before 18:19 *Derfflinger* was hit fourteen times by 15in fire, either from *Valiant* or *Barham*. Her ability to absorb punishment was impressive. No wonder she was nicknamed 'the iron dog' by the British. But just before the hour, at 18:55 she received a hit critically damaging her bow. Within minutes she took on 300 tons of water (equivalent to around 270 cubic metres). She emerged with two main gun turrets out of action and the majority of her turret crews dead. Hase described this moment when the Germans were '*im absoluten Wurstkessel*' – right in the frying pan, so to speak.

> A perfect hail of projectiles beat on us. A 15-inch burst in the turret called Caesar. The flames penetrated to the working chamber, where two other cartridges caught fire; flames leapt out of the turret as high as a house, but they did not explode, as the enemy's cartridges had done. The effect was appalling: seventy-three out of seventy-eight men of the turret crew were

---

* The translation of the '*Ran an der Feind. Voll einsetzen*' command is not that straightforward. Irving cited the original nine pendant 'R' flag as 'Battle-cruisers: attack the enemy immediately regardless of the consequences', evolving into 'Close to the enemy and ram. Ships will fight to the death' which he quoted from von Hase (Irving, p158). Bacon's translation is probably more accurate: 'Ships are to attack without regard to consequences' (Bacon, *Scandal*, p118).

killed outright. A 15-inch shell hit the roof of Dora turret; again charges were set fire to, roaring up into the sky from both turrets like funeral pyres. The enemy had our range to an inch.¹¹³

Seydlitz, already low in the water, was hit five more times. Even though she could not add firepower, *Von der Tann* was also hit at the foot of the aft conning tower, although the explosion was felt throughout the ship. Deep in the boiler room the passages were filled with lethal gas and smoke. The combination of not being able to see what you were doing while feeling trapped inside the respirators must have been hellish. And the poor *Lützow* continued to be pounded by *Monarch* and *Orion*, who between them landed another five shells on the dying ship. Only *Moltke* was left relatively unscathed. A grateful Scheer lauded his battle-cruisers: '[Their behaviour] … is specially deserving of the highest praise; crippled in the use of their guns by their numerous casualties, some of them badly damaged, obeying the given signal "at the enemy", they dashed recklessly to the attack'.¹¹⁴

In twenty-five minutes from 19:05 to 19:30, the Germans had taken thirty-seven hits;† the British had taken just two, both on *Colossus*, from *Seydlitz*. Injuries and fatalities among Grand Fleet sailors were miraculously light: there were five wounded on *Colossus* and two dead on *Marlborough*. Over half of the thirty-seven hits on the Germans had come from the guns of five British ships: *Revenge, Royal Oak, Colossus, Barham* and *Valiant*. None had come from Beatty's ships. The idea later put about that the Grand Fleet had been barely engaged, the proof being the light casualties suffered, is not borne out by these engagements, which very nearly destroyed three of Germany's proudest battle-cruisers in the space of a half-hour: Jellicoe's sailors were, understandably, happy that he had not needlessly risked their lives.

After the war, the myth that the Grand Fleet had never really been engaged reared its ugly head early. Admiral Brock (who had been brought over to the Admiralty from the Battle Cruiser Fleet by Beatty as his chief of staff) said that he thought that the Harper record gave the impression that the British came off distinctly worse at Jutland than the Germans:

It does convey to me the impression that not only was a great battle fought between the British and German fleets, but it was one in which we got the

---

† 'Jellicoe's battle fleet and Evan-Thomas's 5th Battle Squadron had scored an estimated thirty-seven direct hits on Scheer's battleships and Hipper battle-cruisers, the majority with 13.5- and 15-inch shells. Beatty's ships had fired at the German battle-cruisers in the latter part of the action, but without any result … *Revenge, Royal Oak, Colossus, Barham* and *Valiant* … registered over half of the thirty-seven hits between them. The only German ship to register any hits during this phase was the *Seydlitz*' (Yates, p175).

worst of it. Neither of these impressions is correct; a great battle was not fought, the opposing battle fleets never really came into action, and far from getting the worst of it, the direct result of the day's fighting was to drive the German fleet ignominiously into its ports.[115]

The fact that there were light casualties on the battleships was now even used as evidence of the minimal role that Jellicoe had played. Temple Patterson highlighted the aggressive and biased style of writing in the *Naval Staff Appreciation*: 'The battle fleet which had put to sea full of hope and ardour, superior to the foe in numbers and gun-power, at least his equal in discipline, individual skill and courage, returned home with two killed and five wounded. It had never seriously been in action.'[116]

Beatty insisted on adding his own wording. On 21 June 1920 at an Admiralty meeting, significant text changes to the wording of the Harper record were discussed. Here Beatty suggested adding a foreword that echoed Brock's earlier sentiments. The wording was a very deliberate attempt to play down any role that the Grand Fleet might have played:

> [This] narrative of events … shows that the enemy's advanced forces were reinforced by their main fleet some hours before the British fleet was able to reach the scene of the action. During this period, therefore, the British were in greatly inferior force. *On hearing of the approach of the British main fleet the Germans avoided further action and returned to base* [my italics].[117]

It was in many ways extraordinary that Beatty acted as judge and jury of his own actions four years earlier. Jellicoe's position had always been that there should be no blurring of the lines, that mixing these roles should be avoided at all costs – the temptation to write your own history in its best light is always too great.

Now it is the Grand Fleet that turns away

Scheer still had significant destroyer resources at his disposal: six flotillas with around 224 torpedoes.[118] He had started the day with sixty-one destroyers and had most of these still intact (save for the early losses of *V.4, V.27, V.29* and *V.48*).

Such an attack covering a German withdrawal was what Jellicoe had always expected and, because he had fully calculated its potential risk, he was fearful of its potential to wreak havoc on his dreadnought line. In fact, it was clear that Jellicoe had over-estimated the numbers. He had assumed there would be seventy-eight destroyers at sea and thought that if that fully half of them would mount six torpedo tubes apiece they would, if fired at a line of ships simultaneously, be expected to have a 40 per cent chance of a successful hit.* Those were pretty high odds when so many British lives were at risk.

But the added numbers actually probably did not make that much difference. A speeding torpedo in the water was a huge threat to a lumbering dreadnought whichever way you looked at it. The standard German 19.7in torpedoes carried a large, 440lb hexanite charge and, like British torpedoes, were fast – the latest G7 model was capable of 35 knots at around 5,500yds (5,000m). They were also numerous – German destroyers at Jutland mounted 326 tubes.[119] What they were not, which Jellicoe was wrongly informed about, was wake-less. The telltale bubble line would still give its position away.

Scheer signalled his flotilla commanders his intentions: use these remaining elements and throw these fast forces into a last manoeuvre that would allow the main battle fleet elements to get away. That he would do so was not a surprise to Jellicoe. The timing was. For what happened was that the attacks were initiated before Scheer came to his own decision. From the bridge of the *Iron Duke*, destroyer groups could already be seen gathering around *Regensburg* at 19:12 (*Rostock*, the other light cruiser flotilla leader, was not visible).[120]

Heinrich and Michelsen reacted immediately to Scheer's signal because at least one of the two, Heinrich, had already started the actions that would turn out to be fundamental for the eventual escape of the German fleet.

Kommodore Heinrich's 6th and 9th Flotillas had come back from the attack on the 3rd BCS, the 2nd from the attacks on *Canterbury* and was regrouping around the *Regensburg*. He was missing quite a large number of his boats. *V.45* and *G.37* from the 12th Flotilla had been taken by Michelsen to protect *Lützow* and three other boats (*V.69*, *V.46* and *S.50*) had stayed with 2nd Flotilla (which had not been sent the attack orders).† He was left with four boats from the 6th Flotilla – *G.41*, the leader, *V.44*, *V.86* and *V.87*. The 9th had already lost *V.27* and *V.29* in the afternoon actions so was left with nine boats: thirteen in total.

For Kommodore Michelsen, it was a similar picture. The 3rd Flotilla was back with *Rostock* after the attempt to rescue crew from the sinking *Wiesbaden*, but *S.54* and *G.42* had not yet come back. The flotilla was only four boats strong and the group was now well out to the starboard of the 3rd Squadron. So, between the three immediate attacking flotillas (the 6th, 9th and 3rd) there was only a total of seventeen boats.

---

* Irving calculated that 50 per cent of seventy-eight destroyers with six torpedoes apiece would mean a total of 239 launches. To reduce the 40 per cent probability of a hit, Jellicoe, in Irving's words, 'preferred to manoeuvre his line by subdivisions of two ships thereby vastly increasing the ratio of water-space to ship-target and thus reducing the experts' estimated assessment of 40 per cent obtainable hits to rather less than 2 per cent' (Irving, pp166–8).

† Frost, p367, 'It is a curious fact that there is on record no signal ordering Flotilla II to attack'.

The attack would eventually be launched in waves from behind the curtain of smoke that had been laid as a protective screen around *Lützow*. The smoke masked what they were up to, but the wave attack was odd. It might have been better to overwhelm the British line and concentrate the release of a devastating fan of torpedoes simultaneously to reduce the odds for the British. It stems from the fact that Heinrich was acting independently of Scheer and had anticipated the latter's orders by around six minutes.* His independent actions 'contributed largely to saving the High Seas Fleet from very serious losses'.[121]

Heinrich's first attack was launched at 19:15 by the thirteen boats out of the greatly reduced combined strength of the 6th and 9th Flotillas. As soon as they broke through the smoke screen it got rough and *G.41* was hit by a 6in shell around 7,000yds (6,400m) distance from the British line. The forecastle exploded and two officers and ratings were killed but the boat's severely wounded torpedo officer, Leutnant Wagner, still managed to launch two torpedoes. Next hit was *G.86*: there was carnage after a heavy calibre shell hit her bow around 19:25. Nine men and the captain, Korvettenkapitän Grimm, were seriously wounded and the radio room completely destroyed. From the front of the V formation, *G.41*'s commander, Fregattenkapitän Max Schultz,† ordered a launch at around 7,500yds as the attackers turned and sped off, under long-range fire from the guns of the 4th LCS. Between 19:22 and 19:24, eleven tubes hissed, delivered their torpedoes into the water and all got away, including *G.86* and *G.41*, even if the former's speed had been cut to 25 knots (*G.41*'s even more).

Right behind Schultz came the 9th Flotilla led by Fregattenkapitän Goehle on *V.28*. The flotilla came in some way under the protection of 6th Flotilla's smokescreen, but it then seemed that the entire firepower of the British line had been switched from the damaged German battle-cruisers to the real threat of the attacking boats. *V.28* was damaged by a direct hit from British secondary armament fire holing her bow at the waterline. Every boat managed to launch – eighteen torpedoes between 19:26 and 19:28 and another two around 19:30 (calculated from the time they passed through the British line). From around 7,000yds, twenty torpedoes streaked towards the British line. Three only managed a one-torpedo launch (*V.28*, *S.51* and *S.36*), but *S.51* got off two and the remainder three apiece. They were not as lucky as the 6th Flotilla had been.

---

* Scheer's orders were for the battle-cruisers to attack the British line (at 19:13) followed by the 19:21 orders for the torpedo boats to do the same. Heinrich had already left at 19:15 with the thirteen boats of the 6th and 9th Flotillas.

† Max Schultz, who died later in January 1917, had known John Jellicoe in China during the Boxer Revolution. In fact, I was told a lovely story by his grandson, Jürgen Schultz-Siemens. Apparently Max had not eaten anything for two days, other than some sardines. He and Jellicoe ended up sharing what Jellicoe had – two eggs. They became friends and, with their wives, spent time together at the Kiel Week Regatta in 1910.

Korvettenkapitän Ihn's *S.35* (which also had on board the rescued crew from *V.29*), was heavily hit and sank when she split into two. *S.51* got hit at 19:30, putting her boiler and steering engine out of action. Both *V.58* and *S.51* got back, limping, *V.58* at a dangerously vulnerable 17 knots.

In total, Heinrich's independently launched attack managed to get thirty-one torpedoes through to the Grand Fleet battle line, mostly concentrated around the ships of the 6th Division (*Marlborough*, *Revenge*, *Hercules* and *Agincourt*). His boats had braved a hail of fire to do so. Of the thirteen boats, one was sunk and four badly hit.

The British line had no other choice now, but to concentrate on the immediate destroyer threat. Heavy secondary, and then primary, fire had been opened up as the boats came within range running up the line. At 19:15 *Royal Oak* had opened up; two minutes later *Agincourt*, *Marlborough*, *Temeraire* and *Vanguard*. The same group – four torpedo boats – were spotted from *Iron Duke* approaching from 40 degrees before the starboard beam at around 19:20. Spotting became increasingly difficult for the British gunners. Between 19:17 and 19:25 the German smoke started to drift across the waters in front of the British fleet. *Iron Duke* opened secondary fire at 19:24 at a range of around 10,000yds (9,100m) and within four salvos registered a hit, and then saw one of the destroyers sinking after she had been hit another three times.[122]

Jellicoe had already decided two years prior what his overall tactic would be: to turn away. At 19:21 he felt the moment had come. At 7,500yds he felt that Heinrich's torpedo boats were in their optimal firing position. Now he gave the order.

He was criticised for the basis of the order. Surprisingly, Frost put the blame fairly and squarely with the Admiralty: 'If that was not what the situation demanded, the fault lies with the Admiralty not with Jellicoe. If the Admiralty desired to carry on a Nelsonian plan of campaign, it should have relieved Jellicoe upon the receipt of his letter on October 30th, 1914.'[123] Where Frost is damning was on Jellicoe's handling of the manoeuvre: 'In that confusing tactical situation, Jellicoe was well served by his division commanders. They brought the battle line into order despite his confusing and conflicting signals.'[124] He had slowed the battle line to 15 knots at 19:20, after his series of orders from 19:12 reallocating positions had clearly created confusion.

At 19:22 Jellicoe had signalled Le Mesurier's 4th Light Cruiser Squadron to 'proceed with the utmost speed and attack the enemy's torpedo vessels', but initially their fire was not that effective as they were not yet in the best position. When they went to meet Heinrich's first attacks, they were 9,000yds (8,200m) off, but aboard *Calliope*, the squadron's leader, Commodore Le Mesurier, was himself nearly caught by torpedoes. Four of them passed right beside his ship.

Why Jellicoe had to resort to signalling this order does raise a question: why did Le Mesurier even need to be told? It was curious that the Grand Fleet did not have an amply prepared destroyer and light cruiser screen out on the engaged side. Especially after seeing the proximity of the destroyer groups at 19:12. It was also, but this can only really be seen in retrospect, that at the times of the first launches, the Grand Fleet was actually turning towards the threat by turning west 3 points and only then, four minutes later, resuming a southern course. This was the nature of the invisible threat that torpedo attack under these conditions represented.

Irving concluded: 'That the battle fleet should have been left to its own gun-fire and manoeuvring capacity to defend itself against these last two attacks is quite incomprehensible'.[125] Maybe here was a more telling indictment of Jellicoe: that he had left his engaged side too open?

Eight minutes after Heinrich had initiated the decisive destroyer action, at 19:23 came a third wave. This one was made up of the five remaining boats from the 3rd Flotilla led by Fregattenkapitän Wilhelm Hollmann's boat, the Schichau-type S.53. The conditions were becoming very difficult indeed. The mixture of drifting chemical smoke, the mass of shell splash and the sombre, shifting North Sea fog banks all made for almost minimum visibility. This was going to be a lightning fast game, a blindman's bluff, except that it was not even dark yet. The flotilla had been even further north than either the 6th or 9th Flotilla attacks, so maybe it was not so surprising that the targets were not there. The only boat that was in the end able to discern any real shapes on the British line was Korvettenkapitän Karlowa's S.54. His boat had been lagging behind the others by around 1,000yds, but had passed the rest of the group as they launched and turned and had ventured far deeper to the east. Nevertheless, it was still almost 10,000yds off when she fired her tubes at 19:45. The group was then, in turn, hunted by British destroyers from Stirling's 12th Destroyer Flotilla. Additional chemical smoke billowed out in their wake as they tried to lose their pursuers. One of the German torpedo boats, G.88, even tried unsuc-cessfully to torpedo them.[126]

The 5th and 7th Flotilla attacks were, in Groos's opinion, 'more difficult'. Koch thought that he was too far away (they had been around five miles down the line protecting the 2nd Squadron) and decided to hold his position. So he kept his 7th Flotilla stationed off the 2nd Squadron's port bow to maintain the protective shield. Oskar Heinecke, however, pulled the 5th Flotilla back to Rostock when Scheer's attack signal came through and prepared his group's attack. He started heading east, leading the flotilla from G.11, but by the time he was in position it was already 19:50 and, like Hollman, he could not find any capital ship targets and did not want to waste his torpedoes. After two minutes he headed back.

The 2nd Flotilla attack was assembled, set in motion, but was never con-summated. With Schuur's *B.98* as the leader, the ten-destroyer group would have been a powerful force.[127] They had been following the 6th Half-Flotilla (3rd Flotilla) through the German line, when their view of the British line was completely obscured. Ironically, it was their own force's smoke that was caus-ing the problems.

Back on *Regensburg* Kommodore Heinrich now decided that the attacks were not going to achieve anything more. The critical objective – taking British pressure off the main battle line – had been achieved. The signal 'Follow the leader' was hoisted and brought in any destroyers which had not made the run. With the signal he was calling back thirteen boats (ten from the 2nd Flotilla and the three from the 6th Half-Flotilla) which had been carrying sixty-three torpedoes. The British were lucky.

Fire from the British line had significantly diminished, so he had concluded that Jellicoe must also have turned away. So not only had the gunnery pressure on the main German battle line and the battle-cruisers been much alleviated by his anticipated execution of Scheer's tactics, but he had also bought precious time for the night.

Reginald Bacon suggested that the approach of the day, the dividing point between the two options of either 'turn-away' or 'turn-towards', was to choose the former method 'if the torpedoes were fired from any position between abeam and half-way to right-ahead'.[128] Complying with these pre-agreed op-tions, Jellicoe at 19:22 ordered the Grand Fleet to turn away from the threat by going 2 points to port. Three minutes later a further 2-point turn-away was ordered, making 44 degrees in total.

It was standard procedure in the French, Italian, American and, indeed, German fleets to turn away in the face of a massed torpedo attack. It was also something that Jellicoe had said he would do in these precise circumstances and that the Lords of the Admiralty had approved, but the seemingly indecisive outcome of Jutland made this turn-away very controversial.

Jellicoe said that this supposedly new manoeuvre had actually been prac-tised by the Grand Fleet when the war broke out. He felt that in following the tactic he gained a number of critical advantages and avoided another threat. By turning away he altered the silhouettes from that of a full, side-on battleship to the beam of a battleship; from an object that was, taking *Malaya* as an exam-ple, 646ft long if presented broadside to a reduced silhouette of 95ft stern or bow on. Furthermore, the torpedo's range was around 10,000yds (9,100m). If a battleship could use its full speed to get to that critical 10,000yd line before a strike, it had outrun it. A turn-towards gave the same advantage of silhouette, but increased the rate of closure and introduced a further unknown.[129]

Jellicoe's assumption had always been that the Germans would do what the Japanese at Tsushima had already demonstrated: to sow mines in the track of an oncoming enemy.[130] He was – as he knew would happen – severely criticised. By the Second World War, the more usually adopted response to a torpedo launch was to turn towards its source, always diminishing the target profile, but 'combing the tracks' rather than outrunning them. In his 1932 appreciation, Jellicoe wrote confidently that he had taken the right decision: 'Experience since the war has shown what a large number of hits may be scored by torpedoes on ships that turn towards or hold their course. These experiences have not been published but they are known to me.'[131]

Jellicoe's position – and, it must be said, Beatty's too, if one looks more closely at his 1917 revised post-Jutland GFBOs – was usually more in favour of the turn-away. This was the case for quite a number of commanders at the time.[132] Beatty stressed that he would pursue but stay outside the effective range of 10,000–12,000yds (9,100–10,000m). At the strategic level, Jellicoe's priority was clear: the continued domination of the North Sea. He did not intend to put that objective at risk – in any form.

Quite a number of historians take a different view. Admiral Lord West, for example, feels that the turn-away 'was a lost opportunity ... [had Jellicoe] turned towards the Germans he would not have lost them', adding that 'he could afford to lose ships'.[133] In another series (on Admiral Cunningham and the Mediterranean war), West continues the same thought:

> This was all very different from the First World War. Then, too many senior commanders seemed risk-averse, reluctant to attack for fear of losing the battle, losing ships, losing men. Twenty years later, many junior commanders from the First World War, men like Cunningham himself ... had risen to the top and wanted, and demanded a much more Nelsonian approach: 'Engage the enemy more closely'. Without the shock of the First World War it is hard to imagine the Royal Navy achieving the same dramatic success as in the Second.

The point that I believe is missed is that it was not a battle that was at stake. It was the war. However, the shock of the First World War was definitely needed to shake the Navy out of its reverie. Despite Fisher's energetic reforms, the Navy was a deeply stagnated institution.

Many historians – Andrew Gordon or Eric Grove would be just two examples – feel that Jellicoe's decision was the one, albeit unforgivable, error of the day, one born from timidity; a deep-seated fear of the destructive power of the torpedo on a dreadnought.

I hold a different point of view. If Jellicoe had stated that this is what he would do, if his reasons for doing so were to protect the critical dreadnought balance between the two opposing fleets and if having done so he achieved this objective, then surely those who approved such a premeditated and calculated manoeuvre (including Churchill) share just as much 'blame' if the desired outcome shifts to keeping contact?

Of the thirty-one torpedoes fired, twenty-one still reached the British line and were spotted at 19:33.[134] *Marlborough*, previously hit, spotted three and avoided them. She first steered to port and then starboard, and they passed ahead and astern of her. *Revenge* turned to port and also avoided two torpedoes, the first passing 10yds (9m) from the bow, the second passing 20yds from her stern. *Hercules* and *Agincourt* also spotted torpedoes and broke out of the line with a 60-degree turn. *Agincourt* had one torpedo pass either side of her. One torpedo ran between *Iron Duke* and *Thunderer*. One passed close to *Collingwood*'s stern. One followed *Neptune*'s track. Two torpedoes narrowly missed *Valiant*, 'one about 20 yards ahead and one about five yards astern'.[135]

It seemed that the turn-away had been executed just in time. 'It was only sharp lookouts, skilful manoeuvring and a measure of good fortune, however, which preserved several ships from damage'.[136] Had a turn-towards been made, the time taken would have been considerably longer and might have presented an even more dangerous battleship silhouette to the attacking German torpedo boats. The Dewar brothers' criticism of Jellicoe's turn-away was based on massive hindsight and went largely in the face of accepted naval policy of the day. Marder pithily commented that 'Crystal balls, alas, are not standard issue in the Royal Navy'.[137] Nevertheless, a chapter heading from Carlyon Bellairs's book, *The Battle of Jutland*, sarcastically jibed: 'Eleven Destroyers Dismiss 27 Battleships'.

An emotional, perhaps subconscious desire to win a crushing annihilation rather than maintain a strategic supremacy may just cloud our collective appraisal of Jellicoe's reasoning. If 'leaving something to chance' had resulted in heavy dreadnought losses and he had still not been able to maintain contact, what would the verdict be now? Should not faster fleet elements be used for maintaining contact, in any case, not behemoth battleships?

Did Jellicoe make the right decision? Undoubtedly yes: 'though this manoeuvre has been hotly debated ever since, most modern writers see it as correct, even inevitable'.[138]

For Kemp, Jutland was 'the story, largely, of a new and still untried weapon', that 'the new weapon, in its then state of development, had failed'.[139] The German attacks were very well-executed.

These two salvos were fired almost simultaneously, from good target angles and at firing ranges within effective range. The spread, as measured from a single firing destroyer, was approximately thirteen and a half degrees in one case and nine degrees in the other. About 42 per cent of the torpedoes fired passed through the target formation, but unfortunately the density was not enough. It averaged about one torpedo to 500 yards in one salvo and one to 200 yards in the other.[140]

The turn-away seemed to have been at 90 degrees to the strike origin but on a lesser, and indeed decreasing, angle to the van of the German fleet, meaning that the weight of gunnery – should there have been an opportunity to fire a broadside – would not have been totally compromised.

The Torpedo at Jutland

According to Farquharson-Roberts, Jutland 'showed that the torpedo had been over-rated as a weapon. Before the war', he continued, 'it was seen as a battle winner; indeed there were some, such as the French *jeune école*, who felt it was all a navy needed.'[141] The torpedo was one of the newest of the untried weapons. Though it had 'largely failed to live up to its reputation, at any rate against heavily armoured ships',[142] the weapon should not be minimised in hindsight. It was a very real perceived threat at the time. It is clear that weapons systems can only be best exploited once sufficient knowledge has been garnered from experience in battle and that was lacking. The course of the battle was heavily influenced by the weapon: 'Jellicoe had declined a night action largely through the fear of a torpedo attack on his fleet at night, though confident that he would still meet the enemy in daylight on 1 June. Scheer, on the other hand, had braved torpedo attack through fear of having to meet Jellicoe's guns in daylight.'[143]

Its development was rapid: effective range increased from 5,000yds (4,500m) (1906) to 10,000 (1914) and around 17,000yds (15,500m) in 1917. Nevertheless, the successful threat of the torpedo lay in a well-spread launch. Bacon calculated that for a typical line of dreadnoughts (say twenty-four, the length at Jutland), a ship target area of 4,800yds (4,400m) with 6,900 non-target yards (6,300m) would result (using 300yds (275m) to be the non-target space between ship). The chance of a single torpedo hitting a target ship would be 40 per cent. But the density of the torpedo launch was also important.

At Jutland there were 826 'tubed' torpedoes (of which 426 were German). Looking at destroyer actions alone (the most important torpedo activity), the Germans fired more torpedoes (89, or 56 per cent of the day's total). They also fired them in different circumstances, by far the largest proportion in daylight hours rather than during the night action. The British torpedo performance later came in for criticism by the Germans, who said that they often fired at too fine an angle, making a turn easier as well as while still closing, and that the attacks were not organised as flotillas to create a 'fan', rather they were usually individual, unco-ordinated attacks.

The performance of the torpedoes on both sides was fairly similar. The standard

British torpedo at Jutland was the Mark II, with a hitting charge of 400lbs of amatol. The latest version available at Jutland could, on a high-speed setting of 45 knots, travel its 4,200yds (3,800m) effective range in just three minutes (1,500yds a minute). Its medium 29 knots setting would let it travel 10,750yds (9,800m) at a slightly cut-down speed of 1,000yds a minute. Battleships and battle-cruisers were actually equipped with a slower speed 18-knot version that could reach up to 17,000yds but at 600yds (550m) a minute they would strike only after having run for 28 minutes.

German torpedoes were fairly similar in capability, although Jellicoe was, mistakenly, under the impression that there had been great advances made on hiding the bubble track. The Germans had a larger 23.6in version with a 540lb hexanite charge but none scored any hits in the battle. The smaller 19.7in G7 version carried a smaller 440lb charge and was the staple torpedo. At its 35- and 28-knot settings it was slightly slower to its maximum ranges than the Mark II: 5,450yds in 4.7 minutes and 10,950 in 11.8.

The British escaped with only *Marlborough* suffering any torpedo damage. The British hit on *Seydlitz* could have been decisive had she been re-engaged in the night action. The number of close-run torpedo misses was alarmingly high and maybe, had the Germans not used up so many when it was still light enough to spot tracks, the results would have been different. Six months after Jutland, at the Horns Reef, the British submarine *J.1* achieved four hits on a four-torpedo spread. Three hit *Großer Kurfürst* aft and the last one *Kronprinz* on the bow. Jellicoe's predictions about the lethal potential of the submarine came true, although this time it was to the benefit of the British.

See Table 'Torpedo Hits at Jutland' in Chapter 13.

Scheer's attempts to charge the British line were costly: there was severe damage to the battle-cruisers and five destroyers were lost. But the destroyer actions, forcing Jellicoe to turn away, had gained Scheer critical miles from the Grand Fleet and used up the last fighting daylight. Many see this as Scheer's genius as a commander:

It was not due to any merit of Jellicoe that the 'crossing of the T' position was attained. It was a matter of chance due to low visibility which was entirely in favour of the British ... Scheer proved himself a master of the situation. His confidence in the discipline and navigational skill of the fleet justified him in repeatedly turning as he liked in the midst of the heaviest of enemy fire. By his repeated rushes at the British line he determined the course of action and his achievement was 'glorious enough to place him among the greatest commanders of all time'.[144]

Macintyre goes on to say:

Thus ... the British Commander-in-Chief, with the enemy fleet tactically beaten and in flight, relinquished the possibility of crowning the success his previous tactics had given him. Now the two fleets were opening out at a speed of 20 knots from each other with sunset half an hour away, the chances of a further full-scale clash were drifting away with every second. Twenty-eight torpedoes and a fixed determination to take no chances with his battle fleet had robbed Jellicoe of decisive victory.[145]

Jellicoe did not know that Scheer had himself turned away; many of his subordinate commanders did and Jellicoe was ill-served by their not keeping him as fully informed as possible.[146]

On *Friedrich der Große* reports started to come in about how badly the fleet had been hit. Heavy damage to *Markgraf*'s boiler room would reduce the fleet's speed. Conditions for the sailors were appalling:

> Feverish labour was going on in the damaged ships – burned and torn human bodies were being lifted on to stretchers and carried below to the over-taxed surgeons and their assistants in ill-ventilated battle-dressing stations. Among the wounded seamen the suffering from picric-acid burns was heartrending; the blind, the scalded, the mangled lay in agony. Nauseating smells penetrated the close, stuffy decks – the sweetish reek of blood, the strangling stink of cordite, of burned paint and linoleum and electrical insulation, the stifling hazy atmosphere of charred corpses.[147]

Scheer was not in a good position. Jellicoe was. 'None of [Scheer's] purposes had been accomplished. He had not rescued the *Wiesbaden*. He had sunk no enemy battleships. He had not surprised Jellicoe, nor affected the latter's plans for the night. He had not gained the easterly position, with its advantages of visibility and its open line of retreat.'[148] Scheer's own flag lieutenant, Ernst von Weizsäcker, described the atmosphere of almost panic on the German flagship: 'Scheer had but the foggiest idea of what was happening during the action and … his movements were not in the least dictated by superior tactical considerations. On the contrary, he had only two definite ideas: to protect the *Wiesbaden* and, when that was no good, to disentangle himself and go home'.[149]

British scouting after the turn-away

Jellicoe was blind again. He could only guess where his adversary was. This was the downside. He had his forces intact but he had lost contact with his foe. Holding off the German flotilla attacks, as Jellicoe had outlined in his GFBOs, and not scouting was the destroyer flotillas' primary function.[150] Only in bad weather, or when the fleet was turning away, would Jellicoe not just permit, but dictate, that the roles be reversed and that attacking the German battle fleet (that implicitly supported scouting) be enforced.

What of his scouting elements? Napier (3rd LCS) had kept his station. Alexander-Sinclair (1st LCS) was busy trying to re-form his squadron on the battle-cruisers, and Le Mesurier (4th LCS) was still heavily engaged in holding off the remnants of the three German torpedo attacks.

Our first chance came soon after 7.30 when they slipped some destroyers at our leading battle squadron: we got two German TBDs on that occasion. And luckily all their torpedoes missed us (four close to *Calliope*) – our second little excursion came soon after eight o/c: another German destroyer attack. This time I only took out three ships: we pushed the German destroyers back, when suddenly, out of the haze, loomed large the High Seas Fleet about four miles off: we held on a bit and fired torpedoes at 'em – *Calliope* had good ground for thinking that hers got home – and then ran billy-oh for shelter – with at least three big battleships plunking at us. A most uncomfortable five or 10 minutes, as their shooting was 100 A1 – we were hit, in *Calliope*, three times, and lost, I am sorry to say, close on a dozen killed and many wounded.[151]

Goodenough's reconnaissance skills now failed him. At 19:45 he misleadingly reported that the enemy had detached a number of ships that were heading northwest. 'Urgent. Enemy has detached unknown number of ships, type unknown, which are steering NW at 19:15. My position Lat. 56° 50' N, Long. 6° 27' E.' The reason for this erroneous message from Goodenough, who, up to now, had been notable for his brilliant, timely and accurate scouting reports, is a mystery.[152]

The Grand Fleet had been steering 135 degrees off Scheer's course to the west. At 19:35 Jellicoe, believing that the Germans were six or seven miles to his west behind the shroud of mist and fog, ordered another 5 points to starboard, south-by-west. 'Alter course leading ships together rest in succession to S by W.'

At 19:45 Jellicoe recalled *Castor* (leading the 11th Destroyer flotilla) and he turned his force, by divisions, another 3 points to starboard (southwest).[153] Sunset was twenty-five minutes away. Beatty was around six miles ahead of *King George V* in the van of the Grand Fleet. He was frustrated by the turn-away and wanted to find a way to pursue the High Seas Fleet – with the eight dreadnoughts of Admiral Jerram's 2nd Battle Squadron at the head of the Grand Fleet.

At 19:47, dispatched at 19:50, Beatty issued what was to become a much-quoted (and much-criticised) signal: 'Submit van of battleships follow van of battle-cruisers. We can then cut off whole of enemy's battle fleet.'[154] The message was perplexing to Jellicoe but 'coming from his chief subordinate commander, it demanded consideration.'[155] Why the 'whole of' the enemy fleet 'cut off'? From where? The Germans were already cut off from their bases. Where exactly was

Beatty, anyway? Jellicoe later termed Beatty's signal as 'bordering on insubordination'. It seemed now that when Jellicoe read it, it was Jellicoe who was actually closer to the High Seas Fleet than the signal implied.

Many still see this as symbolising Beatty's Nelsonian spirit. However, he may not have been able to see the enemy. His own battle-cruisers were, at the time, 'at least thirteen miles from the nearest enemy battle-cruiser and more than seventeen miles from any of Scheer's battleships – much too far away to be in visual contact with the German fleet'.[156] There is, as is always the case, disagreement on the relative distances. The maps, done for the official German Groos narrative, put the distances closer, but with Beatty still only slightly nearer than the 1st Division of the British battle fleet.[157] Five minutes before, he had said that he had lost sight of the Germans: 'The destroyers at the head of the enemy line emitted volumes of grey smoke covering their capital ships as well as with a pall, under cover of which they undoubtedly turned away, and at 7.45 pm we lost sight of them'.[158]

For some reason Jellicoe submitted to Beatty's signal and signalled Jerram at 20:01: 'Follow our battle-cruisers'. Jerram received Jellicoe's signal but he, too, could see neither Beatty nor the Germans. He consequently turned south. It was an impossible order to follow and it is not to Jellicoe's credit that he issued the order given the total lack of clarity of the situation and Beatty's signalling ambiguity, as well as Jellicoe's general distrust of Beatty's judgement on issues like this. The question remains: could Beatty have maintained visual contact at this point? The Battle Cruiser Fleet was far from the Germans and with visibility being what it was, it is doubtful that he could have.

At 19:40 Beatty had given Jellicoe an indication of the Germans' whereabouts, the information that he needed, saying that the German battle fleet – its leading elements – 'bears from me north-west-by-west distant 10 to 11 miles'.[159] It was now, as Beatty stated in his dispatches, that he 'lost sight' of the enemy. At 19:59, Beatty's second signal arrived, this one by searchlight – so there was less of a time lag – saying that the course of the leading battleship was 'south-west'. Unfortunately, it was a confused report: Beatty was not only thirteen miles from the nearest enemy ships; the battleship that had been spotted was in reality a battle-cruiser. Jellicoe realised that he was too far from the enemy fleet. He thus ordered the Grand Fleet, at the time cruising at 17 knots on a course change of 4 points by divisions, to a course that was directly westerly. It was 20:00. *Lion* was out of sight of *Iron Duke*, making it difficult for Jellicoe to get an exact position. No course was referred to either. Jellicoe assumed that Beatty was six miles ahead of his van and slightly to the southwest. John Brooks points to this episode as yet another case where Beatty, keen to avoid any criticism of his own actions, shifts the blame to the commander-in-chief:

It is unlikely to be a coincidence that at 08:00, Jellicoe ordered the guides of all his divisions to turn west. This put the battleships on a steeper approach than the battle-cruisers. At the same time, Beatty ordered his light cruisers to sweep to the Westward. But he did not order the battle-cruisers to follow until about 18:15. Almost immediately, they sighted German ships and, for the last time, opened fire with their heavy guns. More hits were made on the battered 1st Scouting Group and even on a pre-dreadnought, *Schleswig-Holstein*. Unable to see their assailants, the BCF did not follow them but also followed a course SW. Meanwhile Jellicoe's battleships had not sighted the enemy and, at 20:20, also turned SW ... Beatty's course (SW, then WSW) and speed (only 18 knots) were too cautious to close an enemy last seen some ten miles NW by W on a course SW. It was Jellicoe who turned boldly West at 20:00, even though, as we now know, he risked the Germans crossing the 'T's' of his columns ... Yet again, the criticism of Jellicoe, for not responding immediately to the 'Follow me' signal, has distracted attention away from Beatty's own failure to keep in contact with the enemy.[160]

Scheer decided to steer for the Horns Reef. He reversed the German line with the old pre-dreadnoughts becoming the van, then the 1st and 3rd Squadrons at the rear. Goodenough's second report arrived at the same time. For Scheer, the real damage had been confined to three ships: *Markgraf*, *Großer Kurfürst* and *König*. The second had shipped 800 tons of water, *König* close to 1,000. But Scheer also had important information, a little more than Jellicoe had. He had heard from the crippled *Lützow*, through a message passed on at 19:49 that the British fleet's van – based on their earlier position – bore south-southeast at 20:02.[161]

Heading for the Horns Reef, Scheer knew that every four miles that he was pushed westward would add a further half-hour's steaming time to reach his goal. So at 19:52 he ordered his fleet to steer directly south at 16 knots. He positioned destroyers from the 2nd Flotilla and the 12th Half-Flotilla to take station around five miles to his east, to give early warning of a possible encounter with Jellicoe or Beatty. Ahead of the fleet were the cruisers of Bödicker's 2nd (with *Frankfurt*) and the 4th Scouting Groups. Along with *Frankfurt* sailed five light cruisers: *Stettin*, *München*, *Frauenlob*, *Stuttgart* and *Hamburg* under the command of Commodore Ludwig von Reuter on *Stettin*.

Beatty sent out scouting forces almost immediately after his battle-cruisers lost visual contact: 'Sweep the westward and locate the head of the enemy's line before dark'.[162] *Falmouth* and *Inconstant* ran southwestward to try to find the van of the German battle line, with a mile between each of the five ships of the 3rd Light Cruiser Squadron spread northeast to southwest. At 20:09

Falmouth spotted a group of enemy ships to the northwest and one minute later these were positively identified as the five German screening light cruisers that Scheer had sent ahead.[163]

Falmouth opened fire and was quickly supported by fire from Le Mesurier's 4th Light Cruiser Squadron to his north. The fire caused the enemy ships to swing back off to their starboard. Moments before, at 20:00 Goodenough on *Southampton* signalled Jellicoe confirming that the High Seas Fleet was heading west. Goodenough's feeling was that the Germans were doing this to break up and scatter. But while he was still fifteen miles to the northeast, Jellicoe felt that by heading south he would stand a better chance of cutting the Germans off from their goal, which he had assumed to be the Jade Basin rather than the Horns Reef.

Roughly ten minutes later, at 20:12 Beatty resighted the German battle-cruisers. They were about 10,000yds off and drifting in and out of visibility.* Beatty's ships opened fire at around 20:20. All four German battle-cruisers were hit hard, *Seydlitz* probably the hardest – twice by shells from *Princess Royal*, one of which hit the bridge, killing all and drenching the navigation charts in blood.

Hipper was about to board *Moltke*, which he had ordered to heave-to. A 12in shell landed nearby and the transfer of the flag was abruptly halted so that *Moltke* could get under way. *Lion* hit *Derfflinger* once, and reported her listing and turning away. Her last turret was inoperable. But at the rear neither *Tiger* nor *Indomitable* made any hits. Hipper was left with little choice. His ships sheered off westward and in doing so caused confusion with Mauve's pre-dreadnoughts in the van of the battleships. *Schleswig-Holstein*, *Pommern* and *Schlesien* were all damaged. If ever there was a time for strong and well-organised reconnaissance, it was now, but not even the Zeppelin (*L.14*) that had been cruising overhead could see much. The battle area below was completely hidden in the murkiness of the North Sea.

On *Castor*, James R P Hawksley, the overall commodore of the British destroyers, spotted smoke to the west and pushed forward to investigate, with eight boats from the 11th Destroyer Flotilla. Le Mesurier, with cruisers *Calliope*, *Comus* and *Constance*, followed. Very quickly they spotted twelve torpedo boats of the German 5th Flotilla and after chasing them to the west, Scheer's 3rd Battleship Squadron came into sight. *Calliope* fired off a torpedo at 7,000yds but, as described earlier, was badly damaged in the action, taking five hits and coming back with ten dead and twenty-three wounded.

---

* During this period, visibility played a critical role: according to Irving it was between 10,500 and 9,000yds in a north and south direction and 13,000–15,000yds to the west (Irving, p180). I saw this at first hand on the 2015 expedition with Innes McCartney. Visibility could close down to less than 2,000yds in minutes, while shifting around the compass could produce completely different ends of the spectrum in terms of visibility.

At 20:38 Jellicoe received some information from *Comus*: 'Enemy battle fleet bearing west'. This seemed to comply with what Goodenough had reported half an hour before, but it was still frustratingly light on information. When Jellicoe queried Napier as to the enemy position at around the same time (20:25) he received the same exasperatingly scanty reply: Napier gave no bearing, distance or course, and it was only at 20:46 that he made a report.

Daylight Scouting at Jutland

At Jutland, the British fought as two fleets, the Grand Fleet and the Battle Cruiser Fleet; the Germans as one. Hipper's battle-cruiser forces – appropriately named *Entdeckungsflotte*, or scouting groups – acted, first and foremost, as an extension of the High Seas Fleet, leading the way for, and communicating back vital information to, the main battle fleet. It has been said that Jellicoe was wary of too much use of WT, but his concerns were its use primarily prior to action being joined; it was too transparent and could give away too much information to the enemy. The implication of this, however, was that forces were possibly more bunched to keep within effective visual signalling distance and that limited the effectiveness of throwing out wide nets of scouting forces.

How well was Jellicoe supported by battlefield intelligence? In brief – with the exception of Commodore Goodenough (*Southampton*), whose performance was exemplary – appallingly. Beatty's updates, which were vital to Jellicoe, were minimal. Even after the battle Jellicoe was told of the loss of *Invincible* and *Queen Mary* at 11:00 on 1 June, but only when the question was repeatedly put to Beatty. Scheer, by contrast, had been told of these critical losses the night before around 20:00.

During the tense minutes leading up to the deployment, the battle-cruisers failed in their primary mission: they were bringing the enemy to Jellicoe, for sure, but not telling Jellicoe anything to aid his decisions. Beatty's first signal to Jellicoe (at 16:45) was wrong on the enemy disposition as well as location. Between 16:48 (when fire was first opened) and 17:00, Jellicoe received five reports of the whereabouts of the HSF: three were from Goodenough, though they all varied on the actual enemy position. The Admiralty's signal referring to a directional intercept at 16:09 was discarded as being outrun by events. Beatty's only signal was scrambled in transmission, and when Beatty finally closed with the Grand Fleet, he then lost sight of Scheer. At 18:01 Jellicoe signalled Beatty, asking for updates. The reply came back: 'Enemy battle-cruisers bearing south-east' (there was nothing about the enemy battle fleet). Finally, at 18:14 Beatty signalled to Jellicoe: 'Have sighted enemy's battle fleet bearing south-south-west'.

Jellicoe's decision to deploy to port was made in the space of two minutes with practically useless information from his key commander. That the dead reckoning was out by eleven miles – *Iron Duke*'s by four miles and *Lion*'s by seven – might suggest that almost any information coming through would be fairly misleading but the frustration in Jellicoe's final signals to Beatty was glaringly clear from their wording. The deployment was based on pure intellectual deduction, taken under extreme pressure, weighing up the assumed course and speed of the enemy, the

> setting sun's position in the west, wind direction, deployment time and Scheer's
> possible escape routes.
>
> On the other hand, it should be pointed out that Jellicoe was not uncritical of his
> own actions. He wrote (in his 1932 notes 'Errors at Jutland'), that he should have
> sent Commodore Le Mesurier ahead of the Grand Fleet when he was not getting the
> information that he needed.
>
> See also 'Lost Opportunities in the Night Action', p257.

There were a few patches of better visibility just before darkness. Even on
Iron Duke, an officer in B turret caught a glimpse of Scheer's 1st Squadron in
the distance at 20:25, while on *Orion* the German capital ships were momentarily spotted to the west. Beatty himself was also in action against Hipper's
battle-cruisers and similarly did not report until 20:40. It is interesting that his
later battle instructions made such a point of commanders on the spot reporting
back such intelligence – it was one of the major lessons of the day – but Beatty's information, passing through *Galatea*, did not reach *Iron Duke* until 21:04.

Two other of his ships – the light cruisers *Caroline* and *Royalist* – did spot
three battleships to their west at around 20:45, and Captain Ralph Crooke on
Caroline turned west to investigate. He immediately told Admiral Jerram that
he had seen *Westfalen*, but Jerram was concerned that they were Beatty's ships
and called *Caroline* back.[164] Crooke stood his ground and would not take no
for an answer. He signalled back for permission to open fire. 'If you are quite
sure, attack', was the reply.

Confirming what *Caroline* and *Royalist* thought, while they were launching
a torpedo they were heavily shelled by *Nassau* and *Westfalen*. The torpedo ran
true but too deep and passed harmlessly under *Westfalen*.[165] Incredibly, despite
everything, Jerram did nothing to back up *Caroline* and *Royalist*; he could have
lent supporting fire. Instead, when Jellicoe signalled the preparations for night
cruising, with 'staggering lack of initiative', Jerram led his squadron round to
comply.* There was enough light, Macintyre maintains, for 'deliberate shooting
for another fifteen minutes'.[166]

These – the lack of initiative, of inquisitiveness and of fighting spirit, and not
Jellicoe's turn-away, which more than likely saved quite a few of his dreadnoughts
from assured hits – were the last chances conceded by the British at Jutland.

---

* Sir Shane Leslie said that it was that single moment which caused Beatty to change his opinion
about Jerram. From then on Beatty had nothing but contempt. When Beatty later saw him in
Scapa, after the battle, he was stony cold. In Leslie's words, he 'markedly cut Jerram dead' when
he was attending a concert on *King George V*. He did not utter a single word to the other man. He
even maintained that Beatty asked Jellicoe to have Jerram court-martialled (Macintyre, p151). It
was certainly a failure to support strong battlefield intelligence with action, though the ensuing
darkness still came too quickly.

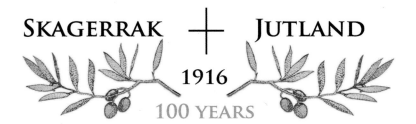

SKAGERRAK ✝ JUTLAND
1916
100 YEARS

The SMS *Lützow* memorial at the *Ehrenfriedhof* in Wilhelmshaven. (Author's photograph)

Admiral Sir John Jellicoe (later Earl Jellicoe of Scapa), commander of the Grand Fleet. Painting by Sir Arthur Stockdale Cope (1857–1949) in 1921. (Private collection)

Admiral Reinhard Scheer, commander of the German High Seas Fleet. (Private collection)

Vice Admiral Sir David Beatty (later Earl Beatty of the North Sea), commander of the Battle Cruiser Fleet. Painting by Sir Arthur Stockdale Cope (1857–1949) in 1921. (BHC2537 © National Maritime Museum, Greenwich, London)

Vice Admiral Franz (later Ritter Franz von) Hipper, commander of the German scouting forces. (Courtesy of Laboe Marine Memorial Collection)

Scapa Flow, the Grand Fleet's base in the remote but relatively safe Orkneys. In the foreground is the 12in-gunned dreadnought *Colossus*. (Courtesy of Martin Bourdillon)

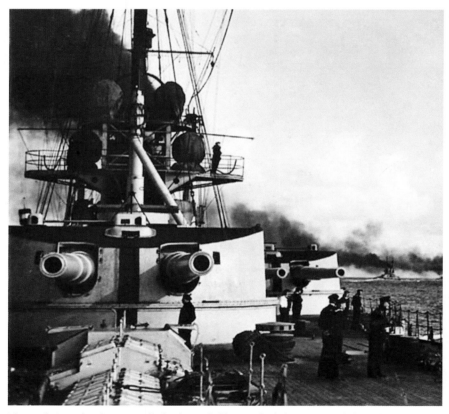

The High Seas Fleet leaving Wilhelmshaven led by *Friedrich der Grösse* and the 3rd Squadron, as seen from *Ostfriesland*. (Courtesy of the German Bundesarchiv)

The three *Lion*-class ships, known as the 'Splendid Cats', were the pride of Beatty's Battle Cruiser Fleet. (Private collection)

Warspite and *Malaya* on 31 May, around 14:00 GMT, seen from *Valiant*. The four 15in-gunned *Queen Elizabeth*-class ships of the 5th Battle Squadron attached to the Battle Cruiser Fleet should have given Beatty a decisive advantage over Hipper's 1st Scouting Group. (Courtesy of Martin Bourdillon)

Jellicoe's flagship, *Iron Duke*, opening fire at Jutland, painted by William L Wyllie (1851–1931). (Private collection)

Claus Bergen's (1885–1964) depiction of the 'crossing of the T', in Prof Arthur Marder's words, 'the greatest concentration of naval gunfire any fleet commander had ever faced.' (Courtesy of Laboe Naval Memorial Museum © 2016, ProLiterris, Zürich)

Powered by the revolutionary Parsons steam turbine, *Von der Tann*, the first German battle-cruiser, reached 24.75 knots during her speed trials. (Courtesy of Blohm und Voss, Hamburg)

The forward 11in SK L/45 guns of *Von der Tann*. British battle-cruisers were more heavily armed, and faster, but the German ships were better protected and could withstand heavy damage. (Courtesy of Blohm und Voss, Hamburg)

The German flag hoist for torpedo attack, the red pennant of the 'Stander-Z' by Willy Stöwer
(1864–1931). Flotilla torpedo attacks were thoroughly rehearsed by the German navy.
(Courtesy of Hamburg International Maritime Museum © 2016, ProLiterris, Zürich)

In Jellicoe's mind, the chief function of British destroyers was to fend off German torpedo-boat
attacks, and in an attempt to obtain a degree of control the flotillas were commanded from
larger 'leaders' like *Broke* seen here. However, during the confusion of the night actions on
1 June, *Broke* collided with *Sparrowhawk,* one of her own 4th Destroyer Flotilla.
(N03104 © National Maritime Museum, Greenwich, London)

The 935-ton destroyer *Spitfire* colliding with the 20,000-ton battleship *Nassau* in the early hours of 1 June. (Courtesy of Alan Bush)

The heavily damaged *Spitfire* entering the Tyne at 14:00 GMT on 2 June. (Courtesy of Alan Bush)

The battleship *Malaya* burying her dead at sea, 1 June. (Author's collection)

The German poet Johann Kinau (1880–1916), is better known under his nom de plume Gorch Fock. He died on the light cruiser *Wiesbaden*.

Repairing *Warspite*'s battle damage at Rosyth. Shown is a 12in shell hit beneath the after Y turret. (N16494 © National Maritime Museum, Greenwich, London)

A lone sailor stands silhouetted in the gaping shell hole on *Derfflinger*, one of the German ships most heavily damaged at Jutland. (Courtesy of the German Bundesarchiv)

Sir John Jellicoe
bidding farewell to
the Grand Fleet,
leaving to take up
the position of
First Sea Lord, 29
November 1916.
(Author's collection)

Sir Hugh Evan-
Thomas (*left*) with
Admiral Beatty
after being awarded
the KCB by King
George V using
Beatty's sword,
25 June 1917.
(Courtesy of
Martin Bourdillon)

John Jellicoe was laid to rest on 3 December 1935 in Nelson's shadow in the crypt of St Paul's. The procession passing Ludgate Hill. (Courtesy *Illustrated London News*)

On the news of Jellicoe's death, the flags of three nations' navies, including that of Hitler's Kriegsmarine, were lowered. (Author's collection)

10

David and Goliath:
Scheer's Escape

Night was falling. Even if Jellicoe was reasonably pleased with the situation – he did not yet know about the calamities of *Queen Mary* or *Indefatigable* – and felt that he had a good chance of keeping the High Seas Fleet caged in, he did not want to be drawn into a night action, partly because he did not think the British either well enough equipped or adequately trained for such, but also because of the very high degree of faulty identification of ships at night. Jellicoe put his trust in his destroyers alerting him if Scheer were to attempt to break through astern of the British battle fleet.[1]

Jellicoe's mind was made up. He would not go looking for a night action. In his words, it was 'far too fluky an affair' in these days of 'destroyers and long-range torpedoes'. He went on:

> The result of night actions between heavy ships must always be very largely
> a matter of chance, as there is little opportunity for skill on either side. Such
> an action must be fought at very close range, the decision depending on
> the course of events in the first few minutes … The greater efficiency of
> German searchlights at the time of the Jutland action, and the greater number
> of torpedo tubes fitted in enemy ships, combined with [the Germans']
> superiority in destroyers, would I knew give [them] the opportunity of
> scoring heavily at the commencement of such an action.[2]

Jellicoe felt that he would have lost the advantage if too much was left to chance. Most of his admirals agreed. The critical question before him was to decide in which direction to take the battle fleet. He estimated there to be four possible routes home open to the Germans.

First, there was the 350-mile route over the northern edge of Denmark into the Baltic. This would be the longest route and, though there would be few British ships around, Scheer's fleet had been significantly slowed down by the damaged battle-cruisers: Scheer feared that they would not make it back at all and Jellicoe assumed that this was his position.

THE NIGHT ACTION
22:00 on 31 May to 02:45 on 1 June 1916

1. 22:00–22:15. Hawksley's 11th Destroyer Flotilla (DF) clashes with Bödicker's 2nd Scouting Group (SG), the light cruisers *Frankfurt*, *Pillau*, with *Hamburg* and *Elbing* at the rear of the 4th SG. There are torpedo launches from *Castor*, *Marne* and *Magic* but no hits. Torpedoes aimed at *Elbing* run harmlessly underneath.

2. 22:30. *Southampton* and *Dublin* of Goodenough's 2nd Light Cruiser Squadron (LCS) clash with Reuter's 4th SG after they are pushed over to port by *Seydlitz* and *Moltke* which are steaming too close to the British lines. *Frauenlob* is torpedoed and sunk by *Southampton*.

3. 23:20. After several short skirmishes, Wintour's 4th DF comes into contact with the German van. *Westfalen* damages the flotilla leader *Tipperary*, which sinks later. In the turn away, the light cruiser *Elbing* is accidentally rammed by *Posen* (and might have also been torpedoed). The destroyer *Spitfire* and *Nassau* collide in another ramming incident as *Nassau* resumes the course needed to break through the British line. 23:40. After this clash, *Broke*, *Sparrowhawk* and *Contest* collide with each other.

4. 23:25. Attacks by a group made up of British destroyers from the 4th, 9th, 10th and 13th Flotillas hit the German van as they pass behind the track of the 5th Battle Squadron. The destroyer *Turbulent* sinks after being rammed by *Rheinland*.

5. 02:10. The 12th DF attack causes another German turn-away but it is too late for the pre-dreadnought *Pommern*, which is torpedoed and sinks.

6. 02:40. Roaming ships of Captain Fairie's 13th DF and two 12th DF boats make an unsuccessful run at *Von der Tann* when *Moresby* launches a torpedo which only narrowly misses *Schleswig-Holstein*.

7. 02:45. Jellicoe turns the Grand Fleet back north.

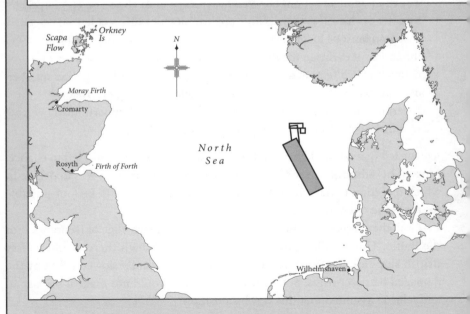

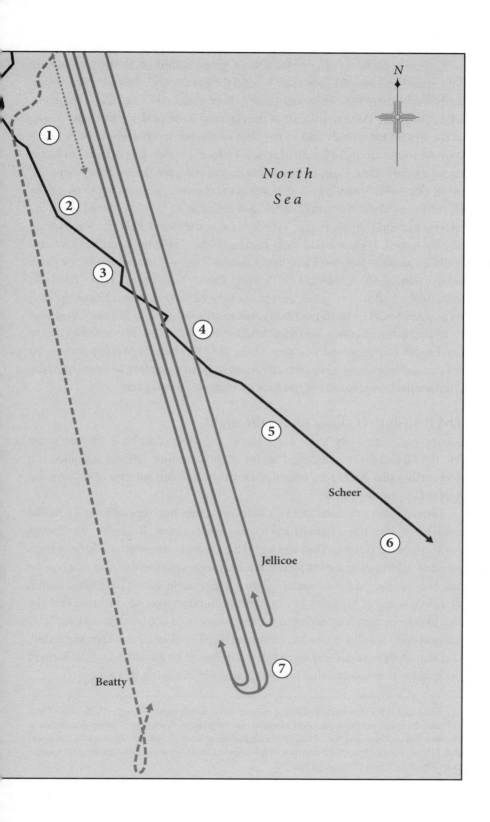

N

North
Sea

①

②

③

④

⑤

Scheer

⑥

Jellicoe

⑦

Beatty

Secondly, there was the possibility of going southeast to the Horns Reef light-vessel and into the Jade river behind the British-laid Amrum Bank mine-fields. From there Jellicoe thought that Scheer could take one of two channels, either the Lister Deep to the east of the Amrum Bank or through a known gap in the British minefields and to the west of the bank. This would be Scheer's shortest route: around a hundred miles. Jellicoe doubted that Scheer could get ahead of the Grand Fleet to make this route, but later that night he sent the minelayer *Abdiel* steaming off at 31 knots to lay mines, just in case, to cover the Horns Reef and the Amrum channel.[3] Setting off at 22:15, she reduced speed fif-teen miles from the lightship at Vyl where, as at the Horns Reef, the waters were heavily mined. Here she laid forty mines, ten to a mile on a southeast course and then another forty on a southwest course. This was in addition to the three submarines –*E.50*, *E.26* and *D.1* – that had already been positioned respectively four, twelve and twenty miles west of the lightship. By 02:00 on 1 June the task was completed. The third possibility was to go southwest to Ems and then east to Wilhelmshaven, again behind a British minefield. The last possibility was to head south to Heligoland and then to the Jade Bay behind Wilhelmshaven. In the end, Jellicoe chose to sail directly south to be in a position to intercept if the German fleet went for either the Ems or Heligoland entrances.

The British fleet closes up for the night

Sunset was at 20:00. By 21:00 it was night. A quarter of an hour after darkness fell, the Grand Fleet was closed up for night steaming. Jellicoe signalled the fleet, saying that he had no intentions for the night but gave no update on the fleet's status or disposition.[4]

Some officers criticised this lack of information, but one can imagine he did not want to give the Germans any leading information. In theory, the known positions of the German fleet elements (they were to the west) could have been valuable information for his forces, but his captains knew about as much as he did. Maybe more clarification of his own deployment would have been useful, as indeed some of his destroyer captains in the rear were so confused that the lack of information only added to the risks associated with a night action.* Jelli-coe may have felt that it was 'axiomatic', as Nigel Steel and Peter Hart suggested, that if an enemy vessel was encountered it should be attacked, but the facts of the night action showed that many captains did not think this way.

---

* Commander R B C Hutchinson DSC of *Achates* wrote in his report: 'I respectfully submit that in future the maximum amount of information may be given to destroyers as to the disposition of our own forces, observing the difficulty of recognition at night'. It was politely phrased but it was also, I think, a strongly implied criticism of Jellicoe's failure to bring his subordinate commanders more into the picture (Taffrail, p155).

The battle fleet was divided into four parallel columns, each a mile apart; three were planned, but with *Marlborough* lagging back and barely managing 16 knots, it became four.[5] As *Marlborough* could not keep up the pace, she and her three 6th Division companion ships steadily fell back behind the 5th. Again, Jellicoe probably should have risked sending *Marlborough* back out of the line, so as not to compromise the rest of his fleet. But it was a large risk and he would have had to further deplete his already stretched destroyer flotillas.

At the westernmost flank were the eight battleships of the 2nd Battle Squadron headed by Vice Admiral Jerram. Next in line, to the east, was the 4th Battle Squadron led by *Iron Duke*, with his second-in-command, Vice Admiral Sturdee on *Benbow*. In the third line was the wounded *Marlborough* leading the 1st Battle Squadron under the command of Vice Admiral Sir Cecil Burney. The last line, Evan-Thomas's 5th Battle Squadron, held the easternmost flank.

As they pushed south they could see no light in the dark murk, except the screened lanterns directed astern of each ship, a barely visible guide for the next ship in line. The concentration on each ship was intense as visibility was extremely bad.† The fifty-eight destroyers attached to the fleet, under the overall command of Commodore Hawksley (who at the same time commanded the 11th Destroyer Flotilla) were placed by flotilla around five miles astern in five parallel columns. At 21:27 they started to move to their allocated areas.[6] Their role would be to guard against the anticipated German torpedo attacks, keep German destroyers from attacking the rear of the British fleet, and safeguard against any German ships crossing the rear of the fleet and making for the Horns Reef. The protection of the rear of the fleet would turn out to be critical, as this was where the Germans would eventually probe and – one by one – cross over the lines of British destroyer groups disposed west to east.

Ahead, and on the flanks, were the cruiser forces. To port of the head of the battle fleet was Le Mesurier's 4th Light Cruiser Squadron (LCS), with Goodenough's 2nd LCS on the western flank, near the end of the line, about six and a half miles from the starboard quarter of the *King George V*, then at the van of the battle line. Three cruiser groups went forward to join up with Beatty's battle-cruisers ahead of the battleships: Rear Admiral H L Heath's 2nd CS, the 1st LCS under Edwyn Alexander-Sinclair and Napier's 3rd LCS.

At 21:00 someone on *Lion* made a bad mistake. At the time she was about fifteen miles west-southwest of *Iron Duke*. In earlier fighting, the signals covering identification and challenge had been lost. Now she flashed *Princess Royal*: 'SO [senior officer] BCF to *Princess Royal*. Please give me challenge and reply

---

† At this point, visibility was appalling, barely 1,300yds (1,200m). 'As the six destroyer flotillas took up their station astern of the battle fleet the visibility was down to three-quarters of a mile' (Kemp, p91).

now in force as they [the signals] have been lost.'[7] The original signal was seen by *Castor* (seven miles from *Lion*) and the reply by *Manners*. The Germans were even closer. The 2nd Squadron was only four miles away and ships of the 2nd Scouting Group, *Elbing*, *Rostock* and *Frankfurt*, saw the exchange and caught part of *Princess Royal*'s response. While they were able to find out only that the response to a challenge should begin with the letters 'UA', it was enough to cause some dangerous confusion later in the night.

At 00:30 the van of Mauve's pre-dreadnought squadrons, the 3rd and 4th Divisions, were able to see burning embers glowing red in the funnel smoke of the 2nd Cruiser Squadron, as well as a masthead light from *Shannon*. As the squadron joined the rear of Beatty's battle-cruisers, it had inadvertently been left on.

In front of Scheer now stood a twenty-three by eight mile armoured block. Jellicoe hoped that he could keep him contained as the German battle fleet moved southwards. 'The night formation of the British fleet was like the mighty British lion – head, body and claws. The course was south, the speed was 17 knots, the general arrangement was roughly a reversed "L", with the Germans caught within the angle.'[8]

With the night formation laid out, Jellicoe signalled *Iron Duke*'s position as a reference point to the fleet. It was 21.45: 'Latitude 56 degrees, 26 minutes north, longitude five degrees, 47 minutes east, course south, speed 17 knots'. It was a crucial signal that, if properly understood at the time of communication, would have avoided a lot of the later confusion. And after having deployed the fleet for the night, Jellicoe fell into a fitful sleep, fully clothed, on the bridge of his flagship.

The German fleet night deployment

As the darkness of the night fell, Scheer was in bad shape, even if his fleet was – in Jellicoe's eyes at least – more skilled at the necessary tactics, and better equipped, for this stage of the battle. He had started it with 101 ships. Now he had ninety-five afloat, very few torpedoes left in the destroyer tubes and, after damage inflicted, his fleet had lost 'between a fifth and a quarter of its fighting value'.[9]

> He had lost one battle-cruiser, the *Lützow*, one light cruiser, the *Wiesbaden*, and four destroyers from the line. Had this been the only damage, his situation would have been less serious; but of his four battle-cruisers still in company, only one was fit for action. Three of his dreadnoughts had sustained marked injuries, and six pre-dreadnoughts were a liability rather than an asset. He had only 17 effective capital ships to meet the enemy's 33–38.[10]

Unlike Jellicoe's force dispersal, Scheer's fleet was kept in a single 'column-ahead' formation steaming at 16 knots. At 21:10 he signalled: 'Battle fleet's course south, south-east by a ¼ east. The course is to be maintained. Speed 16 knots.' The German word that he used was '*durchhalten*' (to hold out to the end of something, or stay the course), which made it very clear that the formation and direction were to be maintained. Scheer also ordered airship reconnaissance off the Horns Reef. Both messages were intercepted by the Admiralty's Room 40 but, with their significance to Jellicoe's planning completely underrated, they languished in the corridors of the Admiralty for hours.

Jellicoe looked forward to daylight; Scheer needed to avoid it. A daylight encounter with the Grand Fleet in his condition would be disastrous. If he failed to avoid the action, he would be annihilated; hence his decision to head for the Horns Reef gap – his closest safe port – and target of his air-reconnaissance request.

Scheer redeployed. He put the slower dreadnoughts *Westfalen*, *Nassau*, *Rheinland* and *Posen* in the van. *Friedrich der Große* remained in the centre. Many of the *König* class were in bad shape: *König* herself had been hit ten times; *Großer Kurfürst*, *Markgraf* and *Kaiser* had received fifteen heavy shell hits between them. *Wiesbaden*, long ago left behind, was sinking. Four destroyers had been sunk.

Trotha, Scheer's chief of staff on *Friedrich der Große*, told of the palpable sense of tension on the German ships: 'Not a word sounded, only whispers, no light was shown. Silent darkness! Tense attentiveness! Each sector of the dark horizon was searched with night glasses under the direction of an officer.'[11] Despite the extreme fatigue that prolonged action brings, few could sleep. Each ship followed the dark silhouette of the next in line, the only light, as one officer described it, the 'weak shimmering light of his stern lantern playing on the foam of the propeller wash'.

Scheer began to adjust the order of the line. The pre-dreadnoughts of the 2nd Squadron were ordered to the rear at 21:50, although their move was delayed by the sighting of *Shannon*. *Westfalen*'s 1st Squadron was now led by the 3rd Squadron, with the 2nd Squadron eventually taking up position in the rear at 22:10. And finally, behind the pre-dreadnoughts, came the badly damaged battle-cruisers.

Von der Tann and *Derfflinger* could only manage a minimal 18 knots: the former's boilers were being cleaned, while astern the latter had been badly holed and had taken on around 3,400 tons of water.

A stubborn struggle [on *Derfflinger*] was being waged against fire and water. Although as far as possible everything inflammable had been taken out of the ship, the fire continued to spread, fed principally by linoleum, the wooden decks, clothing and oil paints. At about eight o'clock we had practically mastered the flames, the fire now smouldering in only a few isolated places. Caesar and Dora turrets were still smoking and giving out clouds of thick yellow gas from time to time, but this gradually ceased after the ammunition chambers had been flooded. No one could ever have believed that a ship could endure so much heavy fire.[12]

In fact, hardly any guns on her port side were working; only two 15cm guns were still intact. On her starboard she still had use of all six secondary guns.

When Scheer had ordered Hipper to take his battle-cruisers to the rear, initially his orders did not get through to the Aufklärungsgruppe chief, who raced *Moltke* to the head of the line at 20 knots with *Lützow* and *Seydlitz* struggling along astern. Both were badly mauled by this stage: *Seydlitz* had suffered twenty-four large-calibre hits, *Lützow* around forty. When the order did finally get through, Hipper took *Moltke* and *Seydlitz* back to join Mauve's slow pre-dreadnoughts. Quickly *Lützow* fell further and further behind. By 21:13 she was out of sight. Scheer could not jeopardise the rest of his fleet for one damaged battle-cruiser.[13]

The 2nd Squadron's move to the rear was very delayed. This is why, when *Friedrich der Große* arrived at the turning point at 21:45, Scheer had to amend his orders in order to maintain the Horns Reef as the target: *Westfalen* did not respond fast enough and a new course of 137 degrees (against the first of 142 degrees) was ordered at 21:46: 'Battle fleet's course south, south-east-by-¾-east'.

The creation of a giant 'V' had been set in motion, with the British fleet heading down the right character stroke south and the High Seas Fleet sailing on the left, at a slightly slower speed – of about one knot, southeast – towards the Horns Reef. Over the dark hours ahead, the 'V' would become an 'X' as the High Seas Fleet crossed over the wake of the British line's rear.

Scheer later proposed, without much credibility, that the move to get to the Horns Reef was so that he could be in a better position to challenge the British when battle resumed in the daylight of 1 June:

> It might safely be expected that in the twilight the enemy would endeavour, by attacking with strong forces and during the night with destroyers, to force us over to the west in order to open battle with us when it was light. He was strong enough to do so. If we could succeed in warding off the enemy's encircling movement, and could be the first to reach the Horns Reef, then the liberty of decision for next morning's fight was assured to us.[14]

Major German ships were spotted by the British, but the critical information was not passed on to Jellicoe. Most commanders thought he probably knew the situation already. Nor was the opportunity taken to attack. Many commanders thought that either they should receive direct orders to that effect or that, in attacking on their own initiative, they might compromise the fleet.

Both *Malaya* and *Valiant* saw large ships without informing Jellicoe. *Thunderer* saw *Moltke* pass by, but her captain thought it would be 'inadvisable' to give his position away. The battleships *Agincourt*, *Revenge*, *Marlborough* and *Thunderer* let the dim outline of the mortally crippled *Seydlitz* fade from sight. Again, with no action. The cruisers *Boadicea* and *Fearless* decided not to loose torpedoes without more positive identification. Having found the van, *Champion* did the same. Only *Faulknor* tried to signal the flagship, alas, unsuccessfully. It was, all in all, a lamentable performance with absolutely no initiative taken.

The last report that Jellicoe had received before the 02:15 deadline (the time by which he needed to have changed direction in order to be in a suitable position to catch the Germans before they reached the safety of the Horns Reef) had been from *Birmingham* at 23:30. However, the report was grossly misleading. It had stated that the enemy was steering south, ie parallel to the Grand Fleet.[15] It was unfortunate that Jellicoe chose to put more faith in this signal than the 22:41 one from the Admiralty, which stated that Scheer was steaming for the Horns Reef.

Jellicoe knew only the rough position of the High Seas Fleet. He had received a signal at around 21:05 that he should expect attacks from three flotilla groups in the night, then at 21:58 information that gave the position of the rear of the German fleet that he did not believe. Room 40 had not erred: the *Regensburg* had; the ship was ten miles out in its dead reckoning. *Iron Duke* got further important information about the German fleet disposition at around 23:05, namely that the Admiralty had received signals intelligence about the Germans' course and speed: 'German battle fleet ordered home at 21:14. Battle-cruisers in the rear. Course south-south-east-¾-east. Speed 16 knots.'

The length of time taken for the signal to get through to Jellicoe is significant. The 21:14 (German time) signal from Scheer was sent through to Admiral Oliver in the Operations Division at 21:55. Signalled back out to Jellicoe at 20:41 GMT, it reached him on the *Iron Duke* only at 23:30.[16] Just fifteen minutes after getting this information, Room 40 decrypted Scheer's telltale signal requesting air reconnaissance of the Horns Reef early on the morning of 1 June. This second vital piece of information – sent through to Oliver at 20:10 – was never passed through to Jellicoe.

Furthermore, Room 40 sent other vital signals to the Operations Division in the Admiralty that: (a) at 20:10 the fleet was steering south-southeast by ¾-east; (b) at 23:15 – southeast by east; (c) all torpedo boats had been ordered by Commodore Michelsen to the Horns Reef to make a 04:00 rendezvous;[17] and (d) the 23:50 course signalled by Scheer was southeast by ¾-east. 'These signals were all in the Operations Division within three-quarters of an hour of their being made. But none of them was passed on to Jellicoe.' For Beatty's biographer, Stephen Roskill, it showed 'the staggeringly bad co-operation between the Admiralty War Staff and Room 40'.[18]

Decryption and Intelligence

The quality and timeliness of battlefield intelligence are fundamental for command. Jutland revealed many instances of wretched intelligence and communications failures; there was a myriad of mistakes and oversights in information management between London and the fleets. During the night of 31 May and the early morning of 1 June, Room 40 intercepted various pieces of intelligence, including a signal that the German torpedo flotillas had been ordered to meet at the Horns Reef. But after signalling that the Germans would take the Horns Reef route, Jellicoe was not given any subsequent intelligence that would have restored his faith after the earlier blunder. He was not told that Michelsen's destroyers were to rendezvous there, nor that Scheer had ordered Zeppelin reconnaissance. He was inclined to trust his own judgement and local intelligence more and chose the Jade route.

The confidence of both Jellicoe and Beatty was severely shaken earlier in the day, as he had heard from the Admiralty at 12:48 that *Friedrich der Große* still appeared to be in the Jade Basin. The illusion was shattered when Goodenough, leading Beatty's scouting arm to the south, saw sixteen dreadnoughts of the HSF steaming up north towards the *Southampton* at speed. Later, there was another Admiralty signal that only increased Jellicoe's distrust. He received a message based on Kommodore Heinrich's 20:13 signal to the 2nd and 6th Flotillas ('Our own battle fleet is square 165 epsilon, lower part, at 20:00, Course South') showing *Regensburg*'s dead reckoning to be around about ten miles out. It certainly did not help that Jellicoe himself was at that exact position at the very same time stated. (This was received by Jellicoe at 20:45, giving the rearmost position of the German line as 56° 33' N, 5° 30' E on a southern course).[19]

Scheer, by contrast, knew that the British destroyers had been placed at the Grand Fleet's rear, and running into them confirmed that he was breaking through at the right point.

It was only years after the war ended that Jellicoe found out the full extent of the information that had been held back. He commented:

> The lamentable part of the whole business is that had the Admiralty sent all the information which they had acquired ... there would have been little or no doubt in my mind as to the route by which Scheer intended to return to base. As early as 10.10 pm, Scheer's message to the airship detachment ... was in the possession of the Admiralty. This was practically a certain indication of his route but it was not passed to me.[20]

Between 21:55 on 31 May and 03:00 on 1 June, sixteen decodes were passed from Room 40 to the Operations Division. Of these sixteen, only three were passed on to Jellicoe. He knew from them that the British and German fleets were on a converging course, and that he was steaming slightly faster than they. 'It is therefore puzzling that, when gunfire, searchlights and star-shells were seen at intervals astern of the main body, as was to happen during the rest of the night, it did not occur to Jellicoe or his staff that these were indications that this was just what was happening.'[21]

Commodore Michelsen on *Rostock* commanded the destroyers attached to the High Seas Fleet. He was given the task of organising diversionary attacks on the British to prevent them blocking the main fleet getting across. *Rostock* joined up with Rear Admiral Bödicker's 2nd Scouting Group, *Frankfurt* and *Pillau* (but not *Elbing*), which were posted out in front on the port wing.[22] Michelsen co-operated with Commodore Paul Heinrich, who commanded the battle-cruisers' torpedo-boat flotillas from *Regensburg*, in night-time probes on the British line. The two men organised the tasks for each group. Ahead of the armoured mass, the torpedo-boat flotillas were laid out in a fan. Korvettenkapitän Heinecke's 5th Flotilla was responsible for searching ahead of the main fleet to the south-southwest and south-southeast (he found little sign of the British and returned to *Westfalen*). To Heinricke's west was the 18th Half-Flotilla, while Korvettenkapitän von Koch's 7th Flotilla was responsible for searching the south by east and southeast sectors.

The night manoeuvring of the torpedo flotillas was dangerous work, partly because the groups had to make frequent crossings of the battleship line – there had been so many changes, of course, but it was also inevitable that they would enter the operating zone of another flotilla. Identifying friend from foe was nerve-racking and stressful for both sides.

British destroyer deployments
Jellicoe's strong destroyer screen, five miles behind the Grand Fleet, stretched out an armoured wall between the Germans and their home ports.

The fifty-eight destroyers were arranged in five parallel columns by flotilla. Positioned at the extreme west, in other words closest to the German scouting forces, was Hawksley's 11th Destroyer Flotilla (with his flag on *Castor*). The other flotillas were spread between the reorganised battle squadron lines cruising in night formation. Between the two lines of battle ships, one led by *King George V*, the other by *Iron Duke*, was the 4th Flotilla. And between the two battleship lines headed by *Colossus* and *Marlborough* came the 13th, the 9th and the 10th joint flotillas positioned on *Marlborough*'s port side. At the extreme east was the 12th Flotilla. Between the 4th and the 13th, which were running south with parts of the 9th and 10th, was a fairly wide gap of about four and a half miles. Behind these five destroyer groups came Goodenough's 2nd Light Cruiser Squadron which acted as a mobile rear scouting group.

Initial Night-time Organisation of the British Destroyer Flotillas

Flotilla	11th DF	4th DF	13th DF	9th/10th DF	12th DF
Leader	Castor	Tipperary	Champion	Lydiard	Faulknor
Commander	Hawksley	Wintour	Farie	Goldsmith	Stirling
	Kempenfelt	Acasta	Moresby	Landrail	Maenad
	Magic	Achates	Narborough	Laurel	Marksman
	Mandate	Ambuscade	Nerissa	Liberty	Marvel
	Manners	Ardent	Nestor	Moorsom	Mary Rose
	Marne	Broke	Nicator	Morris	Menace
	Martial	Christopher*	Nomad	Termagant	Mindful
	Michael	Contest	Obdurate	Turbulent	Mischief
	Milbrook	Fortune	Onslow		Munster
	Mons	Garland	Pelican		Narwhal
	Moon	Hardy	Petard		Nessus
	Morning Star	Midge			Noble
	Mounsey	Ophelia*			Nonsuch
	Mystic	Owl			Obedient
	Ossory	Porpoise			Onslaught
		Shark			Opal
		Sparrowhawk			
		Spitfire			
		Unity			

*Attached to the Battle Cruiser Fleet.
Sources: Taffrail, *Dispatches*, Kemp et al (see Bibliography).

Once again *Marlborough's* continued presence had adverse effects. Because she had been slowing her division down, the destroyer screens had also been pushed back and were more to the north of their station than they should have been, so in front of the 12th Flotilla was part of the 9th Flotilla (four destroyers headed by *Lydiard*). By 01:00 *Marlborough* had slowed to 12 knots and it was then absolutely clear that she could no longer stay in the line.[23]

Scheer's idea was to push through the British line, using his destroyers out in front to gauge where the Grand Fleet was, so that he could slip across its wake west to east. He knew that he had to be relentless. It was a bold plan, but succeeded more because of poor British intelligence, reporting and communications than because of its audacity.

Jellicoe had been warned by the Admiralty of what to expect after he had received a 21:05 signal: 'Three destroyer flotillas have been ordered to attack you during the night'. He wanted confirmation that the gunfire that had been heard was indeed from destroyer attacks and signalled *Castor* at 20:43: 'Urgent. Are you engaging enemy destroyers?' To this he received a negative, via *Kempenfelt*, the 11th Flotilla's leader. That reply should have been of more significance to Jellicoe. It is surprising that there was no follow-up signal.

Around the time that Jellicoe was questioning *Castor*, Scheer was coming to a clearer understanding of the British deployment. At some point in the night Scheer probably received the Neumünster signal which had picked up Jellicoe's 21:17 destroyer-deployment orders. That he did so was denied in the German official history and later allowed to pass in Sir Julian Corbett's account, but it seems to be the case that the signal at least got to the flagship. Now – if he indeed saw the signal – Scheer understood how he could avoid a fleet action, and realised the significance of Koch's and Friedrich Bödicker's engagements.[24] Many of these night-time clashes were about the encounters between the probing units of the German scouting groups and the British flotillas laid out west to east; Scheer now decided that his fleet should head southeast by east, with the emphasis – '*durchhalten*' – that this course was to be maintained without regard to consequences.

Scheer's Route Home

Using a combination of Tarrant, Hines and Koever,[25] the following sequence of signals seems to represent the most critical that could have significantly influenced the closing stages of the battle. In sum, they highlight failures of intelligence co-ordination, carelessness but, alternatively according to Hines,[26] a policy of secrecy designed to protect continued British signals access:

- 21:06. C-in-C to airship detachment: 'Early air reconnaissance at Horns Riff is urgently requested'. Decrypted at 22:10 but not passed to Oliver and not sent to the Grand Fleet. Considered by historians to be one of the key signals of the battle since it clearly showed Scheer's intended route.[27]
- 21:14. C-in-C: 'Our own main body is to proceed in, maintain course SSE¼E, speed 16 knots'. Decrypted/passed to Oliver/Operations at 21:55 but seen by Jellicoe after 23:30. From this point Beesly contends that 'no fewer than sixteen decodes, all of which would have added in some degree to Jellicoe's knowledge, were passed by Room 40 to Operations Division. *Only three of them were sent to Jellicoe*'.[28]
- 21:46. C-in-C to HS Fleet: 'Our own main body course SSE¾E'. Decrypt passed to Operations at 22:10 and signal sent to Jellicoe at 22:41, a full hour later reading 'German battle fleet ordered home at 21:14, cruisers in the rear, Speed 16 knots.

Course SSE¾E'. This signal combined the information gleaned from the 21:14, 21:29 and 21:46 signals but left out the 21:06 signal (on air reconnaissance). The 22:41 transmission was received in the cipher room on the *Iron Duke* around 00:05. Jellicoe saw the signal between 00:15 and 00:30. *Almost four hours had elapsed.* A chart plot at 22:00 would have shown Horns Reef as the destination, even if it was not named.

- 23:06. C-in-C to High Seas Fleet: 'Our own main body at 23:00 12 epsilon (56° 15' – 5° 42' E), Course SE¾E'. Deciphered at 23:50 but not passed to Jellicoe.

23:14. Flag to the *Nassau* and the *Westfalen*: 'Course SE¾S in the direction of Horns Reef'. Intercepted by the *Fearless* (see Hines) but only decrypted after the battle.

- 22:32. OC 1st TD to all TBD flotillas: 'Be assembled *with our main fleet* [my italics] at 04:00 at Horns Reef or course round Skaw'. Deciphered at 23:15 but not passed to Jellicoe and the vital phrase 'with our main fleet' was even carelessly left out of the version passed to the Operations Division.

- 00:31 (1 June). AC 2nd SG: 'Where is the head of our main fleet at 12:30? My own position is 106 alpha centre (56° 3' – 6° 42' E)'. Deciphered and passed to Operations at 01:05

- 00:43 (1 June). C-in-C to *Lützow*: 'Our main body's position at 12:30 073 alpha'. The response was not passed to Jellicoe.

- 01:03 (1 June). C-in-C to AC 2nd SG: 'Head of our own main fleet at 01:00, bottom of alpha (55° 50' – 6° 25' E)'. Deciphered and passed to Operations at 01:25. Not passed to Jellicoe.

- 02:30. C-in-C: 'Main fleet in 101 alpha right middle (55° 33' – 6° 50') course SE by S. Speed 16 knots'. Deciphered and passed to Operations at 03:05. This was passed to Jellicoe at 03:29.

Jason Hines holds that while Captain Thomas Jackson – usually portrayed as having been one of the principal 'problems' of the Room 40 saga – was not a likeable character, what happened was by design, not error. The British simply did not want to give themselves away by sending information through to Jellicoe, which would have been picked up by the Germans, thus revealing that it had clearly been decoded. Harley says that Oliver had taken on an inexperienced officer, Captain Allan Everett (naval assistant to the First Sea Lord), and used him as a replacement for Captain Jackson while the latter slept, saying that it was this that caused the problems, not what Hines suggests. According to Lieutenant Commander William Clarke, 'Jellicoe was the only 1st Sea Lord' to visit Room 40 regularly.[29]

In conclusion, as Massie summed up:

All of this vital information made it plain where Scheer was going, yet incredibly none of it was passed on to the Commander-in-Chief by the Operations Department. The tragic result of this lamentable performance – criminal neglect is not too strong a term – was that Jellicoe was left completely in the dark, when he might have turned north to intercept Scheer at daybreak and inscribed another Glorious First of June in the Annals of the Royal Navy.[30]

The first night encounter: small boat action between the British 4th Flotilla and the German 7th Flotilla

Lieutenant Commander Gottlieb von Koch pushed the eastern reconnaissance wing of torpedo boats, the 7th Flotilla, further east. On the British side, Captain Charles Wintour on *Tipperary* was in the process of leading the destroyers of the 4th Flotilla around to take them up north to protect the rear of the British fleet as Jellicoe had instructed. The time was 21:59. From *Garland*, the fourth ship in the British destroyer line (which also included *Contest* and *Fortune*), Koch's nine-boat flotilla was spotted coming in at a slow 17 knots.[31] The British did not see them immediately, but at 500yds (460m) *S.24* flashed the recognition signal. Getting nothing in return, the British opened fire. Four boats (*S.24, S.16, S.18* and *S.15*) each launched one torpedo.[32] Nothing came of the encounter, as the British turned away, though *Garland* opened fire and was only narrowly missed by a torpedo passing her stern by 10ft.[33] *Contest*'s captain, Lieutenant Commander Master, reported the encounter, but no further signals were made. *Garland,* at the rear of the line, had also seen the four torpedoes pass harmlessly behind the destroyer line and had similarly reported to Wintour.[34]

Koch fell back to avoid fire and eventually, later in the small hours, decided that there was nothing better for him to do than go directly to the Horns Reef rendezvous point. Many other German destroyers gave up the search as well and also proceeded to the same destination.

The second night encounter: German cruiser engagement with the 11th Flotilla

The next flotilla to see action was Hawksley's 11th Destroyer Flotilla. Hawksley, on *Castor*, was also proceeding north as Wintour had done, aiming to take up position at the extreme west of the destroyer flotilla line behind the fleet. At around 22:05 *Castor* and *Kempenfelt* (the 11th DF divisional leader, captained by Commander Sulivan) spotted and were spotted by, two cruisers of Bödicker's 2nd Scouting Group, the *Frankfurt* and the *Pillau*. From around 1,200yds (1,100m), the Germans fired two torpedoes, thinking that they had spotted cruisers rather than destroyers. The torpedoes harmlessly passed the five-destroyer flotilla and the Germans turned away so as not to reveal their own positions.[35]

Bödicker was biding his time, but after ten minutes he came in closer, supported by *Elbing* and *Hamburg*. This time the German boats tried a different tactic. From *Castor*, Hawksley saw two dark silhouettes on his starboard. They flashed the correct 'UA' British recognition signal, but followed it with some erroneous letters. When Hawksley saw the two random letters in the 'UA' flash, he knew that something was not right. The Germans closed in to around 1,000m

(1,100yds) and then, in one second, the German searchlights pierced the moon-less night.* From the back, behind the 4th Scouting Group, *Hamburg* and *Elbing* opened fire on *Castor*.[36] It was around 20:13.

> In the dark we saw, in an easterly direction, the shadows of English ships, the *Castor* with the 11th Flotilla. We showed them English recognition signals, which they acknowledged. As we were sure it was the enemy, we opened up heavy fire from around 1,000 metres distance. The *Castor* returned fire immediately and turned back.[37]

Castor was caught in a blizzard of shell at point-blank range.[38] She was by herself. Her accompanying destroyers thought that these were, indeed, other British ships and did not open fire, so convinced were they 'that a mistake had been made and that we were firing upon our own ships'.[39] It was an example of how terrifyingly confusing night fighting could be.

Castor hit back with her 6in guns, managing to score some hits, but within minutes she had suffered severe loss and damage, twelve killed and twenty-three wounded.[40] Her electrics were smashed up and, more importantly, her wireless shot away. The very first hit had set the motor barge on fire and brightly illu-minated her as a very easy target for her assailants.

Before turning, *Castor*, as well as the two following destroyers, *Marne* and *Magic*, had fired off torpedoes at *Elbing*, only missing her when the weapons ran too deep. Again, the unreliability of British torpedoes was to blame. *Marne* nearly got into trouble, which she avoided as, instead of accelerating forward, she came to a dead stop. Intense enemy fire opened up but mostly fell ahead of her, over-anticipating her intended course. None of the British torpedoes hit but, then, neither did the single torpedoes from *Pillau* or *Frankfurt*. Coming back to help *Marne*, *Castor* fired off a torpedo and opened up with her 6in guns. For her troubles, she ended up getting holed forward.

When the action was reported to Scheer, he pulled back the main fleet and angled off slightly more by turning one point to starboard at 22:06, even though the two fleets were still converging. But Jellicoe misinterpreted Hawksley's 23:00 signal telling him they had engaged enemy cruisers. He thought it meant that these were likely to have been supporting the destroyer attacks, not the main body of the German battle fleet itself.

---

* German searchlights were very much more efficient than British ones. The German searchlight had an iris shutter, allowing it to reach full power before opening up at full blaze on a target. The light could also be switched off in a second should the situation require it. By contrast, British searchlights were very basic: when '[we] switched off our searchlights we had to find tarpaulins to throw over them to hide the glowing carbons that stood out like full moons and gave the enemy the chance to have a bang at us'.

The third night encounter: 2nd Light Cruiser Squadron engagements

Commodore Goodenough's 2nd Light Cruiser Squadron was at the rear, in the westernmost position, far behind Hawksley's 11th Flotilla group. At around 20:15 the Light Cruiser Squadron spotted five unknown ships to starboard, at around 1,500yds (1,400m) and to their front.[41] The ships were Commodore Reuter's 4th Scouting Group – *Stettin*, *München*, *Hamburg*, *Frauenlob* and *Stuttgart*.

In their push to the front of the van, the two battle-cruisers *Moltke* and *Seydlitz* had cut far too close to *Stettin*, forcing her to slow and in turn forcing *München*, *Frauenlob* and *Stuttgart* to pull away to port. In doing so they become visible to Goodenough's ships. The two adversaries steamed in parallel to each other, only slowly converging from a gap of around 1,500yds to a minimal one of 800yds (730m). To starboard were five German light cruisers; on the port side four British equivalents. Each side must have been looking at the other and wondering: 'Friend or foe?'. 'The Commodore looked at them through night glasses, and I heard a whispered discussion going on as to whether they were the enemy.'[42]

Despite the uncertainty, Goodenough ordered 'open fire', but as soon as *Dublin*'s captain, A C Scott, gave the same order, both ships were caught in the fierce dazzle of German searchlights and instantaneously caught in the witheringly concentrated fire of Reuter's ships. But British fire was also on target. *Dublin*'s shells burst on the side of the enemy ship with such effect that one officer on *Southampton* had 'a nightmare glimpse of her interior'[43] – a scene that 'remained photographed in my mind to this day. I said to myself, "My God, they're alongside us!"'[44]

Dublin and *Southampton* received most of the enemy's fire while the two rear ships, *Nottingham* and *Birmingham*, wisely kept their searchlights off and escaped unscathed. They could add their firepower without being fired upon. Both Commander Rebensburg's cruiser, *Stettin*, and Commander Böcker's *München* were each hit twice, the latter before she could even get her torpedo tubes to bear. *Stettin* had a gun put out of action and her steam pipe was fractured. The escaping steam scalded and blinded the torpedo team. Even though *Hamburg* was only hit once, ten of Commander von Gaudecker's men were killed, including the captain and navigating officer, while others on the signal platform were badly wounded.

The British ships were thoroughly peppered by enemy shell. In the five-minute encounter, *Southampton* alone was hit by twenty 4.1in and 5.9in shells. Three guns and two searchlights were knocked out, and the ship's radio destroyed; on her decks lay the bodies of thirty-five dead and forty-one wounded, and on *Dublin* there were a further three dead and twenty-four wounded. Both ships were on fire.

Dublin had managed to avoid heavier casualties because she had turned 3 points to port when she had taken the first hit. Nevertheless, she was to be hit thirteen times and the navigating officer killed, along with two other men. It was sheer bad luck that all her charts and WT equipment were also destroyed. However, as *Southampton* turned, her torpedo officer was able to fire one salvo from the bridge firing position, aiming for the searchlight sources. The torpedo ran true and hit *Frauenlob* in the port auxiliary machinery space.

The German cruiser's engines stopped the moment she was hit, 'probably owing to damage in the propeller shafts'.[45] At 20:40 all the lights went out. The confusion was overwhelming. The scene was as hellish for one midshipman, Stolzmann, as it was for the sailors on *Southampton*: 'I at once switched on both available searchlights at the cruiser opposite us. The guns immediately opened fire. This was followed by such a furious rain of shell, which nearly all hit the after part of the ship, that it looked as if several enemy ships were concentrating their fire on us.'[46]

The torpedo detonation caused pandemonium. *Stuttgart* swerved out of the German line and only just managed to avoid a collision. As a result she became separated but *Frauenlob*'s crew bravely fought on:

> The electric lights went out, the ammunition hoist machinery failed, and while the cruiser heeled so far over to port that the projectiles in the shell room were dislodged, shells hitting the ship started a fire aft. But nothing could daunt the ship's company. Up to their waists in water, the crew of the No. 4 gun, under Petty Officer Schmidt, continued to engage the enemy until fire and water put an end to the fighting. The *Frauenlob* capsized, and with three cheers for the Kaiser and the German Empire, the captain [Georg Hoffmann], eleven officers and 308 men attested with their deaths their loyalty to the Fatherland.[47]

Somewhere in the five minutes before 22:30 she sank. Between the two British light cruisers, *Southampton* and *Dublin* had also managed to hit *Stettin* twice, *München* five times and *Hamburg* four. After her fight to the death, *Frauenlob* left only seven survivors.[48] For *Southampton*, the torpedo had been an extremely lucky launch, as it had been fired from one of her submerged tubes, which did not have the capability for flexible aiming, but a launch from her deck tubes would probably not have been possible because of the amount of damage from earlier German fire.[49]

Without radio, Goodenough was unable to contact Jellicoe directly and the latter only had an inkling of what was going on. The commodore relayed a message back to the flagship through *Nottingham*, but given Goodenough's pre-vious record of regularly updating his commander-in-chief, the radio damage could not have come at a more critical moment in the battle. Goodenough's message, via *Nottingham*'s, reading, 'Urgent. Have engaged enemy cruisers 22:15 bearing west-south-west (10.40)', did reach *Iron Duke* but not until 23:38.

The action may only have lasted a bare three and a half minutes but in that short time the carnage had been terrible and one of *Southampton*'s officers com-mented: 'The general effect was as if a handful of splinters had been thrown at the upper works of the ship'.[50] As Stephen King-Hall remembered, 75 per cent of the upper deck men on *Southampton* had been killed or wounded. It had been point-blank engagement. *Southampton* was burning so badly that 'a friend of mine ... who was five miles away on one of the 5th Battle Squadron ships read a signal on the bridge by the light of our fires'.[51] Thirty-five men had died outright or later from wounds, while fifty-five more were wounded. The ship herself had sustained around eighteen hits and her five broadside 6in guns had been reduced to two.

King-Hall was sent down the so-called 'tuppenny tube', a passage running down the centre of the ship above the boilers and engine rooms.* He had been asked by Goodenough to check on the number of dead and wounded. The car-nage he found left him profoundly shocked. He found the surgeon operating in the stoker's bathroom, a small room only 8ft high and 12ft square. The doctor would continue his vital work to help save whomever he could for eleven hours straight.

An hour after Goodenough's signal had gone off, *Birmingham* spotted enemy battle-cruisers heading west by south around 23:15, but her report con-flicted with Admiralty signals suggesting the course was east-southeast.

Another effect of the near collision between *Stettin* and *Moltke* was that she and *Seydlitz* had now lost contact with each other. *Moltke* headed towards her port, *Seydlitz* starboard. Kapitän von Karpf on *Moltke* edged his ship progres-sively closer to the British line but had to turn back three times, and only finally passed the line at around 01:00.

The fourth night encounter and 4th Destroyer Flotilla actions: *Tipperary*, *Broke*, *Spitfire* and *Sparrowhawk* – and the loss of SMS *Elbing*

Some time around 23:00 the German van was approaching the rear of the

---

* I am indebted to the Cayzer archivist, Susan Scott, for an explanation of the 'Tuppenny Tube'. Apparently, it was the familiar term around 1900 for an early stretch of London's Central Line underground system (ie long, dark, windowless tunnel). Sailors clearly adopted this nickname for their own long, dark, windowless corridor!

Grand Fleet. Imagine two lines of ants moving down from the top of the two sides of a large X, steadily converging on each other. This is what was happening. The German main battle fleet sailing down from left to right; at the top, the rear, on the extreme east, was the 6th Division (of the 1st Battle Squadron) running roughly parallel with HMS *Marlborough*, which was steaming at reduced speed as a result of the earlier torpedo damage. And further east still of the 6th Division was Farie's 13th Flotilla, along with the 12th, the 9th and the 10th. As the two forces converged, it could have been a monumental collision of armoured steel.

Six miles southwest of the 12th Flotilla, and slightly to the east of Hawksley's 11th Destroyer Flotilla, Captain Wintour on *Tipperary* was leading the eleven remaining K-class destroyers of the 4th Destroyer Flotilla.[52] The 4th was aware something was afoot. They had heard the sounds of the battles involving Hawksley's flotilla and Goodenough's 2nd Light Cruiser Squadron. Wintour was closest to the German van.

At 21:58 the 4th Flotilla encountered nine destroyers of Koch's 7th Flotilla approaching from the west at 17 knots. All but one were of the same class as the lead boat, *S.13*. *S.24* was followed by *S.15*, *S.17*, *S.20*, *S.16*, *S.18*, *S.19* and *S.23*. The last, *V.189*, was an older, bigger class. The German commander assumed that the 4th Flotilla's line of destroyers was actually part of Bödicker's 2nd Flotilla and flashed his recognition signal.[53] When no response was received, four of the line, *S.24*, *S.16*, *S.18* and *S.15*, attacked with a single-tube launch. Wintour had not seen the German signal and was turning his flotilla southwards and, as a result, three of the four torpedoes streamed past harmlessly behind their wake. The Germans fell back.

Half an hour later at 22:35 *Garland*, the fourth ship in the line, sighted an enemy vessel on her starboard quarter and reported the sighting of a *Graudenz*-class cruiser to *Tipperary*. At 22:40 *Boadicea*, one of Jerram's attached light cruisers, also spotted what she believed to be an enemy cruiser. Then five minutes later (at around 22:45), *Unity*, the last in line, spotted a another group of destroyers on her starboard. The leading German destroyer launched torpedoes and then turned away. Lieutenant Commander Arthur Macaulay Lecky on *Unity* turned the ship straight into the direction of the torpedo attack and avoided a hit. Fire on the German line, now fast disappearing from sight, was only opened up from *Garland*, from whose bridge Lieutenant Commander R S Goff had seen the attack.

Scheer, now armed with Neumünster signals intelligence, felt that he had found the approximate point in the British line at which his ships could be pushed through to safety. Contacts with the destroyers and the lack of enemy British battleships, coupled with the knowledge that the destroyer screen was five miles behind the Grand Fleet, had led Scheer to conclude that this was the spot for which he had been searching. Jellicoe, on the other hand, had received no reports of any of these actions and concluded that he was correct to stick to his original plan.

Between 23:15 and 23:20 a lookout on *Garland*, Torpedoman Cox, saw what he thought to be enemy ships on the starboard quarter. *Tipperary*, the flotilla leader, thought that they might actually be British, ships of Hawksley's 11th Flotilla. After ten minutes the recognition signal was flashed 700yds (640m) out and, almost immediately, *Tipperary* was lit up like a Christmas tree. She was caught in the searchlights of *Westfalen*, *Nassau* and *Rheinland*, plus those of the light cruisers *Hamburg*, *Rostock* and *Elbing*. The German line opened up very heavy fire. A young sub lieutenant on *Tipperary* commented on the intensity:

> They were so close that I could remember the guns seemed to be firing from some appreciable height above us ... The three ships of the enemy that were firing ... could not have fired more than four salvos before they gave us up as done for, and the whole thing had happened so suddenly and was over so quickly that I think we were all quite dazed.[54]

Tipperary was very badly hit. The bridge was damaged, communications were cut and just about everyone up forward was killed or wounded. But she still managed to fire both starboard torpedoes and the acting sub lieutenant, N J W William-Powlett, ordered fire from the aft guns. But when the steam pipes were also hit, the ship was literally hidden in a cloud of steam, at a dead stop. In just over four minutes, *Westfalen*, accompanied by *Nassau*, had together fired 150 5.9in shells at *Tipperary* (*Westfalen* alone, ninety-two rounds of 5.9in and forty-five of 3.5in).[55] The British ship had 'defended herself with noteworthy heroism',[56] but the oil that had spilled soon ignited and she was caught in a ghastly inferno. Later at around 02:00 *Tipperary* was abandoned and eventually sank. Throughout actions like these, the strain on ships' captains and the lookouts must have been enormous. Despite the hail of enemy fire, there was still hesitation whether it was a friend or foe in your own gun's sight; *Broke*'s captain had held fire until he could see with his own ship's searchlight that these really were Germans.

Once the line of eleven British destroyers had passed across the German van, the group disintegrated. Three of the leading four – *Sparrowhawk*, *Contest* and *Broke* – each, at really close range, fired a single torpedo and then peeled off to port. The rest (*Achates*, *Ardent*, *Fortune*, *Porpoise* and *Unity*) did not open fire or launch torpedoes. Only *Ambuscade* did. At the end, *Broke* gathered up the stragglers (minus *Garland*) and headed south.

Broke's group was not left alone for long.

Almost as soon as the ship was steadied on her course south, the hull of a large ship was sighted on the starboard bow on a more or less parallel course, but this time well before the beam and not more than half a mile away. The captain immediately gave the order to challenge but almost as soon as he spoke the stranger switched on a vertical string of coloured lights, some green and some red, an unknown signal in our service.[57]

There was not enough space in which Captain Allen could launch a torpedo attack. He was already at point-blank range, around 150yds (140m) off. *Broke* ran into a wall of fire. She was heavily shelled by the combined firepower of the light cruiser *Rostock* (which was on the port beam of the battleships), and the dreadnoughts *Westfalen* and *Rheinland*.

She tried to get a torpedo into the water, but the gear was out of action: the wheel and the engine telegraphs had been destroyed. In the few minutes of *Broke*'s daring attack, fifty of her crew were killed and another thirty injured. One of the dead was the helmsman and the ship, running at a full 28 knots, swerved to her port when the helm jammed, on a collision course with *Sparrowhawk*. The latter was heading back northeast. On *Sparrowhawk* a young sub lieutenant, Percy Wood, saw what was happening and shouted warnings, to no avail. *Broke* hit *Sparrowhawk* at full speed on the starboard side. The force of the collision must have been enormous. Twenty-three crew members were catapulted from *Sparrowhawk* and landed hard on the decks of *Broke*. There was mass confusion as each commander ordered his own crew to abandon ship and move to the other vessel. Twenty men from *Sparrowhawk* transferred to *Broke*, fifteen from *Broke* to *Sparrowhawk*. The scene was chaotic.

The twisted and heavily damaged *Broke* was reversing engines to disengage when *Contest*, steering close astern of *Sparrowhawk*, now also came in at full speed, ramming the unfortunate *Sparrowhawk* once again, this time on her port side. Five or six feet was cut from her stern structure and the rudder jammed hard to port.[58] It took half an hour but eventually *Broke* and *Contest* were able to disentangle themselves, while *Sparrowhawk* – without either a bow or a stern – could only sit where she was and gently drift. With thirty of *Sparrowhawk*'s crew taken on board, *Broke* headed off. The scene on board *Broke* could symbolise what had happened to the whole flotilla:

When we could see and I had time to think it dawned on me what a terrible scene had been enacted. We thought of the 'Honour' and the 'Glory', which so many people in their ignorance say is attached to warfare. You should have seen the decks of HMS *Broke* at 4.00 am, 1 June 1916. There you would have seen an exhibition of 'Honour' and 'Glory' in reality. Forty-eight of our crew lay dead and most of them shattered beyond recognition; another 40 were wounded very badly. We were about five hours finding all our dead chums, dragging them out of the wrecked mess deck and throwing their bodies over the side to be buried in the deep ocean … You wonder how men can have the audacity, for if we stopped to think of what we were going to do we should never fight at all.[59]

Unfortunately, *Broke*'s suffering was not over. Around 01:30 she came upon more enemy ships, this time a group of destroyers. Despite being badly damaged (she had lost her own bow), she managed to get off one shot in answer to the six that the Germans fired at her. Miraculously, she made it back into the Tyne, two and a half days after the battle ended.

Now it was Hutchinson's turn to take over the lead of what remained of the 4th Flotilla, after Wintour and Allan before. On *Achates* Hutchinson led the remaining ships in the flotilla, *Ambuscade*, *Ardent*, *Fortune*, *Porpoise* and *Garland* (the last having just rejoined the group) into a renewed attack on the leading German ships.

Turning away, *Achates* fired her torpedoes at *Rostock*, which, while manoeuvring desperately to avoid the incoming track, ran through her own line between *Westfalen* and *Rheinland*, only still to be hit in the no. 4 boiler room. She was badly holed and took on 930 tons of water and in minutes was listing 5 degrees. The next day she was scuttled.[60]

An ever-decreasing group of British destroyers now came around to launch more torpedoes at the huge German battleships. It really was a matter of many Davids against a Goliath, but with little of the success and a large loss of life. A hit on *Elbing* was claimed, but later denied by the Germans. Three cruisers, *Elbing*, *Frankfurt* and *Pillau*, desperate to avoid the British torpedoes, threaded their way through the line. *Elbing*'s luck did not hold. She was rammed by one of her own, the battleship *Posen*. Both her engine rooms flooded; the lighting plant and the steering engine room were damaged. The stricken *Elbing* took on an 18-degree list and 'then drifted down the starboard side of the German line, incapable of manoeuvring or fighting'.[61] Her crew was taken off by *S.53*, but Madlung and some officers stayed aboard, trying to see if they could get the vessel back in to German waters using a jury-rigged sail. When enemy ships were spotted around 03:00, *Elbing* was finally abandoned. Her last moments could be seen from *Sparrowhawk* and *Tipperary*. She sank after explosive charges had been laid and the order to abandon ship given by her captain, Commander Rudolf Madlung. From the small cutter that they were in they rescued one of their foes, the surgeon from *Tipperary*.

Eleven small British destroyers had just come into direct contact with, and taken hostile fire from, the van of the German battle fleet. Taffrail said that the British then spotted what were 'seen to be light cruisers with four funnels' 'coming up abaft the beam'.[62] First impressions were that they were British.

The head of the line had turned away from the torpedo threat, *Westfalen* out in front, *Nassau*, *Rheinland* and *Elbing* following closely her lead. *Spitfire* had been just behind *Tipperary*. She fired off two torpedoes at the second ship in the German line. Lieutenant Commander Clarence W E Trelawny on *Spitfire* wrote in his official report: 'The torpedo struck her between the second funnel and the foremast. She appeared to catch fire fore and aft simultaneously, and heeled right over to starboard and undoubtedly sank.'[63] What ship it actually was is hard to say now. He had identified her as having four funnels, so it could not have been *Nassau* (which only had two).

After letting loose the torpedoes, *Spitfire* hauled out of line to port and swung around westwards to reload, hoping to launch a further salvo. She could not. 'Unfortunately, as we turned back the torpedo davit was struck in three places ... and the torpedo could not be got into the tube'.[64] The gunner and two torpedo ratings had also been wounded. Trelawny decided to take his 935-ton destroyer back around to see if he could help the crippled *Tipperary* which was by now 'a mass of burning wreckage and looking a very sorry sight indeed'.[65] On his way there, the story goes, *Spitfire* literally ran into the *Nassau*.

The story of the collision is one of those that still today continues to stoke a heated debate over what really happened. The ships' identities could have been mistaken. Given the conditions, the speed of the engagement and the darkness, different stories were bound to emerge. At the worst there is the accusation of the truth being hidden.

There were quite a few people from both sides whose accounts can be used, from the captain of *Spitfire*, Lieutenant Commander Clarence Trelawny, one of his officers on the bridge and First Lieutenant Athelstan P Bush. On the German side, there were Sepp Schlager, who used his contemporary notes to write about the action forty years later, Rupert Berger, an able seaman who later became the mayor of Traunstein in southern Germany and a parliamentary figure,[66] Heinz Bonatz, a cadet, and Otto Thomas, a junior officer in one of the 5.9in casemates.[67] Only Bonatz's account is well-known.[68]

Berger's first thought was that *Nassau* had been torpedoed, but later realised that there had been a collision in which the bow of the enemy ship penetrated the hull of *Nassau* by more than 2m. At that point, apparently, there was a huge explosion on the destroyer. It was right up against *Nassau*, so the carnage on both ships was gruesome. Instantly, three sailors on the *Nassau* were killed; there was blood everywhere. Berger thought that an English sailor must have slipped along that gun barrel and smashed against the turret as there were bloody pieces of flesh and skin still hanging from the turret. There was a gruesome reminder of another unknown sailor, a kid glove on the blooded deck with part of a severed hand inside. A letter was next to it with a curl of hair. His child? The enemy ship's flags had ended up on the German ship. On the port side, Bonatz had been in the casemate and had survived:

> We sustained a direct hit on the forward group of lights and, soon after, rammed HMS *Spitfire*, which had not seen us. The destroyer brushed against the 15cm gun in my casemate, and ripped it and its carriage from the deck. Just a few seconds before the collision, I had been looking through the telescopic sight on the right side of the gun but was then called away to my proper battle station of the starboard side, because destroyers were reported there. Thus I stood right in the doorway of the middle casemate that lay between the two 15cm gun casemates. With the tilt of the ship, the armour-plated door struck me on the right foot and the back. We believed the British ship to be destroyed at the time, especially as a great number of pieces of wreckage, both great and small, were floating round us.[69]

Trelawny's own account of the encounter was gripping.[70] The German battleship, he said, opened fire, but could not depress her guns far enough; still, the blast from *Nassau*'s guns knocked *Spitfire*'s bridge, funnels, boats and searchlight platform clean off. Trelawny had a close shave as a shell passed through the bridge screen, blowing his cap off and leaving a bad gash on his head. It was nothing short of miraculous, as the pressure wave created by a heavy calibre shell would normally have killed him. In the words of Athelstan Bush:

> She was coming at us full speed across our port bow. The captain ordered, 'Hard a starboard: full speed ahead both', and leaning over the bridge screen, shouted 'Clear the fo'c'sle'. It wasn't a minute too soon, as with an awful crash the two ships met end on, port bow to port bow, we steaming at almost 27 knots, she steaming not less than 10 knots (perhaps 20 or more).[71]

Spitfire was almost rolled over by the collision. His actions crumpled her bow, but saved his ship, but none had any idea that what they were ramming was a 20,000-ton battleship. On the bridge, Trelawny had taken much of the impact full-on. He discovered, as he was being supported by his chief stoker, Weavers, that he had broken his jaw. Bush added some further detail:

> Fires started breaking out forward and to make matters worse all the lights were short-circuited, so that anyone going up to the bridge received strong electric shocks. Moreover, all the electric bells in the ship were ringing, which made things feel rather creepy. It was extraordinary the way the fire spread, burning strongly in places where one thought there was hardly anything

inflammable, such as on the forebridge and the decks, but flags, signal halyards and the coconut matting on the deck all caught fire, and sparks from the latter were flying about everywhere. We thought the light would be sure to draw some enemy fire upon us, but fortunately it didn't. There was a large hole in the base of the second funnel through which flames were pouring out, and every single hosepipe in the ship seemed to be cut by splinters and useless.

So far it seemed that the incident was a case of last-minute manoeuvring under battle conditions from which neither ship could avoid a collision. But then the questions start to appear.

It was not *Nassau* that rammed *Spitfire* as she claimed. In his book, Scheer still upheld *Nassau*'s story and talked about the signal that she sent when she was 'standing by the Vyl lightship at the Horns reef and that during the night had rammed and cut through a destroyer'.[72] In reality it was the other way around. It was *Spitfire* that rammed *Nassau*. The German repair yard photos show *Nassau*'s bow perfectly intact and the war log also confirmed that the destroyer's crumpled metal bow was lodged in her side. Who in their right mind would charge a 20,000-ton battleship with a puny destroyer displacing less than a twentieth? It was an unintentional ramming, at best. *Spitfire* slammed into the port bow section, metres from the bow.

One can see little evidence of the deep horizontal gashing that would have occurred if the impact really had been 'port to port'. While *Spitfire* would have slid along the battleship, it might be true to say that it is more likely that the damage would be more extensive on the thin skin of a destroyer rather than on the armour-plated side of a battleship; nevertheless one would also expect to see telltale signs. It suggests that the initial impact might have been closer to 90 degrees than 45 degrees.

The German accounts include torpedo explosions. The British accounts from *Spitfire* do not mention anything about this, only that the davit was damaged so the tubes could not be reloaded. Indeed, Schlager maintained that there were multiple explosions and Berger recalled that there were British dead strewn on the foredeck. Had they been blown there by the blast of the explosion? Was it this explosion that really caused the huge carnage on board *Nassau*?

What is not visible in the surviving German damage plan is the huge waterline hole that had been blown in the *Nassau*'s port bow ('*durch Rammen und Torpedoexplosion großes Loch im Backbord Vorschiff*') documented in the official damage report and in the war log. The damage report said that 'the bow section was torn open at about a length of 20 metres and the gaping hole reached from the waterline up to the deck', although this is not shown in the surviving photographs.

If *Nassau* heeled 5–10 degrees to starboard as Campbell maintains, what on earth would have happened to a small destroyer, especially with the enormous suction that would have been present between *Nassau* and the destroyer?

Most of the German accounts maintain that either the British destroyer sank or that at least one half did. This is true for Berger, *Nassau*'s war log and for the cadet, Heinz Bonatz, as well as Schlager, who was on the bridge at the time. If that was the case, what was the identity of the ship that caused the damage? If the ship that was involved sank and *Spitfire* arrived back in the Tyne thirty-six hours later, it could not have been *Spitfire*. Only Bonatz's account was a little less sure. He only said that they '*believed the British ship to be destroyed at the time*, especially as a great number of pieces of wreckage, both great and small, were floating round us'. *Spitfire*'s account maintains that the 'cruiser passed down the length of us, cleared us astern and disappeared, leaving us still afloat, but drifting and in a somewhat pitiful condition'.

Both the crews of *Spitfire* and *Nassau* steadfastly maintain details about the opponent ship that do not square with *Nassau* and *Spitfire* as being the two ships in question. *Nassau*'s war log recorded details such as that the destroyer that rammed them 'had a triangle pointing upwards and a flotilla flag on her mast' – but made no mention of the very visible '41' painted on *Spitfire*'s hull.* In fact, a photograph exists of *Spitfire*'s upward-pointing triangle and her flotilla flag taken at 17:00 earlier that same evening.[73] Berger also said that the navigation officer had seen a '*big British four-funnel destroyer*', but *Spitfire* was an *Acasta*-class destroyer, which only had three funnels. So was it *Spitfire* or was the navigation officer wrong? And when Trelawny saw *Nassau* looming out of the dark, he swung *Spitfire* over so that she would not be cut in half. As *Nassau* loomed up closer and closer, 'those aft noted that the enemy had *three funnels with a red band on each* [author's italics]. On the bridge we were blinded by the flashes of our fo'c'sle gun. All I recall is that she had a large crane amidships, and looked big.' Trelawny was right about the crane, but *Nassau* had two funnels, not three.†

---

* *Spitfire*'s official pendant number was 'H41' but only the '41' is shown in the famous photo of her re-entering the Tyne, while there is also a 'K' painted on the rear funnel. After repairs had been carried out she was redesignated 'H1A' (Stern, p74). See special volume for 31 May–1 June 1916 and damage report of the Schiffbau-Ressort of the Kaiserliche Werft, Wilhelmshaven. The report held that the ramming destroyer left a portion of its bow in *Nassau*, but that instead of a painted number (the famous '41') witnesses had seen a triangle on the destroyer mast and a flotilla flag: '*die backbord Ankerklüse und ein großer Teil zusammengeschrumpfter Bordwand waren völlig in die Kante vom Backsdeck eingekeilt. Eine Nummer des Bootes war nicht zu sehen*'.

† Initially, Trelawny had reported that he had probably been involved with an older ship type, a *Freya* (*Dispatches*, p306). Four-funnelled destroyers that took part at Jutland included *Faulknor*, *Broke*, *Marksman* and *Tipperary*. *Nassau* had two funnels not three. She did have a large crane amidships, one on each side.

Crippled, *Spitfire* limped along at 6 knots and somehow was able to get back to the Tyne thirty-six hours later, at around 16:30 on 2 June. She had suffered six dead and a further three officers and six ratings wounded. She also brought a remarkable battle trophy with her: 20ft of planking from *Nassau*. The story goes that *Spitfire*'s crew were given small mementoes cut up from *Nassau*'s strake, part of her hull. Trelawny said later that a portion of *Nassau*'s strake was sent to America as part of a propaganda campaign.[74]

She had left her own trophy on *Nassau*: 'part of her bridge hanging on the torpedo net'.[75] Trelawny was out cold on the deck and command was taken over by Bush. When Trelawny came to, he found the six men with whom he had been on the bridge dead or wounded. 'The coxswain and one other able seaman were later found trapped in the wreckage. To be released, the unfortunate seaman subsequently had to have his leg amputated without any anaesthetic, whilst lying amongst the tangled ruins of the bridge.'[76] Bush was steering from the emergency helm aft.

When the ships had apparently disengaged, planking from *Nassau* was supposedly ripped off and entangled with *Spitfire*, the latter having lost 60ft of her own hull siding. Later, on inspection, Trelawny wrote that *Nassau* had to be an older ship, as the paint was '3/32nds of an inch' thick. The 20,000-ton vessel sailed away with a 3.4m (11ft) long gash in her hull, and claimed later that she had rammed and sunk her comparatively small opponent. An unidentified officer on *Spitfire* recalled:

> You can imagine how the 1/8th inch plates of a destroyer would feel under such a blow. I can recollect a fearful crash, then being hurled across the deck, and feeling the *Spitfire* rolling over to starboard as no sea ever made her roll. As we bumped, the enemy opened fire with their fo'c'sle guns, though luckily they could not depress them to hit us, but the blast literally cleared everything before it. Our foremast came tumbling down, our for'ard searchlight found its way from its platform above the forebridge down to the deck, and the foremost funnel was blown back until it rested neatly between the two foremost ventilation cowls, like the hinged funnel of a penny river steamboat.[77]

The story of the meeting of *Nassau* and *Spitfire* for the moment remains a shrouded mystery. It may never be solved.

The turn away by the German van was not in line with Scheer's strict orders. '*Durchhalten*', he had time and again stressed. To break through the British line, the German van had to be single-minded. As soon as possible, the ships swung back around to port to head back. Now they were heading towards each other again.

Around midnight, after the *Nassau* had dropped back along the port side of the line, *Thüringen* spotted another probable British target around 1,000yds (900m) off. A hailstorm of close-range shelling ensued and 'every one of the twenty-seven medium-calibre and twenty-four light-calibre shells hit the target, raking the cruiser from after to forward as she was turning away'.[78]

Out of the pitch-black night, the armoured cruiser *Black Prince* roared past the crippled *Spitfire*. She came so close that the guns of the former, which were pointing out on the beam, passed clean over the destroyer's wake. 'She tore past us with a roar, rather like a motor roaring uphill in low gear, and the very crackling and heat of the flames could be heard and felt. She was a mass of fire from foremast to mainmast, on deck and between decks. Flames were issuing out of her every corner.'[79]

She had been heading south to rejoin the fleet after she had lost contact when *Defence* had blown up earlier. Steaming across the head of Beatty's line, astern of *Defence*, she mistimed her pass and had to veer off. And later, in her search for her squadron companions, instead of joining the rear of the Grand Fleet, she ran right into the German battle fleet as they were cutting across the wake of Jellicoe's ships. Stumbling into the very centre of Scheer's battle line, she faced the guns of *Thüringen*, *Ostfriesland* and *Friedrich der Große*. After flashing the recognition signal, fire from *Thüringen* and *Ostfriesland* had rained down on her, knocking two of her funnels clean off. She was so close to the German ships that they could see crewmen 'rushing backwards and forwards on the burning deck'.[80] She drifted out of control down the enemy battleship line, taking more fire from each great ship in turn: from *Thüringen* and *Ost-friesland*, as well as *Nassau* and *Friedrich der Große*.[81] 'She presented a terrible and awe-inspiring spectacle as she drifted down the line, blazing furiously until, after several minor detonations, she disappeared below the surface with the whole of her crew in one tremendous explosion.'[82] Fire had found its way to *Black Prince*'s magazines. When she blew up, she took the entire crew of 857 officers and men to their graves.

Earlier, after *Sparrowhawk* and *Broke* had collided, part of the 4th Destroyer Flotilla took off to the east led by Hutchinson on *Achates*; *Ambuscade*, *Ardent*, *Fortune*, *Porpoise* and *Garland* joined. *Contest* could not keep up, and lost touch. Hutchinson's group soon turned southward hoping to rejoin the British line, but in the run north, *Ardent* and *Fortune* had already become separated. Then *Ardent*'s captain, Lieutenant Commander Arthur Marsden, thought that he spotted *Ambuscade*. Instead, he had run into four German ships crossing from starboard to port. He fired a torpedo at the lead ship and was caught in the enemy's search-lights. They flashed the usual German recognition signal. Immediately, *Fortune*, just astern of *Ardent*, was illuminated, and heavy German fire opened up.

Returning fire against their larger aggressors, the two destroyers managed to cause havoc in the command of *Oldenburg*, where Kapitän zur See Wilhelm Höpfner, though badly wounded, was obliged to take over the wheel after the bridge staff were killed.[83] Fritz Otto Busch, the searchlight officer on *Oldenburg*, described how a 4in shell fired by *Fortune* exploded on the battleship's bridge. The hit caused wide-scale damage and death. Among the dead were Kapitänleutnant Rabius, the fire control officer, signals officers, the second searchlight officer, the officer of the watch, the helmsman and four other men. Kapitän Höpfner, along with a further three officers and nine men, were badly wounded, Höpfner critically. After he had come back to man the helm, just avoiding a collision with another ship, he collapsed from his two wounds. Busch was astonished by the small British ships' will to fight: 'It was the most gallant fight that I had ever seen. She [HMS *Fortune*] was literally riddled with shell; but clear in the glare of our searchlights, I could see a petty officer and two seamen leading and firing her after gun until she disappeared.'[84]

Now it was *Ardent*'s turn. Within minutes she was a fiery wreck, riddled by '22 rounds of 5.9" and 18 of 3.5" fire'.[85] *Westfalen*'s first salvo destroyed her bridge and in twenty-eight seconds, after fifteen shells of secondary battery fire, *Fortune* was completely ablaze.[86] *Ardent* was badly shot up and unable to fire back on her attacker. After five minutes, during which time Marsden managed to dispose of the confidential documents, the Germans moved on. The boat was sinking; the life rafts were useless and the men, forty or fifty of them, lowered themselves into the freezing sea. One by one, they died. In Marsden's words, 'they just seemed to lie back and go to sleep'.[87]

> I spoke to many men and saw most of them die [continued Marsden] … Not a man of them showed any fear of death, and there was not a murmur, complaint or cry for help from a single soul. Their joy was – and they talked about it to the end – that they and the *Ardent* had 'done their bit' as they put it.[88]

When Marsden was rescued – at around 06:00, by the *Marksman* – he was among three who had survived up to then. The other two were picked up by *Obdurate*, but one more died on board. Of a crew of four officers and seventy-eight men, these two were the only survivors.

Turning off their searchlights, the German van continued, leaving behind the trail of wreckage. At around 00:10 the line passed a number of burning hulks. Kommodore Heinrich sent boats to rescue survivors. *S.53* and *G.88* found *Tipperary*, *S.53* managing to bring in nine men who were still floating near the wreck in a raft. *S.54* found and stayed by the crippled *Rostock*. On the way back, *S.53* and *G.88* found another ship, *Elbing*, but before they could help another British destroyer turned up: the *Broke*. Walter Allen had taken over the command with six ships in his line: *Sparrowhawk, Ardent, Porpoise, Garland, Contest* and *Fortune*. In total darkness, at around 00:40, they fell in silently beside the rear of the German line. *Broke* was in very bad shape: 'forty-two of her crew had already been killed, six more were missing, and fourteen were seriously and twenty slightly wounded'.[89] At 500yds (460m), the two German torpedo boats suddenly engaged her and she received two more hits, but then just as abruptly they broke off the action, deeming the mission to help *Elbing* more important. *Broke* turned north and made the Tyne on 3 June in the afternoon.

The equally damaged *Sparrowhawk* was still slowly circling near the stranded *Tipperary*. Around 02:00 a lone German destroyer approached. It came in close, to around 100yds, then nothing. It sat there, watching; the ship moved off without firing. Maybe the Germans did not want to waste more ammunition on an enemy ship that they felt was already doomed.

Three hours later at 06:10 a raft was seen from *Sparrowhawk* with twenty-three survivors from *Tipperary*. They were taken on board, but two had already died and five more would die before reaching England. An attempt was then made to tow *Sparrowhawk* by *Marksman*, the 12th Flotilla's leader, but the hawsers could not hold her. Eventually, *Marksman* fired eighteen rounds to sink her. One of *Tipperary*'s officers, the surgeon, was picked up by the survivors of *Elbing* and transferred to a Dutch boat.

The last action at night in which a 4th Flotilla destroyer participated took place at around 03:10, when a mixed group of fourteen destroyers made up from four different flotillas encountered the German van. *Westfalen* struck again and, having hit *Petard*, picked up the last ship in the line, *Turbulent*, almost under her bow: she was almost blown out of the water.

In the night-time encounters, the 4th Flotilla suffered a 67 per cent casualty rate, but could show little for it. Sadly, especially given the night's extraordinary heroism, not a single report of these encounters got back – at the time – to the bridge of *Iron Duke*. Doubly sad and frustrating was the fact that massive power was so close at hand, yet never intervened:

> At times [the British] battleships had been so near to the engagements in which their own light forces were involved that the *Vanguard*, the rear ship of the 4th Battle Squadron, on one occasion thought that she could make out an attack on the 2nd Battle Squadron on her port side, while the *Thunderer*, the rear ship of the 2nd Battle Squadron, could actually have intervened with her guns several times had she not been afraid of disclosing the position of the battle fleet.[90]

The fifth night encounter: death on *Petard* and the loss of *Turbulent*

Just astern of the German battle fleet's 6th Division, Captain Farie was leading the nine destroyers of the 13th Flotilla from his light cruiser *Champion*. On his port beam was Commander Malcolm L Goldsmith, leading the 9th/10th Flotillas on *Lydiard*, and behind Goldsmith's group came Captain Stirling, with another flotilla leader and thirteen destroyers of the 12th Destroyer Flotilla. The 13th was around four miles northeast of Stirling's group, which *Tipperary* was leading.[91] All combined, it was a sizeable force. Farie had heard the sounds of battle coming from the earlier destroyer engagements taking place to his starboard:

> Heavy firing was opened on our starboard beam, apparently at some of our destroyers between the 13th Flotilla and the enemy. I hauled out to the eastward, as I was unable to attack with any of our flotilla, our own forces being between me and the enemy.[92]

At around 23:30 salvos started falling around them. Nobody was quite certain whence they came – whether they were the enemy's or from their own forces. Goldsmith thought them 'to be our own'.[93] *Landrail*, his third ship in line, thought the same.

Champion's reaction was to swerve violently eastward. It was such a sudden movement that only two destroyers, *Obdurate* and *Moresby*, were able to follow. *Nicator*, *Termagant*, *Narborough*, *Pelican*, *Petard* and *Turbulent* all stayed in line with Goldsmith's destroyers. *Nerissa*, the last ship, became separated, and her place was taken by *Unity*, separated after the 4th Flotilla's earlier actions. Farie cut straight across *Faulknor*'s bows and in doing so pushed her eastwards. *Menace* and *Nonsuch* also took evasive action, *Nonsuch* accelerating hard and heading off eastward. *Faulknor* and the 12th Flotilla ended up heading northeast. At that point, Stirling estimated that he was ten miles behind the Grand Fleet; in fact, it was closer to twenty-four.

On *Lydiard* Goldsmith reassembled the forces he could find to form a makeshift group of twelve ships.[94] The time was approximately 01:00. With the remnants of the 9th and 10th DF were five ships from the 13th Flotilla and *Petard* from the 4th. Goldsmith led his little force back southwest at 30 knots towards where he thought he would find the Germans. In his mind, he would first need to cross what he assumed were ships of the 5th Battle Squadron. Most of his line got across, but the last four did not. They had run in 'head to head' with the van of the German line, across the bows of *Westfalen*.

Geoffrey Corlett's destroyer *Narborough* spotted 'a large vessel making a lot of smoke'. Thinking that she was British, he signalled her. The response was instantaneous. Searchlights flashed on. Small armament fire started hitting the rear of the line. Behind Corlett, Lieutenant Commander K A Beattie on *Pelican* spotted two ships and he too thought that they were British, until fire was opened. Second from last in line was *Petard*. At around 01:25 she spotted large battleship silhouettes 6 points of her starboard bow and practically on top of her at 500yds, but she had no more ordnance, not a single torpedo left after her earlier actions against *Seydlitz* and *V.27*. Lieutenant Commander Thompson, her captain, took the boat right across *Westfalen's* bow. He cleared by 200yds, but was caught in the battleship's searchlights. Before she could get away, *Petard* was hit six times on the stern. In these flashes of combat, two officers (Lieutenant Charles Sperling, who was manning the aft 4in gun, and the surgeon probationer, Hugh Dingle) and seven men were killed: one officer and five men were also wounded. *Petard* was able to get away, but after all the punishment he had taken and the significance of what had just happened, it did not occur to Thompson to send a report back to Jellicoe.

The last destroyer was not as lucky as *Petard*. *Turbulent's* path was blocked by two huge German dreadnoughts – *Westfalen* and *Rheinland* – and she could not get through. *Westfalen* steered slightly to starboard to get more guns to bear on *Turbulent*. The small destroyer had turned away and was trying to outrun the line in parallel. She took a massive broadside of secondary armament fire – twenty-nine 5.9in and sixteen 3.5in shells ripped through her. *Turbulent* was completely disabled and was then rammed by *Rheinland* and split in two. Of the British crew, the Germans only managed to rescue thirteen; five officers and eighty-five men, including her captain, Lieutenant Commander Dudley Stuart, died.

Neither Goldsmith nor the 5th Battle Squadron, four miles to the north, made any report to Jellicoe.

The sixth night encounter: the 12th Destroyer Flotilla attack and the loss of *Pommern*

Earlier in the destroyer attacks, Captain Anselan Stirling's 12th Flotilla had been forced northeast during the confused engagements. From the bridge of *Faulknor*, he decided to resume his search and started heading south looking for more German targets. To his north, two 13th Flotilla destroyers, *Obdurate* and *Moresby*, and the light cruiser *Champion* had started their run south just after midnight.

Faulknor was with the two flotilla leaders and twelve M-class destroyers of the 12th Destroyer Flotilla running parallel to the German van at around 25 knots. At 01:43 *Obedient* caught sight of enemy battleships steering southeast. They were soon identified as *Kaiser*-class. Stirling saw one of the German ships flash the wrong recognition signal – the letter 'K' – and correctly guessed that

German ships were trying to get around the back of the Grand Fleet's destroyer screen. The ships were, in fact, a mixture of Mauve's pre-dreadnoughts and Behncke's super-dreadnoughts, attempting to do just that.

At 01:45 Stirling attacked. With him he had the ships of the 1st Division – *Mindful, Marvel, Onslaught, Faulknor* and *Obedient*, the last a divisional leader, commanded by George William McOran Campbell. But almost immediately, as they swung round, the battleships disappeared behind layers of mist. Stirling realigned his destroyers and tried to radio-signal the valuable information to Jellicoe three times with the low-power destroyer transmitter:[95] 'Enemy battle fleet is steering south-east, approximate bearing south-west. My position is 10 miles astern of the 1st Battle Squadron.'[96] The one commander who took the initiative to give Jellicoe 'eyes' was jammed by German *Telefunken* and no signal got through. Only *Marksman* received Stirling's signal.

Stirling was absolutely convinced that the German line would re-form on its original course and so held on for a while, pushing forward at 25 knots, then turning his small force around 16 points to starboard at 01:06. His adversary came back into view. But now he was caught on the wrong side of the German line, to the northwest, on the Germans' port beam.

At the same time as *Faulknor*, German torpedo boats from the 9th and 5th Flotillas were approaching the main battle line and, in the exchange of recognition signals, *Faulknor*'s second group of attackers were thought to be 'friendlies'. Both *Markgraf* and *Kronprinz* held fire as they were unsure of their targets.[97] It was 02:00. Not so the third ship in the line, the *Großer Kurfürst*. Her guns targeted the third, fourth and fifth boats at a range of around 1,500yds (1,400m). *König* and *Deutschland* also fired, but their targets were less easily made out.

Faulknor fired at the second and third ships in line. *Obedient* fired two torpedoes, and *Marvel* and *Onslaught* four each. *Mindful* made the run several times, but her speed was limited (as one of her boilers was out of action), and in the end she was not able to launch. One torpedo crossed ahead of *Großer Kurfürst*, another about 100yds astern of *Kronprinz*. *Markgraf* turned to avoid two more, while *Hessen* was also successful as a torpedo passed harmlessly by. It was 02:07. But luck was not with *Pommern*.

> The pre-dreadnought was the third ship in line: right amidships in the *Pommern* appeared a dull red ball of fire. It spread fore and aft, and flared up in the masts in big red tongues of flames, uniting in a black cloud of smoke and sparks. Then one saw the ends of the ship come up as though her back was broken before the mist shut her out of view.[98]

It is thought that the explosion had set off one of *Pommern*'s 6.7in magazines.[99] Huge pieces of debris fell near *Deutschland*, maybe a turret roof,[100] and as *Hannover*, the next ship in line, passed, *Pommern* was going under, propellers high out of the water, still turning. An officer described her last moments: 'We saw a huge pillar of fire shoot up to the sky. It looked to us like the trail of a gigantic rocket. The ship must have literally blown to atoms, for a few minutes later not the slightest trace of her could be seen.'[101]

In the attack *Onslaught* was seriously hit. As she was turning away, her bridge was completely destroyed after a box of cordite ignited in the chart house. Lieutenant Commander Onslow, two officers, the coxswain, both quartermasters and both signalmen were either killed or mortally wounded. It was left to a junior sub lieutenant, Harry Kemmis, to take over command and get her back to port. *Onslaught* was the last British vessel to be attacked that day; none of the others in her group had been hit. Of *Pommern*, only the bows remained afloat. All 845 of her crew went down with her, but the other 5th Division ships – *König, Großer Kurfürst, Kronprinz* and *Markgraf* – escaped.

The 2nd division's destroyers could now only count on *Maenad* and *Narwhal* to attack. Three more torpedoes were fired: one from *Maenad*, two from *Narwhal*. Neither *Noble* nor *Nessus* fired.[102] As the enemy steamed the other way, *Maenad*'s commander, John Pelham Champion, tried two last stern shots at ranges of between 4,000 and 5,000yds (3,700–4,600m). The effort was for naught.

The High Seas Fleet was now only sixteen miles from the safety of the Horns Reef entrance. It was too late for Jellicoe to be able to do anything.

The seventh and last night encounter

By this point there was only one destroyer group left to challenge the advancing German van.

Captain Farie on *Champion*, along with *Obdurate* and *Moresby*, were some miles east of the 12th Destroyer Flotilla when they had attacked *Pommern*. They had become detached and were gradually moving south hoping to catch up with the fleet. At 02:15 they heard the sounds of gunfire and turned in its direction. At 02:20 *Marksman* was sighted and a signal made: 'What are ships bearing south?' *Champion* replied, 'They are Germans, I think', then turned away eastward, at 02:34.[103] They too were detached and lost after the last night encounter.

At that moment, around 02:35, Roger Alison on *Moresby*, following *Obdurate*, spotted four German battleships about 4,000yds off. Alison fired a single torpedo at 02:37 and two minutes later felt the concussion wave of an explosion. He was sure he had hit the battle-cruiser but, in fact, had missed. *Von der Tann* had managed a sharp starboard turn-away to avoid the short-fused torpedo. The German line continued inexorably on its southeast course at 18 knots. One destroyer guard, *V.4*, was lost en route. She seemed to blow up for no obvious reason.[104] Scheer later maintained that she had struck a drifting mine.

One other opportunity was missed. While *Champion* was heading back north, leading *Marksman, Maenad* and four destroyers, German torpedo boats were spotted close by to port. They had gathered there to guard the mortally wounded *Lützow* and help remove her crew. Fire was opened but after two minutes the Germans – *G.37, G.38, G.40* and *V.45* – were gone.

The time now was roughly 03:25. It was the last of the confusing, dangerous and incredibly courageous night actions.

Peter Kemp praises the individual courage and persistence of the British destroyers, but one is left with an awful sense of frustration that more did not materialise from these dangerous skirmishes:

> The destroyers had done what they could, had claimed a battleship, two light cruisers and two destroyers as their victims … but had been unable to deflect the German battleships from their homeward course. Only heavy ships could have done that, and the heavy ships were not there.[105]

For their part, the assessment by the Germans is more critical, not of the evident bravery of the destroyer flotillas, but of their tactics, particularly the failure to attack as an organised group in order to launch fans of torpedoes, the evasion of which was far more difficult than individual runs, one after the other. The commanding officer of *Westfalen*, Kapitän Redich, reported that:

> All attacks of British destroyers showed very little training in the methods of making the approach to the attack, inability to estimate the situation and the counter manoeuvres of the vessel attacked. All attacks were executed individually and after approach, and even though it is not in accordance with British tactics to fire during the approach, the destroyers came too close to the German ships before turning and were thus picked up and fired on before they were able to get into action.[106]

The British fleet

The night, even if there was little action on the battleships and battle-cruisers, was not restful. The men were exhausted, there were scenes of the day's carnage all around, the decks slippery with blood and the remains of bodies shredded beyond recognition. One grisly sight aboard *Lion*, made light of by the badly wounded sailor, was described by Able Seaman Alec Tempest:

> Passing along the stoker's mess deck, first-aid parties were bringing wounded stokers up from the engine room. One of them had his leg blown off at the knee. He was yelling his head off, 'Where's my bloody leg?' Repeatedly. The leg was eventually recovered and was found to have the

stoker's roll of bank notes tucked into the sock. The money was obviously of more importance than the leg.[107]

In Q turret, Private Wilson had gone back with the chief gunner to see what ammunition could be salvaged. The scene was almost frozen in the moment of *Lion's* near-death: 'The handling room, switchboard flat and shell room were completely burned out, and the crew were lying in all directions, some still hanging on the ladder in a last attempt to get out ... The major [Hervey] was in the range-finder position close by the voice pipe.'[108]

The three anticipated German destroyer attacks had not materialised. The 2nd Flotilla and 12th Half-Flotilla could not find targets and, after receiving Heinrich's 20:08 signal, headed back around midnight through the Skagerrak. Koch's 7th Flotilla briefly skirmished with the 4th Flotilla and then started to search an area in which they were never to make contact with Jellicoe's ships.[109]

One young commander of a flotilla torpedo boat, Leutnant Edgar Luchting* on *S.23*, recalled how bad the conditions of visibility were that day. After they had been out to try to find the British ships, they had come back 'and looked for our own ships. There were none. There was smoke. Clouds but no German ships.' He continued: 'suddenly the *Derfflinger* appeared ... and our leader boat made a breakthrough behind the *Derfflinger*'. They were dangerously close, 'damn near, as a matter of fact 10–12 metres away'. They scraped up against *Moltke*. The 5th Flotilla held close to the starboard side of the German battle-fleet van, so near that they were fired on by their own ships; *G.11* was even nearly torpedoed by one of the 4th Flotilla attacks.

In daylight Jellicoe would realise how dispersed the fleet had become. Neither Vice Admiral Burney's division nor Beatty's battle-cruisers were anywhere to be seen. At 02:30 Jellicoe had ordered the Grand Fleet north. Only at 03:20 was shooting heard off to the southwest: it was *Indomitable*, unsuccessfully trying to down the Zeppelin *L.11*, which could not see much in any case.

The High Seas Fleet struggles back to safety

By 02:30 Scheer had reached the Horns Reef. Already, starting at 01:30, elements of the fleet had arrived back in the safety of the Jade and by 01:45 the main body was there.[110] He waited for *Lützow*, but heard that she had had to be abandoned. Many of his ships were in poor condition. *König* was unable to pass through the Amrum channel until high tide, since she was drawing too

---

* Luchting talked of the performance of the small torpedo boats. The 570-ton *S.23* had seventy-five crew and was a 'pretty fast boat, had done 37 knots in her trials'. The average age of her crew was only just over twenty-one (Imperial War Museum Collection, no 4168 BBC *The Great War*, Lt Edgar Luchting, German destroyer officer, recorded 1964).

much water from damage forward. Only three light cruisers, *Frankfurt*, *Pillau* and *Regensburg*, were 'available'.

At 04:13 the Grand Fleet re-formed into daylight-cruising formation – lines of four battleships. *Marlborough* was missing. Just after midnight she had asked for help, and to leave the line. Escorts and trawlers from Hull and Grimsby would be standing by ready to take off her entire crew, should she not make it. At one point they came right alongside – there was real fear that she might go down.[111] Later *U.46* fired at her, but missed by about 50yds. *Marlborough* made it back.

Two minutes after the fleet re-formed, Jellicoe was handed the Admiralty signal saying that the High Seas Fleet was – at 03:00 – within sixteen miles of its home base. You could just imagine his frustration at its tardy arrival, compounded by the frustration of reading Beatty's signal a quarter of a hour later: 'Damage yesterday was heavy on both sides. We hope to cut off and annihilate the whole German fleet. Every man must do his utmost. The *Lützow* is sinking and another German battle-cruiser expected to have sunk.' Hopeful of claiming another enemy ship, Jellicoe immediately asked them to concentrate on finding and sinking *Lützow*.

The German battle-cruiser escape

With incredible luck, but also some sheer incompetence on the part of the British, the three heavily wounded German battle-cruisers *Moltke*, *Lützow* and *Seydlitz* got back to the Horns Reef. At one point during their escape, as darkness fell, they had spotted four ships on their port bow. The Germans did not know whose ships they were, but after considerable discussion the idea of launching torpedoes was dropped; the torpedo officer was unconvinced.

It had been clear for some time that *Lützow* was not going to make it. The destroyer *G.39* went alongside and her commander, Oberleutnant Franz-Ferdinand von Löfen, finally succeeded in getting Hipper and Commander Prentzel off and into the safety of the less damaged *Moltke* – a third attempt to do so. *Moltke* continued back to port without further fighting, but had some close calls. At one point, Kapitän Johannes von Karpf saw the threatening shadows of some of the rear dreadnoughts of Jerram's 2nd Battle Squadron. They were around 2,000yds (1,800m) off. It was not that he had not been seen; a British captain, hesitating about giving his own position away, *let* him escape.

On board *Lützow* the situation was really grim. By 00:30 there was so much water in the hull (around 8,300 tons) that Kapitän von Harder decided to get the crew off. He was very worried that she could capsize at any moment. When the fore and middle bulkheads gave out, things were further complicated by the news that a sizeable British force was bearing down on them: two cruisers and five destroyers. It was now around 02:00.

One thousand and forty of her crew transferred to smaller craft but many were still not able to escape despite the orders to abandon ship.[112] Some stayed by choice, others because they had no choice. Twenty-seven men continued working in the diesel-dynamo chamber, keeping the ship supplied with light, giving their comrades the means to find their way out. Trapped, around one hundred heroic, dedicated men worked through to the end.

Lost Opportunities in the Night Action

- Captain A D Doyle (*Malaya*) and Captain M Woollcombe (*Valiant*) both spotted 'significant ships' passing. Neither did anything about it, nor did Captains Farie (*Champion*) and Stirling (*Faulknor*) also, though the latter did tried to pass on information but was jammed.
- *Thunderer* allowed *Moltke* to pass by and did nothing. As the captain later said: 'It was inadvisable to show up the battle fleet unless obvious attack was intended'.[113] At 22:30 she had edged over to the port towards the Grand Fleet and been seen as a dim outline from the ships of Rear Admiral Jerram's 2nd Battle Squadron.
- *Seydlitz* had a miraculous escape, maybe more so as she passed three British dreadnoughts without getting fired upon, apparently – according to some accounts – using the British recognition signal 'J' and even being answered. She had even passed down the starboard side of the British battle line, seen by *Agincourt* and then *Marlborough*, who later reported seeing 'a large ship', but did not fire. The gunnery officer, Lieutenant Commander Guy Royle, lamented: 'I missed the chance of a lifetime on this occasion. I saw the dim outline of this ship from the top and had the main armament trained on it and put a range of 4,000 yards on the sights and a deflection of 24 right, then asked the Captain (George Ross), who was in the conning tower, for permission to open fire. He replied, "No", as he thought that it was one of our ships. Of course, what I ought to have done was to have opened fire and blown the ship out of the water and then said, "Sorry".'[114]
- Again *Thunderer*. This time apparently thinking *Seydlitz* to be a destroyer. No report. She did not want to give her own position away was the later explanation. The scout cruisers *Boadicea* and *Fearless* decided not to attack: 'It was too late to fire a torpedo when she could be identified'.[115] *Seydlitz* was also seen by *Revenge*. Her 6in gun crews were given orders to fire but they were not at their stations. They had been watching the night action as though they were at a fireworks display; by the time they were back at their posts, it was too late.
- But the lack of reporting was not just confined to the night action. Observers on the *Canterbury* and the *Falmouth* saw Scheer's first battle turn and reported nothing.
- One of the few ships that did try to get intelligence back was *Faulknor*. Despite Stirling's efforts, his signals were jammed. Three separate signals from *Faulknor* to *Iron Duke* were sent at 01:56, 02:08 and 02:13. Even if *Faulknor*'s position was wrong it would have given Jellicoe an important indication of what was occurring behind the fleet (see Macintyre, p179).

At around 02:45 the decision was taken to put an end to the stricken *Lützow*. A destroyer, *G.38*, fired two torpedoes into the twisted mass of steel that was once a proud and powerful battle-cruiser. At the very same moment of the torpedo launch, seven men were seen running, desperately trying to get to the quarterdeck. Two other destroyers, *V.2* and *V.6*, came to help take crew off. *V.4* was also there, but had had its bow blown off. A torpedo from *V.2* finally sank Hipper's brave but crippled flagship. *Lützow* went under and took 597 lives. The wreck rests today at a depth of 44m (144ft). Much was picked over by commercial dive operations in the 1960s, but around her, a hundred years later, divers can still find a mass of her 12in shells with their characteristic 5ft-long shell cases.

On *Seydlitz* Kapitän zur See Moritz von Egidy's intention was to follow *Moltke*, but she lost contact and very nearly lost her way entirely. Nothing was working. The compasses were broken, the charts covered in blood and even the spare charts inaccessible. But she escaped. At 01:40 she managed, somehow, to reach the Horns Reef, running aground twice and Egidy twice going astern to refloat her.

By the afternoon of 1 June, at around 13:30 *Seydlitz* was finally able to turn around and reverse in stern first. Her list was now at 8 degrees. *Pillau* had tried a tow, but the hawser lines broke. They found another way. As the wind started to blow more strongly, *Pillau* opened up her sea-cocks to let out oil, calming the furious waters. The *Seydlitz* then ran aground on the Weser river sandbank; in the end she was carrying around 5,300 tons of water inside her hull. When she had reached the Horns Reef she was so badly flooded forward that the middle fish (of the three stacked one on top of the other in her bow crest) was in the water, and to prevent her stern lifting out of the water entirely with the immense forward weight, a significant amount of counter-flooding was implemented in the after sections. Over the next four days two 11in guns were taken off to lighten her more, as well as armour from her forward turrets.

On 6 June at 15:30 *Seydlitz* finally made it back inside the sluice gates. She still could not get into the dry dock itself but she was now safe. Egidy and First Officer Commander von Alvensleben's efforts to get her back to Wilhelmshaven had been extraordinary. She had received hits from 'around 21 heavy and two medium' shells, as well as having been hit by a torpedo. A full week later on the 13th she was finally secure inside the dry dock. Of her crew, ninety-eight were dead and a further fifty-five wounded: the figures were lower than at Dogger Bank, but this time she herself could almost be counted amongst the dead. She was little more than a floating husk.

Beatty gives Jellicoe the bad news

By 06:00 the light cruisers had rejoined the Grand Fleet, and by 09:00 most of its destroyer screens. Jellicoe started to radio for reports. Just after 10:00 Beatty signalled Jellicoe the position of the wrecks of *Queen Mary* and *Indefatigable*, but he had not preceded this with any explanation of why they were 'wrecks' at all. It was a bombshell for Jellicoe.

One hour later, replying to Jellicoe's continued inquiry as to when they had gone down, Beatty said: '*Indefatigable* sank at 4 pm, *Queen Mary* at 4.30 pm'. Jellicoe was mystified. The commander-in-chief almost had to coax the information out. The exchange of signals had been astonishing: 2,200 British sailors had perished and Jellicoe was only now finding out for the first time.

Jellicoe to Beatty: 'Was the cause sinking mines, torpedoes or gunfire?'

Beatty to Jellicoe: 'I do not think it was mines or torpedoes because both explosions immediately followed hits by salvos.'

For a few hours, British ships continued looking around for wounded in the battle debris. One of *Tipperary's* crew members blessed his luck that day as he was spotted from the *Dublin*. One sailor remembered:

There's something in the water. It looks like a figure waving … a German…
To everyone's surprise he shouted, 'Thank God!' He had one arm on a tea
box. We dropped a Jacob's ladder over the side for him to climb up, but he was
so exhausted and nearly dead. All we could do was send a man down with a
heaving line.[116]

Others were not so lucky. As the ships made their way back to their home ports, the sad duty of 'calling the roll', to account for all crews, had to be carried out. On *Barham*, the scene was as it must have been on many other ships:

I was horrified to come on deck and see our fore mess deck gone, sick-
bay patients and staff wiped out, as the sick bay had received a direct hit. I
thought to myself, 'I must be lucky!' Because nine of us boys who had not
been vaccinated during the last five years were attended to on 30 May. On the
morning of the 31st, eight went sick and were detained in the sick bay: I put
up with my sore arm and remained alive.[117]

The dead sailors were laid out on deal planks, sewn up in a hammock with a 6in shell tied between their feet and a Union Jack draped over them. To the sound of the bugle and hushed prayers, accompanied by mumbled and choked responses, the dead slid out, each splashing into the grey-brown waters of the North Sea.

Many did not sink immediately, but kind of floated in a horizontal position for a time until the weights took effect, when they gradually righted themselves to an upright position with about half of the canvas showing above the surface before finally disappearing beneath the waves. It was an eerie scene, as though they wanted to take one last look at their old ships before they went under.[118]

On *Lion*, Beatty was so overcome that he could not carry on. Fighting back tears, he handed the prayer book to Ernle Chatfield to honour the dead sinking to their graves.

Homecoming: what a difference a day makes

Tuesday	Wednesday	Thursday	Friday	Saturday	Sunday
30 May	31 May	1 June	2 June	3 June	4 June

Monday	Tuesday	Wednesday	Thursday	Friday	Saturday	Sunday
5 June	6 June	7 June	8 June	9 June	10 June	11 June

As Scheer was entering the Jade river, he ordered champagne up to the bridge of *Friedrich der Große*. It must have tasted good: maybe not quite the victory drink that he had foreseen, but Scheer had successfully brought most of his fleet home against huge odds. The outcome had nearly been very different.

Getting back to port first, the Germans were able – critically, as it turned out – to get word out about the battle in the way they wanted. A communiqué from the Admiralstab was prepared and released mid-afternoon on Thursday, 1 June. A Reuters dispatch, based wholly on what the Germans wanted to appear, led to newspapers around the world carrying their story while Jellicoe and Beatty were still at sea.

The German announcement suggested a great sea victory off the Skagerrak, without mentioning the word 'victory'; it talked rather of there having been 'a successful engagement':

> During the afternoon a series of heavy engagements developed between the Skagerrak and the Horns Reef that were successful for us and continued throughout the night. In three engagements, so far as has been learnt to the present, the large British battleship *Warspite* and the battle-cruisers *Queen Mary* and *Indefatigable* were destroyed, as were two armoured cruisers apparently of the *Achilles* type, one light cruiser, the new destroyer flotilla leaders *Turbulent*, *Nestor* and *Acasta*, a large number of torpedo-boat destroyers, and one submarine. Through observations beyond challenge, it is known that a large number of English battleships suffered damage from our

ships' artillery and from the attacks of our torpedo-boat flotillas during the day and night engagements. Among others, the large battleship *Marlborough* was struck by a torpedo, as has been confirmed by prisoners. Several of our ships rescued portions of the crews of sunken English ships, among them being the only two survivors of the *Indefatigable*. On our side the light cruiser *Wiesbaden* was sunk by hostile artillery fire during the day engagements and the *Pommern* during the night by a torpedo. The fate of the *Frauenlob*, which is missing, and of some torpedo boats which have not returned home, is unknown. The High Seas Fleet returned to our ports during the day.[119]

In part, Scheer's report on the British losses was correct or even understated. Three British battle-cruisers had been sunk, not two. Two armoured cruisers had also been sunk but a third, *Warrior*, sank on the way back to port; Scheer nonetheless vastly overestimated the number of destroyers – thirteen against the actual eight – and misled in his statement that 'a large number of English battleships suffered damage from our ships' artillery'.[120]

The extensive damage that had been inflicted on the High Seas Fleet was entirely covered up. There was no mention of the severe damage to *Seydlitz*, *Derfflinger* or *Von der Tann*, or, indeed, of the actual loss of the most modern battle-cruiser, Hipper's flagship *Lützow*. The pre-dreadnoughts also were all in bad shape and even ships of the first line were badly holed. *König* was drawing 10m (32ft) of water. When the loss of *Lützow* finally leaked out, the secrecy backfired. Their recounting of events, not questioned until then, now came under intense scrutiny. So it was with *Rostock* and *Elbing*. To use the expression 'missing' when talking about *Frauenlob*, or of other ships (*S.35*, *V.4*, *V.27*, *V.29* and *V.48*) as not having 'returned home', were similar untruths that backfired.

The afternoon Scheer arrived back in harbour, just after he had sent out a communiqué to the fleet with the words '*Deutschland und unser Kaiser über alles*', he received a written note of congratulations from the Kaiser: 'I am proud of our mighty fleet, which has proved by this feat of arms that it is a match for a superior enemy'.[121] With such announcements it was hardly surprising that there was celebration all over Germany, flags flying wildly on Berlin's Unter den Linden and headlines extolling the Trafalgar that Germany had won.

The British, in total contrast, bungled the handling of the story from the first. In the Admiralty's Room 37 the Royal Navy's official censor, Captain Sir Douglas Brownrigg, received the text of the German communiqué; Jellicoe was radioed the text and asked for his response to the claimed British losses. Jellicoe responded openly, not thinking that his words would be used for any outside communication. He was alarmingly frank about the British losses and his words contained no spin.

One of the first of Beatty's battle-scarred ships back at Rosyth was the heavily damaged *Warspite*. Still on fire, she passed the Forth Bridge on 1 June at around 15:00, greeted by 'loud cheers from the men at work on the bridge'.[122] On the way back, once out of the battle area, the turret crews had been allowed to stretch their legs. It was the first sight that many had of the damage that their ship had sustained:

> When I got out [on top of the turret] I was amazed at what I saw. Part of the bridge was alight, a store of lifebelts under the bridge was in flames; I could see there was a fire raging in the 6-inch battery where the cordite was alight; the upper deck was riddled with shell; the funnels were holed, every boat on the ship had a hole in it and the ship looked really bad.[123]

Warspite's hull was 4ft 6in lower in the water than it should have been. A lucky escape she might have had, but she still had fighting spirit: she had spotted *U.63* on the journey back and had tried to ram her. (Luckily for the submarine, which had engine trouble, it was able to crash-dive fast.) As soon as she docked, nurses from the hospital ship *Plassey* went to work bringing the wounded ashore.

At 08:30 on Friday, 2 June, as the scraps of news about the battle were starting to leak out, the Battle Cruiser Fleet made home waters, sailing into the Firth of Forth. Families lined the banks. Admiral Hood's family, unaware of what had happened to *Invincible*, stood and waved the fleet in as enthusiastically as the rest. Only later that night, when an Admiralty communiqué was released, did they discover the news of the death of the 1,019 souls, including the head of the family, the Hon Horace Hood, who had gone down with the battle-cruiser two days previously.

One sailor from *Malaya* was totally shell-shocked. He had endured appalling conditions and thought that he was still in his turret station:

> After landing at base we were taken by hospital train to Queensferry. Ladies on the train handed us cigarettes. I kept shouting, 'Pass up Lyddite, pass up shrapnel'. A lady put a spoonful of jelly in my mouth to shut it. One chap said, 'Do you know who that lady was?' I said, 'Haven't the slightest.' He said, 'That was Lady Jellicoe!'[124]

Not everything about the battle-cruiser homecoming was welcoming. As *Lion* returned to her berth at around 09:00, a black moment came for those who had fought so valiantly over the previous two days: the memory remained with them for many years after. Dock workers, hearing the news that the Reuters report had given out and that had started to spread, jeered the sailors; later, they spat on them in the streets. By late afternoon, the news was everywhere and crowds began to form, heckling sailors:

My job in harbour was to run the second picket boat, so I took the steward in to a pier just underneath the Forth Bridge, at the bottom of the hill, South Queensferry. There was not a very big crowd of about 30 people and their attitude was one of, 'Here, what do you think you are doing? What do you think we pay the navy for?' Remarks like that. We said, 'Well, we have just had a battle!' 'Yes,' they said, 'fine battle that was. The Germans beat you, didn't they? We read about it in the papers.' Now that was really a complete surprise to us and a great shock.[125]

Before the Grand Fleet had made port at Scapa Flow the Admiralty, while doing nothing to help form a response from the British commanders, released the text of the German communiqué to the British public. It was a very strange thing to do. Jellicoe's no-spin report, made in response to Admiralty requests for information, was signalled at 10:35 after the release of the German communiqué had started circulating. Jellicoe's words were factual and talked of the known British losses, and of some of the assumed German casualties and sinkings.

The way that he dealt with the information set the tone: 'VAC BCF reports *Queen Mary*, *Indefatigable* blown up by enemy shell exploding in magazine. *Invincible* blown up, probably same cause but might be due to mine or submarine. She was blown in half. *Defence* similarly blown up'.[126]

Three hours after the battle-cruisers had arrived in the Forth at 11:30, the Grand Fleet also made it home to the protection of Scapa Flow to a very different scene. No one was there. Nobody welcomed or cheered the battle-weary sailors as they slid silently through the cold grey waters of the flow. Almost before anything else was the business of re-coaling and restocking, accompanied by the duties of burying the dead on the island of Hoy.

The British were clearly in a quandary. The Reuters radio reports were circulating furiously and rumours were growing. The battle-cruiser crews had been subjected to a baffling reception, in their minds, after coming out of a fierce and bloody fight. The Admiralty had to do something.

The first communiqué was most likely written by First Lord of the Admiralty, Arthur Balfour, assisted by Admiral Sir Henry Jackson (1SL), and Vice Admiral Sir Henry Oliver (Chief of Staff). Douglas Brownrigg claimed that Jellicoe had been asked for a statement for publication, but this was not so: had Jellicoe known how his information was going to be used, he would probably have signalled none at all.

The final text for the first Admiralty communiqué – several were to be released over the following days – was only concluded and handed to the British press that evening, at 19:00, more than forty-eight hours after the battle had started. It played right into German hands by not claiming the victory that

Jutland was: like the German communiqué, the British one did not use the word 'victory'. It talked instead of the losses among the British battle-cruisers as having been 'heavy', while saying that the enemy losses were only 'serious'. Sir Shane Leslie described the net result pretty memorably: 'It was so impartial it might have been issued from the planet Neptune'.[127]

At 19:20 Brownrigg said that the Admiralty had to make a statement, as the 'ports were full of damaged ships and our hospitals full of wounded men', with no thought that it might not have got the statement right. Seventeen British ships were named as sunk or lost; no mention that the Royal Navy had been left with control of the North Sea, or that a flotilla had been sent out to ascertain this the next morning, was made. The overall impression on the British public was that a terrible defeat had been suffered. News vendors cried out the dreadful headline.

Balfour tried to explain his position in a personal meeting with the same Major Claude Wallace of the 14th Hussars, aboard the *St Vincent* when she set sail for the fleet rendezvous. Wallace had witnessed the battle (and wrote about it later): 'As I had received no definite news from the fleet as to the German losses I could not very well say anything about them. Something had to be issued in reply to the German account in order to allay anxiety at home.'[128]

Saturday, 3 June 1916 was George V's birthday. Jellicoe wrote to him on behalf of the fleets to offer their congratulations. The King's response was a fine spin on the events that had robbed the British admiral of a more obviously understandable victory:

> I am deeply touched by the message which you have sent me … it reaches me on the morrow of a battle which has once more displayed the splendid gallantry of the officers and men under your command … I mourn for the loss of brave men, many of them personal friends of my own, who have fallen in their country's cause. Yet even more do I regret that the German High Seas Fleet, in spite of its heavy losses, was enabled by the misty weather to evade the full consequences of an encounter which they have always professed to desire, but for which, when the opportunity arrived, they showed no inclination …[129]

A second communiqué, increasing the known German losses, was issued at 01:15 Saturday morning after Jellicoe had updated the Admiralty three times on the evening of Friday the 2nd. It was also 'shortly after midnight' when Beatty had added his own long report.[130]

Beatty's perspective was that the Grand Fleet had only been 'a short time in action'. While he offered – and would retain – the public image of support for his commander-in-chief, it is clear from early accounts that he was unhappy. Hubert Dannreuther, the *Invincible*'s gunnery officer who had magically

survived, remembered visiting him and said that Beatty 'firmly believed that
he had been deserted'.[131] Finally came some added – albeit guarded – details of
the presumed enemy losses: 'of three enemy battle-cruisers (two of them believed to be the *Derfflinger* and the *Lützow*), one had been blown up, another
was seen to be disabled and the third was observed to be seriously damaged
… one German light cruiser and six German destroyers were sunk … repeated
hits had been observed on three of the German battleships.'[132] More and more
it seemed that the public was willing to accept that Beatty had suffered heavy
losses; the fact that the Germans had been allowed to escape and that Jellicoe
had suffered no losses at all seemed to suggest that he had let Beatty down and
not tried to engage the enemy.

In Germany, by 2 June the propaganda machine was at full tilt. Wilhelm
II visited the docks, building on a picture of a great victory. Surrounded by
cheering sailors, he decorated the men with Iron Crosses. Each ship had a
quota of awards. Scheer and Hipper were offered elevation to the nobility,
although only Hipper accepted the Kaiser's gift. He became Franz, Ritter von
Hipper. Scheer was promoted to admiral (Hipper also accepted his own elevation to vice admiral). Both received the '*Pour le Mérite*', Germany's highest
military honour.

Jellicoe, meanwhile, communicated his displeasure at the first communiqué.
His comments were received at the Admiralty at around 14:00 on Saturday, 3
June. By now there was a sense of desperation in senior British political and
naval circles, and a realisation that they had seriously erred in communicating
in the way that they had. Winston Churchill was called on for his journalistic
skills. Brownrigg thought that he would be credible as he had always been seen
as a 'somewhat keen critic of the Admiralty'.[133] He was given wide access to
many confidential papers on the Saturday afternoon and asked to write for the
Sundays. His main point was that 'The British margin of superiority at sea remained in no way impaired', and that it was the 'hazy weather, the fall of night,
and the retreat of the enemy'[134] that frustrated the efforts of both Jellicoe and
Beatty. But damage had been inflicted. 'Seventy-two hours of confusion had
done the mischief' was how Langhorne Gibson and Vice Admiral J E T Harper
put it in 1936 in *The Riddle of Jutland*.[135]

The British press now complained that it had not been given the same kind
of access that Churchill had had. While the Germans had been first back to harbour and publicised their side of events immediately, the British had dithered.
Rumours about the battle swirled around London society. Admiralty communiqués showing a complete inability to manage wartime spin did not help
convince the British public of the facts. What had taken the British days had
taken their adversaries hours.

On the morning of Monday, 5 June a third communiqué from the Admiralty got to the point: 'Sir John Jellicoe, having driven the enemy into port, returned to the main scene of the action and scanned the sea in search of disabled vessels'.[136] What did the Admiralty now do? It opened up many of the files on the battle (except the secret ones dealing with the details of the loss of the three battle-cruisers) to all journalists; Jellicoe was, of course, astonished. He complained. The Admiralty reimposed censorship – from one extreme to the other. And with censorship thus reimposed, Jellicoe won a point, but only further angered his enemies in the press.

On 7 June the Germans admitted to the loss of *Lützow* and *Rostock*. That same day, a Wednesday, saw other news that eroded the credibility of the Royal Navy: namely, Lord Kitchener's death after *Hampshire* sank. She had been hit by a mine laid earlier by *U.75*, to the west of the Orkney Islands.

Jellicoe worked on his dispatch now that he was able, back on dry land, to talk with his admirals. The issues in writing it were considerable: for example, could he mention the names of all the destroyers, including many new ones, that were unknown to the Germans? Another way had to be found, which was to mention only the ones that had rendered outstanding action during the battle.

Some of the admiral's less public reactions, written only days after the battle had ended, only became available for the first time in 2015.* He said it had been 'next to impossible to make out the situation' before the deployment. Quite surprisingly he said that he was 'not quite sure if the firing ahead of me was *at* [my italics] the battle fleet' and before making his decision, he 'considered this point at the time'. When *Iron Duke* opened fire, 'we could only just see the ship' around 11,500yds (10,500m) distant that turned out to be *König*. He recognised that the bad visibility might have been the reason for the battle-cruiser losses when he was told about the action by Evan-Thomas, but he added that it was also 'the fact that the enemy's battle-cruisers have the protection of battleships whereas ours are most indifferently protected'. This private thought was very different from some of Jellicoe's later, public statement, clearly written to maintain BCF morale and a faith in their own ships. At first light, visibility was down to 'three or four miles' and he concluded around 10:00 that 'the enemy had cleared out'. He concluded saying that he 'could not conceive of an action being fought under more difficult circumstances'. Mention has been made already of the fact that Beatty's plot was twelve miles out; Goodenough's was even more – twenty:

---

* The letter (and the accompanying typed report) which was sent to Rear Admiral Warrender in June 1916, were then purchased by a private collector from whom we tried, unsuccessfully, to acquire them for the Cayzer family archives. Very generously the same man has provided copies to the family.

consequently it was impossible for me to say where I was going to meet their fleet, or on what bearing, or where our ships were. That and the gathering mist and darkness gave a very difficult problem to solve. It was really bad luck striking them under such conditions. Had it not been for this bad luck, I think business must have been decisive.[137]

Jellicoe was, at this point, under the impression that 'three battleships and three battle-cruisers 'were certainly sunk', but he found public perception of the battle was like a yo-yo. 'I am only annoyed', he wrote in his covering letter, 'because first the country looked on it as a defeat and now they are inclined to look on it as a 2nd Trafalgar' [*underlining in the original*].

By the time Jellicoe released the dispatch on 6 July, other concerns were in the air. The Somme offensive on the first day of the month had begun as an unmitigated disaster and so, even if Jutland could be seen in a better light, its moment in the light as a victory had now passed.

Changing the guard

In the days following the battle, the disappointment that Jellicoe felt was crushing. He felt let down by circumstances, subordinates and events. He was, according to Beatty, sick that he had missed this great chance. Jellicoe came to see Beatty: Beatty reported that he sank into a chair in his cabin, his head in his hands. For Beatty, it was about more than disappointment. He seethed at what he saw as Jellicoe's caution that had, in his opinion, allowed Scheer and Hipper to slip away after they had been so brilliantly delivered into his hands.

The admirals' camps divided. The officers and men of the battleships and the battle-cruisers were never that close anyway. An unhealthy rivalry had taken the place of earlier friendlier times. The battle-cruiser crews serving on Jacky Fisher's greyhounds regarded their battleship counterparts as dinosaurs whose time was well past. Louis Mountbatten talked of how strong these attitudes were:

I completely changed the immature emotional views I had absorbed about Jellicoe when I was a midshipman. I now realised what an outstandingly competent, brave and brilliant man he was, though I could still have wished that he had steered for the Horns Reef.[138]

In his youth, Mountbatten, had been less than enthusiastic about Jellicoe: Jellicoe, in his words, was 'without style and looking like a frightened tapir. Beatty had dash, élan and loads of style.'[139]

The camp-followers exacerbated the debate in the weeks and months that followed, spurred on by press and politicians responding to the public clamour and search for scapegoats in the absence of the wild expectations of another Trafalgar. Jellicoe was sad to hand over command of the Grand Fleet, for sure, but as the new First Sea Lord, he felt that he could help find an answer to the increasingly pressing problem of the submarine threat. He was also very tired. But he would never have chosen Beatty as his successor – he had wanted Madden to take the position.

When he was asked on 24 November 1916 by Balfour to take the position, Jellicoe arranged to meet him three days later in Rosyth, and accepted. Jellicoe felt that his services commanding the Grand Fleet could be spared and that Scheer would not attempt another sortie while he was repairing his fleet and while he focused all his efforts on the increasingly dangerous submarine campaign. He was, in Gibson and Harper's words, 'almost uncannily accurate in his predictions'. A day later on the 28th, Beatty wrote to his old friend Walter Cowan, from the very first day of his new command, expressing the opinion from which he never wavered: that the battle fleet had not been engaged: 'As you will know, my heart will always be with the battle-cruisers who can get some speed but I'll take good care that when they are next in it, up to the neck, this old Battle Fleet shall be in it too'.[140]

Scheer had actually just been censured by the Kaiser for the further damage done to his beloved fleet. This was not only about *Westfalen*'s torpedo damage from *E.23*; on 4 November 1916 British torpedoes damaged *Große Kurfürst* and *Kronprinz* as well. The light cruisers *Stettin* and *München* had also been damaged on 10 October. Scheer promised to keep the High Seas Fleet behind the safety of defensive minefields while the submarine war was being played out.

On 5 December Jellicoe took up his new role at the Admiralty. On the very same day the Asquith government resigned. This was a double blow. Jellicoe had lost an important political ally just when the vital challenges of, and vision for, his new position needed to be emphasised. 'The duties of the First Sea Lord', writes James Goldrick, 'were monumental in both peace and war, and required enormous energy'.[141] Jellicoe, despite being a very keen sportsman, was already exhausted after two gruelling years of command of the Grand Fleet. His move to a desk job was misunderstood – interpreted as some sort of public pillorying, especially in the light of Beatty's moving into the position that Jellicoe had just vacated. With the change of government, however, and Lloyd George's becoming prime minister, Jellicoe's position became increasingly shaky. He and Lloyd George had never seen eye to eye: not, anyway, since their public confrontations over the 1909 Naval Estimates.

THE
AFTERMATH

—

11

Opening Pandora's Box:
Unrestricted Submarine War

———

'You kill him. I'll bury him.'
Lloyd George to Lord Northcliffe, talking about Jellicoe's future,
quoted in Robert Massie, *Castles of Steel*

On 19 November 1916 the American president, Woodrow Wilson, put forward a plan for peace talks. His ideas fell on deaf ears. Lloyd George's new government was already opposed to the secret German proposals which had been received just three days previously. Consequently, the prime minister was quick to reject Wilson's olive branch, preferring, as he expressed it, to 'put our trust rather in an unbroken army than in broken faith'.

In fact, the situation was improving for Germany, particularly in the east. Pressure on Romania had come to a head and on 6 December Bucharest fell. Romanian oil came under German control. In one campaign, the Germans had gained an essential war commodity, abundant wheat supplies and an opportunity to shift much needed troops back to the Western Front where, under the new commanders, Paul von Hindenburg and Erich von Ludendorf, a new defensive line was being built, literally setting in concrete the terrible stalemate of war in the trenches.

It was different in Germany itself. Morale was deteriorating. The effects of the British blockade were hitting the population hard. Many had barely survived the 'Turnip Winter' of 1916 and the feeling was one of near desperation.* The moment had come for Germany to boldly throw one last roll of the dice to try to win the war, rather than negotiate its ending. Holtzendorf's plan for unrestricted submarine warfare was the key to the gamble.

With a victory in her pocket, Germany now felt she could open negotiations. In a speech in the Reichstag on 12 December, Chancellor Theobald von Bethmann-Hollweg outlined a proposal, but put practically nothing on the

---

* The staple diet became 'turnips and herb tea, potato bread, very little meat' (Gibson and Harper, p322).

table. Rather, it read as though it would be the Allies' fault if the war dragged on because the Allies did not wish to negotiate. Three days later the French launched a strong counter-attack and pushed the Germans back from Verdun to where they had started. With the Tsar also rejecting the idea on the 20th, Wilson suggested that the Allies make their own proposals directly to the Germans. The German olive branch had fallen on very stony ground.

Bethmann-Hollweg's speech was not popular with either the army or the navy. In a memorandum dated 22 December, Holtzendorf outlined his thoughts on Britain's vulnerability: 'Now England's mainstay is her shipping, which brings to the British Isles the necessary supplies of food and materials for war industries and ensures their solvency abroad'.[1] Not only by directly hitting British and Allied shipping, but also in the belief that 'at least two-fifths of neutral sea traffic will at once be terrorised into ceasing their journeys', Holtzendorf calculated that within five months all shipping to and from England would be reduced by a massive 39 per cent. With the army now backing him, the last barriers to the chancellor's opposition to Holtzendorf's plan were removed. Scheer's conclusive remarks to the Kaiser in June 1916 had finally found fertile ground.†

On 1 February the new campaign was launched. Starting with around 142 submarines, the Germans were able to sink more than 2,000,000 tons of Allied shipping in the first three months.[2] For the British, the prospect of a successful outcome to the war suddenly became very bleak indeed. But the German navy had not planned well for this sudden change of strategy – well enough, that is, to give the level of certainty that Holtzendorf needed‡ – even if new boats were being launched at a furious pace. While the campaign's immediate successes secured political, financial and naval support and more than 250 new submarine orders were placed with German yards in 1917 (fifty-one in February, ninety-five in June and 120 in December)[3], the question really was, would these new assets arrive too late?

---

† Scheer had written to the Kaiser shortly after the Battle of Jutland saying that 'A victorious end to the war in the foreseeable future can only be achieved by wearing down the British economy, therefore by setting the U-boats against the British trade routes ... I strongly advise your Majesty not to opt for any milder form of U-boat warfare ... which would force us into humiliating loss of face if we could not act without total ruthlessness (*mit voller Schärfe*)', quoted in Nicolas Wolz, *From Imperial Splendour to Internment. The German Navy in the First World War* (Seaforth, 2015).

‡ A German study before the war had been done by Korvettenkapitän Blum on what numbers of submarines would be needed to make an economic blockade of Britain successful. He reckoned 222, so the second unrestricted submarine campaign would be launched with half of what he calculated was necessary. Fregattenkapitän Hermann Bauer, who led the North Sea submarines at the start of the war, said that of the twenty-one submarines stationed there in 1914, only three or four could be maintained on patrol (Terraine, p9).

German Submarines Active in Primary Theatres, 1917

Group	Feb	March	April	May	June	July	Nov
HSF	46	52	54	56	59	59	
Pola	23	24	25	26			31
Flanders	23	32	33	34			29
Total	92	108	112	116			

Source: Karau, *Naval Flank of the Western Front, The German MarineKorps Flandern 1914–1918*, p115.

As the campaign progressed, by design so did 'sinkings without warning'. The sinking of still mostly unarmed merchant ships without surfacing and issuing a warning rose from 37 per cent to 60 per cent in the first three months.[4] British outrage strengthened, and neutral opinion shifted sharply in favour of the Allied cause, fed by press stories of the atrocities of the total war at sea. It strengthened, rather than weakened, Allied resolve.

Even before the new German submarine initiative was announced, Jellicoe acted. It was well 'before either Lloyd George or Geddes would have been the reason'.[5] It may have been that in 1914 'the Admirals of the Royal Navy remained contemptuous of the potential of the submarine'.[6] Even Churchill, in writing to Fisher, argued against the latter's case, though I'm sure he would later say that he qualified his conclusion: 'There are a few points on which I am not convinced. Of these, the greatest is the question of the use of submarines to sink merchant vessels. I do not believe that this would ever be done by a civilized power.'[7] For him it was also unlikely that the Germans would use unrestricted submarine war. In *The World Crisis*, he wrote: 'Neither the First Lord (Battenberg) nor I shared Lord Fisher's belief that the Germans would use submarines for sinking unarmed merchantmen without challenge or any means of rescuing crews. It was abhorrent to the moral law and practice of the sea.'

Since he was writing in 1923 with the benefit of hindsight, I think Churchill's inclusion of this correspondence was merely to emphasise that Germany was not a civilised nation and that she possessed no moral code of any worth. It should be pointed out, however, that Fisher anticipated this kind of total war with Germany in 1913.

From the beginning, Jellicoe was of a very different ilk. He very clearly saw the dangers even if he did immediately not have the answers. He was clear that finding them would take time:

> The Admiralty can hold out little hope that there will be any reduction in the rate of loss … unless new methods which have been and are in the process of being adopted … result in the destruction of enemy submarines at a greater

rate than that at which they are being constructed ... On the latter point it would not be safe to anticipate benefit during the next two or three months.[8]

Britain's anti-submarine warfare (ASW) efforts had been floundering. Admiral Sir Henry Jackson, Jellicoe's predecessor, wrote to Balfour, then First Lord, voicing his concern in 1916: 'the methods which have been used in the past for attacking submarines are now not meeting with the success which had hitherto attended them'.[9] Following his memo, Balfour gave him the position of First Sea Lord (1SL) in the hopes that he would find the solution with the help of 'young officers who (were) prolific in ideas', as Jackson had requested.

Criticism of Jackson and the previous regime was strong. To Andrew Gordon, Jackson was 'lacklustre', and the Admiralty 'comatose'.[10] Even Jellicoe complained. In a letter to Beatty at the start of 1917 he said, 'Everything has been left to the wait and see principle. The late government is to blame'.[11] This kind of accusatory tone was unusual for Jellicoe and showed his mounting concern. Asquith finally moved: Arthur Balfour was out; in came Sir Edward Carson. The Ulster Unionist Member of Parliament joked, 'I am here, gentlemen, because I know nothing at all about the job. My only great qualification for being put at the head of the Navy is that I am very much at sea'. He and Jellicoe would work well together from the first meeting.[12]

Jellicoe was appointed to 'sweep its hallowed corridors with (what was anticipated as) a stimulating sea-breeze'.[13] And on 13 December Jellicoe set up the new Anti-Submarine Division under Rear Admiral Alexander Duff.[14] A staff was added comprising of four commanders, three lieutenant commanders and two engineering officers, all from the Grand Fleet. Jellicoe himself then combined the role of First Sea Lord with Chief of Naval Staff. With him came Sir Henry Oliver (up till that point the Chief of the War Staff) serving as his Deputy Chief of Naval Staff (DCNS) with responsibility for operations while Duff became Assistant Chief of Naval Staff (ACNS) with the added responsibilities for the minesweeping and trade and convoys sections.*

For Jellicoe, 'there were only three ways of dealing with the submarine menace'. 'The first, naturally, was to prevent the vessels from putting to sea; the second was to sink them after they were at sea; and the third was to protect the merchant ships from their attack.'[15] At a War Cabinet meeting in February 1917 he outlined some of his major findings and initiatives.

In January 1917 Britain 'did not possess a mine that was very effective against submarines'.[16] One author described the British mine as 'a cheap and

---

* Jellicoe brought the bulk of his trusted officers from the Grand Fleet when he moved to the Admiralty. Duff had been 2IC of the 4th BS, Captain W W Fisher became the director of the Anti-Submarine Division itself, RA Hope became Jellicoe's deputy, and RA Lionel Halsey, Third Sea Lord.

ineffectual machine' that, in addition to often not exploding, often sank. In fact, one-third failed to explode at all and in April 1917 a large number (20,000) had been kept back from use because their mooring systems were found to be faulty.[17] Even Beatty was deeply despondent: urging Jellicoe to push for fast and effective research and development, he added, 'we must think of it on the largest scale possible or we shall be done in and it will be the lack of foresight of the Navy that has caused our defeat'.[18] The fastest means to improving the situation was to copy an effective mine. The answer was to adopt the German Herz horn type. By November 1917, after 100,000 of the new Mark H mines had been ordered, delivery of significant quantities started, and by the year end, around 20,000 were sown in the Heligoland Bight and in the Dover Straits.

A second solution was to use an underwater net barrage, in combination with mines, to block the Dover Straits. This was tried early in the war but the difficulties attached to moorings and protection against the heavy channel storms were not inconsiderable; even heavy 3in cabling would be torn apart in bad weather.[19] Until the arrival of effective mines, the barrage in itself was an abject failure. Ludwig von Schöder, admiral commanding the Flandern MarineKorps, found his submarines could quite easily get through the barrage.[20] Between February and May 1917, U-boats successfully passed the barrier 122 times and on only two occasions (both because of destroyers) were their submarines lost.[21]

The 1910 Admiralty Submarine Committee (SAC) looked at the idea of a 'dropping bomb', 'launched over the stern of the attacking vessel and exploded at a pre-determined depth.'[22] By June 1916 the central idea, that of incorporating a pre-determined explosion depth, was a reality, a simple hydrostatic valve making it possible. The results of these early 'depth charges' were good and, with increased availability, related submarine sinkings steadily increased from two in 1916, to twelve in 1917 and twenty-four in the first eleven months of 1918.[23] What took considerably longer was finding a way to fire the bomb far enough away from the attacking vessel so that the latter would not suffer collateral damage. The pistol-fired Type D thrower overcame that problem. Even if with a 300lb (135kg) charge, the damage caused to a submerged boat was still minimal unless the targeting was spot on.[24] In July 1917 the first depth-charge throwers capable of firing the charge 40yds (35m) were delivered, while, separately, ASW 'howitzers' which could reach between 1,200 and 2,600yds (1,100–2,400m) also started delivery,[25] but in extremely small numbers. By the end of 1917 only 377 had been delivered. The high potential value of this system would be seen much later, in 1942, when it became the basis for the Royal Navy's 'hedgehog' depth charge mortar.[26]

Early efforts at 'listening' for enemy submarines yielded very poor results, partly because at the start only boats lying absolutely still in the water could be used, to avoid noise interruption. More importantly, the capability was only directional. It could not even roughly pinpoint a submarine's position. Marder was rightly critical of the wartime results, but the system was only introduced at the very end of the conflict in November 1918. A mere seven ships were fitted and, as a result, only three sinkings and twenty-two cases of submarines being damaged were attributable to hydrophone detection. Again, it was the foundation for very successful future systems, in this case, ASDIC (supposedly named after the Allied Submarine Detection Investigation Committee, but this is now disputed).[27]

There were some pretty unconventional ideas given airtime as well. Training seagulls to land on periscopes was one. Duff, for example, was extremely critical of the idea of training sea lions to track German submarines: 'Valuable time, personnel and money had in fact to be wasted to prove the futility and childishness of this contention.'[28] Clearly, no stone was left unturned.

The use of aircraft for spotting did not start well either, although when America entered the war, they came with a seaplane which changed the game considerably. The Curtiss H12 flying boat had a six-hour endurance and soon began flying ASW patrols out of Felixstowe and then Yarmouth.* A new search pattern was developed and was able to effectively cover an area so large that German submarines would be exposed to observation for the ten hours they took to pass through the area. The new pattern was the so-called the 'spider's web', a search pattern flown in an ever-decreasing circle. By August 1917 the British added kite balloons towed by destroyers. Like aircraft, balloons were able to spot an enemy submarine at long distances, allowing a convoy's accompanying destroyers to either peel off and attack the submarine at a safe distance from the convoy itself, or for the convoy to alter its track around the submarine's assumed path.[29]

The increased arming of civilian ships such as trawlers and so-called Q-ships – armed merchantmen with their weapons disguised, a tactic introduced earlier in the war – continued. By the start of 1917 1,420 merchantmen had been armed; by July it was 3,001.[30] Throughout the war, the number of submarine sinkings directly attributable to Q-ships was only around thirteen, but in his book *The Submarine Peril*, Jellicoe shows that the fact of being armed increased the ship's chances of survival dramatically.[31] In 1916 both Q-ships or otherwise armed ships were more successful in escaping a submarine attack than an unarmed ship – in fact, more than doubly likely to escape.

---

* The Short Type 184, the type flown by Rutland before the battle of Jutland, became the RNAS's principal aircraft and around 650 were built, but the endurance was only around two and a half hours compared to the H12's six.

Submarines Attacks January 1916 – January 1917

	Attacked	Escaped	Sunk by torpedo	Sunk by gun
Armed ships	810	326	62	12
Percentage		40.2%		16.2%
Unarmed ships	302	67	30	205
Percentage		21.8%		87.3%

Source: Jellicoe, *The Submarine Peril*, p5.

In 1917 alone sixty-three duels were fought between Q-ships and submarines, so one would imagine the impact on tactics to be quite high. It has, in fact, been argued that the Q-ship increasingly encouraged unrestricted warfare and, overall, that could benefit the Allies. The existence of guns, whether hidden or in sight, would force the submarine to use its limited supply of torpedoes instead of surfacing to use its deck guns, and so necessitate more harbour runs for torpedo rearming.

Q-ships in Operation and Duels 1915–1917

	In operation	Duels
1915	'approx a dozen in use'	8
Percentage		66%
1917	180	63
Percentage		35%

Source: Gibson and Pendergast, *The German Submarine War 1914–1918*, p55.

Not much is said about British submarines being used as sub-killers, but around seventeen German submarines were sunk by their British counterparts during the war. Had it not been for the unreliability of British torpedoes, 'not running straight, or passing under even large ships, and failing to explode even when they did make a hit', the number could have been substantially greater.[32]

Convoy may have become one of the mainstays of the ASW effort, but 'it was not just the introduction of the convoy system that ultimately thwarted the U-boat threat'. Mcfarlane writes that 'it was a combination of that and the offensive measures developed by the Anti-Submarine Division that ultimately solved the problem, which in turn gives credence to Jellicoe's leadership and effectiveness as First Sea Lord'. It also became the most controversial.

At the time it was believed that the destroyer was the only effective anti-submarine hunter, but when it came to destroyers, Britain 'could not possibly produce the necessary escort vessels and that, until this difficulty was overcome, we should have to postpone the introduction of a convoy system'. But again,

Jellicoe held his options open; Temple Patterson said 'he appears to have been somewhat holding his judgement.'[33] He went on immediately to say that the havoc that the German raider *Möwe* was wreaking might mean that the system might have to be introduced in the Atlantic to protect trade and that 'the question must be borne in mind'.* Convoy protection had to be evaluated in the light of the country's overall naval strategy, particularly the role and well-being of the Grand Fleet itself: 'The Grand Fleet is the centre and the pivot on which all naval operations depend ... The safety and efficiency of the Grand Fleet to a very large extent depend ... on its destroyers and to carry out any policy that involves a reduction in (their) numbers increases the already considerable risks we now take.'[34]

In a private letter to his father-in-law Sir Charles Cayzer in May 1915, Jellicoe shows that he already recognised the importance of destroyers in an ASW role: 'We could finish the submarines off pretty successfully if we had double the number of destroyers we have now. I hope it will be a lesson for the future, but I expect all will be forgotten in five years time.'[35]

There are a number of considerations that need to be borne in mind when looking to answer the question of how many destroyers were actually needed. First, how many destroyers were available after the needs of the Grand Fleet and the destroyer flotilla commands were met; secondly, what was the effective ratio of covering destroyers to merchantmen; and, thirdly, what types of vessels were available. Finally, it would need to be decided how many merchantmen would have to be escorted. This issue became a matter of contention.

In February 1917 Jellicoe calculated that around forty destroyers or sloops were available from what Terraine estimates were the 283 in 'home waters'.[36] As mentioned, in coming to this number Jellicoe was adamant about not reducing the destroyer fleets of Harwich, Dover, the east coast or the Portsmouth commands. He still felt – like Beatty – that the destroyer protection for the Grand Fleet itself was weak: 'It was not until late 1915 that the number of destroyers attached to the Grand Fleet available was sufficient to screen the battle fleet adequately. An Anti-Submarine screen for cruisers was not available until the end of 1916.'[37]

---

* Jellicoe, *The Submarine Peril*, p111. The *Möwe*, built in 1914, was originally employed as a minelayer by the German navy. At the end of 1915 she was converted and began her life as an armed merchant ship under Swedish colours. *Möwe*'s operational success was impressive – and dangerous. When attacking, her Swedish colours would be lowered and the German Imperial flag hoisted before the main armament of four SK L/45 5.9in (15cm) guns were brought to bear. In addition, she was armed with two 50cm torpedo tubes and carried a very large number of mines (500). She was not fast – at best she could manage around 13 knots – but at that sort of speed she was able to cover 8,700 nautical miles. By war's end her guns had sunk forty-five merchantmen.

The American president sent Admiral Sims, an old friend of Jellicoe's since his China days, on a secret mission to London to understand the gravity of Britain's position. He travelled in civilian clothes, but was nevertheless a well-known officer, so his arrival was not kept totally secret. Sims understood the critical dilemma in which Jellicoe found himself: 'The British Navy in 1917 did not possess destroyers enough both to guard the main fighting fleet and to protect its commerce from submarines'.[38] 'At our average moment ... we could not expect more than seventy destroyers and eight leaders would be with the Fleet', around the same number that were at Jutland.[39] Beatty told Jellicoe that 'we are so very short of them ... if we have to go to sea, we could not screen efficiently the squadrons.' With the destroyer question, Jellicoe was walking on the edge of a razor.[40]

It may be that Jellicoe overstated needs. At one end of the spectrum, Oliver was comfortable with one destroyer for every twenty merchantmen, thinking it sufficient,[41] but at the other, the 1917 Convoy Committee's conclusion may seem high: eight destroyers for a convoy over twenty-two ships, seven for between sixteen and twenty-two, and six for under sixteen ships.

Until he could get his hands on more destroyers, Jellicoe was of the opinion that the adoption of convoy for the transatlantic routes would have to be 'postponed'. This, maybe, is as close as one gets to what I feel is a misleading conclusion that Jellicoe was 'resolutely opposed' to convoy.[42] It is interesting to pause for a moment here to emphasise that, even though Scheer had changed strategy and was now keeping the battle fleet more or less leashed in harbour, the High Seas Fleet still represented the threat of a 'fleet in being', in that the eighty-strong Grand Fleet destroyer screen could not easily be released from Scapa Flow for other duties in anticipation of possible action. Having been impounded, the German fleet was, in fact, rusting away. Boredom and frustration set in; already starkly hierarchical social divisions became more acute. The fleet had become a cancerous sore in the German military machine. Jutland had unleashed not just one, but three, evil genies: unrestricted U-boat warfare, locking up the destroyer screens in Scapa Flow and the fomenting of eventual German mutiny.

At this point Jellicoe was deeply fearful that Britain was losing the war and he did not hesitate from saying so, even if he sounded defeatist. But he was still able to persuade the Americans, as newly allied partners, to help solve what he probably saw as the most pressing obstacle: the destroyer shortage. Within four days of Sims's arrival in Liverpool on 9 April 1917, Jellicoe had persuaded the American to help with the immediate delivery of destroyers.[43]

Jellicoe was not quick to embrace the idea of transatlantic convoy but, unlike many others in the Admiralty, he certainly did not reject it out of hand.[44] In fact, Winton found his attitude to convoy 'curiously difficult to define. He was doubtful about its efficacy, but he never voiced those doubts strongly enough to suggest that he was a real opponent.'[45] True to his professional nature and his character, he always wanted his decision to be based on a careful analysis of what was and was not working, on what the options were, and on what the limitations and considerations were, rather than on a hunch. For one of his biographers, Altham, this meant that he 'constantly emphasised that there was no single specific antidote to the submarine'. The solution lay in a multi-layered approach to the problem.[46]

In *The Submarine Peril* Jellicoe later wrote that the convoy question was receiving 'constant consideration' at the Admiralty in early 1917, but that 'objections to it were, until a later date, far too strong to admit of its adoption.'[47] I think his phrasing is wrong here. It would have been more precise if he talked about the 'implications surrounding the introduction of convoy on the *Atlantic* [my italics] trade routes'. There were significant obstacles to getting a successful convoy system in place: first, the lack of destroyers; then the impossibility of assembling convoys in the neutral harbours or even the territorial waters of the United States (until, that is, the American declaration of war on 6 April);[48] the difficulty in keeping station; darkening ship; the very large lack of bridge to engine room voice pipes needed for frequent changes of speed; of new port facilities to handle very large simultaneous arrivals of shipping; the new communications and procedures between Merchant Navy and Royal Navy ships; the concern of convoys running into minefields en masse and the new training and schedules that were needed. As a totally integrated system, convoy was a daunting task.

When looking at the specifics of the transatlantic trade routes one can add the narrowing 'cone' effect of the three major trade routes converging on the British Isles: the southern routes converging off the Scilly Isles for ships heading for either the Channel ports or for Bristol, the lower western trade from the Caribbean converging on the Fastnet rock and turning to Bristol or Liverpool, and the North American and Canadian trade heading past Tory Island and heading to the northern ports of Liverpool and the Clyde. Jellicoe added a fourth route, which narrowed after passing around northern Scotland at the Orkneys. The natural choke-points made any attacker's task much easier.

In Cabinet Sir Maurice Hankey had always been a strong proponent of a system of convoy. His only real concern was that a concentration of ships might actually increase the ease of their being found by an enemy submarine, to which Churchill later correctly pointed out that the very concentration of ships reduced the probability of chance sightings by a patrolling enemy submarine. Escort was the obvious answer but, with the shortfall in the numbers needed for individual escort, difficult to realise. So grouping merchant ships together into a convoy was an immediate route to a solution. Hankey claims to have been the person who persuaded Lloyd George of the solution and he had already met early in 1917, on 11 February, with Jellicoe and Duff, where the civilian explained what he called his 'brainwave' to the two admirals as though they had never thought about the subject.

A week or so later, on 23 February, Jellicoe met with ten shipmasters. They were 'firmly of the opinion that they would prefer to sail alone rather than in company and under convoy.'[49] That Jellicoe went out of his way to put the questions as impartially as possible was confirmed by Captain Bertram Smith, a member of the Mercantile Movements Division at the Admiralty. Why wouldn't he? What's more, Jellicoe's connections with the merchant marine were strong. His father had been a captain of the Southampton Royal Mail Steam Packet Company, and had gone to sea aged twelve. John Jellicoe had married Gwen Cayzer, whose father, Sir Charles Cayzer, owned one of the largest commercial shipping fleets of his age, the Clan Line.[50] Jellicoe, in short, would most likely have been hearing a lot about the difficulties of the merchant fleets at first hand.

Lloyd George loved to hark back to the days of Nelson, so it is all the more ironic that even the revered Nelson was a little less taken by civilian sailors than he might have been: 'They behaved, as all convoys that I ever saw, shamefully ill; parting company every day.'[51] There is often surprise at the idea that convoy, such an established method of protecting civilian ships that had been used so extensively in the Napoleonic wars, was not taken up without further ado. The point has often been missed. The times and challenges were remarkably different. The submarine war of 1917 was the first naval war fought with an unseen enemy, the new technologies of W/T and hydrophone, as well as new weapons such as mines, torpedoes and the submarine itself. Speeds could touch 38 knots for fast torpedo boats or 8 knots submerged for submarines rather than the 2 or 3 knots as was the case at Trafalgar.

But the numbers with which the Admiralty argued their case – how many merchantmen needed to be escorted – were, apparently, wrong. A young commander, Reginald Henderson, had given Lloyd George different numbers. The prime minister later wrote in his autobiography that it was 'a fatal error in accountantship which nearly lost us the war' and one that would not have been made 'by an ordinary clerk in a shipping office'. The real number of departures, he announced, was forty ships a day, not seven hundred. Supposedly, the Admiralty had counted all the small inshore movements in its figures. But, just maybe, the Admiralty had been caught in a trap of its own making. So as to not alarm the British public, the much higher, all-inclusive Customs returns data had been used in public communiqués so that the sinking ratios would look better. It happens in every war when the public is fed only what is deemed safe.

Actually, it now seems that the Admiralty not only had, but also used, the correct data. Captain Bertram Smith showed that the figure of ships leaving for just the American ports would have been around ten a day, a number which fits very closely with Reginald Henderson's overall forty a day estimate.[52] Certainly, if the Admiralty was really basing policy on the much higher numbers, it would not only have been utterly incomprehensible, it would have been scandalous. But there is surprisingly little material on this point, which Lloyd George tried to turn into a press story.* Colvin, writing Carson's biography in 1936, wrote scathingly about the whole affair: 'Nor was it true to say, as has been alleged by several writers who ought to know better, that the Admiralty was deceived by a weekly return of entrances and clearances supplied by the Customs authorities, which included small craft and coast-wise traffic. This fable is on the face of it grotesque'.[53]

It is certainly the case that the staff and bureaucracy of the Admiralty were strongly against the concept of convoy: 'The system of several ships sailing together in a convoy is not recommended in any area where submarine attack is a possibility. It is evident that the larger the number of ships forming the convoy, the greater is the chance of a submarine being enabled to attack successfully'.[54] Did the fact of his new association with an institution with which he had often disagreed, make Jellicoe guilty of the same position per se? Lloyd George assumed that Jellicoe was strongly against convoy because he had not immediately and openly come out in support of his policy before having made his own evaluation. At the War Cabinet of 2 November 1916 the prime minister had vigorously proposed the convoy system where he had not been supported by Carson, Jellicoe or Duff.

Jellicoe had implemented convoy for ammunition supplies to the Western Front. This had already been done by December 1916. The French coal trade, vital for the continuation of French factory production after a significant number of coalfields had been lost to German territorial gain, and the Scandinavian trade were also both under convoy protection. The French convoys were approved by Jellicoe on 17 January and, as a measure of success, of the 2,600 ships involved in this trade in April, only five were sunk by U-boats.[55] Significantly, the Admiralty preferred not to use the word 'convoy' and called it a system of 'controlled sailings', as protection was given to the shipping lanes not groups of ships. The same Reginald Henderson who produced the estimates of sailings was the senior officer of the French convoy system, so the experience,

* Allan Macfarlane told me, in personal correspondence, that he could find no further detailed discussion of these statistics in the papers of Jellicoe, Duff, Lloyd George (in the Parliamentary Archives) and Carson, nor was there anything that he could find in the Admiralty records at The National Archives.

the basis from which he spoke, was strong. At the end of January a system of protection was also implemented for the Scandinavian trade, but it was not that successful and by April high losses of 25 per cent were being sustained. After Duff and Oliver had themselves both approved, Jellicoe signed off on the findings of the resulting Longhope Conference on 21 April 1917.* It had concluded that a system of convoy should be used:

> in preference to a scheme of continuous stream of traffic, i.e. assembling groups of ships to be convoyed rather than trying to protect sea lanes. In the first month of operation, May, the rate of loss was dramatically cut to 0.24 per cent of the April figure, a rate that was very close to that of the French Coal trade's 0.19 per cent the same month.

To further underline the impact on the Grand Fleet's destroyers, Jellicoe was obliged to 'postulate the laying-up of one of his [Beatty's] battle squadrons in order to obtain destroyers for the work'.[56]

Jellicoe spent much of a Cabinet meeting of 25 April, during which the subject of convoy was discussed, writing a letter to a friend. It was not wise, though understandable maybe, to so overtly show his frustration. The signal that he conveyed by this type of behaviour did not help his standing with many of his colleagues. In truth, he hated the frequency of the meetings when he felt he should be on the job with his staff at the Admiralty. Then, at a War Council meeting on the 27th, he launched into what can only be described as a tirade on the submarine issue. Goodenough said that Jellicoe was not good at presenting his case and this presentation is, perhaps, a good example of his sounding too negative:

> In my opinion, the War Council fails entirely to realise the position, in spite of the repeated efforts I have made to explain its gravity ... The only result has been the appointment of committees to investigate various features ... but I must point out with all the force at my command that all this is only playing with the situation ... It is now almost too late, but it is not quite too late ... we are carrying on in this war ... as if we had the absolute command of the sea. We have not ... and have not had for many months ... If we do not recognise this fact and shape our policy accordingly, it is my firm conviction that we shall lose the war by the starvation of our country.[57]

---

* Beatty had been at the Longhope Conference (in the Orkneys) and made his strong support of convoy known, but in this context he was talking about the Scandinavian convoy, not the transatlantic. Dreyer quotes the findings, also saying that 'The conference unanimously agreed that a system of convoy should be tried, but the representatives were unable to state whether the necessary vessels could be spared from their respective areas' (Dreyer, *Sea Heritage*, p218).

Jellicoe's pessimism was stark. To Lloyd George in particular, his words smacked of something worse: defeatism. Jellicoe's lack of strong, immediate and optimistic backing of the convoy system left him open to Lloyd George portraying him, along with the 'old men' of the Admiralty, as being in opposition to the idea. In truth, he was not.

The month of April was a turning point of the naval war. Even if the news of America's entry was good news, the last two weeks of the month were catastrophic and became known as the 'black fortnight'. Almost one million tons of shipping was sunk or damaged (in *The Naval Flank*, Karau's figures show that with the latter consideration the total figure is 964,000 tons). Sims wrote about Jellicoe's intent on this trial: 'The Admiralty had not definitely decided that the Convoy system should be adopted but that there was every intention of giving it a thorough and fair trial'.[58] In the meeting of 26 April Duff presented his findings. They were 'detailed, and contained so many considered points and tabulated conclusions, that it suggested that Duff, or somebody, must have been working on it for some time beforehand'.[59] Winton would say that 'it is difficult to believe that Duff was the sole author of the memorandum, the views expressed in it are so at variance to his previous statements', but if he knew that Jellicoe wanted to keep his mind open to the possibilities, this must have had an impact.[60] Jellicoe's key point was that he had to postpone convoy until more destroyers could be found. That was now the case.

Duff more than likely changed his position and, therefore, his recommendations to Jellicoe on the convoy system were based on two important considerations: America's entry to the war with the immediate (by 4 May) supply of the first additional destroyers, and the appalling figures of the last weeks of April. He proposed a large-scale test based on a Gibraltar sailing on 10 May. Jellicoe agreed and signed off. For these reasons, I think it is going too far to suggest that Duff was an officer 'who shared his [Jellicoe's] scepticism'.[61] Jellicoe was not sceptical, just very cautious, an approach which Lloyd George told his biographer that he understood.† At the beginning, Jellicoe certainly did not appear to have been an overt supporter of the system: 'Differences of speed, loss of the safety afforded by zigzagging, and the inevitable tendency of merchant ships to straggle at night are some of the reasons against an organised system of convoy'.

Jellicoe had, in fact, indicated soon after his appointment that some form of convoy might become necessary for the North American trade routes.

---

† Colvin writes that 'He (Lloyd George) had worked – so he told his biographers – in complete harmony with Sir John Jellicoe and the other Sea Lords; he had understood the reason for their cautions and delays in the matter of convoy; they were due entirely, in his opinion, to practical difficulties which had to be overcome.' (Colvin, *Carson*, p261). This does not sound like the public Lloyd George, but might have been his real view.

According to the official British historian, Sir Julian Corbett, 'even after Admiral Jellicoe had read [Chief of Staff] Admiral Oliver's catalogue of difficulties, he minuted the paper with the remark that the whole question must be borne in mind and be brought up again later if needs be. That is, he still withheld judgement.'[62] The success of the surface raider *Möwe* had left a very strong impression on Jellicoe.

It is most probable that this memorandum was not the result of hearing that Lloyd George would visit the Admiralty on the 30th. Jellicoe maintained that for most of the first part of 1917 the Admiralty had already been actively weighing the pros and cons. Following the declaration of war by America on 6 April, the first American destroyers arrived on 4 May, so given this timing, 'It was, then, the approach of the American destroyers in Queenstown (Ireland) rather than the approach of Mr Lloyd George to Whitehall that "galvanised" the Admiralty.'[63] By July, there were a further twenty-seven American destroyers in British waters.[64]

At the meeting with Lloyd George at the Admiralty on 30 April, Jellicoe, much to the prime minister's surprise, announced that the Admiralty had changed its opinion and was now ready to test convoy on a large scale. The two had a very pleasant lunch during which, apparently, Lloyd George doted on Jellicoe's youngest daughter (my Aunt Prudie).

The meeting was productive, in Terraine's eyes, because 'a set of useful agreements' was 'cordially arrived at between the two men', including the appointment of Sir Eric Geddes as Controller. His move into the Admiralty was speedy and he took up his post on 9 May.[65] Lloyd George liked to boast later that he had 'beat compliance' out of the Admiralty, but 'It is good stuff for the port and brandy or the gossip columns, but for nothing else. The decisions were already taken three days before.'[66] On the issue of whether the Admiralty or he had been strongly influenced by Lloyd George's position or by his intention to come to the Admiralty, Jellicoe was equally clear. He said that Lloyd George's visit had nothing to do with Duff's recommendation, approved four days earlier. Even Hankey put a diary entry on the day before, 29 April, saying that the Admiralty's ideas on convoy had, at this point, been developed 'on their own initiative'.[67] Earlier, on 30 March he noted that he was finding it difficult to get convoy onto Lloyd George's agenda till late April: 'I have so many ideas on the matter, but cannot get at Ll. George in regard to it, as he is so full of politics'. The minutes themselves are neutral. They merely say the visit was made 'with a view to investigating all the means at present in use in regard to anti-submarine warfare'.

On 10 May a large convoy left Gibraltar. It was to be used as a test case and its success led to the decision to implement the system more widely. It arrived in Britain on the 20th without casualties. Two weeks later, on 24 May the first transatlantic convoy from America left Hampton Roads, arriving in Britain on 7 June.[68]

Jellicoe was never against convoy. Rather, he knew that in order to make the convoy system work the most important thing he needed was sufficient destroyers. Jellicoe worried that – whatever the merits of the convoy system – Britain did not have available the required levels of escort vessels; this was one of the first, essential issues to solve. To that end, in the War Council he argued for the reduction of the number of routes, trade or military, that the Navy was being asked to cover, saying, for example, that land campaigns – such as one then being undertaken in Salonika – should be considered 'sideshows' and as a consequence no longer be supported; there should be a strict reduction in the amount imported into Great Britain by restricting luxuries or inessentials; and whenever troops were transported, foodstuffs and munitions should be carried on the same vessels. 'In the light of the amended figures, the position with regard to destroyers now became that between 20 and 30 of the 70 or more needed for a really comprehensive convoy system could be found immediately.'[69] The newly arrived American destroyers helped.

By September Jellicoe was starting to feel some of the extreme pressure of the first three months dissipate. Ten German submarines had been sunk in the month and the losses were moving in the right direction. But Jellicoe wrote to Beatty about the continuing political problems that he was facing: 'I have got myself much disliked by the Prime Minister and others. I fancy there is a scheme afoot to get rid of me. The way they are doing it is to say that I am too pessimistic … I expect it will be done by first discrediting me with the press.'[70] He was right. Beatty's response was described by Massie as not just 'ambivalent' but, maybe unfairly, as 'hypocritical'[71] – Beatty urged Jellicoe to hang on: 'And you must stick at all intentions to your not volunteering to go, that would be fatal. Do not be goaded into any step of the kind no matter what the press or anybody else says.'[72]

Lady Beatty was another matter. She appeared to hold Jellicoe almost personally responsible for her husband not receiving the level of national accolade that she would have liked him to have after Jutland, and was openly antagonistic. She was meeting as many people as she could to stir things up – naval inventor turned journalist Arthur Pollen, Rear Admiral Sims, and others within government and naval circles.[73] Her dislike of Jellicoe was deep and vehement. It is difficult to see Gwen Cayzer and Ethel Beatty as wives who would have much in common. In July 1916 Ethel wrote that all she could do, now that the battle was over, was 'curse Jellicoe', saying that she thought the real truth was that 'he was in a *deadly* funk and of course it makes one perfectly sick with the

286 JUTLAND: THE UNFINISHED BATTLE

Admiralty trying to make out he is a great man … He failed hopelessly and not only that but he does not tell the truth in his dispatch'.[74] She tried to, but did not convince Sims. The American had a great deal of respect for John Jellicoe, with whom he had served in China during the Boxer Rebellion. He was to write in 1939 of his old friend: 'The admiration which I had then conceived for the Admiral's intelligence and character I have never lost … Simplicity and direct-ness were his two most outstanding points … success had only made him more quiet, soft-spoken and unostentatiously dignified'.* Pollen, who had been quite close to Jellicoe at one point, was maybe an easier target now that Dreyer's di-rector system had been chosen over his. He was angry at Jellicoe for not giving him continued access after Dreyer's system became the front-runner.

The introduction of convoy did not immediately dramatically shift the num-bers. Tonnage sunk did not suddenly, magically, decline. Till the end of 1917, the average monthly total remained around 300,000 tons. It took till May 1918 for the average to fall below the 200,000 mark. But what was seen as a decline was as much due to reduced submarine activity as to the British 'winning' the battle.

'Sinking submarines is a bonus, not a necessity': what Marder meant by this dictum was that what counted was whether the food and war materiel was getting through in the required quantities.[75] And while the number of German submarines sunk doubled from the first to the second half of 1917, from twenty-one to forty-two, the Germans had added huge capacity with new submarines becoming operational at an ever-increasing rate. But the privations of war, although very tough, were never for the British as severe or on such a wide scale as they became for German families.

British commanders were most uncomfortable with the Flanders harbour triangle and, increasingly, Jellicoe felt that destroyers from these ports would pose an even larger threat than that of the submarine if the Germans were to use these forward Belgian bases to support larger naval activity in the Chan-nel.[76] He had unsuccessfully lobbied for the capture or destruction of the ports since 1915 when the army had, against the Navy's advice, not demolished the facilities when retreating. But the proposed operations were repeatedly opposed and delayed by the French, who only concurred when British participation in the Somme offensive was agreed upon.[77] A major result of the success of the early operations was, as both Holtzendorf and Schröder had predicted, an in-creasing concentration of British naval assets in the south.

Holtzendorf had promised victory in six months: 'Victory before the harvest,'

---

* Sims held Jellicoe in high regard even where the anti-submarine war was concerned: 'The whole scheme which has defeated the German submarine campaign was conceived by Admiral Jellicoe just before he was fired' (see Altham, p149, also Temple Patterson, p169).

he had proclaimed. The first three months had delivered results beyond expectations, especially April, and even more when one took into consideration damage as well as actual sinkings. But by July there was absolutely no sign that the British were about to throw in the towel and what the German naval staff already knew, the politicians were beginning to suspect – that the claim was not going to be delivered and that, in fact, slowly but surely the tide was starting to turn. Matthias Erzberger, the leader of the Catholic Centre party, openly challenged the navy's continued public optimism. The debate which it triggered ended with the Peace Resolution of 19 July and Bethmann-Hollweg's replacement as chancellor by the exceedingly weak Georg Michaelis. The change effectively put the army in control. Then August saw unrest in the fleet and the execution of five sailors. The rocky road to the German revolution was open.

Then the astonishing rate of early sinkings started to taper off, again slowly but discernibly. July's total of 555,514 tons was reduced to 472,372 in August and 353,602 in September. While October's figure increased again to 446,542 tons, the losses suffered by the submarine flotillas were high. The Flanders Flotilla itself lost five boats. By November the German results fell again, dramatically, to 302,599, the worst result of the year. April had been the peak of a slightly unevenly distributed bell curve which was now rapidly falling to a monthly average of 300,000 tons, which would then cut below 200,000 tons shortly into 1918.

British and Total Allied Sinkings 1914–18

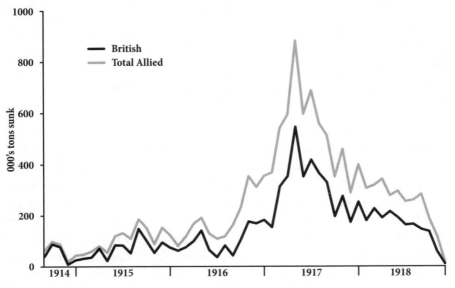

Source: C E Fayle, *Seaborne Trade*, III, p465, Table 1(a) (John Murray, 1924).

British and Allied Merchant Shipping Loses by Torpedo 1914–18

	1914	1914	1915	1915	1916
	British	Total Allied	British	Total Allied	British
January			32,054	47,981	62,288
February			36,372	59,921	75,860
March			71,479	80,775	99,089
April			22,453	55,725	141,193
May			84,025	120,058	64,521
June			83,198	131,428	36,976
July			52,847	109,640	82,423
August	40,254	62,767	148,464	185,866	43,354
September	88,219	98,378	101,690	151,884	104,572
October	77,805	87,917	54,156	88,534	176,248
November	8,888	19,413	94,493	153,043	168,809
December	26,035	44,197	74,490	123,141	182,292
	1916	1917	1917	1918	1918
	Total Allied	British	Total Allied	British	Total Allied
January	81,259	153,666	368,521	179,973	306,658
February	117,547	313,486	540,006	226,896	318,957
March	167,097	353,478	593,841	190,458	342,597
April	191,667	545,282	881,027	215,543	278,719
May	129,175	352,289	596,629	192,436	295,520
June	108,855	417,925	687,507	162,990	255,587
July	118,215	364,858	557,988	165,449	260,967
August	162,744	329,810	511,730	145,721	283,815
September	230,460	196,212	351,748	136,859	187,881
October	353,660	276,132	458,558	59,229	118,559
November	311,508	173,560	289,212	10,215	17,682
December	355,139	253,087	399,111		

Source: C E Fayle, *Seaborne Trade*, III, p465, Table 1(a) (John Murray, 1924).

The increasing success of the British anti-submarine campaign prompted Holtzendorf to evolve new tactics, such as teaming up two boats against a convoy. While he was not able to implement the idea, it would be the basis of the feared submarine 'wolf packs' in the battle of the Atlantic twenty years later.

As if the submarine threat were not enough, Jellicoe's time at the Admiralty was dogged by political back-stabbing and dark-corridor politics of the most insidious nature on the part of Lloyd George, Eric Geddes (his appointee as Controller) and from the press baron, Lord Northcliffe, the prime minister's political supporter and friend. But Jellicoe also faced opposition from a less likely quarter: from Sir Douglas Haig, with whom he had been closely allied in the War Cabinet over the need to keep resources focused on the Western Front.

Lloyd George had most likely made up his mind to get rid of Jellicoe quite early on – earlier than the summer as he said in his diaries. He had never liked him; in the War Cabinet he found what he perceived to be his now established pessimism too much to take. So serious were losses becoming, that in June Jellicoe made the comment in the War Cabinet that it was 'no use' talking about plans for 'spring next year' if they had already lost the war by that point. The previous year in October 1916, he had already speculated that the Allies might be forced into accepting peace terms and talked about the 'serious effect' he anticipated 'by early summer 1917'.[78] Jellicoe accurately predicted the bleakness of Britain's situation in the opening months of 1917.

Jellicoe had thought about resigning several times. He was incensed at just how rudely not just he, but also other senior commanders, had been treated by Lloyd George.[79] When Jellicoe was asked by the prime minister to get rid of both Oliver and Cecil Burney, he demurred, saying that if he had to he would dismiss the latter, but so far as Oliver was concerned he threatened his own resignation if it were to come about. 'You will obey orders like any midshipman', retorted the prime minister, to which Jellicoe calmly responded: 'You don't know what you're talking about.' Since the Sea Lords were civil appointments, Jellicoe added, they 'came under no act of discipline'. This was the moment in June 1917 when the prime minister said that he 'made up his mind to effect a change at the top of the Admiralty', and told Geddes that he would give him six months to see if he concurred.[80] Lloyd George was not giving Geddes the decision, merely the time to come around to his own point of view that Jellicoe had to go.

In John Winton's words, the conclusion of the 1909 Naval Estimates debate was a 'pyrrhic victory' for Jellicoe (and Fisher). Lloyd George did not trust that Jellicoe really had secret information about accelerated German naval construction from 'private sources'. In his own notes of a meeting in Sir Edward Grey's office, the former Foreign Secretary, Jellicoe says that Lloyd George had made a remark about the information: 'I think it shows extraordinary neglect on the part of the Admiralty that all this should not have been found out before. I don't think much of any of you Admirals and I should like to see Lord Charles Beresford at the Admiralty and the sooner the better.'[81] Lloyd George held that it was 'all contractor's gossip'.

Neither Lloyd George nor Jellicoe had the kind of character that made it easy for them to work closely together as colleagues. Lloyd George was a man of action, the more unusual or unexpected, the better for the media-savvy politician. Jellicoe was the consummate professional, cautious, modest and analytical, but he was also a 'results' man. He spoke with a frank realism that was often misunderstood. Jellicoe's War Cabinet presentations may have been purposefully pessimistic: 'It was necessary', he later said, 'to be very outspoken to the War Cabinet on the subject of the Submarine danger even at the risk of being accused of pessimistic views, for it was very difficult during the first half of 1917 to get the magnitude of the danger realised'.[82]

As characters, Jellicoe and Lloyd George could not have been more different. Strategically, they were at loggerheads: the 'westerner' versus an 'easterner'. Jellicoe wanted focus on the Western Front; Lloyd George eastern Europe or the Middle East. Jellicoe wanted to reduce the number of war theatres; Lloyd George was always looking for another opportunity. In Jellicoe's words, another 'sideshow' that would stretch the Navy's thin resources even further.

Not without some justification, Lloyd George held a grudge against Jellicoe. He was, in part, responsible for the collapse of the Liberal government's agenda of social reform. Lloyd George's character did not lend itself to bowing down gracefully. He would engineer his revenge when the right moment presented itself.

> His faults had been pretty glaring and pretty constant ... He bullied; he fibbed; he blustered; he wheedled. He could be outrageously intolerant. He engaged in wholesale misrepresentation and chicanery on a grand scale. He was selfish, vain and boastful. He attributed mean motives to his opponents and splendid intentions to himself. He was devious and cunning ... He was a rogue, a trickster, an opportunist, a will of the wisp.[83]

Colvin's biography of Carson, who was, like Jellicoe, targeted by Lloyd George, has a wonderful turn of phrase: Lloyd George 'succumbs to the temptation, so strong in the hearts of us all, to be the hero of every fight, the Jack who kills every giant'.[84]

Sir Eric Geddes, was a man whose personal manner – gruff and pushy, with an insatiable appetite for statistics – could test many a man's patience. At first, Jellicoe had not only welcomed the appointment of Geddes as Controller, he even wrote to Beatty extolling Geddes, though Beatty was rather more opposed to the idea of a civilian in the Admiralty. Buoyed up by vanity, Geddes demanded that he be given not only military rank (so that he would be taken seriously by the men of arms) but also that he wear the uniform of either a major general or a vice admiral. To many, Geddes' behaviour was laughable, but he loved his power and he loved using it. The appointment of a civilian with no experience in shipbuilding annoyed many industry men. Sir Joseph Maclay, the Shipping Controller, said that 'L.G. has made a mistake in not appointing a shipbuilder or someone who understands shipbuilding'. Maclay was as equally pessimistic as Jellicoe was at this juncture of the war. Using May 1917 shipping losses as the basis of his calculations, he felt that Britain would not be able to feed its population or supply overseas military needs beyond the end of the year. It would not be till the second quarter of 1918 that new shipbuilding would be able to catch up and overtake the losses.

Sir Eric Geddes was an Edinburgh-born businessman whose extensive experience in managing rail systems in America, India and Great Britain had made him a brilliant logistics aid to Douglas Haig. The field marshal thought so highly of him that when he transferred to the Admiralty he still kept him on as a 'consultant'. Sims talked equally highly of Geddes: 'A man after Roosevelt's heart – big, athletic, energetic, with a genius for reaching the kernel of a question and of getting things done'.[85] However, one was a businessman; the other, a thoroughly naval man with deep respect for the traditions of the service: oil and water. Privately, Geddes had complained to Haig about Jellicoe calling him 'feeble to a degree and vacillating'.[86]

Lloyd George wanted both Carson and Jellicoe out, but could not move against both men at the same time. He would have not only lost the support of the Navy, he would also have lost the right wing of the Conservative party and put his coalition government in jeopardy. Right from the start, Carson was under pressure from Lloyd George to get rid of Jellicoe.

He had to get rid of Carson first and Geddes' appointment was the manoeuvre by which the First Lord's replacement hungrily took up the reins of power. Already, by 2 May the Northcliffe press had started the whispering campaign, making it look like neutral commentary: 'renewed rumours of Sir Edward Carson's impending resignation circulated last night – probably by those political agencies which see in the German submarine a weapon for striking at the government'.[87] A month later, on 20 June Geddes was openly complaining about Carson's lack of effectiveness to his old protector, Haig.[88] The prime minister's solution was to 'kick him upstairs'. He made Carson a member of the War Cabinet in June 1917 and moved Geddes right into his place as the new First Lord. At the same time, the insinuations of the Northcliffe press changed target. Without Carson as his political ally and defender, the barbs were now clearly aimed at Jellicoe himself. Carson did not stay long in the War Cabinet. He resigned in January 1918, part of the wave of mostly suppressed protest at Jellicoe's own dismissal at the end of December.

Discord eventually boiled over into conflict. A minor disagreement was on Jellicoe's recommendation of honours for Duff whose 'manner' Geddes disliked. Jellicoe defended his choice saying that the honour was for Duff's services, not his demeanour. A more serious disagreement, however, was over Jellicoe's defence of Admiral Bacon, and Marder wrote that he felt this was the immediate cause of Jellicoe's dismissal. Admiral Wemyss, Jellicoe's deputy, wanted to replace Bacon, who was the architect of the Dover barrage through which enemy submarines seemed to have little difficulty passing. Geddes agreed – Jellicoe did not.

Bacon had asked the Admiralty back in February 1917 to strengthen the original September 1916 barrage, but additional mines were only supplied at the end of 1917, in November. Leading up to the disagreement, Geddes had not acted with any great tact. For example, Bacon had not been appointed to the Channel Barrage Committee by Geddes. One of the committee's recommendations was that there be additional patrols of the submarine dive areas and that the same area be illuminated at night. Bacon did not agree, claiming that he did not have the resources for the first and that he found the second potentially very dangerous to the patrol vessels themselves.

Bacon, like Geddes perhaps not best known for diplomacy, wrote a very critical letter to Geddes: 'The above statement put, as politely as I possibly could, the obvious fact that it was better to leave the defence of the Straits to the Admiral who had local knowledge, experience, and the whole responsibility entailed by the command at Dover, than to allow dabbling by a committee who had no local knowledge, experience or responsibility.'[89] Jellicoe defended a fellow admiral: 'I am not able to accept the sweeping indictment of the work of the V.A. [Vice Admiral] Dover, as stated by the Director of Plans. The V.A's dispositions are based on experience, not only of submarine action but of destroyer attacks, and he is naturally reluctant to ignore the latter in the attempt to deal with the former'.[90] Nevertheless, Jellicoe then supported Roger Keyes on the idea of strengthening the patrolling and the illumination. It was a diplomatic censure of Bacon's position, while at the same time letting it be known that there was a preferred manner in which to handle these kinds of situations. Geddes was too impatient to get 'to the point'.

Keyes, however, was complimentary about what Bacon had achieved: 'The activities of the Dover Patrol were immense and Admiral Bacon had built up an enormous organization, which carried out its daily duties with great regularity and efficiency'.[91] During the time that Bacon had commanded the barrage, 125,100 merchant ships had passed through with only seventy-three sunk.[92] Bacon was eventually dismissed a week after Jellicoe himself, but what he had feared did, in fact, come to pass. On 14 February 1918 the Germans exploited the illumination and severely mauled almost a dozen trawlers and drifters.

The other serious disagreement was over the handling of the aftermath of the two Scandinavian convoy disasters. The first was in October 1917. Two German light cruisers attacked a twelve-ship convoy that was protected by four British escorts. Nine of the twelve ships were sunk. Then there was a repeat, in mid December. This time five merchantmen accompanied by a strong escort (two destroyers and four armed trawlers) were attacked by four German destroyers. All British ships except one destroyer were sunk.

Geddes sent Jellicoe a very curt note saying that he was calling a court of enquiry and that if Jellicoe refused it he would send the matter up to Fisher. It was, frankly, a bizarre suggestion to make and a very provocative notion. Jellicoe wrote back that he could 'hardly believe that the suggestion is serious', as Lord Fisher was no longer in the Navy and that, therefore, the Navy 'would not trust his judgement & impartiality'.[93] Geddes then went on to alter the wording of a draft telegram to Beatty, inserting the idea that the Admiralty would approve the names of the officers on the enquiry. Jellicoe first saw the offending telegram when he visited Beatty on 22 December and found him, understandably, fuming. Jellicoe told Geddes that the telegrams were 'insulting'. Geddes concluded that he 'did not like Jellicoe's frankness.'[94] While Geddes subsequently wrote an apology to Beatty, which the commander-in-chief read out to his flag officers, this caused a lot of bad blood with Jellicoe.

Geddes then sent over a draft of what he proposed to say in Parliament, clearly pointing the finger at Beatty. Jellicoe would have none of it, especially regarding a fellow officer like Beatty. He wrote of the incident:

> On Sunday he sent over to me a draft of an announcement to make in Parliament. It was worded so as to throw blame on Sir D Beatty, and in such a way as to give the idea that the loss of convoy was a disaster of the greatest magnitude as well as preventable. I objected to this wording, altered it a great deal and sent it back. Most of my alterations were adopted, but not all and the announcement was not a happy one.[95]

Nevertheless, there is one piece of writing from Sir Eric Geddes to David Lloyd George, meant as a draft response for the prime minister's use in the House (but never used) that states Geddes' point of view but not the detail: 'The Cabinet – the great majority of the Cabinet – felt however great Lord Jellicoe's services may have been as Commander-in-Chief afloat, which position he held under great strain for 28 months, he lacked certain qualities as the Chief of Naval Staff and as the Chief Naval Advisor of the Government ... I was dissatisfied with Lord Jellicoe'.[96] Even if Haig also said that the War Cabinet was disenchanted with Jellicoe, there was little evidence that his ideas had been refuted or discredited. Lloyd George did not discuss the firing of a War Cabinet colleague within the War Cabinet.

Geddes' brother claimed that during the War Cabinet meeting of 21 December 1917 the question of Jellicoe's dismissal was discussed. There is no mention in the War Cabinet minutes of the 21st, nor those of the 24th, nor the 26th when Wemyss was present as deputy First Sea Lord. It is doubtful then, that

Lloyd George, as he later said, 'knew the views of (my) colleagues.'⁹⁷ Wemyss, who had made it known that he did not want to stay on at the Admiralty, was then asked by Geddes on 22 December if he would take over Jellicoe's spot.

The creation of the War Cabinet was one of the very first actions taken by David Lloyd George when he became prime minister in December 1916; its composition comprised selected cabinet members and senior military commanders and was chaired by Lloyd George himself. Haig, Robertson and Jellicoe were members. Jellicoe found himself allied to Haig and Robertson in their requests that efforts should be focused on the Western Front rather than be diluted with attacks through the Austro-Hungarian Empire. The vast pressure on naval resources springing from the many commitments on multiple fronts – for example, from Salonika to Egypt – was wearing a thinly spread Navy even thinner. Jellicoe argued in the War Cabinet that there should be an effort made to limit the number of 'sideshows', 'so that more adequate protection be given to ships bringing supplies to our country and to our allies.'⁹⁸ In this vein he wrote to Carson in April: 'It is a continual fight to prevent more side-shows being started. He [Lloyd George] is at present mad on one in Palestine, fed from the sea.'⁹⁹ In July 1917 the War Cabinet supported the Jellicoe–Haig–Robertson triumvirate and the Flanders campaign was given the 'go ahead'. Jellicoe's hopes of sealing off the Flanders Flotilla's bases of Ostend and Zeebrugge evaporated, as the disastrous Passchendaele campaign ground to standstill with the loss of 250,000 British soldiers.

With this background, it is curious that Haig fomented anti-Jellicoe feelings. It might simply have been that 'attack is the best form of defence', because Haig was concerned that otherwise he might become a target of the prime minister himself, as did Robertson. On 18 April Lord Derby spoke to Haig, repeating what Jellicoe had already told the War Cabinet: 'we have lost command of the sea.' A month later, the prime minister's special envoy to Paris, Lord Esher, certainly complained about Jellicoe to Haig: 'It is time that something was done at the Admiralty. There has been no critical or creative movement within its antique walls since the war began.'¹⁰⁰ This was around the same time that Lloyd George made his decision on Jellicoe, the latter putting it down to a midsummer conversation with Haig.

Haig was a great supporter of Sir Eric Geddes, who had helped solve the land armies' monumental logistics issues, and Lloyd George now wanted his expertise to be refocused on speeding up the shipbuilding programme as well as getting faster delivery of the anti-submarine weapons. When Geddes was proposed as the Controller, Jellicoe said – according to Arbuthnot Geddes – that he would prefer a naval man. Lloyd George promptly made Geddes a vice admiral. Jellicoe disputed this and maintains that he actually said he would try to smooth things over with the existing Admiralty officials. Apparently Geddes turned to Haig for advice and complained about Carson, whom he thought a man who 'is very tired and leaves everything to a number of incompetent sailors.'[101] A few days later on 25 June, Haig openly spoke to Lloyd George and Lord Curzon about what he termed the 'seriously deficient state of the Admiralty', adding that he thought both of them 'much perturbed already.'[102] At breakfast the next day Lloyd George suggested replacing Carson with Robertson and also replacing Jellicoe and other 'numbskulls' on the Board. Lord Beaverbrook thought the attack a 'well organised and thoroughly considered' campaign to remove Jellicoe and that its motives were clear: 'It is interesting to speculate on Haig's motives. Certainly, it may have been that he was moved by genuine concern about Jellicoe's continued ability to serve in the role of 1SL. He had informed Lady Haig as early as May that he looked on the admiral as an "old woman".' Or again, it is possible that that he may have been 'interested in diverting the lightning from striking at himself, for the dismissal of Haig had been a principal objective of Lloyd George for many months.'[103]

Speaking before Parliament in 1918, Lord Carson not only praised Jellicoe, he accusingly addressed the press:

> I saw no one and I knew no one in the Navy who could advise me of anybody who was at all equal to Sir John Jellicoe for the particular position he occupied. When I made that speech at the Constitutional Club (in November 1917) ... I was smarting under constant and persistent efforts of a section of the Press to try and get Lord Jellicoe turned out of his post.[104]

Jellicoe had come close to accurately predicting his own demise. On the very first day that he entered the Admiralty, 5 December, he told Douglas Brownrigg, when the latter suggested helping him with his press image, that 'he did not expect to last twelve months and had no time to read the newspapers'.[105] In June 1917 he wrote to Beatty about his concerns: 'I fancy there is a scheme on foot to get rid of me ... I expect it will be done first by discrediting me in the Press. That is the usual political move and I have seen signs of it already'. [106]

The 'press' was essentially one man: Arthur Harmsworth, Viscount Northcliffe, sole proprietor of both *The Times* and the *Daily Mail*, a powerful portfolio that appealed to both ends of the British social spectrum. Northcliffe was also 'a man corrupted by power and wealth, who desecrated journalistic standards and became dominated by the pursuit of political power, unguided by political prescience.'[107] Even in Churchill's eyes, Northcliffe was dangerous, someone who 'wielded personal power without official responsibility.'[108]

Lloyd George carefully cultivated Northcliffe, knowing that the latter could give him access to and support from the British public. It was said that Lloyd

George had agreed with the newspaper magnate that they should act in concert regarding Jellicoe: 'You kill him. I'll bury him.' In July, Hankey had remarked that 'the PM is hot for getting rid of Jellicoe', and even King George V had said that Lloyd George 'had the knife into him (Jellicoe) *for some time*' [my italics].[109] Yet nothing could be done about removing Jellicoe himself until Lloyd George had found a way to rid himself of Edward Carson, a consistent supporter of Jellicoe. This he managed by bringing Carson into the Cabinet. He then left the odious task of actually firing Jellicoe to someone else.

Press opinion in Northcliffe's papers abruptly turned against Jellicoe in the summer. In January 1917 the Northcliffe press was full of support: 'We must be content to accept the firm assurances of Sir Edward Carson and Admiral Jellicoe given on Friday to the Navy League, that steps which it is hoped will be adequate are being taken to counter the depredations of enemy submarines. The pity is that the late Board of the Admiralty lacked foresight.'[110] In May there was another example of positive support: 'A good beginning at the Admiralty … After a thousand days of war we are beginning to return to the system that existed in Nelson's day.'[111] Three days later another complimentary article:

> The figures [for shipping losses] which were published yesterday show that for the week ending May 13 there had been a very marked reduction in the number of ships sunk by submarines. That is all to the good and though we cannot as yet be certain that the improvement will be maintained, we congratulate the officers and men of the Navy very warmly upon it.[112]

Then things suddenly turned sour and the reporting took on a strongly negative tone: 'Ships and men will not be rashly and foolishly sacrificed if we have strategists in charge who know what war is … The recent changes as Mr Lovat Fraser has pointed out did not go far enough or high enough.'[113] The attacks clamoured for more accurate information on losses and for better strategic thinkers at the Admiralty. After the first Scandinavian convoy disaster, the press pointed the finger at the Admiralty: 'The British Navy is an incomparable weapon if only it is placed in hands with the skill to wield it. It is not the fleet at sea that is concerned – for no one blames our seamen – but the Admiralty in London.'[114] And days before, when the Germans captured Riga, the *Daily Mail* wrote that the paper 'will also naturally expect him (Sir Eric Geddes) to consider very seriously whether the recent changes in high command in Whitehall have gone far enough.'[115] On the 25th, titled 'Weaknesses at the Admiralty', 'we have not yet found a man or set of men at the Admiralty with the instinctive genius for carrying on our naval share of the war.'[116] And in November, a more personal attack on Jellicoe: 'The best Navy in the world may be paralysed by feeble control – our strategical direction for which our First

Sea Lord is primarily responsible – has shown weakness in three various thea-tres of war.'[117] The attacks became so bad that even Geddes was at the point of seeking legal advice from the Attorney General on whether these articles were damaging to the nation's war effort, in possible contravention of the Defence of the Realm Act.

Lloyd George had told Geddes that he had six months to make up his mind if he agreed with getting rid of Jellicoe. Now Geddes agreed. He could not work with Jellicoe but, rather than act sooner while the press attacks were at their height, he had decided to wait, possibly to show that it was his decision and not pressure from the press that was forcing his hand. When Geddes decided to act, he did so by letter on 24 December 1917. Jellicoe was still at his office, having just met a group of officers from *Iron Duke*, who had presented him with a silver model of the ship containing a scroll with all their signatures on it.[118] At around six,* as he was about to leave, a messenger arrived from Geddes:

> My dear Sir John Jellicoe
> After very careful consideration, I have come to the conclusion that a change
> is desirable in the post of the First Sea Lord. I have not, I can assure you,
> arrived at this view hastily or without personal regret and reluctance. I have
> consulted the Prime Minister and with his concurrence, I am asking to see the
> King to make this recommendation to him.[119]

Jellicoe replied instantly saying that he would be glad to be relieved as soon as possible. The strain of the workload of the last few years, and particularly the amount of time that he was having to devote to Cabinet, had become very great. A letter from Lloyd George, awarding Jellicoe a title, arrived on Christ-mas morning. It was one sentence long: 'Dear Sir, I have the honour to inform you that His Majesty has been pleased to approve of my recommendation that the dignity of a peerage of the United Kingdom be conferred upon you. Yours faithfully, D Lloyd George.'[120] Later, the prime minister referred to the 'courteous letter' that he had written to Sir John Jellicoe.

It was a curt manner in which to end such an illustrious career. 'A strange curtain-line for the most brilliant officer of his time' was how William Jameson put it.[121] And well-timed: it avoided any effective outcry; Parliament had ad-journed for the Christmas recess and there were no newspapers over the Christmas–Boxing Day holidays. And though the prime minister made out that this was not the case, the sacking *had* been carefully co-ordinated with Lloyd George to minimise political fallout. The line in the letter saying that he

---

* Massie, p743. Massie says that Geddes' letter arrived marked 'Personal and Strictly Private'. Gibson and Harper, rather theatrically, p327, have it a little later, at 9pm. 'The strokes of Big Ben's chimes floated through the still wintry night … eight … nine o'clock.'

had wanted to get the prime minister's 'concurrence' was transparent. Sir Auckland Geddes made it plain that he saw David Lloyd George as the puppeteer who pulled his brother's strings, as the instrument through which he could rid himself of Jellicoe.[122]

The reaction after Christmas was ferocious. Prince Louis of Battenberg was livid: 'I cannot find the words to express my disgust and indignation'.[123] Goodenough said: 'Never a man stood higher in the estimation of his friends, his brother officers and every man and boy in the Service'.[124] Asquith said what Lloyd George should have had the courtesy to have written: 'No one knows better – perhaps no one as well as I do – what the State and the Allied cause owes you'.[125] Messages from the fleet demanding his return poured in, but of course he could not go back.

On 1 January the Sea Lords met (except Wemyss, Duff and Oliver),* saying they 'had full confidence in Sir John Jellicoe's ability and fitness to perform his responsible duties ... (that) they were most gravely concerned and disturbed by this sudden removal of a most able and distinguished officer'.[126] They threatened resignation en masse if they did not get a satisfactory explanation from Geddes on his reasons. That they would have resigned is highly doubtful; nevertheless, Jellicoe asked them to back down: 'I advised Halsey that the Sea Lords should not resign as it would do no good and be bad for the country'.[127] John Winton said that the point of resignation in protest was more a figure of speech than real intention.[128] Added to that, it would never have been in Jellicoe's character to publicly bandstand his obvious bitterness.†

As always, Geddes was slippery. He claimed that others had been in favour of the dismissal, Carson in particular. Carson flatly denied it and said that when Geddes raised the issue in October of what he should do his reply was crystal clear: 'Do? Why stand beside him and think no more about it'.[129] Carson and Jellicoe had been close and, indeed, Sir Edward later made it clear to the Commons that Jellicoe had been targeted by Lloyd George for months.

It was a sad affair, after a lifetime of service to his country and the Navy. No reason was given for the dismissal. Jellicoe had been Asquith's choice for the position, not Lloyd George's. But there is ample evidence to speculate as to the immediate causes.

---

* Duff's offer of resignation on 28 December was accepted by Geddes, even if the latter asked him to come back to the post when he realised how much experience was being lost. Carson also resigned, but later, on 22 January 1918.

† Just the opposite. Jameson talks about him meeting the Bishop of London as he was strolling on the Embankment. 'This is the first time, Bishop, I've been sacked in my life' (Jameson, p204) was his rather self-effacing comment.

Marder believed it was Jellicoe's refusal to approve of the dismissal of Bacon that was 'the catalyst that prompted (his) dismissal'; Temple Patterson because of the accumulated strain of twenty-eight months of command at sea and eleven months at the Admiralty during Britain's most dire time. Jellicoe himself thought that it was as a result of Lord Northcliffe's press campaign carefully orchestrated with his close ally David Lloyd George.

Jellicoe had always held the press at arm's length (while Beatty, wisely, learnt how to use and befriend journalists). In *The Submarine Peril* he explained his reasons for not letting journalists onto *Iron Duke*: 'it was not advisable to give full details of our methods' to the press. Jellicoe, according to Thompson, had heard that Northcliffe had spoken with Carson in late February or March 1917 and 'complained personally to Carson' about the 'ineptitude of the Navy' after his Essex house had been hit by German destroyer fire.[130] Carson experienced the typical Lloyd George over a breakfast meeting: 'Sack the lot of them', 'why do you not get fresh men with sea experience?'[131] Equally, Carson became deeply respected in the Navy for his determination not to let the politicians overrule them.[132] He was very conscious that his role was one of defending naval officers from Lloyd George's constant attacks, even reminding Jellicoe on one occasion when the latter had come to see him about resigning, that he was his boss, not Lloyd George, and that, as is the way in the Navy, he should 'carry on'.

Admiral Rosslyn 'Rosie' Wemyss took over the post of First Sea Lord. In the words of his biographer, his wife, 'Confidence and cheerfulness took the place of uncertainty and gloom at the Admiralty', and that he had 'not been seated many weeks in the First Sea Lord's chair before I had the pleasure of knowing that the machine was running more smoothly and efficiently than before.'[133] The King was conscious of Wemyss's intellectual shortcomings, and even Wemyss himself made no bones about it, but at the same time the King was very confident of his friend's suitability for the role that Jellicoe had vacated. He trusted Wemyss's ability with people and his practical mind. Beatty worked closely with Wemyss from the start, taken by his easy way, but later came to disagree more fundamentally on policy. Most importantly on destroyers: 'to counter the submarine menace defence only has been used. To me it appeared absolutely necessary that the tables be turned and we must hunt the enemy submarines instead of them hunting us'.[134] His ideas for submarine hunting groups never came to fruition as 'senior members of the Staff chose not to reduce the readiness of the Grand Fleet in the face of opposition from Beatty'.[135] Others, like Madden, Jellicoe's brother-in-law, were not so happy. He wrote that he was 'full of fear for the future; the Grand Fleet is all right as Beatty is strong enough to refuse to throw it away on wild cat schemes, but the wider field of operations is not in such able hands.'[136]

Andrew Gordon wrote that 'Jellicoe had gone to the Admiralty partly to get to grips with the submarine menace. He failed.'[137] I disagree. Through the creation of the Anti-Submarine Division he laid solid foundations for the future success of the submarine war. Sims's letter said as much: 'I am distressed to hear of your leaving the Admiralty when the effects of all your anti-submarine measures are showing such great success.'[138]

In the same vein, Jameson put much in balance: 'He may have been slow to decide (when there was no evidence to help him) that convoy would thwart the U-boat, and stubborn in concentrating on the so-called "offensive" methods. But it was he who had given "teeth" to the anti-submarine organization without which convoys could not have enjoyed their present success.'[139] Even Lloyd George would write in his memoirs that 'the greatest allied triumph' and the 'real decision of the war' was meeting and defeating the U-boat threat in 1917.[140]

12

From Kiel to Scapa Flow

——

German sorties after Jutland

One of the myths that somehow gained traction in the post-Jutland years was that Germany's High Seas Fleet never put to sea again after the battle. This is simply not true. Not counting the North Sea crossing to internment at Scapa Flow, the fleet, in fact, came out a further three times, even if its role was significantly different.

Jutland had changed Scheer's thinking fundamentally. He wrote to the Kaiser that 'a victorious termination of the war can only be obtained by the employment of the submarine'.[1] Two weeks later he added: 'We have proved to the world that the British fleet is not invincible … Yet if, in our present situation, we are not ultimately to bleed to death materially, we must make unrestricted use of the submarine to paralyse England's vital nerve.'[2] Effectively, Scheer argued, 'even the happiest outcome of a battle on the high seas will not force Britain to sue for peace in this war'. The Kaiser put his thoughts down in the margin. He only wrote one word: 'Right'.[3] Scheer's major opposition came from Bethmann-Hollweg, who feared that the result of such a policy would be America's entry into the war.

While *Derfflinger* and *Seydlitz* were still in dry dock undergoing much-needed repairs, *Großer Kurfürst*, *Markgraf* and the new eight 15in-gunned *Bayern* were used to reinforce Hipper's 1st Scouting Group. The slow-moving pre-dreadnoughts were taken out of the battle line but the dreadnought *König Albert*, which had been in dry dock during Jutland, was now available. Hipper's idea was similar to the pre-Jutland planning. His force would bombard the town of Sunderland, pull Beatty out and across a waiting submarine line, while the High Seas Fleet would be lurking a safe distance away, hoping to achieve the same surprise that was the case in the middle of the battle-cruiser action at Jutland. Submarines would play a stronger role. Scheer increased their number from the seventeen he had deployed at Jutland to twenty-four.

On 18 August 1916 an intercepted signal gave warning that the High Seas Fleet was preparing another sortie, and the Grand Fleet was at sea before the Germans sailed. Its margin was even more overwhelming this time: thirty-five dreadnoughts against nineteen. And this time Jellicoe and Beatty would also be supported by the Harwich Force of light cruisers and destroyers. Jellicoe joined the fleet late as he had been ill. The stress of the last two years of command had started to catch up with him. It would temporarily render him deaf. The light cruiser *Royalist* took him out to his command.

The German fleet itself went back to sea on the night of 18 August 1916. Hipper's five capital ships led Scheer's fourteen dreadnoughts and supporting forces. Each side now was well-supported by airborne reconnaissance. Scheer had allocated eight Zeppelins – four to the north, four to the west – while the British used kite balloons. Towed behind a dreadnought, the balloons would give them a view from 1,000ft above the battlefield. Their first use gave the fleet's reconnaissance capability an enormous forward stride.

Goodenough's scouts were also out ahead. *Dublin* first spotted activity but thought it to be a fishing-boat sail.* Very soon after, *Nottingham* was hit by two torpedo explosions and when *Dublin* came back to help, she was also attacked. At 06:25 yet another torpedo hit. This time *Nottingham*'s crew were taken off by two destroyers.[4] Jellicoe was now even more worried that the Germans had perfected the weapon that he had so needlessly feared at Jutland. He ordered that the Grand Fleet should not be put at risk and, consequently, not cross a line that roughly ran south of Scotland or east of Belgium, unless there was a real chance of catching the German battle fleet: he turned his fleet north, thinking it 'prudent to avoid this locality … until it was ascertained that the damage was due to torpedoes'.[5]

It was now becoming abundantly clear to Jellicoe that the submarine was coming into its own. In fact, he had laid a similar trap for his German counterparts, positioning five submarines along the access points to the Heligoland Bight. At 800yds (730m), the commander of *E.23*, Lieutenant Commander Turner, was able to launch and successfully hit the battleship *Westfalen* after an abortive first effort on a battle-cruiser and a second miss at Scheer's main battleship line, but he only damaged her. Scheer ordered the wounded ship, along with five escorting destroyers, to return home to port. Turner was able, however, to surface and let Jellicoe know what he had seen.

By 09:50 Scheer's position was estimated to be 150 miles off the British coast. The British had guessed that Sunderland was the target. Jellicoe turned his ships back south as he learned that it had not been a minefield that had caused the *Nottingham*'s sinking, rather a submarine attack. Meanwhile, Commodore Tyrwhitt raced north to join him. By noon Scheer closed in to around seventy miles. Beatty was close by, only thirty miles from Scheer at 12:15, while Jellicoe was sixty miles away.

---

* The 'fishing boat sail' later actually turned out to be a cleverly camouflaged German submarine, *U.52*, whose commander, Leutnant Hans, had used the disguise as a way of secretly watching the British movements.

Then an extraordinary twist of fate saved the German forces from the closing trap. A report came in from one of Scheer's Zeppelins, *L.13*. They had
mistaken Tyrwhitt's forces coming from the south to be major fleet elements
and, what is more, including dreadnoughts. Immediately, Scheer turned his
fleet around and headed south. Meanwhile, Tyrwhitt had done the very same,
since he had not seen any German forces. What could have been the closing
round of the battle of Jutland had been narrowly lost for the most unpredicta-
ble of causes.

Scheer found out from reports from one of his submarines, *U.53*, and two
other Zeppelin reports that the Grand Fleet was in fact to his north. Now he knew
that he had nearly been outwitted and that his radio transmissions had been intercepted. At 16:00 Jellicoe turned the Grand Fleet around. He had just received
news from the Admiralty that Scheer had escaped south: first to the southeast and
then east through the minefields to the safety of Wilhelmshaven. Tyrwhitt did
manage to spot the Germans at around 17:00 and tried to outrun them, but Jellicoe, knowing that he could not give any support, ordered him back to Harwich.

Mutiny

Back in the monotonous safety of Wilhelmshaven, but confined throughout
the long grey winter months with no apparent purpose, crews became restless.
Morale plummeted and the officers were soon openly ignored and increasingly
felt under threat. The extreme danger of the submarine service was the only way
out of the monotony of shore barrack life for those sailors who still yearned for
action. For most, it was a dangerously Faustian deal.

The daily diet on ships was abysmal: turnips and herb tea, potato bread and
hardly any meat.[6] In fact, the quality and quantity of the food was so poor that
it became a dangerous source of tension. Richard Stumpf described one typical
item, a concoction that was derisively called '*Drahtverhau*' or (translated literally) 'chopped barbed wire': 75 per cent water, 10 per cent Oldenburger sausage,
3 per cent potatoes, 2 per cent peas, 1 per cent yellow turnips, 0.5 per cent beef,
0.5 per cent vinegar, 0.25 per cent fat and that little '*je ne sais quoi*' that nobody
could describe.[7] Horn noted that German battleships had three galleys. In one
vivid picture, that symbolised the rigid social divisions: one galley for staff officers, one for deck officers and one for the men. It was small wonder that the
men and officers who messed together on torpedo boats had far higher morale
and officers were almost never challenged.

By December 1916 the food was already so bad that Kapitän Schramm, the
liaison officer with the war food production department, complained that the
calorific intake could not be cut any further – and this was even before the so-
called 'turnip winter' that followed. Few officers looked after their men, but one

who did was Kapitän Langemak, the commander of *Thüringen*, who realised that there was a close connection between the quality of food and the morale of his men.

Throughout 1917 conditions deteriorated and by 1918, after months of inaction, the disgruntlement turned to open insurrection. In June the first hunger strike occurred and a sailors' union was created in the fleet. Each ship had a sailors' council, a kind of soviet. The chairman of the fleet council was a petty stoker on *Friedrich der Große*, known by sailors as 'Big Fritz'.

Much of Germany's eventual defeat could be blamed on the officer class, on its 'bungling incompetence and abdication of responsibility'.[8] The resentment between ranks – never a major issue on most British battleships – was tangible. When First Officer Korvettenkapitän Herzbruch passed a group of sailors on the deck of *Prinzregent Luitpold*, 'the silence of hate followed him'.[9] So it was with Kapitän zur See Thorbecke of the *König Albert*. Late one evening in July 1918, as he was returning from a drinking session, he was pushed overboard by sailors and drowned.[10]

At the end of July things were getting out of hand: 350 crew from *Prinzregent Luitpold* went ashore and demonstrated on the streets of Wilhelmshaven. Already angry about the short leave and the poor quality of the food, the cancelling of a cinema show (so that infantry training could be carried on) ignited the fuelled-up fury and protest broke out. Fifty stokers went ashore. When they returned, Kapitän zur See Karl von Hornhardt arrested eleven. The revolutionary leadership that had previously been established in *Friedrich der Große*'s soviet was now overshadowed by the unrest on *Prinzregent Luitpold*. On 1 August the brimming tension overflowed. The protest did not seem to be about a major issue. It was about the rights of ordinary sailors and in particular the rights of a stoker to enjoy, like an officer, the simple pleasure of visiting a cinema, but for crews that had been so thoroughly badly treated, it was absolutely the last straw.

For three days the fleet was in turmoil. Then Scheer stepped in decisively. The two ships were sent off to the Schillig Roads, at the North Sea entrance to the Jade basin, to isolate them so the contagion would not spread, and two of the ringleaders were executed on 5 September in Cologne. Others were imprisoned in the hope that they would give up information about revolutionary comrades in Berlin. If they did so, their death sentences would be commuted to either fifteen years' penal servitude or to duty at the Western Front with a naval brigade.* The 'best distraction', in Scheer's opinion, was 'active warfare' but, under the circumstances, active war was quite out of the question.[11]

---

* Reichpietsch and Köbis were the two mutineers who were executed. Sachse, Weber and Beckers all had their sentences commuted to fifteen years' penal servitude (see Horn, p163).

Generally speaking, naval officers did not defend the honour which they had promised to defend. During the uprising, only three risked their lives: *König*'s Kapitän Weniger along with two staff officers, Korvettenkapitän Heinemann and Leutnant Zenker.[12]

In late October 1918 Hipper decided on one last, and what looked to many like an almost suicidal, attack on the British. But when his orders for Operation Plan 19 was passed to the ships anchored off Wilhelmshaven on 29 October the sailors chose not to obey it. Some of the crews refused to raise anchor and on two ships full mutiny broke out. While the mutineers ultimately backed down and surrendered after a group of small torpedo boats threatened to sink them the next day, Operation Plan 19 was cancelled and the ships returned to Kiel. The last offensive sortie of the Imperial German navy was over.

There a further mutiny was planned. It was to be supported by workers sympathetic to their cause and influenced by the radical Independent Socialist Democratic Party of Germany (the *Unabhängige Sozialdemokratische Partei Deutschlands*, or USPD). On 3 November 1918 thousands of sailors, led by Karl Artelt and Lothar Popp, both USPD members, held a large rally. As protest banners inscribed with '*Frieden und Brot*' (peace and bread) were raised, the crowd shouted their demands for the release of the Wilhelmshaven mutineers. When they reached the military prison where the mutineers were being held, they were met with gunfire. This provoked a further swelling of the ranks and the next day thousands of sailors joined in to take over the control of Kiel.

The pressure on the monarchy was immense and finally, on 9 November, the Kaiser accepted the inevitable and announced his planned abdication and exile to a teary-eyed General von Hindenburg. The reins of power were handed over to Friedrich Ebert, the leader of the Social Democratic Party (*Sozialdemokratische Partei Deutschlands*, or SPD), and Germany was declared a republic. Three days later, on 11 November, the Armistice was signed.

Internment at Scapa Flow

As part of the Armistice terms, Germany's U-boat fleet was disarmed and 200 vessels were handed over to the Allies.[13] The German battle fleet was to be interned at Scapa Flow, under the guns of the Royal Navy.[14] A decision on the fate of the main fleet itself – under Article XXIII – was not so easy. America suggested that while a solution was being sought the fleet should be interned in a neutral port; two proposals, one in Spain, one in Norway, were turned down. It is doubtful that the Allies really pursued all avenues to find a neutral port solution.

The preliminary arrangements had been made on the night of 15 November 1918, when Rear Admiral Hugo Meurer, Hipper's representative, met Beatty on *Queen Elizabeth* to hear the terms (on taking command of the Grand Fleet, Beatty had moved the C-in-C's flag to this faster and more powerful battleship, in preference to *Iron Duke*, declaring that there was 'too much of Jellicoe in her'). The U-boats were to surrender to Tyrwhitt, now a rear admiral, at Harwich, while the main fleet was to sail three days later to the internment location – Scapa Flow – that had been suggested by Jellicoe's immediate successor at the Admiralty, 1SL Sir Rosslyn Wemyss.

The meeting between Beatty and Meurer did not go well. Beatty was convinced that he needed to show a stern and cold exterior, and the courtesies that normally existed between officers were not extended. Quite the opposite. Guards had fixed bayonets. Lighting was purposely as bright as possible. Meurer asked for more time as he was concerned for the morale of his men – especially so, as they were still in a visibly mutinous mood. Beatty would brook no delay and at midnight the agreement was signed.

Four days later, on the 19th, the first German fleet elements set sail for Britain, but not before the British had checked to make sure that all ammunition had been landed. On the morning of the 21st the Germans arrived off the Firth of Forth where they were met by an Allied force of 250 ships. This included the Grand Fleet, as well as an American battleship squadron and ships from other Allied navies, including from the French navy. In total, there were forty-four capital ships. By the 27th the remnants arrived at Scapa Flow, save the torpedo boat, *V.30*, which had strayed off course and paid for her folly, striking a mine and sinking in the open sea.

Beatty took no chances. British and Allied guns – fore and aft – were trained on the German ships as they steamed into internment. A postcard of the time shows British sailors wearing flash-protection headgear, stating that 'they would not trust the Hun even at the last'. At 15:57 the German flag was ordered to be hauled down. As the German ships came into the Flow they were watched by Beatty, but not by Jellicoe. Neither he nor Churchill had been invited, nor Fisher or Battenberg. Had such an invitation been extended, it would have been, in Oliver Warner's words, a 'gracious gesture'.[15]

Months went by without any resolution amongst the victors over the division of the spoils. For Britain, the question was not an easy one, as any likely resolution was bound to upset the balance of naval power between Britain, France and America. Any additional ships being allocated to Britain's allies would cut back her overall lead in the ratio between her Navy and those that could one day become challengers.

For the Germans, internment was an unpleasant experience. Separated from their families, the daily routine was gruelling in its relentless monotony. Food came from Germany twice a month. Predictably, it was mediocre.

There was nothing for the men to do, so they supplemented their diets with fish and seagulls. They were not allowed ashore or to visit any other ship. Each ship was a floating prison. There were doctors but not a single dentist on the ships. The British refusal to provide dental care was an unnecessary and cruel hardship. It cannot be a surprise that the mood amongst the crews became dangerous. There was no way to blow off steam. Things got so bad on *Friedrich der Große* that Ludwig von Reuter, the fleet's commander, even transferred his flag in March to the cruiser *Emden* so that he could get some sleep. A group of sailors who called themselves 'the red guard' used to jump up and down on the deckhead above his cabin each night, denying the poor man any rest.

Admiral Sir Charles Madden saw the extent of the disintegrating chain of command among the German ships' companies: 'All proposed orders are considered and countersigned by the men's committee before they are executed and then they are carried out as convenient'.[16] Gradually, the number of sailors was reduced as men were repatriated to Germany. By December their number had shrunk from 20,000 to just under 5,000.* The British had encouraged the reduction to allow only minimal skeleton crews on the ships: 200 for a battle-cruiser, 175 for a battleship, eighty for a light cruiser and twenty for a destroyer, leaving a nominal total of 4,565, plus 250 officers and warrant officers (although the exact figures are thought to be higher). Even this minimal complement was more than the British wanted.

Reuter increasingly considered scuttling the fleet as the means of avoiding handing the Allies any more ready-made naval power. As early as January 1919 he was actively drawing up detailed plans with his staff on how a scuttling could actually be carried out. With the months going by and peace negotiations dragging on in Versailles, the Germans became increasingly distrustful of Allied intentions. On 18 June Reuter sent out the critical message to the close circle of officers whom he felt could be trusted: 'It is my intention to sink the ships only if the enemy should attempt to obtain possession of them without the assent of our government. Should our government agree in the peace terms to the surrender of the ships, then the ships will be handed over, to the lasting disgrace of those who have placed us in this position'.[17]

Only three days after first announcing his intentions, Reuter acted. At 10.00 on 21 June the stand-by signal was given. An hour later, at 11:20, a flag signal was hoisted and repeated in semaphore and with searchlight to all ships. The scuttling plan went into action. 'To all commanding officers and the leader of

---

* 4,000 sailors returned to Germany on 3 December, 6,000 on 6 December and 5,000 on 12 December, leaving 4,815, of whom approximately 100 continued to be repatriated each month (see Massie, p784 and p786).

the torpedo boats. Paragraph 11 of today's date. Acknowledge. Chief of the interned squadron.'[18]

To British guards everything seemed normal. But within the ships' hulls the crews set about their appointed tasks with a practised but ordered frenzy. Sea-cocks were opened, water pipes smashed and bulkhead doors left open. Portholes were opened, condenser covers also left open and even holes bored through compartment bulkheads to accelerate the intake of water. All the threads had been well lubricated to make sure there would be no last-minute glitch. It was only around noon, when *Friedrich der Große* started to take on a pronounced list, that the alarm was raised. Even then the scuttling signal had not succeeded in getting around the whole fleet and it was an hour before all ships acknowledged it.

At 12:20 the British finally took action. But it was too late and too little. The only British warships present were the destroyers *Vesper* and *Vega*; there were also a couple of depot ships, and various trawlers and drifters. While they signalled Vice Admiral Sydney Fremantle's 1st Battle Squadron, which returned to base at full speed, it was a lost cause. Over the course of the afternoon fifty-two German warships – including fourteen battleships – went down. It was the greatest loss of shipping that had ever occurred in a single day.

Wemyss's reaction to the news reflected a larger perspective. The scuttling had actually rid the British of a major challenge. 'I look upon the sinking of the German fleet as a real blessing. It disposes, once and for all, the thorny question of the redistribution of the German ships. When the facts become known, everybody will probably think, like me, "Thank the Lord"'[19] – in other words, that handing them over to either or both the American and French navies had been averted; the French, in particular, felt that they deserved a navy for their role in the war. The British managed to save a few ships from sinking – by running them aground – but by 17:00 the last major ship, *Hindenburg*, slowly sank beneath the cold dark waters of the Flow.

Vice Admiral Fremantle delivered a speech to Reuter on the quarterdeck of the *Revenge* once the scuttling operation was concluded:

Admiral von Reuter: I cannot permit you and your officers to leave naval custody without expressing to you my sense of the manner in which you have violated common honour and the honourable traditions of seamen of all nations. With an armistice in full operation you recommenced hostilities without notice by hoisting the German flag in the interned ships and proceeding to sink and destroy them. You have informed my interpreter that you considered the Armistice had terminated. You had no justification whatever for that assumption. You would have been informed by me of the termination of the Armistice and whether the representatives of your nation had or had not signed the Treaty of Peace. Indeed, letters in readiness to send to you to that effect as soon as I had received official intimation from my Government were written and signed. Further, can you possibly suppose that my squadron would have been out of harbour at the moment of the termination of the Armistice? By your conduct you have added one more to the breaches of faith and honour of which Germany has been guilty in this war. Begun with a breach of military honour in the invasion of Belgium, it bids fair to terminate with a breach of naval honour. You have proved to the few who doubted it that the word of the New Germany is no more to be trusted than that of the old. What opinion your country will form of your action I do not know. I can only express what I believe to be the opinion of the British navy, and indeed of all seamen except those of your nation. I now transfer you to the custody of the British military authorities as prisoners of war guilty of a flagrant violation of Armistice.[20]

Privately Fremantle felt very differently: 'I could not resist feeling some sympathy for Reuter, who had preserved his dignity when placed against his will in a highly unpleasant and invidious position.'[21]

Most of the wrecks were salvaged by the British but seven still remain on the bed of the Flow. They include three battleships, *König*, *Markgraf* and *Kronprinz Wilhelm*, and the light cruisers *Brummer*, *Köln*, *Dresden* and *Karlsruhe*. Between 1924, when salvage began, and 1931, the majority of the work was carried out by the British company, Cox and Danks. Ernest Cox bought the salvage rights from the Admiralty for £40,000, raised twenty-six destroyers, one light cruiser, four battle-cruisers and two battleships.

Cox took considerable risks and only just managed to break even on the operations.[22] Raising *Hindenburg*, for example, cost him around £30,000. *Seydlitz* was an equally difficult and expensive operation, and was actually raised twice: the first time, while Cox was away on holiday, unsuccessfully; he immediately ordered her re-sunk to await his return.

Nine German sailors were killed during the scuttling and around sixteen wounded. These nine German sailors were the last fatalities of the First World War.

13

Counting Up After the Battle

It seems to me that the criticism of Jellicoe's tactics, even when a *prima facie* case can be made (notably with regard to Jellicoe's turn-away in the face of flotilla attack), ignores the basic principle of war, namely, that tactics are governed by strategy. That is, battles are ancillary to the main strategy of war. *Jellicoe's primary object was the retention of command of the sea, and this was accomplished.* His secondary object was the destruction of the High Seas Fleet; it was highly desirable, but not essential.

Arthur Marder, *From the Dreadnought to Scapa Flow*

The Battle of Jutland should not have become as controversial as it did. The Navy's limited and controlled objectives of blockade were greatly overshadowed by the nation's unrealistic desire, fuelled by the press, for another Trafalgar. The German fleet was not annihilated. It came away with serious damage and the realisation that it could not achieve its ends in a fleet-to-fleet engagement, but politicians answer to the public, and the hunt for scapegoats began early.

The comparisons with Trafalgar were inevitable, yet the contrast between 1916 and 1805 cannot be more stark. Nelson's enemy at Trafalgar was not a single nation's navy. It was actually two fleets: a French force with a Spanish component. They shared neither common language nor signals, and they had little experience in operating together. Their morale and fitness for battle was questionable; the French and Spanish sailors had been holed up in Cadiz for the long, hot summer of 1805 on poor rations. The harvest of 1804 had failed. Morale in the British fleet, after a decade of victories – notably Cape St Vincent, the Nile and Copenhagen – was exceptionally high.

The fleets that fought at Trafalgar were significantly smaller in absolute numbers and as a ratio to the total naval forces available at the time.* While only around a quarter of the Royal Navy's ships of the line were engaged at

---

* Nelson's fleet comprised twenty-seven ships of the line (of which HMS *Victory* was one of three First Rate ships), but if had been a catastrophic battle, a loss at Trafalgar would still have left Britain with an adequate number of ships for its strategic requirements. Not so Jutland. I am very much indebted to my cousin, Richard Latham, for his extensive knowledge of Trafalgar which he was happy to share.

Trafalgar, Jellicoe's fleet comprised all the modern capital ships that the Navy could muster to maintain the critical dreadnought margin on the North Sea. A defeat for the British in 1916 would have had dire consequences. Jellicoe knew this, hence his aversion to unnecessary risk. Beatty's Battle Cruiser Fleet had run the gauntlet at around 26 knots; *Abdiel* was sent off at 31 knots. Nelson took five hours in bright sunshine, approaching his opponents at speeds of around 1–3 knots. At Jutland, with the antagonists' fleets approaching each other at about thirty-five miles an hour, eighteen minutes passed between initial sighting and battle-cruiser action. At Trafalgar, while the French opened fire at around 1,000yds (900m), most of the most destructive fighting was within 10–50yds (9–45m).

Tactically, Jutland was a bad blow for British prestige, the nation's morale and, most importantly, for the standing of the Royal Navy. The British came off worse in terms of lives and tonnage lost. British losses of life – including three admirals – was three times that of their enemy. Tonnage was twice as much. In the post-war tally, the Germans focused on the sinking of ships and the thousands of dead. In terms of materiel and human loss they rightly claimed victory, but numbers rarely tell the complete story.

Almost 200,000 tons of ships were sunk in less than a day. The two really significant losses were those of *Queen Mary* and *Lützow*. The German battle-cruiser was fresh out of the shipyard and Hipper had just transferred his flag to her. Most of the other British and German ships – *Invincible, Indefatigable, Black Prince, Warrior, Defence* and *Pommern* – were outdated, even if the British battle-cruisers' sister ships continued to serve until the end of the war.

British and German Losses

Ship Type	British	German
Battle-cruisers	Three *(Invincible, Queen Mary, Indefatigable)*	One *(Lützow)*
Pre-dreadnoughts		One *(Pommern)*
Armoured cruisers	Three *(Defence, Warrior, Black Prince)*	
Light cruisers		Four *(Elbing, Frauenlob, Rostock, Wiesbaden)*
Destroyers	Eight *(Ardent, Fortune, Nestor, Nomad, Shark, Sparrowhawk, Tipperary, Turbulent)*	Five *(S.35, V.4, V.27, V.29, V.48)*

Self-Inflicted Sinkings and Damage

SMS *Elbing*	Hit and sunk by SMS *Posen*
HMS *Broke*	Rammed by HMS *Sparrowhawk*
HMS *Sparrowhawk*	Rammed by HMS *Contest*

Mistakes in fleet composition were clearly made by both sides and these errors of judgement produced easy casualties once the fighting started. Neither *Frauenlob* nor Rear Admiral Mauve's 2nd Squadron of 17-knot pre-dreadnoughts should have been there. *Indefatigable*'s and *New Zealand*'s slower speed (by 5 knots) and shorter range (by around 5,000yds) made their inclusion in the Battle Cruiser Fleet a risk. Both sides paid for these misjudgements with the death of thousands on the day.

Returning to their ports, the British had eight capital ships damaged, the Germans fifteen; and at the end of the action Jellicoe still had twenty-six un-damaged capital ships against Scheer's five. At home Jellicoe had another five in reserve, while Scheer had just two. Jellicoe's fleet was ready to sail again on the day that it got back to Scapa Flow – at 22:30 on 2 June. Scheer's dry-dock repairs immobilised the High Seas Fleet for considerably longer than the British. The number of dry-dock repair days* needed to get both fleets back fully operational was in the German case almost 50 per cent higher: 550 days against 367 for the British. *Derfflinger* needed 135 days in dock, the *Seydlitz*, 106. The only British ship that required such lengthy repairs was *Lion* – 103 days. Otherwise fewer British ships needed major repairs.

Comparative Dry-Dock Repair Days

German	Individual ship Tonnage	Cumulative Tonnage	Date back in line	Tonnage still under repair	Total Repair Days	Tonnage Days
Helgoland	22,800	22,800	16 June	14,208,115	15	342,000
Großer Kurfürst	25,391	48,191	16 July	13,801,859	16	406,256
Markgraf	25,391	73,582	20 July	12,557,700	49	1,244,159
König	25,391	98,973	21 July	11,288,150	50	1,269,550
Ostfriesland	22,800	121,773	26 July	8,741,800	56	1,276,800
Moltke	25,300	147,073	30 July	8,493,350	60	1,518,000

* A 'dry-dock repair day' is defined as the total of all the days for each individual ship that went into repair. With the information I had at hand I was not able to calculate the dry-dock repair *man*-days. This would have been a more instructive comparative measure.

	Individual ship Tonnage	Cumulative Tonnage	Date back in line	Tonnage still under repair	Total Repair Days	Tonnage Days
Von der Tann	21,750	168,823	2 August	7,123,100	63	1,370,250
Seydlitz	28,100	196,923	16 September	4,144,500	106	2,978,600
Derfflinger	30,700	227,623	15 October		135	4,144,500
TOTALS					550	14,550,115

British	Individual ship Tonnage	Cumulative Tonnage	Date back in line	Tonnage still under repair	Total Repair Days	Tonnage Days
Tiger	35,000	35,000	1 July	10,274,600	30	1,050,000
Barham	32,000	67,000	4 July	9,218,600	33	1,056,000
Malaya	32,000	99,000	10 July	7,970,600	39	1,248,000
Warspite	32,000	131,000	20 July	6,402,600	49	1,568,000
Princess Royal	29,700	160,700	21 July	3,349,600	50	1,485,000
Marlborough	29,500	190,200	2 August	3,059,100	63	1,858,500
Lion	29,700	219,900	13 September		103	3,059,100
TOTALS					367	11,324,600

Sources: Tarrant, *Jutland: The German Perspective*, p249, Dates of completion.

There was also a question with the amount of out-of-action tonnage.[1] For the Germans, with a much smaller fleet, the amount was 30 per cent higher than that of the British: 14.5 million tonnage days against 11.3 million. A disproportionate amount of damage had been suffered by the Germans and could not be absorbed. The British had lost three battle-cruisers, but six remained. The Germans were left with the same number of battle-cruisers as they had when the war started. Jellicoe also still had twenty-six dreadnought battleships at his disposal.

Beatty's failure to concentrate his forces caused the greatest losses at the start of the run to the south. Even though Evan-Thomas had to manage a fighting rearguard action in the run to the north, his four battleships holding off nine German capital ships, the damage was heavy. The loss of life resulting from the battle-cruiser sinkings was horrendous. On these three ships alone – *Invincible*, *Indefatigable* and *Queen Mary* – 3,309 men died, 2,283 in the run to the south. This was not primarily caused by bad design – for example, a lack of armour where needed or of better compartmentalisation – but more directly by faulty and dangerous ammunition-handling practices.

Jellicoe never underrated German shipbuilding qualities: ship design reflects the planned role a fleet is envisioned to play. One of the British fleet's primary tasks was to defend her empire's sea trade routes. The German fleet was opti-mised for short-distance operations, a close action in the North Sea. Jellicoe had seen the extensive facilities that allowed the Germans, unlike the British, to build broader-beamed battleships. Jellicoe was well aware of these qualities:

> … if in ships of equal displacement British guns were of greater calibre than German guns, more weight being thus expended in gun armament, it was obvious that in some other direction the German ships possessed advantages; and the advantage they did possess was that of far greater protection both in the way of armour above and below water, and in more complete watertight subdivision below water as protection against torpedo or mine attack. This more complete subdivision and underwater protection in German capital ships was facilitated by the greater beam of the ships as compared with that of our own, our vessels being limited in beam by the width of existing docks and the difficulty of persuading our government to construct new and wider docks. Any naval officer who inspected the German ships salvaged from Scapa Flow, when in dock at Rosyth (as I did), could see clearly the immense under-water protection of these ships due to their great beam and wonderfully complete watertight subdivision. I certainly – as Second Sea Lord before the War – pointed out to Mr Churchill the fallacy of his argument …[2]

Nor did Jellicoe underrate German naval professionalism:

> I had, ever since my experiences of the German navy in China during the Boxer troubles, conceived a decided admiration and considerable liking for German naval officers and men. I had taken every opportunity of meeting them, and personally knew a great many of the senior officers, including those obviously destined for high command. I felt, too, a great respect for the efficiency of the German navy.[3]

Before he died in 1935, Jellicoe was planning to visit Germany to inspect the new navy.

Beatty's contribution to Jellicoe's battlefield intelligence was, as we have seen, poor. Air and/or submarine reconnaissance could have played a significant role, but *Engadine*'s four messages from Rutland were never passed to Jellicoe (or, for that matter, even to Beatty).[4] Nor could Scheer employ Zeppelins. None of his carefully placed U-boats passed back any significant intelligence (as neither did Jellicoe's submarines at the Amrum minefield). By 1917 British dreadnoughts would not only tow kite balloons that gave them a 1,000ft high vantage point above sea level; so would many platform-launched aircraft that perched on the main armament turrets.

Jellicoe assumed that the Germans would not be able to break through his forces without his knowledge. He was wrong. The battleships *Malaya* and *Valiant*, the cruiser *Champion* and five smaller warships all failed to pass on information that they had sighted major German elements. Only *Faulknor* tried, but her signals were jammed. The escape of both *Seydlitz* and *Derfflinger* was a startling blunder by the British.

After signalling Jellicoe that the Germans would take the Horns Reef route, Jellicoe was given no subsequent signals intelligence that would have restored his confidence in the information coming from the Admiralty. He was not told that Kommodore Michelsen's destroyers were to rally there, nor that Scheer had ordered Zeppelin reconnaissance. Scheer, by contrast, knew that the sixty-four British destroyers had been placed at the Grand Fleet's rear and running into them confirmed that he was breaking through at the weakest point of the British line. In later years, the Admiralty was keen to protect its own. Not until 1940 (when the relevant *Naval Operations* volumes were completed by Sir Henry Newbolt, who was given access by the Admiralty to all the signals) was the series of errors in not relaying important intelligence from Room 40 raised – a quarter of a century after the battle.

German signals and communications within the fleet were exemplary, while those of the British were lamentable – with some exceptions, of course. The difficulties for British signalling – a mixture of flag, semaphore, searchlight and, the least used, wireless telegraphy – were evident. The two flag failures that led to the misuse of the 5th Battle Squadron at the start of the action and to the near-fatal lack of co-ordination at the beginning of the run to the north clearly demonstrated this. Having endlessly lobbied to have the powerful 15in guns of the 5th Battle Squadron under his command, Beatty failed to use them properly in the very first action.

Jellicoe was criticised for his over-use of signals. Scheer, more like Hipper and Beatty, believed in his officers being imbued with strong guiding principles with minimum distracting detail. But belief in principles is one thing; training in, and the communication of them, quite another. At a capital-ship level, Jellicoe did not support individual initiative, for the simple reason that the large number of ships would have risked chaos under battle conditions. The Royal Navy that fought at Jutland still bore the vestiges of its Victorian past. While Jacky Fisher's reforms had dramatically pulled it out of its deepest slumbers, the lack of initiative without orders, the poor performance under battle conditions and the lingering social system that limited advancement to the officer class all continued to hold it back.[5]

Given the slow speed of flag signalling (and maybe also the lack of initiative), Jellicoe no doubt felt that he had no other option but to keep a tight rein on the fleet. His tactics were to make the Grand Fleet fight as a tightly co-ordinated and centralised force. In 1914 he had held a rather different point of view, which left more room for independent squadron initiative and manoeuvre, but he had changed his thinking when he realised how little initiative there really was in the fleet.* And his experiences on pre-war manoeuvres with Callaghan, his predecessor as C-in-C, definitely showed a different Jellicoe. On the other hand, Beatty lost tactical control of the small number of ships that he commanded and made little effort to use the skills of experienced officers, preferring younger men, often with strong social connections.

The myth survives that the Grand Fleet was not really engaged at Jutland and that Jellicoe's timidity lost the battle. The gunnery record gives a very different picture. Records have probably been distorted by both adversaries but probably also by the increasingly ill-tempered battle-cruiser/battleship rivalry. The Germans certainly felt that they had a better record and presented copious statistics to prove their case. The Admiralstab accounts state that the accuracy of their gunners far exceeded that of the British: a hit rate of 3.3 per cent against 2.17 per cent.[6] Yet the logic is faulty at best. As with all statistics, it depends on definitions. Much smaller-calibre hits, for example, were included in the German assessment, which grossly distorted the final impression.

In the last hour before sunset on 31 May 1916, when the Grand Fleet was engaged, the British landed forty-nine heavy calibre hits against three from enemy gunners. The Grand Fleet's performance was – during its limited (and much closer-range) engagement – demonstrably better than that of the 1st or 2nd Battle Cruiser Squadrons, but this was successfully buried at the time. The elements of the Grand Fleet that did open fire were able to concentrate twice on the enemy 'T'. Beatty's battle-cruisers fired 1,469 rounds. Excluding the 15in guns of Evan-Thomas's 5th Battle Squadron (technically part of Beatty's Battle Cruiser Fleet), the Grand Fleet fired 1,593. The Grand Fleet suffered amazingly few casualties but managed to score fifty-seven hits; by contrast, some of the battle-cruisers' performance was woeful.[7] The 1st and 2nd Battle Cruiser Squadrons expended an average of seventy shells per hit; the 1st, 2nd and 4th Battle Squadrons twenty-seven. For the Germans it was similar: the 1st Scouting Group twenty-six, the 1st, 2nd and 3rd Battle Squadrons thirty-four. In both cases, however, the visibility conditions had a major impact on the gunnery performance of both sides.

The quality of British ordnance might have left much to be desired but it was also easy to turn this discussion against Jellicoe, as he had – briefly – been Controller. Blaming the poor quality of shells took much of the focus away

---

* Initially, Jellicoe agreed with his predecessor Sir George Callaghan's position on the need for independent divisional action. By 1916 he strongly opposed such independence, presumably after seeing the lack of initiative within the Grand Fleet.

from gunnery skill and training. The fact is that Jellicoe had lobbied strongly but ineffectively – the cost was deemed too high – for more realistic trials of ammunition in October 1910. Most British testing was done at long range, with plunging shells hitting deck armour rather than at side-belt armour, so the effect of hitting at the oblique was not highlighted. As Jellicoe put it:

> In order to determine the effectiveness against armoured ships of the shell supplied for the various guns I arranged for extensive firing trials to be carried out in 1910 against the old battleship *Edinburgh*, which had been specially prepared by the addition of modern armour plates. As a result of these trials, before the end of my Office as Controller, the Ordnance Board were asked on the 18th October 1910 to endeavour to produce an armour-piercing shell which would perforate armour at oblique impact and go on in a fit state for bursting.
>
> I left the Admiralty in December 1910, to take command of the Atlantic Fleet; and unfortunately the production of such efficient armour-piercing shell was not sufficiently pressed and our shell continued to be proved only at normal impact to the plate. As a result, during the War, in the various actions in which the shell naturally struck at oblique impact, due *inter alia* to the angle of descent, our armour-piercing shell did not achieve the results they ought to have against the well-armoured German capital ships. Our shell, though in many cases they knocked holes in the enemy's armour by their momentum, broke up at oblique impact instead of going on and bursting in the vitals of the enemy ships.
>
> We thus lost the advantage we ought to have enjoyed in offensive power due to the greater weight of our projectiles, while suffering the accepted disadvantage in the protection of our ships due to the heavy weights of our guns and ammunition which reduced the total weight available for armour plating.[8]

British coincidence range-finders proved difficult even in ideal conditions. German Zeiss stereoscopic range-finders were found to be more accurate for initial range-finding, but the Barr and Stroud split screen, if provided with a hard, well-defined edge, worked well, causing less strain. It was said that while German initial ranging was excellent, its accuracy did tend to fall off over time.

The German 'ladder' approach to firing required salvos being rapidly fired from successive turrets, while the shells from the previous turret were still in flight at ranges separated by around 400yds (370m). They were then able rapidly to 'ladder' up or down, depending on 'spotting' the shell fall. 'Laddering' up was obviously easier to read and it was probably significant here that the initial fire of the British battle-cruisers fell very long. The British often relied more on speed than careful calculation, and even if Jellicoe himself was not of the 'speed school', Beatty was.* Jellicoe is still much criticised for his seemingly exaggerated respect for the new weapons of the day – torpedoes and mines – but he was dealing with mostly untried technologies. He clearly stated that he would not pursue an enemy that executed a turn-away, especially at night, as he was concerned at being led over mines dropped by the retreating force. As it turned out, the effect of mines in the battle was negligible. Nevertheless, the threat led to the later introduction of the paravane (a type of towed underwater kite which cut the cables of anchored mines), affording a fleet steaming into a minefield some protection.

The torpedo was a different matter. Scheer and Hipper were torpedo specialists. Jellicoe and Beatty were both concerned to keep any engagement outside of torpedo range, at roughly 14,000yds (12,800m). This makes it a little ironic that the British scored more torpedo hits and escaped with battleship torpedo damage only to *Marlborough*. The British hits on *Seydlitz* could have been exploited had she been re-engaged in the night action. Additionally, German torpedo activity at night was significantly less than what had been feared by Jellicoe.†

Torpedo Hits at Jutland (*sunk)

	German	British
Battleships	*Pommern**	*Marlborough*
Battle-cruisers	*Seydlitz*	
Light cruisers	*Wiesbaden*	
	*Frauenlob**	
Destroyers		*Shark**
		Porpoise
Torpedo boats	*V.29**	
	V.35	

Source: Brown, 'Torpedoes at Jutland'.

During the turn-away, the number of near-misses was high. The likelihood of serious damage to the battle fleet had Jellicoe not turned away was almost

---

* It may be no coincidence that the fastest-firing ships in the BCF were *Invincible* and *Queen Mary*. On both ships, stacking additional cordite outside of the protected magazines ready to feed to the guns faster was standard practice.

† 'The irony is that the German destroyer flotillas, the element of the High Seas Fleet that Jellicoe most feared and that had loomed so large in his night dispositions, played no part in the night-time battle. Ten German destroyers actually left the battlefield early and returned to Kiel around the northern tip of Denmark. Through the rest of the night, the remaining German destroyers searched in vain for the British battle fleet.' (Massie, p649).

certain. But even with the turn-away, had the Germans increased the number of torpedoes within the fan, the results, it has been suggested, might also have been very different. Both sides tended to conserve torpedoes rather than use quantity when the opportunity presented itself. As an example of what might have been achieved, six months after Jutland, at the Horns Reef, the British submarine *J.1.* scored four hits in a four-torpedo spread. The fact that German torpedoes did not inflict heavier damage should not lead one to conclude that the threat itself was non-existent or, indeed, question the wisdom of the turn-away manoeuvre practised by almost every navy at the time. It is sometimes not the actual success of a weapon in use, but rather the effect of the threat that shows its potential.

The importance of flash protection was quickly understood by the Germans after the loss of *Blücher* and *Seydlitz*'s near-fatal turret fire at Dogger Bank. The British did not have quite the same experience from which to learn and after Jutland, Beatty remained quiet on the subject. He owed much to his gunnery officer, Warrant Officer Gunner Alexander Grant, who had been brought up in the practices of the Grand Fleet, and who limited the open stacking of cordite and imposed tighter procedure when he joined *Lion*. Grant was not popular for his actions but it might have been some of his efforts (as well, of course, Major Harvey's) that saved *Lion*. Jellicoe had always been worried that the system of anti-flash doors would be compromised by the emphasis on gunnery speed. In the event, the concerns he expressed in late 1915, telling Beatty that he felt it [gunnery speed] was 'being carried to excess', were completely justified.

After the disappointment of Dogger Bank, Beatty concluded that the ideal gunnery range for battle-cruiser action would be 12,000–14,000yds (11,000–12,800m): this would be at the extremes of torpedo effectiveness and out of range of German secondary armament. He also concluded that the problem was too few hits, but he concentrated on speed of fire rather than on accuracy. Within a year of Dogger Bank, the safety granted by the 'flash-tight interlocks from the ammunition hoists that carried the cordite charges from the magazine, safe in the bowels of the ship, to the exposed gun mountings' was removed on all the ships of the Battle Cruiser Fleet.[9] Ironically, the only exception was *Lion*, where Alexander Grant had ordered them to be replaced, in direct opposition to both Chatfield's and Beatty's preference. Chatfield remarked: 'whoever gets the biggest volume of fire short or hitting will gain the ascendancy and keep it as the other person can't see to reply'.[10] Maybe this is why the gunnery results of the battle-cruiser practice shoots were not good. In the spring 1916 exercises, for example, 'the *Tiger*'s [was] so bad her captain was censured'.[11]

On 2 June 1916, after the battle-cruiser bloodletting of Jutland, Beatty quietly ordered the flash-tight interlocks to be restored.* The Grand Fleet had not found a solution to, in Andrew Lambert's wonderfully visual description, 'a fleet steaming off the bottom of the page'. 'They [the Germans] were meant to steam along in parallel courses and obligingly be sunk. They didn't do that. Why on earth should they?'[12]

The debate on dogma: the Grand Fleet Battle Orders

The British fleet that fought at Jutland was steeped in traditions and etiquette that had been built over centuries, while the ships and weapons technologies they were to fight in and fight with had completely changed in twenty short years. With war, direct experience was garnered, and this knowledge from battle then applied. Apart from Tsushima, a decade previously, since Trafalgar there had been no fleet action experience from which to develop any new tactics. All commentary was supposition, a purely hypothetical guessing game. Jutland was the first opportunity for both the Germans and British to test their thinking. Jellicoe's approach to tactics has to be looked at within a fast-changing environment. It could not have been more different from our own age, where the Western powers have been almost continuously engaged in military or naval actions somewhere around the globe.

The launch of HMS *Dreadnought* instantly rendered all other battleships obsolete, including much of the existing British fleet. Fisher's battle-cruiser concept was supposed to have a similar impact but ended up costing his country's Navy dearly. In the space of thirty years accurate naval gunnery had increased from ranges of 1,600–2,000yds (1,460–1,830m) to the *Queen Elizabeth* class that could hurl a shell weighing almost a ton over a distance of 24,400yds (22,300m): just under fourteen miles.[13] Torpedoes, which had a range of over 1,000yds just before the start of the twentieth century, were, at Jutland, able to cover 17,000yds (15,500m) in twenty-eight minutes: a speed of 600yds a minute.[14] Mines had become more sophisticated. They now started to incorporate variable depth settings, multiple launch platforms, and later even a magnetic fusing type.

In other complementary areas, systems had not kept pace, notably in communications. Flags, a system that was developed at the time of Nelson, was still the primary method of sending orders up and down a battle line. Visual contact and good visibility were fundamental to their efficacy. WT, still in its infancy, was discouraged before any fleet engagement for fear of giving the enemy one's position and even, because of the nature and strength of signal, an indication of one's force strength.

---

* On 2 June 1916, following Jutland, Beatty, in Lambert's words 'tacitly admitted his responsibility for the three battle-cruiser losses … symbolically ordering that the flash-tight interlocks be restored' (Lambert, p360).

British fleet doctrine on how to engage with the Germans was first codi-
fied by Jellicoe in what were known as the Grand Fleet Battle Orders, usually
referred to by their initials, the GFBOs. These were detailed instructions to
commanders as to what actions were appropriate or mandated under the widest
possible range of circumstances, most of which – unfortunately, but by necessity
– had been tested out only in manoeuvres and not in battle conditions. To say
that the orders did not leave much to individual initiative is an understatement.

Later rewritten when Beatty commanded the Grand Fleet, the GFBOs were
a constantly changing body of tactical thinking. Consequently, quoting the
GFBOs *in general* as a single source of validating support for Jellicoe or Beatty
is often a very misleading exercise but – with the caveat that I am not a naval
man – I will try to highlight some of the issues on which the two admirals were
at variance.

The GFBO print-run was around 250 copies. This suggests that circula-
tion reached captain level. However, there were issues, often important and
significant ones, not dealt with in the main body of orders that were handled
in memoranda marked 'Most Secret', personally delivered by Jellicoe to his admirals and commodores: a group of fourteen people. Jellicoe's starting point
was the overall strategy that he needed to pursue. His primary objective was
not defeat of the High Seas Fleet; it was retention of the command of the seas.
Marder spoke of the annihilation of the enemy as a 'nice to have', not a primary,
objective.

> It is not, in my opinion, wise to risk unduly the heavy ships of the Grand
> Fleet in an attempt to hasten the end of the High Seas Fleet, particularly if
> the risks come, not from the High Seas Fleet itself but from such attributes as
> mines and submarines. There is no doubt that, provided there is a chance of
> destroying some of the enemy's heavy ships, it is right and proper to run risks
> with our own heavy ships, but unless the chances are reasonably great, I do
> not think that such risks should be run, seeing that any real disaster to our
> heavy ships lays the country open to invasion.[15]

It is this kind of thinking that Arthur Marder points to when he talks about
the 'subordination of the offensive spirit to defensive precautions, especially
against the torpedo'.[16] Jellicoe's outlook had been derived from an almost purely
technical perspective, but it was fought over in the most emotional manner.
The clear risk for Jellicoe was not so much the High Seas Fleet as the torpedo
and mine. This fear supported a long-range plan of battle because the torpedo's danger and the assumed German superiority in this weapon made Jellicoe
extremely conscious of the downside potential for any error on his part. In 'subordination of the offensive spirit', Marder cited the adherence to the 'single line,

parallel course, and long range of the plan of battle; and centralised command'. All of these Jellicoe, and the Admiralty, believed in.

A summing-up by an adversary says it well:

> The greatness of personality of a Jellicoe perhaps rests in the fact that he did not yield to fighting impulse, but evinced a statesmanlike mind ... To him it was more important to keep his country's fleet intact at all costs for the main strategic task – remote blockade of the German Bight. A total victory over the High Seas Fleet might well have hastened the defeat of Germany ... but the risk inherent in such an attempt was not justified when the blockade, slowly but with deadly certainty, achieved the same end.[17]

The single line was the only known deployment of battleships that allowed him to concentrate fire in some manoeuvres, for example, that of crossing the enemy's 'T'. With decentralised command, he felt that the very power of the Grand Fleet would be dissipated by too much independent action and that it might leave isolated squadrons open to effective enemy counter-attack. Maintaining the *controlled* fighting effectiveness of his fleet under battle conditions would be difficult; without effective communications and signalling, near impossible. Signalling and communications were not great strengths with either the battle-cruisers or the battle fleet.

The pressure on Jellicoe on the day was enormous and was well-summed up in Churchill's oft-quoted phrase, that he was the only man who 'could lose the war in an afternoon', but not – I stress – 'the only man who could *win* the war in an afternoon'.[18] In today's armed services, individual initiative and delegated authority are accepted practice. But you cannot use today's standards with yesterday's context. P Wayne Hughes wrote in 1986:

> It does not do simply to dismiss Jellicoe as lacking the Nelsonian will to win. The analyses that reach this conclusion also compare his fleet's quality and gunnery unfavourably with the German fleet's; some authors go so far as to say Scheer had a chance to win. One cannot have it both ways. Either Jellicoe retained sole power to destroy, provided he exercised no imprudence, or his caution was justified because he in fact might have lost, in which case the consequences were incalculable.[19]

Looking at the main body of the GFBOs that were in place on the eve of Jutland,[20] major doctrinal issues of difference between Jellicoe and Beatty existed.

- *Independence of action*: Jellicoe held onto the previous position that the commander-in-chief 'controls' before and on deployment except in cases of low visibility,[21] but he stressed that after deployment – with ships at speed, and with smoke and gunfire – that 'the vice-admirals commanding squadrons have discretionary power to manoeuvre their squadrons independently while conforming generally with the movements of the Commander-in-Chief and complying with his known intentions'. In spirit this was also Beatty's position. Nevertheless, the dreadnought fleet would move 'as a whole' to avoid 'isolation of ships',[22] although independent action would be called for in case of destroyer or submarine attacks, mines, sudden, unsignalled moves by the commander-in-chief or moves by the enemy, such as closing with a portion of the British line.

- *Signalling*: 'Signalling may be indistinguishable or they may take too long to get through a large fleet. This does not mean that they will not be made, but the movement signal may be commenced before the executive is given. It is hoped that difficulties in signalling will be largely overcome by the use of wireless telegraphy.'[23]
- *Reconnaissance and signalling*: 'Ships having to make a report of sightings or of the movements of the enemy must pass the message to the admiral as well as to their own senior officers'.[24] Jellicoe went on to stress that positions should be reported based on the 'Commander-in-Chief's reference position'.
- *Opening range*: In these instructions Jellicoe was clear. 'I attach great importance to making full use of the fire of our heavier guns in the early stages at long range.'[25] This idea was much influenced by Jellicoe wishing to maintain as much range as he could from possible attack by torpedo, a weapon in whose use he felt the Germans probably had the upper hand. He was – wrongly, as it turned out – under the impression that the Germans had developed a new torpedo that did not leave a stream of telltale surface bubbles. With that in mind he did not wish to close 'much inside 14,000 yards'[26] and felt that opening ranges should be between 10,000–15,000yds (9,100–13,700m) in 'weather of good visibility'.* This was very similar to Beatty's preference for action between 12,000 and 14,000yds (11,000–15,300m).
- *Speed of fire*: Jellicoe's focus was that 'at all ranges, the early development of accurate rapid fire is the object'[27] or not firing 'too soon'.[28] This was very similar to Fisher's position: 'It is not numbers, it is solely "gunnery efficiency" that will win the fight … no excess of numbers, however inordinate, [will be] of any use whatever if the guns don't hit the target!'[29]

---

* Confusingly, however, Jellicoe later talks about 18,000yds as being the probable distance and in any case these rules applied 'unless the enemy does so earlier'. This is within the same GFBOs.

- *Use of destroyers*: Jellicoe firmly believed that the role of attacking enemy ships was secondary to their role of defending the Grand Fleet's capital ships. Beatty had always been in favour of the opposite: 'I am a firm believer in getting our TBD attack with the torpedo in first, which would place them admirably for frustrating a counter-attack of enemy craft. ... I believe that if the enemy torpedo craft attack first, ours would never get into a position in sufficient time to enable them to frustrate it.'[30]
- *An enemy turn-away*: Jellicoe held to his previous point of view that this manoeuvre's purpose would be for 'drawing our fleet over mines or submarines'.[31] Following a withdrawing enemy without a decisive speed advantage merely put the Grand Fleet at risk for an extended period.
- *Destroyer-launched torpedo attack*: Beatty's views on the destroyer were very different from Jellicoe's. Beatty was of the older May-Callaghan school, whose doctrinal ranks Jellicoe deserted in 1912. 'Admiral Sims relates that it was generally reported that Beatty had memorably ordered all torpedo flags, an emblem displayed to warn ships to change course if torpedoes were seen, to be destroyed.'[32]

Beatty's strong belief in a more proactive, aggressive role for the destroyer was incorporated into his own GFBOs:

> The best counter to the German torpedo tactics [torpedo attacks on the British battle line by destroyers and light cruisers] ... is for our destroyers to attack the enemy's battle fleet with torpedoes first, and therefore our flotillas are to commence their attacks as soon as the heavy ships are engaged. They should not attack earlier as they will be driven off by the gun fire of the enemy battleships and light cruisers, and the attack will be ineffective.[33]

Jellicoe's GFBOs have been used by some historians to attack their author and cited as an example of his over-attention to detail. By Jutland, Jellicoe's GFBOs consisted of around fifty-two foolscap pages of main text, with additional pages for very detailed deployments.

Months after Jutland, when Beatty had become commander-in-chief, he reduced the GFBOs again – some said theatrically. On 12 March 1917 he issued a two-page memorandum that he called the Grand Fleet Battle Instructions or GFBIs. While the eventual instructions were of similar length to Jellicoe's GFBOs, the main difference was not in length but in flavour. The orders and instructions reflect the very different characters of the two admirals.*

Did Jellicoe's GFBOs leave too little room for disagreement, or was his position that a concerted, unified action was always better than continued debate, discord and possible open disunity in the command structure? Maybe there is a bigger issue at stake here: Jellicoe's command style. Unlike Hipper (and Scheer), he did not like to have his orders questioned or even to discuss the evolution of his orders with subordinates. I would hazard a guess that Beatty was not so far from Jellicoe's mindset here. Jellicoe was, in fact, far from rigid. He was nervous of divergence, because it could fatally weaken the concerted power of the Grand Fleet *in action*. He actually constantly revised his tactics, based on experience and action, and this showed an intellectual flexibility not rigidity.

The problem, of course, with dissecting documents such as the GFBOs and the GFBIs is that behaviour in action is always different. On the day, things are always different – 'no plan survives contact with the enemy' as von Moltke expressed it – and many say that the best commanders think that their plans should be considered obsolete once the first shot is fired. In this respect, Jellicoe was different. He maintained the principles he had set out when he had the luxury of calm reflection.

> Throughout the war it had been our policy to cause our battle-cruisers, with their attendant light cruisers, to occupy when at sea an advanced position, often at a considerable distance from the Battle Fleet. Battle-cruisers were designed and built in order that they might keep in touch with the enemy and report his movements when he had been found; hence the heavy guns which they carried.[34]

On reconnaissance and reporting, I would hold that Beatty failed in this primary role for his Battle Cruiser Fleet. But where the responsibility for that lies is a different matter. I would say that this is just as much Jellicoe's fault, for not only failing to make this absolutely clear, but also for failing to practise these separate roles for the two fleets whenever they could. It is easier said than done, maybe, when waters are potentially mined or patrolled by enemy submarines

On the day, Jellicoe was woefully ill-informed by subordinates of battle conditions out of his direct line of sight. It remains extraordinary that what Scheer had been informed of by Hipper at 20:00 on 31 May (the losses of *Indefatigable*

---

* Comments like Sir Julian Thompson's that the GFBOs were 'voluminous' are rather misleading. It was not the length but the over-obsession with detail and the lack of a visible over-arching strategy that present any reader problems. Beatty's GFBIs are much more to the point, but of roughly equal length. Incidentally, the first GFBOs published by Jellicoe in August 1914 were also three pages (see the introduction in Brad Golding's work). Do depth and detail come with experience? (see Bachrach, *Jutland Letters*).

and *Queen Mary*), Jellicoe was only told the following day. There were many other examples of poor communications, such as the sightings of German capital ships that were never reported to Jellicoe, or even acted upon by the commander on the spot. Commanders such as Goodenough were exceptional, but they were just that: exceptions. And if that was not enough, at the top there were intelligence failures from Room 40.

So how did the GFBOs change after Jutland? Committees were set up to collect evidence on the experiences of both officers and men, the first one on 4 June. Dreyer headed possibly the most important, on gunnery and shell for the battleships. Chatfield headed up the equivalent committee for the battle-cruisers. There were also committees on battleship protection (Rear Admiral Arthur Leveson), cruiser protection (Captain John Dumaresq), and others 'on torpedo, wireless, anti-flame and gas, signals, searchlights, engineering'.[35]

'In the light of the lessons learned at the Battle of Jutland,' Jellicoe reissued the pre-Jutland GFBOs on 11 September 1916, and on 15 September the Admiralty brought out a revised signals book.[36] An important change was the introduction of a new signal: 'MP'. This was to be applied when weather conditions made it 'very difficult to control the movements of the whole battle fleet'. Flag officers were now permitted to 'manoeuvre their squadrons independently while acting in support of the squadron or division to which the fleet flagship is attached. It is in no way intended to imply that such a de-centralisation is not to take place unless the signal "MP" is made. If made it merely points out that decentralisation has become essential for the time being'.[37] Given Jellicoe's considerable baggage after the Tryon affair (when *Camperdown* had rammed *Victoria* off the coast of Tripoli in 1893 and Jellicoe, sick below decks, had nearly been drowned), Gordon calls this the admiral taking 'an uncertain step into doctrinal schizophrenia'.[38]

How did the GFBOs change under the new regime of David Beatty? His were issued as 'instructions', suggesting that they were more guides to action than orders that had to be obeyed. The GFBIs were about half the length of Jellicoe's GFBOs; more importantly, they were to the point and they were readable. All the minutiae of the GFBOs was relegated to a less familiar volume called the Grand Fleet Manoeuvring Orders (GFMOs) on which little is ever said, and which seems to have largely disappeared from the discussion on the GFBOs.[39] Beatty made it quite clear what the fleet's role was. He encouraged independent action and he encouraged communicating battlefield intelligence.

The instructions' first page clearly laid out quite a number of intentions: to gain a position between the enemy and its harbour; to concentrate fire on weaker elements at least to annihilate some elements of the enemy fleet; and to seek an engagement from the van at no less than 16,000yds, allowing the longer-range ships further down the line to be engaged at around the same time. Independence of action would be, just as Jellicoe believed, curtailed in the approach but then given from the deployment and after; that is a slight change.

Further differences were notable: 'The commander of a wing column under these conditions has full authority to act without waiting for orders. He should decide and turn as necessary … When action is joined the flag officers commanding battle squadrons have full discretionary power to manoeuvre their squadrons independently whilst conforming generally to the movements of the Commander-in-Chief.' This was not a question of only under certain circumstances, such as fog.

However, when it came to the actual conduct of the fleet throughout the rest of the war it was, it turned out, very similar to Jellicoe's. 'Aside from this important change in tactics, Beatty's overall North Sea strategy became almost more cautious than Jellicoe's.'[40] Not very long after Jellicoe had been dismissed, Beatty attended a conference at the Admiralty: 'On January 2nd 1918, when the general situation in the North Sea was discussed … Sir David Beatty informed the conference that it was, in his opinion, no longer desirable to provoke a fleet action even if the opportunity should occur.' This was surprising, given that Beatty's numerical advantages over his adversary had swung heavily in his favour.

Commenting on volumes IV and V of *Naval Operations*, Jellicoe said that in 1918 he:

should never have accepted this view had I been at the Admiralty, for the following reasons: (1) The greatly increased strength of the Grand Fleet since Jutland. In addition to the reinforcement of four battleships from the United States, two British battleships have been added, bringing the Grand Fleet strength up to thirty-four as against twenty-eight at the time of Jutland. Twenty-five light cruisers were available as against twenty-three, and at least one hundred destroyers as against a total of about seventy at the time of Jutland. As regards battle-cruisers, even if the *Mackensen* and *Hindenberg* were added to the High Seas Fleet, the disparity in force was not very serious, nor was it so important in a fleet action, no doubt adding somewhat to our scouting difficulties. (2) Even if Beatty detached a complete battle squadron (which he never did) to protect the convoy, there was no reason whatever why this squadron should not join the Grand Fleet if it went to sea. The squadron would obviously have plenty of fuel, and it could reach a point, say, in Lat. 56° 30' N, Long. 5° E. at least as soon as the Grand Fleet from Rosyth could do so, the distance in each case being about the same and the squadron on convoy duty having the advantage of having steam ready. The only disadvantage would be a slight shortage of fuel on the part of the escorting destroyers, but this shortage could not be very serious unless the battle squadron had been on escort work for two or three days. It is obvious if the High Seas Fleet was expected by the Admiralty to move, there was no danger to the convoy in withdrawing the protecting battle squadron and the C-in-C Grand Fleet would not be 'seeking action' unless the High Seas Fleet was on the move.[41]

Already, nine months before, in March 1917 Beatty had thirty-one dread-noughts (including the three new 15in *Resolution* class) against Scheer's twenty-one, while the battle-cruiser ratio was seven to four (after replacing the three that were lost by the British at Jutland with one).

Jellicoe could be criticised for many things but his GFBOs, while not in the least easy to read and clearly over-detailed, did try to tackle the most im-portant issues in a thoroughly professional and unemotional manner. They displayed a cold, pragmatic approach to assessing an opponent's strength and weaknesses, and a disregard for the role that luck would or might play in the frantic, disorganised turmoil of battle. Jellicoe's lack of Nelsonian charisma should not lessen the importance of what he did accomplish. Again, while there is a tendency to see black and white between the two commanders, for Beatty 'there was no question of overthrowing, with one stroke of the pen, the ideas of his predecessors'.[42]

Jutland was an extremely complex battle fought under very difficult condi-tions for both navies. Gibson and Harper's conclusion on the ebb and flow of the battle is as fair and balanced a judgement as any that I know of:

> The initial meeting between Hipper and Beatty had been a decided German victory – so had the brief engagement between *Lützow*, *Derfflinger* and *Invincible* and the night contact between the High Seas Fleet and the destroyer formation led by *Lydiard* ... There had been a number of equally decisive British victories – in particular the second, third and fourth meetings between Beatty and the German battle-cruisers; the 5th Battle Squadron's run to the north in the face of a much superior enemy concentration; the actual contacts between the main fleets; and the day and night torpedo attacks which sank *Pommern* and *Frauenlob*, torpedoed *Seydlitz* and *Rostock*, and caused the ramming of *Elbing* ... The crux of the battle had been the actual meetings between the fleets – very brief, but both finding Jellicoe ready with every bit of his power concentrated and brought to bear, while Scheer, numerically inferior to begin with, was employing his ships in such a manner that only a fraction of his gun-power could be directed at the enemy.[43]

Should not the conclusion of the battle over Jutland be a little more straight-forward than it has become after the hundred years or so of occasionally vitriolic debate? 'The issue at stake had been sea power – sea power which one of the contestants exercised and wished to keep, which the other lacked and wished to wrest – and command of the seas within and beyond the war area, and of the arteries of maritime traffic and commerce vital to the destinies of both nations – the maritime highways which meant national life or death to both peoples.'[44]

In the short term the battle might still be seen as a German tactical victory, though the British were ready for action again within four hours of reaching port. Hipper's leadership had been brilliant, Scheer's escape remarkable. In the medium term, however, the British maintained the blockade. The irony remains that Jutland persuaded Scheer to alter strategy to the very successful U-boat campaign against which only the convoy system would in time prevail. Jellicoe's success at Jutland, or at least his maintenance of the status quo during the battle, unfortunately sowed the seeds of his demise two years later.

Jellicoe's reforms before Beatty took over

Before Jellicoe handed command of his beloved Grand Fleet to Sir David Beatty on 29 November 1916, important changes began to be made in the way that the Navy did battle.

One important area was in gunnery efficiency. 'It is no exaggeration to say that the average time to find the gun range of the enemy with these new methods was about one half of that previously required.'[45] Dreyer explained: the time to get 'on target' was 'by "laddering up and down", when our shots were in line with the target for direction. We introduced the firing of rapid double salvos in the ladders. These were incorporated in new standardised spotting rules.'[46]

The range-finders at Jutland were mostly 9ft-long Barr and Stroud models with the 15ft version available in only 'the most modern ships'. In fact, when war was declared, 'the overwhelming majority of units composing the battle line' only had two 9ft units. During the next twelve months there was a concerted effort to install further (9ft) units. But the chosen tactics and equipment were at odds. For longer range gunnery only the 15ft Barr and Stroud was accurate enough for distances of up to 15,000yds. According to Sumida, only around forty-five of the 15ft versions had been delivered to the fleet by August 1916,[47] it generally being the 15in-gunned *Queen Elizabeth*s and the battle-cruisers that received them. By 1917 range-finder lengths were increasing to 25ft, and even 30ft.[48]

At the outbreak of war only one 12in-gunned dreadnought in the Grand Fleet had a Dreyer table. While the table was installed on more ships over the next two years, the Dreyer Mark I was found to be superior in combination with Arthur Pollen's Argo clock (the Mark II used a Vickers clock that was

found to be inferior). In May 1916 one-third of the battleships and half of
its battle-cruisers were using the inferior combination (for details of British
fire-control systems, go to Jutland1916.com). In August 1914 only eight British
dreadnoughts were equipped with directors.[49] Shore bombardment units were
receiving more than the fleet at sea, but by December 1915 twenty-four dreadnoughts were equipped with directors.

Dreyer complained that 'we have many people engaged in trying to make
out that our AP shell filled with Lyddite, which burst half-way through the
plate, are just as good as German shell filled with Trotyl with delay-action fuse,
which burst their shell way inside our ships. It seems a pity not to be willing to
learn.'[50] Jellicoe's request on 25 July 1916 for a copy of the German shell was not
taken on and it was only when he went to the Admiralty at the end of 1916 that
serious work resumed.

Certainly, Scheer had commented on the quality of British shell as a factor
in the battle:

> It was astonishing that the ships had remained navigable in the state they
> were in. This was chiefly attributable to the faulty exploding charge of the
> English heavy calibre shells, their explosive effect being out of all proportion
> to their size. A number of bits of shell picked up clearly showed that powder
> only had been used in the charge. Many shells of 34cm and 38cm calibres had
> burst into such large pieces that, even when picked up, they were easily fitted
> together again.[51]

In May 1917 new shell started to appear. Whereas the 1,920lb shell used
at Jutland would break up on a 6in armour plate at 20° to the normal at about
16,000 yards, the vastly improved 15in shell (known as 'green boys'), with a
thicker head and a thicker and harder cap, and much better bursters and fuses,
would carry their bursters through 10–12in plate under the above conditions
and burst 20–30 ft beyond. The shame of it was that they did not arrive in quantity in the fleet until April 1918.

Jellicoe's instructions on which shell to use are not easy to understand. He
regarded AP as near useless for ranges over 10,000yds, so it seems that he must
have felt that the real gunnery duel would take place at medium range. Yet there
is really room for a lot of confusion here, given what he says in his GFBOs about
not wanting to fight 'much inside 14,000 yards'. The German tactical orders,
which were made available to Jellicoe and others such as Dreyer and Madden,
stated that the German fleet desired range of engagement was 'from 8,800 to
6,600 yards'.[52] In April 1916, based on intelligence that he had received about
new German torpedo performance, Jellicoe ordered the longer-range settings
of 18,000yds at 19 to 20 knots.[53] The torpedo emerged from Jutland decidedly

pushed off its pedestal, only to regain its position in the submarine war years of 1917.

Jellicoe talked of the 'indifferent armour of our cruisers particularly as regards turret armour and deck plating'.[54] The experiences of 31 May also prompted Beatty to write to the Admiralty that 'either our methods of ship construction are seriously at fault or the nature of the ammunition we use is not sufficiently stable to ensure safety'.[55] Of the nine British ships sunk by German gunfire at Jutland, six had blown up; of the fourteen enemy vessels, none.[56] Maybe one of the most fundamental reforms, given the design defects of the battle-cruiser, was the introduction of strengthened anti-flash protection. It was a 'drastic change in the system at the stage when cordite was being passed out of the magazines'.[57] Magazine doors would now operate 'like revolving doors in a hotel entrance (except that they were horizontal), so that they were always sealed against a tongue of flame'.[58]

Tirpitz always maintained that ruggedness of construction and the ability to take punishment were *the* primary considerations of ship construction: 'The supreme quality of a ship is that she should remain afloat and continue to put up a good fight; in this respect the English navy was so much behind ours that the difference in quality alone might decide the issue of an engagement'.[59]

Deck armour was increased. The issue was discussed at an Admiralty conference on 25 June 1916. The Director of Naval Construction, Eustace Tennyson d'Eyncourt, supported by the 3SL (Admiral Tudor), disputed Jellicoe's and Beatty's points of view, but they were eventually overruled and a weight-saving committee was established to see where it could compensate for the added armour protection. HMS *Hood*, laid down on the same day as the battle, received an additional 5,000 tons of armour protection (though this still did not prove adequate for its survival). And finally, in 1917, Jellicoe was able to give the fleet the star-shell that he had so lacked for night fighting.

14

The Controversy: An Unfinished Battle

———

It may be deemed a refusal of battle … might possibly result in failure to bring the enemy to action as soon as is expected and hoped. Such a result would be absolutely repugnant to all the feelings of all British naval officers and men, but with new and untried methods of warfare new tactics must be devised to meet them. I feel that such tactics, if not understood, may bring odium upon me, but so long as I have the confidence of their Lordships, I intend to pursue, what is in my considered opinion, the proper course to defeat and annihilate the enemy's battle fleet.

Jellicoe to the Secretary of the Admiralty, *Iron Duke*, 20 October 1914

Most historians of the battle have felt that controversy was inevitable. In the Beatty papers, Bryan Ranft quoted William Scott Chalmers:

After the war, with the inevitable post-mortem, the controversy reached its height, because the bird's-eye view depicted on diagrams could not always be identified with the situation as seen by those in command when they made their decisions. Owing to low visibility, no two commanders got the same view of the action, and although 250 ships took part, there were never more than three or four enemy capital ships in sight at the same time from any point on the British line.[1]

Geoffrey Bennett, himself a naval officer before turning historian, mentioned that there was a strong, simmering distaste for Beatty among a lot of senior officers. Many of them had been passed over during Beatty's meteoric rise on Churchill's coat-tails. At forty-four he was commander-in-chief of the Royal Navy. But his flamboyance courted dislike. There was his self-permission to have two three-button rows on his uniform, the only man in the Navy to do so. There was also the occasion when he was seen on the deck of *Queen Elizabeth* talking to his King – whom he regarded as his friend, too – with his hands in his pockets. 'Soon the press, which had already built up Beatty's panache into a heroic image against which Jellicoe's quiet personality counted for little, was distorting Jutland into a victory for the Battle-Cruiser Fleet, and ascribing Scheer's escape to Jellicoe's failure to handle his Grand Fleet with comparable skill.'[2]

Another ex-Navy historian, Captain Stephen Roskill, wrote:

> Many perfectly genuine uncertainties existed regarding the movements of ships and what combatants saw. Or thought they saw. By modern standards the plotting of ships' movements were then archaic … and on 31 May 1916 weather conditions were such that few, if any, opportunities existed for navigating officers to establish observed positions from celestial bodies … Thus when it came to drawing maps of the various phases of the battle, historians have inevitably to rely on the deck and signal logs of ships and on the diaries kept on their bridges or at their plots.[3]

Roskill also said that officers would naturally try to intervene to give what they felt was a truer picture of the battle.

The debate was drawn out. Positions hardened and bitterness at the sense of not having achieved a recognised victory over the Germans made things turn into increasingly personal and partisan attacks, as the lines formed between politicians, officers and men of the Battle Cruiser and Grand Fleets, press and historians. Soon it was as if the Navy was as divided as it had been in the days of the Beresford–Fisher era. The controversial extension of life to the Jutland story started with the ill-fated Harper record, with the vitriol heating up with the Dewar brothers' *Naval Staff Appreciation* and its later, re-edited public version, the *Narrative of the Battle of Jutland* (see below). In between, the forays of the likes of Jellicoe's biographer Bacon, of Filson Young and even Churchill in *The World Crisis* added oxygen to the fire. Others, such as Sir Julian Corbett, and later Arthur Marder and Correlli Barnett, tended to quieten the debate.

Roskill, Bennett and now also the equally respected naval historian, Dr Andrew Gordon (*Rules of the Game*), all reopened the wounds of the Jutland debate.

Before the Harper Record

The official dispatches of the battle were released in 1919. Their initial appearance, in July 1916, bore, as Le Mesurier noted, 'signs of careful editing for public consumption.'[4] That would seem all too obvious. Yates rightly complains that they were very badly presented: 'a stupefying mass of undigested documents, dispatches and ships reports'.[5] Indeed, in his opinion, it was 'an exercise in official obfuscation'. They are difficult to read and to use. All of Jellicoe's comments and insights on superior German ship design, ordnance, communications and searchlights were taken out: they could have been useful to the Germans.

In 1919 Jellicoe published *The Grand Fleet*, described by Keith Yates as 'long-winded, dull and self-effacing',[6] an assessment with which I, sadly, rather agree. It is a shame that Cassell, Jellicoe's publisher, did not persuade him to take on a ghost-writer. The next year, 1920, saw one of the first accounts for the Beatty school, *The Battle of Jutland: The Sowing and the Reaping*, by Carlyon Bellairs. A chapter heading in the book – along with the one quoted earlier – said it all: 'I came, I saw, I turned away'.*

The Harper Record
The First Sea Lord, Rosslyn Wemyss, wanted an official report on the battle completed, to try to assemble the known facts. He was persuaded that he needed to do this when he learnt that Jellicoe had been preparing a history of the Grand Fleet through the war. He worried that this would be partisan and therefore start considerable debate. He was wrong about Jellicoe's approach, but he decided to set up his own marshalling of the facts.

On 23 January 1919 New Zealand-born Captain (as he then was) John Harper was appointed to 'prepare a record, with plans, showing in chronological order what actually occurred in the battle'.[7] Harper had four junior officers working with him as research assistants. He had no experience of command at sea – which would plague him later – but having been Director of Navigation at the Admiralty, he chose to start with the track charts to establish the known positions of the wrecks. He decided to locate that of *Invincible*, which he then verified with divers. The idea was to create a base of documentary information for the Admiralty without any added commentary or interpretation.

The report was presented to Wemyss and had reached proof stage, but sat on his desk while he was on holiday. His deputy chief of staff, Admiral Brock, who had commanded the 1st Battle Cruiser Squadron at Jutland, read the piece and announced that he was delaying a decision: 'As Lord Beatty is assuming office as First Sea Lord in a few days it must wait for his approval'.[8] This was the first intimation of Beatty's battle-cruiser influence in the Admiralty. There were wider changes. It was as if – in Temple Patterson's quoting of a comment made at the time – 'the battle-cruiser people took over the Admiralty'.[9]

It was immediately clear that Harper had actually exceeded his brief and, in one critical account of the battle-cruiser action, had added commentary that was purely personal interpretation. He talked of what he supposed were some of the things that could have caused higher British damage, such as indifferent

---

* Commander Carlyon Wilfroy Bellairs (1871–1955) was a very strong critic of Jellicoe. He had both a naval and parliamentary career. After leaving the Navy in 1902 he entered politics and served as the MP for King's Lynn from 1906 to 1910 after having done a short stint as a lecturer for naval officers.

armour protection, or – a particular nettle to Beatty's sensitivities – the very high standard of the German battle-cruisers' gunnery. At the same time, even if he overextended himself, he tried where possible to strike the balance and, in talking about the battleship duel, said that the British had 'something of an advantage in the way of light'.[10]

Beatty claimed that the wording in Harper's report 'implies that the Commander-in-Chief was badly served and that many errors were being made which prevented him from receiving [information] such as he could have reasonably expected'.[11] Beatty also commented on the section of the record referring to 'Reports on the progress of the Action', saying that they 'might as well be omitted as they come in the category of criticisms which serve no useful purpose'.[12]

Harper told Beatty that he refused to make any changes; he would only make them if he received written orders to do so from the 1SL. Beatty wanted to add his own reports, and those of Scheer and Jellicoe, as well as all the signals from the battle. The Admiralty position, however, was that too much detail would give a sense of defeat, not overwhelming victory.†

Brock commented that it lacked 'the note and tone of victory, and [read] rather as a record of disasters and misfortunes'.[13] Chatfield felt the same. But they could not have it both ways: a neutral report of the 'chronological order of what actually occurred in the battle' *and* one that would strike a 'tone of victory'. There was evidently a belief within the Admiralty that it was preferable not to explain the greater losses of the British fleet, even though the battle was felt to have been a strategic victory. Jellicoe's astonishment at this is expressed in a letter written to Beatty in response to his criticisms: 'the publication should take place without any alteration by the Board, myself or by any other person'.[14]

Harper was understandably becoming testy – he was increasingly caught in the middle of powerful forces. He demanded that he be able to put a comment of his own in the introduction, saying that this was only a record that did not wholly accord with the facts.[15] Jellicoe became aware of the duel between Beatty and Harper; he broke his own rule and asked to see the report for himself.

Sir Walter Long, First Lord of the Admiralty, met Harper, asking him what was holding up the report's publication. Harper told him about his issues with Beatty. Long was in strong disagreement with Beatty's interference – direct or indirect – and told the latter his position. Shortly thereafter, Beatty withdrew his

---

† The First Lord, Walter Long was extremely perturbed about where the affair was heading. In his diary for 15 March 1920 he made the following entry: '(Harper) tells me the Jutland Report is held up because Beatty wants alterations made. I'm sorry. I wish Beatty would leave it alone. He has made Harper alter some things which did "injustice" to the battle-cruisers' shooting, also a part of the track which H has put in from the evidence. But Beatty says he doesn't care about all the evidence in the world ... as it can't alter "facts" ... A pity this, as it will open the way to controversy afterwards' (Temple Patterson, *Jellicoe*, p232, footnotes).

objections and publication was scheduled for 14 May1919, even though there were still differences from the original, and alterations.

When Jellicoe saw the original and the amended reports, he was incensed. He wrote to Walter Long with his complaint and threatened not to take up his new position as governor general of New Zealand unless his comments were taken on board. The impression given by Beatty's interference with the report was that the Grand Fleet arrived so late that it had no impact on the battle.

The situation was very difficult. Irreconcilable positions were being taken by Jellicoe and Beatty. Harper, trapped in the middle, offered to resign. This was refused. He then said that he would like to add a statement to the report, saying that he was not responsible for materials that were not aligned with the documentary evidence that he knew was shortly to be published as the *Jutland Dispatches*. This was also refused. However, with the latter's publication in December 1920, questions started to be raised in Parliament as to why the Harper Record had not yet seen the light of day. Harper himself had come to the conclusion that Beatty was now merely trying to delay publication.

Finally, Walter Long, who had not been aware of Beatty's efforts to change Harper's conclusions, found a way out by saying that Julian Corbett's official history would soon appear and that there was no longer need for a separate report. Harper was asked to hand over all his documents to Corbett.

The outcome was ironic. Beatty had at one point asked Corbett to write an introduction to the report that would talk about gunnery at Jutland and in particular about the poor quality of ordnance. This could throw the focus off the poor quality of gunnery at the start of the run to the south.[16] Corbett refused, saying that he was already commissioned to write the official history.

Harper finally placed copies of his report in safekeeping with the Royal United Services Institution, fearing its suppression and destruction.[17] One copy is today in the British Library. One remained in the possession of Jellicoe's family. Included inside is the famous sketch of the disputed 360-degree turn by *Lion* that Beatty had so vehemently denied. Even though the words, 'Published by HMSO, 1920', appear on the front, the full report was never actually published and has never, as the author would have intended, seen the light of day outside its life in the British Library archives.[18]

By the mid 1920s Harper was thoroughly disgruntled at the treatment that his report had received and decided to produce his own account, *The Truth about Jutland*, published with considerable commercial success in 1927. His attack here on Beatty was full of vitriol. Though Harper could no longer be said to be writing without bias, some of his points were valid: 'It is an indisputable fact that, in the first phase of this battle, a British squadron, greatly superior in numbers and gun-power, not only failed to defeat a weaker enemy who made no effort to avoid action, but, in the space of 50 minutes, suffered what can only be described as a partial defeat'.[19] It is no surprise that a rebuttal was published under the title, *The Truth about Harper*. I have never seen a copy.

While Harper was made a rear admiral in 1924, his position was highly vulnerable and Beatty certainly did not want him around. In 1926 Harper was advised that he would take command of a dockyard, but this was withdrawn a year later at the request of Chatfield in February 1927, when he was retired from the service, though he had by then been promoted to vice admiral. Even after he had left because of ill-health, his report came back to haunt Beatty: between 1919 and 1927 the delayed publication of the Harper Record 'was raised on at least twenty-two occasions in Parliament'.[20]

The threat of dividing the service: the *Naval Staff Appreciation*

Beatty took things into his own hands and ordered the compiling of yet another report on the battle. The Director of Training and Staff Duties, Captain Ellerton, asked Captain Alfred Dewar in November 1920 to start work on a staff appreciation of the battle using some of Harper's own findings, one that would clearly be a battle-cruiser point of view.

In November 1920 Alfred and his brother, Captain Kenneth Dewar,* set to work. Kenneth Dewar had crossed paths with Jellicoe before, when he had worked at the operations and then at the plans divisions of the Admiralty. Temple Patterson maintained that the 'conservatively minded' Jellicoe took exception to Kenneth Dewar, 'the iconoclast with a chip on his shoulder'.[21] Jellicoe regarded the older brother, Alfred, as 'a retired Lieutenant of but little sea experience' and Kenneth 'a recently promoted Captain [who] had never as yet commanded a ship at sea'.[22] There seemed no love lost. 'Jellicoe', Dewar wrote, 'instinctively mistrusted mental independence in his subordinates'.[23] After two years they published what was to be the most contentious criticism of Jellicoe in the *Naval Staff Appreciation* (officially titled 'CB0938' – that is, a confidential Admiralty book not intended for general distribution).

On 27 September 1920 Jellicoe, accompanied by his wife, four daughters and his young son George, stepped onto New Zealand soil to take up the post of governor general. At the same time, he received a copy of the completed *Appreciation* from Walter Long. At the very moment when he should have been

---

* Kenneth Gilbert Balmain Dewar, later Admiral, CBE, RN (1879–1964]. He had served in the Operations Division of the Naval Staff under Jellicoe and then the Weymss Boards of the Admiralty. He had been a brilliant cadet and student. Later, in 1912 he wrote an essay entitled 'What is the war value of oversea commerce? How did it affect our naval policy in the past and how does it in the present day?' in which he quite correctly predicted the distant blockade. The relevant chapter was censored by the Admiralty. Jellicoe's opinion of both Dewar brothers was not that complimentary; quoted in Roskill, *The Last Naval Hero*, p332, from the Evan-Thomas Papers.

fully focused on his new colonial role, Jellicoe instead commenced a lengthy correspondence pointing out inaccuracies and misleading conclusions.

Jellicoe eventually summarised his concerns to the Admiralty in a letter in November 1922, saying that if he could not have his own thoughts incorporated into the *Appreciation*, he would at least like his comments published alongside. He waited quite a while before being replied to with a series of amendments to the original text. He was not satisfied and requested the Admiralty hold up publication while he sent back his comments. The Admiralty refused and published a redacted version of the report, now being called the *Admiralty Narrative of the Battle of Jutland*, in 1924.

The conclusions and the writing of the original *Staff Appreciation* were widely criticised. Julian Corbett, who was on first-name terms with Jellicoe, wrote that the 'facts were ... very loose'; he read it (he said) 'with increasing wonder till at last I felt it my duty to convey to the Admiralty that such a grotesque account of the battle certainly ought not to go out as their considered verdict'. In a letter to Jellicoe he lambasted the *Staff Appreciation*, saying that 'To call it a "Staff Account" is nothing but a bad joke'.[24] Ernle Chatfield and Roger Keyes – Keyes was later known as the father of combined operations – wrote to Beatty saying that they felt publication would not be in the interests of the Navy, and that going ahead would only cause a public airing of the most vindictive quarrel.

When the *Narrative* was used in 1922 during a number of lectures to twenty officers on the senior officers' war course at the Royal Naval College Greenwich (one of which Harper attended), Kenneth Dewar was 'severely' heckled.[25] Even Captain Ellerton's successor, Rear Admiral W H Haggard, was very critical of the Dewars' work: 'The mental attitude of the writer [*sic*] was rather that of the counsel for the prosecution than of an impartial appraiser of the facts ... an obvious bias animates his statements throughout ... leading to satirical observations and a certain amount of misrepresentation'.[26]

The Dewars even maintained that the staff of *Iron Duke* had forged or manipulated the signals logs. Jellicoe had produced an ink copy for review when the policy at the time was to write signals text in pencil.[27] In fact, as was also normal at the time, a second, personal, copy had been made for him in ink. The report also pointed the finger at Evan-Thomas's responsibility for the signals muddle and Jellicoe's reaction was predictable: to defend staunchly the actions of his old friend (with whom he used to punt in his junior-officer days; the families were close). The report had not been shown to Evan-Thomas beforehand to get his reactions or at least his own version of events. Evan-Thomas did manage to see the then First Lord of the Admiralty, Leo Amery, in July 1923, but to no avail.

Evan-Thomas tried a second time to get a fair hearing at the Admiralty, but was cut off by Beatty before he could get started. Later the same day, Evan-Thomas suffered a stroke. He retired the following March, too ill even to attend a meeting with the King, who had been saddened by the way he had been treated. When he did finally see the King in May 1925, the latter felt that he could not publicly support his old friend: the controversy had – in the King's view – to end.

Such was the early furore around the report that by August 1922 even Beatty was questioning whether the *Naval Staff Appreciation* should be distributed as had been intended. He put the question to Roger Keyes and Ernle Chatfield. Their reaction was recorded in the 22 August minutes of their meeting:

> While not approving the tone in which the book is written … nor [agreeing] in all respects with the criticisms of the tactics of the Commander-in-Chief, e.g. the criticism of the single line, we are in entire agreement with the main conclusions … both as regards the failure of Lord Jellicoe to seize the great opportunity before him on the afternoon of 31 May, and his failure to make any dispositions or give any instructions that would bring the enemy to action at dawn on 1 June.
>
> It is not considered, however, that any sufficient cause exists at the moment to justify the issue to the Fleet of a book that would rend the Service to its foundation …[28]

It was the Dewars' criticism of the single line and the embodying doctrine of centralised command, and not the criticism of his former commander-in-chief, that persuaded Beatty to call back copies. Having reached proof stage, work was stopped by Beatty and later, in 1928, Admiral Charles Madden – married, like Jellicoe, to a daughter of Sir Charles Cayzer – ordered all copies of the report destroyed. Copies do exist, but are hard to come by.[29] Roskill received one from Jellicoe's secretary and Churchill referred to it in *The World Crisis*.* Beatty's copy also survived and is signed by him.[30]

Ranft also said that Beatty had ordered the destruction of all the Harper charts. One copy, rolled up on a dusty shelf and thought to have been spare wallpaper, was recently found at my father's house in the UK.[31] It was another copy of the set of Harper maps which are in the British Library in the Jellicoe Papers. The British Library sets are marked up in pencil with the original track of *Lion* before Beatty altered it. The Jellicoe set is a completely clean copy.† Beatty was not persuaded to stop the work of revision, however, that Rear Admiral Haggard undertook on the *Naval Staff Appreciation*. That version

---

* Roskill's copy is amongst his papers held at the Churchill Archives at the University of Cambridge and shown to the author by the very helpful staff.

† Dr Innes McCartney, underwater archaeologist, helped sort out this mystery. I had hoped that the maps might have proved to have been as significant a find as the circumstances of their finding were.

appeared later in what Marder termed a 'de-venomised' form, as the aforementioned *Narrative of the Battle of Jutland*.

The official history: Corbett's *Naval Operations*

It was known that Sir Julian Corbett, who had been given the task of writing the official history of the Navy in the Great War, was on friendly terms with Wemyss. His especially close friendship with Jellicoe, from whom he had received ample commentary and advice, rendered him untrustworthy in Beatty's mind.[32] Officially the history was sponsored by the Committee on Imperial Defence, but Wemyss had actually asked Corbett to write it, as he feared that Jellicoe's own book would be too biased; it was not especially so.

Beatty was eventually able to harness this mistrust into a decision by the Board of the Admiralty to issue a disclaimer on the third volume of Corbett's *Official History of the Great War Naval Operations* – the volume that dealt with Jutland and which was published in 1923 – stating that 'The Lords Commissioners of the Admiralty have given the author access to official documents in the preparation of this work, but they are in no way responsible for its production or for the accuracy of its statements'. In the earlier 1923 edition there was an additional paragraph that was subsequently taken out of the revised 1940 edition. It was a pretty damning statement: 'Their Lordships find that some of the principles advocated in the book, especially the tendency to minimise the importance of seeking battle and of forcing it to a conclusion, are directly in conflict with their views'.

Because he was also a civilian, Corbett was attacked by Navy professionals on the basis of not having had the experience at sea to give credibility to his commentary. Chatfield simply called his account of Jutland 'an outrage'.[33] Dewar wrote equally disparagingly. Talking of his own work and Corbett's:

> The real and essential difference between the two is that the *Narrative*
> confines itself to a statement of events whereas Corbett's, while adopting
> its sequence and material, has woven into it a long sustained apologia for
> British tactics. He illuminated the battle in a historical glow of soft sunlight,
> providing a good narrative, based on the *Staff Appreciation*, set in a frame of
> general congratulation.[34]

That Corbett's history of the battle should have been attacked by the Beatty faction for being too supportive of Jellicoe was quite expected, but it was strange that even so eminent a historian as Corbett was also hampered in what he was allowed to use as documentation. He was not, for example, permitted to quote any of the deciphered German signal traffic that had been passed on so late in the battle to Jellicoe, an act that made it look as if the Admiralty was protecting its own. As Roskill himself commented in a letter to *The Times*: '[Corbett] was prevented from placing a share, and perhaps the chief share, of the responsibility for the escape of the High Seas Fleet where it properly belonged' – presumably with Admiralty operations.[35]

Only by 1940, eighteen years after Corbett's death, had the revised *Naval Operations* volumes been completed, by Henry Newbolt: twenty-four years after the battle the series of errors in not passing on important Admiralty intelligence from Room 40 was actually noted.* And on this, of course, there was, too, an Admiralty disclaimer!

The Admiralty's *Narrative of the Battle of Jutland*

The draft of the Dewars' modified *Narrative*, as edited by Haggard, was sent to Jellicoe – still in New Zealand. Again Jellicoe, who lacked appropriate staff, set to work, personally going through the material in great detail. He replied to the Admiralty on 27 November.

Again, he asked that the Admiralty either agree with some of his requests for changes or at the very least publish his own comments along with the *Narrative*. For a full ten months – almost twice the time that Jellicoe himself had actually worked on the revisions – the Admiralty did not bother to reply. When it did, only a very few of his comments were accepted, but he was still asked to cable his acceptance of the latest version of the book. The approach was coercive.

Quite reasonably, Bacon made the following comment on the *Narrative*: 'To the technical reader, versed in naval operations and terms, as well as in the sentiment of the Navy, a nasty flavour pervades the whole narrative.'[36] Bacon presented some examples. First, 'Hardly had the columns turned south than the sound of heavy firing indicated the close proximity of the enemy's heavy ships and the *Lion* signalled (6.6) that the enemy's battle-cruisers bore south-east ... About 6.14 pm and almost simultaneously, a signal came in from the *Lion* reporting that [enemy battleships] had been "sighted bearing south-south-west"'.[37] This gave the impression of a fast relay of information from Beatty to Jellicoe. The facts on the day were very different from Jellicoe's 'Where is the enemy?' signal, abysmally absent from the description. Bacon could scarcely contain himself: 'That is all. Nothing more. The whole episode is glossed over and the important facts are never mentioned.'[38] In Bacon's words, these reports 'did no more than deepen the obscurity'.[39]

He continued with a second example: 'A few minutes later the guns of the *Calliope* and the 4th Light Cruiser Squadron could be heard to the westward.

---

* Churchill, apparently, also took exception to Corbett. He worked against him in delaying the publication by insisting that other official documents should be published with the history.

Touch had evidently been regained, and at 6.21 pm the Commander-in-Chief altered course to west-south-west *2 points away from the enemy*' (Bacon's italics).[40] In fact, the sound of the guns was to Jellicoe's west; hence his turn was actually *towards* the enemy and not away.

Bacon then talked of the night action: 'Admiral Beatty was still in ignorance of the enemy's course to the south-eastward, and imagined him to be the westward. The battle-cruisers had been too far ahead to observe the route of the High Seas Fleet *as indicated by destroyer actions*.'[41] Bacon highlighted in italics the last phrase as the destroyer actions, per se, did nothing more than indicate action. Since such an interpretation was not clear to the two admirals, Evan-Thomas and Burney, four miles nearer the fighting, he found it strange that Jellicoe should have arrived at another conclusion different from the admirals closest to the action.[42]

Jellicoe cabled back his disagreement on the major points, saying that he would send his full comments by mail and requested that the Admiralty hold back publication until they had been reviewed. Instead, in 1924, the Admiralty went ahead with the publication, using only Jellicoe's cabled highlighted comments. These were relegated to Appendix G while the Admiralty's comments – which Jellicoe had not even seen – dismissed his assessment at the outset. Much had been lifted from the earlier *Appreciation* and Jellicoe felt it like a slap in the face. He was also furious about the treatment meted out to Evan-Thomas. Blame for the heavy losses incurred in the run to the south was being squarely laid at his door.

The Jutland Scandal

In many ways, Admiral Reginald Bacon's 1925 *The Jutland Scandal* exemplified the 'Jellicoe school' in defending what the admiral had done at the battle. The book appeared early in the New Year, but it was actually written to rebuff an article that Filson Young had written the previous year, and that appeared on 10 August 1924 in the *Sunday Express*. It was Alexander Filson Young who had been 'embedded' on *Lion* by Beatty and had written the glowing account of Beatty in *With the Battle-cruisers* in 1921. Filson Young had also written the *Encyclopedia Britannica* entries on Jutland and Beatty the following year.

Reinhard Scheer had been quoted in another, earlier, article on the battle. Scheer claimed that he had been badly quoted:

The account in the 'Daily Express', published without my foreknowledge, is a gross misrepresentation of a conversation that I had with an English correspondent in 1922. In the report the English correspondent does not completely express the explanations given by me, but in a not very gentlemanly manner he has not hesitated to deceive the English reader by the misleading title 'How I escaped at Jutland' and by a false date.[43]

The article made out that Scheer claimed that Jellicoe had lost the perfect opportunity to annihilate the High Seas Fleet. At the time, Jellicoe reacted angrily to the article which claimed that the Grand Fleet had been first to 'turn away'.

Jellicoe did not support the deep divisions that these partisan attacks were creating within the service. Bacon's book was, in the opinion of one author, 'vitriolic'. Temple Patterson called it 'belligerently partisan'.[44] I can understand his frustration. Bacon's text, like Filson Young's, often became too sarcastic for such a serious subject. Beatty wrote in fury: 'that bloody Bacon book annoys me, and has added to my despondency, and the difficulties I am having with the government are not so easily overcome, and I think they don't pay so much attention to my advice as in the past'.[45]

Kenneth Dewar had let Beatty know that he had written about it in the *Naval Review* and had also mentioned the *Staff Appreciation*. Beatty told him to take out any reference to CB0938 as, of course, it was a restricted publication. It was not surprising: so much bad blood now existed between the factions.

Bacon's points, however, are that Beatty failed in his primary mission, the reconnaissance role, and in his secondary role of meeting and defeating an enemy battle-cruiser challenge.[46] Bacon asserts that Beatty neither managed nor concentrated his fleet but, rather, dispersed his strength, and then tried to put the blame on Evan-Thomas and not on the signals officer, Ralph Seymour. Bacon was relentlessly critical of the notion of Beatty's giving the High Seas Fleet to Jellicoe on a platter; as we know, he had lost visual contact.

But in the end Bacon's assessment of Jutland was not unrealistic: 'No one wishes to pretend that Jutland was a glorious victory. It was not. No glorious victory was possible under the daylight conditions that prevailed on 31 May.'[47] Bacon was, nevertheless, taken to court and found guilty of having infringed the 1911 copyright law as he had quoted so extensively from Filson Young's articles, allowing the latter to claim that he was diminishing his (Filson Young's) future revenues from this work.

Churchill's *The World Crisis*

In 1927 Churchill weighed in on Beatty's side with his two-chapter account of the battle in *The World Crisis*. It was no surprise that he would favour Beatty; the latter had worked closely with Churchill and through Churchill's patronage had, again as we know, risen meteorically.* Churchill liked the proximity of a national icon such as Beatty. It put him in a good light. As Margot Asquith, wife of Herbert Asquith, quipped: 'Winston wrote a book about himself, and called it *The World Crisis*.'[48]

Jellicoe, he wrote – to reiterate a well-known quotation we have encountered more than once – was the only man 'who could lose the war in an afternoon'.[49] The words, here, are worth a moment's pause. Churchill did not say that he was the man who could win the war, but implied that his action could lead to a British defeat. If the Grand Fleet had been defeated, Britain's trade lifeline would have been instantly severed and the nation's economy crippled.

This was why, on the day, Jellicoe had to favour caution above all else. He saw the bigger picture and that the blockade of Germany had to be preserved. He was also aware of the status quo: that an out-and-out victory would not necessarily bring much more to the table. Some have argued that just such a decisive British victory at Jutland would have considerably shortened the war. This is conjecture. Yet most of Churchill's attack on Jellicoe highlighted what he cited as his excessive caution and rigidity, and, Churchill added, obsessive fear of the mine and torpedo.

Churchill's account is gravely inaccurate in places, especially about Scheer's evening battle turn: 'At 6.35 pm he ... turned his whole fleet about ... launching a flotilla to cover his retirement by torpedo attack ... Jellicoe, threatened by the torpedo stream, turned away according to his long-resolved policy.'[50] Jellicoe did not, in fact, turn away at this point: he closed with his adversary. The famous Jellicoe turn-away took place almost an hour later.

Churchill's book soon provoked responses, one example being *Winston Churchill: The World Crisis. A Criticism*.[51] Churchill's book had acknowledged the huge burden on Jellicoe, but at the same time – with the full benefit of historical hindsight and the accumulated knowledge of the post-battle debate – roundly criticised his decision to deploy the fleet to port and the subsequent battleship engagements.

Churchill was also highly critical of Evan-Thomas and blamed him for the failure to turn south, despite the 14:32 signal not having been seen. He placed no blame on Beatty for not having used the time before the 'turn south-south-east' signal to pull back the 5th Battle Squadron into the general battle-cruiser line. For Jellicoe, Churchill's blaming of Evan-Thomas was inexcusable. 'That they [the 5th Battle Squadron] were not 5,000 yards closer was due entirely to

* Kenneth Dewar also worked as a naval adviser to Churchill, so Dewar's work re-emerged in *The World Crisis* (see below for more on this). Many of the charts that Churchill used were found in the *Staff Appreciation*; Churchill's idea of a deployment on the centre was directly influenced by Dewar's thinking, even if the latter thought the manoeuvre was far too complicated.

their slowness in grasping the situation was made with the first contact with the enemy.'[52] Bacon's assertion is that Beatty did not use the twelve minutes, between 14:20 and 14:32, from sighting the enemy fleet to close up his two fleets: the battle-cruisers and Evan-Thomas's *Queen Elizabeth*s.

Churchill's account elicited silent criticism from Jellicoe; privately, as was his style. On the fly jacket of a family copy of *The Criticism* is a pencilled, handwritten note by Jellicoe: 'No one should read Churchill's book *The World Crisis* without reading also this volume which shows so clearly how grossly inaccurate are Churchill's writings'.

An eminently more readable account of the battle was Langhorne Gibson's and Vice Admiral Harper's *The Riddle of Jutland*, published over a decade after Churchill's. Then, nearly seventy years later, Robert Massie's *Castles of Steel*, along with Nigel Steel's and Peter Hart's *Jutland 1916: Death in the Grey Wastes*, became classics. Both are lucid and involving, and full of gripping personal accounts.

Der Krieg zur See: the 'official' German point of view

The German official history, *Der Krieg zur See 1914–1918*, was written to legitimise the role of the Imperial Navy in the war: 'Every volume should make the German people conscious of what deeds were performed on all seas by its navy and the men who created and led it and what it (the German people) has lost through the loss of its sea power'.[53] It was a very political document indeed, and Tirpitz consulted closely with Captain Eberhard von Mantey, the head of the Marinearchiv, on each volume in the series. Edited by Otto Groos (who served at Jutland as a navigating officer), 'the purpose of the series was to foster the rebirth of the navy and to propagate a narrative to that end'. Both Ingenohl and Müller objected to the pro-Tirpitz stance. Neither's opinion was taken account of, and Eric Raeder, later to become head of Hitler's navy, wrote the foreword to the series.

What is interesting about the German official histories, in comparison to the British, was that the writers were all serving or former officers.

Newbolt's *A Naval History of the War*

As a successor to Julian Corbett, Sir Henry Newbolt was an odd choice. He was known as a poet and writer, but not as a naval historian. When Corbett died in September 1922, Newbolt took over the work and immediately was able to bring attention to the lack of signals intelligence passed to Jellicoe during the battle. This was not possible in Corbett's earlier history. It pointed the finger perhaps too directly at the Admiralty.

Volume II of the Jellicoe Papers

In 1966, on the fiftieth anniversary of the battle, it seemed as if we had suddenly returned to the acrimony of the 1920s. The second volume of Jellicoe's papers, which included a full account of the Harper story, was released. A copy went to *The Times*. On Saturday, 14 December a review of the work by Basil Gringell appeared under the unnecessarily provocative headline, 'Beatty shown as falsifier of the Jutland record'.[54] Beatty was portrayed in the worst light: as a commander who consciously doctored documents that would enter into the historical record of the battle. The 2nd Earl Beatty replied to the piece in a letter to the newspaper. Even the young Nicholas Beatty ('aged seven and a half at the time') wrote a letter of objection.[55]

The papers were speedily followed by American naval professor Arthur Marder's five-volume opus, *From the Dreadnought to Scapa Flow*, whose third volume is often regarded as the seminal work on Jutland. He was greatly helped by Stephen Roskill, who not only agreed not to bring out a rival work at the same time, but to hand Marder much of his research, including one file of the decipher transcripts for the days and nights of the Jutland action that he had been given by Edward Clarke of Room 40, as well as a rare copy of the *Appreciation* that he had received from Jellicoe's secretary. (The subsequent fall-out between the two historians was described in Barry Gough's *Historical Dreadnoughts: Arthur Marder, Stephen Roskill and Battles for Naval History*, which appeared in 2010.)

Marder ended up criticising Beatty and, to a lesser extent Jellicoe, in different ways, but was also full of approval when he saw fit. He was critical of the failure to concentrate the 5th Battle Squadron into the initial battle-cruiser line, but strongly praised Beatty's performance when he led the German battle-cruisers, closely followed by the High Seas Fleet, to Jellicoe in the run to the north. Yet for the most part, Marder was outraged at how Jellicoe had been treated post-war: He was 'most unfairly blamed for not doing miracles at Jutland. He was as brave and enterprising as the best of them, and did the best that was possible.'[56]

The pendulum soon tipped the other way. In Pan Books' popular Grand Strategy Series, Geoffrey Bennett published *Naval Battles of the First World War* that gave the British credit for Beatty's tactical victory in the run to the north by bringing Hipper and Scheer unsuspectingly into Jellicoe's hands; but then he fully criticised Jellicoe when, after the deployment, 'he twice failed to follow his opponent when he recoiled, the second time being after the German C-in-C's ill judged return to the east'.[57]

Bennett was at least sympathetic to Jellicoe's difficulties. He gave my father a copy of his book, *Jutland*, inscribed with a very clear message of support[58] and quoted Jellicoe's frustration at the amount of armchair theorising done after the battle by the likes of Churchill: 'None of my critics appear to have realised the extent to which the absence of information regarding the High Seas Fleet, and the lack of visibility, affected my handling of our fleet'.[59] 'If it had only been about 6pm instead of nearly dark,' Jellicoe later said, 'and clear instead of thick, we should have had a second Trafalgar'.[60] At the end, however, Bennett got caught up with the idea that Jellicoe's caution, combined with exhaustion, made him unsuitable as a war leader. He needed to be replaced, but was not so convinced that the replacement should be Beatty: 'If Jellicoe lacked fire in his belly, Beatty had it to excess: if the High Seas Fleet had come out he might have been as reckless in handling the whole Grand Fleet as he was with the Battle Cruiser Fleet during the initial stages of Jutland'.[61]

Richard Hough's *The Great War at Sea: 1914–1918* tried to be less partisan than Bennett's account. Hough's central focus was what he saw as the inflexibility of the Grand Fleet Battle Orders; he compared Jellicoe's 'orders' with Beatty's Grand Fleet Battle Instructions, written in 1917. The mere use of the word 'instructions' in place of 'orders' encapsulates much of the difference between his and Jellicoe's style of fleet command. It suggested that individual commanders in action had more flexibility and independence of decision-making. In particular, independent, proactive initiative was encouraged from destroyer commanders. 'By definition rules restrict, and they restrict initiative as much as they define conduct and lead to centralisation and leader dependence ... The GFBOs reveal in almost every line the subordination of offensive spirit to the defensive spirit'.[62]

As Jellicoe himself explained, the policy of centralisation was necessary. Unlike Nelson at Trafalgar, he doubted the abilities of individual commanders and ships raised in the tradition of the Victorian Navy to function effectively. In the battle conditions on the day, when even close-quarter combat was often carried out with serious questions as to whether indeed the target being engaged was an enemy, the risk of ensuing chaos was just too high.

Only one admiral took exception to the deployment to port (and, by inference, the single line of battle). That was Sturdee, who also openly tried to change Jellicoe's opinions about following a retreating enemy. It seems that Jellicoe was misinformed on German destroyers potentially laying minefields in front of any chase: 'German destroyers did not in fact carry mines at Jutland'.[63] Hough got closer to the truth when he said that there was 'a tragic irony in the fact that Jellicoe commanded a fleet built on the calculated policy of risk: more and bigger guns to destroy the enemy at the cost of protection from enemy gunfire'.[64]

There was substance in this; but the real truth lay in the disjuncture between Jacky Fisher's vision and the time that was needed to change a hundred years of a culture that came increasingly to reinforce the complete opposite. Gunnery technology was still not up to par (with the exception of the director system), and training was underrated and under-utilised (especially in the Battle Cruiser Fleet – also to Beatty's concern). The much newer German navy did not have to overcome the stultifying effects of this nineteenth-century legacy. Its superior efficiency and co-ordination in night-fighting equipment (star-shells and iris-shutter lenses), as well as the co-ordination between searchlight and secondary armament gun crews, was a notable example of the high level of training in the High Seas Fleet.

Andrew Gordon's *The Rules of the Game: Jutland and British Naval Command* was published in 1996. This fascinating and extremely readable book reignited the decades-old debate. To Keith Yates, the fact that a review of the book in the *Sunday Times* could so naively repeat hook, line and sinker the untruths of the *Appreciation* was astonishing: 'Admiral Jellicoe's Grand Fleet was barely engaged, was not struck by a single shell and suffered only two dead and five wounded from shrapnel. Most of the fighting ... was between the subordinate Battle Cruiser Fleet and elements of the High Seas Fleet.'[65]

In *Flawed Victory: Jutland, 1916* (2000), Keith Yates gets straight to the point: 'It is nothing less than amazing that this canard is still being perpetuated 80 years after the battle. The facts remain that Jellicoe's battleships fired more heavy shells at the enemy in their two brief engagements than Beatty's battle-cruisers did all day, and moreover scored nearly as many as three times as many direct hits on the ships of the High Seas Fleet. Scheer's fleet may have only had to face the full might of Jellicoe's Grand Fleet for less than an hour altogether, but that was quite long enough for Scheer to decide never to risk it again.'[66]

In 2005 John Brooks finally added a very detailed technical discussion in *Dreadnought Gunnery at the Battle of Jutland: The Question of Fire Control*. With the level of technical expertise that Brooks brings as an engineer to the subject, it was and will remain a seminal work.

Meanwhile, using the letters of Commander Le Mesurier as her source, Harriet Bachrach wrote on the battle in 2006, in *Jutland Letters: June–October 1916*, and picked up one of the self-criticisms that Jellicoe himself made in 1932. This was his decision not to send Le Mesurier's 4th Light Cruiser Squadron ahead to scout the forward German fleet elements before the deployment to port decision.

There have been numerous German accounts of the battle, but very few have made it into English (which is not true the other way around). The official German war account, *Der Krieg zur See 1914–1918* by Kapitän Otto Groos, was not written until after the war and only translated into English in 1926; it was never *published* in English (although it was translated both by the ONI, the American Office of Naval Intelligence, as well as by the RN). It was a far more balanced affair, critical of Beatty's performance, but nevertheless not conceding any overall victory to Jellicoe or the British. Hough commented that this work was 'stately and irreplaceable'; Scheer's *Germany's High Seas Fleet in the World War* was 'egocentric, idiosyncratic, unreliable and execrably translated but should be read'.[67]

Hase's account of the battle from his perspective as the chief gunnery officer of *Derfflinger* long continued to serve as an anchor for the German version of events. Beatty's fire control and fire allocation were much criticised. The effectiveness of the firing from Evan-Thomas's ships was singled out by Hase as causing them considerable alarm – but this was only one man's point of view.

The battle was, of course, an excellent propaganda platform for Germany. The simple arithmetic of the battle supported the easy claim that Britain's centuries-long dominance of the seas had been broken by the German navy. Jutland may have been the start of the decline of the British Navy, but not for Scheer's stated reasons: it was not because he had defeated the Royal Navy in a great sea fight, but because he had failed to do so. More to the point, Scheer correctly concluded that a decisive change in strategy was needed. The balance of material losses (111,000 tons against Germany's 62,000) and casualties (6,784 officers and men killed and wounded on the British side against German losses of 3,058) was always the mainstay of the German case. However, in his report to the Kaiser on 4 July 1916, Scheer came close to what he really thought: 'There can be no doubt that even the most successful outcome of a fleet action in this war will not force England to make peace'. The real effort, he added, should be aimed at 'the defeat of British economic life – that is, by using the U-boats against British trade'.[68]

Jellicoe's and Beatty's mistakes

In 1932 John Jellicoe, with the benefit of sixteen years of hindsight, wrote about what he felt had gone wrong on the day. He had also tried to update and re-release a new version of his 1919 *The Grand Fleet*, but his publisher, Cassell, was not interested. To my knowledge Beatty never wrote a self-critique, neither did Scheer nor Hipper.

Jellicoe was not above apportioning some of the blame to himself, though he was clear that Beatty had failed on many fronts and had gone on to blame others. In the main, he identified his own failure not as the one for which he has been most criticised, the turn-away. It was in not using his scouting capabilities fully, or making it clear that battlefield intelligence was of the utmost importance. He felt that he should have sent Le Mesurier's force ahead (as per

Bachrach above), as Beatty had so successfully used Goodenough's 2nd Light Cruiser Squadron in the opening battle-cruiser actions. He also felt that he had made a mistake in placing his scouting forces on the disengaged side of the line of battle after he had successfully crossed Scheer's 'T', twice. On both occasions this disposition had left him less reaction time and could have been used immediately before or during the turn-away.

The night actions proved to be one lost opportunity after another. Jellicoe had no 'night-fighting intentions'. A synopsis to his captains of what his intentions were and the need for instantaneous communication of information and the permission to break WT silence would have had important consequences. Even if he did not want to fight a night action, it was critical, if he were to resume action at dawn, that he prevent the Germans breaking through his blocking line. To do that he needed to know where they would probe. None of the destroyer captains, bar one, made it a priority to get that information back to *Iron Duke*.

Like Scheer and Beatty, he made some mistakes in the disposition of his forces and particularly in the inclusion of slower, more vulnerable ships such as *Defence*, *Warrior* and *Black Prince* with the battle fleet. They should not have been there. Similarly, the torpedoed *Marlborough* only slowed the line – she should have been sent back immediately after she had been hit, though I imagine Jellicoe did not like the idea of losing the destroyers that she would have required as escorts.

Something that Jellicoe himself never commented on (as far as I am aware) was the question of why he submitted to Beatty's signal that he could bag the entire German fleet. He was not even sure that Beatty had contact. The day had already shown that this was not one of Beatty's strong points. Yet Beatty's biggest shortcoming was his character. Fierce independence of thinking led to too many battlefield decisions that reduced the overall effectiveness of a *combined* Grand Fleet and Battle Cruiser Fleet working in tandem.

Beatty's failure to pass on vital intelligence has been well documented. It led to the fleets fighting almost as two independent entities, rather than as one. The failure to send any scouting intelligence back to his commander-in-chief was especially the case before the deployment and during the critical hours up to darkness. No contact information was transmitted at 20:20. Beatty's not communicating the loss of *Indefatigable* and *Queen Mary* still leaves many questions. Had he done so, he would not have been giving the Germans anything that they did not know. Surely he should have let Jellicoe know earlier?

There also seems to have been the issue of how Beatty communicated with his captains – how he communicated his intentions on the battlefield. For Evan-Thomas, communication was non-existent. Others might have been, but

Evan-Thomas was certainly not treated as one of a 'band of brothers'. After Beatty had fought so hard to get the 5th BS within his command, he ignored its rear admiral. For the others it was built only around the concept of 'conforming on the flagship', *Lion*, but Evan-Thomas was not sure about what his role was supposed to be at that point.

Beatty's most fundamental errors were, then, based on allowing his aggressive character to take precedence over more considered decision. Not consolidating his forces before taking on Hipper in the first battle-cruiser engagement was the example of what Jellicoe had feared. Beatty's main difference from Jellicoe lay in his aversion to centralisation and in his placing 'a higher premium of initiative and individual action'. Often, this boldness translated into ill-prepared action. The Germans knew his character and that they could probably rely on this weakness. Jellicoe was happy to take risks that were carefully calculated. By contrast, he saw in Beatty character flaws that he feared could be exploited. In a letter to him after Dogger Bank, Jellicoe warned him of what would, as it turned out, happen at Jutland:

> I imagine that the Germans will try to entrap you by risking their battle-cruisers as a decoy. They know that the odds are that you will be 100 miles away from me, and can draw you down to the Heligoland Bight without my being in effective support. This is all right if you keep your speed, but if some of your ships have their speed badly reduced in a fight with their battle-cruisers, or by submarines, their loss seems inevitable if you are drawn into the High Seas Fleet with me too far off to extricate them before dark. The Germans know you very well and will try to take advantage of that quality of not letting go when you have once got hold, which you possess, thank God. But one must concern oneself with the result to the country of a serious decrease in relative strength. If the game looks worth the candle the risks can be taken. If not, one's duty is to be cautious. I believe you will see what is the proper course and pursue it victoriously.[69]

Having the 5th Battle Squadron in the line, covering the longer range from the rear, would have given him near-impregnability. It is quite possible that Beatty would not have survived the episode without very courageous support from Evan-Thomas's 5th Battle Squadron.

The failure to engage with the range advantage, even if the gunnery conditions were not what he had hoped for on the day, is debatable. Certainly it seemed that Chatfield wanted to fire much earlier. Later, in his Battle Cruiser Fleet Instructions, Beatty specifically talked about using the range advantage of the *Queen Elizabeth*s. Maybe this was one of the things that Beatty himself learnt from the day.

Appalling signalling practices at Jutland have been much discussed. Beatty himself said that Seymour had cost him 'three battles', despite which he kept him on as his signals officer.[70] Why, at least, was he not better supported if his capabilities were not trusted? Ironically, Beatty was very clear that not being able to choose good people was one of Jellicoe's problems. A year after Jutland, he wrote that Jellicoe was 'absolutely incapable of selecting good men because he dislike[d] men of character who ha[d] independent views of their own'.[71] This was not accurate. Jellicoe was eminently capable of working with men of 'independent views', although Dewar said this about him as well.

The two men, great and courageous admirals, died within months of each other and now lie almost side by side, in St Paul's Cathedral. Jellicoe had been loved by the men around him, especially the ranks. He had been seen as kind, fair, strikingly intelligent, but modest; Beatty had been admired for his style, good looks and charisma.

On 14 May 1916, two weeks before Jutland, Beatty was interviewed by a journalist, Cecil Roberts, in Rosyth:

> There we now met the legendary figure, Vice-Admiral Sir David Beatty. He was to be the last spectacular figure in British naval history. Never again would the service touch such a height of power and glory. He was a lion of a man with his handsome, strong-jawed face, bulldog air and his habit of wearing his peaked admiral's cap at a rakish angle. He was the perfect image of the public's idea of a daring sea-dog in the Drake tradition. His postcard photo was in every newsagent's window.

When Roberts visited Jellicoe a few weeks later in Scapa Flow, the picture that he painted was a little different. Here was a small man. A rather weather-beaten, kind – but not strong – face with sparkling warm eyes. Jellicoe had the style of another generation but with an air of quiet confidence.

> Jellicoe was tight-lipped in what might have been a drawing room except for a large chart on the wall by the fireplace. Could this be a battleship? It was so peaceful and homelike. There were easy chairs and a divan covered in flowered chintz. French windows opened onto a stern walk bright with potted geraniums. I was astonished to see in one corner a baby grand piano with open keyboard and sheet music on its rack. A silver photograph of Lady Jellicoe stood on its flat top. Near a divan chair was a revolving bookcase. A large carpet, curtained windows and a log fire burning in the open grate, completed the domestic scene ... Admiral Jellicoe himself, apart from the heavy gold lace on his sleeves and his ribbon decorations, contributed to the illusion (of the indestructibility of

such great ships). Sturdy, medium in height [he was five-and-a-half feet tall], with a smiling round face and twinkling eyes, in other garb he might have been a country vicar like his brother. He had nothing of Beatty's leonine appearance. He had the reputation of being a quick worker who never showed any temper.[72]

The two men's matrimonial lives were very different. Beatty's marriage to Ethel was tough. For weeks at a time, Beatty would share his home ashore, Aberdour House, with his mistress Eugénie Godfrey-Faussett. Jellicoe's family was a happy and close-knit one. Their personal styles were also quite distinct. Jellicoe was low-key; it was easy to see why he was so loved below deck. I cannot imagine the wives getting along for one minute.

Joe Cockburn, a young torpedoman on *Iron Duke*, who used to make ships' models for Jellicoe, gave a very endearing description of how he remembered his commanding officer: 'at sea Sir John, a figure in a duffle coat and sometimes wearing a white cap cover, would come through the mess decks with an "excuse me", and that would be Sir John making his way to the bridge. When Beatty came on board, it was "CLEAR LOWER DECKS" and a file of marines wearing short arms with Beatty in the middle. We never liked him.'[73]

For many, however, this is what made David Beatty the kind of leader of men he was. Goodenough, who worshipped both admirals, said it well: 'It was not his great brains ... it was his spirit, combined with comprehension of really big issues ... The spirit of resolute, at times it would almost seem careless advance'. He then pinned it down: 'I don't mean without taking care; I mean without care of consequence'.[74]

Jellicoe, on the other hand, was a cerebral leader who played the fleet as if it were a chessboard, calculating moves and probabilities. 'It is difficult to believe that Jellicoe was wrong to centralise his battle fleet and its tactics', Correlli Barnett summarised, 'The truth was that the Grand Fleet was only capable of rigid textbook manoeuvres; and Jellicoe was cool-headed enough to realise it.'[75] He was not one, as much as some historians might have liked him to have been, keen to leave *anything* to chance.[76]

The admirals' deaths and their memorials

John Jellicoe died on 20 November 1935. The flags of the navies of three nations – Britain, France and Germany – flew at half-mast, honouring a man who, twenty years previously, had commanded the British Navy in what is still acknowledged as one of the greatest – and most controversial – fleet actions of all time. His death was honoured by friend and foe alike as the news was flashed around the empire.

George, my father – then only eighteen – had temporarily left the family house at No. 9 Egerton Gardens in Chelsea for a short walk down the King's Road. He had thought that his father was recovering. When he got to Sloane Square tube station he was struck by an awful premonition and rushed back. It was too late. Once home, the butler told him his father had just died.

Jellicoe's body lay in state in Westminster Abbey, in the Henry VII chapel. On the morning of 25 November 1935, a grey, foggy Monday, the coffin was taken to Horse Guards Parade, from where a procession started down Northumberland Avenue, along the Embankment, up New Bridge Street and Ludgate Hill, to arrive at St Paul's fifty minutes later. Seven Admirals of the Fleet, among them one French and one German, Vice Admiral Förster, and one field marshal and one marshal of the Royal Air Force accompanied the gun carriage. From his Jutland comrades-in-arms were Goodenough, Chatfield and Beatty.

Behind the coffin was my father. I have watched the Pathé News footage of him as he walked silently, looking bewildered and lost behind the cortège, mounting the steps to St Paul's, flicking his falling hair to one side. He was just sitting his exams at Winchester. Behind him were the admiral's three sons-in-law, Major Latham, Lieutenant Wingfield and Lionel Balfour. The Prince of Wales and the Duke of York followed the family, and were in turn followed by 158 admirals (*The Times* reported that another 130 admirals were in the abbey itself). The prominent display of a swastika flag placed near Jellicoe's coffin, sent by Admiral Erich Raeder, Scheer's chief of staff at Jutland, bore a strange witness to the camaraderie of those who fought against each other in the North Sea, but alongside each other in northern China. Jellicoe had planned to visit the new, young German navy and it had been their intention that he should have been invited to the opening of the Laboe Memorial on 31 May 1936, *Skagerrakstag*. Whenever I've been there I've wondered whether he would actually have gone. Despite the old friendships, he would not have wanted to have his name associated with the new German politics. Admiral Förster, who had been *Seydlitz*'s gunnery commander at Jutland, represented the German navy. The ex-crown prince's son, Prince Frederick, 'Fritzi', represented his great uncle, the former Kaiser, who sent a large wreath.

Beatty served as one of the pallbearers. 'What would the Navy say?' he was heard to ask. I feel that it was a last act of the warm friendship that the two had sometimes shared before Jutland. It was sad that the battle had so twisted a fair bond: 'Self-appointed champions poured forth a stream of calumny and uninformed criticism upon one or other of the two admirals. This was deplorable and gave a false impression of the relationship that actually existed between the two men'.[77] Beatty's tribute to his old comrade-in-arms was warm and heartfelt:

Jellicoe, he said, 'had epitomised the highest ideals for which the British Navy stands. The country owes (him) a great debt of gratitude for the valiant work he did during the war ... He was an upright man and a model of integrity in everything he undertook.'[78]

Even Lloyd George had warm words: 'Although we had our differences during the war as to the best method of dealing with the submarine attack on our shipping, our personal relations were always of the very best. I never doubted that the view he took was prompted by the very highest sense of duty.'[79]

Captain Henry Taprell Dorling's eulogy was very human. He was the writer who wrote about the Jutland night actions under the pseudonym of 'Taffrail.'

The nation and the Empire regret the passing of a very great public servant. But the Navy mourns more than that – the death of a great seaman and leader who was a loved and respected friend and whose life and character are a pattern of integrity, industry, courage and devotion to duty to those who come after him. His heart was a heart of gold.[80]

In his article was a wonderful image of the admiral. On Flotta, where the fleet had built an eighteen-hole golf course, John Jellicoe was the only man allowed to play through, but rather than walk the holes, he ran between every stroke!

Strangely, Beatty predicted his own death, which was only months away: 'So Jellicoe is gone,' he announced. 'I feel I will be the next to be summoned. I don't think the call will be long. I'm tired. Very tired.'[81]

In the spring of 1936, just before midnight on 10 March, Earl Beatty died. He had been getting worse since the previous November, yet against doctor's orders he had insisted in January on attending the funeral of George V, his friend and king. Onlookers said that he looked grey by then and one, a journalist, thought he looked so ill he offered him some brandy.[82] Raeder did not want to send a deputation to Beatty's funeral. There was still so much acrimony after the way in which the High Seas Fleet had been treated during the post-Armistice internment. Only the German naval attaché in London represented Germany.

In the month of Beatty's death, Ernle Chatfield became embroiled in a squabble with the Office of Public Works when it suggested that there was no more room in central London for statues: those of Beatty and Jellicoe should be placed in Greenwich, rather than in the centre of the British capital. Chatfield wrote to the office saying that 'Trafalgar Square should become a naval memorial' – because, except for those of Nelson, John Franklin and Captain Scott, there were no other statues of naval heroes *in* the middle of London.* To my knowledge, there is not even a bust or statue of Jacky Fisher.[83]

It was a shame that in Sir Edwin Lutyens's final proposal of lining the square with the great names of Francis Drake, George Rodney and St Vincent, among others, never came to pass. Ten years later, in 1948, the two British Jutland admirals were finally honoured on Trafalgar Day (21 October), when their busts were unveiled by the Duke of Gloucester. They are there today on the northeastern side of Trafalgar Square.

In the Pathé News archive there is also footage of my thirty-year-old father, dressed in the uniform of the Coldstream Guards, briefly meeting Churchill, my grandmother looking on from the side. I do not think, from the expression on her face, that there was any love lost between them, given what Churchill had written about her husband. Whenever I can, I walk through the square towards the National Portrait Gallery to share a few quiet moments with my grandfather.

Over the next few years the undercurrent of the controversy continued to swirl. When two new *King George V*-class battleships were to have been named *Jellicoe* and *Beatty*, Churchill vetoed the names in February 1940, and they were launched instead as *Anson* and *Howe*. The closest that the navy got to honouring the admirals by name was to launch a destroyer, *Jutland*, in 1943. A small memento of her is now in my library: a copy of Bacon's book dedicated to the ship by my paternal grandmother, Gwen Jellicoe.

Fittingly, in 2014 Sir Arthur Stockdale Cope's huge (17ft-wide) 1921 portrait of twenty-two of the great naval officers of the war had pride of place at the top of the stairs leading into the galleries of the National Portrait Gallery in London. Sadly, I have never come across a photo of David Beatty and John Jellicoe, fellow officers and commanders of the same Grand Fleet, together. Yet in this portrait the body language speaks loudly. Charles Madden, looking at Jellicoe, has his back to Beatty. Jellicoe, pushed off to the right of the canvas, is in thought – one of seven officers sitting. Beatty is centre stage. Some of the officers could not be there. They had been killed in action: at Jutland, Hood and

---

* 'Later, the problem of memorials to Lord Jellicoe and to Lord Beatty arose for discussion; I felt strongly that they should have statues erected in London. The Office of Works, however, to my astonishment suggested that there was no room in London for more statues and asked if they could not be placed at Greenwich ... Almost would it appear that we had had but a short naval history. Great soldiers' monuments, fortunately, were everywhere ... I claimed for the Navy that Trafalgar Square should become a naval memorial' (Chatfield, p131).

Arbuthnot; at the Battle of Coronel, Cradock. Notably absent from the group was Jacky Fisher.

Both Jutland's admirals were soon after the Great War honoured nationally by the country that they served with valour. Beatty was elevated to the peerage and became Earl Beatty, Viscount Borodale of Wexford and Baron of the North Sea. On his return from New Zealand Jellicoe was also offered and accepted an earldom. In tribute to the men with whom he had spent so many lonely wintery months in Scapa Flow, he became the 1st Earl Jellicoe of Scapa.

'Where are you going, my Johnny-o?'
'I'm joining a ship in Scapa Flow,
That's where I'm going, my Nancy,
I'm joining the *Black Prince*, Nancy-o,
Joining the *Black Prince*, Nancy-o,
She's bristling with guns and ready to go,
To sail to glory with Jellicoe!'
But where is the *Black Prince*? Gone now!
And where is the glory? Gone now!
And six thousand sailors? Gone now!
They have gone to the bottom at Jutland.

Ob sturm uns bedroht hoch vom Norden,
Ob Heimweh im Herzen auch glüht;
Wir sind Kameraden geworden,
Und wenn es zur Hölle auch geht.
Matrosen die wissen zu sterben,
Wie immer das Schicksal auch spielt,
Und geht uns're Trommel in Scherben,
Dann singt uns der Nordwind ein Lied:

Auf einem Seemansgrab,
Da blühen keine Rosen,
Auf eine Seemansgrab,
Da blüht kein Blühelein,
Der einz'ge Gruß, das sind die weißen Möwen
Und eine Träne die ein kleines Mädel weint.†

---

† 'The U-Boat Sailor's Song': Whether high storms threaten us from the north / Whether homesickness glows in the heart / We have become comrades / And when it also comes to hell / Sailors know how to die / As always fate also plays / And goes our drum in pieces / Then the north wind sings us a song / REFRAIN: On a seaman's grave / No roses bloom / On a seaman's grave / No flowers bloom / The single greeting is the white seagulls / And a tear which a small maiden cries.

Notes

Introduction

1 Bennett, p236, quoting Captain Herbert (later Admiral Sir Herbert) Richmond.
2 Dr Andrew Gordon, BBC Scotland, *Scotland's War at Sea*, 2015.
3 Jameson, *The Most Formidable Thing*, p207.

1 The Emergence of German Economic and Naval Power

1 Steinberg, *Tirpitz*, p131, quoting Marder.
2 MacMillan, p67.
3 Kelly, *Tirpitz*, p103.
4 Ibid, p2.
5 Kaiser Wilhelm II, *My Early Life*, p229.
6 MacMillan, p72.
7 Herwig, p23.
8 Epkenhans, *Tirpitz*, p19.
9 Ibid, p21.
10 Rear Admiral Alfred Tirpitz was appointed on 18 June 1897 as Secretary of State to the Navy Office, the RMA.

2 The Fleet Builders: Fisher and Tirpitz

1 Jameson, p90.
2 Wragg, p39.
3 Ibid, p42.
4 Mackay, quoted in Wragg, p44, and Hough, p38.
5 Hough, *First Sea Lord*, p43.
6 Wragg, p52.
7 The six were Wilhelm Büchsel, Oscar Klausa, Iwan Oldekop, Otto von Diederichs, Richard Geißler and Oscar Boeters.
8 Kelly, p25.
9 Kelly, p33.
10 Kelly, p42.
11 Steinberg, p69.
12 Kelly, p48.
13 Jameson, p97.
14 Jameson, p98.
15 Kelly, p52.
16 Hough, *First Lord*, p66.
17 Kelly, p76.
18 Alfred Tirpitz: 'Reasons for the Retention of an Oberkommando with a Powerful Competence', 'Our Further Maritime and Military Development' and 'Manuscripts about the Organisation of our Armoured Fleet'.
19 The German Admiralty was divided into two main branches, one executive, the Oberkommando der Marine (OK), the other administrative, the Reichsmarineamt (RMA). When Wilhelm ascended the throne, he immediately took steps to dismantle the unified power of the navy so that he could direct policy.

The operational command of the navy had till then been unified under the chief of the Admiralty, who was answerable to the emperor and liaised with the Reichstag while at the same time being its military head. Wilhelm now split the organisation into three parts – the Oberkommando (OK), the Reichsmarineamt (RMA) and the Marinekabinett (MK). His overriding objective was to bolster his power of decision-making – *Kommandogewalt* – in the development of his navy.

20 Woodward, p19.
21 Kelly, pp92–3.
22 As Fisher had asked the Director of Naval Construction, William White, in 1892 (Wragg, p95).
23 Tirpitz, *My Memoirs*, pp118–19.
24 Ibid, p126.
25 Ibid, p126.
26 The new news section was officially called Section for News and General Parliamentary Affairs (M II) under the leadership of Korvettenkapitän August von Heeringen.
27 Kelly, p11.
28 Steinberg, p145.
29 Kelly, p134.
30 German personnel who had served in the torpedo arm of the Imperial Navy in the formative years came to be known as the 'torpedo gang'. There were many prominent names on the list: Tirpitz, Scheer, Hipper, Ingenohl, Heeringen, Müller, Pohl and Bachmann.
31 Within the conservatives were various factions of the agrarian parties and the Catholic centre parties, the latter formed in 1870 to counter the Prussian state's attacks on the Catholic Church.
32 Kelly, p171.
33 Ibid, p277.
34 Wragg, p99.
35 Hough, p115.
36 Wragg, p100.
37 Jamieson, p106.
38 Massie, *Dreadnought*, p438, quoting Lord Hankey.
39 Kelly, p179.
40 Hawkins, p2.
41 Kelly, p166.
42 Ibid, p166.
43 Ibid, p167.
44 Ibid, p168.
45 Massie, *Dreadnought*, p184, quoting Lord Selborne.
46 Ibid.
47 Wragg, p177.

48   MacMillan, p. 360
49   Hough, *First Lord*, p238, and Morris, p146.
50   Morris, p146.
51   Ibid, p152.
52   Ibid, p148.
53   Herwig, p39.
54   Kelly, p261.
55   Ibid, p257.
56   Furthermore, Arthur Marder maintained that there was not 'a scrap of evidence' indicating that Fisher had pushed the dreadnought project because it would mean that Germany would have to widen the Kiel Canal.
57   I am indebted to Peter Schenk for signposting a discussion on the *Nassau* class in *Warship International* by Dirk Nottelmann. The German building of wider beam ships was to provide added protection against torpedo attack and, as a secondary consideration, a more stable gun platform. The hexagonal distribution of the turrets, according to Dieter Thomaier of the Groener group, was also chosen because of the battle doctrine which included a possible melee during the battle requiring firepower to both sides.
58   Kelly, p280.
59   The cry came about because of a mounting fear in the Admiralty that Germany was accelerating her shipbuilding programme. According to a memo from the Sea Lords to Sir Reginald McKenna, the First Sea Lord, 'we concur with the statement of the First Lord that there is a possibility that Germany, by the spring of 1912, will have completed 21 dreadnoughts (including large cruisers) and that there is a practical certainty that she will have 17 by that date; whereas, presuming we lay down six in the coming year, we shall only have 18 … We therefore consider it of the utmost importance that power should be taken to lay down two more armoured ships in 1909–1910, making it eight in all.' (Memorandum, Sea Lords to McKenna, BL, Add MSS 48990).
60   Massie, *Dreadnought*, p618, quoting Churchill.
61   Wragg, p197; Asquith to Fisher, 26 October 1909.
62   The second Moroccan Crisis, known as the Agadir Crisis (or, to the Germans, the *Panthersprung*), had its roots in Wilhelm's continued efforts to split France and Great Britain, although it was set off initially by the French deploying troops to the interior in April 1911 to quash a local rebellion against the new sultan, Abdelhafid. It was a perfect opportunity, Wilhelm thought, to show that Germany must protect its citizens and trade interests. The French action in sending troops was against the terms of the 1906 Treaty of Algeciras, and German Chancellor Bethmann-Hollweg and Foreign Secretary Alfred von Kiderlen-Wächter decided to state an objection to the French move. The Kaiser agreed. Tirpitz, however, was not informed and would probably have been opposed to such 'sabre-rattling'. A gunboat, *Panther*, was diverted to Agadir. She arrived on 1 July 1911, supported a few days later by the cruiser SMS *Berlin*. It turned out that there was a sole German civilian, an employee of the Warburg Bank (who, at the time, was nowhere near Agadir but seventy miles away), to be picked up. France reacted sternly and sent troops to Fez, despite the British foreign secretary, Sir Edward Grey, trying to restrain them. Fisher feared that the Germans would build a naval base or, at the very least, a coaling station opposite Gibraltar. The Germans were stopped by a run on their banks: the market lost 30 per cent of its value in a single day (see Liaquat Ahamed, *Lords of Finance*, p43). They demanded compensation from France in the form of a territorial exchange and France's promise to allow equal commercial access to the Germans to Morocco. Eventually, Germany backed down when the British started sending signals of their intention to back the French. With the signing of the Treaty of Fez in November 1911, Germany accepted territories from France that became part of Neukamerun. Four months later, the French extended a full protectorate over Morocco. Far from splitting the British and the French, once again Germany's clumsy threats had only succeeded in solidifying the Entente Cordiale.

3   A Contradiction, Not a Team: Jellicoe and Beatty

1   Yates, p232.
2   Other biographers included Stephen Roskill and Admiral Chalmers.
3   Less reverently, Jellicoe's flagship was later known as the 'Iron Duck' or 'Tin Duck', after the 1922 Washington Treaty prompted her conversion to a fleet training ship, with her 13.5in guns and armour belt removed.
4   Herwig, p48.
5   Roskill, p21. There is some confusion here, as Beatty's nephew Charles Beatty, and biographer, talks about him 'passing in' '10th out of 32'.
6   Lambert, p338.
7   Roskill, p21.
8   *Monarch* was 'as successful combination of sails and turrets as could be obtained but most of her 12-inch muzzle-loading rifles would have been a significant professional challenge to Jellicoe.' (private correspondence with Prof Eric Grove).
9   Lambert, p338.
10   Temple Patterson, *Jellicoe*, p23.
11   In seamanship, gunnery and pilotage Beatty took a second and in navigation a third.
12   Hough, *Admirals in Collision*, pp98–9.
13   *Kind Hearts and Coronets* (1949).
14   Beatty, p23.
15   Sir Michael Culme-Seymour, the commander

of *Ramillies*, was, as Jellicoe wrote in his autobiographical notes, 'a great sportsman, a keen game shot, a good fisherman, fond of boat sailing and a good rackets player. He and I spent many hours playing rackets in Malta while the fleet lay in the Grand Harbour, and one year, playing as partners, we won the Fleet Rackets Cup.'

16 Massie, p85.
17 Lambert, p339.
18 This was a smaller type of battleship specially built for overseas stations in general and to navigate Chinese rivers in particular (private correspondence: E Grove).
19 Roskill, p28.
20 Ibid, p110.
21 Massie, p94.
22 Lambert, p343.
23 Fisher to Lord Selbourne, First Lord of the Admiralty. See letters dated 25 and 29 October, quoted in Marder (*Fear God and Dread Nought*, pp45–7).
24 Roberts, p28.
25 Proceedings of the Ordnance Board, 28 October 1910. 'DNO 18.10.10 states that the trials recommended by the board are approved. He asks them to consider the possibility of increasing the chance that AP shell carry their burster through armour plates when striking obliquely by increasing the thickness of the walls of the shells, or by carrying out trials with shell of various shaped cavities, i.e. ribbed, which might be stronger than the cylindrical cavities, observing that the introduction of Lyddite seems to render this question more feasible than formerly'.
26 Massie, p61.
27 Temple Patterson, *Jellicoe*, p38.
28 Lambert, p345.
29 Temple Patterson, *Jellicoe*, p49.
30 Temple Patterson, *Jellicoe*, p46, quoting Marder, *Fear God and Dread Nought*.
31 For an interesting account of the first tests on *Thunderer*, see John Winton's *Jellicoe*, pp127–8.
32 Massie, p63.
33 BL, MSS 49038.249 Jellicoe Autobiographical Notes.
34 Lambert, p337.
35 Hough, *Mountbatten*. p. 36.

4 Men From the Same Mould: Scheer and Hipper
1 Tolbin, thesis, p23.
2 Waldeyer-Hartz, p27. The Admiralty orders for *Leipzig* are produced in full to show the almost pedantic level of detail that Admiral Stosch had included.
3 Waldeyer-Hartz, p56.
4 Tolbin, p11.
5 Ibid.
6 Waldeyer-Hartz, p60.

7 Sweetman, essay by Gary Weir, 'Rheinhard Scheer: Intuition under Fire', p391.
8 Waldeyer-Hartz, p80.
9 Tolbin, p18.
10 Waldeyer-Hartz, pp85–6.
11 Tolbin, p25.
12 Ibid, p27, quoting Erich Raeder.
13 Massie, p339, quoting von Ingenohl.
14 Massie, p339.
15 Massie, p339, quoting Rear Admiral James Goldrick, RANR.
16 Massie, p359.
17 Sweetman, essay by Gary Weir, p394.
18 Tolbin, p124.
19 Gibson and Harper, pp79–80.
20 Massie, p555, quoting von Trotha.
21 Sweetman, essay by Gary Weir, p394.
22 Ibid.
23 Ibid, p400.
24 Hough, p295.

5 The Naval Non-War
1 Sweetman, essay by Gary Weir, p394.
2 Churchill, *The World Crisis*, quoted in Marder, *FDTSF*, p358.
3 For a quick summary see Hawkins, pp14–15.
4 Hawkins, p15.
5 Osborne, p61; see also Hawkins, p25.
6 Spain and the Netherlands also signed, although they had not had a sitting participant.
7 Hawkins, p85.
8 Ibid, p86.
9 Ibid, p87.
10 Ibid, p89.
11 Grebler, Leo, *The Cost of the World War to Germany and Austria-Hungary*, Yale University Press (1940), p78.
12 Hawkins, p38, quoting Bennett.
13 The fastest of the class, HMS *Indomitable*, burnt around 500 tons of coal a day as well as 120 tons of oil (Hawkins, p41).
14 Hawkins, p46.
15 Ibid, p59.
16 Ibid, p66.
17 Gibson and Harper, p92.
18 Wolz, *From Internment to Scapa Flow*, p122.
19 Terraine, p10.
20 Hawkins, p106, quoting Thomas, p87.
21 Preston, *Wilful Murder*, p423.

6 Prelude to Action
1 Wolz, *Lange Wart*, p100, quoting Firle's *Tagebuch*.
2 Ibid, p100, quoting Knobloch's *Tagebuch*.
3 Ibid, *Hafen*, p148.
4 Ibid.
5 Grove, p53.
6 *U.46* was originally ordered to patrol the Sunderland coast but after mechanical problems was replaced by *U.47*. *U.46* never left harbour.
7 The ten boats were *U.24, U.32, U.43, U.44, U.47,*

U.51, U.52, U.63, U.66 and the *U.70*.

8   *U.72* turned back after an oil leak and *U.27* after she had fouled her propellers on fishing nets. It was *U.75*'s decision to lay mines that later had terrible consequences as HMS *Hampshire*, with Kitchener onboard, struck one.

9   Barnett, p157.

10   Grove, p67.

11   Plivier, p218.

12   Temple Patterson, *TJP*, vol 1, p44.

13   Gibson and Harper, p91.

14   Kemp, p68.

15   During the morning of 31 May, Scheer received a number of reports giving intelligence on his foe, Jellicoe: (a) 05:29. *U.32* reported spotting two battleships, two cruisers and destroyers in 56° 15′ N, 0° 43′ W. (b) 06:00. The signals intercept station at Neumünster reported that a decoded British message indicated that two battleship squadrons had just left Scapa. (c) 06:47. *U.66* spotted and reported eight battleships and light forces 57° 45′ N, 0°, 7′ W. and (d) 10:00. Neumünster reported that a Scottish wireless telegraphy (WT) station had sent out a weather report normally used when the British fleets were at sea (see Koervner, p174.)

16   Massie, p579.

17   Sent at 00:30 by Admiral Oliver in his own hand after Jackson's erroneous conclusions on the 'DK' signal. Jellicoe received the signal at 00:48 (Beesly, p155).

18   Massie, p582.

19   A cable's length equals around 202yds.

20   See Wallace, *From Jungle to Jutland*.

21   Wallace, p237.

22   Thompson, p297.

7   **The Battle-Cruiser Debacle**

1   On board *Galatea* was Commander Frank Marten, father of Tim Marten, my father's oldest childhood friend. They remained friends till their deaths in 2007.

2   Yates states that *Galatea* opened at the maximum range of her forward 6in gun, ie at 14,000yds (p127).

3   Macintyre, p92 (15:31 GMT, 14:31 local German, *Feindliche Panzerkreuzer in Sicht in WzN*).

4   Time of fire 14:34.

5   Letter, Commander Frank Marten, HMS *Galatea*.

6   Beatty signalled *Engadine* before *Galatea* had even sent the second, more detailed signal at 14:51, asking them to 'Send up seaplanes to scout NNE. Am sending two destroyers to you.' *Onslow* and *Moresby* were the two destroyers that Beatty selected to cover her.

7   For interesting film footage on *Engadine* search 'HMS *Engadine*' on YouTube; see also Harper, *The Truth*, p57.

8   In an interview with Grahame Donald, the pilot

who was sitting in the Short ready to fly the first recce mission, Rutland was described as having been 'outstanding', 'quite outstanding' and a 'very good pilot', but Donald, interestingly, remained adamant in refusing to answer what kind of person he was, while he described Trewin as 'a very nice Cornishman' (source: Imperial War Museum Archive, CAT No 18,1972-09-27, Reel 9).

9   Squadron Leader Frederick Rutland was finally arrested in 1942 and was interned in Britain for twenty years but he was never prosecuted, as the British authorities did not want to make public the scandal of a British officer turned enemy spy. It was said that that his aid helped to develop the aircraft carrier force that the Japanese navy used so effectively in their attack against Pearl Harbor in 1941. The MI5 file contained a report from 1922 which states: 'Reliable information was received from a very delicate source to the effect that the Japanese government were communicating regularly with an officer in the RAF'. 'He is an officer who has a unique knowledge of aircraft carriers and deck landing and his experience gained in the RAF will be invaluable to the Japanese,' the file says. In his book *Rutland of Jutland* (1963) Desmond Young made a strong case for Rutland. He concluded, 'The circumstances of his arrest and prolonged "detention", without trial and without charge, in World War II, as well as the refusal of the then Home Secretary to give any explanation in the House of Commons to so senior a member of his own service as Admiral Sir Roger Keyes, were so strange that they make his story as disquieting as it is distressing'. The DSO that Rutland won was rather economically phrased, given the outstanding courage he and Trewin had shown. The citation read, 'Squadron Leader Rutland was awarded the Distinguished Service Cross "for gallantry and persistence in flying in close range of four enemy light cruisers" at the Battle of Jutland' (*Independent*, 10 November 2000: 'Another MI5 file reveals that an RAF First World War hero became a spy for the Japanese') .

10   The time of the turn is put at 15:32–15:33.

11   Gordon, p35. In the ensuing run to the north the assumption proved to be wrong and the *Queen Elizabeths* had a tough time keeping ahead of their pursuers.

12   Bacon's biography of Jellicoe is written as much as a friend as a biographer. Jellicoe defended the vice admiral (as he was then) when he was attacked for his command of the Dover Patrol.

13   Bacon, *Scandal*, p90.

14   Yates, p131.

15   Jellicoe to Jackson, 5 March 1916, Temple Patterson, *TJP*, vol 1, p225.

16   Gordon, p49.

17 The order for Rear Admiral Pakenham's 2nd Battle Cruiser Squadron to fall in behind the 1st was described as being delivered 'somewhat belatedly'. Signal at 15:45: 'Alter course together to ESE' (Steel and Hart, p78).

18 Gordon, p87.

19 Dr Quintin Colville's (of the National Maritime Museum) grandfather was Egerton's flag lieutenant on the bridge of HMS *Barham* on the day of the battle. In 1989 some of the survivors would get together for lunch. Present were Michael Craig-Waller (Arthur Craig's son), Evan-Thomas's two nephews (Martin Bourdillon and his brother), the daughter of the midshipman of the watch and the chief yeoman – who now lives in New Zealand. Also there was Rear Admiral Royer Dick who had been a midshipman on *Barham* at Jutland and had then served on HMS *Valiant* after *Barham* was torpedoed. Sadly, I've been told, there was not any discussion of that crucial moment before the run to the south. Martin very kindly gave me full access to many of the Evan-Thomas papers and photographic records while Quintin has been a constant supporter of the Jutland Centenary Initiative since its first presentation at the NMM in 2011.

20 Rawson, p152.

21 Chalmers, p225: 'the prescribed distance between the battle-cruisers and the 5th Battle Squadron, while cruising as part of the Grand Fleet, was 10 miles'.

22 Rawson, p176.

23 Bacherach, p43.

24 Rawson, p242.

25 Tarrant, *Battle-cruiser Invincible*, p98, 14:33 GMT. The power of transmitters was normally related to the size of a warship. 'Battleships and battle-cruisers normally carried a 14kW set with a range of approximately 500 miles, cruisers a 1.5kW set with a 100 mile range, destroyers a 1kW set with half the range and submarines a set with approximately thirty miles range'. (Kent, p35).

26 Time 15:11.

27 Turn to the SSE, timed 16:06.

28 Signal timed 16:56.

29 A good description of the steps taken during an 'action stations' is given on p170 of Steel and Hart, described by a lieutenant on HMS *Agincourt*.

30 Yates, p133.

31 Steel and Hart, p79; also Chalmers, pp229–30.

32 Hase, p81.

33 King-Hall, p130. Note: this is the 'Etienne' version.

34 Kemp, p70.

35 Staff, p280

36 *Official Dispatches*, p132.

37 Paschen became an outspoken critic of the Nazi regime and was eventually executed. He came from a strong naval background as his father was chief of staff of the Baltic Naval Station and a vice admiral. His mother was also a rear admiral's daughter. Paschen married an English woman and so it was more likely, when the second war came again in 1939, that he might have had some misgivings about the Nazi party. After a show trial he was sentenced to death by the notorious Nazi judge, Roland Freisler. His wife was not even allowed to take his body back to Flensberg, his birthplace, to be buried.

38 Steel and Hart, p80, based on Campbell's *The Fighting at Jutland*. The calculation of 167hm seems too far.

39 *Moltke* was as close as 141hm, while *Von der Tann* reported firing at 162hm.

40 Sumida, 'A Matter of Timing: The Royal Navy and the Matter of Tactics of the Decisive Battle 1912–1916', *Journal of Military History*, 67:1, January 2003.

41 Brooks, p241.

42 Fawcett and Hooper, p34.

43 Private correspondence, Byron Angel, translating Mahrholtz's diaries (*Von der Tann*'s gunnery officer).

44 Steel and Hart, p86.

45 Double fire on *Lützow*, as the enemy flagship, was intentional while this was not the case for *Moltke* (Hawkins, p75).

46 Campbell, p39. Time of straddling 15:52.

47 The signal was based on Nelson's famous signal at Trafalgar, signal no. 16.

48 Born in 1887, after leaving school and joining the Navy, Seymour eventually came to David Beatty's attention, who helped his career, appointing him signals officer on *Lion*. After the war Seymour became engaged to the admiral's niece, Gwendolyn, an engagement to which Beatty's wife, Ethel, strongly objected. Seymour had to break off the engagement and eventually committed suicide in 1922. While Beatty praised his actions at the time in the Jutland battle-cruiser despatches ('In conclusion, I desire to record and bring to your notice … my Flag Lieutenant, Commander R F Seymour, who maintained efficient communications under the most difficult circumstances, despite the fact that his signalling appliances were continually shot away.') and also worked to get him promoted to commander, he blamed his faulty signals for mistakes made at the Scarborough Raid, the Dogger Bank action and Jutland.

49 Massie, p590. This seems to be slightly misquoted, see Steel and Hart, p80, quoting *Lion*'s flag captain, Ernle Chatfield.

50 Campbell, p39.

51 *Moltke* was steaming 30 degrees off her port side at around 15:50.

52 A number of different approaches were used
by navies at this time for identifying turrets.
On British ships these would be letters: to
paraphrase from Wikipedia, A and B were
for the turrets from the front of the ship
backwards, and letters near the end of the
alphabet (ie X and Y, etc) were for turrets in
the rear of the ship. Mountings in the middle
of the ship would be P, Q and R etc. Secondary
mountings were named P and S (port and
starboard), and numbered from fore to aft; eg
P1 was the forward port gun. Obviously, there
were exceptions. For example, *Agincourt* had,
unusually, seven turrets that were named after
the days of the week, 'Monday' up to 'Sunday'.
On a German ship, if all turrets were on the
centre line, turrets were generally A, B, C, D,
and E, going backwards from stem to stern.
Usually the radio alphabet was used on naming
the turrets, eg Anton, Bruno, Berta, Caesar,
Dora. If there were six turrets, as on *Helgoland*
and *Nassau*, they were named alphabetically in
a circle around the ship, starting at the bow and
going counter-clockwise. Similar exceptions
applied to ships with staggered wing turrets
or super-firing aft turrets. There were also
phonetic alphabets that were adopted to suit a
ship more: on *Blücher*, Alsen, Bautzen, Cezille,
Düppel, Eylau and Fehrbellin; on *Von der
Tann*, Alsen, Bautzen, Culm and Düppel; on
Seydlitz, Anna, Berta, Caesar, Dora and Emil;
on *Lützow*, Alsen, Bautzen, Culm and Düppel.

53 Hayward, pp102–3.

54 Hayward, p103.

55 Yates, p134.

56 Yates, p134.

57 Fawcett and Hooper, p35.

58 Grove, p86.

59 Steel and Hart, p89, quoting Kapitän zur See
Moritz von Egidy from *Seydlitz*: 'This time, only
one cartridge caught fire, the flash did not reach
the magazines, and so we lost only 20 dead or
severely burned, and only one turret was put
out of action'.

60 Signal time 15:55.

61 Quoting Captain Walter Cowan's dispatch.
Official Dispatches, p151.

62 Steel and Hart, p85, quoting Sub Lieutenant
Harry Oram, HMS *Obdurate*, 13th Flotilla.

63 Snelling, p113.

64 Massie, p593.

65 Steel and Hart, p91, quoting Commander Alan
Mackenzie-Grieve, HMS *Birmingham*, 2nd
Light Cruiser Squadron.

66 Snelling, p113.

67 Ibid, p114

68 Steel and Hart, p92.

69 Campbell quotes the time as 15:58 (*Jutland,
Analysis of the Fighting*, p69). The shell from
Derfflinger 'hit 6' belt in line with the centre of

'B' barbette, and a little below the main deck' of
Princess Royal (see diagram, p71).

70 Steel and Hart, pp92–3.

71 Private correspondence, Byron Angel,
translating Mahrholtz's diaries.

72 Fawcett and Hooper, pp38–9, navigating officer,
HMS *New Zealand*.

73 Imperial War Museum, interview with
Signalman Falmer (CAT No 4096. BBC. C
Falmer, recorded 1963).

74 Falmer insisted that he was picked up at around
02:30, not 20:00. It is hard to believe that he
could have survived that long in the water, but
his memory about the event was very distinct.
He said that the captain came down and said in
broken English, 'German navy, *alles kaputt*', at
which point, Falmer said, he 'laughed actually.
And I asked him for water. He sent a man up
and he came back with a bottle of whisky and
on the bottle was McAllister of Dundee.'

75 Signalman Falmer, Imperial War Museum,
podcast No 22, Jutland.

76 Imperial War Museum, interview with
Signalman Falmer (CAT No 4096. BBC. C
Falmer, recorded 1963).

77 Between 16:02 and 16:05, *Lion* lost her radio
equipment after a hit (one of around six) from
Lützow at around 20,000yds (182hm).

78 Private correspondence, Byron Angel,
translating Mahrholtz's diaries.

79 Between 15:48 and 16:07, *Lion* fired around
twenty-three salvos, *Lützow* thirty-one
(Campbell); the one regret that Kommodore
Paschen had was that he did not use PAC rather
than uncapped AP.

80 Steel and Hart, p98.

81 *Warspite* at 16:00, *Warspite* at 16:02, *Valiant* at
16:01, *Barham* at 16:11 (Narrative, p17). Harper
in *The Truth* states specifically that *Barham*
opened at 16:06. Campbell put the timing at
16:08 – *Barham* on *Von der Tann*. At 16:10
Barham and *Valiant* open up on *Moltke* while
Warspite and *Malaya* opened up on *Von der
Tann*. In fact, *Valiant* and *Warspite* had joined in
the fight a few minutes earlier, at 15:59, but at this
point firing at nearer targets, *Pillau*, for example.

82 *Warspite* had one refit in 1928 when her
twin funnels were streamlined into one joint
stack. Then, after the 1937 reconstruction,
her ordnance was upgraded to fire the Mk II
1,938lb shell and her guns given 30-degree
elevation. By this point she was able to add
another 10,000yds range, her shells hitting at
32,500yds with a 432lb propellant. The shell
would take a whole minute to arrive on target.

83 Steel and Hart, p98, quoting Seaman Carl
Meims, *Von der Tann*, 1st Scouting Group.

84 Private correspondence, Byron Angel,
translating Mahrholtz's diaries.

85 See *Defence Viewpoints*. Notes by MP Oliver

Colville on his grandfather, Charles Neate, who served on *Valiant*.

86 Ranft, *TBP*, vol 2, p429, written 4 June 1916, HMS *Lion*.

87 Steel and Hart, p102, quoting Midshipman Arthur Lewis, HMS *Lion*.

88 Tarrant, *Jutland: The German Perspective*, p88. Tarrant reports in German time (GMT +1)

89 Hase, p87.

90 Steel and Hart, pp103–4.

91 In his report to his senior officer, Francis, despite the value of the information on his experience within *Queen Mary*'s X turret that he had shared, wrote deprecatingly of himself: 'I am asking that whoever reads this at any time will please remember that the writer is much handier behind a pair of 13.5" turret guns than behind a pen'. His description of the event brought to life much of the horror of being trapped in one of the turrets.

92 Steel and Hart, p104, quoting Petty Officer Ernest Francis, HMS *Queen Mary*, 1st Battle Cruiser Squadron.

93 I was touched to see that the book from which this story was taken (Harold Felix Baker-Wheeler, *Stirring Deeds of Britain's Sea-dogs in the Great War*) was dedicated to my father's remaining sisters, Lucy, Norah, Myrtle and Prudence. Betty had already died seven years earlier of a mastoid infection. Brooks Rowlett, a friend, kindly passed the dedication from the book on to me.

94 Hase, p91. The same description appeared in *The Times* (9 June 1916). Harold Felix Baker-Wheeler, *Stirring Deeds of Britain's Sea-dogs in the Great War*, Eld and Blackham Ltd (1917), pp340–1, identified the *Daily Telegraph* as being the source.

95 Massie, p 595, quoting Hase.

96 Steel and Hart, p106, quoting from Victor Hayward. Fawcett & Hooper, p42 seen from the conning tower of HMS *Tiger*, 1st Battle Cruiser Squadron.

97 Massie, p595, quoting an eyewitness from HMS *Tiger*.

98 On other Royal Navy ships there were other Japanese observers: Commander Suetsugu Nobumasa aboard *Colossus*, Lt Commander Imamura Shinjiro aboard a light cruiser. Nobumasa (1880–1944) later became an admiral and was the Japanese Minister of the Interior in 1937–9. He declared in 1934 that for the navy even war with the US was acceptable 'if it will get us a budget'. Vice Admiral Imamura Shinjiro (1880–1969) became the Chancellor, House of Chichibujn 1936. Hase (p162) substantiates the claim coming from captured prisoners: 'In the course of the day our destroyers picked up two survivors of the *Queen Mary*, a midshipman and a seaman,

and brought them as prisoners of war to Wilhelmshaven. According to their account there were more than 1,400 men on the *Queen Mary*, among whom was a Japanese prince, the Naval Attaché in London.'

99 Harper, *The Truth*, p62.

100 Taffrail, pp138–9.

101 Steel and Hart, p113, quoting Flag Captain Alfred Chatfield, HMS *Lion*. Steel and Hart, pp113–14. Boy Telegraphist Arthur Lewis and Leading Signalman Alec Tempest HMS *Lion*, who were both close at hand each remember a slightly different phrasing: 'What's the matter with our bloody ships today?'

102 Captain Alexander Grant, CBE, DSC, *Through the Hawse Pipe*, unpublished memos held by the Imperial War Museum, which can also be accessed online. Chapter 14 is the relevant chapter on flash protection.

103 Steel and Hart, p114, quoting Private H Willons, Royal Marines Light Infantry, HMS *Lion*.

104 'SMS *Seydlitz* at Jutland' (extract from the book *Warships and Sea Battles of World War I*, edited by Bernard Fitzsimons, BPC Publishing Ltd, 1973), being an account of the Battle of Jutland written by the captain of the German battle-cruiser SMS *Seydlitz*, Kapitän zur See von Egidy.

105 Plivier, p217.

106 Harper, *The Truth*, pp69–70.

107 McCallum, quoting Dreyer, 'Riddle of the Shells: The Approach to War', p18.

108 Ibid.

109 McCallum, part 2, p12.

110 *Inflexible*'s gunnery officer, Commander Vener even wrote 'although our shots were obviously falling all over the *Scharnhorst* … we could not stop her firing … (and) I remember asking my Rate Officer "what the devil shall we do?"' (McCallum, part 2, p11).

111 Massie, p668.

112 Hough, *Great War at Sea*, p277.

113 Tarrant, *Jutland: The German Perspective*, p97. Yates, p142, quotes Campbell, *Jutland: An Analysis of the Fighting*: 'The Germans scored a total of forty-four direct hits by heavy shells in the first hour of the action to only seventeen by the enemy. Six of the British hits were made by the 5th Battle Squadron, so that Hipper's battle-cruisers had outhit Beatty's by a margin of four to one'. *Moltke* alone scored thirteen hits.

114 'The Narrative', p21.

115 Scheer commented on the weather conditions at the time of the sighting: 'The weather was extremely clear, the sky cloudless, a light breeze from the northwest and a calm sea. At 6:30 PM the fighting lines were sighted', Scheer, p147. (Note that 6:30 German time is 4:30 GMT).

116 Massie, p599.

117 Yates, p140.
118 Massie, p598.
119 Etienne, p133 (King-Hall).
120 Yates, p141.
121 Etienne, p137; also Hooper & Fawcett, pp83–4; Extract from *A Naval Lieutenant 1914–1918* (Commander Stephen King-Hall serving on HMS *Southampton* and writing under the nom de plume Etienne).
122 Fawcett and Hooper, p84.
123 This is, by Ralph Seymour, a repeat performance of the signals muddle at the start of the run to the south. The times stated for the signals seem to differ in places. Bacon states that 'at 16:40, when Admiral Beatty swung around from the German battle fleet the signal made by flags could not be seen by Admiral Evan-Thomas, who was eight miles off'. The result was that the 5th BS continued south for a further eight minutes sustaining 'considerable damage'. Bacon likens this episode to the earlier Phase One incident when *Tiger* had reported back that the 14:32 signal had not been passed through to *Barham*.
124 Bacon, *Scandal*, p167.
125 Gordon, pp139–140.
126 'Is it an unacceptable slur on David Beatty to suggest', Gordon asked, 'that the loss of the primary record of the *Lion*'s outgoing flag signals might have been assisted? ... The truth about the Rough Signal Log's fate will probably never be known' (Gordon, p140).
127 Massie, pp600–1.
128 Waldeyer-Hartz, p220.
129 Ibid, p208.
130 Scheer, p149.
131 Fawcett and Hooper, p80, Extract from Naval Lieutenant on HMS *Southampton* (Etienne); also King-Hall, p120.
132 Beatty also signalled back intelligence. (Jellicoe 16:45). 'Urgent Priority. Have sighted Enemy's battle fleet bearing S.E. My position Lat 56° 36′ N Long. 6° 04′ E.' (Received by C-in-C as '26-30 Battleships, probably hostile, bearing S.S.E. steering S.E.'). How it could have come through as 'probably hostile' is a mystery!
133 Massie, p599. Ten German battleships were firing at the *Southampton* at this point.
134 Steel and Hart, p150, Lt Stephen King-Hall (Etienne).
135 Gordon, pp407–8, 'half drowned by spray from shots falling in the water alongside the ship. The spray rises about 80 or 100 feet and then we steam through the column of falling water. We seemed to have a charmed life.'
136 Steel and Hart, p149, quoting Lt Commander Stephen Tillard, HMS *Barham*.
137 Massie, p602.
138 Fawcett and Hooper, p79, narrative of an officer on the forebridge of HMS *Southampton*.
139 Steel and Hart, p154, quoting Lieutenant Desmond Duffy, HMS *Valiant*, 5th Battle Squadron.
140 Fawcett and Hooper, p120, report from HMS *Malaya*.
141 Massie, p602, quoted the rate only; also Fawcett and Hooper, p120, report from HMS *Malaya*.
142 Steel and Hart, pp156–7, quoting Private John Harris, Royal Marines Light Infantry, HMS *Malaya*.
143 Massie, p602.
144 Steel and Hart, p155, quoting Sub Lieutenant Clifford Carlson, HMS *Malaya*.
145 Tarrant, *Jutland: The German Perpective*, p107.
146 Gordon, p407.
147 Ibid, p406.
148 Ibid, p406.
149 Ibid, p407.
150 Ibid, pp406–7.
151 Comment by Admiral Sir Charles Madden in 1923 (Madden was married to Jellicoe's wife's sister).
152 Gordon, p408; also Steel and Hart, p150, quoting an officer from the 2nd LCS.
153 Ibid, p409, quoting Sub Lieutenant Haworth-Booth.
154 Massie, p604, quoting the Hipper *Nachlaß*, 31 May, pp5–14.
155 Hase, p97.
156 Cruitwell, p336.
157 Harper, *The Truth about Jutland*, pp69–70; 'Disastrous', p52.
158 Fawcett and Hooper, p36.
159 Wallace, p241.
160 Wallace, pp241–2. Wallace quotes *Le Jutland* by Jaques Amet, suggesting that this must have been just after Jellicoe asked Beatty for the enemy's position. Wallace suggested that this now put the battle-cruisers between the Grand Fleet and the Germans, but that 'in order, I supposed, to get out of the way, the *Lion* changed course 16 points and took them off to the west. Which bore little relation to reality as Beatty went east to take up his position at the van of the Grand Fleet. Jellicoe slowed to make the transition faster.
161 Ibid, p646, quoting Captain Algernon Boyle, HMS *Malaya*.
162 Bacon, *Scandal*, pp97–8.
163 Hase, p99.
164 Harper, pp69–70. In 1950 Harper left copies of his papers both with the Jellicoe family as well as a set revised in 1928 with the United Services institution and the original with the Historical Section of the Committee for Imperial Defence.
165 Quoted in Temple Patterson, *Jellicoe*, pp230–1.

8   The First Destroyer Melee

1   See Taffrail, p132, showing the situation between 16:30 and 17:00 on 31.5.16 with

the approximate tracks of *Nestor* and other destroyers during initial destroyer attacks.

2 *The Narrative*, p21.

3 By 17:30 British destroyers had fired 'twenty two or possibly twenty six, the exact number being uncertain, because the *Turbulent*, which attacked with the *Nerissa*, was sunk in action during the night' (Taffrail, p137), but only two 'went home, and both were fired by the *Petard*'. One hit *V.27*, the other *Seydlitz*.

4 *Petard* should have taken station behind *Pelican* and *Narborough*, but as a result of *Nottingham*'s actions decided to make the run with *Nerissa*, *Turbulent* and *Termagant* instead.

5 He had exchanged her position in the group with *Nicator*.

6 *Turbulent, Termagant, Moorsom* and *Morris* were part of the 10th Flotilla.

7 Taffrail, p130.

8 Hase is quoted in *The Narrative*, p19.

9 Some versions say it was two from *Nestor*, one from *Nicator*.

10 Fawcett and Hooper, diagram p54, outlining 13th Flotilla attack; also p345, *Official Dispatches*.

11 Macintyre, p100. Although Taffrail had a slightly different take on this show of initiative. 'From the German Commander-in-Chief's dispatch we now know that this was launched to relieve the pressure on the *Lützow, Derfflinger, Seydlitz, Moltke* and *von der Tann* which were suffering severely from the accurate fire from the 5th Battle Squadron', see pp129–30.

12 *Official Dispatches*, p347; Taffrail, p133.

13 *Official Dispatches*, pp231–2, *Petard*, commanded by Lieutenant Commander E C O Thompson.

14 *Obdurate* had been about 1,000yds off *Lion* when the signal to attack had been given and was unable to join the rest of the flotilla. *Petard* had been behind *Pelican* and *Narborough* and, because *Nottingham* had cut across, had been cut off as well.

15 No mention of *Petard*'s rescue was made in the relevant *Queen Mary* dispatch where only the actions of *Laurel* were included.

16 Steel and Hart, p120, quoting Sub Lieutenant Harry Oram, HMS *Obdurate*, 13th Flotilla.

17 Signal 16:12, *Onslow* to *Engadine*.

18 *Official Dispatches*, p238. Alison wrote that 'it did not justify further expenditure in view of the night work expected to follow'.

19 *Official Dispatches*, pp238–9.

20 Kemp, p152.

21 Time of fire given as 17:08 for secondary and 17:12 for main armament (*Dispatches*, p239).

22 *Official Dispatches*, p239.

23 Steel and Hart, pp152–3, Sub Lieutenant Anthony de Salis, 13th Destroyer Flotilla.

24 *Dispatches*, p237.

25 SMS *Seydlitz* at Jutland (Egidy).

26 Brown, p25.

27 Kemp, p79.

9   The Deployment

1 Macintyre, p113.

2 Source: *North Sea Pilot* (courtesy of Rear Admiral James Goldrick who has had operational experience on the North Sea).

3 Hawkins, p154

4 John Travers 'Jack' Cornwell became the third youngest recipient of the Victoria Cross in the First World War. He was born on 8 January 1900 at Leyton in Essex. His father, Eli, had spent many years in the Army Medical Corps and then had various jobs that included a tram driver, a milkman and a hospital worker. He had a large family. His first marriage to Alice Carpenter brought two children, the second to Lily (née King) gave him another three sons and another daughter. Jack was a quiet but conscientious boy and, after leaving school aged only fourteen, worked as a delivery boy on a Brooke Bond tea van. He joined the Scouts (the 11th East Hall Scout Troop) in which he excelled. When war broke out Jack (as he was known to the family) tried to enlist. Even with the glowing references he had received, he was refused because he was too young. The next year, on 27 July 1915, he was finally able to join up and went to Keynsham Naval Barracks, Devonport. After ten months of training he joined HMS *Chester* for the final twenty-nine days as Boy Seaman 2nd Class (no. J/42563). After joining *Chester* in Rosyth in April, he was assigned duty at the forward 5.5in gun where he was mortally wounded in the chase north before *Invincible* was blown up.

5 Snelling, p138.

6 Cornwell's case was raised in Parliament by Admiral Lord Charles Beresford, his body exhumed and then given a public funeral in Manor Park on 29 July 1916. Very quickly Cornwell's face became a symbol for the British national war effort. Cornwell's brother, Ernest, stood in as a model for a painting of him standing at his position, steady by his gun. A memorial plaque was erected at Jack's old Walton Street school and 30 September 1916 was recognised as Jack Cornwell Day. Lord Baden-Powell built up Cornwell's position as a role model in the Scout movement. Memorial Homes for Sailors were built in Hornchurch and opened by Admiral Jellicoe in 1929, but the plaque honouring Cornwell that stood opposite was stolen in 2012. The Cayzer family had agreed to pay for a new plaque. Unfortunately, I was never able to find the right people locally though I looked far and wide

and was helped considerably by the Boy Scout Association. The end of the story was as sad as Jack's death. Eli died of a bronchial infection at the end of 1916 and is buried beside Jack's body at the Manor Park Cemetery. Arthur Cornwell, his eldest stepbrother, was killed in France. Almost without any money, Lily had to move out of her home and moved to Stepney. She died in 1919, aged only forty-eight. After her death, the family split up; Alice, his half-sister, went to Canada, where George and Ernest later joined her.

7 Taffrail, p146.

8 Yates, p159.

9 Hayward, p121.

10 Massie, p615, quoting Gibson and Harper.

11 Yates, p160.

12 An archaeological dive that was made on the Defence in 2003 by Dr Innes McCartney, however, found that the wreck was almost intact, suggesting that she did not blow up but, in fact, that something else had happened. What the divers said was that they 'saw an enormous ship which is largely in one piece, the turret roofs blown off suggesting a blast in the passage-way'. I was lucky enough to go with Innes when he went back with Gert Normann Andersen at the end of April 2015. Gert had kindly invited me to join Innes and his crew on his cable-laying ship the L/S Vina on an eight-day expedition to look at the wrecks of Jutland. We had considerably better fortune than the Royal Navy's HMS Echo which was not only delayed right at the start by a Force 8 gale, but also unable to find some of the critical wrecks, like the Wiesbaden or the Rostock. We were lucky enough to see both. We looked again at the Defence but starting from the opposite end from the one on which he had originally dived. He commented that there had been quite a significant amount of degradation. But what was extraordinary for me was that, at one point, I was able to see the fully extended torpedo launch rail in the hull.

13 Harper suggested that Wiesbaden was probably being hit by German fire as well, before also having been torpedoed by Onslow. Iron Duke herself fired on her around 18:23 (Harper, The Truth, p86).

14 Oberheizer Zenne was later picked up by a Norwegian steamer, Willy. It was his testimony that corrected British assumptions that Wiesbaden had gone down at around 18:45. He had had enough time to make a thorough inspection of the ship, bow to stern, and said that it must have been closer to around 03:00 on 1 June. On 12 June his detailed report was presented to the Admiralty Chief of Staff.

15 Wolz, Lange Wart, p129.

16 Gibson and Harper, p163.

17 Beatty Papers, vol 2, p443. Beatty's reaction to Harper's point was that 'errors in dead reckoning were unavoidable, and also that there were errors by cipherers and operators, which, by inference, were avoidable, which was unjust'.

18 On Hercules, the moment was estimated by the Russian observer at 17:55, saying that 'every face was radiant with enthusiasm and delight', Gordon, p433; Massie, p609. At 16:51 Jellicoe informed the admiralty: 'Fleet Action imminent'.

19 Gordon, p433, quoting Roger Kirk Dickson, Acc 13S09/13586 (NLS). The quote is handled slightly differently.

20 Gordon, p433.

21 Bacon, p152, quoting Filson Young.

22 Ranft, TBP, vol 1, p319; Jellicoe to Beatty, Iron Duke 4 June 1916, Beatty Papers, vol 1, BTY/13/22/13.

23 McLaughlin, p130.

24 Brooks, p258.

25 Bacon, Scandal, p83, diagram 28.

26 See p175, 'Comparative Allocation of Broadside Weight at the Deployment 1914–1916'.

27 Massie, p613, quoting Sir Reginald Corbett.

28 Ibid, p613, quoting Prof Arthur Marder.

29 Gordon, p441.

30 Padfield, The Battleship Era, p230.

31 Gibson and Harper, p173.

32 Letter, Commander Frank Marten, HMS Galatea, Dorset County Library records.

33 Wallace, p243.

34 King-Hall, p140.

35 Yates, p159.

36 Thompson, p308, quoting Lieutenant Briand, HMS Malaya.

37 Bacon, p151.

38 Fawcett and Hooper, p134.

39 Thompson, p309, quoting Lieutenant Bowyer-Smith, HMS Marlborough.

40 HMS Bellerophon was fondly known to those who sailed on her as 'Billy Ruffian'.

41 Gordon gives a fascinating account of the court martial explaining the ambiguity of the existing signals, at the time of the sinking of Victoria by Camperdown (Gordon, pp264–74).

42 Gordon, pp435–7, discussion on the complexities of the deployment.

43 Yates quotes this exchange from the 14 July meeting of the Board of the Admiralty. The discussion started when the conversation turned to Hercules getting straddled during the deployment (Yates, p264).

44 Bradford, p88, quoting King George VI.

45 Massie, p621, quoting Scheer's flag lieutenant, Ernst von Weizsäcker.

46 Wallace, pp254–61.

47 Wallace, p258.

48 Fawcett and Hooper, p149.

49 Imperial War Museum, online exhibition.

50 See 'Allocation of Broadside Weight' on p175.
51 Campbell, p155. 'The range finders could not get a range initially, and an estimated 10,000 yards was used and later 13,000 yards'.
52 Harper, *The Truth*, p86.
53 Behncke was hospitalised when the fleet got back to Kiel where the Kaiser visited him.
54 Brown and Meehan, p99.
55 Marder, *FTDTSF*, vol 3, p102. 'His first information of the British Battle fleet was the flash of its guns to the northward'.
56 Groos, p105. The 1926 Admiralty version translated by Lieutenant Commander W T Bagot put it very similarly. 'Ahead of the German column extending from northeast to northwest, nothing could be seen but the flash of gunfire from an unbroken line of enemy ships, while all around us, salvo after salvo struck in the immediate vicinity. The situation appeared all the more grave, as the fire could not be effectively returned since none of the British capital ships were distinguishable in the smoke of battle'.
57 On the site, Jutland1916.com, are some examples of Bergen's paintings.
58 Harper, *The Truth*, pp89–90. The quote is not from Bacon.
59 *St Vincent* herself, one of the last dreadnoughts in the line, engaged the third German ship in the line according to *The Dreadnought Project*. Her captain, William Fisher: 'The German ships opened fire with quick ripples almost simultaneously with *St Vincent*'s first broadside which was directed against their third ship considered to be a *Kaiser* [class]. The third ship was chosen as there were many ships ahead of *St Vincent* who could attack the two leading ships. And this was clearly done, all ships being continuously surrounded by splashes'. *The Dreadnought Project*, on which I am a contributing editor, is a valuable web resource for dreadnought-related information.
60 Tarrant, *Battle-cruiser Invincible*, p103, quoting Captain Kennedy of HMS *Indomitable*.
61 Those who survived were William Griffin, Stoker Petty Officer Charles Filleul, Charles Howell, and Ordinary Seamen Charles Hope, Charles Smith and Thomas W Swann.
62 After the war ended, Margaret Jones took her daughter, Linnette, to see the memorial at Fiskebackskil. Later in the 1960s the grave was moved to Kvivborg Cemetery in Gothenburg.
63 The flag gave the signal: 'Am in danger of sinking of injuries received in action'.
64 Taffrail, p152.
65 Ibid, p152.
66 Kemp, p88.
67 *Invincible*'s fire on *Lützow* caused her serious damage: the damage that later proved fatal to *Lützow* was from five hits from *Invincible*

(nos. 12, 13, 14, 15 and 16) in conjunction with damage from two earlier hits from *Princess Royal* (no. 3 and 4) but either way the fatal damage arose from 12 and 13.5in projectiles (source: Great War Forum).
68 *Source Records of the Great War*, vol IV, ed Charles F Horne (National Alumni, 1923).
69 Gibson and Harper, pp180–1.
70 Massie, p618.
71 Massie, p618.
72 Tarrant, *Battle-cruiser Invincible*, p107.
73 Ibid. Tarrant puts the time at 18:34.
74 Gordon, p455, quoting Roger Kirk Dickson, Acc 13509 /13589 (NLS).
75 Arthur, p52, quoting Midshipman Brian de Courcy-Ireland, HMS *Bellerophon*.
76 James William Fisher, p68.
77 *Official Dispatches*, p79, also reports *Oak* standing by.
78 Massie, p618.
79 Dannreuther, a godson of Richard Wagner, and his father Edward had founded the London Wagner Society in 1872. His son lived to a hundred years later and only died in 1977.
80 Scheer, pp151–2.
81 After the battle, yearning for a real engagement in which he could prove his mettle, the young prince wrote back home: 'life is going on as usual, very dull and monotonous ... the action seems years ago and we are longing for another one' (Bradford, p91).
82 Thompson, p310, quoting Midshipman Hext on HMS *Collingwood*.
83 Anthony Lovell (DreadnoughtProject.com) describes the German signalling for the manoeuvre: 'The German turn-around was effected by a single flag which was green in the upper right half and white in the lower left half ... A flag entirely red would have done the same turn, but to port rather than starboard. The flag being hauled down indicated the lead ship was putting her helm over that moment and that all ships were to turn together. Had the compass course signal been hung beneath either flag, it would have been the heading for the turn rather than the 16 point turn implied by there being no such compass course signal below'. Barnett, p160, maintains that the manoeuvre was 'unknown to the British fleet'. This does not seem to be the case, more that because of the additional cable's length between the German ships, such a manoeuvre was more likely to be executed without mishap or collision, but it also meant that the line became significantly more extended.
84 German ships used a mixture of chemical- and oil-based fires for laying smokescreens. Mostly destroyers employed oil fuel smoke while artificial fog could be created using a mixture of chlorosulphuric acid and sulphur trioxide

(Campbell, p204).

85 For a very readable description of this phase, see Yates, pp166-7.
86 Yates, p167.
87 The number launched was put at six (Harper, *The Truth*, p92).
88 Barnett, *The Swordbearers*, p161.
89 Bacon, *Scandal*, p114.
90 Ibid, p163.
91 Ibid, pp115-16, see explanatory diagrams 34 and 35.
92 Brown, *Torpedoes at Jutland*, p25.
93 Wallace, pp244-5.
94 Goldrick, *Before Jutland*, p25.
95 Ranft, *TBP*, vol 2, pp433-7.
96 Ernle Chatfield, who was on the bridge, later said that he handed over the conn to Beatty's chief of staff, Captain Rudolf Bentinck. In itself this was odd as technically – apparently – the helm should have been handed over to Strutt (Admiral Chalmers memo to Roskill MSS, quoted in Marder and cited by Gordon, p457).
97 Gordon, p457.
98 Gordon, p457.
99 Massie quoted Scheer's later defiant comment after the battle: '*So gehe Ich hier nicht weg!*' (I will not leave here in this manner). (Massie, p625; Marder, p111; quoted by Commander Friedrich Forstmeier, 'Zum Bild der Personalichkeit des Admirals Rheinhard Scheer 1863-1928', *Marine-Rundschau*, April 1963).
100 Massie, p625, quoting Scheer.
101 Massie, p625; also Marder, *FTDTSF*, vol 3, pp110-11. See footnotes quoting Ernst von Weizsäcker, Scheer's flag lieutenant.
102 Yates, p171.
103 *Source Records of the Great War*, vol IV, ed Charles F Horne (National Alumni, 1923).
104 Massie, p619, quoting Erich Raeder, Scheer's chief of staff.
105 Tarrant described the bravery of *Von der Tann* in the following way: 'Zenker, *Von der Tann*'s commanding officer, decided to remain with the squadron so that the enemy, having to take his ship into account, would not be able to concentrate his fire against the other battlecruisers. A steady course requisite for accurate shooting, Zenker was able to manoeuvre *Von der Tann* in such a manner as to avoid enemy salvos', Tarrant, *Jutland: The German Perspective*, p107.
106 Macintyre, p136.
107 Bacon, *Scandal*, p116.
108 Yates, p172.
109 Yates, pp166-7.
110 Irving, p163, quoting Hase.
111 Barnett, p165.
112 Massie, p627.
113 Irving, pp160-1.
114 Scheer, p156.

115 Temple Patterson, *Jellicoe*, p233.
116 Ibid, p236.
117 Temple Patterson, *Jellicoe*, p233; Winton p284.
118 Tarrant, p165.
119 Brown, p25.
120 Irving, p165.
121 Frost, p368.
122 *Dispatches*, p54.
123 Frost, p375.
124 Ibid, p372.
125 Irving, p171.
126 Groos (p133) says that this was *G.68* but it could not have been. *G.88* was part of the 3rd Flotilla. It was probably a transcription error in the ONI copy that I have used.
127 See the ships database on Jutland1916.com for complete details of each of the destroyer types.
128 Bacon, *Scandal*, p53.
129 Jellicoe's letter to Secretary of the Admiralty dated 30 October 1914 cites why he said that he would not be drawn into pursuit of a withdrawing fleet. 'If, for instance, the enemy battle fleet were to turn away from an advancing fleet, I should assume that the intention was to lead us over mines and submarines, and should decline to be so drawn … I feel that these tactics, if not understood, may bring odium upon me, but so long as I have the confidence of their Lordships I intend to pursue, what is, in my opinion, the proper course to defeat and annihilate the enemy's battle fleet, without regard to unrestricted opinion and criticism'. The decision to turn away was also based on presenting a smaller profile and outrunning the enemy's torpedoes (cited in Temple Patterson, *The Jellicoe Papers*, vol 1, pp75-6. Jellicoe put a copy of the letter in his bank as he was convinced that he had to do the right thing. Odium was, indeed, poured upon him). Jellicoe – as it turned out mistakenly – was convinced that all German torpedo boats and destroyers carried mines. Temple Patterson says that at Jutland only twenty-five did (Temple Patterson, *Jellicoe*, footnotes p66).
130 Although I should mention Anthony Lovell's suggestion that the destruction of *Navarin* was not necessarily demonstrative of the tactic of sowing mines in the track of a pursuing enemy since the battle had 'essentially run its course' and that *Navarin* was 'dead in the water' when two Japanese destroyers sensed the opportunity, came in, laid mines and were responsible for her destruction when she eventually got underway (*The Dreadnought Project* private correspondence).
131 Jellicoe, *Errors at Jutland*, 1932, quoted in Dreyer, pp164-91.
132 The GFBOs (Grand Fleet Battle Orders) do not seem to elaborate on this critical point as

neither do Beatty's GFBIs (Grand Fleet Battle Instructions). Bacon's listing was as follows: 'This method of defeating torpedo attacks was used by: Admiral Jellicoe in the Battle of Jutland, Phase III, Admiral Beatty at the Dogger Bank action, again by him on the way out to Jutland, Admiral Sturdee during Phase 3 of Jutland, Vice-Admiral Evan-Thomas, Phase 1 Jutland, Admiral Burney at Jutland, Phase 3, Rear-Admiral Horace Hood Jutland Phase 2 and Admiral Hipper, Jutland Phase 1' (Bacon, pp53–4; see also Dreyer, pp181–2).

133 BBC Radio, *Britain at Sea – The Navy wins*, Admiral Lord West, 2014.

134 Irving comes to a slightly different tally. 'In all these attacks between 7.00 pm. and 7.45 pm., 28 torpedoes had been fired: 23 of them had been seen and avoided – spent at the end of their run; no ships of the Grand Fleet had been so much as grazed, yet the aim had been good. The Germans had lost one destroyer – the *S.35* – and two (*S.52* and *S.36*) – if not three more damaged by shellfire (Irving, pp172–3).

135 Charles Neate, HMS *Valiant* (see *Defence Viewpoints*, 'Notes by Oliver Colvile, MP').

136 Padfield, *Maritime Dominion*, p177.

137 Yates, p230, quoting Marder.

138 Brown, *Torpedoes at Jutland*, p24.

139 Kemp, p102.

140 *Cruisers and Destroyers in the General Action*, Naval War College, Newport RI June 1937.

141 Farquharson-Robert, p131.

142 Kemp, p102.

143 Kemp, p102.

144 Waldayer-Hartz, p221, quoting Corbett, *Naval Operations*, vol 3.

145 Macintyre, p140.

146 It is interesting to look more closely at Irving's footnotes quoting from the Captain's After Action reports: *Marlborough*: 'The enemy battle fleet in sight was observed to turn 8 points until their sterns were toward our line'; *Hercules*: 'They then withdrew'; *St Vincent*: 'The enemy had turned 8 or 10 points away, disappearing into the mist away from us and broke off the action'; *Temeraire*: 'Target showed her port side'; *Royal Oak*: 'enemy turned away into the mist'; *Benbow*. 'Enemy observed turning away to starboard'; *Valiant*: 'enemy's battle fleet now altered course together and on opening fire then turned away until stern on, continued to come round to starboard and then disappeared'; *Malaya*: 'Owing to the battle fleet's having turned away.' (Irving, p177).

147 Gibson and Harper, p206.

148 Ibid, p205.

149 Massie, p672.

150 How Jellicoe defined the role of destroyers in a battle action changed dramatically from when he was subordinate to Sir George Callaghan.

'Unless conditions are very clearly favourable and enable our light-cruisers to deal effectively with the German destroyers, it is impressed upon all destroyer officers that their primary duty is to stop the German destroyers engaging them in close action before they can fire their torpedoes, and that a torpedo attack on the German battle fleet is secondary to a gun attack on their destroyers' (Temple Patterson, *TJP*, vol 2, pp252–3). He had held an opinion which was closer to that of Beatty's when he was with Callaghan, ie that destroyers should actively be used to spoil an attack on our fleet by actively seeking out opportunities to attack an enemy's battle fleet. This is a policy Beatty followed at Jutland, but that Jellicoe did not. I am here of the opinion that Beatty's was the better policy.

151 Bachrach, *Jutland Letters*, p14.

152 *Dispatches*, p466.

153 Just moments before, at 19:31 Jellicoe had ordered *Castor*, at the time to the north westward of *Iron Duke*, not to go 'too near' to the German battle fleet: 'Tell *Castor* to come back. Destroyers recalled' (Irving, p176).

154 *Dispatches*, Beatty to Jellicoe, Time of Dispatch 19:47, Time of Origin 19:50.

155 Gibson and Harper, p209.

156 Yates, p180.

157 See Groos, map 32; note that the German time used is Berlin summer time, ie two hours ahead of GMT.

158 Macintyre's comment comes from Beatty's report but should be looked at in addition to an earlier signal which just said that the bearing was northwest by west. The 19:45 signal added information to say the enemy 'was on a course of about south-west'. This additional data reduced the confusion caused by Goodenough's signal that he (Goodenough) had seen a group of ships detach at 18:15 and head on a northwest course (Macintyre, pp143–5).

159 *Dispatches*, p465, sent by WT via a wireless transmission from *Princess Royal*.

160 Brooks, *Jutland: British Viewpoints*, pp13–14; private correspondence.

161 Macintyre, p144.

162 The 1st and 3rd Light Cruiser Squadrons were ordered by Beatty at 19:50 to try to regain contact which had been lost five minutes earlier (*Dispatches*, 467, Time of Dispatch (TOD) 20:00).

163 The ships that *Falmouth* spotted were *Stettin*, *München*, *Frauenlob*, *Stuttgart* and *Hamburg*.

164 After the battle Jerram wrote to Jellicoe that he had 'negatived the attack with Whitehead torpedoes ordered by *Caroline* as I was certain the vessels seen on our starboard beam were our own battle-cruisers. The Navigating Officer of my Flagship, who had just come from the battle-cruiser Fleet, was also certain that they

were ours and saw them sufficiently clearly to give their approximate course which I reported to you.' (*Power at Sea: The Age of Navalism 1890–1918*, Lisle A Rose). Jerram signalled Jellicoe at the time, 'Our battlecruisers in sight bearing 280 degrees, steering 210 degrees.' (*Jutland. Death in Grey Wastes*, Steel and Hart)

165 *Caroline* was also the target of a torpedo attack according to one crew member, L S Smith. 'The huns sent three torpedoes at the "Carrie" but missed'. He maintained that *Caroline* fired two torpedoes at the enemy ships in the evening 'one of which took effect'.

166 Macintyre, p151.

10   David and Goliath: Scheer's Escape

1   Stern, p56. Jellicoe 'hoped there would be no accidental encounters with friendly forces'.

2   Massie, p636.

3   Steel and Hart, p285, suggests that *Abdiel* was ordered forward at 21:32.

4   The night deployment order to the Grand Fleet was made executive at 21:17: 'Assume 2nd Organisation'.

5   By this point *Warspite* had already returned to port. Eventually, at 22:03 the three battleships of the 5th BS turned back to cover *Marlborough* which was labouring to keep station. Inside, her stokers were working under increasingly difficult conditions, most knee-deep in water. When Jellicoe finally ordered her out of the line, *Fearless* came alongside to take Vice Admiral Sir Cecil Burney off and transfer him to *Revenge*. Then *Revenge, Hercules* and *Agincourt* stayed with *Marlborough*, as did the remaining *Queen Elizabeths* of the 5th BS.

6   Hawksley flew his flag on *Castor*, but only had four of the 11th Flotilla with him; the remainder were commanded from *Kempenfelt* as the divisional flotilla leader.

7   Irving quoted *Lion*'s log which read 'Challenge and reply passed as requested'. The incident was played down as much as possible: the Admiralty said the visual message was made with a flashlight. Massie points out that neither Groos in the official German history nor Corbett in the official British history even mention the incident, while Tarrant (*Battlecruiser Invincible*, p103) suggests that the recognition signals were discovered by the German navy from intercepted *wireless* traffic and lists the WT messages in *Jutland: The German Perspective* in the Signals Appendix. However, *Castor* maintained that a searchlight was actually used (Irving, p205). If this were the case it would be an extremely strong light for a 500yd gap. Yates (pp190–1) outlined how the event itself might have happened, highlighting the traffic from *Elbing* and *Frankfurt* (Yates, p286).

8   Gibson and Harper, p216.

9   Ibid, p218.

10   Ibid, p217.

11   Admiral von Trotha, Steel and Hart, p289.

12   Steel and Hart, p288, quoting Hase, SMS *Derfflinger*, 1st Scouting Group.

13   Tarrant, *Jutland: The German Perspective*, p183.

14   Scheer, p159.

15   Bacon, *Scandal*, p129.

16   James, p119; for an overview see pp118–20.

17   Room 40 had done their work and passed the first message to Vice Admiral Oliver at 19:40, but the signal was not forwarded to Jellicoe on *Iron Duke* for another hour and twenty-five minutes. Similarly, the instructions for the U-boats to advance north and for further destroyer actions (Michelsen's orders to the Horns Reefs rendezvous) were available, respectively, at 20:40 and 20:31, but were not sent to Jellicoe. The failure to pass on intelligence in a timely manner partially resulted from the fear of betraying the success of the decryption operations, but it meant that intelligence that would have put Jellicoe where he wanted to be for a successful morning engagement was withheld (Yates, p198). For a general overview of Room 40 operations and Jutland see Beesly, pp160–1. Beesly unequivocally steers the blame entirely away from Room 40 (Beesly, p160, 'These signals were all in the Operations Division within three-quarters of an hour of their being made. But none of them was passed on to Jellicoe.').

18   Gough, *Dreadnought*, p276.

19   Tarrant, *Jutland: The German Perspective*, p209.

20   Tarrant, *Jutland: The German Perspective*, p210; also see Massie, pp641–2. On another occasion: 'Of course, if the Admiralty had given me this information, I should have altered in that direction during the night'.

21   Macintyre, p163.

22   *Elbing* had fallen out of station with engine trouble and later joined the 4th Scouting Group on the starboard bow.

23   Steel and Hart, p397.

24   'Destroyers take stations five miles astern of battle fleet' (22:15), logged as dispatched from *Iron Duke* at 21:27 (Irving, p207). Admiral Scheer and the official German naval history deny Scheer ever received this signal, a claim that Sir Julian Corbett felt was 'entirely improbable'. Diplomatically, however, in the 1940 revision of the British official history he maintained that while the message must have reached the flagship (*Friedrich der Größe*) it may not have been seen by Scheer himself.

25   Koever, Hans Joachim, *Room 40: German Naval Warfare 1914–1918, vol II, The Fleet in Being* (LIS Reinisch 2009); see appendix pp661–5 for a copy of TNA, PRO HW 7/1.

26   Jason Hines, 'Sins of Omission and
      Commission: A Reassessment of the Role of
      Intelligence in the Battle of Jutland', *Journal of
      Military History* 72 (October 2008). Sources:
      'Records of messages at Jutland', PRO ADM
      137 / 4710, TNA, Transcript list of key German
      signals intercepted during Battle of Jutland,
      included as an appendix to Clark and Birch, *A
      Contribution to the History of German Naval
      Warfare 1914–1918*, vol 1, pp1–3, PRO HW
      7/1, TNA.
27   Hines, p1151. Like Tarrant, the author cites the
      meeting times to have been 04:00. The time
      would have been late for the first arrivals.
28   Beesly, p162.
29   Ibid, p168.
30   Yates, p198.
31   Tarrant maintains that the flotillas had been
      running so fast during the day that 'their
      fires were dirty and their stokers exhausted'
      (Tarrant, *Jutland: The German Perspective*,
      p185), while Groos (p159) says that 'in order,
      however, to get the fires of these coal-burning
      destroyers in condition for smokeless steaming
      preparatory to night operations, after their
      slacking as a result of the daylight attacks, Koch
      was forced to keep the speed below 18 to 21
      knots in steaming up to position at the head of
      the battleship column. Even at 15 knots these
      boats were easily visible on account of the
      sparks and smoke from the stacks'.
32   Tarrant, p192. Groos (p165) puts the time of
      launch at 21:58.
33   Campbell, p279.
34   Groos, p165. He puts the time of signal at
      22:02.
35   Tarrant, p192.
36   *Hamburg* had her radio antenna destroyed
      and the crew of no. 3 gun had been 'severely
      wounded'.
37   Steel and Hart, p298, quoting Leutnant
      Heinrich Bassenge, SMS *Elbing*, 2nd Scouting
      Group, HSF. Groos (p166) states that the ships
      that had opened fire were *Hamburg* and *Elbing*.
38   Taffrail mentions that this could have been as
      close as 1,500yds (p392); Corbett puts it around
      2,000yds.
39   *Official Dispatches*, Report of HMS *Castor*.
40   Steel and Hart, p299.
41   The squadron was composed of HM Ships
      Southampton, Nottingham, Birmingham and
      Dublin.
42   Steel and Hart, p300, Lieutenant Stephen King-
      Hall, HMS *Southampton*, 2nd LCS.
43   Irving, p202.
44   Etienne (King-Hall), p149.
45   Steel and Hart, p303, Machinist Max Müller,
      SMS *Frauenlob*, IV SG.
46   Ibid, p302.
47   Taffrail's summary of the casualties is different.

      Frauenlob – 342 officers and men lost, *Stettin*
      – thirty-six killed and wounded, *München*
      – twenty-six killed and wounded, *Hamburg* –
      thirty-nine killed and wounded. He also noted
      that some of these casualties 'may have been
      inflicted earlier in the day' (sources: Taffrail,
      p158; Tarrant, p194, quoting Groos, *Der Krieg
      in der Nordsee*).
48   Campbell, p281, says there were nine survivors
      after she capsized.
49   Brown, *Torpedoes at Jutland*, p26.
50   Taffrail, p158.
51   King-Hall, p153 (Etienne).
52   *Tipperary* was followed by *Spitfire,
      Sparrowhawk, Garland, Contest, Broke* (the
      divisional leader), *Achates, Ambuscade, Ardent,
      Fortune, Porpoise and Unity*.
53   *S.13*-class destroyers each carried two 88mm
      (3.5in) guns and four 500mm (19.6in) tubes
      and each displaced 568 tons. Campbell (p285)
      quotes Groos saying that the 11th DF 'was
      probably following the German fleet in mistake
      for the British, and it would seem that it passed
      astern of the German line at about the time that
      the leading battleships became engaged with
      the 4th Flotilla'. As a flotilla the 11th still had
      considerable torpedo resources – fifty-seven
      (while the 4th had around twenty-four).
54   Stern, p62.
55   *Westfalen* was firing at ranges, Groos reports
      (p171), of 'between 1,800 and 1,400 metres'
      (Tarrant, *Jutland: The German Perspective*,
      p198).
56   Groos, p172.
57   Stern, p65.
58   Tarrant maintains that 'thirty feet' was sliced
      off, not five (Tarrant, p201).
59   Steel and Hart, p373, quoting Telegraphist J J R
      Croad, HMS *Broke*, 4th Flotilla.
60   Tarrant, *Jutland: The German Perspective*, p201
61   Ibid, p200.
62   Taffrail, p160.
63   Ibid, p160.
64   WO Phillip White, HMS *Spitfire*, as recounted
      by his grandson.
65   Fawcett and Hooper, p322.
66   Rupert Berger was born in 1896 and was only
      sixteen and a half when he joined the Navy in
      1912. After the war he was involved in the CSU
      (*Christliche Soziale Union*) and was even briefly
      imprisoned in Dachau for his opposition to
      the Nazis. After the Second World War, Berger
      became involved in politics, becoming the
      mayor of Traunstein and then serving twice as a
      parliamentary deputy for Munich.
67   See Marinekameradschaft Salzburg newsletter,
      Das Bullauge April/May 2012 edition for
      accounts of Berger, Schlager and Thomas on
      SMS *Nassau*.
68   Heinz Bonatz's account can be found in Nigel

Steel and Peter Hart's *Jutland 1916: Death in the Grey Wastes*. Part of the stories of Rupert Berger, Otto Thomas and Sepp Schlager can be found online in the newsletter of the Salzburg Navy Veterans (*Das Bullauge*, April–May 2012), an account written by Fritz Lahner.

69 Steel and Hart, pp315–16, Cadet Hans Bonatz, SMS *Nassau*, 2nd Division, 1st Battle Squadron (on duty on the port 5.9in battery).

70 Trelawny's and Bush's accounts were written up in the *Strand Magazine*, April 1928, and in the *Official Dispatches*. See also 'Sequel to Jutland', *Evening Post* (Wellington, New Zealand), vol cvi, issue 7, 10 July 1928.

71 Stern (pp63–4) writes that *Spitfire* was doing at least 27 knots. Groos (p172) said that 'The two vessels struck with a speed of twenty metres per second' (ie 38 knots). If, however, one takes *Spitfire*'s probable speed of 27 knots and adds the average speed of the German battle fleet during the night (16 knots) one arrives at a closing rate of 43 knots, around 79km – 49 miles – an hour.

72 Scheer, p162.

73 Alan Bush, Athelstan Bush's grandson, with whom I made contact through the Imperial War Museum's wonderful story-sharing platform, sent me a photo from his collection.

74 'On the Spitfire at Jutland', April 1928 issue of the *Strand Magazine* (vol 75, pp335–42); Trelawny: 'I may mention that this souvenir was later on dispatched to the USA in connection with a propaganda campaign, and there perhaps it still is. I have never been able to trace it.'

75 Groos, p172.

76 'A Narrow Escape: *Spitfire*'s Adventure'.

77 'A Narrow Escape: *Spitfire*'s Adventure' (Wellington), *Evening Post*, vol cvi, issue 7, 10 July 1928, p14.

78 Tarrant, *Jutland: The German Perspective*, p203.

79 Taffrail, p162. Taffrail thought that the damaged ship was either *Derfflinger* or *Seydlitz*, but a footnote corrected the identification to that of *Black Prince*.

80 Massie, p647.

81 Tarrant, p203; *Ostfriesland* at 00:07, *Nassau* at 00:15, and *Friedrich der Größe* at 00:14.

82 Ibid, p203.

83 Along with Kapitän zur See Wilhelm Höpfner, Kapitänleutnant Rabius, the secondary armament fire control officer, the second searchlight officer, the signals officer and four men, and wounding three other officers and nine men, including the helmsman and the officer of the watch (Tarrant, *Jutland: The German Perspective*, p203).

84 Steel and Hart, p323, quoting Fritz Otto Busch.

85 Ibid, p205.

86 Stern refers to the number of rounds fired, not

the time, but differs substantially from Tarrant: 'The *Westfalen* engaged her with around 40 rounds of 3.5-inch and 5.9-inch fire' (see Stern, p70).

87 Taffrail, p169.

88 Ibid, pp167–9.

89 Tarrant, *Jutland: The German Perspective*, p205.

90 Ibid, p207, quoting *Der Krieg in Nordsee*.

91 *Tipperary* was the leader of the 4th Destroyer Flotilla; Stirling himself was on *Faulknor*, the 12th Destroyer Flotilla leader.

92 Taffrail, p177, quoting *Official Dispatches*.

93 Ibid, p178.

94 Tarrant, *Jutland: The German Perspective*, p211.

95 Taffrail, p182; twice at 01:52 and 02:12.

96 Signals *Faulknor* to *Iron Duke* 01:56, 02:08 and 02:13. Even if *Faulknor*'s position was wrong it would have given Jellicoe an important indication of what was occurring astern of the fleet (see Macintyre, p179).

97 Ibid, p219.

98 Report from one of *Obedient*'s officers. Quoted (slightly differently) in Massie, p648. 'Amidships on the waterline of the *Pommern* there appeared a dull, red ball of fire (said an officer of the *Obedient*). Quicker than one can imagine, it spread fore and aft, until, reaching the foremast and mainmast, it flared up the masts in big, red tongue of flames, uniting between the mastheads in a big, black cloud of smoke and sparks. Then we saw the end of the ship come up as if her back had been broken.'

99 Tarrant, *Jutland: The German Perspective*, p221.

100 Ibid, p220.

101 Taffrail, p183, footnotes.

102 *Nessus* had been badly hit and had suffered severe casualties, with two officers and five men killed, and a further seven men wounded.

103 Quoting Sir David Beatty's official dispatch (p139), which was critical of *Champion*'s lack of communications: 'If, as was probable, they were the enemy, an excellent opportunity was missed for an attack in the early morning light. More important still a portion of the enemy might still have been located' (see Tarrant, *Jutland: The German Perspective*, p185).

104 It seems that the detonation was around 02:15. So it must have been a mine or maybe *V.4* hit a submarine.

105 Kemp, p102.

106 Groos, p184.

107 Steel and Hart, p293.

108 Steel and Hart, p293, Private H Wilsons, Royal Marine Light Infantry, HMS *Lion*.

109 'Flotillas to return to Kiel around the Skaw, should return journey to German Bight appear inadvisable' (see Tarrant, *Jutland: The German Perspective*, p215).

110 Tarrant, *Jutland: The German Perspective*, p237.

111 Earlier in the night Burney had been taken

off with his staff and signalman, transferring to *Fearless* (the scout cruiser/flotilla leader attached to the 1st Battle Squadron) and then to *Revenge*.

112 Different sources give different totals. The Record of the Great War cites 1,003 survivors, Wikipedia 1,150.

113 Massie, p652, also Tarrant, p195.

114 Tarrant, *Jutland: The German Perspective*, pp195–6, quoting *Marlborough's* gunnery officer, Lieutenant Commander Guy Royle.

115 Yates, p199, referring to *Seydlitz* being spotted by *Boadicea* and *Fearless*.

116 Steel and Hart, pp398–9, quoting Able Seaman William Cave, HMS *Dublin*, 2nd LCS.

117 Steel and Hart, p402, quoting Boy 1st Class Henry Hawkins, HMS *Barham*, 5th Battle Squadron.

118 Steel and Hart, p409, quoting Signalman John Handley, HMS *Barham*, 5th Battle Squadron.

119 Gibson and Harper, pp254–5.

120 Ibid, p254; see above quotation.

121 Ibid, p237.

122 Steel and Hart, p397, quoting Asst Clerk Gilbert Blakemore, HMS *Warspite*, 5th Battle Squadron.

123 Ibid, p392, quoting J J Hazelwood, HMS *Warspite*, 5th Battle Squadron.

124 Ibid, p413, quoting Private John Harris, Royal Marines Light Infantry, HMS *Malaya*, 5th Battle Squadron.

125 Ibid, p421, quoting Midshipman John Crawford, HMS *Valiant*, 5th Battle Squadron.

126 Winton, p215.

127 SLGF Archives, Churchill College, Cambridge.

128 Wallace, p252.

129 Gibson and Harper, p238.

130 Sir Shane Leslie says that after Beatty had written up his dispatches when back in Rosyth, he then wrote to his sister and to the family chaplain who later became Dean Baillie of Windsor. None of the letters survived, but Ballie was quoted in a letter dated 22 June 1948, as saying that even in this confidential letter, Beatty did not attribute any blame: 'David's letter after Jutland is one of the tragedies of my life. It would certainly have been one of the most remarkable historical letters you could find. On the evening of the day when his emotions were stirred partly by the disappointment and partly by the loss of his dearest friend before his very eyes, I think he must have wanted to let off steam. So he sat down and wrote an account of the battle and his own feelings. In fact, he poured out his whole heart to me. But the letter was so confidential that I felt that at that moment I could not possibly show it to anybody. I didn't even show it to my wife, and I locked it into a cupboard in which I kept nothing else. Not very long after came the move to Windsor and my first thought was the letter. When I opened the cupboard it was empty. I searched everywhere but it has never turned up … I liked to remember in view of the controversies that followed that he cast no blame for his disappointment on Jellicoe. He said that Jellicoe had, as he thought, made a wrong cast. We had always talked together in terms of hunting so it was a natural simile to me. But the impression it made on me was not an impression of bitterness'. Beatty's sister's letter did not survive because she felt it was so confidential that she herself destroyed it (The Leslie papers, Churchill Archives. The reference to when Beatty finished his report is from Gibson and Harper, p264).

131 Steel and Hart, p430.

132 Gibson and Harper, p264.

133 Brownrigg, p54.

134 Gibson and Harper, p270.

135 Ibid, p272.

136 Ibid, pp271–2.

137 Jellicoe, *Narrative*, p6.

138 Lord Louis Mountbatten was the son of Louis, Prince of Battenberg, who was the second son of Princess Victoria, Queen Victoria's granddaughter ('Vicky'). He served in the Grand Fleet as a midshipman, but missed the Battle of Jutland. Apparently, his brother Henry, who was at Jutland, was not allowed out of the turret in which he was stationed to get his cine camera. It is a great shame that the chance of some real footage of the battle was never shot. See Gordon p564, quoted in Adrian Smith's *Mountbatten: Apprentice Warlord*. After Mountbatten met Jellicoe in Malta, shortly before the latter's death in 1935.

139 Hough, *Mountbatten*, p36.

140 Beatty to Cowan, 28 November 1916, SLGF Archives, Cambridge.

141 Goldrick, *Before Jutland*, p19.

11 Opening Pandora's Box: Unrestricted Submarine War

1 Scheer, p248.

2 The exact numbers of submarines available, as has been noted elsewhere, is always difficult to calculate. Terraine uses the figure of 111. That makes the starting submarine number exactly 50 per cent of what Blum had estimated as being needed (see following note). Of these, he estimates forty-nine belonged to the North Sea Flotillas (vs forty-six estimated by Karau), and thirty-three to the Flanders Flotilla (vs twenty-three from Karau who puts the number at thirty-two in February).

3 Depending on the source, there is some variation in the numbers of submarines that Germany was bringing into service. The figures

quoted are from Macfarlane's 2014 thesis on Jellicoe's dismissal.

4   Terraine, p44.

5   Black, pp189 and 191.

6   McKee, Fraser, 'An Explosive Story: The Rise and Fall of the Common Depth Charge', *Northern Mariner*, vol 3, no. 1, Jan 1993, 45, quoted in Macfarlane, p57.

7   Redford, *The Submarine*, p102.

8   Jellicoe, Memorandum to War Cabinet, 21 Feb 1917, NA, PRO ADM 1/8480.

9   Memorandum Admiral Sir Henry Jackson to Balfour, 29 Oct 1916, BL Add MSS 48992.

10   Gordon, *Rules of the Game*, p519.

11   Letter, Jellicoe to Beatty, 25 Jan 1917, Temple Patterson, *TJP*, vol 2, p140.

12   Colvin, p217.

13   Gordon, p519.

14   Rear Admiral Duff had been second in command of the 4th Battle Squadron at Jutland. Grigg says (p50) that when Jellicoe became First Sea Lord 'he brought with him as Anti-Submarine chief an officer who shared his scepticism. Admiral Alexander Duff'. As far as I know there is little evidence to support this particular assertion that suggested that Jellicoe himself was sceptical of convoy. Geddes did not like Duff and objected to Jellicoe's request for a KCB for Duff 'as he did not like his manner on the wording of some minutes' (Temple Patterson, p201). Jellicoe replied that 'he was being recommended for his services, not his manner'.

15   Marder, *FTDTSF*, vol 4, p70.

16   Jellicoe, *Crisis of Naval War*, p50.

17   Macfarlane, p62; Jameson, *The Most Formidable Thing*, p204.

18   Colvin, p225

19   For a quick discussion on the barrage's construction see Admiral Sir Reginald Bacon, *The Concise Story of the Dover Patrol* (Hutchinson, 1932), pp151–5.

20   The Flandern Marine Korps was set up as an integrated military command with air, land and sea assets on the coast of Belgium using the 'triangle' ports of Ostend, Zeebrugge and Bruges as harbour facilities for the destroyers and pens for the submarines. It was under the command of Admiral Ludwig von Schröder.

21   Karau, p118.

22   Macfarlane, p58.

23   When Jellicoe arrived at the Admiralty each ASW vessel had around four 'depth charges' (John Terraine, *Business in Great Waters*, p27). By the end of 1917, the number per vessel was between thirty and forty per ASW vessel (Jellicoe, *The Crisis of Naval War*, p60). The availability had been achieved by steadily increasing production from around 140 per week to 500 per week in October and 800 per

week by the end of year 1917.

24   Jellicoe (*The Crisis of Naval War*, p61) gives some figures for the distances of an exploding charge from a submerged submarine and the expected damage: 'It is necessary to explode within 14 feet of a submarine to ensure destruction; at distances of up to 28 feet from the hull the depth charge might be expected to disable a submarine to the extent of forcing her to surface, when she could be sunk by gun-fire or rammed, and at distance of up to 60 feet the moral effect on the crew would be considerable and might force the submarine to surface'.

25   Terraine, p28.

26   Jellicoe, *The Crisis of Naval War*, p57.

27   Marder, *FTDTSF*, vol 4, pp77–8.

28   Ibid.

29   Because there was some initial concern that balloons aloft over a convoy would actually attract U-boat attention, Beatty at first experimented with an independent submarine-hunting group of balloon-equipped destroyers. It achieved its first success on 19 July 1917 when a balloon tethered to the destroyer *Patriot* (with an observer, F/L O A Butcher) spotted *U.69* from a distance of twenty-eight miles, which *Patriot* then successfully sank.

30   Jellicoe, *Crisis of Naval War*, p69.

31   Duncan Redford, former head of research at the NMRN in Portsmouth, described Jellicoe's book as 'remarkable for its lack of emotive language' (Redford, *The Submarine*, p116).

32   Terraine, p34.

33   Temple Patterson, *Jellicoe*, p150.

34   Jellicoe, Paper to the War Cabinet on the Influence of the Submarine upon Naval Policy and Operations, 18 November 1917, NA, PRO ADM 116/1806.

35   Muir, p267.

36   Jellicoe, *The Crisis of Naval War*, p111 ('forty destroyers and sloops') and Terraine, p25 (283 in 'home waters').

37   Colvin, p228.

38   Ibid, p260.

39   Jellicoe, *The Crisis of Naval War*, p114.

40   Although Sims has also been described as being too diplomatic with the British and letting his friendships cloud his judgement. Morrison's book on Sims (*Admiral Sims and the Modern American Navy*) was dedicated to my grandmother, Gwendoline, in 1949 with the words 'affectionate good wishes and happy memories'. In the same book, Morrison writes that although 'Jellicoe was mistaken in believing that the convoy system was impossible without American assistance, it was true yet that the complete success of the plan rested upon the number of anti-submarine craft our country could send to the dangerous area' (Morrison, p353).

41 Oliver, 20 April 1917, NA, ADM 137 /1322.
42 David Wragg, *The First World War at Sea*, Dr Andrew Gordon, *The Rules of the Game*, quoting from the 2015 BBC Scotland programme, *Scotland at War*.
43 On 13 April Admiral Sims promised the immediate delivery to Beatty of seven destroyers. They arrived in May with a promise of more to come. Sims was shown confidential information by Jellicoe revealing the real level of tonnage lost to be 'four' times as that released in the press.
44 Johnston, Rawlins, and MacFarlane, p546.
45 Winton, p245.
46 Jellicoe's approach was always to try and look at the anti-submarine challenge as multi-faceted: (a) Q-ships to lure enemy submarines into armed traps; (b) howitzers firing shells that would explode under water, depth-charge throwers; (c) coastal motor boats, fast anti-submarine chase boats; (d) mine development; (e) improved smoke-making screening; and (f) hydrophones (Altham, p140).
47 Jellicoe, *The Submarine Peril*, p96.
48 Colvin (*Carson*, p228) actually goes as far as to talk of America as 'the neutral who refused to allow arrangements to be made by the Admiralty in her home waters'.
49 Temple Patterson, *TJP*, vol 2, p150.
50 Unfortunately, Sir Charles Cayzer died September 1916 otherwise I could well have imagined that there would have been extensive conversations and advice from the shipowner to his two sons-in-law, John Jellicoe and Charles Madden. Nevertheless, before his death John Jellicoe had visited many of his shipyards and been on enough of his ships to know his way around sufficiently well. After the outbreak of the First World War, sailings of Clan Line ships had carried on 'as normal' as far as possible, although conscious of the new risks the ships now faced as they transported civilian and wartime commodities across the globe. The enemy threat to merchant shipping duly claimed its first company victim, SS *Clan Matheson*, in September 1914. Additionally, ships could be requisitioned by the Admiralty at any moment: SS *Clan Stuart* was wrecked while on Admiralty business, delivering coal to the naval base at Simonstown in November 1914. Having been unexpectedly requisitioned at Cape Town, she had been forced to transfer her commercial cargo to another Clan Line ship before taking up official duties. HMS *Clan Macnaughton* was commandeered in London by the Admiralty that same November, and lost with nearly three hundred hands in February 1915. Eleven of these were Clan Line ratings who had volunteered to remain with their ship in its naval duty. Soon merchant ships were fitted with defensive guns, but in the earlier years there were rarely enough guns to go round. The brave fight put up by *Clan Mactavish* in July 1916 against the infamous *Möwe*, one of the deadliest German raiders, was made with only one gun. *Mactavish*'s second gun was a wooden dummy, intended to give the outward appearance of a well-armed vessel. At the end of the war, twenty-eight Clan Line ships had been sunk by enemy action, out of a fleet that in 1914 had stood at fifty-six, with the loss of nearly three hundred officers and men. Eleven Clan Line men were decorated, and five received the Lloyd's Medal. The captains of *Clans Macgillivray* and *Macphee* were mentioned in dispatches during the times their steamers were employed as transports, as too was one of Sir Charles' own sons, Major H R Cayzer, for his work in France (Archibald Hurd, *The Clan Line in the Great War*, privately printed for The Clan Line Steamers Ltd, c1921 [commercial edition published by Cassell & Co, 1924]).
51 Captain Mahan, *The Life of Nelson* (Simpson, Low Marston, 1899), p611.
52 Captain Bertram Hornsby Smith, CBE RN (1874–1945) was actually on the retired list in 1915 but became director of the Mercantile Movements Division of the Naval Staff. Smith's calculations were based on the total sailings anticipated for January 1917 of 304 ships (see Smith memorandum, 4 January 1917 NA ADM, 137 /1322).
53 Colvin, p229.
54 Admiralty pamphlet, January 1917.
55 Macfarlane, *Dismissal*, p74.
56 Colvin, pp228–9.
57 Temple Patterson, *Jellicoe*, pp163–4.
58 Sims must have been specifically referring to the all-important transatlantic trade routes.
59 Winton, *Convoy*, p64.
60 Winton, p65.
61 Grigg, p50.
62 See Jellicoe, *The Submarine Peril*, p111.
63 Colvin, p260.
64 After the first six on 4 May, another six arrived on the 17th and a further six on the 24th (Dreyer, *Sea Heritage*, p216).
65 Terraine, p67.
66 Ibid, p59.
67 Ibid.
68 Dreyer, *Sea Heritage*, p220.
69 By the end of July, thirty-four American destroyers were available in British waters, while British shipyards could also produce another fifteen.
70 Massie, p740; Jellicoe to Beatty, 30 June 1916.
71 Ibid, p741.
72 Ibid, Beatty to Jellicoe, 2 July 1916.
73 Arthur Pollen had, unsuccessfully, lobbied the

Navy for his fire-control equipment He later wrote his side of events in *The Great Gunnery Scandal* and followed up with another book, published two weeks after the end of the war, entitled *The Navy in Battle*. Ethel openly schemed with him about Jellicoe: 'I telephoned Mr Pollen to come and see me which he did. He told me that he had declared open warfare and is going to have him removed from office in a month'. Jellicoe was removed from office six months later (see Massie, p742). In some of his later writings he suggested that the Grand Fleet deployment 'must have been dictated, either be some general principle of tactics … as given by the Vice-Admiral (Beatty), or it must have been part of a plan suggested by the Vice-Admiral' (Massie, p677). Massie cites Temple Patterson as describing Pollen's book (*The Navy in Battle*) as 'full of errors, some of them ridiculous' and Winton as saying that his work was 'almost unreadable'.

74 Letter from Lady Beatty, 10 July 1916. Ranft, *TBP*, vol 1, p369.

75 Marder, *FTDTSF*, vol 4, p277.

76 Additionally, these forward bases allowed the Germans to use larger numbers of the smaller and cheaper UB and UC classes of coastal submarines in the 1917 campaign.

77 Admiral Bacon had developed a plan for a combined operations attack on the Flanders batteries with Sir Douglas Haig's staff. The operation never took place and maybe, in the form it was put forward, might not have succeeded, but it became the basis for the later and famous Zeebrugge raid with which Admiral Roger Keyes is now associated.

78 Colvin, p224.

79 Colvin, Sir Edward Carson's biographer, gives some illuminating examples of how Lloyd George would, as is so often done in the business world, undercut the positions of 'direct reports'. Lloyd George had told Sir Douglas Haig at one War Cabinet meeting in 1917 that he did not agree with the general's assessment as he had 'a letter here from a subaltern in the trenches which gives an entirely different opinion' (Colvin, p261). He did the same with Jellicoe, talking behind the Admiralty's backs with officers like Dewar or Henderson, both brilliant minds, but in a manner that was lacking in integrity. In the same way, the prime minister's secretaries would often eat in the canteen underneath the Admiralty to pick up gossip. When he disagreed with Generals Sir Douglas Haig and Sir William Robertson over the proposed attacks through the Julian Alps or his idea to capture Jerusalem, Lloyd George said he would ask the opinions of Sir Henry Wilson and Sir John French on whether they thought what he proposed could be done

(Colvin, p281). So impressed was the prime minister with General Nivelle that he even put British troops under his command, without bothering to so much as consult Haig.

80 Colvin, p274.

81 Memorandum, Jellicoe to McKenna, 24 February 1909, BL Add MSS 48990.

82 Jellicoe, *The Submarine Peril*, p118.

83 Peter Rowland, *Lloyd George* (1975), p799, quoted in Macfarlane.

84 Colvin, p226.

85 Quoted in Colvin, p265.

86 Macfarlane, p142, quoting Haig, diary entry, 20 June 1917, NLS, Acc 3155, 114.

87 Colvin, p268.

88 Ibid.

89 Quoted from Bacon, *Dover Patrol*, in Macfarlane, p113.

90 Memorandum, Jellicoe to Keyes, 14 December 1917.

91 Keyes, *Naval Memoirs*, vol II, p159.

92 Ronald Handley, *The Dover Patrol Memorial* (Dover, 1998), pp8–9.

93 Letter Jellicoe to Geddes, 15 Dec 1917, NA, ADM 116/1806.

94 Jellicoe, *Account of Circumstances of Dismissal*, BL, Add MSS 49039.

95 Ibid.

96 Draft Statement, Geddes, 29 April 1918.

97 Draft Statement, Undated, NA, ADM 116/1806; part of the Geddes Papers outlining possible answers for Lloyd George for parliamentary question time.

98 War Cabinet papers, 21 February 1917, BL, ADM 1/8480.

99 Letter, Jellicoe to Beatty, 12 April 1917, Temple Patterson, *TJP*, vol 2, p156.

100 *Journals and Letters of Reginald, Viscount Esher*, vol 4, p115, quoted in Macfarlane.

101 Haig, diary entry, 20 June 1917, p114, NLS, Acc 3155.113.

102 Ibid.

103 Beaverbrook, *Men and Power 1917–1918* (1956), p166, quoted in Macfarlane, p144.

104 Hansard, Parliamentary Debates, 6 March 1918. The speech at the Constitutional Club was made in November 1917.

105 Brownrigg, pp67–8; see also Temple Patterson, *Jellicoe*, p154.

106 Letter, Jellicoe to Beatty, 30 June 1917, Temple Patterson, *TJP*, vol 2, p173.

107 Quoted, Thompson, Northcliffe, xii.

108 Ibid.

109 According to Massie the words ('You kill him…') are what '… the Prime Minister supposedly said to Northcliffe regarding the admiral' (see Massie, p740).

110 *Daily Mail*, Lovat Fraser, 29 January 1917.

111 *Daily Mail*, 15 May 1917.

112 *Daily Mail*, 18 May 1917.

113 *Daily Mail*, 6 July 1917.
114 *Daily Mail*, 22 October 1917.
115 *Daily Mail*, 19 October 1917.
116 *Daily Mail*, 25 October 1917.
117 *Daily Mail*, 1 November 1917.
118 The model is now in the collection of the National Museum of the Royal Navy in Portsmouth. In June 2011 the model took pride of place on the head table of a formal dinner at the museum to celebrate 100 years since its founding. Guests included HRH The Princess Royal and John McCarthy, a great American friend from Geneva whose mother, the late Lily Lambert McCarthy CBE, donated many of the Nelson artefacts and memorabilia – as well as the famous Fueger portrait of Nelson in full dress uniform – to the NMRN and which are exhibited in the Lambert McCarthy Nelson Gallery.
119 Massie, p743.
120 Ibid.
121 Jameson, *The Fleet that Jack built*, p204.
122 Geddes, p242.
123 Massie, p744.
124 Ibid.
125 Ibid.
126 Memorandum, Sea Lords to Geddes, 2 January 1918, NA, ADM 116/1807.
127 Jellicoe, 'Account of Circumstances of Dismissal', BL, Add MSS 49039.
128 Winton, p262.
129 Colvin, p264.
130 J Lee Thompson, p131, quoted in Macfarlane, p165.
131 Colvin, p162; also in H Montgomery Hyde, *Carson, The Life of Sir Edward Carson, Lord Carson of Duncairn* (London, 1953).
132 On the occasion of Lloyd George's breakfast outburst, Carson took great pleasure in then preparing a list of seventy such officers within the Admiralty who had previous sea experience.
133 Wemyss, p370.
134 Ibid.
135 Black, p219.
136 Letter, Madden to Jellicoe, 27 December 1917, BL MSS 49039.
137 Gordon, *The Rules of the Game*, p531.
138 Letter, Sims to Jellicoe, 29 Dec 1917, BL, Add MSS 49036.
139 Jameson, p237.
140 Ibid, p238.

12 From Kiel to Scapa Flow
1 Gibson and Harper, p279.
2 Ibid, p294.
3 Wolz, *From Imperial Splendour*, p119.
4 HMS *Penn* and HMS *Oracle*. The other British casualty was HMS *Falmouth*, torpedoed by *U.66* on the way back after the fleets failed to engage.
5 Gibson and Harper, p298.
6 Ibid, p322.
7 *Naval Mutinies*, p42.
8 Horn, p235.
9 Schubert and Gibson, p26.
10 Ibid, p42.
11 Scheer, p293.
12 Horn, p245.
13 Under Article XXI.
14 The detailed orders for the guard ship formation was called Plan ZZ. I understand it means the very last operation, but I could not hold back a slight chuckle. A sense of humour?
15 Warner, p183.
16 Admiral Sir Charles Madden to Jellicoe, 29 November 1919.
17 Van der Vat, *The Grand Scuttle*, p167.
18 The text is quoted differently by several authors: see Massie, p787, van der Vat, p170, etc.
19 Howarth, *The Dreadnoughts*, p168.
20 Van der Vat, *The Grand Scuttle*, pp180–1.
21 Howarth, p168.
22 For a fascinating account of Ernest Cox's story, see Tony Booth's *Cox's Navy*.

13 Counting Up After the Battle
1 Out-of-action tonnage is defined as the total cumulative displacement of each individual ship while still in dry dock.
2 When many of the German ships were finally inspected at close quarters, what impressed British officers and officials was the honeycomb of watertight compartments (see Hough, pp273–4 quoting an officer inspecting the *Friedrich der Größe* after salvaging; quote in Temple Patterson, pp42–3).
3 Jellicoe Biographical Notes, British Library Online.
4 Flight Lieutenant Frederick Rutland managed to fly his Short seaplane to within 600m of Hipper's ships.
5 Admiral Fisher once calculated the cost of a naval officer's education at £700 per annum, limiting this career path to a possible 300,000 families in the UK. 'Surely we are drawing our Nelsons from too narrow a class' was his conclusion. With the advent of both new types of vessel as well as new or dramatically improved technologies, as examples, the torpedo, the submarine, long-range gunnery, wireless telegraphy etc, there was an urgent concomitant need for both wider and deeper education.
6 Gibson and Harper, pp242–3. The claim is that German ships fired 3,597 heavy shells with 120 hits while the British fired 4,598 shells with 100 hits. Thirty-seven of the German hits (ie 30 per cent) are actually counted from the fire upon three British ships (*Warrior*, *Defence* and *Black Prince*) that were at extremely short range

and without reply. No hits were allotted to the sinking of *Wiesbaden* (which should have been analysed in the same manner as the cases of *Warrior, Defence* and *Black Prince*, while nine of *Derfflinger*'s twenty-six hits were allocated to smaller calibres and, therefore, discounted. With these changes, they reach a final figure of eighty-eight German hits (versus the original 120 claimed) and a comparative rate of 2.44 per cent vs 2.17 per cent for the British. See also Campbell, *Jutland: An Analysis of the Fighting.*

7   Gibson and Harper, p242. See also 'Summary of British Gunnery Results', Yates, p296.
8   Jellicoe Autobiographical Notes, British Library Online.
9   For some differing points of view, see Temple Patterson, *Jellicoe Papers*, vol 1, pp188–9. Beatty to Jellicoe: 'I should very much like to have a yarn with you about the rapidity of fire. I feel very strongly on this subject and think we should endeavour to quicken up our firing … The Germans certainly *do* fire 5 to our 2, which would be very deuce if we were unlucky …' (21 November 1915). Jellicoe to Beatty: 'I am all for rapidity of fire, but my only fear is that ships may break into rapid fire *too soon*, as *Queen Mary* I think did. It's alright even if not hitting *if short*, but no use *if over…*'. (23 November 1915). [Author's note: Of course, this is exactly what happened with the initial British battle-cruiser fire in the run to the south. The first shots were massive 'longs']. Nevertheless, Jellicoe summed up his position in a letter to Jackson days before the battle (28 May, Temple Patterson, p249): 'At all ranges, the early development of *accurate* rapid fire is the object' [author's italics].
10 Although, as he points out, it was possibly because of Alexander Grant's refusal to obey these directives, that *Lion* survived the fate that *Invincible, Queen Mary* and *Indefatigable* did not (see Gordon, p47).
11 Padfield, *Maritime Dominion*, p155.
12 Andrew Lambert, quoted from the TV programme, *A Clash of Dreadnoughts.*
13 James, p161. Accuracy increasingly depended on sophisticated fire-control arrangements, like centralised director-controlled fire. *Neptune* was fitted with the prototype director system in 1911, even though there was considerable opposition to the scheme (including from Admiral Sir Francis Bridgeman, whose flag was on *Neptune*). Churchill intervened and two ships, *Orion* and *Thunderer,* one with, one without the system, were pitted against each other in variable weather conditions. The results said Jellicoe 'proved most conclusively the superiority of the Director System'.
14 The German navy standard torpedo, the *G.7,* was not able to cover 15,000yds, although

Jellicoe, days before Jutland, had said he had received reliable information to suggest that the Germans had improved the torpedo so that it i) could reach this distance, and ii) would not leave a telltale wake of bubbles on the surface (see Temple Patterson, *TJP*). See also Sueter, *Submarines, Boats, Mines and Torpedoes,* chart on p299 on the evolution of the torpedo between 1876 and 1903. The chart includes Whitehead and Schwarzkopf models (see Brown, *Torpedoes at Jutland*).
15 Temple Patterson, *Jellicoe*, p100.
16 Marder, *FTDTSF*, vol 3, p5.
17 Hough, p290, quoting Korvettenkapitän Friedrich Forstmeier, *Marine Rundschau*, June 1966.
18 Churchill, p112.
19 Hughes, *Fleet Tactics*, pp79–80.
20 Temple Patterson, *TJP*, vol 1, pp243–53.
21 'The Commander-in-Chief controls the whole battle fleet before deployment and on deployment except in the case of low visibility mentioned in paragraph 4, Section VI. He cannot be certain, after deployment, of being able to control the movements of three battle squadrons when steaming fast and making much funnel smoke. With the noise and smoke of battle added, the practicability of exercising general control will be still further reduced.' (see Golding, p13).
22 Ibid, p243.
23 Ibid, p244.
24 Ibid, p250.
25 Ibid, p244.
26 Ibid, p244.
27 Ibid, p249.
28 Ibid, p189.
29 Ibid, p95. Letter: Fisher to Jellicoe, 17 Nov 1914.
30 Jellicoe differed from his predecessor, George Callaghan, on destroyer tactics. Unlike Callaghan, who had strongly endorsed divisional attack and the offensive use of destroyers, Jellicoe believed the primary role of destroyers was the protection of the battleship fleet. Most of the British destroyers' torpedo launches took place at night (when centralised command was non-existent), while the majority of German destroyer-flotilla torpedo launches (in fact more than 80 per cent of them) took place in daylight as a result of centralised command decisions. But at one earlier point in his career, Jellicoe had supported independent and more aggressive destroyer action (see Temple Patterson, vol I, p178, Beatty to Jellicoe, 12 Aug 1915).
31 Ibid, p245.
32 Rawson, p242.
33 Marder, *FTDTSF*, vol 3, p225, quoting Beatty, GFBOs.
34 Jellicoe, *The Grand Fleet*, quoted Rawson, p149.

35   Marder, *FTDTSF*, vol 3, p213.

36   Gordon, p517; Temple Patterson, *TJP*, vol 2, pp47ff.

37   Ibid, p518.

38   Ibid.

39   Gordon, p166, 'Military Transformation in Long Periods of Peace', in Williamson Murray and Richard Sinnreich (eds), *The Past as Prologue: The Importance of History to the Military Profession* (Cambridge University Press, 2006).

40   Massie, p746.

41   Dreyer, *Sea Heritage*, pp223–4.

42   Chalmers, p277.

43   Gibson and Harper, pp240–1.

44   As Arthur Marder put it: 'It seems to me that the criticism of Jellicoe's tactics, even when a *prima facie* case can be made (notably with regard to Jellicoe's turn-away in the face of flotilla attack), ignores the basic principle of war, namely, that tactics are governed by strategy. That is, battles are ancillary to the main strategy of war. *Jellicoe's primary object was the retention of command of the sea, and this was accomplished.* His secondary object was the destruction of the High Seas Fleet; it was highly desirable, but not essential' (Marder's italics; see Gibson and Harper, p245, quote from Marder, vol 3, p185).

45 - Jellicoe, *The Grand Fleet*, p421.

46   Dreyer, *Sea Heritage*, p205.

47   By August 1916 around eighty-four had been delivered (see Sumida, 'A Matter of Timing', p116).

48   Jellicoe, *The Grand Fleet*, p421, regarding the 25ft and 30ft Barr and Stroud range-finders.

49   Sumida, p117.

50   Dreyer to Jellicoe, 25 July 1916.

51   Steel and Hart, p428, quoting Rheinhard Scheer.

52   Sumida, 'A Matter of Timing', p122.

53   Ibid, p118.

54   Ibid, p217.

55   Beatty to Admiralty, 14 July 1916, Naval Staff Monograph, *Home Waters: From June 1916 to November 1916*, p5.

56   Marder, *FTDTSF*, vol 3, p217.

57   James, *Fisher*, p69.

58   Marder, *FTDTSF*, vol 3, p216.

59   Rawson, p180.

14   The Controversy: An Unfinished Battle

1   Ranft, *TBP*, vol 2, p417, quoting W S Chalmers, *Life and Letters of David, Earl Beatty*.

2   Bennett, p239.

3   Roskill, *The Last Naval Hero*, p322.

4   Bachrach, p41.

5   Yates, p266.

6   Yates, p259.

7   Temple Patterson, *TJP*, vol 2, p464.

8   Ibid, p464.

9   Winton, p282.

10   Temple Patterson, *Jellicoe*, pp230–1. The passage is quoted in full at the end of Chapter 7 of this book.

11   Ranft, *TBP*, vol 2, p443.

12   Ibid, p443.

13   Temple Patterson, *TJP*, vol 2, p399; also refers to Chatfield's comments about 'a tone of victory'.

14   Jellicoe 'had hitherto adhered to his view that he ought not to read it (Harper's Report), now asked to see his foreword…' (see Temple Patterson, *Jellicoe*, p233). And Winton: 'When he first commissioned the report, Wemyss had intended that neither Jellicoe nor Beatty should read it before publication, and Jellicoe certainly agreed with this stipulation. But the moment he arrived back in England Jellicoe began to hear rumours that all was not well with the record'. Gough (p257) pointed out that Jellicoe already knew before sailing to New Zealand that Beatty 'intended to make changes'.

15   Temple Patterson, *TJP*, vol 2, p486. One example is Harper's letter to the Secretary of the Admiralty, dated 4 November 1920.

16   Gough, *Historical Dreadnoughts*, p257.

17   Harper left copies of his papers both with the Jellicoe family, as well as a set revised in 1928 with the United Services Institution, and the original with the Historical Section of the Committee for Imperial Defence.

18   What did become available in 1927 was another HMSO publication called the 'Reproduction of the Record of the battle of Jutland, prepared by Captain J E T Harper and other officers by direction of the Admiralty in 1919–1920'. This was a faithful reprinting of the March 1920 printer's proof, but this of course already included alterations to Harper's original text.

19   Harper.

20   Roskill, *The Last Naval Hero*, p324.

21   Temple Patterson, *Jellicoe*, p235.

22   Roskill, p332.

23   Dewar, *The Navy Within*, p242.

24   Corbett had been critical of both the *Naval Staff Appreciation* and the subsequent *Narrative*. He wrote about the former to Jellicoe in March 1922: 'I have now got well into the battle (of Jutland) and find, so far as I have got … that my reading of the whole affair differs materially from the "Staff Appreciation". After I had read it – for they were good enough to let me have a copy – it appears to me that merely as a piece of history it ought not to go out with the Admiralty imprimatur', Add MSS 49037, ff172–3, 10 March 1922 (see Temple Patterson, *TJP*, vol II, pp413–15).

25   Temple Patterson, *Jellicoe*, p237.

26   Ibid, p236.

27   On German ships the log-keeping system was

also an issue. After Lowestoft, Hase introduced a gunnery record as none had existed before: 'It was the custom in our Navy that no gunnery-logs be kept, as every man had to devote all his energies to the action itself'. Hase's gunnery records from Anna and Bertha turrets are the basis for *Derfflinger*'s account of the battle as each shot was recorded for time (to within ten seconds), elevation and direction.

28 Temple Patterson, *Jellicoe*, pp236–7.

29 For many years I tried (unsuccessfully) to get hold of one in the library at the University of Irvine in California, which must have been Arthur Marder's copy. However, an annotated edition is to be published for the first time in 2016, with a commentary and notes by William Schleihauf (Seaforth Publishing, Barnsley).

30 Ranft, *TBP*, vol 2, p425, BTY/22/9

31 Ranft, *TBP*, p425. Footnotes 'and that two sets were sent to the secretary's office which had not been subsequently found'.

32 Beatty's dislike of Corbett was a shame, given that the latter was a far-sighted strategist. In 1911 (*Some Principles of Maritime Strategy*) he had quite clearly seen the Allied blockade's importance: 'Anything, therefore, which we are able to achieve towards crippling our enemy's finance is a direct step to his overthrow, and the most effective means we can employ to this end against a maritime State is to deny him the resources of sea-borne trade'.

33 Prof Paul Halpern, 'The Naval War in Print: A Survey of Official Histories, Memoirs and Other Publications', paper delivered at the Wilhelmshaven Naval History Conference, Oct 2014.

34 Dewar, *The Navy Within*, p268.

35 Roskill, Letter to *The Times Literary Supplement*, 17 June 1960, quoted Temple Patterson, *Jellicoe*, p241.

36 Bacon, *Scandal*, p144.

37 Ibid, pp144–5.

38 Ibid, p145.

39 Ibid, p144.

40 Ibid, p145.

41 Ibid, p145.

42 'It is, therefore, grossly unfair to hint that Admiral Jellicoe should have drawn an inference which was not apparent to the two Admirals four miles nearer to the fighting' (Bacon, *Scandal*, p147).

43 *The Argus*, Melbourne, 25 March 1925.

44 Temple Patterson, *Jellicoe*, p494.

45 Lambert, p374; also see Roskill, p349.

46 'The main reason why the battle-cruisers were originated was to provide the Commander-in-Chief with a cruiser force which could push home a reconnaissance and supply him with accurate information, but Admiral Beatty failed to keep touch with the enemy and was,

therefore, unable to report to his Commander-in-Chief' (Bacon, *Scandal*, p108).

47 Bacon, *Scandal*, p164.

48 Halpern, *The Naval War in Print*.

49 Churchill, *The World Crisis*, p112.

50 'Jellicoe, threatened by the torpedo stream, turned away according to his long resolved policy. The Fleet fell rapidly apart, the Germans faded into a bank of mist, and Scheer found himself alone again' (Churchill, p152).

51 'The points made are frequently telling … Lord Sydenham's treatment of Churchill as a historian, Sir Reginald Bacon's reconsideration of Jutland, and a long general article by Sir Frederick Maurice are among the best things in the book.' (From a note on the book in the April 1928 issue of the New York magazine, *Foreign Affairs*, commenting on *A collection of criticisms of Churchill's third volume* by Lord Sydenham of Combe and others).

52 Bacon, *Scandal*, p179.

53 Halpern, *The Naval War in Print*.

54 Gringell 'doubled' as a correspondent for *The Times* on Church of England/ecclesiastical and Admiralty issues (see Gough *Historical Dreadnoughts*, p264).

55 Gough, *Historical Dreadnoughts*, p265.

56 Marder, *FTDTSF*, vol 3, p187.

57 Bennett, *Naval Battles*, p225.

58 'George Jellicoe, with the author's warmest thanks for your help in the sincere hope that the result does justice to your distinguished father'.

59 Ranft, *TBP*, vol 2, p470, 'Jellicoe's Defence of his Conduct at Jutland', undated. Add 49041; also Bennett, p235.

60 Winton, p203.

61 Bennett, p237.

62 Hough, *Great War at Sea*, p268

63 Ibid, p269.

64 Hough, *Great War at Sea*, p272.

65 Yates, p275, quoting the *Sunday Times* review headlined 'Something wrong with our bloody ships?', 22 September 1966.

66 Yates, p275.

67 Yates, p271.

68 Herwig, p190.

69 Massie, pp420–1.

70 Beatty was referring to the battles of Heligoland, the Dogger Bank and Jutland (quoted Yates, p237).

71 Beatty went further: '(Jellicoe) loves sycophants and toadies' (Roskill, p221).

72 Charles Beatty, pp84–5, quoted from Cecil Roberts, *The Years of Promise*, Hodder, 1968.

73 Gordon, p523.

74 Quoted by Commander Andy Jordan RN, former CO of *Iron Duke*; see Sources.

75 Yates, p229, quoting Correlli Barnett, *The Swordbearers*.

76 I am thinking here of the closing comments in the first of the two-part 2015 BBC Scotland series *Scotland's War at Sea* (2015).
77 Chalmers, p266
78 *Daily Dispatch*, Manchester, 21 November 1935.
79 *Daily Record and Mail*, Glasgow, 21 November 1935.
80 *Observer*, London, 24 November 1935.
81 *St Petersburg Times*, 11 March 1936.
82 Warner, p184.
83 On 20 July 1920 Admiral Sir John Arbuthnot Fisher, Baron Kilverstone, had died of cancer. He was seventy-nine and alone. He too was given a state funeral in Westminster Abbey. He had cast a striking figure in his time. It seems an extraordinary historical wrong for the man who was the creator of the modern British Navy for there to be no monument to him. Instead, his ashes lie beside those of his wife, who had died two year earlier, under a chestnut tree on his family estate, Kilverstone.

Alfred Tirpitz died in March 1930. His grave site is a simple but handsome slab on stone under trees in the Munich town cemetery, the Waldfriedhof. His personal motto, '*Ziel erkannt, Kraft gespannt*' (recognise the goal, pursue it with zeal) is not written there: just his dates and his title – but not his rank. At Mürwik, the German Naval Academy, there is one notably absent bust. That of Alfred Tirpitz. Neither of the two fleet builders were honoured with such public or private memorials.

Sources

BIBLIOGRAPHY
What follows is a guide to the written source material both in English and German many of which, but not all, have been referred to for *Jutland: The Unfinished Battle*. It is there for anyone wishing to delve deeper into broader aspects of the battle, such as the submarine war, and the ships and technology used.

1. Books in English
Unless otherwise stated, all books published in London.

Allison, R S, *HMS Caroline: A Brief Account of Some Warships Bearing the Name, and in Particular of HMS Caroline (1914–1974), and of Her Part in the Development of the Ulster Division, RNVR, and Later RNR*, Blackstaff, Belfast, 1974
Altham, Captain Edward, *Jellicoe*, Blackie and Son, 1938
Applin, Arthur, *Admiral Jellicoe*, C Arthur Pearson, 1915 (facsimile)
Arthur, Max, *Lost Voices of the Royal Navy*, Hodder and Stoughton, 2005 (first published 1996)
Bachrach, Harriet (ed), *Jutland Letters: June–October 1916*, Wessex Books, 2006
Bacon, Admiral Sir Reginald, KCB, KCVO, SO, *The Jutland Scandal*, Hutchinson and Co, 1925 (*Straits Times* review on http://newspapers.nl.sg/Digitised/Article/straitstimes19250212.2.3.aspx)
—, *The Life of Lord Fisher of Kilverstone, Admiral of the Fleet*, vols I and II, Hodder and Stoughton, 1929
—, *The Concise Story of the Dover Patrol*, Hutchinson, 1932
—, *The Life of John Rushworth Earl Jellicoe*, Cassell, 1936
Ballantyne, Iain, *Warspite: From Jutland Hero to Cold War Warrior*, Pen and Sword, Barnsley, 2010

Barnett, Correlli, *The Swordbearers: Supreme Command in the First World War*, William Morrow, New York, 1964
Beatty, Charles, *Our Admiral: A Biography of Admiral of the Fleet Earl Beatty*, W H Allen, 1980
Beesly, Patrick, *Room 40: British Naval Intelligence 1914–1918*, HarcourtBrace Jovanovich, New York, 1982
Bell, Christopher M, *Churchill and Sea Power*, Oxford University Press, 2013
Bellairs, Carlyon, *The Battle of Jutland: The Sowing and the Reaping*, Hodder & Stoughton, c1920
Bennett, Geoffrey, *Naval Battles of the First World War*, Pan Books, London and Sydney, 1983
—, *The Battle of Jutland*, Wordsworth Editions, 1999
Bingham VC, Hon Barry, *Falklands, Jutland and the Bight*, John Murray, 1919
Black, Nicholas, *The British Naval Staff in the First World War*, Boydell Press, 2009
Blyth, Robert J, Lambert, Andrew and Rüger, Jan (eds), *The Dreadnought and the Edwardian Age*, Ashgate, Farnham, for the National Maritime Museum, 2011
Bönker, Dirk, *Militarism in a Global Age: Naval Ambitions in Germany and the United States before World War I*, Cornell University Press, 2012
Bonney, George, *The Battle of Jutland 1916*, Sutton, Stroud, 2002
Booth, Tony, *Cox's Navy: Salvaging the German High Seas Fleet at Scapa Flow 1924–1931*, Pen and Sword, Barnsley, 2005
Bradford, Sarah, *George VI*, Penguin Books, 1989
Brodie, Bernard, *A Layman's Guide to Naval Strategy*, Princeton University Press, 1943
Brooks, John, *Dreadnought Gunnery at the Battle of Jutland: The Question of Fire Control*, Routledge, 2005

Brown, David K, *The Grand Fleet: Warship Design and Development 1906–1922*, Seaforth, Barnsley, 2010

Brown, Malcolm and Meehan, Patricia, *Scapa Flow: The Reminiscences of Men and Women who Served in Scapa Flow in the Two World Wars*, Allen Lane, 1968

Brownrigg, Rear Admiral Sir Douglas, *Indiscretions of a Naval Censor*, Cassell, 1920

Buchan, John, *The Battle of Jutland*, Thomas Nelson, 1938

Burrows, C W, *Scapa and the Camera*, Periscope Publications, 1931 (reprinted in 2007)

Burt, R A, *British Battleships of World War One*, Seaforth, Barnsley, 2012

Butler, Daniel Allen, *Distant Victory: The Battle of Jutland and the Allied Triumph in the First World War*, Praeger Security International, Westport, Connecticut, 2006

Campbell, John, *Jutland: An Analysis of the Fighting*, Conway Maritime Press, 1987

Carradice, Phil, *1914: The First World War at Sea in Photographs: Grand Fleet v German Navy*, Amberley, 2014

Chalmers, Rear Admiral W S, *The Life and Letters of David, Earl Beatty, Admiral of the Fleet*, Hodder and Stoughton, 1951

Chatfield, Lord, *The Navy and Defence*, vol II, Heinemann, 1947

Churchill, Winston S, *The World Crisis 1916–1918*, vol III part i, Thornton Butterworth, 1927

Clark, Christopher, *The Sleepwalkers. How Europe went to War in 1914*, Allen Lane, 2012

Cock, Randolph and Rodger, N A M, *A Guide to the Naval Records in the National Archives of the UK*, University of London, School of Advanced Study, Institute of Historical Research, 2008

Colledge, J J, *Ships and the Royal Navy: An Historical Index*, David and Charles, Newton Abbot, 1969

Colvin, Ian, *The Life of Lord Carson*, vol III, Gollancz, 1936

Corbett, Sir Julian, *History of the Great War: Based on Official Documents by Direction of the Historical Section of the Committee of Imperial Defence: Naval Operations*, vol III – Jutland, Text and Maps, Longmans Green, 1923

Cruttwell, C R M F, *A History of the Great War 1914–1918*, Clarendon Press, Oxford, 1934

Delage, Edmond, *Le Drame du Jutland*, Grasset, Paris, 1929

Dittmar, Frederick J and Colledge, J J, *British Warships 1914–1919*, Ian Allan, 1972

Downing, Taylor, *Secret Warriors: Key Scientists, Code Breakers and Propagandists of the Great War*, Little, Brown, 2014

Dreyer, Admiral Frederic, *The Sea Heritage: A Study of Maritime Warfare*, Museum Press, 1955

Encyclopedia Britannica: These Eventful Years – The Twentieth Century in the Making, includes chapters by von Tirpitz, Jellicoe and Scheer (undated)

Epkenhans, Michael, *Tirpitz: Architect of the German High Seas Fleet*, Potomac Books, Washington DC, 2008

Farquharson-Roberts, Mike, *A History of the Royal Navy in World War 1*, IB Tauris Books, 2014

Fawcett, Harold William and Hooper, G W W (eds), *The Fighting at Jutland: The Personal Experiences of 60 Officers and Men of the British Fleet*, Chatham Publishing, 2001 (first published by MacLure, Macdonald and Company, Glasgow, 1921)

Filson Young, Alexander, *With the Battle-Cruisers*, Naval Institute Press, Annapolis, 1986 (1st edn, Cassell, 1922)

Fisher, Admiral of the Fleet, Lord, *Memories*, Hodder and Stoughton, 1919

Fitzsimmons, Bernard (ed), *Warships and Sea Battles of World War I*, Phoebus, 1973

Freeman, Richard, *Unsinkable: Churchill and the First World War*, History Press, Stroud, 2013

Freiwald, Ludwig, *The Last Days of the German Fleet*, Constable, 1932

Friedman, Norman, *Naval Firepower: Battleship Guns and Gunnery in the Dreadnought Era*, Seaforth, Barnsley, 2008

Frost, Commander Holloway H, *The Battle of Jutland*, US Naval Institute, Annapolis, 1964 (first published in 1936) (The author died suddenly, aged 45, just before completing his Jutland book; Edwin Falk – author of *Togo and the Rise of Japanese Sea Power* – finished it for him.)

Frothingham, Thomas Goddard, Captain (USN), *A True Account of the Battle of Jutland: May 31, 1916*, Military History Society of Massachusetts, Bacon and Brown, 1920

Fullerton, Alexander, *The Blooding of the Guns*, Walker, 1976

Gannon, Paul, *Inside Room 40: The Codebreakers of World War One*, Ian Allan, 2010

Geddes, Sir Auckland, *The Forging of a Family: A Family Story Studied in Its Genetical, Cultural, and Spiritual Aspects, and a testament of Personal Belief Founded Thereon*, Faber & Faber, 1952

George, S C, *From Jutland to Junkyard*, Birlinn, Edinburgh, 1999

Gibson, Langhorne and Harper, Vice Admiral J E T, *The Riddle of Jutland: An Authentic History*, Cassell, 1934

Gibson, R H and Prendergast, Maurice, *The German Submarine War 1914–1918*, Constable, 1931

Gill, Charles Clifford, *What Happened at Jutland: The Tactics of the Battle*, George E Doran, New York, 1921

Golding, Brad, *Grand Fleet Battle Orders vol III: Jutland*, AAD Services, 1997 (facsimile copy)

Goldrick AO, CSC, RANR, Rear Admiral James, *The King's Ships Were at Sea: The War in the North Sea, August 1914–February 1915*, Naval Institute Press, Annapolis, 1984; revised and republished in 2015 entitled *Before Jutland*

(publisher's proof version used)

Gordon, Professor Andrew, *The Rules of the Game: Jutland and British Naval Command*, John Murray, 1996

Gough, Barry, *Historical Dreadnoughts: Arthur Marder, Stephen Roskill and Battles of Naval History*, Seaforth, Barnsley, 2010

Grabler, Leo and Winkler, Wilhelm, *The Cost of the World War to Germany and to Austria–Hungary*, Yale University Press, New Haven, 1940

Grainger, John D, *The Maritime Blockade of Germany in the Great War: The Northern Patrol, 1914–1918*, Ashgate, Farnham, 2003

Grigg, John, *Lloyd George: War Leader*, Allen Lane, 2002

Gröner, Erich, Mickel, Peter and Mrva, Franz, *German Warships 1815–1945 – Volume One: Major Surface Vessels*, Naval Institute Press, Annapolis, 1983

Grove, Professor Eric, *Big Fleet Actions: Tsushima, Jutland, Philippine Sea*, Brockhampton Press, 1961 (also published as *Big Fleet Encounters*)

Hale, John Richard, *Famous Sea Fights: Armada to Jutland*, Mellifont Library (undated)

Harper, Vice Admiral J E T, *The Truth about Jutland*, John Murray, 1927 (third reprint)

Hase, Commander Georg von, *La Bataille du Jutland vue du Derfflinger* (translated by Edmond Delage), Payot, Paris, 1920 (also published as *Kiel and Jutland* in a translation by Arthur Chambers and F A Holt, Skeffington and Son, 1921; NB: in this book times are two hours ahead of GMT)

Hawkins, Nigel, *The Starvation Blockades: Naval Blockades of WWI*, Pen and Sword, Barnsley, 2002

Hayward, Victor, *HMS Tiger at Bay: A Sailor's Memoir 1914–1918*, William Kimber, 1977

Heathcote, T O, *British Admirals of the Fleet 1734–1995: A Biographical Dictionary*, Pen and Sword, Barnsley, 2003

Herman, Arthur, *To Rule the Waves: How the British shaped the Modern World*, Harper, New York, 2004

Herwig, Holger H, *Luxury Fleet*, Humanity Books, New York, 1980 (republished 1987)

Hoerling, A A, *The Great War at Sea: A History of Naval Action 1914–1918*, Thomas Y Crowell, New York, 1965

Horn, Daniel (ed), *War, Mutiny and Revolution in the German Navy: The World War I Diary of Seaman Richard Stumpf*, Rutgers University Press, 1967

—, *The German Naval Mutinies of World War 1*, Rutgers University Press, 1969

Hough, Richard, *Admirals in Collision*, Hamish Hamilton, 1959

—, *The Great Dreadnought*, Harper and Row, New York, 1966

—, *First Sea Lord*, George Allen and Unwin, 1969

—, *Mountbatten. Hero of our Time*, Weidenfeld and Nicholson, 1980

—, *The Great War at Sea*, Oxford University Press, 1983

—, *Former Naval Person: Churchill and the Wars at Sea*, Weidenfeld and Nicholson, 1985

Howarth, David, *The Dreadnoughts*, Time Life Books, Amsterdam, 1979

Hughes, Terry and Costello, John, *Jutland 1916*, Holt, Rinehart and Winston, New York, 1976

Hughes, Wayne P, *Fleet Tactics: Theory and Practice*, Naval Institute Press, Annapolis, 1986

Hurd, Archibald, *The British Fleet in the Great War*, Constable, 1918

Hyde, H Montgomery, *Carson, The life of Sir Edward Carson, Lord Carson of Duncairn*, Heinemann, 1953

Irving, John, *The Smoke Screen of Jutland*, William Kimber, 1966

James, Admiral Sir William, *Admiral Sir William Fisher*, Macmillan, 1943

—, *The Eyes of the Navy: A Biographical Study of Admiral Sir Reginald Hall*, Methuen, 1955

Jameson, William, *The Fleet that Jack Built: Nine Men Who Made a Navy*, Harcourt, Brace and World, 1962

—, *The Most Formidable Thing: The Story of the Submarine from Its Earliest Days to the End of World War I*, Rupert Hart Davis, 1965

Jellicoe, George, 2nd Earl, *The Boxer Rebellion*, Fifth Wellington Lecture, 1993

Jellicoe, Admiral Sir John, *The Grand Fleet 1914–1918: Its Creation, Development and Work*, Cassell, 1919

—, *The Crisis of Naval War*, Cassell, 1920

—, *The Record of the Battle of Jutland*, HMSO, 1927. (Reproduction of the proof that was printed in March 1920, published in its original form 'without correction or amendment')

—, *Errors Made in the Battle of Jutland*, 1932 (transcribed in 1955, Museum Press; also in Dreyer's *The Sea Heritage*)

—, *The Submarine Peril*, Cassell, 1934 (there also exists a publisher's manuscript with personal annotations, in Author's collection)

—, *Grand Fleet Battle Orders: Volume III. Jutland* (originally prepared by Admiralty Naval Staff, 'Training and Staff Duties Division under the Direction of Admiral John Rushworth Jellicoe'; edition prepared by Brad Golding, 1997)

Jones, Geoffrey, *Battleship Barham*, William Kimber, 1979

Johnston, Ian, *Ships for a Nation 1847–1971: John Brown Company, Clydebank*, West Dumbartonshire Libraries and Museums, 2000

—, *Clydebank Battlecruisers: Forgotten Photographs from John Brown's Shipyards*, Seaforth, Barnsley & Naval Institute Press, Annapolis, 2011

Johnston, Ian and Buxton, Ian, *The Battleship Builders: Constructing and Arming British Capital Ships*, Seaforth, Barnsley & Naval Institute Press, Annapolis, 2013

Johnston, William, Rawling, G P and MacFarlane,

John, *The Seabound Coast: The Official History of the Royal Canadian Navy, 1867–1939*, vol I (online)

Kaplan, Philip, *Images of War: Battleships – The First Big Guns*, Pen and Sword, Barnsley 2014

Karau, Mark D, *The Naval Flank of the Western Front. The German Marine Korps Flandern 1914–1918*, Seaforth, Barnsley, 2014

Keegan, John, *The Price of Admiralty: War at Sea from Man of War to Submarine*, Hutchinson, 1988

Kelly, Patrick J, *Tirpitz and the Imperial German Navy*, Indiana University Press, 2011

Kemp, Lieutenant Commander P K, *HM Destroyers*, Herbert Jenkins, 1956

Kemp, Peter, 'Prelude to Jutland' and 'Whose Victory?' in Fitzsimmons, Bernard (ed), *Warships and Sea Battles of World War I*, Phoebus, 1973

Kenworthy, Lieutenant Commander the Honourable J M, *The Real Navy*, Hutchinson, 1932

King-Hall, Commander Stephen, *A North Sea Diary 1914–1918*, Faber and Faber, 1952 (also published under the title *A Naval Lieutenant*, with the nom de plume 'Etienne', Methuen, 1919)

Kipling, Rudyard, *Sea Warfare*, Macmillan, 1916

Koevner, Hans Joachim, *Room 40: German Naval Warfare 1914–1918: vol I: The Fleet in Action; vol II: The Fleet in Being*, LIS Reinisch, 2009

Lambert, Andrew, *Admirals*, Faber and Faber, 2008

Lambert, Nicholas A, *Planning Armageddon: British Economic Warfare and the First World War*, Harvard University Press, 2012

Lavery, Brian, *Able Seamen: The Lower Deck of the Royal Navy 1850–1939*, Conway Maritime Press, 2011

Le Fleming, H M, *Warships of World War*, Ian Allan, 1967

Legg, Stuart, *Jutland: An Eyewitness Account of a Great Battle*, Rupert Hart-Davis, 1966

Leslie, Sir Shane, *The Jutland Epic*, Ernest Benn, 1930

Liddle, Peter H, *The Sailor's War: 1914–1918*, Blandford Press, Poole, 1985

Lloyd George, David, *War Memoirs*, Odhams Press (undated)

London, Charles, *Jutland 1916: Clash of the Dreadnoughts* (illustrated by Gerrard Howard), Osprey, 2000

Macintyre, Captain Donald, *Jutland*, Evans Brothers, 1957

—, 'Night Action: Confusion and Escape' in Fitzsimmons, Bernard (ed), *Warships and Sea Battles of World War I*, Phoebus, 1973

MacMillan, Margaret, *The War that Ended Peace: How Europe Abandoned Peace for the First World War*, Profile, 2013

Marder, Arthur J, *From the Dreadnought to Scapa Flow*, Oxford University Press (vol 1, 1961, vol 2, 1961, vol 3, 1965, vol 4 1969)

—, *Jutland and After, May to December 1916*, Oxford University Press, 1966

— (ed), *Fear God and Dread Nought: The Correspondence of Admiral of the Fleet Lord Fisher of Kilverstone*, Jonathan Cape (vol I: *The Making of an Admiral, 1854–1904*, 1953; vol II: *Years of Power, 1904–1914*, 1956)

—, *The Anatomy of British Sea Power. A History of British Naval Policy in the Pre-Dreadnought Era, 1880–1905*, Frank Cass, 1972 (3rd impression)

Marten, Michael, *Tim Marten: Memories*, Snipe, 2009

Massie, Robert K, *Dreadnought : Britain, Germany and the Coming of the Great War*, Jonathan Cape, 1991

—, *Castles of Steel: Britain, Germany and the Winning of The Great War at Sea*, Jonathan Cape, 2004

Morison, Elting E, *Admiral Sims and the Modern American Navy*, Houghton Mifflin, Boston, 1942

Morris, Jan, *Fisher's Face*, Viking, 1995

Muir, Augustus, *A Victorian shipowner: A portrait of Sir Charles Cayzer, Baronet of Gartmore*, Cayzer, Irvine, and Co Ltd, 1978

Naval Who's Who 1917, The, Hayward, 1981

Newbolt, Henry, *A Naval History of the War 1914–1918*, Hodder and Stoughton (undated)

O'Hara, Vincent, Dickson, W David, and Worth, Richard, *To Crown the Waves: The Great Navies of the First World War*, Naval Institute Press, Annapolis, 2013

Oakeshott, Ewart, *The Blindfold Game: 'The Day' at Jutland*, Pergamon, Oxford, 1969

Osborne, Eric W, *Britain's Economic Blockade of Germany 1914–1919*, Frank Cass, 2004

Owen, Charles, *Plain Yarns from the Fleet*, Sutton, Stroud, 1998

Padfield, Peter, *Aim Straight: A Biography of Sir Percy Scott, the Father of Modern Naval Gunnery*, Hodder and Stoughton, 1966

—, *The Battleship Era*, Rupert Hart-Davis, 1972

—, 'The Battle-cruisers' in Fitzsimmons, Bernard (ed), *Warships and Sea Battles of World War I*, Phoebus, 1973

—, *The Great Naval Race: The Anglo-German Naval Rivalry, 1900–1914*, David McKay, Philadelphia, 1974

—, *Naval Dominion and the Triumph of the Free World*, Overlook Press, New York, 2010

Parratt, Geoffrey, *The Royal Navy: The Sure Shield of the Empire*, Sheldon Press, 1930

Perrett, Bryan, *For Valour: The Victoria Cross and Medal of Honour Battles*, Weidenfeld and Nicholson, 2003

—, *The North Sea Battleground: The War at Sea 1914–18*, Pen and Sword, Barnsley, 2011

Philbin, Tobias Raphael, *Admiral von Hipper: the inconvenient Hero*, B R Grüner (printed in The Netherlands), 1982

Plivier, Theodor, *The Kaiser's Coolies* (translated by William F Clarke), Faber and Faber, 1932

Pollen, Anthony, *The Great Gunnery Scandal: The Mystery of Jutland*, Collins, 1980

Pollen, Arthur Hungerford, *The Navy in Battle*,

Chatto and Windus, 1918

Preston, Antony, *Battleships of World War One: An Illustrated Encyclopedia of the Battleships of All Nations 1914–1918*, Stackpole, Harrisburg, Pennsylvania, 1972

Preston, Diana, *Wilful Murder. The Sinking of the Lusitania*, Doubleday 2002

Ranft, B McL, *The Beatty Papers* (vol 1 1902–1918, Navy Records Society, 1989, vol 2 1916–1927, Navy Records Society, 1993)

Rasor, Eugene L, *The Battle of Jutland: A Bibliography*, Greenwood Press, 1991

Rawson, Geoffrey, *Earl Beatty, Admiral of the Fleet*, Jarrolds, 1930

Ray, Archibald, *General French and Admiral Jellicoe*, Collins, 1915

Redford, Duncan, *The Submarine: A Cultural History from the Great War to Nuclear Combat*, I B Tauris, 2015

Ridley-Kitts, Daniel G, *The Grand Fleet 1914–19: The Royal Navy in the First World War*, History Press, Stroud, 2013

Roberts, John, *The Battleship Dreadnought: Anatomy of the Ship*, Conway Maritime Press, 1992

Roskill, Stephen, *HMS Warspite: The Story of a Famous Battleship*, Collins, 1957

—, *Admiral of the Fleet Earl Beatty: The Last Naval Hero. An Intimate Biography*, Collins, 1980

Ruge, Vice Admiral F, *SMS Seydlitz Großer Kreuzer 1913–1918*, Warship Profile 14, Profile Publications, 1972

—, *Scapa Flow 1919: The End of the German Fleet*, Ian Allan, 1973

Ruge, Friedrich, 'The Fleets Collide', in Fitzsimmons, Bernard (ed), *Warships and Sea Battles of World War I*, Phoebus, 1973

Ruvigny, Marquis de, *Roll of Honour 1914–1918. A Biographical Record of Members of His Majesty's Naval and Military Forces who fell in the Great War 1914–1918*, Anthony Rowe, undated

Sanford, Terry C (ed), *The Battle of Jutland Bank, May 31 – June 1, 1916: The Despatches of Admiral Sir John Jellicoe and Vice-Admiral Sir David Beatty*, Oxford University Press, 1916

Scheer, Admiral Reinhard, *Germany's High Seas Fleet in the World War*, Cassell, 1920

Schubert, Paul and Gibson, Langhorne, *Death of a Fleet 1917–1919*, Hutchinson, 1932

Seligmann, Matthew S, *The Royal Navy and the German Threat 1901–1914*, Oxford University Press, 2012

Sims, Rear Admiral William Snowden (with Hendrick, Burton J), *The Victory at Sea: The Allied Campaign against U-Boats during the First World War 1917–1918*, Leonaur, 2012 (a reissue of a book first published in 1920 as *The Victory at Sea* by Doubleday, Page and Company in New York and John Murray in London)

Sinclair, David, *Uncharted Waters: The Cayzer Family Firm 1916–1987*, Sybaris Books, 2010

Staff, Gary, *German Battleships 1914–1918 (1): Deutschland, Nassau and Helgoland Classes*; *German Battleships 1914–1918 (2): Kaiser, König and Bayern Classes*, Osprey, 2010

—, *Battle on the Seven Seas*, Pen and Sword, Barnsley, 2011

—, *German Battlecruisers of World War One*, Seaforth, Barnsley, 2011

Snelling, Stephen, *The Naval VCs*, History Press, Stroud, 2002

Steel, Nigel and Hart, Peter, *Jutland 1916: Death in the Grey Wastes*, Cassell, 2003

Steinberg, Jonathan, *Tirpitz and the Birth of the German Battle Fleet*, Macdonald, 1965

Stephen, Martin, *The Fighting Admirals*, Pen and Sword, Barnsley, 1991

Stern, Robert C, *Destroyer Battles: Epics of Naval Combat*, Seaforth, Barnsley, 2008

Stille, Mark, *British Dreadnought vs German Dreadnought: Jutland 1916*, Osprey, 2010

Stokesbury, James L, *Navy and Empire: Short History of Four Centuries of British Seapower and the Rise and Decline of British Imperialism from the Armada to the Falklands*. William Morrow, New York, 1983

Sumida, Jon Tetsuro, *In Defence of Naval Supremacy: Finance, Technology and British Naval Policy, 1889–1914*, Unwin Hyman, Boston, 1989

—, *The Pollen Papers*, The Navy Records Society, 1984

Sueter, Murray F, *The Evolution of the Submarine Boat, Mine and Torpedo: from the 16th Century to 1907*, J Griffin, Portsmouth, 1907

Sydenham, Colonel the Lord (and others), *The World Crisis by Winston Churchill: A Criticism*, Hutchinson, 1928

Sweetman, Jack (ed), *The Great Admirals: Command at Sea 1587–1945*, Naval Institute Press, Annapolis, 1976

'Taffrail' (Dorling, Captain Henry Taprell), *Endless Story*, Hodder and Stoughton, 1938

Tarrant, V E, *The Battle-cruiser Invincible*, Naval Institute Press, Annapolis, 1986

—, *Battleship Warspite*, Arms and Armour, 1990

—, *Jutland: The German Perspective*, Brockhampton Press, 1999

Temple Patterson, A, *The Jellicoe Papers* (vol 1) *1893–1916*, Navy Records Society, 1966

—, *The Jellicoe Papers* (vol 2) *1916–1935*, Navy Records Society, 1968

—, *Jellicoe*, Macmillan/St Martin's Press, 1969

Thomas, Roger D and Patterson, Brian, *Dreadnoughts in Camera: Building the Super Dreadnoughts 1905–1920*, Sutton, Stroud, 1998

Thompson, J Lee, *Northcliffe: Press Baron in Politics 1865–1922*, John Murray, 2000

Thompson, Major General Julian, *The War at Sea: 1914–1918*, Sidgwick and Jackson, 2005

Tirpitz, Grand Admiral Alfred von, *My Memoirs*, vols I and II, Dodd, Mead and Company, 1919

Vat, Dan van der, *The Grand Scuttle: The Sinking of*

the German Fleet at Scapa Flow in 1919, Hodder and Stoughton, 1982

Waldeyer-Hartz, Kapitän von, Admiral von Hipper, Rich and Cowan, 1933

Wallace, Major Claude, From Jungle to Jutland, Nisbet, 1932

Walter, John, The Kaiser's Pirates: German Surface Raiders in World War One, Naval Institute Press, Annapolis, 1994

Warner, Oliver, The Battle of Jutland 1916, Luttterworth Press, 1972

—, Command at Sea: Great Fighting Admirals from Hawke to Nimitz, St Martin's Press, New York, 1976

Weir, Gary, Building the Kaiser's Navy: The Imperial Naval Office and German Industry in the von Tirpitz Era, 1890–1919, Naval Institute Press, Annapolis, 1992

Wells, Captain John, The Royal Navy: An Illustrated Social History 1870–1982, Sutton, Stroud, 1994

Wemyss, Lady Wester, The Life and Letters of Lord Wester Wemyss, GCB, CMG, MVO, Admiral of the Fleet, Eyre and Spottiswode, 1935

Westcott, Allan (ed), Mahan on Naval Strategy, Sampson Low, 1919

Williams, Sir John Ernest Hodder, Jack Cornwell: The Story of John Travers Cornwell, VC 'Boy – 1st Class', Hodder and Stoughton, 1917

Wilson, Ben, Empire of the Deep: The Rise and Fall of the British Navy, Weidenfeld and Nicolson, 2013

Wilson, H W, Battleships in Action, vols I and II, reprint Conway Maritime Press, 1995

Winton, John, Jellicoe, Michael Joseph, 1981

—, Convoy: The Defence of Sea Trade 1890–1990, Michael Joseph, 1983

Woodward, M A, Great Britain and the German Navy, Clarendon Press, Oxford, 1935

Wragg, David, Fisher: The Admiral who Reinvented the Royal Navy, History Press, Stroud, 2009

—, The First World War at Sea, Five Minute History Series, The History Press, Stroud, 2014

Wyllie, W L and Wren, M F, Sea Fights of the Great War: Naval Incidents during the First Nine Months, Cassell, 1918

Yates, Keith, Flawed Victory: Jutland, 1916, Chatham Publishing, 2000

Young, Desmond, Rutland of Jutland, Cassell, 1963

2. Magazines, periodicals and papers

Brooks, John, 'Percy Scott and the Director', Warship (1996) (eds David McLean and Antony Preston), Conway Maritime Press

—, 'Dreadnoughts at Jutland: Tactics and Gunnery', private correspondance with author

—, 'The Admiralty Fire Control Tables', Warship (2002/2003) (ed Antony Preston), Conway Maritime Press

—, 'Jutland: British Viewpoints', published under the German title 'Beatty und die Fürung des Schlachtkreuzerverbandes' (pp286–300) in Epkenhans, M, Hillman J and Nägler, F (eds),

Skagerrakschlact. Vorgeschichete, Ereignis, Verarbeitung, München: R Oldenbourg Verlag, 2009

Brown, David K, 'Torpedoes at Jutland', Warship World, vol V, no 2, Spring 1995

Chapman, David Ian, 'One Crowded Hour: Jack Cornwell – The Boy VC', Leyton and Leytonstone Historical Society, 2006

English, Major J A, 'The Trafalgar Syndrome: Jutland and the Indecisiveness of Naval Warfare', Naval War College Review XXXII, 1979

Goldrick, Rear Admiral James, 'The Need for a New Naval History of the First World War', Corbett Paper No 7 King's College London, 2011

—'The Royal Navy and the Offensive 1914–1939. Something must be left to chance', Hudson Lecture

Gordon, Andrew, 'The Best-Laid Staff Work: An Insider's View on Jellicoe's 1919 Naval Mission to the Dominions', Australian Maritime Issues (SPC-A Annual), 2006

Grant, Alexander, 'HMS Lion at the Battle of Jutland 1916', A Naval Miscellany, Navy Records Society, 2008

Healey, Giles, 'Into Battle on Board the Invincible', Naval History, US Naval Institute, February 2012

Hewitt, Nick, 'The Kaiser's Pirates: Hunting Germany's Cruising Raiders 1914–15', Military History, February 2014

Hines, Commander Jason, 'Sins of Omission and Commission: A Re-assessment of the Role of Intelligence in the Battle of Jutland', Journal of Military History, vol 72, October 2008

Johnston, Ian, Newman, Brian and Buxton, Ian, 'Building the Grand Fleet: 1906–1916', Warship (2012) (ed John Jordan), Conway Maritime Press, 2011

Kent, Captain Barrie, FFIAV, FFI, 'Flag Signalling at Sea', XIX International Congress of Vexillology (UK), July–August 2001

Lambert, Nicholas A, 'Our Bloody Ships or Our Bloody System? Jutland and the Loss of the Battle-cruisers, 1916', Journal of Military History, vol 62, January 1998

Latham, Richard, 'Jellicoe and Jutland', presentation to the senior officers of HMS President, Portsmouth, October 2014

McCallum, Iain, 'The Riddle of the Shells, 1914–1918: (part I) The Approach to War, 1882–1914', Warship (2002/2003) (ed Antony Preston), Conway Maritime Press, 2002

—, 'The Riddle of the Shells, 1914–1918: (part II) The Test of Battle, Heligoland to the Dardanelles', Warship (2004) (ed Antony Preston), Conway Maritime Press, 2004

McLaughlin, Stephen, 'Equal Speed Charlie London: Jellicoe's Deployment at Jutland', Warship (2010) (ed John Jordan), Conway Maritime Press, 2010

Marshall, Peter A, 'The Invincible's Explosive Photo', Naval History, US Naval Institute, February 2012

Naval War College (US), 'Cruisers and Destroyers in the General Action', June 1937

Seligman, Matthew, 'A German Preference for a Medium-Range Battle? British Assumptions about German Naval Gunnery, 1914–1915', *War in History*, January 2012

Sumida, Professor Jon Tetsuro, 'The Quest for Reach: The Development of Long-Range Gunnery in the Royal Navy, 1901–1912', *Tooling for War: Military Transformation in the Industrial Age* (ed Stephen D Chiabotti), Imprint Publications, Chicago, 1996

—, 'A Matter of Timing: The Royal Navy and the Tactics of Decisive Battle 1912–1916', *Journal of Military History*, vol 67, 85–136, January 2003

3. Archives
ADM: Admiralty
CID: Committee for Imperial Defence
HMSO: Her Majesty's Stationery Office
SLGF: Shane Leslie/Godfrey-Faussett papers, Churchill Archives, Cambridge University
RNMIN: Liddle Archives, University of Leeds
Add MS: The British Library, London

Add MS 49030 Jellicoe Papers Col XLII Five lectures on the Battle of Jutland, given at the Royal Naval College, Greenwich, by Adm Sir Bertram Home Ramsay, 14–21 June 1929

CAB 45/269 CID Historical Section Various materials on Jutland, including letters from Admiral Sir John Jellicoe and reports by Vice Admiral Scheer and Hipper, 1916–1932 (later, respectively, Admiral of the Fleet Reinhard Scheer and Admiral von Hipper)

MFQ 1 7 366 Message from Kaiser Wilhelm II thanking the High Seas Fleet after the Skagerrakschlacht

ADM/196/20 John Jellicoe, Naval Career
ADM/196/38 John Jellicoe, Naval Career
ADM/196/87 John Jellicoe, Naval Career
ADM 1/8457/114–118 British Ships damage and Casualty Lists at Jutland
ADM 1/8457/122–132 British Ships damage and Casualty Lists at Jutland
ADM 137/3880 German ship damage at Jutland

HMSO *Narrative of the Battle of Jutland*, 1924
HMSO *Official Dispatches. Battle of Jutland*, three vols – narrative, maps and appendices (copy annotated and signed by Admiral Sir John Jellicoe)
HMSO *Official Record of the Battle of Jutland*, 1920 (Lord Jellicoe's signed and annotated copy, with 'The Harper report' written on the flyleaf)

SLGF *Naval Staff Appreciation of Jutland*. With appendices and diagrams, C.B.0938: copy marked

'RSK 3/13. Training and Staff Duties Division January 1922', Churchill Archives, Churchill College, Cambridge University
SLGF Pastfield, The Reverend J L, *New Light on Jutland*, 1933

Personal correspondence
Commander Frank Marten, HMS *Galatea*, Dorset County Library records

4. Newspaper articles
Filson Young, Alexander, 'Admiral Scheer's bombshell', *Daily Express*
Keegan, John, 'When Jack Tar was burned alive', *Sunday Telegraph*, 30 October 1988

OTHER WRITTEN, FILM AND DIGITAL SOURCES
1. Academic theses
Black, Nicholas Duncan, 'The Admiralty War Staff: its influence on the conduct of the naval war between 1914 and 1918', University College London, 2005
Gavigan, Patrick J, 'Alfred Tirpitz and the Origins of the Anglo-German Naval Rivalry 1898–1906', Ball State University, Indiana, 1968
Jordan, Andy (former commander of Type 23 HMS *Iron Duke*), 'Churchill famously said that Jellicoe was the only man on either side "who could lose the war in an afternoon". How did the interpretation of the concept of the decisive battle and the legacy of Trafalgar shape pre-war naval thinking and the behaviour of senior officers at Jutland?' (undated theis, privately circulated)
Loudon, Hugo, 'Why was the Battle of Jutland not another Trafalgar?', BA Hons, University of Durham, 2001
Macfarlane, J Allen C, 'Notes from A Naval Travesty: The Dismissal of Admiral Sir John Jellicoe, 1917', Doctorate, University of St Andrews, 2014
Otto, Nathanial G, 'Battle-cruisers at Jutland: A Comparative Analysis of British and German Warship Design and its Impact on the Naval War', Senior Honours Thesis, Ohio State University, July 2010
Philbin, Tobias Raphael, 'Admiral Hipper as Naval Commander', Thesis for Doctorate in Philosophy of War Studies, University of London, 1973 (an updated and revised version was published in 1975 by King's College, London. The thesis was eventually published as *Admiral von Hipper: The Inconvenient Hero*, see Bibliography)
Whelan, J J, 'Jellicoe: To what extent was Admiral Sir John Jellicoe to blame for the perceived failure of the Battle of Jutland and how fairly was the event reported in official and journalistic accounts?', University of Oxford, 2005
Yates, James Alexander, 'The Jutland controversy: a case study in intra-service politics, with

particular reference to the presentation of the Battle-cruiser Fleet's training, conduct and command', submission to the University of Hull, September 1998

2. Unpublished

Grant, Captain Alexander, CBE, DSC, 'Through the Hawse Pipe' (memoir), Imperial War Museum

Harper, Vice Admiral J E T, Private papers concerning the Battle of Jutland (Harper Papers in private family papers)

Jellicoe, Admiral Sir John, 'Biographical notes': typewritten notes kindly sent to me by Simon Harley, editor, The Dreadnought Project from Jellicoe's notes for Admiral Bacon's biography found in the British Library

Jellicoe, Sir John, Narrative of the Action on May 31st – June 1st 1916. Letter and first reactions to the battle written privately to Sir George Warrender, June 11th 1916 (Private collection)

Leslie, Sir Shane, Unpublished biography of Admiral Sir David Beatty (SLGF, Churchill Archives)

3. Films and YouTube

Allen, Kenneth, *The Battle of Jutland 1916: A Dramatised TV Documentary*, 1977

Battlefield Detectives: World War I: Jutland

Battleships: The Clash of the Dreadnoughts: Jutland, Channel 4

Lost Ships: The Last Broadside, 2000

Royal Cousins at War. Season One. A House Divided, BBC, 2014

Steel, Nigel, *Jutland*, podcast series on WWI, no. 22, Imperial War Museum, London, 2012

Scotland's War at Sea, 2-part series, BBC, 2015

The Battleships: The Darkness of the Future

World War One: Jutland, narrated by Robert Ryan, 1963

World War One, Part 4/4, The Battle of Jutland

4. A selection of books in German (for reference)

Busch, Korvettenkapitän Fritz Otto und Forstner, Korvettenkapitän D Georg, *Unsere Marine im Weltkrieg 1914–1918*, Brunnen, Berlin, 1934

Dohm, Arno, *Skagerrak: Die größte Seeschlacht der Geschichte*, Bertelsmann, Gütersloh, 1936

Epkenhans, Michael (ed), *Mein lieber Schatz!: Briefe von Admiral Reinhard Scheer an seine Ehefrau. August bis November 1918*, Winkler, Bochum, 2006

Epkenhans, Michael, Hillmann, Jörg und Nägler, Frank, *Skagerrakschlacht. Vorgeschichte – Ereignis – Verarbeitung*, Oldenbourg, Munich, 2011

Filcher, Andreas, *Unter Flatternden Fahnen. Dritter Band. Die Seeschlacht vor dem Skagerrak*, Deutscher Wille, Berlin, c1940

Fock, Harald, *Schwarze Gesellen. Torpedoboote bis 1914*, Koehler, Hamburg, 1979

—, *Schwarze Gesellen. Zerstörer bis 1914*, Koehler, Hamburg, 1981

Frost, Holloway H, *Grand Fleet und Hochseeflotte im Weltkrieg*, Verhut Verlag, Berlin, 1938 (foreword by Grand Admiral Dr Erich Raeder; contains many of the same maps as the English edition, with additional illustrations on gunnery allocation)

Groos, Otto, *Der Krieg zur See 1914–1918* (German text published in 1920 by Ernst Siegfried Mittler und Sohn, Berlin, with maps; the 1926 British Admiralty translation was by Lieutenant Commander W T Bagot)

Hanstein, Otfrid von, *Die Seeschlacht am Skagerrak*, Vogel und Vogel, Leipzig, 1916

Hersfeld, E von, *Die Seeschlacht vor dem Skagerrak*, Velhagen und Klasing, Bielefeld/Berlin/Hanover, c1919

Hopman, Admiral Albert, *Das Kriegstagebuch eines deutschen Seeoffiziers*, August Scherl, Berlin, 1925

—, *Das ereignisreiche Leben eines 'Wilhelminers': Tagebücher, Briefe, Aufzeichnungen 1901 bis 1920* (ed Michael Epkenhans), Oldenbourg, Munich, 2004

Hormann, Jörg-Michael und Kliem, Eberhard, *Die kaiserliche Marine im Ersten Weltkrieg. Von Wilhelmshaven nach Scapa Flow*, Bucher, 2014

Kludas, Arnold und Beer, Theo, *Die Kaiserliche Marine auf alten Postkarten*, Gerstenberg, 1983

Kühlwetter, Friedrich von, *Skagerrak: Der Ruhmestag der deutschen Flotte*, Ullstein, Berlin, 1933

Kuntze, Paul H, *Skagerrak*, Hermann Hillger Verlag, Berlin/Leipzig, c1933

Loeff, Wolfgang, *Skagerrak. Die größte Seeschlacht*, B.G. Leubner, Leipzig/Berlin, 1938

Looks, Otto, *Großkampf unter Deck*, Bertelsmann, Gütersloh, 1938

Lützow, A D, *Der Nordseekrieg: Doggerbank–Skagerrak*, Gerhard Stalling, Oldenburg, 1931

Lützow, Friedrich, *Skagerrak*, Langer-Müller, Munich, 1936

Mantey, Eberhard von, *Unsere Marine im Weltkrieg 1914–1918*, Vaterländischer Verlag C A Weller, Berlin, 1927

Pemsel, Helmut, *Seeherrschaft. Eine Maritime Weltgeschichte von der Damfschiffahrt bis zu Gegenwart*, Bernard und Graefe Verlag, Bonn, 1995 (two vols)

Scheer, Admiral Reinhard, *Vom Segelschiff zum U-Boot*, online Salzwasser fascimile of 1925 edition

Scheer, Reinhard and Stöwer, Prof Willy, *Die deutsche Flotte in großer Zeit*, Georg Westermann, Berlin

Scheibe, Korvettenkapitän, *Die Seeschlacht vor dem Skagerrak am 31 Mai bis 1 Juni 1916*, Siegfried Mittler und Sohn, Berlin, 1916

Schultz, Willi, *Linienschiff 'Schleswig-Holstein'*, Koehler, Hamburg, 1991

Simsa, Paul, *Marine Intern. Entwicklung und Fehlenwicklung der deutschen Marine 1888–1939*,

Motorbuch, Stuttgart, 1972

Weyer, Bruno, *Taschenbuch der Kriegflotten XVII. Jahrgang 1916*, J F Lehmans, Munich, 1916

Winkelhagen, J, *Das Rätsel vom Skagerrak. Eine Quellenanalyse*, Theodor Weicher, 1925

Witthöft, Hans Jürgen. *Lexicon zur deutschen Marinegeschichte*, Koehler, Herford, 1977

Wolfslast, Wilhelm. *Skagerrak. Die größte Seeschlacht der Geschichte*, Moewig, Munich, 1958

Wolz, Nicolas, *Das lange Warten. Kriegerfahrungen deutscher und britischer Seeoffiziere 1914 bis 1918*, Schöningh, Paderborn, 2007

—, *Und wir verrosten im Hafen, Deutschland, Großbritannien under der Krieg zur See 1914–1918*, Deutsche Taschenbuch Verlag, 2013

Zenne, Gustav, *Oberheizer Zenne, der Letzte mann der Wiesbaden (Nach Mitteilungen des oberheizers Zenne von Frhr Spiegel von und zu Peckelsheim)*, A Scherl, Berlin 1917

5. War diaries in German

Many of the following are extracts from materials supplied privately to the author. References to published works are made where possible.

Huck, Stephan, Pieken, Gorch und Rogg, Matthias, *Die Flotte schläft im Hafen ein: Kriegsalltag 1914–1918 in Matrosen-Tagebüchern*, Sandstein, Dresden, 2014

Linke, Carl Richard, SMS *Helgoland*

Mahrholtz, Konteradmiral aD, *Der Artillerieoffizier eines Großkampschiffes im Kriege 1914/1918* (Gunnery Officer, SMS *Von der Tann*), M Dv Nr 352, Dienstschrift Nr 10 Fuhrergehilfenausbildung der Marine, Berlin 1930. English translation provided by Michael Behm, excerpts provided courtesy of Byron Angel

Paschen, Commander Günther, SMS *Lützow*, 'German Officer's Vivid Memories of Jutland' (magazine article)

Schinkel, Willy, SMS *Kaiser*

Stumpf, Richard, *Erinnerungen aus dem deutsch-englischen Seekriege auf SMS Helgoland*

Steen, Hans, *habe meine Pflicht getan – Erlebnisberichte*, Adolf Sponholz, Hanover, 1939

Wilhemshaven Marine Museum, exhibition catalogue based on the war diaries of Richard Stumpf and Carl Richard Linke

Index